Teaching the Global Middle Ages

Teaching the Global Middle Ages

Edited by

Geraldine Heng

Modern Language Association of America
New York 2022

85 Broad Street, New York, New York 10004
www.mla.org

To order MLA publications, visit mla.org/books. For wholesale and international orders, see mla.org/bookstore-orders.

The MLA office is located on the island known as Mannahatta (Manhattan) in Lenapehoking, the homeland of the Lenape people. The MLA pays respect to the original stewards of this land and to the diverse and vibrant Native communities that continue to thrive in New York City.

Options for Teaching 54
ISSN 1079-2562

Library of Congress Cataloging-in-Publication Data

Names: Heng, Geraldine, editor.
Title: Teaching the global Middle Ages / edited by Geraldine Heng.
Description: New York : Modern Language Association of America, 2022.
Series: Options for teaching, 1079-2562 ; 54 | Includes bibliographical references.
Identifiers: LCCN 2021062582 (print) | LCCN 2021062583 (e-book) | ISBN 9781603295161 (hardcover) | ISBN 9781603295178 (paperback) | ISBN 9781603295192 (EPUB)
Subjects: LCSH: Literature, Medieval—Study and teaching. | Literature, Medieval—History and criticism. | Middle Ages—Study and teaching. |. Civilization, Medieval—Study and teaching. | LCGFT: Literary criticism.| Essays.
Classification: LCC PN671 .T35 2022 (print) | LCC PN671 (ebook) | DDC 809/.02071—dc23/eng/20220502
LC record available at https://lccn.loc.gov/2021062582
LC e-book record available at https://lccn.loc.gov/2021062583

This volume is dedicated to

the students in the original six-hour-long graduate seminar, Global Interconnections: Imagining the World, 500–1500, in spring 2004 at the University of Texas, Austin;

the participants in the year-long, graduate-postdoctoral-faculty Winton seminar, Early Globalities I: Eurasia and the Asia Pacific and Early Globalities II: Africa, the Mediterranean, and the Atlantic, in 2012–13 at the University of Minnesota, Twin Cities;

and the late Eugene ("Gene") Vance,
whose vision was always already global.

Contents

Acknowledgments

This volume exists because Fiona Somerset, who was a member of the MLA's Publications Committee in 2017, conveyed a request that I edit an MLA Options for Teaching volume on the Global Middle Ages, so instructors in higher education might have a resource with ideas, guidelines, and syllabi for how to teach courses on the literatures, cultures, histories, and materials of early globalism. This volume exists because of her initiative, and the initiative of a forward-looking MLA Publications Committee in 2017 and 2020. I also thank two anonymous reviewers who generously endorsed the manuscript and made suggestions; the MLA's extraordinary acquisitions editor, Jaime Cleland, for her tact, patience, kindness, and skill in shepherding a large and cumbersome project through the long process of preparation; the meticulous, unnamed MLA copyeditor who undertook invaluable work on the manuscript; and, finally, Erika Suffern, the equally extraordinary head of book publications, for taking over the project during the production process and steering it to successful completion.

Since I coined the term and concept of a "Global Middle Ages" in 2003, there have been many remarkable and adventurous colleagues who have collaborated on the Global Middle Ages Project's (GMAP's) research, teaching, conferencing, workshop, and digital initiatives. I wholeheartedly thank them all, even if, regretfully, it is impossible to detail everything adequately on an acknowledgments page. You know who you are and how deep my thanks and appreciation are for your fellowship and your work. Two persons, however, must be singled out for special mention because of their roles in ensuring GMAP's survival and success at key junctures: Susan Noakes of the University of Minnesota minded the store when I was preoccupied with completing a long and difficult book, and Stephen G. Nichols of Johns Hopkins University ensured that GMAP had an online platform to call home.

At various stages, allies working in modern fields have also critically offered their support: special thanks go to David Theo Goldberg, Kevin Franklin, Cathy Davidson, Gayatri Chakravorty Spivak, and the late Hayden White.

After all, it takes a village to raise a global Middle Ages.

Geraldine Heng

Introduction: What Is the Global Middle Ages and Why and How Do We Teach It?

In spring 2004, as the incoming director of medieval studies at the University of Texas in Austin, I decided to experiment with a new kind of teaching. Fresh in the aftermath of September 11, 2001, the West seemed to find itself in an odd temporal wrinkle in which the "Middle Ages"—always defined as European and seen as an interregnum between classical antiquity and its so-called Renaissance—was being invoked by world leaders and Islamist militant extremists alike for phenomena that seemed curiously transportable from the deep past to the contemporary present.

The foremost leader of the Western world, George W. Bush, like the extra-state militant actors he condemned, was expatiating on Crusades and crusaders in the context of international war. A model of empire as a form of governmentality in international affairs was approvingly re-emerging in political theory. Dispositions of race practiced at airport security checkpoints, in the news media, and in public conversation suggested that religion—the magisterial discourse of the European Middle Ages, just as science is the magisterial discourse of the modern eras—was once more on the rise as a mechanism by which absolute and fundamental distinctions could be delivered to set apart human groups and populations by positing strategic essentialisms in a quasi-medieval racialization of religion.[1]

Even as the West was being shadowed by premodern time, however, humanities departments teaching the past in institutions of higher learning continued to be calcified along disciplinary, national literature, national history, and area studies lines that atomized teaching and made almost impossible a broad view across civilizations and systems that could deliver a multilayered, critical sense of the past in our time.

Nor did September 11 decenter the near-exclusive focus on Europe in literature and history departments in which the medieval period was taught. At best, courses like Europe and Its Others continued to be offered, and a new enthusiasm for teaching the Crusades appeared. Area studies programs focusing on other territorial regions—the Middle East, South Asia, East Asia, and so forth—continued not to engage substantively with the teaching and study of other geographic zones and sociopolitical formations of the premodern world outside their regions.

To experiment with an alternative kind of learning, I assembled an instructional team of five faculty members from different departments, centers, and programs on campus, and two visiting faculty, to introduce to graduate students, through our collaborative teaching, an interconnected, decentered world, with points of viewing in the West and in Islamicate civilizations, in trans-Saharan and North Africa, India and South Asia, the Eurasian continent, China and East Asia.

The "Global Middle Ages," a term and concept I coined in 2003 out of curricular and pedagogical necessity (and expediency) in designing and preparing for the spring 2004 course, was born.

It will not surprise anyone in education that the classroom is an important incubator of new concepts and new projects. Faced with keen-eyed students eager to see what a different kind of pedagogy can deliver, the improvisations of instructors rapidly devolve into strategies, and the strategies start to develop pathways through intellectual thickets that carve a path into the future.

To begin with, without privileging any locations, we decided to introduce cultures and vectors as interdependent but also discrete formations to be examined through a linked set of issues, questions, and themes. A decentered world countered the ubiquity of eurocentrism in pedagogy and addressed the concerns of some area studies scholars—like those in Indian Ocean studies who objected to what they saw as the hegemony of Mediterranean studies (see, e.g., Grewal 187). To cultivate new contexts for studying a multilocational past, we also did not descriptively survey but critically assessed the materials with which we conjured.

In this way, we sought not to replicate the descriptive world history surveys beginning to gain traction in the academy at the undergraduate level in lower-division courses. Though world history surveys were, and continue to be, extremely important in delivering a sense of the world, we wanted greater depth of analysis and to sustain from week to week a thickened sense of the complex interrelations that webbed the globe. Fortunately, given that the fields of the instructional faculty included literary studies, social history, art history, architectural history, religious studies, women's studies, the history of science and mathematics, and law and linguistics, interdisciplinarity was an inescapable condition of our teaching.

But rather than codify a priori how interdisciplinarity would function in the course, we worked through the pragmatics of the day-to-day instructional process, each teaching from the disciplinary assumptions and practices most familiar to us while reaching across to address what differed from our practices in the examples offered by our colleagues. We thus aimed for a kind of classroom laboratory: an open-ended process of trial, correction, and experimentation.

Our reasoning was pragmatic. We hoped our experiment would incubate new habits of thinking and working among our students—foster a habit of reaching across cultures and methods, even as individual departments continued to ensure accreditation in local disciplinary training and knowledges—and that the process would produce, in time, a distinctive group identity for our students in a contracting national academic market.

An important aim was also to bring medieval studies, a field that was too often dismissed as concerned with largely obscure interests—with knowledges, it was thought, mainly interesting to academic antiquarians performing custodial functions for archives of little urgency to anyone else—more visibly into conversation with other kinds of teaching and investigation in the twenty-first-century academy.[2]

To the euphoria of all involved, the experiment proved a resounding success. Everyone—from senior faculty members (which included the then dean of liberal arts) to the two undergraduate students who had permission to enroll in a course that met for six intense hours a week in the classroom and many more hours outside—found the experiment exhilarating and unlike any classroom experience we had known.[3] In its wake, as I published and lectured on how to conceptualize and teach a globalized Middle Ages, I was asked, again and again: why can't teaching and learning be more like this? Many of my projects since 2004, including this volume, are a continuing response to that question.

In 2007, Professor Susan Noakes, then director of medieval studies at the University of Minnesota, Twin Cities, and I formally convened the Global Middle Ages Project and cohosted a workshop at the University of Minnesota, inviting participants from institutions of higher learning coast-to-coast, across several disciplines, to thrash out questions of terminology, definitions, concepts, and other challenging problematics.

From 2012 to 2013, we convened the Winton Seminar at the University of Minnesota, reshaping the Texas course as a yearlong seminar with seventeen visiting and on-campus faculty leaders: Early Globalities I: Eurasia and the Asia Pacific and Early Globalities II: Africa, the Mediterranean, and the Atlantic. Two years later, with the aid of a Council on Library and Information Resources (CLIR)–Andrew W. Mellon Foundation grant, we launched a series of digital projects on a new platform, *The Global Middle Ages* (www.globalmiddleages.org), as a cybernetic classroom: a gateway to learning that takes place outside university walls and is open to all.

An Idea Whose Time Has Come: The Global Turn in Medieval Studies

A Global Middle Ages—transhumanities work that asks scholars to step outside their discipline and area specialization to engage with other humanities scholars, social scientists, computer technologists, musicologists, archeologists, designers, and others to make sense of an interconnected past—appears to be an idea whose time has come.

In the nearly two decades since my coining the term, universities and colleges in the United States, the United Kingdom, Europe, and Australia have begun undergraduate concentrations and graduate programs on a Global Middle Ages.[4] Three journals have emerged as the publications of record for this new field, and conferences on the Global Middle Ages now abound.[5] You can even buy flashcards online now on the Global Middle Ages.

As if to confer institutional blessing, the Medieval Academy of America decided that the theme of its 2019 annual meeting would be the Global Turn. Collaborative grants have also been awarded by foundations to universities in the United States, the United Kingdom, and Australia to advance research, teaching, and digital humanities on a Global Middle Ages, and publishers have commissioned texts: this present volume, and a forty-title Cambridge Elements series on the Global Middle Ages are among the publishing initiatives.[6]

The ease and rapidity with which the idea of the Global Middle Ages has spread and the newfound enthusiasm for the global in early studies suggest that teachers and scholars today are looking for something new to drive the transformation of early studies in the twenty-first-century academy.[7] The gains, both for teaching and research, are considerable. I have argued that a global perspective of the deep past can transform our understanding of history and of time itself, enabling us to identify, for instance, not just a single scientific and industrial revolution that occurred once, exclusively in the West, but the recurrence of multiple scientific and industrial revolutions in the non-Western, nonmodern world.

For instance, the industrial mass production of commercial ceramics in China for the international export market during the Tang dynasty in the ninth century and the massive iron and steel industries of eleventh-century Song China—using coal that amounted to seventy percent of the tonnage of coal burnt in the iron and steel industries of early-eighteenth-century industrial Britain—attest to the efflorescence of early, multiple industrial revolutions in China and startlingly reshape our understanding of the past. Our view of the relationship between modernity and premodernity is suddenly transformed, and we see that multiple modernities may have occurred in premodern time, complicating our sense of history and periodization.[8]

Seeing the global in this way yields startling insights and recognitions, but by no means shunts aside study of the national, the local, and the regional. In fact, for those of us who have been trained in particular national literatures, languages, and histories, a global view yields an important perspective of how national and global forces interlock in shaping a country and the world.

For instance, Hispanists can point to Spain's persecution and expulsion of Jews and so-called Moriscos—a moment of self-purification constitutive of the early Spanish nation—as that moment, also, in which Spain's global-colonial ambitions arose and began to spread their umbra across the world. As it forcibly emptied itself of people it saw as belonging elsewhere in the world, not in Spain, Spain under the Catholic monarchs also made its governance bloom elsewhere in the world. The spread of Spain's national boundaries outward in the form of Hispanized colonies around the globe—in the Americas, in the Philippines—thus affirmed the forces of Spanish nationalism and Spanish imperialism-globalism, and Spain's national and global identities, as mutually constitutive and interlocking.

All this, and more, is visible in literature and history once we look globally. Early global studies therefore does not mean the elision of the local nor the end of studying national languages, literatures, and histories. To see how nationalism and colonialism-imperialism are linked and mutually constitutive phenomena requires training and viewing in both local and global perspectives.

In the same way, the study of globalism by no means obviates the continuing and necessary work of regional studies—of Mediterranean studies, Indian Ocean studies, Atlantic studies, and so on—but merely positions a reminder that for the world's inhabitants, every place is the center of the world, and, to multifarious scholars worldwide, there is no single region of supreme historical importance and priority above all others. Indeed, when viewed together, all scales of relation—local, regional, and global—can yield remarkable insights.

Of some importance today, for those of us who were trained as Euromedievalists, is that highlighting the overlap between the local, the regional, and the global undercuts the fantasy that an earlier Europe was the opposite of Europe now, a continent with global populations from everywhere.

The study of international slavery and human trafficking, transnational migration, global commerce, and transnational wars in premodernity foregrounds archives that enable us to bear witness to a premodern Europe that already contained people from everywhere—Jews, Arabs, Turks, Romani (then called "Gypsies"), Africans, Indians, Mongols, steppe peoples, and others—and refuses the fiction that a singular, homogenous, communally unified Caucasian ethnoracial population once existed in Europe when it was Latin Christendom.

The notion that a "white" Europe existed as a historical fact—and not as a concept manufactured by centuries of assiduous identity construction—is thus exposed as the fantasy of contemporary politics and political factions. The study of the global past in deep time can thus speak productively to the racial politics of the contemporary European and Western now.

In the twenty-first century of a post-Trump era, Brexit, and the ascendancy of alt-right and white supremacist movements in the United

States, United Kingdom, and Europe, the study of a Global Middle Ages can thus be an act of intellectual allegiance to ethical responsibility.[9]

What Is the "Global Middle Ages"? Terminology, Concepts, Problematics

I have argued that responsibility to the emerging field called the Global Middle Ages requires commitment to continual critical reflection on its animating terms, frames, concepts, methods, and approaches. Even the use of the term *Middle Ages*, a Eurocentric construct fabricated by Renaissance historiographers to name an interregnum between two glorified ages of empire identified by their putative authenticity and supremacy—Greco-Roman antiquity and its so-called Renaissance—requires critique of its ideological freight, even if alternative names for the past ultimately prove impractical.

For some—like my codirector and collaborator, Susan Noakes, and more particularly for non-Europeanists—even the commonplace term *Middle Ages* should only be embraced under erasure and be accepted but contingently, as a contested Eurocentric construct with little epistemological bearing for the not-Europe cultures of the world, and perhaps with little bearing even for Europe itself.[10]

Definitions: The "Middle Ages" and the World

For Euromedievalists reflexively to export the "Middle Ages" to territories beyond Europe in naming cognate chronologies in other zones of the world would thus inadvertently be a colonizing gesture by Euromedieval studies, the centrality of European time giving its name to asynchronous chronologies elsewhere, so that there is an Indian "Middle Ages," an African "Middle Ages," and so forth. Those eager to embrace a Global Middle Ages must acknowledge that the zones and cultures of the world are asynchronous, following different time lines of description, naming, change, development, recurrence, transformation: differential temporalities characterize the many zones of the world.

In this volume, Emma Flatt's essay exemplifies precisely how problematic it is to port over to South Asian history and culture a Eurocentric template of dividing time into "classical," "medieval," and "modern" periods. Patiently, she shows us how that importation of a Western model of periodicity winds up colluding with Hindutva nationalist interests and British colonial imperialism.

But even as she highlights the problem of naming several centuries of Indian history and culture "medieval," Flatt recognizes the necessity of communicating with readers in terminology of sufficient familiarity so as not to risk an alienation that puts in jeopardy the project of this volume to offer help that encourages, not discourages, readers from finding ways to incorporate the worlds of South Asia in their teaching.

Feeling the tug of contradictions, Flatt's compromise is the logical one: she points to the political stakes of importing a European terminology and naming, and increases our consciousness of what is gained, and what is sacrificed, in her decision to use a terminology familiar to those of us working in Western literatures, histories, and languages.

In similar fashion, some scholars of other non-Western zones—of Africa, or Islamicate civilizations, or Japan, for instance—have also decided to conjure with terms like *medieval* and *Middle Ages* in identifying periods in the historiography of their regions. Their references to the "Islamic Middle Ages," the "Jewish Middle Ages," "medieval Japan," or even the "North American Middle Ages" (as Tim Pauketat, one of the foremost archeologists of Cahokia and the Mississippi basin prefers it) can perhaps be seen both as the hegemonic ineluctability of European studies' dominance in the academy and also as efforts of goodwill on the part of non-Europeanists in positing the utility of structuring overarching heuristic paradigms across geographic zones through attention to features and characteristics that suggest resemblance or analogy.

Needless to say, situated terminology of this kind, issuing from within non-European studies and attached by their scholarly proponents to their own zones and periods of study, carries a different valence from its attachment by Euromedievalists willy-nilly to chronologies and zones around the world.

Some scholars of non-European zones and regions, like Flatt, duly preface the imperfect choices open to them with a discussion that highlights the stakes involved in their decisions of terminology. Terms like the "Islamic Middle Ages" or "medieval India" can thus be seen as crucial compromises that point to academic vocabulary's limitations, and Euromedieval studies' hegemony in the academy, even as they enable and facilitate conversations across a broad spectrum of premodernists.

Compromises of this kind in naming and terminology do not mean that we of the Global Middle Ages Project have not reflected critically on the naming of our own project or have not made conscientious efforts to find alternative names for the "Global Middle Ages." At the 2007 workshop in Minnesota, several attempts were made to rename our collective endeavor, with other names being tried and considered.

"Global Premodernity" seemed to some to retain attention too fixedly on modernity as the focal point of an implicitly linear temporality and had the disadvantage of temporal vagueness. It was pointed out that "Premodernity" could indicate the Bronze and Iron Age, biblical time, and Greco-Roman antiquity all the way through the so-called Renaissance, which is still considered by some as a premodern era.

An inspired suggestion by a graduate student that we call the "Global Middle Ages Project" the "1001 Years Project" met with objections from historians who felt the reference to the *Thousand and One Nights* lent an unfortunate aura of fantasy to the project. My own preferred term, "Early Globalities," was also felt by historian colleagues to signal too strongly the work of literature rather than history departments.

All attempts at naming the past thus pointed to the inescapability of the conceptually and politically freighted nature of the language we had to use in order to participate in academic discourse. In the end, to be able to speak at all among ourselves and to others, we agreed to continue the use of conventional terms, but also to continue to critique and problematize them. In a sense, therefore, we were following in the footsteps of preceding academic movements: poststructuralist critique of logocentrism and feminist critique of phallogocentrism did not work to produce alternate linguistic systems, but a critical highlighting of consciousness of the stakes involved in language use.

Time Lines: From 500 to 1500 CE?

There can be no hard and fixed time line for what we have called, for lack of better nomenclature, and subject to continuing autocritique, the Global Middle Ages. Time across the globe is inexorably asynchronous. Scholars of different zones and regions describe the chronologies and historiographies of their areas in multifarious ways that should not find it necessary to link up with European time nor with the temporalities of other, Western or non-Western, zones and regions. Modernity is defined differentially and begins, ends, and recurs variedly in the miscellaneous chronologies and narrations of time and history in different parts of the world.

The conventional time parameters in the West identified for the "Middle Ages"—neatly adumbrated as 500 to 1500 CE—are themselves little more than a heuristic fiction, of convenience mainly as a way to round off the jagged edges of history and place fantasmatic borders around messy, sticky historical phenomena that do not hew to temporal confinement.

The digital, research, and teaching initiatives of the Global Middle Ages Project have thus foregrounded or critiqued the hegemony of a Europe-based, factitious Roman-calendar periodization hedged at one end by the collapse of the Roman Empire (neatly located as circa 500), and at the other by the incipience of the early modern era or so-called Renaissance in the West (neatly located as circa 1500) and have rejected temporal rigidity in favor of a plethora of time lines around the world.

This does not mean, however, a renunciation of all forms of periodization, as the discussion in the section "Early Globalism versus Globalization Today" below makes plain.

What Does "Global" Mean in Premodernity?

The global is not the same thing as the planetary. A student or teacher of the global should not feel a requirement to address every place on the planet, nor feel a corollary obligation to establish the interconnectivity of each corner of the earth with every other corner of the earth. Early globality is not tantamount to, and should not be equated with, a twenty-first-century globalization that—at least in theory—knits together the inhabitants of all pockets of the planet. The study of a Global Middle Ages is not synonymous with the study of planetarity.

Though Europeans in the form of Greenlanders and Icelanders crossed the Atlantic Ocean to reach the Northern American continent around 1000 CE during the Little Climatic Optimum (or the Medieval Warm Period, or Medieval Climatic Anomaly), they did not cross the Pacific Ocean to reach Austronesia. Though Chinese imperial "treasure ships" helmed by the Muslim admiral Zheng He crossed the South China Sea and Indian Ocean to reach Africa in the fifteenth century, they did not arrive in Austronesia, the Americas, or Antarctica. Extraordinarily, DNA research in plant biology now indicates that Polynesians traversed half the world to reach the South American continent around 1000 CE, but there are no suggestions yet that the inhabitants of Oceania arrived in Siberia or Greenland.

From these simple examples alone, we can see that what constitutes the "global" for the inhabitants of the premodern world differs from place to place and according to their location on the globe. The study of globalism also differs from the study of the world per se: studying the world involves learning about a wide collection of places with individual cultures, histories, and societies. By contrast, the study of globalism addresses the interconnectivity of lands—sometimes distant, and far-flung—whose cultures, stories, religions, languages, art, goods, germs, plants, and technology were braided into relations across distances that were sometimes unimaginable in their time.

The Global Middle Ages thus focuses on interconnectivity—whether of an artistic, commercial, linguistic, technological, religious, scientific, agricultural, political, martial, or epidemiological kind. We see, in this way, that early globalism is not just a concept of *space*—how large geographic spaces and vectors can be seen as interrelated and interconnected—early globalism can also be viewed as a *dynamic*: the forces pushing toward the formation of larger scales of relationship.

The essays in this volume show us early globalism at work when a religion like Islam makes its way out of the Hijaz to South Asia and West Africa, transforming local occupations and personal statuses and reshaping rituals, politics, stories, and roles. We also see globalism at work when Indic culture scatters across island Southeast Asia, spreading architectural styles, languages, mythologies, Buddhism, and Hinduism.

Pax Mongolica famously secured overland trade routes and moved artisans and goods around the vast Eurasian continent from termini to emporia, so that an English King, Edward I, in a far northwestern island of the world was seen to wear Chinese brocade as part of his inaugural robes. In other work, I describe transworld artistic exchanges between Chinese and Iraqi potters and a mass industrialization in China that was fueled by international market demand for Chinese export ceramics—a demand that was met through ocean-going cargo vessels in the form of the Arab dhows that plied the arterial waterways of the ninth-century world ("An Ordinary Ship"). Such are the globalisms of the premodern world.

Early Globalism versus Globalization Today

Lest we in early global studies are accused of naivete, moreover, it is important to distinguish between early *globalism* and today's *globalization*—the specific name that has been attached to the complex processes that characterize our contemporary moment of the twenty-first century, and a name that is sometimes claimed by premodernists for the many forms of globality that have existed across the centuries, and even across millennia.

Scholars who assert that contemporary globalization is not new but exists on a continuum with the past, sans meaningful break, sometimes insist, for example, that the large trading networks of the premodern past are tantamount to globalization,[11] thus denying that the differences of speed, scale, intensity, digital immediacy, technological interconnectivity, and sheer density that characterize our contemporary moment have in fact shaped a specific new kind of globalism today, with a particular new kind of reality.

This is not the kind of exercise in retrieving modalities of globalism across the *longue durée* that we should pursue or endorse.[12] Responsible premodernists should acknowledge that technology makes a difference. A planet alive with social media, the Internet, cell phones, global positioning satellites, fiber optics, and supercomputers produces new outcomes materially different from a time when geographic distance forcibly delayed communication for months and years.

Even for the centuries of modernity, the compression of time and space experienced today, as David Harvey points out, is something new: the result of technological and material transformations of recent duration.

Globalization today points to the complex, often ironic, uneven and contradictory, political-sociocultural-economic outcomes produced by new technologies for which no premodern or early modern antecedents exist; to a post-Fordist, outsourcing, subcontracting, corporatization of the world where production regimes in speed-sensitive economies of flexible accumulation have no precedents in premodernity or early modernity; and to a compression of space-time that ends distance and shrinks the planet, condensing life and interaction to the point where a single event—in the entertainment industry, in business negotiations, or in MOOC pedagogy—can be experienced simultaneously by people in Bangkok, Rio de Janeiro, and Vladivostok; none of this has any premodern or early modern precedent.

Distance, too, no longer exercises the constraints of old on human activity: when a family can video chat instantly around the planet rather than wait for the next monsoon to bring letters and news by ship across the ocean, the world has shrunk in a way that has no precedent in earlier globalisms.

Therefore, even as we rejoice in recalling a declaration once made by Yo-Yo Ma that the Silk Road (really a braided network of several "silk roads," as Susan Whitfield's essay in this volume reminds us) is the "internet of antiquity" (qtd. in Keller), we should bask in the metaphor's resonance while putting aside any temptation to claim the ancient silk roads as evidence of a globalization that the internet signals for us today. The "internet" of the Silk Roads, we understand, is not the same internet that speeds social media, *Wikileaks*, *Reddit*, *8chan*, Anonymous, *Facebook*, *Twitter*, *Instagram*, *WhatsApp*, *Snapchat*, *TikTok*, or the Arab Spring.

Karimi merchants who plied the Red Sea and Indian Ocean trade in the mercantile capitalism of premodernity are not the same thing as a gargantuan corporate Microsoft or Apple outsourcing production and their supply chain to Foxconn, at the other end of the planet in the People's Republic of China, in today's post-Fordist global economy. Post-Fordist, just-in-time capitalism means that the production process itself is now fully global; supply chains are globalized; and the relations of production are globally dispersed.

Transmigrant labor's character, too, has changed with the advent of new technologies: transnational workers can now forge and maintain personal, social, and economic relations across time and space, in their homelands as well as in the host countries where they labor, connecting local and global in new manifestations of diasporic identity and attachments.

The globalism experienced by Guillaume Boucher, the Parisian goldsmith discovered by the Franciscan missionary William of Rubruck at Karakorum in the heart of the thirteenth-century Mongol Empire or made manifest in the lives of Iranian silk workers relocated to Yuan China by their Mongol masters thus differs not only in scale, but also in kind, from the globalization experienced by today's transmigrant labor.

To deploy the term *globalization* as a catch-all across deep geopolitical time is then to empty the term of the significance it bears as a political, economic, social, and cultural analysis of the contemporary present: a moment that manifests not only the distribution of late capitalism and its cultural logic across the world but also the global relations that characterize the flexible, reversible colonizations Alan Liu has correctly called "post-neo-colonialism."

Yet some world history scholars have sometimes suggested that the world has seen an "archaic globalization," a "proto-globalization," and a "modern globalization" in earlier eras.[13] In this kind of taxonomy, the word *globalization* functions largely to name an interconnectivity in earlier eras that links places and peoples around the world in networks of communication and mobility. Such networks were emplaced through trade, war, pilgrimage, missionary activity, diplomacy, and so forth, and occurred at the speed of camel or dhow, horse or wagon: at a pace, that is, quite different from the instantaneity of the Internet, fiber optics, or the electronic speed of global financial circuits—the definitive metaconditions undergirding the process we call globalization today.

Used in a general sense to describe the networks of the past, the term *globalization* is thus really a synonym for the interconnectedness of the world. What is usually intended, then, when premodernists apply the term *globalization* to mean a global interconnectedness, might be better referred to as the *globalisms* of earlier eras, preceding the *globalization* of today, and preceding, also, Europe's *colonial globality* in the era of the European maritime empires of the sixteenth through nineteenth centuries, before the decolonization movements of the twentieth.

To name the world's interconnectivity as forms of *globality*, or as the *globalism* of different eras, better retains a sense of the variety and character of the global connectivity of those earlier eras, without yoking all to a single relation with globalization today and forcing a resemblance. By attesting to the continuing usefulness of periodization in this way, the multiple globalisms of the past are not recruited for a chronology monolithically aimed at the endpoint of the contemporary present.

Just as we would want academic recognition of the existence of more than a single scientific or industrial revolution in the history of the globe, we should concomitantly be willing to afford recognition to our contemporary moment's own technological revolutions, with their particular imprint and signature on our time.

We thus see it is useful to retain and complexify the idea of periods and periodization, so as to honor the differences characterizing the diverse global eras of the deep past across centuries and millennia and to enable the modes and patterns of globality in different eras to be differentiated and disaggregated, so that all need not bear the one name of *globalization* (whether of an antique, archaic, proto-, premodern, or modern kind) in discussing the world's interconnectivity. Honoring the differential character of varied globalisms with attentiveness and recognition, rather than lining up the globalisms of the past as precursor-facsimiles of the globalization of the present, ensures that variety and difference are not collapsed into an invariant chronology issued by a calendar embedded in Western perspectival interests.

To be able to think and reason in this way, we need a form of early global studies that is self-conscious, critical, and analytical, rather than solely descriptive and summative. A critical early global studies also potentiates historiographies of the global that are attentive to histories-from-below, and microhistories—of women; enslaved people; peoples of alternative genders and sexualities; peasants; the old; the poor; the ill; the disabled; the powerless; and the nonhuman worlds of flora and fauna, climate and ecoscape—that can otherwise fall between the cracks of historical *grands récits*.[14]

A critical early global studies allows for the possible recovery of subaltern histories in the deep past to gain traction. It also initiates an academic revisionism that attests that globalism did not begin only when the West began to exercise maritime power, at the start of what became Europe's centuries of colonial globality, but was rather the cumulative, accretional result of the initiatives of ordinary people on the ground in multiple vectors of the world.

How to Use This Book

The question I was asked again and again in 2004 and after—why can't learning be more like this?—is a key reminder of the importance of teaching in efforts to transform the twenty-first-century academy. Alongside the necessity of new research and scholarship, transformation of how present and future generations see and understand the past requires tools, resources, road maps, ideas, and guidelines for classroom and online teaching.

This volume thus reprises, in book form, an expanded version of the teaching examples supplied by the instructional teams in the 2004 and the 2012–13 courses in Texas and Minnesota. Four of the original instructors—Denise A. Spellberg, Susan Whitfield, Gabriela Currie, and myself—also have essays featured here.

The contributions in the volume evince a variety of styles, formats, and approaches. To avoid an empire of style and monotonous homogeneity, contributors were not asked to hew to a single format in writing, just as they do not hew to a single format or style in teaching their courses. As a result, some contributors, like Kavita Mudan Finn and Helen Young, and Eva Haverkamp-Rott, have offered a full syllabus—contextualized and framed by an introduction that raises key questions and issues for students—that readers can import wholesale and immediately use in the classroom.

Yuanfei Wang, Derek Heng, and Lynn Ramey, among others, also offer week-by-week or section-by-section syllabi for classroom use.

Others, like Shahzad Bashir, Emma J. Flatt, Timothy May, Robert W. Barrett, Jr., and Elizabeth Oyler, Marci Freedman, and Kristen Collins and Bryan C. Keene, have narrativized their course content and teaching methods, discussing which materials they have found useful to highlight and what questions to ask, follow, and complicate as a course proceeds. Essays of this kind not only list texts and materials to use in teaching a course but also take the reader in detail through the contents and main issues to conjure with in the texts and materials they treat.

Yet others, like Susan Whitfield, lay out the problems and themes that animate their specialization and discipline and feature a variety of possible texts, images, and data for readers to pick through and selectively incorporate into their own courses, as they wish, or with which to devise brand new courses.

Some essays thus offer materials that are instantly ready for importation into any classroom right away. Others offer thoughtful suggestions of materials and guidelines that can be accommodated within ongoing courses, to vary one's teaching. An essay like Spellberg's on camels, or Wan-Chuan Kao's on hostelry, guides students on how to think about the animals or habitations that students ubiquitously encounter in literary, cultural, and historical texts. Yet others offer careful, detailed readings of texts with which instructors themselves might be unfamiliar or less familiar, enabling these texts to be added to any syllabus by a nonspecialist.

To encourage readers to add *Sundiata*, the epic of Mali, to their courses, for example, Michael A. Gomez offers guidelines for how the epic can be taught, as well as a bibliography and additional resources to supply background and increase understanding; a number of essays also point to the University of California at Berkeley website on *Sundiata*, which is directed at schoolteachers but is likely useful in higher education as well.

Virtually all the essays in this volume contain syllabi, sketched in outline, or described in narrative form, and a "Resources" section, compiled and organized by Colleen C. Ho rounds off the volume.

These essays, of course, treat a wide range of literatures and materials from many parts of the world: Africa, India, China, Southeast Asia, Mongolia, the Jewish diaspora, the Silk Roads, and the Persian and Arab worlds, along with a sprinkling of well-traveled European texts and materials.

Global stories that have traversed large geographic distances and transhistorical time, like the Alexander legend (treated by Adam Miyashiro and Su Fang Ng), the legend of Prester John (by Christopher Taylor, the director of a massive interactive digital database on the legend), and the *Thousand and One Nights* (by Arafat A. Razzaque and Rachel Schine), receive attention, as do themes, motifs, and cruxes—such as inns and habitations (by Kao), beasts of burden like the camel (by Spellberg), disease and disability (by Monica H. Green and Jonathan Hsy), and climate and the environment (by Jeffrey J. Cohen)—that repeat through many literatures in the world.

So popular are certain global stories, like the Alexander and Prester John legends, for teaching in different disciplines that they are mentioned in this volume more than once: the art historians Kristen Collins and Bryan C. Keene also consider both legends in their essay on manuscripts and illuminations.

This volume features the kinds of interdisciplinary approaches and content that seem most adaptable to and useful for coursework likely offered by MLA readers. For readers who want to show their students what the world looked like to its inhabitants located in various parts of the globe, there is an essay on mapping and cartography, coauthored by an authorial team of three specialists in European, Islamic, and Chinese representations of geographic space (Asa Simon Mittman, Karen Pinto, and Cordell D. K. Yee).

For those who find the investigation of soundscapes fruitful to their teaching of culture and literature, there is an essay on music by musicologists Lars Christensen and Gabriela Currie. An essay on manuscripts—always an important subject for medievalists—is coauthored by two curators of the J. Paul Getty Museum, Collins and Keene, who not only teach courses on manuscripts, but have curated a highly successful exhibition on the manifold worlds contained in manuscripts, an exhibition attended by over a million visitors to the Getty Museum. For those who have wondered whether it is possible to stitch together a course on theater with materials from either ends of the earth, a Japanologist (Elizabeth Oyler) and a Middle English scholar (Robert W. Barrett, Jr.) have produced a course they hope to teach together one day.

The importance of two new fields in our time—digital humanities, and the study of popular culture—is recognized in two essays. Lynn Ramey, the technical director of the Global Middle Ages Project, discusses the range of digital media and technology available online today for teaching early globalism; and a coauthored essay by Kavita Mudan Finn and Helen Young, who specialize in medievalism studies (the academic analysis of how postmedieval eras retrieve and present the medieval period) has the authorial pair showing readers how to teach a course on popular culture's retrieval of the global past, a course that shows instructors how to foreground the multiracial and the multicultural.

Despite its range, this volume does not span as many concentrations and disciplines as I would like: partly because of its original remit of a set number of words but also because of the unlikelihood that the materials and methods of certain fields—such as archeology, for instance—can readily be incorporated into the courses of MLA readers, who are likely to be scholars of literature, history, and cultural studies. The volume also has an implicit focus on written texts and images, or texts that eventually came to be set down in writing, in order for the book to be of greatest utility to an MLA readership.

To extend the range of interdisciplinary approaches and content important for the study of a Global Middle Ages beyond this volume, however, Susan Noakes and I are coediting forty titles in a Cambridge University Press Elements series on the Global Middle Ages (forty titles are our original remit, but we are enjoined to continue the series indefinitely as needed). Cambridge Elements are compact, born-digital studies that can embed video, audio, and images and are updatable on an annual basis by their authors. The first ten titles in the inaugural year of the series appear in 2021–22.

Unlike massive tomes of world history that are expensive to purchase for teaching, and have to be repurchased every few years as new editions appear, these compact studies are inexpensive, updated regularly, and can be customized by instructors for their own learning, classroom use, and research, and are discounted when purchased in a cluster.

An expansive series like the Cambridge Elements makes it possible to incorporate the work of archeologists, anthropologists, and other social scientists and scientists, and can feature cultures that are more reliant on oral, epigraphic, and other traditions than textual materials—including traditions from the Native American cultures of the Mississippi basin and Cahokia, for instance, or of those of Oceania and the Pacific worlds.

The Contributors and Their Essays

The contributors featured in this volume are as diverse and multifarious as their approaches, formats, and writing styles. They are literary scholars, historians, art historians, musicologists, museum curators, theater studies scholars, religious studies scholars, area studies scholars, cartography specialists, and digital humanists, and span all academic ranks from full professors with named professorships and endowed chairs to graduate students and independent scholars. Two deans, a program director, and a department chair are among their ranks.

Nearly half of the thirty-three contributors in the volume are scholars of color, representing several ethnoracial groups in the United States and from around the world, and two more are international scholars. I am proud of the fact that this is not a volume on globalism authored only by Caucasian scholars in the United States–United Kingdom academic circuit. Like their work, the contributors are cosmopolitan and global, with countries of origin in different parts of the planet, and they work in a plethora of languages and disciplines.

For the purpose of widening this volume's readership, all the contributors have been asked to write in English, even when their teaching and scholarship has been in other languages. In recommending texts to readers, they have also been asked to use translations in English as far as possible—though all are mindful of the pitfalls of translation—since most of the teaching they outline and courses they recommend in this volume are directed at undergraduate students. In their graduate teaching, of course, the contributors emphasize the use of original languages and are cognizant of the importance of language training and accreditation.

Finally, I share the objective of all the contributors to this volume: that you, the reader, can find ways to incorporate the worlds they know into your own teaching, and that, with your students, you too will find the Global Middle Ages an experiment in learning whose time has come.

Notes

1. On neomedievalism and neoconservatism, see Holsinger; Lampert. On race, see my *Invention of Race*.

2. A 2003 article in the *Chronicle of Higher Education* reports *The Guardian* quoting Charles Clarke, Great Britain's Secretary of Education at the time, declaring unctuously at University College, Worcester: "I don't mind there being some medievalists around for ornamental purposes, but there is no reason for the state to pay for them." While medievalists in the United Kingdom seemed stung by his condescending insult, they also seemed to flounder when attempting to argue for their work's importance. A medievalist from Cambridge University was quoted as falling back on an old academic vagueness, indignantly defending medievalists as "working on clarity and the pursuit of truth." Her lament that Clarke was "someone who doesn't understand what we do" touches on precisely the problem (Galbraith).

3. For detailed descriptions of the syllabus, the students, the problems that had to be overcome, and student conference papers and publications that resulted, as well as other details, see Heng, "Global Middle Ages" and "Experiment." Some of the thoughts and arguments in this introduction have appeared in these and other publications cited in the text and notes.

4. In the United Kingdom, Edinburgh University offers a master's degree in art history on the Global Middle Ages, and Birmingham University a PhD on Borders and Borderlands in the Global Middle Ages. In the United States, the University of Pennsylvania, the University of Minnesota, the University of Connecticut, the University of Texas, the Getty Museum, and Georgetown University, among other institutions, now have courses or programs, undergraduate and graduate, on a Global Middle Ages.

5. The three journals are *The Medieval Globe*, *Medieval Worlds*, and *The Journal of Medieval Worlds* (an older journal, *Medieval Encounters*, has concentrated in the past primarily on interfaith encounters, and primarily in the Mediterranean). Oxford University historians convened a series of workshops on the Global Middle Ages in 2011, and a conference in 2012. Among other venues, conferences on the Global Middle Ages have also been held at the University of Illinois, Urbana-Champaign (2012), the Eastern European University (2014), the University of Wisconsin-Madison (2015), the Medieval Association of the Pacific at the University of California-Davis (2016), Indiana University (2016), the University of California, Los Angeles (2016, in art history), the Getty Museum (2016), the University of Sydney (2016), and the University of Arizona (2014–17). The University of Sydney also created The Global Middle Ages Research Group, a Pan-Australian-New Zealand collaboration, in 2016.

6. In the United States alone, a half-million-dollar Mellon grant was awarded to the University of Minnesota, Twin Cities, for collaborative courses and teaching on the global in premodern and early modern studies; Texas received an NEH digital humanities grant shared with two other projects for training and workshops at the Institute for Computing in Humanities, Arts, and Social Sciences (I-CHASS) and supercomputing centers and a CLIR–Mellon grant for a postdoctoral fellow to create the MappaMundi platform and digital projects at www.globalmiddleages.org; and the University of California system awarded a large collaborative grant to a consortium of historians (at Berkeley, Santa Barbara, and Davis) for research projects, workshops, and a new journal published by the University of California Press: *The Journal of Medieval Worlds*. Oxford's Centre for Global History and Sydney University have also been awarded grants for research and conferences on the Global Middle Ages. Most recently, Vanderbilt University and the University of Colorado, Colorado Springs, were awarded a $250,000 NEH grant in 2022 to teach an immersive Global Middle Ages.

7. Our own projects on early globalism have been heralded by Cathy Davidson in *Academe* and Gayatri Chakravorty Spivak in *PMLA* (166) as new ways to undertake teaching, collaborative work, and reading in the twenty-first-century academy.

8. These are short-form summaries of long and complex arguments. For the long-form versions, see Heng, "Early Globalities" and "Ordinary Ship."

9. That poetic term, "deep time," is Wai Chee Dimock's, adapted from the physical sciences. The Medievalists of Color, an advocacy and activist group, have documented the rise of white supremacy and the alt-right in the United States in a series of blog posts, conference panels, and talks. For a representative sampling, see posts by Kim; and Lomuto. Graduate students are also doing their share to combat neoconservative extremism: at Columbia University, funded by a small Mellon grant, medievalist graduate students in the Art History and History departments have assembled a Medieval Toolkit to furnish the media with information and resources to combat the falsehoods and distortions retailed by the alt-right in public discourse about the premodern past.

10. It has been suggested, for instance, that in place of "the European Middle Ages," we might instead prefer to name the period before modernity "early Europe," "premodern Europe," "Europe (or Latin Christendom) of the twelfth, thirteenth, fourteenth centuries (inter alia)," alongside "modern Europe," "later Europe," "sixteenth-century Europe," "twenty-first-century Europe," and so on.

11. Even modern scholars make the mistake of conflating early globalism with globalization today. See, e.g., Behdad.

12. I have little room in this introduction to discuss Immanuel Wallerstein's world-systems models for the modern eras (*Modern World-System*), and partly adapted by Janet Abu-Lughod to the thirteenth- and fourteenth-century world. For a full discussion, see my *The Global Middle Ages: An Introduction.* One of the problems in world-systems' retrievals of globality is the carving up of the world through an optic of center-periphery relations, a schematic that can seem exclusionary, consigning certain zones of the world—like trans-Saharan Africa—to a status that overrecognizes the extraction of their natural resources and raw materials and underrecognizes their complex economic agency, thus reinforcing the impression of their underperformance relative to the all-important civilizational metropoles located elsewhere. The deck thus can seem stacked against the zones some scholars study, not only by the acknowledged metropoles of the global past but also through the terms adduced, and the definitions set in place, by world-systems models themselves. This emphasizes why we need a critical form of early global studies—precisely to allow us to recognize the stakes involved in various models and schematics of globalism. Wallerstein thoughtfully tries to add that "core" and "periphery" are terms intended to designate production processes, not particular zones, states, regions, countries, or polities (*World-Systems Analysis* 17), but in actual discussion, unfortunately, the distinction tends to be elided.

13. *Globalization* as a term used in a general way is exemplified by Wilkinson's essay in Gills and Thompson's anthology—a volume in which the editors themselves waver over how to define "globalization," "global history," and even something called "world consciousness" (Gills and Thompson 1–17). In another anthology on globalization and world history, "archaic" and "modern" "globalizations" of the eighteenth and nineteenth centuries are discussed by Bayly; Ballantyne conjures with "proto-globalization" and "modern globalization"; and Bennison considers "Western globalization" in the context of "Muslim universalism."

14. The digital projects at www.globalmiddleages.org thus assemble a kaleidoscopic early world in which viewers can immerse themselves, shorn of overarching grand narratives in which empires wax and wane, universal religions spread their mighty umbra around the world, regions rise and fall, or where world-systems models tell viewers what zones are "core" or "peripheral" ones.

Works Cited

Abu-Lughod, Janet L. *Before European Hegemony: The World System, A.D. 1230–1350.* Oxford UP, 1989.

Ballantyne, Tony. "Empire, Knowledge, and Culture: From Proto-Globalization to Modern Globalization." Hopkins, pp. 116–40.

Bayly, C. A. "'Archaic' and 'Modern' Globalization in the Eurasian and African Arena, ca. 1750–1850." Hopkins, pp. 45–72.

Behdad, Ali. "On Globalization, Again!" *Postcolonial Studies and Beyond*, edited by Ania Loomba et al. Duke UP, 2005, pp. 62–79.

Bennison, Amira. "Muslim Universalism and Western Globalization." Hopkins, pp. 73–98.

Davidson, Cathy N. "Strangers on a Train: A Chance Encounter Provides Lessons in Complicity and the Never-Ending Crisis in the Humanities." *Academe*, September–October 2011, www.aaup.org/article/strangers-train#.XUNHWS2ZPOQ.

Dimock, Wai Chee. *Through Other Continents: American Literature across Deep Time*. Princeton UP, 2006.

Galbraith, Kate. "British 'Medievalists' Draw Their Swords." *Chronicle of Higher Education*, 6 June 2003, www.chronicle.com/article/british-medievalists-draw-their-swords/.

Gills, Barry K., and William R. Thompson, editors. *Globalization and Global History.* Routledge, 2006.

Grewal, Inderpal. "Amitav Ghosh: Cosmopolitanisms, Literature, Transnationalisms." *The Postcolonial and the Global*, edited by Revathi Krishnaswamy and John C. Hawley, U of Minnesota P, 2008, pp. 178–90.

Harvey, David. *The Condition of Postmodernity.* Blackwell, 1990.

Heng, Geraldine. "Early Globalities, and Its Questions, Objectives, and Methods: An Inquiry into the State of Theory and Critique." *Exemplaria*, vol. 26, nos. 2–3, 2014, pp. 232–51.

———. "An Experiment in Collaborative Humanities: Imagining the World, 500–1500." *ADFL Bulletin*, vol. 38, no. 3, 2007, pp. 20–28.

———. "The Global Middle Ages." *Experimental Literary Education*, special issue of *English Language Notes*, edited by Jeffrey Robinson, vol. 47, no. 1, 2009, pp. 205–16.

———. *The Global Middle Ages: An Introduction.* Cambridge UP, 2021.

———. *The Invention of Race in the European Middle Ages.* Cambridge UP, 2018.

———. "An Ordinary Ship and Its Stories of Early Globalism: Modernity, Mass Production, and Art in the Global Middle Ages." *The Journal of Medieval Worlds*, vol. 1, no. 1, 2019, pp. 11–54.

Holsinger, Bruce. *Neomedievalism, Neoconservatism, and the War on Terror.* Prickly Paradigm, 2007.

Hopkins, A. G., editor. *Globalization in World History.* W. W. Norton, 2002.

Keller, Johnanna. "Yo-Yo Ma's Edge Effect." *Chronicle of Higher Education*, 23 Mar. 2007, www.chronicle.com/article/yo-yo-mas-edge-effect/.

Kim, Dorothy. "Teaching Medieval Studies in a Time of White Supremacy." *In the Middle*, 28 August 2017, www.inthemedievalmiddle.com/2017/08/teaching-medieval-studies-in-time-of.html.

Lampert, Lisa. "Race, Periodicity, and the (Neo-) Middle Ages." *Modern Language Quarterly*, vol. 65, 2004, pp. 392–421.

Liu, Alan. "The University in the Digital Age: The Big Questions." Keynote lecture, Digital Humanities: Teaching and Learning, Texas Institute for Literary and Textual Studies symposium, 10 Mar. 2011, liu.english.ucsb.edu/the-university-in-the-digital-age-the-big-questions-u-texas-austin/.

Lomuto, Sierra. "White Nationalism and the Ethics of Medieval Studies." *In the Middle*, 5 Dec. 2016, www.inthemedievalmiddle.com/2016/12/white-nationalism-and-ethics-of.html.

Pauketat, Timothy R. "The North American Middle Ages: Big History from the Mississippi Valley to Mexico." *Global Middle Ages*, www.globalmiddleages.org/project/north-american-middle-ages-big-history-mississippi-valley-mexico.

Spivak, Gayatri Chakravorty. "How Do We Write, Now?" *PMLA*, vol. 133, no. 1, 2018, pp. 166–70.

Wallerstein, Immanuel. *The Modern World-System I: Capitalist Agriculture and the Origins of the European World Economy in the Sixteenth Century.* Academic, 1976.

———. *World-Systems Analysis: An Introduction.* Duke UP, 2004.

Wilkinson, David. "Globalizations: The First Ten, Hundred, Five Thousand and Million Years." Gills and Thompson, *Globalization*, pp. 68–78.

Part I

Connectivities, Encounter, and Exchange

Geraldine Heng

The Literatures of the Global Middle Ages

Archaeologists tell us that sometime around the year 1000 CE an expedition of peoples from Greenland and Iceland took advantage of climate change, in what has been called the Little Climatic Optimum or the Medieval Warm Period, and crossed the Atlantic Ocean during the summer months to North America. There, they proceeded to build a settlement at L'Anse aux Meadows in Newfoundland, where over the years, the material record shows, they erected a complex of houses, smelted iron for tools and weapons, hewed trees, repaired ships, slept, socialized, threw away their trash, wove cloth, and did single-needle knitting. The presence of what might have been a child's toy hints that a new generation may even have been born there.[1]

Beyond that, the archeological record is silent. What these northern Europeans saw in the Americas, why they wanted to be there, what happened in their encounters with Native peoples: for worlding of that kind, we must turn to two literary-historical accounts in Old Norse known as the Vinland sagas.

Half a century before such transoceanic forays, an Arab scribe journeyed northward by land along caravan routes from Baghdad to the Volga with an embassy from the Abbasid Empire, headed for the king of the

Bulgars (*Saqaliba*), a vassal of the Abbasid caliph, who had asked for fiscal aid and instruction in the Muslim faith. The traveler from the caliphate, Ahmad ibn Fadlan ibn al-Abbas ibn Rashid ibn Hammad, gifts posterity with the earliest textual account of the Eurasian landmass, complete with details of weather and how time is experienced, and vivid portraits of the Turkic Orghuz and Patzinaks, the Khazars, the Bulgars, and the Rus. Shocked by habits of human hygiene and sexual mores he claims to have encountered for the first time, Ibn Fadlan nonetheless gazes on the aurora borealis with awe and recites the Quran a world away from Baghdad.

On another continent away from Eurasia and the Americas, the founding of the great empire of Mali and the global spread of Islam were embedded into African stories that were transmitted intergenerationally from griot to griot, by word of mouth, until a narrative coalesced in the form of the West African epic we now know as *Sundiata* (*Sunjata*). The Saharan worlds the epic evokes weave together multiple strands of local, regional, and global encounters until intricate stories about individuals, religious beliefs, forms of labor, gender relations, and political and military negotiations are pieced and fitted into narrative form.

Here, then, is why I teach early global literatures: they narrate with precision the intricate interconnectivity of the early world and are produced by a multifarious world and its peoples.

A tenth-century ship captain from Ramhormuz in Khuzistan, Buzurg ibn Shahriyar, vivaciously recounts what sailors have told him about Java and Malaya on the other side of the planet. Abu Zayd al-Sirafi, whose name tells us he was ensconced in Siraf in the Persian Gulf, compiles reports from merchants who plied the Indian ocean trade all the way to China, who tell of the mercantile communities resident there, gripe about the taxes, and are aghast at uprisings in the great port cities of the southern Chinese coast.

Students are deeply curious about these global literary texts, partly because such texts are not constructed as fiction or fantasy but offer themselves as accounts of how ordinary and extraordinary people lived their lives in deep historical time, made their way in their world, and came to understand the environments and the societies they encountered. For a teacher, these texts are an invitation to discuss the intermeshing of facticity and embellishment in the recovery of memory and in the making of narrative, especially when anonymous texts were cocreated by passing through many hands and miscellaneous agents in the course of being transferred intergenerationally across time.

What Is Premodern Global Literature, and Why Should We Teach It?

Global literature, it must be said, is not the same thing as *world literature*, though there are, of course, convergences. World literature courses typically amalgamate a miscellany of texts assembled to represent the many cultures and localities of the world—offering a snapshot of the world's literary creations in the form of best practices. The modus vivendi of world literature courses, when taught, thus requires compiling disparate texts plucked from many countries in many eras (sometimes across millennia) each of which represents a place, people, culture; or era, style, genre; and then, for organizational coherence, asks the instructor to stitch together connections between such texts—which could be as disparate as *Gilgamesh*, Pramoedya Ananta Toer's novels, or Basho's poetry—with a set of themes to connect them (perhaps attitudes to love?), or repeating tropes or motifs (birds as symbols?), generic conventions (realism? the lyric?), and so on.[2]

By contrast, global literatures of the kind I teach already arrive with a theme and connectedness: they thematize the interconnectivities—the globalism, if you like—of an early world. Whether through an account of humans crossing the Atlantic to create new habitations in coastal North America or a retelling of what happens when global Islam migrates to West Africa, the interconnectedness of peoples, cultures, and landscapes shimmers through the social relations, cities, and environments—the lived worlds—that these texts call forth for their audiences. Globalism itself becomes the prism through which audiences receive the worlds that are narrated for them. Literature of this kind thus globalizes in the very process of remembering, and narrating, globalized worlds.

Sometimes, the literature itself is globalized, as it is adopted, added to, changed, and recirculated by peoples in different cultures and societies across time. One example of literature like this is the cocreated tale of *Balaam and Josaphat*, the story of the Buddha's life that over the centuries turns into the story of two Christian saints, in the course of westward travel from India. A more famous example is the *Thousand and One Nights*, *Alf Layla wa-Layla* (also known as *The Arabian Nights*), similarly cocreated for a millennium and more, well into modern time. The example of *Balaam and Josaphat* suggests that *global literature* might not be the same thing as *travel literature* either. Sometimes the text—like this one—does not depict travel or travelers; sometimes the text itself travels and is the traveler, whereas the characters in it do not move around very much.

For those of us concerned with the dominance of eurocentrism in university curricula, an important reason to teach global literature is that by its very nature it loosens and uncenters the grip of the West, provincializing Europe avant la lettre by being produced elsewhere and awarding attention and significance to multifarious lives and places in the world's many vectors.

Most important, it is impossible to read premodern global literature without recognizing that for its texts, every place is the center of the world.

No person or polity in the epic of *Sundiata* considers Mali to be positioned on the periphery of a great world system whose economic and political center is hived elsewhere, not in Mali.[3] The magnificent city of Vijayanagar, the capital of the Indian empire of the same name in Kamaluddin Abdul-Razzaq Samarqandi's *Mission to Calicut and Vijayanagar*, is also the center of the world. Marco Polo and Rustichello da Pisa's Hangzhou—so far surpassing other premodern megalopolises in the immensity of its population, resources, and cosmopolitanism—cannot be anything but the center of the world.

But it is not just size, wealth, fame, or population that decides what gets to be the center of the world. For each text, the world turns on the axis of wherever its people and their concerns are: everywhere is the world's center. Global literature thus undercuts heuristic models like world-systems theories that systematize the world into centers and peripheries through economic or other rationales; dislocating, in the process, assumptions of cultural priority or superiority that might be extrapolated from such organizational schemas.[4] Wherever the people in a text are is always the center of the world.

It needs to be said from the outset that global literature can only be taught through translations. When David Damrosch leads a class through the *Epic of Gilgamesh*, no one is required first to acquire Sumerian or Akkadian. The sample global course I outline below features accounts in Old Norse, Mande/Mandingo, Arabic, Jawi-Malay, Uighur-Mongolian, Latin, Franco-Italian and Hebrew: it is unteachable except through translations.

Of course, since the advent of translation theory in the academy, we have been acclimated to understand that every translation is a rewriting and a re-creation, not a facsimile of the original that has been transposed into another language. A translation is never coidentical with the original text from which it is reconstituted (if, that is, an original text—an urtext—can even be determined, which is no sure thing in premodern literature).

But the success of many translations-as-re-creations—from the King James Bible to Seamus Heaney's *Beowulf*, to name just two famous examples in the West—argues for the value of translations that evince cultural sensitivity, nuance, and tact, as well as literary richness and genius. Therefore, rather than our seeing translation as something that must always detract from a text—and teaching in translation as disseminating imperfect, inexact replicas from which something is always askew or missing—we might see translation instead as the invitational dynamic that allows a text to acquire its fullest audience and its fullest ultimate meaning, as Damrosch urges (*How to Read* 5).

Without translations, premodern texts with few exceptions become isolated and localized, confined to their initial audiences who are distant in time and place. In particular, noncanonized premodern texts are easily ignored and forgotten—especially, let's face it, in contemporary literature departments saturated with a multitude of modern literatures and the alluring creations of popular culture and digital media. By contrast, circulating early literatures through translations conduces to ensuring their continuing reception across time, well into the future, and grants premodern texts long, rich afterlives.

In this way, translation can be seen as imparting "a new stage in a work's life as it moves from its first home out into the world" (Damrosch, *How to Read* 84). We might even say that teaching with translations performs—in a pedagogical register, within the four walls of a classroom, or online—a cultural exchange that parallels and recreates the exchanges that are often foregrounded and thematized in global texts. This is a positive outcome of the fact that there can be no courses on global literatures without translations.[5]

Organizing a Course on Global Literature

There are numerous ways to plan a course on global literature, and I urge continual trial and error experimentation. There are also innumerable texts that can be productively taught in such a course; my selection, designed to combine well-known with less familiar texts, is just one possible concatenation among many. All listed below are in English translation, but instructors located in French, German, Italian, Chinese, Japanese, and other language and literature departments should be able to substitute appropriate translations in their own vernaculars.

I currently teach the following: the Vinland sagas (paired with a novella called *The Ice Hearts*, which imagines how Native Americans might have seen the Greenlanders, as well as online exploration of the "'Discoveries' of the Americas" project on www.globalmiddleages.org); *Sundiata*, the epic of Mali (paired with online exploration of Mali in the Zamani Project at www.zamaniproject.org/, the Timbuktu manuscripts in the Tombouctou Manuscripts Project at www.tombouctoumanuscripts.uct.ac.za/, the Block Museum at Northwestern University's "Caravans of Gold, Fragments in Time" exhibit, and the Berkeley ORIAS web page "Sundiata"); Ibn Fadlan's *Mission to the Volga* (with clips from the film *The Thirteenth Warrior*); Ibn Jubayr's travels around the Mediterranean; selections from Usamah ibn Munqidh (with clips from *Kingdom of Heaven*); selections from the *Thousand and One Nights* (see *The Arabian Nights*); selections from Benjamin of Tudela; Buzurg ibn Shahriyar's *Book of the Wonders of India*; documents from the Cairo Genizah, including "The Slave of MS. H.6" (Ghosh); Amitav Ghosh's *In an Antique Land*; Kamaluddin Abdul-Razzaq Samarqandi's *Mission to Calicut and Vijayanagar*; Abu Zayd al-Sirafi's *Accounts of China and India* (paired with online exploration of the Tang-Belitung Shipwreck in the Asian Civilisations Museum, "The Tang Shipwreck"); selections from the *Malay Annals* (*Sejarah Melayu*); and from *The Secret History of the Mongols* (paired with the film *Mongol: The Rise of Genghis Khan*, directed by Sergei Bodrov); John of Plano Carpini's *History of the Mongols*; William of Rubruck's *Journey*; and Marco Polo's *Description of the World.*

This assemblage of texts for teaching early globalism is organized to track internodal connections of some importance to me. Other instructors, of course, will have different preferences. Some may elect texts that foreground how key religions weave the connective tissue of early globalism or how merchants' manuals and travel literature map traceries of goods, peoples, and encounters around the world. Others may emphasize international artistic exchanges visible in material objects depicted in texts, like fabric, dress, headgear, weapons, tableware; highlight texts that feature the spoor of disease, bacteria, and pandemics around the world; or follow the global pathways traced by food and drink, spices and cuisines in literature.

Yet others may seek out perennial favorites like Ibn Battuta's accounts of his world-traversing journeys, or the ever-popular Mandeville-author's fake ethnographic survey of the world. War as an animating force of globalism can feature a slew of texts from renowned epics to Crusade literature (now commonly taught since September 11, 2001) to literature on the Mongol invasions. A number of essays in this MLA volume offer literatures from China, India, Southeast Asia, and the Persianate, Islamicate, European, and African worlds for teaching; yet other essays in our volume offer content, and points of entry, from a variety of humanities and fine arts disciplines that can be readily intercalated into a global literature course.

Word constraints make it impossible to detail minutely the totality of ways I teach each and every global text listed in my syllabus. As a compromise, I offer some explicit guidelines for one text in particular, and schematic possibilities for teaching, in an interlinking way, a few other texts not discussed by the contributors of this volume.[6] For detailed approaches to teaching *Sundiata*, the *Thousand and One Nights*, Benjamin of Tudela's *Itinerary*, and the *Malay Annals*, I urge readers to consult the essays in this volume specifically treating those texts.

I begin a global literature course by asking students to imagine what would interconnect peoples, animals, plants, and organisms in an early world. We discuss climate, topography, and ecosystems; landmasses with forests, deserts, riverine systems, seas, and oceans as features that connect, not just divide; and human responses to these physical and environmental worlds. The time frame of our texts, loosely 500 to 1500 CE, allows us to reflect on the factitiousness of periodizing chronologies and question a Eurocentric time line traditionally called the "Middle Ages," neatly wedged between two eras thought to possess special authority—Greco-Roman antiquity and its so-called Renaissance. We consider how societies around the world in fact moved at different speeds, with global time being asynchronous, and with each part of the world developing its own vocabulary for how to name and organize its temporalities.

A quick survey of how humans organized their societies—for example, in the form of towns, cities, villages, hinterlands, ports, kingdoms, trade republics, feudal polities, nomad confederations, settler colonies, empires—leaves aside the question of differential economic systems for the moment, to be plumbed in greater detail when we read our texts. But we survey what drives the encounter of peoples and communities in early globalism—imperatives such as trade, commerce, and the ever-powerful profit motive; war, religious pilgrimage, international diplomacy, and politics; migrations, exile, exploration, even marriage—and I ask students to keep track of these and other animating factors as our texts accrue over the semester, so we have points of comparison around the world.

I like to organize courses around a geographic and spatial progression, so students see our literary itinerary moving us around the world. We begin in the West and end in the East—starting with short texts and gradually reading longer texts as the semester proceeds. Others, of course, may organize their courses differently, say, through chronological progression or thematic categories.

Encounters in the Classroom: Teaching the Vinland Sagas as Global Texts

At present, I begin with the Vinland sagas. Good translations of the Greenlanders' Saga and Eirik the Red's Saga abound (see *Eirik the Red, and Other Icelandic Sagas*; *The Norse Atlantic Saga*; *The Sagas of the Icelanders*; and *The Vinland Sagas*), and it seems apposite to initiate a transglobal reading journey by addressing a phenomenon with which students are already intimately familiar, one that profoundly conditions human life, including their lives: climate change.

Unlike the climatological exigency of our current moment in the Anthropocene, however, scientists tell us that the Medieval Warm Period around the end of the tenth century did not impact all parts of the world equally: Mediterranean latitudes were relatively unaffected, but for the circumpolar world of the North Atlantic, the difference of a few degrees made an ocean traversable in the summer months, with real economic and ethnological consequences for communities in encounter.

It is vital, of course, to furnish students with cultural and historical contexts to orient them in each set of texts. This requires beginning with how the naming system works in different cultures, since students will repeatedly encounter names and naming systems they will find alien and strange.

Because they are seldom fluent in the vocabulary of premodern literary categories, it's also necessary to survey the narrative forms they encounter, like Icelandic sagas, or epics, or chronicles, or biographies, or travel literatures incorporating marvels and wonders. This is an opportunity to discuss the complex mix of historicity and embellishment visible in saga narratives, as well as the interplay of memory, desire, convention, and the authorial, scribal, and editorial interventions that shape literary texts, including those offering themselves as historical accounts. It is also an opportunity to discuss what history and historiography mean for different eras and societies.

Classroom discussion should thus treat the tropes and conventions; gender relations; family relations; socioeconomic organization of Iceland and Greenland vis-à-vis Norway and feudal Europe or Latin Christendom; attestation of Christianity and its uneasy relations with a still-palpable pagan past; masculine vaunting, violence, outlawry, and stoic humor; treatment of the supernatural and the uncanny; and Norse-style colonization issuing from the accidental discovery of new lands, exile, and opportunism—this, and more, as seen in saga narratives. I also discuss Norse migrations and invasions, so students are able to situate the settler colonies established in North America against a historical backdrop of invasion and settlement across coastal northern Europe, continental northern and eastern Europe, and the Mediterranean.

Climate, as a starting point when we begin reading the texts, readily conduces to examining the ecoscapes and physical environments that decide what human habitations can be built, the societies that consequently form, and the types of economy that devolve, so that students see Iceland's stubby trees and Greenland's austere ecoscape driving the excitement the Greenlanders and Icelanders feel at their discovery of the lush, tall forests of the North American coast, replete with wild "wheat" and grapes, fish fat in tidal pools, and a weather so mild that livestock thrives even in winter.

This segues into a consideration of valuable, high-status, and luxury agricultural products, and enables students to understand why the first expedition to Vinland returns so triumphantly laden with timber and grapes—not commodities modern students usually consider scarce or important—thus determining future, repeated expeditions across the Atlantic.

At the same time, the animal products the settlers later acquire through barter trade with Indigenous peoples—the furs and pelts they garner in exchange for the drinks of milk and strips of red cloth they proffer the Natives—point toward the global markets for furs and valuable animal goods the settlers know exist, with Norway acting as their conduit to international emporia. The ease with which the colonists amass furs and skins also signals the sagas' awareness that the Natives themselves are not linked to the species of globalism the Europeans experience.

In this way, the theme of profit and commerce as a driving force in globalism can be usefully tracked in the Vinland sagas from beginning to end: from the resource extraction of forest products carried out by the first expeditions to coastal North America, through the episodes of unequal trade relations with Indigenous peoples, all the way to the very close, when

Thorfinn Karlsefni unloads his North American goods in Norway and is able to buy a family farm and homestead in Iceland for future generations—Glaumbær—a site that has been extensively excavated in the modern era, lending significant historicity to the claims made in the saga narratives.

The *Greenlanders' Saga* even buoyantly depicts Karlsefni making a handsome last profit by selling a ship's figurehead carved from North American wood (*mǫsurr*) for half a mark of gold, a small fortune. Transatlantic voyaging has made this enterprising Icelander a rich man, and an important one, lionized by the elites of Norway. He also gets to control the narrative: *Greenlanders' Saga* tells us that it is Karlsefni, the shrewd businessman-as-expedition-leader, more than anyone else, who is responsible for recounting the story of all the voyages to Vinland.

In this way, though students may begin the course by assuming, romantically, that love of adventure drives human exploration through the ages, surfacing the tissue of commercial motivations that power transatlantic encounters in the sagas is a non-naive way of answering that burning question animating all travel literatures: Why do people travel?

Fidelity to the texts prompts us to acknowledge that curiosity, and the desire for fame and reputation that adventure brings are also motivations cited in these sagas, but a concomitant recognition of the power of the profit motive is important because students will encounter again and again in the course of the syllabus the mercantile forces that drive early globalism and propel individuals to hazard life and limb in distant lands. As important, commerce and profit also substantially color the encounters with ethnoracial otherness depicted in the Vinland sagas and in many other texts, including Marco Polo's.

In the *Greenlanders' Saga* and *Eirik the Red's Saga*, the episodes depicting trade differ only in the trade commodity the settler colonists present to the Natives. In one saga, it is milk (which quickly evanesces in the body, the narrative notes with satisfaction, as the settlers reap the rich reward of furs and pelts in return); in the other saga, it is ever more paltry strips of red cloth.

The self-congratulation registered by the sagas in conveying the exploitative nature of the trade relations on the North American continent thus positions groups of childlike, naive Indigenous peoples who can be easily bilked by superior Europeans half a millennium before Columbus. For those who make it a point to follow the spoor of race relations in premodern global texts, it is therefore not just the sagas' depictions of Native physiognomy, faces, height, hair, and clothing alone that convey racialization in these texts, nor even the application of a pejorative name, *Skraelingar*, to the Indigenous: race-making proceeds even here in the group characterization of a people who are easily duped.

Twinned with the absence of business acumen that characterizes a people as living low on the evolutionary ladder of civilization is the depiction of the Indigenous as technological primitives. Both sagas insist on Native fascination with the settlers' iron and steel weapons, which manifest the superior technology of metallurgy, whereas the Natives themselves wield mere Stone Age weapons, long left behind in the dim European past. That the Natives are able to defeat the settlers with stone weapons is ignominious, of course, but the sagas nonetheless take care to insert into descriptions of their lost battles strategic face-saving vignettes about Native ignorance of, and awe at, the doomsday efficacy of metal weaponry.

Textual strategies of this kind can be tracked across all the texts of the syllabus to accrue a composite picture of how global literatures, in presenting encounters with the foreign and the alien, represent otherness. The Vinland sagas' strategy of dealing with Native others by emphasizing the primitivity of the locals is encountered again and again, with variations, through many cultural iterations in other texts.

In the tenth century, Ibn Fadlan represents the Turkic populations of the steppe as primitive and barbaric through their dreadful hygiene and sexual mores. In the thirteenth century, John of Plano Carpini and William of Rubruck do the same with the Mongols, and William adds fellow Christians—those of the Church of the East, also known as Nestorians, whom he deems heretics—to the list of the backward and barbarous.

In the fifteenth century, the supercilious Abdul-Razzaq—sent as ambassador by Shahrukh Mirza, the youngest son of Timur Lenkh ("Tamerlane" to the West), from Central Asia to the subcontinent of India, Al-Hind, and the court of Deva Raya III in the kingdom of Vijayanagar—is appalled by the seeming polytheism of Hindu India, which appears barbarous to his monotheist eyes, even as those eyes are involuntarily bedazzled by the incomparable art and architecture of the polytheists.

We see that the premodern West has no monopoly on Orientalism, when the emissary from Central Asia blithely conjures up South Asia as an object of knowledge against which to define the superior cultural identity of the Timurid Empire that is his home. The ambassador from Samarkand pronounces on South Asians as "[n]aked blacks with loincloths" who are "every ill-proportioned black thing" (Kamaluddin Abdul-Razzaq

Samarqandi 305)—one Asiatic empire gazing on and patronizingly defining another.

A question students can therefore be asked, across all the encounters staged by the syllabus is: Do people only admire, in the other, what they admire in their own culture? This leads logically to follow-up questions: Is cultural otherness an unbridgeable gulf, across which the only structure of connection that can be built is a mirror, through which otherness is transformed into the familiar and the same? Can alterity be acknowledged and respected, if the gazer has no familiar point of reference by which to understand what the gaze falls on?

As a counterexercise, I also have students identify in global literatures the possible existence of potential bridges—of however fantasmatic or fleeting a kind—across differences in global encounter. Differences make up the narrative matrix in premodern texts that thematize encounter and, in order not to enact a pedagogical trajectory in the classroom that totalizes the impossibility, ever, of discovering genuine intercultural sympathy and connectivity across all the global interconnections the texts feature—which would be an irony indeed—it is helpful to ask what does connect people, interculturally, across the panorama of differences encountered, again and again, in these texts?

In Ibn Fadlan's account, a resonant moment of connection occurs when his Quranic recitation is admired by his steppe audience for its beauty and majesty—forming an aural bridge across the chasm between the culture of the Abbasid Empire and the cultures of the steppe. Beauty, however, whether of a cultural or a natural kind, is not easily to be had without a recognition that mediatory layers of interpretation intervene.

When Ibn Fadlan gazes on the beauty and majesty of the aurora borealis, what he sees in the glorious panorama of lights are images of shadow warriors in battle. His hosts, the Bulgars, concur with his figural interpretation of a natural phenomenon—they, too, see in these lights warriors in battle, but they see jinn, not humans, fighting. Here, it is bellicosity, not shared aesthetic wonder, that forms another point of convergence across difference and global interconnectedness.

As limited as these kinds of cultural convergences may be, they rescue pedagogy in the classroom from an unremitting emphasis that might produce existential despair in a student.[7] Interspersing the immoderate ethnoracial pronouncements uttered by Abdul-Razzaq, the ambassador from the Timurid Empire in his account of Vijayanagar, we also find expressions of awe at the intricate complexity of temple carvings in Mangalore and at the beauty of flowers, cypresses, and plane trees that surround a temple there.

The ambassador from Samarkand appreciates beauty, opulence, displays of wealth, craftsmanship, and skilled artisanry. Most striking of all is his resounding praise of female beauty. Unused to women dancers and performers in his own cultural *habitus*, he is enchanted by the supremely talented young women acrobats and dancers who perform at the lavish, three-day imperial festival in Vijayanagar that he documents in fascinated detail.

That women constitute a node of convergence between cultures in encounter, over and over in global literature texts, will not surprise many. In his twelfth-century peregrinations around the Mediterranean, Ibn Jubayr—that pious scholar from Granada who offers vivid portraits of crusader cities and ports juxtaposed against the vanished glories of old Islamicate cities—is enraptured by the resplendent beauty and finery of a Latin Christian European bride during her nuptial procession through the city of Tyre: a vision so ravishing it causes the traveler to exclaim out loud for divine protection against the seductions of enemy cultures and their female representatives. It seems that figures of women in these global texts situate portals to cultural seduction. Ask students what they make of this.

The *Greenlanders' Saga*, too, enacts an intercultural connection accomplished through women that momentarily suspends the greed and bellicosity of the men, with their unequal trade and their pitched battles. Two women meet in a domestic setting at the home of Gudrid Thorbjarnardottir, Karlsefni's wife, who is sitting by the door of her home, rocking her infant child. An unknown woman appears in the doorway, a fleeting exchange of words takes place between the two women, and, just as Gudrid hospitably gestures to the newcomer to sit, more belligerence by the men outside produces a loud commotion and causes the visitor to vanish.

However we might interpret this episode—and I interpret it as a brief, interstitial exchange between a Native American woman and a Norse European woman—we should ask students the following questions: Why does imagining alternatives to war, violence, and killing and to insidiously unequal trade relations require the narrative to stage women specifically? What is gained by staging domesticity, and the intimate environment of a home, as the ground of intercultural encounter? Why is there an infant in the picture—what is made possible by staging children in settings where otherness is encountered?

This is an opportunity to discuss the burden of symbolic signification that women and children bear for cultural systems across the eras—why the vilification of Jews in medieval Europe obsessively fixated for centuries on the lie that Jews mutilated and slaughtered Christian children; and why, even today, a woman in hijab or combat fatigues rouses strong affective responses in so many cultures.

In every text students encounter in the syllabus, women form a symbolic and figural nexus within a sociocultural system that bears close analysis. In the West African epic of *Sundiata*, the forces of globalism are dramatically palpable in how the arrival of Islam has reconfigured traditional identities, occupations, and roles in Mali—the scholarship of Michael Gomez and others has shown—as old ancestral religions are displaced by new, global Islamic forces reshaping society.

Dramatically, the changing positions of women under this form of globalism relegate the women in the epic to roles as sorceresses and mothers, but the retention of supernatural abilities by many women in the epic remains a way of acknowledging the countering power, still, of older systems that have yet to be fully replaced. Owing his life and survival, as well as his ability to overcome his chief enemy in the battlefield, to the women in his life, the hero Sundiata and the narrative of Mali's imperial formation perform their story arcs by a symbolic evocation of a residual tracery of power accruing to women. Ask students this: Why women?

Children are also a key part of the symbolic apparatus on which cultural narrations depend. In the Vinland sagas, the Native Americans the Greenlanders and Icelanders meet resoundingly thrash the outnumbered settlers in pitched battle, forcing the recognition that there is no safety in Vinland (or in steel weapons) and mandating retreat across the sea. But in *Eirik the Red's Saga*, a symbolic victory of sorts is snatched when the colonists successfully abduct and kidnap two Native boys, whom they carry back home to northern Europe with them. These young human prizes, as valuable in their own way as North American furs, pelts, grapes, timber, and burls, are forcibly Christianized, taught Norse, and become Native informants who transmit information about their societies, lands, and cultures.

If depriving Native American society of two of their children is a satisfaction that *Eirik the Red's Saga* registers, we should not hastily assume that symbolism is the only work the saga performs in reporting gains derived from the transatlantic encounters exemplifying early globalism. Scientists today have discovered a shared gene element, the C1e gene element, that is only found in Icelanders and Native Americans and not shared by any other ethnoracial groups in the world. Although scientists rightly hesitate to make conclusive extrapolations from this strange genetic inheritance, we can see the value of teaching early global literatures from this small piece of genetic evidence alone. Be sure to intercalate evidence like this—from DNA science, archeology, art, music, cartography, or other disciplines—into classroom discussions of literary narratives, to complexify the reception by students of these early global literatures.

Teaching Nodes of Interconnection within and among Global Texts

I end this essay with a brief list of broad questions and issues that can be used to scaffold classroom discussion of early globalism in a global literature course. In the Cambridge University Press Elements series in the Global Middle Ages that Susan Noakes and I are editing, there will be one Element apportioned to global literature, and there I will offer detailed guidelines, akin to the guidelines for the Vinland sagas above, for teaching several texts listed in my syllabus.

Meanwhile, here are ten questions and issues to consider:

1. What does globalism look like in a given text? Not all global texts feature travel or depict individuals from different places in direct, interactive encounter. But global religions like Islam, Christianity, and Buddhism set in motion internationalizing forces that have a discernible footprint in culture and society. Literary texts show us that globalism in the form of a religion's arrival hybridizes local cultures; syncretizes old practices with new ones; reconfigures social roles, occupations, and human relations; and links the local and the regional with larger worlds beyond. In similar fashion, languages, too, perform globalizing functions that can be traced and discussed in literature. Trace the globalism of texts that themselves have done the traveling by being cocreated across the world and across time.
2. How is the unknown represented in contexts of global encounter? How are otherness and difference represented? Are there repeating strategies of representation across disparate texts and eras? Do the representations harden into race-making and racialization? into versions of Orientalism? Does "Orientalism" in these texts also signify the Orient gazing on the Orient, as seen in Abdul-Razzaq's commentary

on South Asia, or the Orient gazing on the Occident, as seen in Ibn Fadlan's contemptuous disgust at the unhygienic way the Rus wash themselves? Is there such a thing as "Occidentalism"? If so, what does that tell us about a concept like Orientalism, or premodern processes of racialization, as we critically survey encounters across the globe? Note that Orientalism encompasses modalities of othering that can render the other as not only uncivilized and savage but also exotic, luxurious, opulent, sensuous, lavish, and self-indulgent.

3. Follow the trail of goods, services, commodities, and money to see the pathways of regional and global interconnectivity among material objects, foodstuffs, currency, and artistry. The Mongols moved skilled artisans around the world, so that William of Rubruck finds a Parisian goldsmith, Guillaume Boucher, unironically creating an ornate, European-style silver drinking fountain at Karakorum, in the heart of the Mongol Empire. Sundiata's sister Kolonkan is recognized as someone from distant Mali because of the produce she buys—Baobab leaves—in the marketplace at Mema. The Genizah documents show the Jewish merchant Abraham ben Yizu sending cardamom from India to North Africa through his commercial agent and slave, and ordering household goods in return—including a stone frying pan—from Cairo. Scaling outward, from individual objects in texts, we find international trade, trans-Eurasian military campaigns, and the routes of continental exile webbing the world.
4. Do climate and ecoscapes elicit types of livelihood; styles of habitation; specific diets; or attitudes toward animals, plants, or the elements that emplace internodal forms of comparison around the world? *The Secret History of the Mongols* tells us that the totemic ancestors of the Mongol race were a grey wolf and a fallow deer: Do the mythologies of other nomad systems also feature primordial animal forebears? Why? Do sedentary cultures respond to nomad cultures across the globe in similar ways? What do sedentary cultures around the world share? What do nomad cultures across the world have in common? How does each kind of civilization depict the other? Consider bioglobalities: the track of disease and pandemics, animals and plants around the world through the interactions of nomad societies and sedentary societies.
5. Examine the roles of women across all the global texts taught: Are there similar ways that women are treated? What do women's roles reveal of disparate societies around the globe? How are children

treated? How are the old treated? How are enslaved people and captives treated? What roles do animals play? What is the response to nature? Consider sexuality and sexual mores, customs and behavior, family relations, birth and death rituals, ethical and value systems.

6. Consider the meaning of particular colors and their significance: for example, red in the Vinland sagas; blue in the Mediterranean; white in *The Secret History of the Mongols*. Is the purpose of color to protect, celebrate, symbolize vital relations? Consider the meaning of *directionality* in different texts: which directions are feared (because enemies issue from those directions) or revered (because sacred locations, shrines, or holy books are sited there)? On a microscale, consider how and where openings in dwellings are sited in different cultures. On a macroscale, consider the different directions world maps are oriented, and why.
7. What constitutes treasure in a society? What possessions and gifts are treasured, and why? John of Plano Carpini and William of Rubruck show us that cloth acts as a medium of currency in Eurasia, and that, for Mongol society, rich textiles like silk and brocade are treasure. For nomad societies, wealth can be measured by the numbers of animals possessed. How does the gifting of treasured goods express power relations, aesthetic pleasure, and individual and group identity? Compare and contrast what leaders give retainers across different sociocultural systems. Compare gift economies with tributary economies.
8. Compare political and economic systems: consider the ownership of land, animals, and resources (including environmental features like oases, grazing lands, forests, mines, as well as built landscapes like cities, ports, hinterlands); structures of leadership, loyalty, and obligation; socioeconomic organization (homesteads, settler colonies, republics, kingdoms, empires); rulership and diplomacy; international relations. Compare the depiction of global cities, such as Vijayanagar in Abdul-Razzaq's account, Hangzhou, in Polo and Rustichello's, and the Islamicate cities of the Mediterranean in Ibn Jubayr's.
9. Compare the arts across different societies: Why do some communities invest in fabric, whereas others admire sculpture and statuary? Does music play a social, religious, or political function? Can motifs or patterns be traced in stories or objects transported across the world? What kinds of buildings are mentioned in a text, and why? What kinds of festivals are described, and what do they celebrate? Are there commonalities to all celebrations? How do the food, drink, spices,

herbs, and cooking styles in a society characterize that society and its relations to other societies?

10. Last of all is also the first question of all: How do the world's geographic zones come into contact with one another? Consider wars of invasion at all scales, whether of a religious kind (Crusade or counter-Crusade, religious expansionism) or of a secular kind (raiding, colonization, empire formation); the news and reports issued by traveling pilgrims, diplomats, and missionaries (the Beijing-born Rabban Sauma in the Latin West; Franciscans and Dominicans in Asia and Eurasia); and the assiduous efforts of merchants and traders, sailors and professional seafarers to add to local, regional, and international knowledge of the physical, cultural, and social geographies of the known worlds.

Above all, do not be afraid to experiment, and to undertake incremental learning through trial and error, as you and your students make your way across the terra incognita of the global literature classroom. We, and the academy, have nothing to lose but our provincialism.

Notes

1. There were likely several expeditions to North America. This essay's length restrictions make it impossible to annotate the discussion of the Vinland sagas in detail. Please consult chapter 5 of my *The Invention of Race in the European Middle Ages* for a detailed discussion and comprehensive bibliography on the excavations and the sagas.

2. An anonymous reviewer importantly reminds us that world literature anthologies like the Norton have done yeoman's service for many years in serving those who wished to teach less Western-centric courses, even if the remit of such anthologies is often a mélange of largely modern literatures supplemented by some premodern examples. Damrosch's edited MLA Options for Teaching volume, *Teaching World Literature*, has been important in similar ways.

3. Mali is in fact bypassed altogether in the seven world systems sketched by Abu-Lughod in her quasi application of Wallerstein's world-systems theory to the thirteenth- and fourteenth-century world. Although Abu-Lughod's study remains invaluable, its neglect of Saharan Africa's worlds means that Mali isn't even located on the periphery of any of the seven world systems the study proposes. For a detailed discussion of Wallerstein, Abu-Lughod, and world-systems analysis, see my *The Global Middle Ages: An Introduction* (40–53).

4. Wallerstein's world-systems theory was initially formulated as a critique of capitalism and focused only on the modern world. Indeed, Wallerstein thoughtfully reminds us that "core" and "periphery" in his system of naming were intended to designate production processes, not particular zones, states, countries, regions, or polities (17). As the scholarship that has deployed his world-systems

theory has amply shown, however, the distinction tends to be elided in actual discussion. See note 12 in my introduction to this volume and my *The Global Middle Ages: An Introduction* (51–52) for fuller elaborations.

5. This proactive view of translations as necessary classroom resources applies principally to undergraduate teaching. Lest it is not blazingly obvious, I am not at all suggesting that graduate education in premodern studies—and especially global studies—should cease the imperative of teaching premodern languages. Moreover, it is also important to acknowledge, in translation projects, the untranslatability of certain concepts, formulations, or configurations of perspective, style, and meaning in some literary texts. Acknowledging the presence of the untranslatable, of course, should not mean we jettison translations altogether and abandon the teaching of global literatures unless undergraduates are able first to acquire a dozen premodern languages.

6. Susan Noakes and I are editing the Cambridge Elements in the Global Middle Ages: a series of concise, born-digital studies that can embed video, audio, images, and digital applications of various kinds and are updatable annually. Forty studies are currently planned (though the series is indefinitely expansible)—including one on global literatures, in which I will offer in detail teaching guidelines for a number of the literary texts I list in this essay.

7. When I taught this global literature course at Yale-NUS College in Singapore in fall 2018—a global location, with students of different races who were mostly not North Americans, and who possessed different languages and cultural perspectives from my students in the United States—one especially astute and sensitive student asked in despair, at the end of the semester: "Is there no hope, then? These othering processes have been taking place for hundreds of years! Will it always be like this?" I resolved never again to evoke hopelessness through the kinds of totalizing critique to which many of us in the academy are accustomed.

Works Cited

Abu-Lughod, Janet L. *Before European Hegemony: The World System, A.D. 1250–1350.* Oxford UP, 1989.

Abu Zayd al-Sirafi. *Accounts of China and India.* Edited and translated by Tim Mackintosh-Smith. Kennedy and Toorawa, pp. 4–161.

The Arabian Nights. Translated by Husain Haddawy, W. W. Norton, 1990.

The Arabian Nights. Selected and edited by Daniel Heller-Roazen, translated by Husain Haddawy, Norton Critical Edition, W. W. Norton, 2010.

Benjamin of Tudela. *The Itinerary of Benjamin of Tudela: Critical Text, Translation and Commentary.* Edited and translated by Marcus N. Adler, H. Frowde, 1907.

Buzurg ibn Shahriyar. The Book of the Wonders of India*: Mainland, Sea, and Islands.* Edited and translated by G. S. P. Freeman-Grenville, East-West Publications, 1981.

"Caravans of Gold, Fragments in Time at the Block Museum of Art." *Vimeo*, vimeo.com/307108617.

Damrosch, David. *How to Read World Literature.* 2nd ed., Wiley-Blackwell, 2018.

———, editor. *Teaching World Literature.* Modern Language Association of America, 2009.

de Rachewiltz, Igor, editor and translator. *The Secret History of the Mongols: A Mongolian Epic Chronicle of the Thirteenth Century.* Brill, 2004. 2 vols.

"'Discoveries' of the Americas." *Global Middle Ages*, www.globalmiddleages.org/project/discoveries-americas.

Eirik the Red, and Other Icelandic Sagas. Translated by Gwyn Jones, Oxford UP, 1961.

Ghosh, Amitav. *In an Antique Land: History in the Guise of a Traveler's Tale.* Granta, 1992.

———. "The Slave of MS. H.6." *Writings on South Asian History and Society*, edited by Partha Chatterjee and Gyanendra Pandey, Oxford UP, 1993, pp. 159–220. Vol. 7 of Subaltern Studies.

Gomez, A. Michael. *African Dominion: A New History of Empire in Early and Medieval West Africa.* Princeton UP, 2018.

Heng, Geraldine. *The Global Middle Ages: An Introduction.* Cambridge UP, 2021.

———. *The Invention of Race in the European Middle Ages.* Cambridge UP, 2018.

Ibn Battuta. *The Travels of Ibn Battutah.* Introduction by Tim Mackintosh-Smith, translated by H. A. R. Gibb and C. F. Beckingham, Pan Macmillan, 2002. Abridged from the Hakluyt Society's four volumes.

Ibn Fadlan, Ahmad. *Mission to the Volga.* Edited and translated by James E. Montgomery. Kennedy and Toorawa, pp. 165–297.

Ibn Jubayr. *The Travels of Ibn Jubayr.* Translated by Roland J. C. Broadhurst, reprint ed., Goodwood, 2008. Originally published by Jonathan Cape, 1952.

John of Plano Carpini. *History of the Mongols. Mission to Asia*, edited by Christopher Dawson, U of Toronto P, 1980, pp. 3–76. Medieval Academy Reprints for Teaching.

Kamaluddin Abdul-Razzaq Samarqandi. *Mission to Calicut and Vijayanagar. A Century of Princes: Sources on Timurid History and Art*, translated by W. M. Thackston, Aga Khan Program for Islamic Architecture, 1989, pp. 299–323.

Kennedy, Philip F., and Shawkat M. Toorawa, editors. *Two Arabic Travel Books.* New York UP, 2014. Library of Arabic Literature.

Kingdom of Heaven. Twentieth Century Fox, 2005.

Mongol: The Rise of Genghis Khan. Warner Brothers, 2008.

The Norse Atlantic Saga. Translated by Gwyn Jones. Oxford UP, 1986.

Polo, Marco, [and Rustichello of Pisa]. *Marco Polo:* The Description of the World. Edited and translated by A. C. Moule and Paul Pelliot, Routledge, 1938. 2 vols.

———. *Marco Polo:* The Description of the World. Translated by Sharon Kinoshita, Hackett, 2016.

The Sagas of Icelanders: A Selection. Translated by Keneva Kunz, Penguin 2001.

Sejarah Melayu or Malay Annals. Introduction by R. Roolvink, translated by C. C. Brown, Oxford UP, 1970. Oxford in Asia Historical Reprints.

"Sundiata." Berkeley ORIAS, UC Regents, U of California, Berkeley, 2021, orias.berkeley.edu/sundiata.

Sundiata*: An Epic of Old Mali.* Retold by Djeli Mamoudou Kouyaté, translated into French by Djibril Tamsir Niane, translated into English by G. D. Pickett, Longman, 2007. Longman African Writers.

Sunjata*: A New Prose Version.* Retold by Djanka Tassey Condé, translated by David Conrad, Hackett, 2017.

"The Tang Shipwreck." *Global Middle Ages*, www.globalmiddleages.org/project/tang-shipwreck.

The Thirteenth Warrior. Touchstone Pictures, 1999.

Usamah ibn Munqidh. *The Book of Contemplation: Islam and the Crusades.* Translated by Paul M. Cobb, Penguin, 2008.

The Vinland Sagas: The Norse Discovery of America. Translated by Magnus Magnusson and Hermann Pálsson, Penguin, 1965.

Wallerstein, Immanuel. *World-Systems Analysis: An Introduction.* Duke UP, 2004.

William of Rubruck. *The Journey of William of Rubruck. Mission to Asia*, edited by Christopher Dawson, U Toronto P, 1980, pp. 89–220. Medieval Academy Reprints for Teaching.

———. *The Mission of Friar William of Rubruck: His Journey to the Court of the Great Khan Möngke, 1253–1255.* Edited by Peter Jackson and David Morgan, translated by Jackson, Hakluyt Society Publications, 2009.

Susan Whitfield

Stories of the Silk Roads

Teaching the Silk Roads might seem daunting, but I approach it as an opportunity to challenge persistent ideas about the major players and influences in the story of the global Middle Ages by introducing often underrepresented cultures, showcasing their importance and their influences. Indeed, many of the other essays in this book could easily be incorporated into Silk Road courses.

Teaching the Silk Roads need not involve knowledge across all the geographic or chronological spread but can be based on quite simple story lines such as, for example, discussion of a single object, person, or event. There are now many more resources available to bring this within reach of every educator, from the schoolteacher to the professor. I hope this essay will encourage wider teaching of this subject and its incorporation into existing courses. The resources cited below and in the special section at the end of this volume are not intended for those wanting to know the nuances of the latest academic debates but are chosen as accessible and reliable overviews or discussion pieces. I have also chosen works overwhelmingly in English.

With such a broad scope, the risk in teaching the Silk Road is trying to cover too much and sowing confusion rather than curiosity. For this reason, a thematic approach based on the core of the Silk Road concept—trade and interaction—is how I usually approach the subject, whether giving a public lecture or teaching students. Below I suggest a number of such themes, but first there is the concept of the Silk Road itself.

Defining the Silk Road

Any Silk Road lecture or course will start with a discussion, even if brief, of what is meant by the "Silk Road" (or "Roads"). As the concept has become widespread, and with the adoption of the term by China for a modern political and economic program, I find that students come with existing ideas, some useful and some restricting. Discussing these can provide a useful way into this topic. Alternatively, providing a broad definition at the start and then using the classes to explore the definition is another possible approach. Personally, I find it helpful to give a definition so as to challenge any misconceptions from the start. I suggest something like the following:

> The Silk Roads are a system of substantial and persistent overlapping and evolving interregional trade networks across Afro-Eurasia by land and sea during the first millennium CE, trading in silk and many other raw materials and manufactured items—including, but not limited to, slaves, horses, semiprecious stones, metals, musk, medicines, glass, furs—and resulting in movements and exchanges of peoples, ideas, technologies, faiths, languages, scripts, iconographies, music, dance, stories, and so on.

There are a number of resources that can be used to unpack this definition. For the origins of the term, very much linked to European imperial history, see Tamara T. Chin's "Invention" and Daniel C. Waugh's "Richthofen's 'Silk Roads.'" For how the term has come to be used over the twentieth century and its usefulness see James Millward's *The Silk Road* and my "Was There a Silk Road?" and the introduction to *Life along the Silk Road*. Given that Richthofen's adoption of the term was closely linked to his looking at routes for a trans-Eurasian railway, this can also tie into a discussion of the Belt-Road Initiative and how it compares—and differs—from a concept of a historical "Silk Road." For this, see my "Inscribing and Expanding the Silk Roads" and Emmanuel Lincot and Arnaud Bertrand's "Anciennes et nouvelles 'routes de la soie.'"

The importance—or otherwise—of silk and trade is another opportunity for discussion, with arguments instead for a "Paper Road" by

Jonathan Bloom ("Silk Road"). Valerie Hansen's *The Silk Road: A History* argues that there is little evidence of significant long-distance trade on the eastern Silk Roads. For a summary and response to this, see my "On the Silk Road: Trade in the Tarim." Although there were no maps of the Silk Roads as such, maps are essential to teaching the Silk Roads. In terms of historical political maps, I find Thomas Lessmann's online history maps invaluable (www.worldhistorymaps.info). But I tend not to use detailed political maps for most teaching, as they introduce numerous political regimes unfamiliar to most students. These can prove distracting when looking at the geography—much of which might also be largely unfamiliar to many (see below). I recommend selecting a clear overall map and showing it frequently or giving it as a handout. There are numerous poor ones available which perpetuate the clichés of the Silk Road discussed below, so it is important to choose carefully. Downloadable maps showing routes are given in the Resources section of this volume. Mapping is one of the themes discussed below.

Challenging Misconceptions

The Silk Road now comes along with a baggage of misconceptions that need addressing. I think it is important to make clear that there was no "Silk Road" as such: this is a modern concept that we use to bring together events that spanned a broad range of space and time. It can be compared and contrasted, for example, to terms like *medieval* or *Middle Ages.*

A dichotomous or binary approach has often been taken to the history and geography of this region: China/Rome, East/West, steppe/cultivated, barbarian/civilized. This is diminishing but still permeates much scholarship. The approach has the effect of squeezing out the in-between, and the history and geography of Central Asia are, in many ways, those of the in-between places and peoples. (For critiques of this approach, see Lieberman; and Whitfield, "Expanding Silk Road," "Inscribing," "On the Silk Road," "Perils," "Under," "Was.")

There are several ways of addressing these dichotomies. For instance, consider the supposed steppe-cultivated division (see below under geography and ecology). The debate about the usefulness or otherwise of the term *nomad* has been around for a long time (see, e.g., Humphrey and Sneath). More recent discoveries by Spengler and colleagues have shown the importance of agriculture among nomadic pastoralists and their role in spreading crops across Eurasia, thus challenging lazy dichotomies.

I also find it useful to have class discussions on why a certain culture is defined as barbarian/other by another culture, by looking at major Silk Road empires such as Rome, Sassania, and China. These cultures all built defensive walls, and, given the topicality of walls today, this can form an interesting focus. See my *Silk Roads* for images and captions on the walls, and Arthur Waldron for a critique of the idea of a single Chinese wall intended primarily to act as a barrier (rather than as a border). There is plenty of scope for comparison with the modern world's attitudes toward migrants and refugees. The legend of Gog and Magog provides an interesting case study, as it appears in Jewish, Christian, and Islamic traditions; involves wall-building to keep out the so-called barbarian; and takes the story back to Alexander the Great. I summarize this and Sallam's mission to find the walls and their gates in *Life along the Silk Road* (129–30). For a detailed account, see E. J. van Donzel and Andrea Schmidt. There are many images of wall building from medieval manuscripts available online.

Some more specific misconceptions are as follows:

There was a single route. There was no one route; rather, multiple routes by land, sea and river existed, and goods traveled by one or more of these. Routes varied over time, depending on political and other factors. Parts of these routes have acquired different labels, such as the "tea horse route" or the "musk route."

The route went east to west. Routes did not only go east to west but also north to south: for example, furs and slaves from northern Europe went to Central Asia, Indian textiles to Central Asia, pepper from India to Iran and Europe, frankincense and ivory from Africa to Eurasia. This is an opportunity to raise issues about the limitations of our evidence. Any course on the Silk Road will of necessity use both textual and archaeological sources. Both have an implicit bias. For example, in terms of understanding the movement of goods, most of the organic material has long disappeared, with exceptions surviving in tombs and desert sites. Indian textiles are a striking example. We hear a lot about silk from China, preserved in tombs in the deserts but very little about textile production in India.

Long-distance trade started with the Silk Road. In fact, long-distance trade existed long before the Silk Road. An effective example of this is to show Tutankhamun's mask with its lapis from what is now northeastern Afghanistan (being careful to point out that much of the blue is glass, emulating lapis, indicating the expense and rarity of lapis) and jade from Central Asian Khotan found in the early kingdoms in what is now China, jade again being a highly valued material. A word of caution, however: there are a number of persistent myths about such interactions, such as the story that domesticated silk from China has been found in an Egyptian tomb. This claim was originally published in *Nature* but has since been withdrawn. I nevertheless hear it repeated frequently.

Merchants traveled the whole route. Most merchants did not travel with their goods to their final destination but sold them on at a market en route, to be passed on to other merchants. Sea routes were often the same.

There was ongoing direct contact between Rome and China. This is part of the dichotomous East-West narratives discussed above.

The Silk Roads are Eurasian. Africa was very much part of the trading networks from the start. Whereas resources from the north and east African early trading networks were rather sparse a decade ago, there is an increasing amount of material now that makes incorporating the role and routes of Africa into any Silk Road course much easier.

Structuring a Course

There are now reasonable resources for structuring a course on the Silk Roads and, depending on the class, a number of broad approaches. I look at several of these below. They are not exclusive; I often combine several in a course.

Historical Narrative

This is an obvious approach, but one that is rather unhelpful in terms of this topic: the Silk Roads cover too long a spread of time and too broad a geography. A linear history is more often than not misleading, supporting, for example, the idea that the Silk Road started with the Chinese diplomatic mission of Zhang Qian (of course, it may be interesting to discuss when this narrative emerged and why it is so persistent). A linear history also easily becomes a litany of the great empires. I therefore do not generally use Silk Road histories as primary teaching texts, but rather give students chapters or essays from various texts with different perspectives while using more specialist histories of the various empires, peoples, and periods as background material.

I see teaching the Silk Roads as sneaking history in through the back door, especially the history of cultures and peoples often ignored in traditional curricula. For short, historical introductions to many of the less well-known cultures of the Silk Road, the UNESCO series *A History of Civilizations of Central Asia* (see Asimov and Bosworth) and the *Cambridge History of Early Inner Asia* (see Sinor) remain useful. Some of the cultures, previously little known, have been studied quite extensively over the past two decades. A notable case is that of the Sogdians. As traders and travelers from the heart of Eurasia with documentary and archaeological evidence of their trading activities and diplomatic relations from the Caucasus to China, Sogdians provide a useful way to understand the Silk Roads. Ètienne de La Vaissière's history and, most recently, the Freer-Sackler Gallery's excellent online resource, *The Sogdians: Influencers on the Silk Road* (sogdians.si.edu/), make this one of the most accessible ways to teach the Silk Road.

Another approach that provides a historical framework for the start of the Silk Road is to concentrate on Central Asia and the rise of the Kushan Empire. Long-distance trade by land prior to the Silk Roads was from either side of the great mountain ranges of Central Asia: for example, lapis went west from Afghanistan rather than east, and not much crossed these formidable ranges. But the rise of the Kushan almost certainly encouraged travel across the mountains, east into the Taklamakan, north to Sogdiana and the steppe, west to Iran, and south to India. The idea of Central Asia as a vital hub in world history has been discussed in many sources, notably Andre Gunder Frank's *The Centrality of Central Asia*. This approach orients the "Silk Road" not at the edges, in East Asia or Europe, but in Central Asia.

It was also during the Kushan period that Buddhism spread, probably both east and west, although the western traces are less visible (Liu, *Ancient India*; and Vaziri). See discussion of religions below. The story of the migrants who formed the Kushan Empire is representative of Silk Road interaction. Their pre–Silk Road history is discussed by C. Benjamin (*Yuezhi*) and exemplifies the large-scale movement of peoples in the Bronze Age and before. Some centuries before the Silk Road, the Kushan were found in what is now northwestern China, probably involved in the jade and horse trade with China (see below), and were forced west by the Xiongnu.

They were the object of Zhang Qian's mission to the western regions. Liu Xinru ("Migration") explores their pastoralist origins.

There are almost no extant manuscript primary sources on the Kushan Empire, and our information comes from archaeology, the histories of other empires and, most importantly for reconstructing the chronology, coins (Benjamin, *Empire* 176–203; Cribb, "Sino-Kharosthi Coins" (parts 1 and 2) and "Numismatic Evidence"; Falk). Coins are often neglected in the Silk Road story, which is surprising, given that, as money, they are central to the Silk Road. See discussion on trade and economics below. The entries in the online *Encyclopædia Iranica* are also invaluable for clear short discussions, such as that by Jessie Pons on Kushan art.

Both the Kushan and Sogdians cover the early history of the Silk Road, concentrating on Central Asia. For later periods, the history of the Umayyad and Mongol Empires are useful foundations, both covering a wide spread of Eurasia and having links with cultures on all their borders. The rise of the Mongol Empire also raises the issue of the interactions between the empires of the Silk Roads and their steppe neighbors. I discuss this further below.

Geography and Ecology

Teaching the Silk Road inevitably becomes in part a geography lesson, introducing a plethora of little-known regions and places. Ensuring the student is familiar and comfortable with the broad geographic setting is essential.

Choosing a good map or maps is key (see above). I find it useful to get students to interact with the map or geography to activate knowledge. Waugh's University of Washington Silk Road site has some interactive map exercises. I have also used various other ways of activating knowledge, including

handing out images or lists of places and artifacts students need to identify and locate on the map (they can extend this to look at the interchange of goods and the routes traveled);

using travelogues to discover and map travelers of old; and

discussing the logistics of travel: illustrating, for example, why some routes might not be accessible at certain times, such as mountain passes or rivers in flood; travel through different regions; and the most suitable means of travel—camel, horse, donkey, yak, cart, and so on.

A course can also be structured around the ecological boundary that traverses Eurasia between what David Christian calls "Inner" and "Outer" Eurasia, also sometimes termed "the steppe and the settled." Different ecologies force humans to adapt in different ways, for example, by adopting pastoralism or farming. There is much recent work to show how many early grains developed on the steppe (see, e.g., Frachettiet al.), with descriptions of pastoralist lifestyles. I discuss interactions between the peoples of the steppe and their southern neighbors during the Silk Road period in *Silk Roads*, with suggestions for further reading.

An ecological approach also provides the opportunity to introduce issues of sustainability and climate change. Waugh ("Silk Road") has a useful summary and Philippe Forêt an interesting discussion based on the maps and data from early-twentieth-century explorers. In terms of ecology, there are two examples central to the Silk Road, namely the codomestications of the silkworm and mulberry tree and of the horse and alfalfa or lucerne. For the schoolteacher in particular, the focus offers opportunities to interleave home, classroom, and outside activities, including raising silkworms, identifying local mulberries (see Coles) and weaving. There are many classroom resources available, and this could also involve visits to see silk farms, museums, and traditional weaving. If these are not available locally, there are *YouTube* resources.

The horse—its breeding, uses, and trade—also forms an excellent topic around which to construct a lecture, or indeed a course. Paul Buell, Timothy May, and David Ramey give an overview (Buell et al.); see also my *Silk, Slaves, and Stupas* (157–63) for further references. It can be argued that the horse was as important for Silk Road trade and economics as silk. One of the reasons for this was the constant demand from China and India for horses, especially for military purposes: both countries failed to breed sufficient numbers for their needs, as I discuss in "Alfalfa, Pasture, and the Horse."

Stories of People and Early Travelers

When I first started studying the Silk Roads, I was very much aware of my lack of historical knowledge for most of the places and periods. I found it difficult to find sources that did not defeat me by their detail and complexity. This was one of my primary motivations for writing *Life along the Silk Road*. I approached the history by telling the story of ten individuals along the eastern Silk Road, using the rich primary sources with which I was working. My aim was to make the stories available for teaching by offering navigation through unknown territories and histories. I relied heavily on the research of others, such as Stephen F. Teiser, who uncovered the life of the tenth-century Chinese official in Dunhuang, and Hansen, who through her study of Turfan documents told the story of the dispute between a widow and her supposed nephew (*Negotiating Daily Life* 68–74).

The advantage of teaching the Silk Road through peoples' lives is that students connect easily with human experience, especially the lives of people otherwise unrecorded and largely disregarded in traditional histories, such as women and enslaved people.

The story of slavery on the Silk Road rarely features as a central theme in most histories but there are growing resources that should make it possible to build a course around this. Chapter 10 of my *Silk, Slaves, and Stupas* introduces the themes and incidences of slavery across the Silk Road, especially in the major empires and cultures. Helen Wang has translations of many documents concerning enslaved people, and Paul Finkelman and Joseph Calder Miller provide further information. The forthcoming publication of volume 2 of the *Cambridge World History of Slavery* will cover the Silk Road period for the Afro-Eurasian region.

Also relevant are questions of what is meant by slavery and how slavery is defined. For example, Gwyn Campbell argues that much premodern Indian Ocean slavery is better labeled as "servitude" (137). There are also gender issues involved, given the persistent use of young women as sexually enslaved people, and the trade in castrated men.

Teaching through early geographers and travelers of the Silk Road combines human stories with the geography and logistics of travel, enabling discussion of the different perspectives presented by the travelers and how these perspectives are informed by culture, religion, and other factors. The challenge in teaching all this is to get beyond oft quoted travelers such as Xuanzang and Marco Polo to less well used material. Geographers and travelers such as Ibn Fadlan and Ibn Battuta provide fascinating insights into areas of life not covered elsewhere, such as the culture and society of the Rus. The Seattle Silk Roads website (depts.washington.edu/silkroad/) provides free online access to translations of numerous travelers on the eastern Silk Road. There are also other online and printed sources, most recently, Donald S. Lopez on the journey of the Korean Buddhist pilgrim, Hyecho. Not surprisingly, female voices are few, but not completely absent. In the modern period there are excellent and entertaining accounts by Mildred Cable, Catherine Macartney, Ella Maillart, Ella Sykes, and Irene Vincent, among others.

Archaeology and Exploration

The stories of the explorers and early archaeologists of the Silk Road are compelling, and there are many readily available and accessible resources. Set in the age of empire, these accounts can be used to pose questions on the ethics of archaeology and collecting, issues of provenance, the growth and ethics of museum collections, and the rise and professionalization of archaeology.

Archaeological resources are heavily weighted toward exploration of the eastern section of the Silk Road, notably the oasis kingdoms and routes of the Taklamakan desert in what is now northwestern China. The explorers and archaeologists themselves left both popular accounts and scientific reports and mapped and photographed their routes, and their finds were largely placed in public institutions. Much of this material is now freely accessible online through projects such as the International Dunhuang Project (idp.bl.uk) and Digital Silk Road (dsr.nii.ac.jp). Modern accounts of exploration, such as those of Peter Hopkirk, Justin Jacobs, and Frances Wood, offer different viewpoints that can lead to discussions of issues such as the ethics of archaeology and restitution. Jack A. Dabbs's and Svetlana Gorshenina's respective works are both immensely useful.

There are numerous stories of archaeologists of other parts of the Silk Road, but they are not usually identified as Silk Road archaeology and need tracking down. One excellent resource, but only available in German (and, sadly, with no index), is Charlotte Trümpler's volume on archaeology and politics during the Great Game.

The growth of maritime archaeology is a topic gaining interest, and there are several recent spectacular finds. The involvement and ethics of commercial interests in this field can be explored, with the Belitung Shipwreck comprising a possible case study (see Heng).

Stories of Objects and Material Culture

As Neil MacGregor demonstrated in his *History of the World in One Hundred Objects*, the story of extant old things can be just as compelling as those of long-dead people. Things have the advantage of still being seen, unlike most historical Silk Road people. They allow for the discussion of technologies, science, collection history and ethics, and conservation (see below). And students can be asked to find their own objects, either in local museums, or online, or find modern objects that reflect silk road themes.

There are numerous objects exemplifying what we mean by the Silk Road. I selected nine for *Silk, Slaves, and Stupas* but had a long list of scores more, many of which I featured in *Silk Roads*. Edward H. Schafer's book on Tang "exotics" is indispensable, containing wonderful stories for teaching. Online exhibition catalogues, blog posts, and tweets also provide useful sources. Millward considers the origins and spread of stringed instruments ("The Silk Road"; see also Zeeuw). Thomas T. Allsen discusses Islamic textiles, while Cat Jarman looks at the journey of a carnelian bead into Europe.

John Kieschnick's study of the effect of Buddhism on material culture is divided into chapters discussing different things, including mundane objects, but concentrates on influences coming into East Asia with Buddhism. In *Silk and Religion*, Liu also looks at objects and materials used in Buddhism, concentrating on ritual and votive things, such as relics (see below). Beth Williamson considers the other end of the Eurasian world and the effect of Christianity on material culture.

For the Indian Ocean world, Elizabeth A. Lambourne's study of a luggage list of a Jewish merchant in India considers the social life of things, from travel to food. Food across the Silk Road is also discussed by Spengler.

I have found it interesting to ask students to think of modern objects that exemplify the themes of the Silk Road, for example, a Gucci handbag designed in Italy, made in China, and sold in the United States. Students can also discuss how objects change in value as they travel or are incorporated into different contexts and cultures. It is possible to structure a whole course around one type of object or discuss different representative objects in each class (see also technologies below).

One other obvious and compelling topic is fakes and forgeries. I reviewed this in my introduction to a conference paper on Dunhuang manuscript forgeries.

Religions

Most of the major religions of the world are found in Afro-Eurasia during the Silk Road period and traveled considerable distances during this time, making converts and forming communities in distant lands. The emergence of these religions; their growth and spread across Afro-Eurasia; and their influence on peoples, landscape, architecture, and material culture—and their persecutions—form a solid foundation for teaching the Silk Road.

Richard Foltz's short introduction to these religions is an excellent starting point. Frantz Grenet considers the religious diversity among the Sogdians. My *Silk Roads* also has short accessible entries from leading scholars on all the major religions, illustrated with featured items, including buildings, with extended captions. There are also several online resources and catalogues that explore religious manuscripts, artifacts, and architecture from across the Silk Road.

Other potential themes for teaching include pilgrimage, death and burial rituals, monasticism, book culture, and relic worship.

Money and Economics

The Silk Road is about trade, yet there are surprisingly few resources on its economics. How were prices set? How did people carry money? How did people pay? Were there taxes? How much did goods change in value? Wang's book *Money on the Silk Road* gives examples of contracts, types of money, and the values of goods along the eastern Silk Road. Hansen uses these and other sources in both her books, where contracts and the extent and value of trade are both central concerns. Hansen and Wang's edited Royal Asiatic Society journal volume looks at textiles as money. Allsen and Roberta Tomber each consider different areas of trade.

There are numerous resources—and online images—for coins. The discovery of coin hoards from Central Asia taken by traders to northern Europe has also been discussed widely.

Technologies

The Silk Road was about trade, both in raw materials and finished goods, and thus discussion of the technologies used to extract the raw materials and transform them into finished products can be justifiably incorporated into a Silk Roads course. In addition to sericulture, weaving is another vital technology that developed in different Silk Road regions and that also spread throughout. Other technologies, such as ceramics and glassmaking, are useful for discussing what was needed for new technologies to be adopted and mastered by different cultures and how they were adapted and transformed. Glass is particularly interesting to compare with silk, as a technology developing in different regions, but mainly traveling east. I discuss this in *Silk, Slaves, and Stupas* (ch. 2). Printing is another key technology and leads to the history and materiality of the book.

Texts, Scripts, Languages, and the History of the Book

The development of writing and the book, in its various forms, is a clear way to show how materials, scripts, and book forms traveled along the Silk Road. It is also a useful topic for including India, as Indian book forms and scripts were influential in several important Silk Road regions, such as Gandhara, Tibet, and the Tarim Basin. The curiously persistent view that the codex form was superior to the scroll form, an argument often seen in discussions of the development of the codex in the western parts of the Silk Road, is a useful point for discussion, and brings up the Eurocentrism of many of the resources available in English. Students need to take into account the purpose of the book, the orientation of the script, and the materials. For ideas, see Bloom's *Paper before Print* and the University of Toronto's online resource *The Book and the Silk Roads* (booksilkroads.library.utoronto.ca/). Teaching this topic can also include classroom activities such as making paper, scrolls, and codices, and visits to see original material.

The many histories of printing can also be a useful departure for further discussion of Eurocentrism. Students can find numerous sites and scholarly books on printing history which effectively ignore pre-European developments or dismiss these as a substandard process. T. H. Barrett gives an informative and entertaining response to this. Frances Wood and Mark Barnard focus on the earliest dated printed book in the world, the Dunhuang Diamond Sutra; further contextual information on this iconic document is provided by Joyce Morgan and Conrad Walters. Another interesting Silk Road–wide topic is censorship, for which Derek Jones's *Encyclopaedia* is commendably comprehensive in terms of geographic and chronological coverage.

The use and spread of language—as opposed to scripts—raises the subject of intangible cultural heritage and how we study and preserve this. I have used the example of Welsh and its revival as a case study for how to stop a language from disappearing and then compared the example of Welsh to Silk Road languages and cultures, such as Uyghur, currently under threat. The Endangered Languages Project (www.endangeredlanguages.com/) gives many more examples.

Cultural Heritage

UNESCO has a list of intangible cultural heritage along the Silk Roads that can form a basis for classroom discussion. The music of the Silk Road in particular has received considerable attention through the foundation by Yo-Yo Ma of his project Silkroad (www.silkroad.org).

The inscription in 2014 of a transnational corridor of the Silk Roads by UNESCO was the first in what UNESCO hopes will be many. I have already mentioned the process of how to define the Silk Roads by mapping relevant sites, as discussed by Tim Williams. There are many other resources on this topic, including the UNESCO Silk Road site. In "The Expanding Silk Road," I review the history of the term "Silk Road" in the UNESCO arena, concentrating on the role of Japan in its early promotion, and the growing influence of China. This influence highlights the role of politics in cultural heritage: the trope of the singing and dancing minority is one theme discussed by Rachel Harris.

To structure and focus a course on the Silk Roads is akin to organizing travel on these routes, with many options among major roads and less-traveled byways. Of necessity, I have only been able to provide a guide to a few of these here.

Works Cited

Allsen, Thomas T. *Commodity and Exchange in the Mongol Empire: A Cultural History of Islamic Textiles.* Cambridge UP, 1997.

Asimov, M. S., and C. E. Bosworth, editors. *The Age of Achievement, A.D. 750 to the End of the Fifteenth Century.* UNESCO, 1998. Vol. 4 of *History of Civilizations of Central Asia.*

Barrett, T. H. *The Woman Who Discovered Printing.* Yale UP, 2008.

Benjamin, C. *Empires of Ancient Eurasia: The First Silk Roads Era, 100 BCE–250 CE.* Cambridge UP, 2018.

———. *The Yuezhi: Origins, Migration and the Conquest of Northern Bactria.* Brepols, 2007.

Bloom, Jonathan. *Paper before Print: The History and Impact of Paper in the Islamic World.* Yale UP, 2001.

———. "Silk Road or Paper Road?" *The Silk Road*, vol. 3, no. 2, 2005, pp. 21–26, www.silkroadfoundation.org/newsletter/vol3num2/5_bloom.php.

Buell, Paul, et al. "The Horse and the Silk Road: Movement and Ideas." *Academia*, www.academia.edu/218892/The_Horse_and_the_Silk_Road_Movement_and_Ideas.

Cable, Mildred. *The Gobi Desert.* With Francesca French, Hodder and Stoughton, 1950.

Campbell, Gwyn. "The Question of Slavery in Indian Ocean World History." *The Indian Ocean: Oceanic Connections and the Creation of New Societies*, edited by Abdul Sheriff and Engseng Ho, Hurst, 2014, pp. 123–49.

Chin, Tamara T. "The Invention of the Silk Road, 1877." *Critical Inquiry*, vol. 40, no. 1, 2013, pp. 194–219.

Christian, David. "Inner Eurasia as a Unit of World History." *Journal of World History*, vol. 5, no. 2, 1994, pp. 173–211.

Coles, Peter. *Mulberry*. Reaktion Books, 2019.

Cribb, Joe. "Numismatic Evidence and the Date of Kaniṣka I." *Problems of Chronology in Gandharan Art*, edited by Wannaporn Rienjang and Peter Stewart, Archaeopress Archaeology, 2018, pp. 17–34.

———. "The Sino-Kharsothi Coins of Khotan: Their Attribution and Relevance to Kushan Chronology: Part 1." *The Numismatic Chronicle*, vol. 144, 1984, pp. 128–52.

———. "The Sino-Kharosthi Coins of Khotan: Their Attribution and Relevance to Kushan Chronology: Part 2." *The Numismatic Chronicle*, vol. 145, 1985, pp. 136–49.

Dabbs, Jack A. *History of the Discovery and Exploration of Chinese Turkestan*. Mouton, 1963.

Donzel, E. J. van, and Andrea Schmidt. *Gog and Magog in Early Eastern Christian and Islamic Sources: Sallam's Quest for Alexander's Wall*. Brill, 2009.

Falk, Harry. "Ancient Indian Eras: An Overview." *Bulletin of the Asia Institute*, vol. 21, 2012, pp. 131–45.

Finkelman, Paul, and Joseph Calder Miller. *Macmillan Encyclopedia of World Slavery*. Vol. 2, Macmillan Reference, 1998.

Foltz, Richard. *Religions of the Silk Road: Premodern Patterns of Globalization*. Palgrave Macmillan, 2010.

Forêt, Philippe. "Sven Hedin and the Invention of Climate Change." *Sven Hedin and Eurasia: Knowledge, Adventure and Geopolitics*, edited by Ingmar Oldberg, Sällskapet för studier av Ryssland, Central-och Osteuropa samt Centralasien, 2018, pp. 29–34.

Frachetti, Michael D., et al. "Earliest Direct Evidence for Broomcorn Millet and Wheat in the Central Eurasian Steppe Region." *Antiquity*, vol. 84, no. 326, 2010, pp. 993–1010, https://doi.org/10.1017/S0003598X0006703X.

Gorshenina, Svetlana. *Explorateurs en Asie centrale: Voyageurs et aventuriers de Marco Polo à Ella Maillart*, Olizane, 2003.

Grenet, Frantz. "Religious Diversity among Sogdian Merchants in Sixth-Century China: Zoroastrianism, Buddhism, Manichaeism, and Hinduism." *Comparative Studies of South Asia, Africa and the Middle East*, vol. 27, no. 2, 2007, pp. 463–78.

Gunder Frank, Andre. *The Centrality of Central Asia*. VU UP, 1992.

Hansen, Valerie. *Negotiating Daily Life in Traditional China: How Ordinary People Used Contracts, 600–1400*. Yale UP, 1995.

———. *The Silk Road: A New History*. Yale UP, 2013.

Hansen, Valerie, and Helen Wang, editors. *Textiles as Money on the Silk Road*, special issue of *Journal of the Royal Asiatic Society*, vol. 23, no. 2, 2013.

Harris, Rachel. "The New Battleground: Song-and-Dance in China's Muslim Borderlands." *The World of Music*, vol. 6, no. 2, 2017, pp. 35–55. *JSTOR*, www.jstor.org/stable/44841945.

Heng, Geraldine. "An Ordinary Ship and Its Stories of Early Globalism: Modernity, Mass Production, and Art in the Global Middle Ages." *The Journal of Medieval Worlds*, vol. 1, no. 1, 2019, pp. 11–54.

Hopkirk, Peter. *Foreign Devils on the Silk Road.* John Murray, 2011.

Humphrey, Caroline, and David Sneath. *The End of Nomadism? Society, State and the Environment in Inner Asia.* Duke UP, 1999.

Jacobs, Justin M. *The Compensations of Plunder: How China Lost Its Treasures.* U of Chicago P, 2020.

Jarman, Cat. *River Kings: A New History of Vikings from Scandanavia to the Silk Roads.* William Collins, 2021.

Jones, Derek, editor. *Censorship: A World Encyclopedia.* Fitzroy Dearborn Publishers, 2001.

Kieschnick, John. *The Impact of Buddhism on Chinese Material Culture.* Princeton UP, 2003.

Lambourne, Elizabeth A. *Abraham's Luggage: A Social Life of Things in the Medieval Indian Ocean World.* Cambridge UP, 2018.

La Vaissière, Ètienne de. *Sogdian Traders: A History.* Translated by James Ward, Brill Academic Publishers, 2005.

Lieberman, Victor. "Transcending East-West Dichotomies: State and Culture Formation in Six Ostensibly Disparate Areas." *Modern Asian Studies*, vol. 31, no. 3, 1997, pp. 463–546.

Lincot, Emmanuel, and Arnaud Bertrand. "Anciennes et nouvelles 'routes de la soie': Pour une déconstruction d'une appellation." *Asia Focus*, no. 155, www.iris-france.org/wp-content/uploads/2021/02/Asia-Focus-155.pdf.

Liu Xinru. *Ancient India and Ancient China: Trade and Religious Exchanges, AD 1–600.* Oxford UP, 1988.

———. "The Migration and Settlement of the Yuezhi-Kushan: Interaction and Interdependence of Nomadic and Sedentary Societies." *Journal of World History*, vol. 12, no. 2, 2001, pp. 261–92.

———. *Silk and Religion: An Exploration of Material Life and the Thought of People, AD 600–1200.* Oxford UP, 1996.

Lopez, Donald S. *Hyecho's Journey: The World of Buddhism.* U of Chicago P, 2018.

Macartney, [Catherine]. *An English Lady in Chinese Turkestan.* Oxford Paperbacks, 1986.

MacGregor, Neil. *A History of the World in One Hundred Objects.* Penguin, 2012.

Maillart, Ella. *Turkestan Solo: One Woman's Expedition from the Tien Shan to the Kizil Kum.* Heinemann, 1938.

Millward, James. "The Silk Road and the Sitar: Finding Centuries of Sociocultural Exchange in the History of an Instrument." *Journal of Social History*, vol. 52, no. 2, 2018, pp. 206–33. *Oxford Academic*, https://doi.org/10.1093/jsh/shy050.

———. *The Silk Road: A Very Short Introduction.* Oxford UP, 2013.

Morgan, Joyce, and Conrad Walters. *Journeys on the Silk Road.* Picador, 2011.

Pons, Jessie. "Kushan Dynasty 9: Art of the Kushans." *Encyclopædia Iranica*, online edition, 2016, www.iranicaonline.org/articles/kushan-dynasty-09-art.

Schafer, Edward H. *The Golden Peaches of Samarkand: A Study of Tang Exotics.* U of California P, 1963.

Sinor, Denis, editor. *The Cambridge History of Early Inner Asia.* Cambridge UP, 2008, https://doi.org/10.1017/CHOL9780521243049.

Spengler, Robert N. *Fruit from the Sands: The Silk Road Origins of the Food We Eat.* U of California P, 2019.

Spengler, Robert, et al. "Early Agriculture and Crop Transmission Among Bronze Age Mobile Pastoralists of Central Eurasia." *Proceedings of the Biological Society*, vol. 281, no. 1783, 2014, https://doi.org/10.1098/rspb.2013.3382.

Sykes, Ella C. *Through Persia on a Side-saddle.* A. D. Innes, 1898.

Teiser, Stephen F. *The Scripture of the Ten Kings and the Making of Purgatory in Medieval China.* U of Hawai'i P, 1994.

Tomber, Roberta. *Indo-Roman Trade: From Pots to Pepper.* Duckworth, 2008.

Trümpler, Charlotte, et al., editors. *Das grosse Spiel: Archäologie und Politik zur Zeit des Kolonialismus (1860–1940).* DuMont, 2008.

Vaziri, M. *Buddhism in Iran: An Anthropological Approach to Traces and Influences.* Palgrave Macmillan, 2012.

Vincent, Irene Vongehr. *The Sacred Oasis.* Ulan Press, 2012.

Waldron, Arthur. *The Great Wall of China: From History to Myth.* Cambridge UP, 2008.

Wang, Helen. *Money on the Silk Road.* British Museum Press, 2004.

Waugh, Daniel C. "Richthofen's 'Silk Roads': Toward the Archaeology of a Concept." *The Silk Road*, vol. 5, no.1, 2007, pp. 1–10.

———. "The Silk Road and Eurasian Geography." 2008, depts.washington.edu/silkroad/geography/geography.html.

Whitfield, Susan. "Alfalfa, Pasture, and the Horse in China: A Review Article." *Sino-Iranica Centennial: Between East and West, Exchanges of Material and Ideational Culture*, edited by Ephraim Nissan, Quaderni di studi Indo-Mediterranei, vol. 12, 2019, pp. 227–45.

———. "The Expanding Silk Road: UNESCO and OBOR." *Bulletin of the Museum of Far Eastern Antiquities*, vol. 81, 2020.

———. "Inscribing and Expanding the Silk Roads: From UNESCO to OBOR." *"One Belt One Road" and China's Westward Pivot*, edited by Lev Andersen at al., Danish Institute for International Studies 2018, dro.dur.ac.uk/23758/.

———. Introduction. *Dunhuang Manuscript Forgeries*, edited by Whitfield, British Library, 2002, idp.bl.uk/downloads/Forgeries.pdf. British Library Studies on Conservation Science.

———. *Life along the Silk Road*. U of California P, 2015.

———. "On the Silk Road: Trade in the Tarim." *Trade and Civilization: Economic Networks and Cultural Ties, from Prehistory to the Early Modern Era*, edited by Kristian Kristiansen et al., Cambridge UP, 2018, pp. 251–78.

———. "The Perils of Dichotomous Thinking: Ebb and Flow rather than East and West." *Marco Polo and the Encounter of East and West*, edited by Suzanne Akbari and Amilcare A. Iannucci, U of Toronto P, 2008. *Academia*, www.academia.edu/2645165/The_Perils_of_Dichotomous_Thinking_Ebb_and_flow_rather_than_east_and_west.

———, editor. *The Silk Roads: Landscapes, Cultures, Peoples*. Thames and Hudson, 2019.

———. *Silk, Slaves, and Stupas: Material Culture of the Silk Road*. U of California P, 2018.

———. "Under the Censor's Eye: Printed Almanacs and Censorship in Ninth-Century China." *British Library Journal*, vol. 24, no. 1, 1998, pp. 4–22.

———. "Was There a Silk Road?" *Asian Medicine*, vol. 3, 2007, pp. 201–13. Brill, https://doi.org/10.1163/157342008X307839.

Williams, Tim. "Mapping the Silk Roads." *Long-distance Trade, Culture and Society*, edited by Mariko Namba Walter and James P. Ito-Adler, Cambridge Institutes Press, 2015, pp. 1–42. Vol. 1 of *The Silk Road: Interwoven History*.

Williamson, Beth. *Material Culture and Medieval Christianity*. Oxford UP, 2014.

Wood, Frances. *The Silk Road: Two Thousand Years in the Heart of Asia*. U of California P, 2002.

Wood, Frances, and Mark Barnard. The Diamond Sutra*: The Story of the World's Earliest Dated Printed Book*. British Library, 2010.

Zeeuw, Hans de. *Tanbûr Long-Necked Lutes Along the Silk Road and Beyond*. Archaeopress, 2019.

Arafat A. Razzaque and Rachel Schine

Teaching the Worlds of the *Thousand and One Nights*

When speaking of the *Thousand and One Nights* (*Alf Layla wa-Layla*), the byword for both the globality that the text internally conveys and the ethic of worldly reading that it advances has often been "cosmopolitanism." The identification with cosmopolitanism is at least as old as the tales' most famous English translator, Sir Richard Francis Burton. Burton regarded himself as a true cosmopolite who believed in the intrinsic value of the many cultures into which he attempted to "go native" and who advocated for translation as a project of cultivating a worldlier English literature, as Paulo Horta has highlighted. Burton found the *Nights* to mirror this worldliness, seeing in the tales a cosmopolitan disposition, and in Baghdad under Harun al-Rashid "a meeting place of nations" (Horta 77). The perspective is by no means unique to Burton, even though few today would dare venture, as he did in the notorious *Terminal Essay* appending his translation, to use the *Nights* as a basis for musings on nothing short of civilizations and their differences, on what he deemed "the mediæval Arab at his best and, perhaps, at his worst" (Burton 10: 63).

Many readers are still struck by the particular ways in which the worlds of the *Thousand and One Nights* are delivered to us in the text—concentrated in great cities like Cairo and Baghdad, and anchored in a vision of multiple realms layered upon one another through travel, trade, and the *mise en abyme* structure of the narrative itself. For some, dubbing this phenomenon cosmopolitanism may help destabilize Western modernity's seeming monopoly of the concept; for others, it simply best captures the time and place under consideration. The term's centrality in contemporary receptions of the *Nights* seems to divulge something about the nature of the tales themselves and also, as we are assured by Horta, about their translators and readers throughout history. Since our pedagogical task entails developing best practices of language through which to guide our students' understanding, we would like to ask here what it means when we rely on cosmopolitanism as an orienting concept in describing the domain of the *Nights*. Does the idea of cosmopolitanism illuminate something significant that we can teach—or perhaps unteach—about the medieval Islamic world in the classroom?

In its original sense, *cosmopolitanism* stems from the notion of world citizenship. This has become bound up over time with philosophical worldliness, the ability to appreciate other cultures and thought-worlds or to envisage oneself as part of a geographically extensive human enterprise; it has also been equally implicated in ideas of property and power, in that to cultivate world citizenship means to be free to move about and experience the world.[1] Historically, many imperial projects have, to varying degrees, idealized cosmopolitanism, performing entitlement to the globe's territories and knowledge of their cultural productions. Yet at the same time, self-identifying as cosmopolitan has often also indicated a moral stance, in which the nonlocal "other" is as valid, real, and knowledge-producing as the provincial "us," and in which one remains intellectually open to what the world has on offer.[2] Nonetheless, according to Mana Kia, *cosmopolitanism* in modern parlance has become a uniquely and unreflexively European byword for celebrating the consumption of difference that is perhaps incommensurable with other locales (Kia, "Space" 259).

Cosmopolitanism is at base a term derived from antiquity and given new life in the Enlightenment, and when it is used particularly to describe the medieval Islamic world, it can have the effect of reifying both the idea of a comparatively insular medieval Europe and the zero-sum narrative of modern Western ascent and Eastern decline. Similarly, as Kevin van Bladel has recently noted, the word *civilization* has also gained new currency since the eighteenth century, and its use to describe the Islamic world "implies at least one other (Western) civilization, the assumption of which was the precondition of its existence" (155). So it is perhaps little wonder that from his self-proclaimed cosmopolitan vantage point at the height of the British Empire in the nineteenth century, Burton looked to the illustrious ʿAbbasid setting of the *Arabian Nights* and identified a world that was at least as familiar as it was foreign. The tensions arising from the multiple resonances of cosmopolitanism hearken to the very origins of the *Nights* as a work of cultural translation, at a time when the imperial reach of Baghdad under the caliphate stretched from the Indus River in the east to Ifriqiyya in the west (formerly Roman North Africa), with the reach of Islam extending yet farther.

Which Nights, Which Worlds

Anyone taking an interest in the *Thousand and One Nights* must soon confront the question it seems to pose more emphatically than many other familiar works of literature: which version? The choice of text is not only an issue of literary criticism but also of historical context, since the early modern developments that launched the *Nights* onto the world stage affected in turn what was still a living tradition in the Middle East. After over two centuries of copious, intensive scholarship on the *Nights*, to this day the field continues to yield fresh discoveries that change our understanding of its genealogy, composition, and transmission.[3]

It has been customary among specialists to conceptually divide the *Nights* corpus into the periods before and after the first French translation by Antoine Galland in the early 1700s. Pivoting its history on the many editors and translators from Galland to Burton and numerous others reveals the work (as we now know it) to be largely a product of the eighteenth and nineteenth centuries, made and remade as much in Europe or its colonial outposts as in the ancient and exotic parts of the world that many generations of Western readers have sought and seen within it. There is an inherent teaching moment in that the iconic story by which students are most likely to be familiar with the *Nights*, the hugely popular "Aladdin," was never a part of the Arabic text but one of a number of imaginative tales that Galland obtained from the Maronite Syrian raconteur Ḥannā Diyāb. Besides Galland's journals, which first betrayed this collaboration, Diyāb's own recently discovered autobiography helps further recuperate his almost unsung role as the curator-cum-composer of these so-called "orphan tales."[4] A discussion of provenance for the variegated collection that is the *Nights* compels us then to be aware of the conditions of our own inheritance and reading of a text that thwarts binarized ways of thinking about periodization: as though one is never quite sure if the text is truly medieval or mixed with later incorporations, which themselves may be inherited from and assuredly conjuring a medieval past.

These considerations of reception history can also help illuminate why many critics disavow the *Nights* as inescapably trapped in the legacy of Orientalism, and even alien to the corpus of classical Arabic literature. This literary judgment in a sense echoes the occasional dismissal by medieval learned elites of what they regarded as silly tales vis-à-vis the didactic category of *adab*, or belles-lettres, etymologically rooted in ideas of self-discipline and refinement. Language is an important factor here, because the *Nights* is written in the so-called Middle Arabic register that incorporates many colloquial features and often deviates from the grammatical rules of standard literary Arabic. Texts in Middle Arabic thus rarely belonged to the category of classical *adab*.

Such critical engagements also pose a salient counterpoint to perceptions of the *Nights* as eminently cosmopolitan; some have noted that it is *adab* as a set of literary and ethical practices—set forth by *udabāʾ*, or the lettered class—that may be most fruitfully compared with the cosmopolitanism of antiquity. Despite her aforementioned focus on cosmopolitanism and *adab*'s incongruities, Mana Kia characterizes Persianate *adab* in ways that harmonize with the definition of cosmopolitanism given above, as a mode of simultaneous self-making and worldly connectivity that functions through geographic or conceptual aporias. *Adab*, in other words, works to blur the boundaries between various forms of social belonging and between self and other (Kia, *Persianate Selves*). In his pathbreaking book *What Is Islam?*, Shahab Ahmed takes a more explicit stance in favor of understanding *adab* as cosmopolitan, though in a way that not only places the individual in a posture of openness to the world, but also to the otherworldly. Ahmed refers to *adab* as a "literary expression of a larger sensibility" that envisions a "cosmological communicative inter-course" (Ahmed 236). In this fashion, he critiques representations of Islamic cosmopolitanism as secular, this-worldly, or purely cultural. The *Nights*, though, insofar as they were not considered *adab*, were typically not perceived by the literati as having the capacity to edify about the grand concepts Ahmed raises.

It is therefore worth recalling that another connection *adab* bears with cosmopolitanism is its exclusivity: openness to the world entails being poised to take advantage of the privileges of empire, including freedom of movement and access to education; the people who have decided what is or is not *adab* throughout history have been predominantly status-conscious, elite men. In many ways, the *Nights*' positioning outside of *adab* is more a remark on the material facts of its production and circulation largely by people outside courtly patronage structures than on its pre-Orientalist obscurity in the Arabic-speaking world. And, to be sure, Konrad Hirschler has noted that "hegemonic groups" have apparently engaged more happily with the *Nights* than with other popular literature. As discussed below, many of its tales play a supporting role to *adab* and its modes of inclusion and exclusion by "broadly support[ing] the status quo" and not posing "an alternative to, or escape from, existent political structures" (Hirschler 175).

As such, to overemphasize the relatively recent literary success of the *Nights* as purely the outcome of Western obsession reifies a Eurocentric narrative of discovery and fails to do justice to the layers of cultural memory and practice buried in the tales, as well as to the ways the text is still a product of the medieval Islamic world and symptomatic of its literary trajectories. Moreover, to associate the hybrid and heterogeneous nature of the collection with only or mainly its transformations post-Galland risks a potentially misleading originalist reading, canonizing some tales as the authentic "core" of the corpus while discarding others as extraneous accretions. This is the interpretation adopted somewhat controversially by no less an authority than Muhsin Mahdi, who gave us the now standard scholarly edition of the *Nights* in Arabic, based on the early manuscript that was acquired by Galland. For use in an English-speaking medieval studies classroom, at least until the eagerly awaited, forthcoming translation by Yasmine Seale, we still favor Husain Haddawy's translation of the Mahdi edition, not because it represents an established text or a perfect translation, but rather because it illustrates so well the vagaries and complexity of the *Nights* tradition.

Even in its earliest known forms, the *Nights* belonged to multiple worlds. Its emergence in Arabic letters was already an act of retelling, possibly dating back as early as the eighth century to the efflorescence of translations in ʿAbbasid Baghdad and the voracious appetite for appropriating the intellectual heritage of empires prior to and beyond their own. The putative Persian original called *Hazār Afsāneh* (*Thousand Tales*) does not survive, though traces of it seem to linger in the frame tale of the *Nights*, given its claimed Sasanian setting and the Middle Persian names of its protagonists, Shahriyār and Shahrāzād. That Shahriyār is said to be the ruler of India (as well as China) becomes all the more tantalizing in view of the fact that key motifs of the frame tale and a number of the embedded stories are found in ancient Sanskrit literature—significantly also a known source through Pahlavi for another major Arabic classic, *Kalīla wa-Dimna*, translated into Arabic less than a century before the earliest surviving material evidence for the *Nights* from the ninth century (Marzolph and van Leeuwen 2: 603–04, 671–72).

Regardless of their diverse origins and unknown paths of transmission, it was in the urban heartlands of the Middle East that those early seeds would sprout and fully bloom into the *Nights*, grounding the tales mostly in Baghdad, Cairo, and Damascus while also elevating these cities to a mythic plane. We know rather little of its textual history during that long period between the remarkable fragment of waste paper dated 879 CE, but from a text likely produced decades earlier that bears the title *Alf Layla* (*Thousand Nights*), and the oldest surviving manuscripts from the very end of the Middle Ages as conventionally defined (Abbott 130; Marzolph and van Leeuwen 1: 17–21).[5] Scattered references allude to the book's existence and circulation in these intervening centuries, such as a mention of the title *Alf Layla wa-Layla* in a twelfth-century Jewish bookseller's lending records found in the Cairo Geniza (Marzolph and van Leeuwen 1: 44–45).

We can also speculate on the tales' life as oral text, by which both professional and dilettante reciters exchanged popular narratives in public and private spaces throughout the medieval Islamic world. Traditions of reciting the *Nights* in storytelling sessions endure today (Slyomovics). Gaps in material evidence, meanwhile, are emblematic of popular literature circulated in the Arabic-speaking Middle Ages, particularly as compared to texts of obvious religious or scholarly value that were diligently copied, loaned, and preserved, and to which more robust paper trails could therefore often accrue. Nevertheless, new research in Ottoman Turkish, Persian, and Syriac sources is helping fill the gaps by identifying some promising intertextual evidence that resituates our perspective on the tales beyond their life in Arabic.[6] The *Nights* existed in several Turkish translations since the fifteenth century, and its influence in the Ottoman Empire may have been a crucial backdrop to its European discovery (see Birkalan-Gedik). Posing the tales against all these broader contexts can encourage classroom debate on both the history of a text and on textuality itself, as well as discussions of multilingualism and vernacularity, oral literature and world folklore, the rise and recycling of paper in the Middle East, and the economy and materiality of premodern books.

The so-called Galland manuscript that made its way from Aleppo to Paris in 1701 dates to around the mid-fifteenth century and remains our earliest known copy of the *Thousand and One Nights* collection. It belongs to a small family of manuscripts that make up the incomplete Syrian recension of the tales (with 282 nights), compared to a more extended Egyptian version available only through much later copies. Indeed, of the hundred or so Arabic manuscripts of the *Nights*, more than half date to the nineteenth century—often understood to be a result of insatiable European demand, and along with it an ever-looming possibility of textual cross contaminations. But we should not underestimate local interest either, since a similar trajectory pertains to manuscripts of Arabic "popular epic" (*sīra shaʿbiyya*) literature, which had relatively less appeal in the West.[7] The related collection of stories known as the *Hundred and One Nights*, substantively different from but no less intriguing than the *Thousand and One Nights*, may date to fairly early manuscripts and retains some older literary elements, including a more ancient version of the frame tale, but seems to have developed as a textual tradition almost exclusively in the Maghreb or "Islamic West," that is, North Africa and the Iberian Peninsula (see Fudge xiv–xxiii).

Notwithstanding Mahdi's critical edition of the *Alf Layla wa-Layla* based on the Galland manuscript, the stemmata have proven difficult to reconstruct with much certainty, and the exact provenance of and relationship between the Syrian and Egyptian recensions (and for that matter, manuscripts that do not fit either classification) remain open to debate. One might assume the oldest copy to be closer to a presumed original, but Aboubakr Chraïbi has now shown that in at least some respects, the text of the fifteenth-century manuscript reflects a more developed literary composition compared with other versions, along with a higher degree of "Islamised" language—including especially the motif of *ʿajab*, or wonder (50–58), discussed further below. In other words, our fifteenth-century text is not so much the oldest as it is coterminous with the literary dispositions and movements of the Islamic Middle Ages. As if looking centuries ahead from her pre-Islamic Persian staging ground, Shahrāzād appears to narrate stories in which the world has only ever known the caliphates of medieval Islam. Examining the layered temporalities of the *Nights*, evoked from its first pages, organically leads us to discuss the social worlds the text traversed as it transformed, crossing empires, confessional communities, and classes.

Cosmopolitanism: Anthropological Truth or Imperial Fantasy?

The mobility and worldliness of the *Thousand and One Nights* may explain the widespread appeal of "cosmopolitanism" as an interpretive framework for both the text and the contents of the tales themselves, to which we now turn. In its most basic contemporary usage, cosmopolitanism has moved away from denoting the aspiration of world citizenship per se, and instead come to connote a form of sociopolitical reality, namely the coexistence within one space of many peoples and cultures. The latter can of course be said to be a precondition of the former. To be sure, in the *Nights* one is introduced to many peoples incorporated into the Islamic realm, either in the form of local archetypes emanating from historical facticity (the Christian broker or Jewish physician, for instance), or who gain admission through the more far-reaching threads of storytelling that disclose manifold—if thin—local recognitions of the global (like the figmentary presence of the king of China).

Taking the "Tale of the Three Apples" as an example in this light, one can uncover a number of key types and figures who existed in the medieval Islamic world that suggest a cosmopolitan scope (Haddawy 181–248). One encounters a Jew; a Black enslaved person; presumably Turkish *mamlūks* (elite enslaved soldiers); an Arab caliph; and Persian courtiers, represented here by the Barmakid family hailing originally from Balkh, in today's Afghanistan. One finds wealthy potentates traveling freely between Iraq, Syria, and Egypt, and, in an embedded tale of wondrous coincidences, two estranged brothers in Basra and in Cairo who happen to get married at the same time. Odes to nubile boys and buxom girls alike are interpolated off the cuff into the text, bearing aesthetic intimations about both one's ideal lovers and poetry itself. We are also introduced into the parallel realm of the demons by the presence of a female jinn.

The material sensorium of the text is likewise global, with the very span of it often adumbrated by the accretive genre of the list: people feast on fruits from humidity-reliant apples to drought-tolerant pomegranates and festoon themselves with dyed silk and gold brocade, wool and doubled viziers' turbans; multiethnic courtesans play on ʿouds and tambourines; lapis, beryl, and ruby encrust wealthy women's wardrobes—all producing the effect of a dizzying opulence that seems to pull from every mine and trade route in the known world. A reader of the *Nights* realizes soon enough that this technique recurs throughout the book, occasionally even shifting from the generic to the specific, populating the narrative with toponymic details that serve to veraciously locate the cosmopolis on the global crossroads.

This is notably the case in the "Story of the Porter and the Three Ladies," which opens in Baghdad with one of the three ladies appearing at the market in a cloak of Mosul silk (the etymological root of *muslin* in English, as Burton makes sure to note) and proceeding to collect the world in her shopping basket, the decadent array of which is conveyed through the common Arabic form of the massive, internally rhymed list (Burton 1: 82). Starting at the fruit seller's stall, she picks up Hebron peaches (*tuffāḥ fatḥī*), Levantine apples (*tuffāḥ miskī*), Aleppo jasmine, Damascus lilies, and so on. Moving from one specialized store to another, she gets Syrian cheese, Iraqi sugarcane, Aleppo raisins, a Baalbek sweet, and many more eclectic items that leave her porter dazzled and "wondering" (*taʿajjaba*) at all that the lady has amassed (Haddawy 81; Mahdi 127). The porter's wonder (*ʿajab*) itself evokes both an appreciation of cosmographic complexity and a form of medieval Arabic literature, the *ʿajāʾib al-makhlūqāt*, that anthologizes the world's exotica in a manner cognate to the wonders, or *mirabilia*, literature of the Latin West (Zadeh 25–26). The wondrous affect punctuates the shopping list's geographic sprawl.

Burton's pedantic footnotes to his translation notwithstanding, linguistic difficulties or archaic terminology can result in some of the orienting details in this scene getting muddled, misrendered, or elided entirely in available versions of the *Nights*, even when translators rightly convey the spirit of the text. The types of apples mentioned in the list both hail from the Levant, with *fatḥī* apples sometimes also known as *Shāmī*, meaning from places like modern Lebanon, Syria, Jordan, and Palestine, and *miskī*, or musk, apples even spawning their own folk etymology in relation to the region. According to the great twelfth-century Arabic geographer Yāqūt al-Ḥamawī, himself a freedman of Byzantine Greek origin, *miskī* apples were said to be associated with the Palestinian village of Miska—homonymous with "musk" in Arabic (128). But Haddawy's English renders the varieties named in the text as simply "yellow and red apples" (81). Even as this anticipates his readers' prior knowledge, and plausibly interprets the underlying words while navigating a philological challenge, the rendering in visual terms breaks from the structuring principle of the shopping list, which is pronouncedly geographic. Students should therefore be invited to reflect on translation as an enterprise that is both cross-cultural and temporal—keeping in mind as well the Middle Arabic register of the *Nights*, a hybridization of classical and colloquial

Arabic in which most popular literature was composed by and for those who often did not belong to the educated elite.

Furthermore, as Anny Gaul has recently pointed out, specific elements of the text can have a discursive logic beneath or beyond literary design: identifying the various exotic flowers purchased during this shopping spree as known medieval aphrodisiacs and abortifacients, she offers an insightful reading of "The Porter and the Three Ladies" in light of Mamluk-era pharmacology and the Galenic principles underpinning Islamic medicine. Gaul reminds us that in approaching the *Nights* as a medieval text, we have to balance between attention to its literariness and more historicist interpretations. Pairing the text with another primary source like the ninth-century *Accounts of China and India* by Abū Zayd al-Sīrāfī or the much later universal encyclopedia of Shihāb al-Dīn al-Nuwayrī is a fruitful way of getting students to compare, contrast, and overlay the tales' imaginary onto a map of the world as known at different points in time.

The expansive, almost unruly quality of the "map" of the *Arabian Nights* calls to mind another dimension of its ostensible cosmopolitanism, namely that of being able to move about the world, beyond being able to conjure the world into the local. This second form of cosmopolitanism, which invokes exploration abroad as well as inclusion at home, emerges especially in the "Story of Jullanar of the Sea" (Haddawy 464–518). We begin the tale in well-trod terrain, the land of Khurasan, the capital of an erstwhile Persian kingdom. At first, the city seems a cosmopolis of a similar ilk to Baghdad or Cairo, with the king's court at its center. Concubines from "various provinces and countries" are all brought before the sonless king, and one day, a man who claims to have traveled three years to reach him brings along the most beautiful bride of all (465).

The king's new wife eventually discloses her identity as Jullanar of the Sea, a princess from the underwater world. She informs an astounded monarch that his concept of the globe and its diversity is yet smaller than what is found in the sea world, saying, "in the sea there are people of all types and creatures of all kinds, just as there are on land, and more" (Haddawy 473). Through Jullanar, the story then pans outward, and rather than the entire world and its maidens being called before the king in Khurasan, his son Badr—half of the land and half of the sea—will go on a quest that spans region and realm.

The story of Prince Badr follows a trajectory that is similar to a range of other premodern adventure tales. It shares several qualities with the far-ranging "City of Brass" story that came to be part of the Egyptian recension of the *Nights*, as well as with the Alexander romance tradition, which has myriad iterations in Greek, Persian, Arabic, Hebrew, and so on; indeed, scholars have already noted the rich intertextuality between the "City of Brass" tale and Alexander's adventures (Marzolph and van Leeuwen 1: 146–50).[8] In its Islamicate context, Alexander can be seen traveling beneath the sea with the aid of al-Khiḍr (the "Green Man" who assists Moses in the Qur'ān), meeting the legendary *sīmorgh* bird of *Shahnameh* fame, encountering a society of Amazonian women, and building walls around the fabled land of Gog and Magog.[9]

Likewise in the *Nights*, Prince Badr explores widely, evading dark magic, encountering wonders, and at times being shepherded along by well-meaning older male guides. All the while, he moves between water and land, the two domains that describe literally the entire world, which his unique genealogy predestines him to inherit. His adventures take him across several islands—implicitly in the southern Indian Ocean and therefore at the edges of the known earth, as Jullanar at one point summons her relatives using a bead of Cambodian aloeswood (*al-ʿūd al-qamārī*, literally "of Khmer," though conflated with Java in a number of medieval texts and thus also by Haddawy).[10]

Badr initially sets out seeking a wife, and along the way discovers much about the world. In what might be read as a restatement of the central themes of the *Nights*' frame tale, he discovers much in particular about the nature of women. Tellingly, even as the textual imaginary expands in space, its conceptualization of human nature is largely unchanged: on a faraway island to which Badr flees after escaping a spell cast on him by his would-be betrothed, there dwells a menagerie of animals, all of whom are men turned into beasts after a stint as playthings of the island's sexually voracious enchantress-queen. Eventually, Badr comes back to where his journey began, suggesting a geographic and figurative full circle, and returns contentedly to his original betrothed.

If cosmopolitanism is to rest not only on worldly wisdom but also on the ethical principles that entail contemplating the cosmos, transcending categories, or encouraging one to reach across the world's varied, collocated constituent parts—a "moral regard for difference" in the words of Siby K. George (66)—the above stories will perhaps leave us wanting. The Black enslaved person in the "Tale of the Three Apples" is referred to as ugly and pursued as a criminal; a temperamental Harun al-Rashid curses and threatens his Persian viziers; and the bejeweled bride is abortively wed to a derided hunchback who literally spends his wedding night face down in shit. Even within the more fantastic ambit of "Jullanar of the Sea," expanding one's world does not necessarily conduce to expanding the mind.

Moreover, from our current vantage point it is at times easy to overstate the seeming facts of cosmopolitanism displayed in such stories, both by stretching their temporal implications and by overreading the text's apparent verisimilitude. This is something we have often seen done with an apologetic force behind it: when confronted with Western media representations of a modern Middle East supposedly plagued by a fatal inability to handle its heterogeneity, the countervailing myth-busting impulse is to emphasize the region's long (uninterrupted?) history of ethnic, religious, sexual, or ideological pluralism. We are starkly reminded of the pitfalls of fetishizing the region as a diverse crossroads and collapsing its chronology by glancing at the writings of Lady Mary Wortley Montagu, who muses in a letter of 10 March 1718 during her Ottoman travels:

> Now do I fancy that you imagine I have entertain'd you all this while with a relation that has (at least) receiv'd many Embellishments from my hand. This is but too like (says you) the Arabian tales; these embrodier'd Napkins, and a jewel as large as a Turkey's egg!—You forget, dear Sister, those very tales were writ by an Author of this Country and (excepting the Enchantments) are a real representation of the manners here. . . . But what would you say if I told you that I have been in a Haram where the winter Apartment was wainscoted with inlaid work of Mother of Pearl, Ivory of different Colours and olive wood, exactly like the little Boxes you have seen brought out of this Country; and those rooms design'd for Summer, the walls all crusted with Japan china, the roofs gilt, and the floors spread with the finest Persian carpets. Yet there is nothing more true; such is the Palace of my Lovely freind, the fair Fatima, who I was acquainted with at Adrianople. (Halsband 385)

This passage could have come straight out of an "Orientalism 101" crash course, and we can readily refer ourselves to Edward Said's discussion of the treatment of the Middle East as a venue of eternal, sacred ancientness overlaid by arrested, decadent medievalism—a rhetorical device contrived to legitimate the effects of civilizing missions and undying claims to an unchanging Holy Land.

The greater challenge, though, is parsing the historical slipperiness that the *Nights* admits in its own pages, which lends Montagu's statements an uncanny air: as the foregoing discussion notes, the text toggles between several chronological frames, perhaps all the more so in its later manuscripts.

In the words of Daniel Beaumont, "[D]espite the antiquity of many of the plots in the *Thousand and One Nights*, the stories as we have them now seem to wear the garb of the late medieval period in the Arab-Islamic world; that is, the eras of the Mamluks and the Ottomans" (25). In other words, the prism through which the ʿAbbasid milieu of many of the core tales is presented may visit at least five hundred years of hindsight on those scenes.

This aspect of the text can, however, serve as an excellent basis for critical reflections on historiography instead of merely classifying the *Nights* as anachronistic. As we have proposed here, the text's layered temporalities open up a conversation about social and political implications. In this case, it calls for us to address the importance for later Muslim societies of articulating their imaginary of the ʿAbbasid period: that is, it prompts us to consider what motivates the text's would-be cosmopolitan representation of its particular world, as well as the more general appeal such representations have popularly held. This gives readers a chance to ask not only what the world of the *Nights* is, but also why it is so.

In an essay on al-Andalus (Muslim Iberia) as a "chronotope" in modern narratives that propound Arab nationalism, William Granara speaks of the collective memory engaged by authors mythologizing the past in order to craft a vision for the present. Though he discusses individual novels with individuated authorial stakes when assessing how al-Andalus has grown into an imaginary landscape marked by religious coexistence, Arab efflorescence on European soil, and the Muslim world's ultimate territorial extent, Granara notes that the works are unified by "a grand mythology with a shared language, reference, allusion, belief, and tradition" (58). We know of few specifics concerning the acephalous, collective authorship of the *Nights*, but there is a unifying tone—a "shared language"—among many of the pieces, and guiding students to this means showing them how the world under discussion, with its putatively historical skeleton, is being strategically, selectively, and creatively remembered by people in the region as a space and time of cultural import and global access.

We can also use cosmopolitanism's many double edges—at once imperial and universal, exclusive and inclusive, and aspirational and nostalgic—to unearth and probe the cynical tendencies of some of the tales, even as the *Nights* more generally evinces that storytellers and historians alike have long colluded around pretty notions of civilizations' alleged golden ages and golden cities (as ʿAbbasid Baghdad has long been held to be).[11] Many of the tales poke fun from below at the ruling elites who enjoy the greatest jurisdiction while also circumscribing the lives of the unfree, disabled, and minoritized. Meanwhile, for everyone else, the tales idealize the simultaneously central and arterial status of the *Nights*' stomping grounds, and of moving among them without any "sense of foreignness" and alienation, as Muhsin Jasim al-Musawi has put it (152). In weaving its motivated fantasy, the text participates in a mode of self-promoting world-building that nearly every culture shares. Comparative study thus becomes particularly useful here. Pairing the *Nights* with related works of literature from other contexts, from the Persian prestige epic, the *Shāhnāmeh* (*Book of Kings*), to the satirical Middle English *Canterbury Tales*, encourages students to think about the work that storytelling does in relation to history, identity, and worldview across a number of regional and sociopolitical gradients in the medieval period.

Critically broaching these rememberings of thriving ʿAbbasid cosmopolises ultimately impels us to address that which is forgotten or overlooked. As al-Musawi notes in his discussion of enslaved people and slave markets in the *Nights*, the mercantile implications of the global access available to an imperial center are utopian for some and radically disadvantaging for others, such that:

> The city [of Baghdad] brought people together, accumulated merchandise from all over the globe, and made countless achievements in science, architecture, and culture. However, along with this enormous growth, the assimilated communities also had to struggle for recognition. Even in the efflorescent cosmopolitan atmosphere, there remained hierarchical and racial gradations and prejudices. (al-Musawi 133)

This reality pertains to portions of the *Nights* that take place outside of Baghdad as well: in Jullanar's tale, the merchandise that draw the greatest narrative focus for their sheer number and global reach are the king's concubines. In other words, we can think with cosmopolitanism to question what it means for one place or people to desire the world, to become its consumer and its epicenter, with all the exploitation and commodification that this entails.

In this essay, we have considered the pedagogical implications of committing ourselves, in a reading of the *Thousand and One Nights*, to the lens of worldliness, which has been often coded as cosmopolitanism where our text is concerned. We have discussed this in the context of historicity, empire, and identity and memory. In simultaneously centering and critiquing the idea that the *Nights*' world is a cosmopolitan one, students are prompted to think about the material, social, and even spiritual implications of global interconnectedness as it manifested itself in the medieval period.

As we have seen, the *Nights* contains many worlds and has also long been of many worlds. Beginning as it did with an Indo-Persian kernel, it changed and expanded greatly—often under what we might call world consciousness, be it nostalgic, imperial, transcultural and translational, or otherwise—into a piece of world literature par excellence. Acknowledging these facts about the *Nights* and taking their implications seriously can lead us to disrupt not only its status as a text that is medieval but also as a unified text that is of any one time and any one place. Moreover, at a time when the medieval in popular discourse can symbolize both civilizational alterity—that is, the unmodern other—and a fantasized preglobal Europe, the *Nights* can help us question the cultural and temporal assumptions of medievalism (after all, we would do well to recall, the *Nights*' pioneering modern European translator Galland was far closer in time to his Arabic manuscript sources than we are to him).

To suggest what it may look like to read in a way that rejects atavistic medievalism while also critiquing cosmopolitanism as it has typically been used to describe the Islamic world, we may look to Eduardo Mendieta's thoughts on the shape of cosmopolitanism to come—an ethics of imaginative and self-reflexive worldly engagement beyond the universalizing telos of imperial desire:

> We are always more and less than what we are imagined to be, which is why we must allow others to challenge our "images" and "imagination" of them, and conversely, to allow ourselves to correct our own self-understanding in light of those challenges. Thus, this imagination internalizes the other, alterity, in a non-imperial and non-obliterating way, in order to reconstitute itself. There is no single cosmopolitan vision, but a process of arriving at it through an engagement with a dialogical imagination that opens up the spaces of mutual transformation. (254)

Ultimately, in teaching the *Thousand and One Nights* in this spirit, we can show the world and its heritage to be at once far bigger and far smaller than it seems, and this is perhaps the key ingredient for generating the sort of considered cosmopolitanism that hews to the term's ethical desiderata within our own classrooms.

Notes

1. On the origins and evolution of the concept of imperial or statist cosmopolitanism, see Chin.

2. On the recent history of cosmopolitan ethics, see Mendieta.

3. Ulrich Marzolph, a doyen of the field, maintains a current bibliography of studies on the *Thousand and One Nights* available online.

4. Ḥannā Diyāb's contributions to the *Nights*, arguably making him the most influential storyteller of the modern era, are now the subject of a growing body of scholarship, thanks to both his newfound memoir/travelogue in a manuscript at the Vatican library and the recent critical edition of Galland's journals. See Marzolph ("Man"). Diyab's book has just been translated into English by Elias Muhanna.

5. For an excellent, concise, and relatively up-to-date account of the textual history of the *Nights*, see also Newman.

6. For instance, Marzolph has recently identified a twelfth-century Persian precursor to part of the tale of Sindbād the Sailor, for which the oldest known Arabic manuscripts date to the seventeenth century ("Early Persian Precursor"). On the place of the *Thousand and One Nights* in the Persian and Turkish literary traditions respectively, including folk narratives, see Marzolph, "Persian Nights"; Birkalan-Gedik.

7. On the reception of the *sīra* corpus in the West from the eighteenth century onward in both scholarly and popular circles, see Heath (3–22). More recently, Magidow has discussed the use of the term "epic" in translating *sīra* in her work on *Sīrat Dhāt al-Himma* (5–8).

8. For a detailed summary of the history, plotline, and broader literary context of the Persian editions (both poetry and prose) of the Alexander romance (or *Eskandar-nāma*), see Hannaway. See also the essay on the Alexander legend by Adam Miyashiro and Su Fang Ng in this volume.

9. Al-Khiḍr is not named as such in the Qur'ān, but there is a longstanding exegetical and apocryphal tradition describing him as Moses's guide based on Qur'ān 18.65–82.

10. For an early medieval Arabic account of the "land of al-Qamār," including a reference to its aloeswood export, see al-Sīrāfī (44–47; 2.7).

11. On the noir aspects of the *Nights*, particularly with respect to social hierarchies and prejudices, see Irwin.

Works Cited

Abbott, Nabia. "A Ninth-Century Fragment of the 'Thousand Nights': New Light on the Early History of the Arabian Nights." *Journal of Near Eastern Studies*, vol. 8, no. 3, 1949, pp. 129–64.

Ahmed, Shahab. *What Is Islam? The Importance of Being Islamic*. Princeton UP, 2016.

Beaumont, Daniel. *Slave of Desire: Sex, Love, and Death in the* Thousand and One Nights. Farleigh Dickinson, 2002.

Birkalan-Gedik, Hande A. "The *Thousand and One Nights* in Turkish: Translations, Adaptations, and Related Issues." Marzolph, *The* Arabian Nights *in Transnational Perspective*, pp. 201–20.

Burton, Richard F. *A Plain and Literal Translation of the* Arabian Nights' Entertainments, *Now Entituled the Book of the* Thousand Nights and a Night. Burton Club, 1885. 10 vols.

Chin, Tamara. "What Is Imperial Cosmopolitanism? Revisiting *Kosmopolitēs* and *Mundanus*." *Cosmopolitanism and Empire: Universal Rulers, Local Elites, and Cultural Integration in the Ancient Near East and Mediterranean*, edited by Myles Lavan et al., Oxford UP, 2016, pp. 129–51.

Chraïbi, Aboubakr, editor. *Arabic Manuscripts of the* Thousand and One Nights*: Presentation and Critical Editions of Four Noteworthy Texts: Observations on Some Osmanli Translations*. Espaces et signes, 2016.

Diyāb, Ḥannā. *The Book of Travels*. Translated by Elias Muhanna, edited by Johannes Stephan, New York UP, 2021. 2 vols.

Fudge, Bruce, translator. *A Hundred and One Nights*. New York UP, 2016.

Gaul, Anny. "Shahrazad's Pharmacy: Women's Bodies of Knowledge in 'The Tale of the Porter and the Three Ladies.'" *Middle Eastern Literatures*, vol. 19, no. 2, 2016, pp. 185–205.

George, Siby K. "The Cosmopolitan Self and the Fetishism of Identity." *Questioning Cosmopolitanism*, edited by Stan van Hooft and Wim Vandekerckhove, Springer, 2010, pp. 63–82.

Granara, William. "Nostalgia, Arab Nationalism, and the Andalusian Chronotope in the Evolution of the Modern Arabic Novel." *Journal of Arabic Literature*, vol. 36, no. 1, 2005, pp. 57–73.

Haddawy, Husain, translator. *The Arabian Nights*. W. W. Norton, 2008.

Halsband, Robert, editor. *The Complete Letters of Lady Mary Wortley Montagu*. Vol. 1, Oxford UP, 1965.

Ḥamawī, Yāqūt al-. *Muʿjam al-buldān*. Vol. 5, Dār Ṣādir, 1977.

Hannaway, William L. "Eskandar-Nāma." *Encyclopædia Iranica*, edited by Ehsan Yarshater et al., www.iranicaonline.org/articles/eskandar-nama.

Heath, Peter. *The Thirsty Sword: Sīrat ʿAntar and the Arabic Popular Epic*. U of Utah P, 1996.

Hirschler, Konrad. *The Written Word in Medieval Arabic Lands*. Edinburgh UP, 2013.

Horta, Paulo. "The Collector of Worlds: Richard Burton, Cosmopolitan Translator of the *Nights*." *Scheherazade's Children: Global Encounters with the* Arabian Nights, edited by Philip Kennedy and Marina Warner, New York UP, 2013, pp. 70–89.

Irwin, Robert. "The Dark Side of the 'Arabian Nights.'" *Critical Muslim*, vol. 13, 2015, www.criticalmuslim.io/the-dark-side-of-the-arabian-nights/.

Kia, Mana. *Persianate Selves: Memories of Place and Origin Before Nationalism.* Stanford UP, 2020.

———. "Space, Sociality, and Sources of Pleasure: A Response to Sanjay Subrahmanyam." *Journal of the Economic and Social History of the Orient*, vol. 61, 2018, pp. 256–76.

Magidow, Melanie. "Epic of the Commander Dhat Al-Himma." *Medieval Feminist Forum, Subsidia Series*, vol. 9, 2019, pp. 1–62. Medieval Texts in Translation 6.

Mahdi, Muhsin, editor. *Kitāb alf layla wa-layla: min uṣūlihi al-ʿArabīya al-ūlā.* Vol. 1, Brill, 1984.

Marzolph, Ulrich. "The *Arabian Nights* Bibliography." *Ulirch Marzolph: Exploring the Narrative Culture of the Muslim World*, 2015, wwwuser .gwdg.de/~umarzol/arabiannights.html.

———, editor. *The* Arabian Nights *in Transnational Perspective.* Wayne State UP, 2007.

———. "An Early Persian Precursor to the Tales of Sindbād the Seafaring Merchant." *Zeitschrift der Deutschen Morgenländischen Gesellschaft*, vol. 167, no. 1, 2017, pp. 127–41.

———. "The Man Who Made the *Nights* Immortal: The Tales of the Syrian Maronite Storyteller Ḥannā Diyāb." *Marvels and Tales*, vol. 32, no. 1, 2018, pp. 114–25.

———. "The Persian Nights: Links between the *Arabian Nights* and Persian Culture." Marzolph, *The* Arabian Nights *in Transnational Perspective*, pp. 221–43.

Marzolph, Ulrich, and Richard van Leeuwen. *The* Arabian Nights *Encyclopedia.* ABC-CLIO, 2004. 2 vols.

Mendieta, Eduardo. "From Imperial to Dialogical Cosmopolitanism." *Ethics and Global Politics*, vol. 2, 2009, pp. 241–58.

Musawi, Muhsin J. al-. *The Islamic Context of the* Thousand and One Nights. Columbia UP, 2009.

Newman, Daniel L. "Wandering Nights: Shahrazād's Mutations." *The Life of Texts: Evidence in Textual Production, Transmission, and Reception*, edited by Carlo Caruso, Bloomsbury, 2018, pp. 62–93.

Nuwayrī, Shihāb al-Dīn al-. *The Ultimate Ambition in the Arts of Erudition.* Translated by Elias Muhanna, Penguin Books, 2016.

Said, Edward. *Orientalism.* Vintage Books, 1978.

Seale, Yasmine, translator. *The Annotated* Arabian Nights*: Tales from the* Thousand and One Nights. Edited by Paulo Lemos Horta, Liveright Publishing, forthcoming.

Sīrāfī, Abū Zayd al-. *Accounts of China and India.* Translated by Tim Mackintosh-Smith, New York UP, 2017.

Slyomovics, Susan. "Performing *A Thousand and One Nights* in Egypt." *Oral Tradition*, vol. 9, no. 2, 1994, pp. 390–419.

van Bladel, Kevin. "A Brief History of Islamic Civilization from Its Genesis in the Late Nineteenth Century to Its Institutional Entrenchment." *Al-ʿUṣūr al-Wusṭā*, vol. 28, 2020, pp. 150–73.

Zadeh, Travis. "The Wiles of Creation: Philosophy, Fiction, and the *ʿAjāʾib* Tradition." *Middle Eastern Literatures*, vol. 13 no. 1, 2010, pp. 21–48.

Marci Freedman

Teaching Benjamin of Tudela's *Book of Travels* and the Jewish Middle Ages

Within the small corpus of Jewish travel literature, few works are more celebrated than that of Benjamin of Tudela's *Book of Travels* (*Sefer Masa'ot*). Its author has even been dubbed the Jewish Marco Polo by many scholars. This little work, of some eighty pages in Hebrew prose, details a journey that begins in Spain, across Mediterranean Europe, to the Middle East, down to Egypt and across North Africa. The narrative also offers descriptions of India and the Far East, as well as Russian, northern, and eastern Europe; whether Benjamin of Tudela visited these regions himself is debated. The anonymously authored prologue states that the *Book of Travels* recorded "all the things which he saw or heard from trustworthy men."[1] And yet, the *Book of Travels* is far from a riveting narrative. The majority of entries detail the distance between destinations, whether the given location contained a Jewish community, and, if so, its size and the names of the leaders of the community. Still, it remains one of the most mined medieval Jewish texts for nuggets of information relating to the twelfth-century Jewish world, and as a valuable resource for the non-Jewish world.

We know nothing about the person known as Benjamin of Tudela—when he lived, why he traveled, or why he wrote the account (if he is even the author). The narrative offers no biography or explicit statements about his motivations to travel, or what he sought to accomplish. All of these remain open questions, and ones which have occupied the pens of scholars since the nineteenth century. The only firm information that we possess is a name, Benjamin ben ("son of") Yonah, and the date that Benjamin is said to have returned to Castile—1173. Both are found in the prologue. Barring the opening sentence, the narrative is written in the third person. How, then, can we begin to understand a text when the author himself is so elusive? For students unfamiliar with studying the Middle Ages and the inevitable gaps in the historical record, the *Book of Travels* may prove a frustrating text; it lacks all the contextual information students traditionally use on which to hang their analyses. And yet, it is for this reason that the *Book of Travels* is an exemplary text for the pedagogical process. Here we can introduce students to a text without its usual framing and illustrate how much can still be gained from texts even when little contextual information survives.

This essay presents four thematic strands—ranging from the Jewish Diaspora to pilgrimage to shared sacred space to encountering the other—through which the *Book of Travels* can be studied. Each strand illuminates how the rich, if succinct, data of the *Book of Travels* can be used as a primary source in a variety of contexts. Although we cannot reach any firm conclusions about the person of Benjamin of Tudela or his motivations to travel, let alone precisely where he traveled, this essay demonstrates how we can move beyond unanswerable questions and still engage with the *Book of Travels* in meaningful ways. Each section offers a brief background of the theme or specific passages from the travelogue, as well as suggestions for readings that can be paired with the *Book of Travels* as supplementary or background readings. Here I must note that this essay draws heavily on Martin Jacobs's *Reorienting the East: Jewish Travelers to the Medieval Muslim World*, and frequent references are made to its many helpful chapters.

Which Version?

The *Book of Travels* has survived in four medieval manuscripts: the first roughly dates to the late thirteenth or early fourteenth century (British Library, London, MS Add. 27089), the second is a fifteenth-century fragment, where approximately the first third of the text is missing (Bodleian Library, Oxford, MS Oppenheim Add. 8° 36), the third dates to 1428 (Biblioteca Casanatense, Rome, MS 3097), and the fourth is from circa 1520 (National Library of Israel, Jerusalem, MS Heb. 82647). The British Library has digitized their copy, and the National Library of Israel has digitized copies of both the Casanatense copy and their own.[2] Each manuscript is its own textual witness; across the manuscripts' transmission history, copyists have produced slightly different versions of the text through scribal error, deliberate omissions and interpolations, and self-censorship.

In the age of print, the *Book of Travels* appeared in Hebrew editions in quite rapid succession—1543, 1556, and 1583. All three Hebrew editions are closely related to the circa 1520 manuscript. Latin editions also followed in 1575, first by the Spanish humanist Benito Arias Montano, and then the Dutch Protestant theologian Constantijn L'Empereur in 1633. Various European vernaculars followed from the seventeenth century onward. This brief overview of the *Book of Travels*' textual transmission offers a sense of the interest in Benjamin of Tudela's travelogue, which went well beyond the confines of the twelfth-century Jewish world: this is a text that has survived centuries in different cultural and linguistic contexts.

At present, there is no good, updated critical edition of the narrative in English. The two most recent editions are Adolf Asher's two-volume 1841 translation, and the only slightly more recent 1907 edition by Marcus Nathan Adler. Asher's edition relies solely on the 1556 Hebrew edition, as he did not have access to any of the extant manuscripts. Adler's edition is the far superior of the two, as the text and translation are based on the British Library manuscript and includes a critical apparatus. Adler's edition comprises an English part and a Hebrew part (rather than a facing-page translation). The footnotes to the English section qualify and elucidate the text with additional historical and geographic information. The Hebrew portion is more technical; here the Hebrew footnotes comprise a textual comparison of the extant manuscripts, and of Asher's edition. Adler logs everything from variations in the spelling of names and places to omissions and interpolations to a number of significant instances where the manuscripts disagree. Neither edition is ideal to set as a teaching text; the Asher because of its textual deficiencies, and the Adler because of its copious, if archaic, notes, as well as its reliance on the Hebrew text.

The most accessible text for students is Michael A. Signer's 1983 edition. Here Signer has reproduced Adler's translation with minimal intratextual notes interspersed. A smaller section of endnotes also helps elucidate the most essential sections of the narrative. Equally helpful is that each location named is printed in the margin, which allows for easy navigation through the text. Included in Signer's edition are three separate introductions—Asher's, Adler's, and Signer's own—offering ample contextual information (if even for comparison). Where passages from the *Book of Travels* are discussed throughout this chapter, page numbers refer to Signer's edition.

Writing Diaspora

In many ways, the *Book of Travels* is a book about diaspora. It surveys the extant Jewish communities, and their size and leadership, across the medieval Jewish world.[3] Here again it must be stressed that our Tudelan narrator did not visit every single location named. Irrespective of this, the given locations that do receive mention are usually afforded a mere few lines, with some places receiving as much as a full paragraph. The *Book of Travels* is not known for its verbosity. Five descriptions do, however, stand out for their length and depth: Rome (Signer 63–64), Constantinople (70–72), Jerusalem (82–86), Baghdad (95–102), and Cairo (128–31). It is not always apparent why these big five receive special treatment by Benjamin of Tudela, Jerusalem being the obvious exception. Rome has received some treatment by Marie Thérèse Champagne and Paul Borchardt. Baghdad (and by extension the Middle East and Far East, where Jews are under Islamic dominion) can be viewed as an idealized version of a glorious past, both for the city itself and its Jewish community. In the framework of crescent versus cross, the *Book of Travels* extols Baghdad, suggesting that Jews fared significantly better in Islamic lands as opposed to Christian ones (Jacobs, *Reorienting the East* 131–37). Likewise, Cairo is home to a sizeable Jewish community in the famed neighborhood of Fustat. Here the *Book of Travels* would be nicely complemented by the vast treasure trove that is the Cairo Genizah.

Embedded in all the locations' descriptions is essentially a descriptive census of the twelfth-century world's Jewish communities. In western Europe, the size of the communities is in the tens and hundreds; as the narrative moves further east, with the exception of the Holy Land, the size of the Jewish communities increases into the tens of thousands (see more below). We simply do not know whether the quoted size of the Jewish communities refers to individuals, just Jewish males (possibly over a certain age), or the number of Jewish households in any given location. Despite an implied precision, the numbers simply cannot be taken at face value.

Nonetheless, they are integral to the text. First, they are an indication of where Benjamin believed Jewish communities could be found in the twelfth century. Second, and more important, they highlight the dispersion of medieval Jewry.

Why Benjamin chose to include this census is an irresolvable debate. The whereabouts and size of Jewish communities does, however, lend itself to a number of discussion points related to Jews being a minority in the medieval world. Although the numbers remain unsubstantiated, they are a historical benchmark for a Jewish presence in any given locale, and the *Book of Travels* is an oft quoted source for those who seek to establish the historicity of Jewish settlement in a particular place. How and under what conditions Jews came to settle in these locations, and their ever-changing economic and social statuses, in addition to the threat and actualization of expulsion, is one set of thematics that the description of these Jewish communities can enable for classroom study. The information derived from the descriptions can, in turn, be compared to any standard medieval Jewish history textbook, with the *Book of Travels* further complementing the historical record. A few good starting points to supplement classroom discussion are textbooks by Anna Sapir Abulafia, Robert Chazan, and Mark R. Cohen, respectively.

Coupled with every Jewish community are the names of its leading rabbis, or in the case of the Far East the *nasi* ("prince"). Some of these rabbinic names have been identified, whereas others are well-known names such as Rabbi Yechiel in Rome and Rabbi Abraham ben David in Posquières.[4] For the most part, however, the rabbinic names listed in the *Book of Travels* are too generic for the identification of specific individuals. Similar to Benjamin's population census, the inclusion of communal leaders raises more questions than it answers. The rabbis can be made meaningful by studying them in the context of what they represent: Jewish autonomy and self-government, and also as chains of tradition for Torah Judaism. Often listed in groups of three, these rabbis represent the communal leadership of any given community; perhaps they can even be understood as a *Beit Din* (a Jewish court of law). Here students can be introduced to the often thriving inner workings of Jewish communities and the autonomy they maintained over their day-to-day lives as overseen by the *Beit Din*. As the perpetual minority in the Middle Ages, especially in Christendom, Jewish self-government demonstrates how these communities continued to operate irrespective of their relationships with their non-Jewish neighbors.

Rabbis and scholars also stand as the pillars of Torah in their respective communities. A *Beit Din*, or *nasi* ("prince") applies Torah law to their specific communities, establishing a code of practice rooted in *halachah* (Jewish law) suitable for that community. In this way they act as links in the chain of Torah, leading back to the revelation at Mount Sinai. Therefore, despite the Jewish exilic state, authentic Torah Judaism continues to flourish within the Diaspora, and it is this adherence to the Torah that connects communities across the Diaspora, with the rabbis as the Torah's arbiters. Chain of Tradition texts were popular in the Middle Ages (in part, as a polemical exercise against the influence of Karaism, the subscriptions of a Jewish sect that only adhered to the written rather than the oral Torah; for more on the Karaites, see below). This is yet another context that the *Book of Travels* can be applied to—rabbinic leadership as pillars of Torah. One of the most accessible Chain of Tradition texts is Abraham ibn Daud's *Sefer Ha-Qabbalah*.

Themes of Jewish sovereignty, exile, messianic hope, and redemption are threaded throughout the *Book of Travels*. The still relatively obscure twelfth-century Far East allowed the *Book of Travels* to portray an idealized world: Teima, Tilmas (Signer 106–07) and Mulahid (110), India (124), where Jews retained their sovereignty; Isfahan (114) and Katifa (119), where Jews were held in high esteem; and Gilan (110) and, of course, Baghdad (which is graced by a lengthy description), where Jews maintained good relationships with those who ruled over them. It is for this reason that the Jewish populations increase in size as Benjamin journeys further east. The hundreds of thousands of Jews said to be living in these Far Eastern locations reflects an idealized stability and success of Diasporic Jewry that the *Book of Travels* contrasts with the less stable Jewish communities in the Christian West.

The above themes are also intrinsically linked with the theme of the ten lost tribes. Three of the tribes are mentioned in the description of Kheibar (107), whereas a further four are found in Naisabur (114–15). These tribes also embody ideas of Jewish sovereignty—both from when the ancient kingdom of Israel was extant and as the representation of the future messianic redemption. One of the harbingers for the arrival of the Jewish Messiah will be the ingathering of the exiles from across the Jewish Diaspora, including the ten lost tribes. This offers yet another explanation for the *Book of Travels*' descriptive census, the precise location of all of the world's Jews, including the ten lost tribes, all of whom can be gathered and moved to the Land of Israel at the end of days for the messianic age to follow. Here, Alanna E. Cooper is a good starting point to use as a supplementary text.

To summarize, students introduced to the *Book of Travels* for the first time will invariably latch on to the precision of the descriptions with respect to the distance between locations, the travelogue's census of the Jewish communities, why certain cities receive more than a cursory treatment, and the listing of communal leaders. In the absence of any records that explain why the narrative was written in the style that it is, students' attention can be redirected to the ways the *Book of Travels*' information may have resonated with medieval Jewish readers (and beyond) with regard to questions about the states of the twelfth-century world's Jewish communities, their perceptions of self-government and autonomy, the Jewish messianic future, and the *Book of Travels*' contrasting views of Jews under Christianity and Islam.

Jews on the Move

The *Book of Travels* is silent on why Benjamin left his native Tudela and traveled through much of the known world. As mentioned above, a range of motivations have been suggested from the most likely—the narrator is a pilgrim, or even a merchant-pilgrim—to the dubious: the narrator is a physician. It is not my intention here to substantiate or refute any one of these motivations; I address the plausibility of each in a forthcoming article. But we should note that if the *Book of Travels* cannot be read strictly as a pilgrim's narrative, it can still be read as a pious journey to the Holy Land and its surrounding sacred environs throughout the Levant.

There is no medieval Jewish concept of pilgrimage comparable to the Christian sense of *peregrinatio*, since a cult of holy places never developed, nor can Jewish pilgrimage be equated with the Islamic *Hajj*. True, Torah Judaism does have a pilgrimage practice known as the *shalosh regalim* ("three foot festivals"), where Jewish males with the means to do so traveled to the Temple at Jerusalem to bring offerings on the holidays of Passover, *Shavuot* ("Pentecost"), and *Sukkot* ("Tabernacles"), as commanded in Exodus 23.14–17 and Deuteronomy 16.16. Once the Temple was destroyed by the Romans in 70 CE, this biblical precept no longer applied. Medieval Jews who journeyed to the Holy Land did so as a personal pilgrimage in the mode of an individual spiritual accomplishment.

To get a sense of the various experiences of Jewish travelers to the Holy Land (and beyond), the *Book of Travels* can be used in conjunction with other medieval and early modern Jewish travelogues. Petachia of Regensburg (or Ratisbon) is a near contemporary of Benjamin of Tudela and probably traveled in the 1170s and 1180s. Whereas Benjamin's account can be read as a Sephardic travelogue, Petachia's is that of an Ashkenazi Jew's journey. For another Spanish perspective, there is the account of the noted poet Judah ha'Levi (see Malkiel; Scheindlin), which predates both Benjamin and Petachia. Ha'levi arrived in Alexandria in 1140 and traveled on to the Holy Land in 1141; his account primarily details his time in Egypt. Moving into the fifteenth century, the travel letters of Ovadia of Bertinoro reflect an Italian rabbi's journey to, and settlement in Jerusalem, and then Hebron 1468/9 (see Shulman). The letters are, however, of a later date. Finally, Moses Basola's account relates his travels from Venice to the Levant between 1521 and 1523 and recounts his travels among the tombs in the Land of Israel (see David). In addition to the detailed itinerary of this "tomb tour" (see below), an appendix notes which prayers should be recited at various sacred sites. Jacobs supplies brief overviews of each with further references. Of some use might also be Elkan N. Adler's *Jewish Travellers*, which contains excerpts of the accounts of the above travelers. As Jacobs notes, however, these excerpts are uncritical abridgments (Jacobs, *Reorienting the East* 228). Other useful sources for background information include Yosef Levanon ("Holy Place," *Jewish Travellers*), Joshua Prawer, and David Jacoby.

The *Book of Travels* can also be taught alongside Christian and Muslim travel accounts. Two near contemporaries include John of Würzburg and Ibn Jubayr. John of Würzburg was a German priest who traveled to the Holy Land around 1160 and recorded his journey in an account entitled *Description of the Holy Land*. Like Benjamin of Tudela, we know little about the author. Ibn Jubayr (1145–1217) is a more documented figure. He made a pilgrimage to Mecca in the years 1183–85, recording the journey and his experiences along the way.

Armed with multiple perspectives, comparisons between other travelogues and the *Book of Travels* can go in any number of directions: first, why the journey is made, the route, and the conditions of the actual trek to the Holy Land. Second, which sites remain stable sacred spaces to visit, and which ones are added or dropped over the centuries? Can Jewish sacred sites even be accessed, and if so how? What are the travelers doing (if anything) at these sites? Third, how do Diasporic Jews experience and view the Holy Land over a number of centuries? In the premodern world, Jews are never politically in possession of the Holy Land; how then do they interact with or perceive those who are in control at any given time, whether such people be Christian or Muslim? Many travelers also comment on the state of the Jewish world, another fruitful avenue for comparison on the state of medieval and early modern Jewry.

If the intention is to discuss the *Book of Travels* in the context of a personal pilgrimage or pious journey, it might be useful to think about the transmission of Jewish collective memory at sacred sites in the Holy Land and the Levant. Three main sites in Jerusalem that attracted Jewish devotional activity are the Temple Mount (Mount Moriah), the Mount of Olives, and the Tombs of the House of David on Mount Zion. The *Book of Travels* mentions all three in quick succession (Signer 82–86). Outside Jerusalem, the Cave of the Patriarchs at Hebron (86–87) is treated in some detail; the Cave of Elijah on Mount Carmel in Haifa was another favored destination (80). All these sites formed part of a collective Jewish historical memory, derived from the Torah and Talmud.

By visiting these sites, Jewish travelers reimposed a Jewish biblical past on the present Christian-Muslim Holy Land, and recreated the biblical landscape, both in their minds and in their accounts, for Diasporic readers. In turn, a Jewish so-called pilgrim could look up on the ruins of the Temple and the Jewish Holy Land and take hope that their redemption had not yet arrived. Through this, the Jewish traveler reaffirmed their belief in a messianic future—that God's presence will return to Jerusalem at the time of the Jewish redemption, when the Temple will be rebuilt, and Jews will once again be in possession of their ancient Holy Land. Whereas Christians hoped for a personal salvation on their pilgrimage, Jews looked toward a collective salvation, making Jewish pilgrimage an eschatological exercise, symbolic of a messianic future (Jacobs, *Reorienting the East* 83–107).

Although Jerusalem, and to some extent Hebron, were always the ultimate destinations for the medieval Jewish traveler, these destinations were not always possible, given the political landscape. Even when Jews were permitted into Jerusalem, the Galilee region, with its numerous tombs of prophets and revered scholars, also became integral to the medieval Jewish itinerary. Here our Tudelan visits cities such as Seopphoris, Tiberius, and Meron (Signer 89). The work of Nurit Lissovsky has explored the development of some of these sites. The graves of these holy and righteous individuals from the biblical and postbiblical past were sites at which Jews could pray, since graveyards offered a greater chance of connecting with the divine presence. Although one could inform the dead of one's hardships, requests and prayers were still directed to God rather than to the deceased, as one must not address the dead directly. It is difficult to ascertain if a cult of holy sites developed in medieval Judaism, especially since the rabbinic literature offers a spectrum of opinions regarding visiting graves (see Freedman). What is clear is that the literary evidence, from Jewish travelers like Benjamin of Tudela and later itineraries, does record a sacred topography and "tomb tour" for travelers to follow.

Shared Sacred Space

"Tomb tours" also extended beyond the borders of the Holy Land and into other regions around the Levant. Ancient Jewry was exiled twice: after the destruction of the first Jerusalem Temple in 586 BCE by Nebuchadnezzar II, when the Jewish population was exiled to Babylonia (known as the Babylonian Captivity); and again after the Roman destruction of the Second Temple in 70 CE. Both exiles resulted in the transference of the seat of Judaism and Jewish learning to Babylonia. There are a number of Jewish sacred sites enumerated in the *Book of Travels* from the biblical Noah's Ark (Signer 94) and Tower of Babel (103) to various tombs of prophets and rabbinic sages. The two most detailed descriptions are that of the Synagogue of Ezekiel (103–05) and Daniel (108–09). The *Book of Travels*' interest in sacred spaces out of the Holy Land is an expression and confirmation of ancient and medieval Jewry's diasporic identity.

A second theme that emerges from the *Book of Travels*' Holy Land travels and "tomb tours" is that of shared sacred space. There is a long tradition of travel narratives including holy sites that are sacred to one or more of the main monotheistic religions. The abovementioned Temple Mount or Mount Moriah changed hands multiple times, reflecting the political landscape of Jerusalem throughout late antiquity and the Middle Ages. Of course, the Holy Land itself, and Jerusalem, are examples *par excellence* of shared sacred spaces, and much has been written on this topic (as a starting point, see Levine). The study of shared sacred space in the *Book of Travels* is relevant for two reasons: first, it reveals what the Tudelan took an interest in and deemed worthy of recording; second, it offers an insight into which sites were venerated by Jews and Muslims in the late twelfth century, and, in particular, how Muslims frequently appropriated these sites through building projects.

Mention of Christian sites are few and far between in the *Book of Travels*, but some do get a passing mention, such as Saint John in the Lateran in Rome (Signer 64), the Hagia Sophia (70), and the Church of the Holy Sepulchre in Jerusalem (83). There is only one mention of a mosque—not in connection with an existing Jewish site—in the description of Damascus (90). The *Book of Travels*, however, notes five significant sites shared by Jews and Muslims: Hebron (86–87), Harran (93–94), the abovementioned sites of Ezekiel and Daniel, and, finally, the grave of Ezra the Scribe in Persia (108). There is a significant body of scholarship on the subject of shared sacred space. Jacobs is yet again a good starting point; other works of use include Josef W. Meri (*Cult* and "Re-appropriating"), Ora Limor, Elka Weber ("Sharing"), Daniel Boušek, and Pamela Berger, respectively.

The Other Within and Without

No discussion of travel literature is complete without reference to authors' observations about whom they meet or observe along the way. This is a long and complicated subject that cannot be given full justice here. The *Book of Travels* is not just a census of Jewish communities and rabbis, it also records differences in Jewish practice and various Jewish sects, as well as Christians, Muslims, and pagans, all of which are too numerous to list here. These groups represent the other both within and without and are mostly observed with marked detachment (see Blanks).

Both Karaites (Signer 72, 75, 89, 91) and Samaritans (80–82, 88, 91) feature as sects beyond the pale of accepted medieval rabbinic Judaism. In Cairo, the travelogue notes the difference in synagogue practice based on the traditions of Israel and those of Babylon (129). Muslims, as seen above, are either noted for their benevolence towards Jewish communities under their rule or recorded as caretakers of shared sacred sites. Pagans are mentioned in Sidon (78), Khulam (120), and Ceylon (121), whereas the Black population of Assuan is portrayed in a less than flattering light (127). Part 3 of Jacobs's *Reorienting the East* offers an excellent foundation to explore the other both within and without that are encountered in the *Book of Travels.*

The world of medieval Jewish travel literature is, as a corpus, understudied. This essay has hopefully gone some way in helping integrate Benjamin of Tudela's *Book of Travels* into the genre of medieval travel writing, showing readers how Benjamin's account can be taught. Like many travel narratives written for particular audiences, the *Book of Travels* is a reflection of cultural and historical allusions that would have resonated with medieval

Jewish readers. Because some of these references may not be so readily apparent in the modern classroom, I have singled out and highlighted some of the main themes that can be drawn from the text and offered ways the *Book of Travels* can function in a variety of classroom contexts and teaching. I hope this essay encourages readers to include the *Book of Travels* as a primary source in a diverse range of contexts.

Notes

1. The translation is my own.

2. For the British Library, see bl.uk/manuscripts/Viewer.aspx?ref=add_ms_27089. For the National Library of Israel, see nli.org.il/he/manuscripts/NNL_ALEPH000095881/NLI#$FL60270115; and nli.org.il/en/manuscripts/NNL_ALEPH000043997/NLI#$FL9690984.

3. The third, data-specific element of the *Book of Travels* is the descriptive geography of distances between places: see Jacobs, "'A Day's Journey.'"

4. One commonly raised question is why Maimonides is omitted from the *Book of Travels*'s description of Cairo. There is currently no satisfactory answer to this question.

Works Cited and Consulted

Abulafia, Anna Sapir. *Christian Jewish Relations, 1000–1300: Jews in the Service of Medieval Christendom*. Routledge, 2014.

Adler, Elkan N. *Jewish Travellers in the Middle Ages: Nineteen Firsthand Accounts*. Dover, 1987.

Adler, Marcus Nathan, editor and translator. *The Itinerary of Benjamin of Tudela: Critical Text, Translation and Commentary*. Henry Frowde, 1907.

Asher, Adolf, et al. *The Itinerary of Rabbi Benjamin of Tudela*. Vol. 1, A. Asher, 1841.

Ben-Dor Benite, Zvi. *The Ten Lost Tribes: A World History*. Oxford UP, 2009.

Berger, Pamela. "Jewish-Muslim Veneration at Pilgrimage Places in the Holy Land." *Religion and the Arts*, vol. 15, 2011, pp. 1–60.

Blanks, David. "The Sense of Distance and the Perception of the Other." *Journal of Medieval Worlds*, vol. 1, no. 3, 2019, pp. 21–44.

Borchardt, Paul. "The Sculpture in Front of the Lateran as Described by Benjamin of Tudela and Magister Gregorius." *Journal of Roman Studies*, vol. 26, 1936, pp. 68–70.

Boušek, Daniel. "'. . . And the Ishmaelites Honour the Site': Images of Encounters between Jews and Muslims at Jewish Sacred Places in Medieval Hebrew Travelogues." *Archiv Orientální*, vol. 86, 2018, pp. 23–51.

Champagne, Marie Thérèse. "Treasures of the Temple and Claims to Authority in Twelfth-Century Rome." *Aspects of Power and Authority in the Middle Ages*, edited by Brenda Bolton and Christine Meek, Brepols, 2007, pp. 107–18.

Chazan, Robert. *The Jews of Medieval Western Christendom, 1000–1500.* Cambridge UP, 2006.

Cohen, Mark R. *Under Crescent and Cross: The Jews in the Middle Ages.* Princeton UP, 1994.

Cooper, Alanna E. "Conceptualizing Diaspora: Tales of Jewish Travelers in Search of the Lost Tribes." *AJS Review*, vol. 30, no. 1, 2006, pp. 95–117.

David, Abraham. *In Zion and Jerusalem: The Itinerary of Rabbi Moses Basola (1521–1523).* Bar-Ilan UP, 1999.

Encyclopedia of the Jewish Diaspora: Origins, Experiences and Culture. Edited by M. Avrum Ehrlich, ABC-CLIO 2009.

Freedman, Marci. "Moving Away from the 'Historical' Benjamin of Tudela." *A Companion to Medieval Pilgrimage*, edited by William Purkis and Andrew Jotischky, Arc Humanities Press (forthcoming).

Goitein, S. D., editor. *A Mediterranean Society.* U of California P, 1967. 5 vols.

Ibn Daud, Abraham. *Sefer Ha-Qabbalah (The Book of Tradition).* Translated by Gerson D. Cohen, Jewish Publication Society, 1967.

Ibn Jubayr. *The Travels of Ibn Jubayr.* Translated by R. J. C Broadhurst, J. Cape, 1952.

Jacobs, Martin. "'A Days's Journey': Spatial Perceptions and Geographic Imagination in Benjamin of Tudela's *Book of Travels.*" *Jewish Quarterly Review*, vol. 109, no. 2, 2019, pp. 203–32.

———. "From Lofty Caliphs to Uncivilized 'Orientals': Images of the Muslim in Medieval Jewish Travel Literature." *Jewish Studies Quarterly*, vol. 18, no. 1, 2011, pp. 64–90.

———. *Reorienting the East: Jewish Travelers to the Medieval Muslim World.* U of Pennsylvania P, 2014.

Jacoby, David. "Jewish Travelers from Europe to the East, Twelfth–Fifteenth Centuries." *Miscelánea de Estudios Árabes y Hebraicos: Sección Hebreo*, vol. 62, 2013, pp. 11–39.

John of Würzburg. "Description of the Holy Land." *Jerusalem Pilgrimage, 1099–1185*, edited by John Wilkinson and Joyce Hill, Hakluyt Society, 1988, pp. 244–73.

Knobler, Adam. "Jews and the Search for the Ten Lost Tribes." *Mythology and Diplomacy in the Age of Exploration*, by Knobler, Brill, 2016, pp. 96–104.

Levanon, Yosef. "The Holy Place in Jewish Piety: Evidence of Two Twelfth-Century Jewish Itineraries." *Review of Rabbinic Judaism*, vol. 1, no. 1, 1998, pp. 103–18.

———. *Jewish Travellers in the Twelfth Century.* UP of America, 1980.

Levine, Lee I., editor. *Jerusalem: Its Sanctity and Centrality in Judaism, Christianity, and Islam.* Continuum, 1999.

Limor, Ora. "Sharing Sacred Space: Holy Places in Jerusalem between Christianity, Judaism and Islam." *Laudem Hierosolymitani: Studies in Crusades and Medieval Culture in Honour of Benjamin Z. Kedar*, edited by Iris Shagrir et al., Ashgate, 2007, pp. 219–31.

Limor, Ora, and Elchanan Reiner, editors. *Pilgrimage: Jews, Christians, Muslims.* Open UP of Israel, 2005.

Lissovsky, Nurit. "From Travelers' Descriptions of the Holy Land to the Survey of Western Palestine: An Integrative Approach for the Study of Sacred Sites in the Galilee." *Revue des études juives*, vol. 171, nos. 1–2, 2012, p. 61–102.

Malkiel, David J. "Three Perspectives on Judah Halevi's Voyage to Palestine." *Mediterranean Historical Review*, vol. 25, no. 1, 2010, pp. 1–15.

Meri, Josef W. *The Cult of Saints among Muslims and Jews in Medieval Syria.* Oxford UP, 2002.

———. "Re-appropriating Sacred Space: Medieval Jews and Muslims Seeking Elijah and al-Khaḍir." *Medieval Encounters*, vol. 5, no. 3, 1999, pp. 237–64.

Petachia of Regensburg. *The Travels of Rabbi Petachia of Ratisbon.* Edited and translated by Abraham Penisch. Trübner, 1856.

Prawer, Joshua. *The History of the Jews in the Latin Kingdom of Jerusalem.* Oxford UP, 1988.

Scheindlin, Raymond P. *The Song of the Distant Dove: Judah Halevi's Pilgrimage.* Oxford UP, 2008.

Shatzmiller, Joseph. "Jews, Pilgrimage, and the Christian Cult of Saints: Benjamin of Tudela and His Contemporaries." *After Rome's Fall: Narrators and Sources of Early Medieval History: Essays Presented to Walter Goffart*, edited by Alexander Callander Murray, U of Toronto P, 1998, pp. 337–47.

Shulman, Yaakov D. *Pathway to Jerusalem: The Travel Letters of Rabbi Ovadiah of Bartenurah, Written between 1488–1490.* CIS, 1992.

Signer, Michael A., editor. *The Itinerary of Benjamin of Tudela: Travels in the Middle Ages.* Translated by Marcus N. Adler [1907], NightinGale Resources, 1983.

Weber, Elka. "Sharing the Sites: Medieval Jewish Travellers to the Land of Israel." *Eastward Bound: Travel and Travellers, 1050–1550*, edited by Rosamund Allen, Manchester UP, 2004, pp. 35–52.

———. *Traveling Through Text: Message and Method in Late Medieval Pilgrimage Accounts.* Routledge, 2005.

Yahalom, Joseph. *Yehudah Halevi: Poetry and Pilgrimage.* Translated by Gabriel Levin. Magnus Press, 2009.

Adam Miyashiro and Su Fang Ng

Teaching the World through the Alexander Legend, a Global Story

Teaching the Alexander romance in today's literature classroom is both a challenge and an opportunity to put into practice the global turn in literary studies, especially in a medieval studies context. The Alexander romance lends itself to truly interdisciplinary approaches that bridge multiple periodizations, a variety of humanities disciplines, and many literary traditions. This late antique Greek romance, a fantastical account of Alexander the Great's conquests and travels, is, according to Ken Dowden, "antiquity's most successful novel" (650).

In its origin, the *Alexander Romance* came out of a heterogeneous cultural environment. Composed in Alexandria, Egypt around the third century CE and misattributed to Alexander's historian Callisthenes, it belongs to the genre of Hellenistic novels, many of which were written by authors from such places as Egypt, Syria, and Turkey; for some, Greek was a second language. Not only was the *Alexander Romance* the literary product of a culturally diverse ancient world it also became an important work of world literature, defined by David Damrosch as works that "circulate beyond their culture of origin" (4). The *Alexander Romance*'s extraordinary translatability offers a special opportunity to teach premodern globalism.

Scholars of the late antique world in the eastern Mediterranean have given us much of the context for the early spread of the Alexander romance. Daniel L. Selden notes that "the Alexander Romance [was] the single most popular narrative for roughly a millennium and a half [and] alone among fictions of the period, it was of sufficient stature to figure in all the major sacred texts that Christians, Muslims, Zoroastrians, and Jews produced during this era" (32–33). Beyond the robust ancient literary networks in the Mediterranean and Red Sea cultures, the work had a long afterlife in the Middle Ages and beyond.

The fictional story of Alexander the Great was told in every major civilization in Asia, Africa, and Europe, and spread through the Indian Ocean with the spread of Islam. The worlding of the Alexander romance was made possible by its transmission, as Selden notes, through networks of "tributary empires of the Mediterranean and Middle East—Iran, Makedonia, Rome, Byzantion, the Caliphates—where it [the Alexander romance] achieved both its greatest artistic complexity and its widest geographic diffusion between the second and twelfth centuries CE" (19). Alexander the Great is mentioned in the Qur'an, and texts from as far as Mongolia to Iceland have been translated and copied. Translated into the world's languages, from Indo-European to Semitic to Turkic to Austronesian tongues, Alexander's legend reached even Southeast Asia and China.

As Geoffrey Chaucer noted in The Monk's Tale, "The storie of Alisaundre is so commune / That every wight that hath discrecioun / Hath herd somewhat or al of his fortune" ("The story of Alexander is so common / That every person of discretion / Has heard of some or all his fortune"; 2631–33). This worlding of the Alexander romance reached into the early modern period and beyond. Su Fang Ng argues that in the early modern period, the Alexander romance was part of a shared classical inheritance that became part of an intensifying cross-cultural engagement in East-West encounters. In the European Enlightenment, Pierre Briant argues, Alexander was a key figure, depicted as a civilizing force in imperial discourse. Alexander's bridging of literary traditions across multiple periods invites not only comparative pedagogical approaches but also approaches that consider questions of periodization and, especially, the relation between our contemporary moment and the past.

Teaching the Alexander Romance

The Alexander romance is ideal for showing how premodern texts move within a text network, to borrow Selden's term, as the legend circulated through imperial capital cities such as Samarkand, Baghdad, Damascus, Cairo, Istanbul or Byzantium, Rome, Cordoba, and Paris at the interstices of a variety of empires, each time appropriating elements of the host culture. Adam Miyashiro's senior seminar focuses on the Alexander romance precisely to chart this medieval text network. It begins with the early Hellenistic Egyptian origins of the Alexander romance in Alexandria to understand the syncretic religion forged between Greek and Egyptian cultures. Then, moving from ancient accounts of Alexander's life and conquests to the variety of literary iterations in the fictional accounts in the Alexander romance, the course explores the interimperial imaginations from Greco-Egyptian syncretic cultures to the Islamic Mediterranean to Christian Europe, employing such texts as Leo the Archpriest's Latin translation, *Historia de preliis Alexandro Magni*, the work that becomes the primary source for versions of the Alexander romance found in medieval Europe, and an Iberian Arabic version, *Qiṣṣat Dhulqarnayn*. Through these versions, the course considers the historical and economic background of tributary empires along the Silk Road, the Mediterranean, and the Indian Ocean, as well as the modern implications for reading the Alexander romance as an example of globalism in the Middle Ages. Reading Greek, Latin, and Arabic texts (all available in English translation), the class is invited to consider medieval Mediterranean circuits of transmission.

As teaching texts, various versions of the Alexander romance are appropriate for undergraduates as well as more advanced students and graduate students. The Greek *Alexander Romance* is conveniently available in a Penguin translation by Richard Stoneman. Also easily available are editions in a variety of commonly taught medieval western European languages, such as Anglo-Norman French, Middle English, and Latin. There is a robust tradition of Alexander stories in Arabic and Persian versions; Arabic translations, such as ʿUmara's *Dhulqarnayn* were being made in the ninth century. Non-Western versions in English translation include Dick Davis's translation of Ferdowsi's *Shahnameh*, Minoo Southgate's translation of an anonymous twelfth- to fourteenth-century Persian prose romance (*Iskandarnamah*), David Zuwiyya's translation of *Qiṣṣat Dhulqarnayn*, as well as older translations of the Syriac and Ethiopic versions by E. A. Wallis Budge (*History* and *Life*). In addition, one part of Niẓāmī's

Sikandar Nama is available in a nineteenth-century translation by Henry Wilberforce Clarke, and a fragmentary version of a Mongolian Alexander romance has been translated and published in a journal (Cleaves). Stoneman's *Legends of Alexander the Great* handily collects selections on Alexander's legendary adventures in the East from Greek and Latin texts, alongside excerpts from a number of medieval English versions of the legend.

The numerous cultural appropriations and remediations of Alexander make his legends eminently suited for teaching world cultures and cross-cultural encounters. The Alexander romance's range and diversity allow for a radical defamiliarization. Key issues include literary transmission and reception, religious difference, cross-cultural encounters, and race, among others. To teach the literary history of the Alexander legend is to teach a history of strong readings. Although the contrast between the European and the Islamic traditions may be the most obvious, the traditions themselves can be quite multifarious, molding Alexander in their own image.

One approach to this textual diversity is to teach the many fathers of the legendary Alexander. In the Pseudo-Callisthenes original, Alexander is the secret son of the last pharaoh, Nectanebo, and that was the version that entered Europe. But the Syriac version that spawned the eastern branch to enter the Perso-Arabic world extending even to Southeast Asia produced an Islamic Alexander who was the secret son of Darius. The Islamic Alexander makes for a fruitful contrast with Alexander the "first European," as Briant terms him. Iskandar Dhulqarnayn, Alexander's Arabic name, meaning "Alexander the Two-Horned," might be called the First Muslim, for this Alexander conquers the world to convert its peoples to Islam. When read in tandem with the European versions, this Islamicized Alexander can better highlight the literary construction of the European Alexander.

In the European tradition, Alexander is Christianized, but his Christianizing had already occurred in the production of the Syriac Alexander some four centuries before Archpriest Leo's version (Gero 3–9). The Alexander legend could be taught through a variety of texts. These include Old and Middle English texts of the *Letter of Alexander to Aristotle* circulating in English scriptoria (Khalaf; DiMarco and Perelman); or Walter of Châtillon's *Alexandreis* and later, the twelfth- or thirteenth-century *Roman de toute chevalerie*, by Thomas of Kent, which gained popularity in francophone Europe, was eventually translated into Middle English by the fourteenth century as *Kyng Alisaunder* (see Smithers), and came to be thought of as ethnographic literary texts in Europe that described populations in the Eastern Hemisphere. In contrast, the Alexander romance's transmission to Southeast Asia by the fifteenth century offers a perspective on the West—in this case the Iberian Peninsula and the Maghreb—as a foreign place.

Rather than a singular story, we have one of multiple identities and perspectives, a multiplicity that simultaneously calls attention to what is specific to the particular culture and its history. Whereas Alexander's genealogy was important to the Persians who recast him as Persian, for others, it is the Alexandrian inheritance that becomes important to their narrative and identity. In Southeast Asia a number of royal houses traced their descent back to Alexander. Kings of Melaka, Aceh, and elsewhere took the name Iskandar Zulkarnain. Such dynastic concerns point to the cosmopolitan nature of materials that make up national literary canons. The many fathers of Alexander and his many literary offspring point to culturally divergent yet interconnected worlds. Although the Malay Alexander romance, titled *Hikayat Iskandar Zulkarnain*, a long prose work much influenced by Persian, is not available in English translation, a summary version of the story is incorporated into an important Malay chronicle, which has been translated, *Sejarah Melayu* (*Malay Annals*), also discussed by Derek Heng in this volume.

This chronicle of the fifteenth-century Melakan sultanate, a port kingdom on the Malay Peninsula that mediated the trade between India and China, offers a glimpse at late medieval global connections on the other side of the world. Although only a paraphrase, this Alexander story is a fine example of the localization of a global story, as Alexander is inserted into the genealogy of the sultans of Melaka. Moreover, in its focus on an Alexander figure—one of Alexander's Malay descendants, Raja Culan, like his legendary forebear, explores the ocean in a diving bell—the work usefully presents an example of literary imitation in an Alexander story transposed into a different context and genre.

Given the plethora of versions, one natural approach to the varieties of Alexander romances is to read parallel episodes across versions, particularly episodes that have gained cross-cultural popularity. Some of these include the Persian embassy sent by Darius to demand tribute with an ensuing exchange of letters and insults between Darius and Alexander, Alexander's aerial flight and his underwater exploration in a diving bell, his encounter with the gymnosophists, his walling up of the supposedly barbarian tribes of Gog and Magog, his journey through the land of darkness and his search for the water of life, his journey to Paradise and the eyestone, and the lamentations of the philosophers at his death. The next section of our essay suggests ways to consider race and Alexander's death in a pair of Alexander texts.

The many versions invite foregrounding translation in our pedagogy. In an assignment designed by Adam Miyashiro, students translate the Middle English *Kyng Alisaunder* into modern English as an experimental group project. After reading several versions of the Alexander romance, the students get a crash course in Middle English. The poem *Kyng Alisaunder* is divided among students to work on over three weeks; they are armed with the necessary apparatus for studying Middle English, including the glossary in the second volume of the Early English Text Society edition (Smithers) and the online Middle English Dictionary (quod.lib.umich.edu/m/middle-english-dictionary/dictionary).

Because Miyashiro's students knew the general outline of the romance components—Nectanebo and Alexander's conception, the conquest of Egypt and Persia, the battles against Darius and Porus, Alexander's marriage to Roxane and the subterfuge with Candace, and his death—they were able to match their sections with earlier versions of the text. They noted how different the Middle English text was from the others they had read: how Alexander became a crusading Christian king, while Darius and the Persians had become "Saracens." They also learned to perform high-level close reading analyses, as they wrote reflections on their translations, the process of learning and translating an earlier version of English into modern English, and the cultural changes that occur in premodern narrative adaptations.

In a course that might only include one Alexander work, such as a world literature survey, the fourth edition of the *Norton Anthology of World Literature* includes a selection—the *Book of Iskandar* (*Iskandarnameh*)—from Ferdowsi's *Shahnameh*, or *Book of Kings*, that can be usefully incorporated into a syllabus emphasizing literary interconnectedness between Europe and the Middle East. In such a course the Alexander romance is only one among a number of global stories that circulated, starting with *Gilgamesh*.

The Alexander romance could thus be taught in relation to other such traveling texts, especially a group of medieval texts that traversed long distances across the trade zones of the premodern world, circulating among Afro-Asian imperial capitals and westward to Europe, including *The Thousand and One Nights* (*Alf Layla wa-Layla*), *Kalila wa Dimna* (originally the *Panchatantra*), and *Vis and Ramin* (an analogue to the Tristan legends) (Kinoshita). These texts reframe the premodern world as already globalized.

Our next section considers in detail how cross-cultural ideas could be introduced through an Alexander text.

Race and Death in the *Qiṣṣat Dhulqarnayn* and *Kyng Alisaunder*

In around the fourteenth century, as versions of the Alexander romance were translated or authored in Europe, the Arabic *Qiṣṣat Dhulqarnayn* (*Tales of the Two-Horned One*), was being translated and copied in al-Andalus. This text, contained in two manuscripts from the fourteenth century in Madrid, will serve here as a counterpoint in formulating a broader perspective of this text network in western Europe. Presumably copied in Granada during the late Nasrid period, the *Qiṣṣat Dhulqarnayn* differs markedly from the European Alexander romance tradition in its representation of the East. Descending from a ninth-century translation of the Syriac version, it chronicles the travels of Dhulqarnayn ("The Two-Horned One"), Alexander's name in the Qur'an in the *Surat al-Kahf* (*The Cave*). The *Qiṣṣat Dhulqarnayn* represents the Alexander romance as it moves into one Arabic tradition in the Middle Ages. The text, deriving from Pseudo-Callisthenes and the Syriac version, also adds a strong Islamic element to the Alexander narrative, like its northern European counterparts who convert Alexander to Western Christianity. David Zuwiyya's edition, with English translation, makes for a useful teaching text. When taught alongside more familiar European versions, this text can introduce cross-cultural perspectives on race.

Formally, the *Qiṣṣat Dhulqarnayn* utilizes the Islamic citation method of *isnad* (or *sanad*), the chain of attributions most commonly found in the hadith tradition of Islamic commentary and apocryphal information about the Prophet Muhammad that is also represented in the classical Arabic literary tradition. Dhulqarnayn, whose Arabic name in the text is Ahmad (sharing a triconsonantal root with Muhammad) becomes an early avatar of Islam, spreading the monotheistic faith through conquest, in similar fashion to that of the *Roman de toute chevalerie* and *Kyng Alisaunder*.

The *Qiṣṣat Dhulqarnayn* shares many episodes with other versions of the Alexander romance: for example, Dhulqarnayn's descriptions of dog-headed peoples and supposedly primitive populations found in Africa and India appear, although with less detail. In Africa, for instance, Dhulqarnayn encounters "a people with fangs and faces like dogs and whose color was black like the crow" (Zuwiyya 153). These people are further described as wearing skins and not being Muslim. The descriptions of Ethiopia and its population, however, become even more profoundly different from the descriptions in the European accounts, which rely on texts like Pliny's *Natural History* and Isidore's *Etymologies* to fill in the fantastical ethnography of Ethiopia.

After encountering the local population, and seeing their fear of horses, Dhulqarnayn asks the people to explain who they are:

> They said, "We are the Abyssinians from Kush." Dhulqarnayn asked, "What brought you to this island?" "Our people came here during the time of our grandfather, Kush, whom Noah ordered to live here. We are their descendants. Until you have arrived, we had never before seen men that differ from us with respect to appearance and skin color. Who are you?" "We are from the Rum. God ordered us to make war on mankind until they acknowledge Him as their Lord and testify to his oneness." They agreed to his terms and became believers. He asked them, "Do you bury your dead?" "We eat them." "You are an atrocious people." He ordered them to bury their dead and departed from there. (Zuwiyya 153–54)

Two things are striking about this exchange: the first is that the Ethiopians are called by their own endonym (*habash*); the second is the linguistic ineptitude of the local population, represented in the Arabic text as grammatical and syntactic errors, something that Zuwiyya also points out in his edition. They speak an ungrammatical Arabic, and, unlike the majority of the European Alexander narratives, the spectacle in this text is not the dark skin color of the Abyssinians but rather the color of Dhul-Qarnayn and his men.

The racialization of African bodies through skin color is stressed in later medieval European romances, such as the Anglo-Norman *Roman de toute chevalerie* and the Middle English *Kyng Alisaunder*. Encyclopedic knowledge is imported into the fictional realm only gradually, as the textual output of encyclopedias grew over the course of the thirteenth century in Europe. Skin color, however, is stressed in the *Roman de toute chevalerie*, and even more so in the Middle English *Kyng Alisaunder*:

Al d[e] rein de Ethiope, droit en orient,
Ad mostres contrefez e mult orible gent.
La face ont tote plein[e], noir[e] cum arrement.
Ils n'ont nies en lour vis, mes boche ont nequedent.
(Thomas de Kent 6751–54)

At the end of Ethiopia, right in the east,
There are many hideous monsters and terrifying people.
They have completely flat faces, black like ink.
They don't have noses on their face, but they have mouths nevertheless.
(our trans.)

In *Kyng Alisaunder*, the Middle English translator tells us that "faire folk woneþ in Ethiope in þe est" ("fair folk lives in Ethiopia in the east"; Smithers 6364)—"faire" here presumably meaning "pleasing" rather than "white," but also perhaps an ironic play on words—and goes on to portray Black men in northeast Ethiopia, whose visage and "lych" ("body") are "blake . . . / als it were grounden pych" ("black . . . just as it if were ground-up pitch"; 6406–07). They also have eyes of ink, and no nose (6408–09). The negative attribution of blackness is evident in the narrator's remark that "[v]nlouerede is þat kynrede" ("hideous is that race"; 6413).

The stark contrast between the Middle English *Kyng Alisaunder*, for example, and the *Qiṣṣat Dhulqarnayn*—two fourteenth-century texts—highlights the different aspects of Alexander's travel conquests. Although the European versions of the Alexander romance emphasize racial differences among the peoples of the East, we would argue that it is the Ethiopian wonder at the "Romans" that inverts the assumed subject position of Alexander as imperial figurehead. Where the western European narratives use Alexander to envision fantastic populations and landscapes of the East, the *Qiṣṣat Dhulqarnayn* repositions Alexander as the figure to be marveled at by the Ethiopians.

One of the central motifs in the Alexander romance is his *Soma* ("mausoleum"), which many early texts take to be in Alexandria, Egypt. Here, Dhulqarnayn's death and burial depart drastically from its contemporaries. The *Qiṣṣat Dhulqarnayn* converts Alexander into a proto-Muslim in many parts of the text, most notably in the prophecy of his death. Likewise, as seen in the quotation below, the Islamic citation method of *isnad* is used to provide authority for the account—a technique most employed in the hadith traditions of Islamic stories.

Just before his death, Alexander becomes the first person to perform hajj, the ritual pilgrimage to Mecca:

> The second account was according to Wathima b. Musa as told by Sufyan b. ʿUyayna. Abraham and Ismael made pilgrimages to the Kaʾba on foot. So Dhulqarnayn desired and prayed for the Almighty God to allow him to meet Abraham so he could ask him about it. When this was granted, Abraham said to him, "O Dhulqarnayn! The Holy Kaʾba is being desecrated." Dhulqarnayn denied this and said "O Friend of God! Its desecration is not my doing. Nobody ever told me this before." The Dhulqarnayn stepped forward, set down his arms, and performed the circumambulation of the Kaʾba. Abraham gave him cows and sheep. Soon Dhulqarnayn realized that he was dying. (Zuwiyya 160–61)

Here, Alexander becomes the first to circumambulate the Kaʾba in Mecca before his death, not in Babylon but in Mecca, and only senses his death after making the hajj pilgrimage. In fact, however, the *Qiṣṣat Dhulqarnayn* gives four separate accounts of Alexander's death, each told by a different source. Unlike most other Alexander romances of this time, Alexander's body is not returned to Alexandria but is buried in a Temple of Apollo, as *Kyng Alisaunder* has it:

> Þat body richely hij kepte,
> And ledden it in to Egipte,
> And leiden hym in gold fyne,
> In a temple of Apolyne.
> (Smithers 8002–05)

> They maintained the body lavishly,
> And led it into Egypt
> And laid him in fine gold
> In a temple of Apollo.
> (our trans.)

In the third and fourth accounts of his death, Dhulqarnayn dies in "Bayt al-muqaddas"—a medieval variant on the name of Jerusalem—or in Dawma al-Jandal, an ancient town in northwestern Arabia (now in al-Jawf province of Saudi Arabia, near the Jordan border). After Alexander's death, the author of the *Qiṣṣat Dhulqarnayn* includes an unusual explanation of why Alexander should not be considered a prophet, despite performing hajj, conquering the world, and appearing in the Qurʾan.

Just as the juxtaposition of *Qiṣṣat Dhulqarnayn* and *Kyng Alisaunder* highlight their diverging racial ideologies, so too their differing accounts of Alexander's death emphasize the story's notable localizations. The topic of Alexander's death is particularly rich in not just ancient accounts but also a Syriac work on the Lamentations of the Philosophers that entered a number of later texts, including the *Historia de preliis.* Such comparisons and cultural analyses across literary traditions can be performed with a range of Alexander texts, ancient to modern.

Alexander across Disciplines: Classics and Asian Studies

An excellent site for globalizing the Middle Ages, Alexander the Great is already a fairly popular course in college curricula, most often taught in classics or history departments, though these courses largely focus on historical works, such as Quintus Curtius, Arrian, and Plutarch. The Alexander romance's reception into the non-Western world offers ample opportunity to diversify courses on Alexander the Great in classics as well. Since some of these courses also attend to modern or contemporary representations (Rudyard Kipling's *Man Who Would be King*, for instance, or Hollywood Alexanders), representations of Alexander beyond the Western world can expand and diversify the syllabi of such standard courses. In addition, such reconceived courses can forge links across departments that are not usually connected. This section highlights one such course, taught by Thomas Martin, professor of classics at the College of the Holy Cross, as a case study.[1]

Martin's course on Alexander the Great and Asia bridges classics and Asian studies. Beginning with the historical Alexander, this course first considers Alexander's Persian and Indian conquests before turning to his afterlives in Asia. Martin's syllabus design is exemplary in going beyond European representations. The historical background is supplied through an accessible introduction to Alexander's life that Martin and Christopher Blackwell coauthored, read alongside excerpts from Arrian and Plutarch, as well as selections from other scholarship, such as Matt Waters' history, *Ancient Persia*. In expanding beyond the usual historical accounts, such popular episodes as Alexander's encounter with the gymnosophists or naked philosophers are examined not only in the Greek *Alexander Romance* but also in Arrian's and Plutarch's accounts. Given the topical focus on Alexander's encounter with Asia, these selections emphasize Alexander's confrontation with Achaemenid Persia, his exploration of Afghanistan, and his encounter with India.

The second half of Martin's syllabus is an expansive exploration of the reception of the Alexander legend in a variety of cultures that would be highly adaptable for medieval literature courses. Beginning with an examination of images of Alexander on coins and in art, the second half explores accounts of Alexander from other perspectives. These include Flavius Josephus's account of Alexander's visit to Jerusalem in *Jewish Antiquities.* Josephus's account is supplemented by a selection from the *Talmud Bavli* (Babylonian Talmud), which includes several episodes from the Eastern branch of the Alexander legend, including Alexander's questions to the sages of the South, his journey to the regions of darkness, and his encounter with Amazons.

The transformation of Alexander into the Islamic Iskandar Dhulqarnayn is examined, focusing on Sura 18 (*Surat al-Kahf*, or *The Cave*) of the Qur'an, which also includes a version of the Syriac story of the seven sleepers of Ephesus that circulated in medieval Europe through the *Golden Legend.* Study of Alexander in his Islamic guise can be explored in depth with readings in Ferdowsi's "Iskandarnameh" from his *Shahnameh*, which is readily available in Davis's translation. This section emphasizes not only Alexander's religious transformation into a Muslim king but also his ethnic transformation into a Persian king, as the Persian tradition (which also influences the Malay Alexander) makes him the secret child of a Persian king and thus half brother to Darius. The course ends with a film representation of Alexander, a Japanese-Korean anime called *Reign the Conqueror*, for another non-Western view of Alexander in Asia.

Alexander on Film

Film depictions of Alexander can engage students more immediately in how an ancient story acquires new resonances. Aside from Hollywood films like the 1956 Richard Burton *Alexander the Great* or Oliver Stone's *Alexander*, a course can use versions from other film traditions—whether *Reign*, mentioned above, or Bollywood productions like *Sikandar* (1941), directed by Sohrab Modi, and *Sikandar-E-Azam* (1965), directed by Kedar Kapoor, or the Egyptian director Youssef Chahine's *Iskandariyya kaman wa kaman* (*Alexandria Again and Forever*) (1989).

Chahine's film, for instance, reveals how productions from outside Hollywood add a more layered perspective to challenge a western narrative. The third of his four films centered on the city of Alexandria in Egypt, Chahine's *Alexandria Again and Forever* is interspersed with triumphalist scenes of Alexander the Great's conquest and founding of the city in

331 BCE. Chahine's portrayal of Alexander as a European conqueror of Africa is linked to the pervasiveness of global capitalism in contemporary Egypt under the rule of Hosni Mubarak, the American-sponsored dictator of Egypt who was deposed by popular revolt in 2011. Deploying the image of a distinctly white European Alexander, reminiscent of other twentieth-century films, such as the 1956 *Alexander the Great*, starring Richard Burton, Chahine critiques the colonial and neocolonial symbol of empire in Egypt, the city of Alexandria, so frequently associated with both the founding and the absent presence of Alexander's *Soma* ("mausoleum"), that haunts it (Chahine and Massad 80).

In the discovery of Alexander's *Soma* at the end, Chahine produces a "Hellenistic syncretism" combining, among other things, hieroglyphics, Greek statuary, and "Alexander in the aspect of Pharaoh" (Halim). The film, on the making of a musical biopic of Alexander, turns into a metafictional commentary on Alexandria as a cultural crossroad. So pervasive is Chahine's focus on collapsing ancient and modern times that Viola Shafik suggests Alexandria's periods run fluidly between "the past, present, and future as part of a seamless web, since there is no notion of a final development towards a perfect end" (95). This seamless web, contends Hala Halim, is the expression of "the sense of loss associated with the city, witnessed in the perpetual search for anteriority, bolstered by the absence of the city's legendary monuments and the fact of Alexandria being built on several older Alexandrias destroyed on a daily basis."

When set in contrast to Chahine, Stone's *Alexander*, portraying a queer emperor and locating the "queer royal flesh" as a *translatio* of West to East, can be more readily seen as standing in for the cultural politics of Western identities in the Arab-Muslim world. The modern film history of Alexander comes full circle in the theological-political order of Western capitalist globalization: from the petrodollar of Chahine's Egyptian film industry to Stone's neoliberalism of pinkwashing Alexander's empire, Alexander has undergone the full conversion from the pre-Christianizing figure of medieval European romances to a secular hellenizer of Africa and Asia.

The modern curriculum that formed in tandem with the rise of the nation-state emphasizes nationalist authors like Chaucer and nationalist heroes like King Arthur. The Alexander romance is fundamentally transnational, its many authors global. It is thus ideal for a twenty-first-century classroom emphasizing the interconnectedness of literary traditions and religious cultures across the boundaries of language and nation. As new media versions of Alexander's legend show, his is a living tradition with ever more new interlocuters. Our students can be among them.

Note

1. We thank Professor Martin for sharing his syllabus with us.

Works Cited

Alexander. Directed by Oliver Stone, Warner Bros., 2004.

Alexander the Great. Directed by Robert Rossen, C.B. Films S.A., 1956.

Alexandria Again and Forever. Directed by Youssef Chahine, La Sept / Mirs International Films, 1990.

Briant, Pierre. *The First European: A History of Alexander in the Age of Empire.* Translated by Nicholas Elliott, Harvard UP, 2017.

Budge, Ernest A. Wallis, editor and translator. *The History of Alexander the Great, Being the Syriac Version of the Pseudo Callisthenes.* Cambridge UP, 1889.

———, editor and translator. *The Life and Exploits of Alexander the Great, Being a Series of Translations of the Ethiopic Histories of Alexander by the Pseudo-Callisthenes and Other Writers.* London, 1896.

Chahine, Youssef, and Joseph Massad. "Art and Politics in the Cinema of Youssef Chahine." *Journal of Palestine Studies*, vol. 28, no. 2, 1 Jan. 1999, pp. 77–93.

Chaucer, Geoffrey. *The Riverside Chaucer.* Edited by Larry Benson, 3rd ed., Houghton Mifflin, 1987.

Cleaves, Francis Woodman. "An Early Mongolian Version of the Alexander Romance." *Harvard Journal of Asiatic Studies*, vol. 22, 1959, pp. 1–99.

Damrosch, David. *What Is World Literature?* Princeton UP, 2003.

DiMarco, Vincent, and Leslie Perelman. *The Middle English Letter of Alexander to Aristotle.* Editions Rodopi, 1978.

Dowden, Ken. "Pseudo-Callisthenes: *Alexander Romance.*" *Collected Ancient Greek Novels*, edited by B. P. Reardon, U of California P, 1989, pp. 650–54.

Ferdowsi, Abolqasem. *Shahnameh: The Persian Book of Kings.* Translated by Dick Davis, Viking Penguin, 2006.

———. *Shahnameh* (selections). *Norton Anthology of World Literature*, edited by Martin Puchner et al., 4th ed., W. W. Norton, 2018, pp. 195–219.

Gero, Stephen. "The Legend of Alexander the Great in the Christian Orient." *Bulletin of the John Rylands Library*, vol. 75, no. 1, 1993, pp. 3–9.

Halim, Hala. "On Being an Alexandrian." *Al-Ahram Weekly Online*, 11 Apr. 2002.

Iskandarnamah: A Persian Medieval Alexander-Romance. Translated by Minoo S. Southgate, Columbia UP, 1978.

Josephus, Flavius. *Jewish Antiquities.* Translated by Ralph Marcus, Harvard UP, 1937. Vol. 4, books IX–XI.

Khalaf, Omar. "The Old English Alexander's Letter to Aristotle: Monsters and Hybris in the Service of Exemplarity." *English Studies*, vol. 94, no. 6, Oct. 2013, pp. 659–67. *Taylor and Francis*, https://doi.org/10.1080/0013838X.2013.814324.

Kinoshita, Sharon. "Translatio/n, Empire, and the Worlding of Medieval Literature: The Travels of *Kalila wa Dimna*." *Postcolonial Studies*, vol. 11, no. 4, Dec. 2008, pp. 371–85.

Martin, Thomas R., and Christopher W. Blackwell. *Alexander the Great: The Story of an Ancient Life*. Cambridge UP, 2012.

Ng, Su Fang. *Alexander the Great from Britain to Southeast Asia: Peripheral Empires in the Global Renaissance*. Oxford UP, 2019.

Niẓāmī Ganjavī. *The Sikandar Nama, e bara, or book of Alexander the Great, written A.D. 1200*. Translated by Henry Wilberforce Clarke, London, 1881.

Reign: The Conqueror. Directed by Yoshinori Kanemori Rintaro, Madhouse, 2000.

Sejarah Melayu, or Malay Annals. Translated by C. C. Brown, Oxford UP, 1970.

Selden, Daniel L. "Mapping the Alexander Romance." *The Alexander Romance in Persia and the East*, edited by Richard Stoneman et al. Barkhuis Publishing / Groningen University Library, 2012, pp. 19–59.

Shafik, Viola. "Egyptian Cinema." *The Companion Encyclopedia of Middle Eastern and North African Film*, Routledge, 2001, pp. 23–129.

Sikandar. Directed by Sohrab Modi, Minerva Movietone, 1941.

Sikandar-E-Azam. Directed by Kedar Kapoor, N.C. Films, 1965.

Smithers, G. V., editor. *Kyng Alisaunder*. Reprint ed., Oxford UP, 1961.

Stoneman, Richard, translator. *Legends of Alexander the Great*. I. B. Tauris, 2011.

———, translator. *The Greek Alexander Romance*. Penguin Books, 1991.

Thomas de Kent. *Le roman d'Alexandre ou Le roman de toute chevalerie*. Edited by Brian Foster and Ian Short, translated by Catherine Gaullier-Bougassas and Laurence Harf-Lancner, Honoré Champion, 2003.

Walter of Chatillon. *The* Alexandreis*: A Twelfth-Century Epic*. Edited by David Townsend, Broadview Press, 2006.

Waters, Thomas. *Ancient Persia: A Concise History of the Achaemenid Empire, 550–330 BCE*. Cambridge UP, 2014.

Zuwiyya, Z. David, editor and translator. *Islamic Legends Concerning Alexander the Great*. Global Publications, 2001.

Shahzad Bashir

The Persian World: A Literary Language in Motion

A few years ago, during a trip to Iran, a local guide with whom I had become friendly said something to me that seemed like a contradiction. Although intensely proud of being Iranian, he reflected that the region corresponding to modern Iran has been home to a diverse and ever-changing variety of peoples for millennia. I wondered: if cultural variety and variability are acknowledged as facts, what exactly is the source of his native pride? The question is not unique to Iran and can be addressed through complex sociohistorical arguments. But for this case, the root of the matter was my friend's attachment to Persian as a literary language and a source for cultural identity. The sentiment I heard in Iran can be observed identically today in neighboring Afghanistan and Tajikistan. In muffled echoes, we can find it farther afield in the larger Iranian sphere, in Central and South Asia, the Caucasus, and Anatolia. This expansive geography has been the heartland of Persian language and literature for more than a thousand years.

Persian has a vast literary corpus that has been accumulating since approximately 1000 CE. Spoken Persian has various dialects, the most prominent today being Farsi, Dari, and Tajik. Literary Persian has also seen much change over time. Attentive readers can periodize and localize on the basis of diction, etymology, style, complexity, citation, and so on. But it is emblematically true that a person literate in the language today can read (although not necessarily fully comprehend) a text written in the year 1000. This historical continuity signifies Persian's extraordinary potential as a carrier of forms and values. Literary Persian's inner distinctiveness is such that we can think of it as containing a shared world of cultural expression.

The story of Persian can be told chronologically and geographically, interlaced with the rise and evolution of poetic and prose genres. An extensive academic literature is available that provides such mapping, allowing us to place thousands of surviving works that range between the proficient and the brilliant (De Bruijn, *General Introduction*). Rather than abbreviating this specialized scholarship, my approach in this essay is thematic, illustrated by poignant examples. This will, I hope, engage readers with no previous knowledge of matters related to Persian. It should also provide a running start for thinking comparatively across the global Middle Ages.

I have chosen four themes that encompass broad literary-cultural phenomena pertaining to Persian. First, I begin with the intuitive sense of placement—the cultural mise-en-scène—of the Persian world that was established early on and continued to affect literary expression over the centuries. Distinctively Persian senses of space and time permeate cultural material through assumption and implication.

Second, I focus on storytelling, covering genres touching on romance and cosmological and religious understanding. Works in this category started to proliferate in the period 1000 to 1300 and were concerned to fashion self and society.

Third, I discuss history and hagiography, modes of narration that make realist claims about states and societal classes and the lives of rulers, dynasties, and extraordinary individuals. This field expanded significantly after 1250, when political and religious elites adopted Persian ever more as the language to represent themselves.

My fourth theme is the expression of sentiment, which saturates emotive moments within all narratives and gives voice to love and desire while privileging timelessness and universality. This theme encompasses distinctive lyrical forms that acquired great prestige after 1300. In the ensuing discussion, I take up the four themes successively, illustrating them through reference to prominent examples available in English translation.

Cultural Placement

Persian (sometimes called New Persian in specialized literature) emerged as a literary language in Iran and Central Asia in the tenth century CE. This region was home to numerous ancient literary cultures that were supplanted by Arabic during the establishment of Muslim rule from the middle of the seventh century onward. While this occurred, a majority of the region's peoples continued to use Iranian vernaculars as their spoken language. For various reasons, the spoken language gradually became a vehicle for written culture as well. Crucially, this occurred through the adoption of the Arabic script to represent the vernacular. The two languages had no genealogical relationship (Arabic is a Semitic language while Persian is Indo-European). Adoption of the script, however, resulted in a commonality that has guaranteed the status of Arabic as a precursor and a continuing resource.

Over the centuries, Arabic has functioned as a vast storehouse of vocabulary, and, to a lesser extent, other linguistic elements for Persian. Most sophisticated authors who wrote in Persian during the Middle Ages possessed significant competence in Arabic as well. Authors chose to write in one or the other language for a variety of reasons: presumed availability of a technical lexicon, affirmation of sociocultural affiliation, the emotional texture of a genre particular to one language, specifics of the desired audience, and so on. The key thing to note is that although expression in Persian is interlaced with Arabic, Persian has a separate cultural and literary history, with its own prosody, genres, and intellectual and aesthetic momentum.

The works of Abolqasem Ferdowsi and Moshrefoddin Saʿdi have left indelible marks on Persian literature. I focus on them here to highlight the distinctive sense of cultural placement that permeates this literary world. Ferdowsi composed the famous *Shahnameh* (*Book of Kings*) at the turn of the first millennium CE. This work puts into Persian verse the memory of pre-Islamic Iranian kings as this was available among Persian speakers at the time (Lewis). Patronized by courts invested in Persian as a vehicle for culture, Ferdowsi's project was literary and cultural rather than historical. It resulted in a grand epic whose particulars have become proverbial with the passage of time.

The *Shahnameh* progresses along a loose chronology that is tied to celebrated kings and dynasties ruling from various locales in a vague geography consisting of Iran and Turan (Iran's often antagonistic alter ego). In the work, shared cultural principles coalesce to form a world inhabited by a great variety of people. *Shahnameh*'s long list of characters includes men and women of varying ethnic identities (Iranians, Turks, Arabs, Armenians, etc.). Over time, personal names from the work have become stand-ins for qualities particular to various types of human beings.

The *Shahnameh* glorifies a highly curated past as the patrimony of those invested in Persian ethnic identity or Persian language as a carrier of political and cultural prestige. Its lasting significance is due also to Ferdowsi's virtuosity in telling tales of heroes and villains who sometimes transform into one another and are perpetually shown subject to human virtues and failings. Although divine powers make occasional appearances, the work portrays the Iranian past as a thoroughly human affair. An exemplary case in point is the encounter between Rostam, unmatched as a warrior and champion, and his son Sohrab, born to the princess Tahmineh without his knowledge. In this tale with many twists, the end comes when Rostam kills his child while being unaware of his identity. Alerting the reader to the tragedy in advance, Ferdowsi states:

> Oh world! How strange your workings are! From you
> Comes both what's broken and what's whole as well.
> Of these two men, neither was stirred by love.
> Wisdom was far off, the face of love not seen.
> From fishes in the sea to wild horses on
> The plain, all beasts can recognize their young.
> But man who's blinded by his wretched pride,
> Cannot distinguish son from foe.
> (*Tragedy*, verses 685–88)

The tragedy's dramatic arc engages matters such as fate, love, erotic desire, pride, valor, stubbornness, regret, and existential desperation. The *Shahnameh* as a whole consists of moving verses that correlate between specific circumstances within a narrative and the human condition. This combination has been greatly generative, rendering the *Shahnameh* a source of inspiration for performance (Davidson), illustration (Brend and Melville), and literary imitation (Melville and Van den Berg) for more than a millennium.

Moshrefoddin Sa'di was born about two centuries after Ferdowsi's death, at a time when Persian was an established literary lingua franca. His life coincided with the Mongol conquest, which culminated in the Middle

East in the destruction of Baghdad (and the Abbasid Caliphate) in 1258. Saʿdi is famous both as a poet and as the author of two celebrated prosimetric collections: *Golistan* (*The Rose Garden*) and *Bostan* (*The Orchard*). Autobiographical comments pepper Saʿdi's works (we have virtually no other personal information about him), describing an itinerant life spanning the present-day Middle East and Central and South Asia. The circumstances he describes portray a world that is, on the one hand, in great political and military turmoil, and on the other, a vibrant cultural sphere densely interconnected through commonality of ideals and literary motifs (Katouzian 9–45).

Ferdowsi's *Shahnameh* became hugely influential in part because it was composed concurrently with Persian's birth as a high prestige literary medium. More than two centuries later, Saʿdi's work had a similar advantage because of a reenergization of the language. The Mongols who took over Iran and Central Asia in the middle of the thirteenth century adopted Persian as their vehicle of administration, diplomacy, and high culture. Significant resources were poured into providing instruction in Persian letters and patronizing its cultivation among the elites. In this milieu, Saʿdi's *Golistan* became regarded as a model for wise discourse meant to cultivate the proper self. Perhaps the most widely read Persian text of all time, this work was a staple for teaching literacy across Iran and Central and South Asia between the thirteenth and the twentieth centuries. Consequently, Saʿdi was well known to almost all authors who came after him, and his mixture of wisdom, irony, and amusement echoes in later works.

As with Ferdowsi, Saʿdi's significance is not merely due to the accident of being born at the right time. Credit is due to his aesthetic and rhetorical sophistication, which invites readers to see themselves in his representations. The conclusion to the *Golistan* contains a reflection on his method:

> Mostly Saʿdi's speech is entertaining and amusing, and for this reason the tongues of some shortsighted people have grown long in criticizing me, saying that to "squeeze the brain in vain and to swallow smoke from a lamp for no gain is not what intelligent people do." However, it is not hidden from the enlightened minds of *sahibdils* ["the stout-hearted"], who are primarily addressed here, that pearls of healing counsel have been drawn into strings of expression, and the bitter medicine of advice has been mixed with the honey of wit, so that their

weary natures may not be deprived of the good fortune of receptivity. Praise be to God, Lord of the Universe.

We made advice for ourselves; we spent a long time in this labor.

If it is not listened to avidly, the messenger has only to deliver the message. (*Gulistan* 173)

Ferdowsi and Saʿdi are important baselines for all Persian literature. The two articulated concerns relevant for their contexts: Ferdowsi memorialized pre-Islamic Iran as a consequential past in the tenth century, whereas Saʿdi gave eloquent voice to the established high culture of the thirteenth century. In centuries after their deaths, the perspectives of Ferdowsi and Saʿdi permeated the work of others by being treated as the very definition of the proper way to evoke the Persian ethos in politics, manners, and literature (e.g., Kaykavus b. Iskandar; Nizam al-Mulk; Najm Sani; Tusi; Yavari). Appreciating these authors as exemplars provides a qualitative sense for notions of space, time, and cultural identity that permeate Persian worlds.

Storytelling

Persian literature burgeoned during the period 1000 to 1300 CE, as the language began covering topics that had earlier been the preserve of Arabic. The expansion led to rapid evolution of genres and a movement toward universality. An author such as Ferdowsi had represented himself as a preserver of Persian exclusivity. While self-consciously indebted to him and his contemporaries, Ferdowsi's successors generated narratives in which Persian carried the duties of a lingua franca for storytelling in the service of an ever wider set of topics. The language continued its close association with courtly culture, a connection that became even stronger when the Mongols chose Persian as their preferred language for administration and historiography in the thirteenth century (Meisami 3–39).

From the eleventh century onward, a second powerful engine added to the development of Persian. This was the great expansion of the influence of Sufi ideas and practices throughout Islamic lands. In Iran and Central and South Asia, Persian was the medium par excellence for Sufi philosophies, mystical expression in verse and prose, accounts of the lives of great saintly figures, and guidebooks for conduct. From this period, literary expression in Persian has been imbued with Sufi ideas at the level of vocabulary and tropes, irrespective of authors identifying themselves as Sufis (De Bruijn, *Persian Sufi Poetry*).

The instinct to encompass the world in Persian is evident in the work of Nezami Ganjavi, a poet from the Caucasus region. His quintet of long narrative poems called *Panj Ganj* (*The Five Treasures*) inspired hundreds of later imitations in Persian and other languages such as Turkish and Hindi-Urdu. Three of these five poems share their subject and some details with Ferdowsi's *Shahnameh* (*Khosrow va Shirin*, *Eskandarnameh*, and *Haft Paykar*). Of the remaining two, one is generally ethicophilosophical (*Makhzan al-Asrar*) and the other has an Arabic precedent (*Layli va Majnun*).

The *Haft Paykar* (*The Seven Portraits* or *Beauties*) is Nezami's most complex work in terms of both the story line and the underlying message. Ostensibly the life of Bahram Gur, a Sassanian king in the *Shahnameh*, the intricate work combines love, eroticism, royal heroism, ethics, cosmology, numerology, and the alchemical transformation of the self for high spiritual ends. Its celebrated central section describes Bahram listening to stories told by seven beautiful princesses whom he had acquired as spouses through assiduous pursuit after earlier coming across their portraits. The princesses come from seven climes of the world (India, China, Khwarazm, Slavonia, North Africa, Byzantium, and Persia) and are placed under different colored domes (black, sandalwood, red, yellow, white, turquoise, green) that are governed by the seven planets (Saturn, Jupiter, Mars, Sun, Venus, Mercury, Moon). The symmetry of sevens recurs in other parts of the narrative, signifying a perspective in which knowledge of the earth and the heavens is correlated to the mind, emotions, and moral obligations of human beings.

Although successful in his many adventures, Bahram eventually forsakes all pleasures, and the domes housing the seven princesses are turned into fire temples entrusted to priests. The king then disappears into a cave forever while pursuing an onager during a hunt. As the reader is reminded throughout the work, remembering the inevitability of death should temper all actions and understandings during life. Near the end of the work, Nezami writes:

> All that which, in these Seven Domes
> of mystery, I have adorned
> With length and width, 'twas that the eyes,
> from full adornment, might find ease.
> All that you see, in this broad space,
> that I've thrown wide to ears and eyes,

Are meaning's beauties, narrow-eyed,
their faces veiled from narrow sight;
Each bride a treasury shut fast,
the golden key beneath her locks.
He will find gold who opes this mine;
who finds the door fair pearls will gain. (267)

The intricate stories Nezami tells are often nested within one another, requiring assiduous attention to keep straight while reading. Gleaning their meanings requires working through the implications of the actors' actions. Although hardly a reluctant didact, Nezami makes the narrative aesthetically attractive while mirroring the complexity of the underlying message.

While Nezami did not self-identify as a Sufi, the heavy focus on death and moralism that permeates his work has much in common with the Sufi narratives that came to dominate Persian literary production from the twelfth century onward. A prominent case is the work of Jalaloddin Rumi who was born in Balkh (Afghanistan) but spent his adult life in Konya (Turkey). Rumi's *Masnavi* is a monumental (but unstructured) collection of stories of all manner of origins, put into service for Sufi ideology.

A narrative poem in rhymed couplets, it begins with the reed flute, a plaintive musical instrument. The flute's sound, produced when its hollow interior is infused with air, is compared to the human voice seeking the species' origins. The desire is supposed to recall an affirmation of God by all human spirits, made at the origin of creation but subsequently forgotten. Rumi's poetic voice takes up the functions of the flute, narrating hundreds of stories that circle around the imperative to make life's choices in the shadow of acknowledging and remembering God's love and commandments (Papan-Matin).

Rumi's stories are compelling and entertaining, but unlike Nezami, he is not interested in weaving them together into a minutely planned verbal tapestry. He acknowledges that stories are necessary to capture attention but is, at least in some measure, always distrustful of them because they can seduce away from the lesson he wishes to impart. Sometimes a story's ostensible conclusion is purposefully subverted in order to startle the reader out of the narrative and toward the work's didactic purpose. The *Masnavi* was composed over a long period and includes reactions to its critics. Rumi writes that some complain that it contains "no mention of [theosophical] investigation and the sublime mysteries towards which the saints make their steeds gallop" (*Mathnawi* 4: 237).

His response is that the same criticism was leveled against the Quran and reflects the spiritual poverty of the critics rather than a deficiency in his work. The comparison to scripture gives us a view of Rumi's sense of his work's significance. Rumi's evaluation was shared by ʿAbdorrahman Jami, a fifteenth-century author, who popularized calling the work the Quran in the Persian Language. Aside from the conceit, the comparison is apt inasmuch as, like the Quran, the *Masnavi* contains a consistent and coherent religious message articulated in an unsystematized and repetitive way.

Nezami and Rumi wrote in the same poetical form, and both are superb narrators. The stories they tell are never trivial, being keyed to larger intellectual and ethical purposes. Yet they mold the form and the contents of the stories to quite different ends. Nezami privileges extreme symmetry, whereas Rumi creates jarring disjuncture to make the reader come back to his religious message. Persian literature includes thousands of other works that fall somewhere in between these two ends of the spectrum (e.g., Attar, *Conference*; Gorgani; Jamali).

History and Hagiography

ʿAta Malek Jovayni composed his monumental *Tarikh-e Jahangoshay* (*The History of the World Conqueror*) during the period 1250 to 1260. The work's title refers to Genghis (Chinggis) Khan, whose descendants were masters over the Persian world at the time Jovayni was writing. Together with many prior generations of his family, Jovayni belonged to an elite of learned secretaries who formed the backbone of imperial administrations throughout the Middle East and Central Asia for centuries. For people like Jovayni, being a high-level bureaucrat in a grand empire went hand in hand with writing chronicles, administrative manuals, and mirrors for princes. Both jobs required training in pragmatic matters and the literary arts that went into their roles as mediators between the rulers and the population.

Teeming with references to Ferdowsi, Nezami, and other Persian and Arabic poets, Jovayni's work describes the Mongol conquest and its aftermath, framed by moral deliberation on society. Reflecting the circumstances of his employment, he is full of adulation for the Mongols' phenomenal military success. But his image of the Mongol rulers constantly recalls ancient Iranian kings known for their military prowess as well as justice. At one level, the narrative accommodates the Mongols as newcomers into the established world of Persian kingship through literary suturing. This makes the rulers legible to readers of Persian while infusing aspects of Persian political culture into Mongol understandings. Jovayni's work also inaugurates Persian's close association with the Mongol Empire's prestige, scale, and ambition. Jovayni and the many chroniclers who followed him generated a massive Persian historical literature that is distinctive for how it combines reportage, nostalgia for the past, and literary creativity (Thackston).

Reading Jovayni, one can be sure of his Muslim identity. He follows in the line of chroniclers with a triumphalist understanding of Islam's role in universal historical development. This commitment stood at odds with the fact that the Mongol rulers he eulogized were not Muslim and yet had clearly been granted providential kingship on a grand scale. An instance where we can glimpse Jovayni's resolution of the situation is his account of Sorqoqtani Beki, a wife and mother to Mongol kings who acted as a kingmaker at a crucial time in the empire's history. General information about Sorqoqtani depicts a complex power broker, a fierce competitor in the court not averse to acting brutally toward opponents (Broadbridge 195–224). But Jovayni describes her as a pure embodiment of wisdom and charity, loved by all:

> Her hand was ever open in munificence and benefaction, and although she was a follower and devotee of the religion of Jesus she would bestow alms and presents upon *imams* and *shaikhs* and strove also to revive the sacred observances of the faith of Mohammad. . . . And the token and proof of this statement is that she gave 1000 silver *balish* that a college (*madrasa*) might be built in Bokhara, of which pious foundation the *shaikh-al-islam* Sa'd-ad-Din of Bakharz should be administrator and superintendent; and she commanded that villages should be bought, and endowment made and teachers and students accommodated [in the college]. And always she would send alms to all parts to be distributed among the poor and needy of the Moslems. (Juvaini 551–52)

We see here a Mongol woman, professing Nestorian Christianity, supporting Muslims and promoting Islamic institutions. Jovayni's amalgamations in such cases focus on his patrons' universally positive qualities, such as justice, valor, good organization, and patronage of religion and high culture. If God had exalted the Mongols despite being non-Muslim, that was meant as a lesson for the Muslims who had squandered their advantages by acting venally and irresponsibly. The complex cultural maneuvering we see in Jovayni's work can be found in a plethora of versions in the vast Persian historiographical literature produced in the Middle East and Central and South Asia throughout the Middle Ages (Melville).

In the Persian context, hagiography—elaborate description of the lives of saintly persons—is an important counterpart to historiography. From the eleventh century onward, Sufi masters started to acquire fame for their esoteric knowledge and miracles, leading to the formation of communities and spiritual lineages. Religious prestige soon transferred to the sociopolitical sphere, resulting in close connections to courts. Although a living Sufi master could acquire great influence on the basis of personal charisma, a person or family's lasting legacy depended on posthumous developments, such as shrines patronized by the political elite and hagiographies that canonized the memory of the sacred presence and ensured it would remain in circulation through reading and performance.

Persian hagiographical accounts present their saintly subjects wielding God's limitless power through miraculous interventions in the material sphere. Descriptions of kings of old acted as literary models for conveying the presence of such persons. Consequently, images from works like the *Shahnameh* and the *Haft Paykar* were easily adapted to hagiography, especially given that they included tropes about kings' wisdom and a concern with morality. Within this general framework, Persian hagiographical works exhibit great internal diversity when it comes to length and form (Bashir 75–80).

A number of major Persian hagiographies are available in English translation (e.g., Aflaki; Attar, *Farid ad-Din 'Attar's* Memorial; Ebn-e Monavvar; Moayyad and Lewis). Of these, I highlight the *Fava'id al-Fu'ad* (*Morals for the Heart*), dedicated to Nizamoddin Awliya, who belonged to the Chishti Sufi lineage. His shrine in Delhi, India, remains a major pilgrimage site to this day. This work recounts a series of assemblies in which the compiler, Amir Hasan Sijzi, asks questions of the saint and informs us of the answers. He states that the saint approved that he write the work based on a request:

> "For more than a year," I explained, "I have been continuously in your service. Every moment that I have obtained the blessing of kissing your feet, I have also derived counsels (*fawa'id*) from your elegant words. What exhortation and advice and inducement to obedience, what stories about the saints and their spiritual states have I heard from you! Every kind of soul-inspiring discourse has fallen on my ears, and I wanted to make that the foundation for my own life—

> indeed, to use it as guide on the Path for this broken person, at least to the extent that I could record with the pen what I understood. Also, I have heard the Shaykh say many times that the novice must consult a book on the Sufi masters and their guidelines for spiritual progress. (Auliya 113)

The hagiography's purpose was to record the teachings and manners of the saint for dissemination. Like history, it memorialized the past with the intent to affect the behavior of readers. Persian Sufi literature includes elaborate manuals of conduct and detailed descriptions of an aspirant's progress along the religious path (e.g., Daya; Hujviri; Shabistari). Hagiographic narratives dramatize abstract advice by depicting its implementation in the actions of saintly exemplars.

Sentiment

In modern Western languages, translations of Persian poetry containing evocative sentimental expression have proliferated since the nineteenth century. Seen as a counterpart to the lyric form in European languages, such poetry works on the basis of highly stylized tropes that can be put to use for purposes as varied as amorous pursuit, panegyric, and ekphrasis. Major figures such as Sir William Jones, Johann Wolfgang von Goethe, and Ralph Waldo Emerson attempted to emulate what they understood to be the distinctive affect of Persian poetry (Aminrazavi; Dabashi).

The greatest (although accidental) success on this score fell to Edward FitzGerald, whose rendering, first published in 1859, of the quatrains of Omar Khayyam became a bestseller in English in the nineteenth century. Khayyam was not counted among the best known or admired poets in Persian in the Middle Ages, and FitzGerald's interpretations are too colored by a predetermined ideology to be regarded as translations. Yet his mixture of artful language, ruefulness, and philosophical introspection is rooted in the atmosphere one encounters in Persian poetry.

In poetry attuned to sentiment, tropes describing the beloved play a key role. The work of Rudaki, an early Central Asian poet, was influential in setting this pattern:

> This wind that blows my way from Bukhara
> Smells of roses and musk, a jasmine breeze.
> Any man or woman caressed by this wind
> Says: maybe this wind blows from Khotan.

No, no. Such luscious wind could not blow from Khotan.
This wind blows from the bosom of my love.
Each night I look to Yemen until you appear
Because you are Canopus rising from Yemen.
My dear, I try to hide your name from people,
Keep it from falling in the public mouth.
Want to or not, with whomever I speak,
When I speak, it's your name that comes to mouth.
(Tabatabai 86)

This poem can be seen to effect transferences between the beloved (the ostensible topic) and the cosmos. The description of the object of desire invokes earthly places (Bukhara, Khotan, Yemen), the sky (Canopus), the world apprehended through the bodily senses (flowers, musk, wind, night), society, and the speaker's psychological state. As we know from the works of thousands of poets in later centuries, all these elements were open to endless further elaboration.

Persian poetry could also paint a sharper, more combative picture of the lover-beloved relationship. Amir Khusrau, a disciple of the aforementioned Sufi master Nizamoddin Awliya, says the following of young men made objects of desire in his home city:

Delhi and its fine lads
with their turbans and twisted beards
openly drinking lovers' blood
while secretly sipping wine.
Wilful and full of airs
they pay no heed to anyone.
So close to the heart, they rob
your soul and tuck it safely away.
When they are out for a stroll
rose bushes bloom in the street.
When the breeze strikes them from behind,
see how the turbans topple from their heads.
When they walk, the lovers follow,
blood gushing from their eyes.
(Khusrau 52)

This description is strongly emotional, emphasizing the destruction and psychological turmoil that accompanies love and desire. Special attention is focused on the beloved's body and comportment, elements that were part of an elaborate allegorization of the human form. Although these verses are explicit that the objects of desire are male, Persian grammar has the benefit that personal pronouns do not indicate gender. The resulting ambiguity means that the vast majority of Persian poetry can be read as referring equally to male or female. The language's androgyny has been a source of much poetic creativity over the centuries (Brookshaw 125–54).

Saʿdi and Rumi, discussed above, are regarded as masters at the expression of sentiment (Saʿdi, Saʿdi *in Love*; Rumi, *Swallowing the Sun*). They were equaled or surpassed by Shamsoddin Hafez, whose verses describe love as a complex game involving enchantment by the beloved, the pain of rejection, and ironies generated by the fickleness of fate. Working almost exclusively in the ghazel, a short form with an end rhyme, Hafez conveys complex images and ideas in the most economical way:

> If I go after him, he [or she] kicks up a tremendous fuss,
> But if I retire from the chase, he rises in high dudgeon.
> And if out of desiring, like dust under his feet,
> At a passing-place, I fall down a moment, he's off like the wind!
> And if I seek half a kiss, a hundred derisions
> From the crucible of his mouth like sugar he pours out.
> That deception I see in your eye
> Had reduced many a reputation to the level of dust on the road.
> The steeps and slopes of the desert of love are calamity's snare;
> Where is the lion-heart that is not wary of the ordeal?
> Ask you for a long life and patience, because the juggling sphere
> A thousand games more novel than this conjures up.
> Place your head, Hafiz, on the threshold of submission,
> Because if you kick over the traces, Fate will kick back.
>
> (Hafiz 206)

Two aspects of this poem can highlight the character of Hafez's art. On the side of imagery and content, the poet takes the tension inherent in love for granted and turns this into musing on the human condition. Pushed and pulled by the beloved, the poetic self is driven to matters such as predestination and fate. Hafez's ingenuity lies in conjuring the complex transition between the intensely personal and generally human repeatedly into new images as the poem progresses. The ghazel works like a pendulum, crossing the same focal point in each verse or iteration while traversing a different image or path. Parsimonious in vocabulary and direct imagery, the verses pack dense reflections on matters such as human psychology, religious and social ideology, and the existential realities of ecstasy, suffering, and death.

Hafez's poetry has sometimes been seen to exemplify the essence of Persian identity. The thought is justifiable, but for understanding the Middle Ages, one would have to be emphatic about disconnecting social identity from modern notions of ethnicity and the nation-state. Rather, Hafez's work embodies a socioliterary aesthetic that was deeply meaningful in most spheres of life in a vast geographic area during the Middle Ages. Developed in Persian, this aesthetic was foundational for literary traditions in languages such as Kurdish, Pashto, Urdu, and many varieties of Turkic. At a longer remove, it affected literary developments in modern European languages. The themes I have explored—placement, storytelling, history and hagiography, and sentiment—contain a vivid realm of human expression equal to the world's other great literary traditions.

Works Cited

Aflaki, Shams al-Din Ahmad. *The Feats of the Knowers of God: Manaqeb al-ʿarifin.* Translated by John O'Kane, E. J. Brill, 2002.

Aminrazavi, Mehdi, editor. *Sufism and American Literary Masters.* State U of New York P, 2014.

Attar, Fariduddin. *The Conference of the Birds.* Translated by Sholeh Wolpé, W. W. Norton, 2017.

———. *Farid ad-Din ʿAttar's* Memorial of God's Friends*: Lives and Sayings of Sufis.* Translated by Paul Losensky, Paulist Press, 2009.

Auliya, Nizamuddin. *Morals for the Heart.* Translated by Bruce Lawrence, Paulist Press, 1992.

Bashir, Shahzad. "Naqshband's Lives: Sufi Hagiography Between Manuscripts and Genre." In *Sufism in Central Asia: New Perspectives on Sufi Traditions, Fifteenth–Twenty-First Centuries*, edited by Jo-Ann Gross and Devin DeWeese, Brill, 2018, pp. 75–97.

Brend, Barbara, and Charles Melville, editors. *Epic of the Persian Kings: The Art of Ferdowsi's* Shahnameh. I. B. Tauris, 2010.

Broadbridge, Anne F. *Women and the Making of the Mongol Empire.* Cambridge UP, 2018.

Brookshaw, Dominic P. *Hafiz and His Contemporaries: Poetry, Performance and Patronage in Fourteenth Century Iran.* I. B. Tauris, 2019.

Bruijn, J. T. P. de, editor. *General Introduction to Persian Literature.* I. B. Tauris, 2008.

———. *Persian Sufi Poetry: An Introduction to the Mystical Use of Classical Persian Poems.* Curzon, 1997.

Dabashi, Hamid. *Persophilia: Persian Culture on the Global Scene.* Harvard UP, 2015.

Davidson, Olga M. *Poet and Hero in the Persian* Book of Kings. Cornell UP, 1994.

Daya, Najm al-Din Razi. *The Path of God's Bondsmen from Origin to Return: A Sufi Compendium.* Translated by Hamid Algar, Islamic Publication International, 2003.

Ebn-e Monavvar, Muhammad. *The Secrets of God's Mystical Oneness; or, The Spiritual Stations of Shaikh Abu Sa'id.* Translated by John O'Kane, Mazda, 1992.

Ferdowsi, Abolqasem. Shahnameh*: The Persian* Book of Kings. Translated by Dick Davis, Penguin Classics, 2007.

———. *The Tragedy of Sohráb and Rostám: From the Persian National Epic, the* Shahname *of Abol-Qasem Ferdowsi.* Translated by Jerome Clinton, U of Washington P, 1996.

Gorgani, Fakhraddin. *Vis and Ramin.* Translated by Dick Davis, Mage Publishers, 2008.

Hafiz, Shamsoddin. *The Collected Lyrics of Hafiz of Shiraz.* Translated by Peter Avery, Archetype, 2007.

Hujviri, 'Ali b. Usman. *The* Kashf al maḥjúb*: The Oldest Persian Treatise on Súfism.* Translated by R. A. Nicholson, Luzac, 1936.

Jamali, Hamid b. Fazlallah. *The* Mirror of Meanings*: A Parallel English-Persian Text.* Translated by A. A. Seyed-Gohrab, edited by N. Pourjavady, Mazda, 2002.

Juvaini, 'Ala-ad-Din 'Ata Malik. *Genghis Khan: The History of the World Conqueror.* Translated by J. A. Boyle, Manchester UP, 1997.

Katouzian, Homa. *Sa'di: The Poet of Life, Love and Compassion.* Oneworld, 2006.

Kaykavus b. Iskandar. *A Mirror for Princes: The* Qabusnama. Translated by Reuben Levy, E. P. Dutton, 1951.

Khusrau, Amir. *In the Bazaar of Love: The Selected Poetry of Amir Khusrau.* Translated by Paul Losensky and Sunil Sharma, Penguin, 2013.

Lewis, Franklin. "The *Shahnameh* of Ferdowsi as World Literature." *Iranian Studies*, vol. 48, no. 3, 2015, pp. 313–36.

Meisami, Julie Scott. *Medieval Persian Court Poetry.* Princeton UP, 1987.

Melville, Charles, editor. *Persian Historiography.* I. B. Tauris, 2012.

Melville, Charles, and Gabrielle van den Berg, editors. Shahnama *Studies II: The Reception of Firdausi's* Shahnama. Brill, 2011.

Moayyad, Heshmat, and Franklin Lewis, translators. *The Colossal Elephant and His Spiritual Feats: Shaykh Ahmad-e Jam.* Mazda Publishers, 2004.

Najm Sani, Muhammad Baqir. *Advice on the Art of Governance: An Indo-Islamic Mirror for Princes: Mau'izah-i Jahangiri of Najm-i Sani.* Translated by Sajida Sultana Alvi, State U of New York P, 1989.

Nezami Ganjavi. *The* Haft Paykar*: A Medieval Persian Romance.* Translated by Julie Scott Meisami, Oxford UP, 1995.

Nizam al-Mulk. *The* Book of Government*; or,* Rules for Kings*: The* Siyar al-Muluk*; or,* Siyasat-nama *of Nizam al-Mulk.* Translated by Hubert Darke, Persian Heritage Foundation, 2002.

Papan-Matin, Firoozeh. "The Crisis of Identity in Rumi's 'Tale of the Reed.'" *Comparative Studies of South Asia, Africa and the Middle East*, vol. 23, nos. 1–2, 2003, pp. 246–53.

Rumi, Jalaloddin. *The* Mathnawi *of Jalalu'ddin Rumi.* Translated by Reynold Nicholson, 6 vols., Gibb Memorial Series, 1925.

———. *Rumi: Swallowing the Sun.* Translated by Franklin Lewis, Oneworld, 2013.

Sa'di, Moshrefoddin. *The* Gulistan *(*Rose Garden*) of Sa'di: Bilingual English and Persian Edition with Vocabulary.* Translated by Wheeler Thackston, Ibex, 2017.

———. *Sa'di in Love: The Lyrical Verses of Persia's Master Poet.* I. B. Tauris, 2016.

Shabistari, Mahmud. *Garden of Mystery: The* Gulshan-i Raz *of Shabistari.* Translated by Robert Darr, Archetype, 2007.

Tabatabai, Sassan. *Father of Persian Verse: Rudaki and His Poetry.* Leiden UP, 2015.

Thackston, Wheeler, translator. *Classical Writings of the Medieval Islamic World: Persian Histories of the Mongol Dynasties.* I. B. Tauris, 2012.

Tusi, Nasir al-Din. *The Nasirean Ethics.* Translated by G. M. Wickens, Allen and Unwin, 1964.

Yavari, Neguin. *Advice for the Sultan: Prophetic Voices and Secular Politics in Medieval Islam.* Hurst, 2012.

Christopher Taylor

Teaching Prester John, a Global Legend

Of all the legendary material produced during the era of the Crusades, the boundless, exotic kingdom of Prester John has proven unmatched in its influence on the European imagination. In a tradition born between the Second and Third Crusades, an imagined eastern priest-king called Prester John (*presbyter Iohannes*) emerged as a potential savior of Christendom. According to a mysterious mid-twelfth-century letter, this self-described devout Christian ruler writes that he has domesticated much of the vast East and created a kingdom notable for its superior wealth and diverse, sometimes monstrous inhabitants.

Within a dominion that "crosses from Farther India, in which rests the body of St. Thomas the apostle, through the desert, and proceeds towards the sunrise, and returns down into the Babylonian desert," John rules over significant sites of Christian history and well-known markers of the East, including the Tower of Babel; Mount Olympus; the tomb of the Old Testament prophet Daniel; the fountain of youth; and the dwelling places of the Amazons, Brahmans, and the ten lost tribes of Israel (Brewer 68). Most essentially, Prester John announces his intentions to visit the Holy Sepulcher and help vanquish the threat of Islam once and for all.

This letter—known now as the Letter of Prester John (LOPJ)—circulated across Europe with remarkable urgency. Although Prester John never arrived, the promise of his strange Christian kingdom did not fade from the minds of Europeans. During the medieval and early modern periods, the desire to legitimate the contents of the letter influenced military tactics and papal policy while serving as a cultural touchstone for medieval maps, travel narratives, and romance tales. Travelers sought the mythic kingdom throughout the Asian steppe and eventually expanded the search to Africa. Rather than another political hoax fading from historical memory, LOPJ grew into a legend on which generations of Europeans continued to draw.

For the past six years, I have attempted to collect and organize six centuries' worth of Prester John lore for a digital platform hosted by the Global Middle Ages Project, entitled "The International Prester John Project." This work began as an attempt to better understand the transmission and translation of this important medieval legend that encompassed the reaches of the world as its stamping ground. The research enabled me to understand the astonishing degree to which the legend transcended the original textual tradition in which it was produced. I have now catalogued hundreds of authors of varied backgrounds and hundreds of texts of diverse genres, each attempting to add a sliver of clarity to the mystery and promise teased within LOPJ. I learned that, whereas the legend of Prester John meant many things to many people, nearly every invocation shares a common hope: to extend the horizon of the known world.

Yet despite its impact on the minds and maps of medieval and early modern Europeans, the legend of Prester John is sometimes relegated to the status of mere curiosity or hoax, a footnote in a seminar on medieval travel literature, a vestige of a superstitious and gullible dark age. Because its primary artifact escapes easy categorization, its historical and literary significance has long been overlooked in medieval studies. By presenting the strange contents of LOPJ and telling the story of John's imagined travels across the globe, teachers can demonstrate how medieval myth influenced global exchanges between western Europe and the rest of the world. In what follows, I offer what I believe are the most salient reasons for teaching the letter and legend of Prester John, along with a discussion of methods for doing such teaching.

Why Teach the Legend of Prester John

I outline five points of emphasis for teaching the legend of Prester John: its popularity, the desires it reflected and inspired, its global impact, the elasticity with which it transformed in response to historical and cultural pressures, and its durability and influence. I then offer suggestions on what matter to teach, how to teach it, and where Prester John might fit into course syllabi.

Popularity

Versions of LOPJ survive in 469 documented manuscripts (234 Latin and 235 vernacular) across eighteen versions (in two traditions) composed in eighteen different languages.[1] The popularity of this text simply cannot be overstated: it was regularly read, copied, and disseminated across Europe from the early thirteenth through the seventeenth centuries. By sheer number of surviving manuscripts, LOPJ outpaces nearly every canonical medieval text.

The reasons for LOPJ's appeal have been speculated on for centuries. These discussions circle back to a fundamental question: How did the legend of Prester John survive for so long despite an absence of evidence to support John's existence? To this end, two features of the legend's popularity merit comment: the quickness with which LOPJ extends beyond the cultural sphere in which it was produced and the liberties that so-called translators took with the hypothetical urtext.

Although its precise origins remain a mystery, scholars agree that the legend of a distant Eastern Christian priest-king begins with a brief conversation recorded in Otto of Freising's 1145 universal history, the *Historia de duabus civitatibus.* Otto's text furnishes an anecdote about a Nestorian Christian prince, Iohannes, hailing from the distant East of the Magi, who had recently conquered Persia and headed West to help crusaders in their defense of the Holy Land. Unfortunately, a flooded Tigris River prevented him from aiding his Latin Christian brethren.

A respected historian and uncle to the Holy Roman emperor Frederick I, Otto creates optimism for Latin Christendom at a moment of crisis. At the time, with the loss of Edessa (the first of the Latin colonies established by the First Crusade) in 1144, the instability of the church (there were four popes in the 1140s alone), and a looming Second Crusade, the rumor of a Christian king from the Orient galvanized European leaders.

Twenty years later, when a letter purportedly authored by Prester John arrived in Germany, not only did John seem a valuable ally uniquely suited to aid Europe in the war against Islam, but his status as a priest and king also neatly resolved Europe's investiture struggle by offering a vision of temporal and spiritual power mingled in the person of a single ruler. Early copies of the letter addressed to Frederick Barbarossa shifted the dynamic between emperor and pope enough for the pope to write to John himself requesting support.[2]

Given that Prester John's kingdom was purportedly situated in a realm in which heretics, pagans, and monsters coexisted, LOPJ acquired a surplus value for the legend far beyond the political intrigues of the twelfth century. This text allowed centuries of readers and writers to speculate on Prester John's location and what his existence meant for the future of Europe.

The letter began circulating in Europe around 1165. Until circa 1190, LOPJ was copied exclusively in Latin. By the beginning of the thirteenth century, however, when its initial political utility began to wane, vernacular copies of LOPJ begin to emerge at a rapid pace. By the end of the century, there was even an Anglo-Norman rhyming version of the letter, retrofitted with a prologue and an epilogue as if it were a romance. In both Latin and vernacular copies, LOPJ became a living text, accruing legendary material as it moved from place to place. Scholars have since classified the different redactions (A–E) into eighteen versions in two traditions, though there is variance even within these recensions. Such variety in the descriptions of John's kingdom suggests that the text's abiding popularity owes something to its ability to be perennially made new to its readers. Indeed, the adaptability of the legend helped successive generations of writers integrate Prester John into political, historical, literary, and prophetic traditions, as versions of what might more accurately be called the letters of Prester John continued to circulate.

Desire

Prester John emerged in the second half of the twelfth century, seeming to promise help for Latin Christendom to recuperate the losses of the First Crusade. Yet as the Second, Third, and even Fourth Crusades were waged, this priest-king failed to materialize. Buried under such a burden of historical expectation, John seemed destined to disappoint for any number of reasons, not least that he did not actually exist. Envoys were sent to make contact with him, but despite boasting the world's largest and richest kingdom, John continued to elude his European devotees.

Auspiciously, the leaders of the Fifth Crusade unearthed a prophecy that predicted the arrival of some great Eastern king, a discovery that convinced the Crusade's military leaders to abandon the recently captured Damietta and march south instead to await John's arrival in Cairo. After all, in LOPJ John had promised to come to defend Christendom against all enemies of the cross of Christ, "inimicos crucis Christi" (Brewer 46). However, on their way, the Nile rises, turning a sure victory against Muslim forces into a ruinous defeat. The crusader armies surrender to Sultan Al-Kamil a few weeks later.

With victory in sight at Damietta, the strange ending of the Fifth Crusade has long puzzled scholars: How is it possible for so many people not only to believe in Prester John but also to have faith that he would materialize at a time of need? The tactical disasters of the Fifth Crusade strongly suggested the patience of those who believed in John's messianic arrival. This patience, in turn, testified to an intense desire; but toward what end was this desire aimed? The deep disappointment and military disaster of the Fifth Crusade should have put an end to the legend of Prester John, yet the legend continued to flourish.

It seems that the desire for Prester John was not strictly bound up with the expectations of his arrival. After all, it is only after the disastrous Fifth Crusade's ending in 1221 that Europeans began to search in earnest for the kingdom of Prester John. Of the 469 extant copies of LOPJ, the majority were copied after the end of the Fifth Crusade. The persistent faith in Prester John attests to a complex set of desires that continued to anchor belief in John's existence. The surging popularity of this text; the dozens of expeditions seeking John's kingdom; and the legend's subsequent integration into other literary, historical, and prophetic traditions show that Prester John continued to produce meaning well after even the most optimistic estimates of his possible lifespan passed. What survives is the legend's avowal of familiarity and sameness even in the most remote, unknowable parts of the world.

Part of the legend's persistence seems to rest on its ability to link the impulse to explore a global landscape with the desire for this landscape to be revealed as a continuation of, rather than a departure from, the known—for a foreign land to be revealed as in fact already Christian. That Prester John reveal his existence matters less than what his potential existence signifies about the nature of the wider world. Powerful yet pious, doctrinally rigid yet tolerant, Prester John represented Christianity at its best. Over the course of the legend, Pope Alexander III (1177), Pope Honorius III (1221), Pope Eugenius IV (1438), Pope Calixtus III (1456), Pope Sixtus IV (1482), and Pope Leo X (1521) all wrote letters either to or about Prester John.

Cast in this light, we can see how LOPJ does not so much provide readers with new information about the world as it mobilizes centuries of accumulated lore about the East toward a specific, political purpose: the globalization of Christianity. Thus, when Prester John fails to arrive, missionaries, merchants, and explorers begin to seek him out in the places where Europeans desired Christianity to flourish. As a result, Prester John's kingdom migrated around the globe, positioned and repositioned at sites that inspired the attention of Latin Christendom for religious, political, or economic reasons.

Globality

Beginning in the mid–thirteenth century, when Europeans begin to search for the kingdom of Prester John in earnest, the legend of John becomes global in scope. By the sixteenth century, three hundred years later, the legend would reach nearly all of Europe and much of Asia and Africa. Writers from at least sixteen countries commented on the legend, whether in the form of a full treatise or through passing comments recorded in travel narratives. I have documented texts from writers hailing from Germany, France, Italy, Spain, Portugal, England, Scotland, Greece, Belgium, Netherlands, Flanders, Norway, Iceland, Syria, Morocco, and Ethiopia.

Writers postulated the existence of Prester John's kingdom in Syria, Iraq, Turkey, India, China, Mongolia, Russia, Ethiopia, Benin, Nubia, and Japan, among other places. Directly or indirectly, the desire to find the kingdom of Prester John helped shape Europe's notion of what the rest of the world actually looked like. Among the many places Europeans sought out John's mythical land of plenty, two peoples of particular interest commanded the bulk of attention: Mongols and Ethiopian Christians.

The association between Prester John and the Mongols dates back to Otto of Freising's mid-twelfth-century vignette and informs John's backstory through the prophecies of the Fifth Crusade. When Europeans finally began to realize the immensity of the Mongol Empire, linking Prester John with the Mongols was then a natural fit. In addition, although not explicitly mentioned in LOPJ, John had long been speculated to be a Nestorian Christian, and the existence of Nestorian churches in Asia was well known in Europe. As European leaders would come to learn, Nestorians commonly held important positions in the Mongol government.

European medieval travel narratives that were focused on converting or studying the Mongols all mention Prester John, including the writing of John of Plano Carpini (1246), Simon of Saint Quentin (1240s), William of Rubruck (1253), Marco Polo (circa 1299), and John of Monte Corvino (1305). Although the intent of these travelers was to return to the Latin West with accurate, firsthand intelligence about the Mongols, it appears that none could resist integrating the lore of Prester John into their reports.

In these texts Prester John becomes, respectively, the Christian king of what was known as Greater India who successfully repels a Mongol army; the long-dead King of India (and lord of the so-called Tartars), whose son, King David, had been murdered by Genghis (Chinggis) Khan (who then wedded John's only surviving daughter); "a pastoral-herder chieftain defeated by Genghis [Khan]" whose reputation had been exaggerated by Nestorian Christians (Heng 315); a figure called Unc Can, also murdered by Genghis Khan; and the ancestor of a Nestorian Christian "King George," whom John of Monte Corvino converts to Catholicism. Having investigated the source of the initial rumors about the kingdom of Prester John, each of these travelers returns to Europe carrying sobering news of the nonexistence of a powerful Christian kingdom in the East, but with knowledge of a different, factual, and even more powerful empire: that of the Mongols.

Not ten years after Marco Polo returns to the West with confirmation of the death of the legend of John, a group of Ethiopian emissaries arrives in Europe and shifts the search for Prester John toward Africa. From 1306 to 1310, a delegation of Ethiopian Christians travels to Spain, Portugal, Genoa, Rome, and finally to Avignon to visit Pope Clement V. These ambassadors greet their European brethren with a request from the Ethiopian emperor to join forces against Islam and return to the true doctrine of the Christian Church (Beckingham). Cartographer Giovanni Da Carignano, apparent witness to one of these meetings, records a now lost report on the meeting and produces an updated world map, the first of its kind in Europe to correctly situate Ethiopia between the Blue and White Nile Rivers. At the center of this territory, Da Carignano depicts Prester John.

These events preserve the legend of Prester John in two important ways. First, they turn Europe's attention toward African Christianity. Within twenty-five years of the embassy visit, Friar Jordanus of Séverac (circa 1330) revives the magical, dragon-filled kingdom of Prester John but places it in Ethiopia. Second, Prester John transforms from a name into a title, making the legend more durable. In the following centuries, as sea exploration arms Europe's imperialism with a more mercantile bent, Prester John remains firmly fixed in Africa. Impervious to tales debunking the story of his vast kingdom, Prester John remains central to Western conceptions of a global Christendom for six centuries.

Adaptability

Presbyter Iohannes, Patriarch John, King John, Prete Ianni, Presto Giovanni, Preste Juan, Prestre Johan, Presbytero-Johanides, Tsar-Priest John, Prete Ianne, Johannes Africanus, Bel Gian, Praeciosus Iohannes, Preste Ioam, Belul Jan, Jonanam, Presbyter Bedigian, Prestigian, Precious John are just some of the names ascribed to the mythical priest-king in the medieval and early modern periods.

Prester John's nomadic journey around the world was perhaps outpaced only by what we might call his textual migrations. The ability of Prester John to rove from location to location might be best understood by analyzing the malleability of the narrative tradition that produced him. From the accumulations and distortions found in the redactions of LOPJ to its central figure's mobility across genres, languages, and contexts, the legend of Prester John exhibits an elasticity that not only absorbs contradictions but also encourages revision.

In practice, LOPJ reads like a series of disconnected fantasies. Because its fragmentary structure tolerated unusual juxtapositions, the text could readily assimilate new material and thus "functioned almost as a genre of a text rather than as a single piece of writing" (Brewer 10). Scholars have traditionally organized LOPJ's multiplicity by theorizing a hypothetical urtext with five distinct interpolations (traditionally labeled A–E), though Bettina Wagner has updated this theory to eighteen separate versions. Regardless of which version of the legend is accessed, the narrative's organization has the following elements: "the presentation of Prester John, with a salutation and invitation to the recipient; a statement of intentions, concerning a proposed military expedition; geographic, geologic, zoological, botanical, mineralogical, sociological and ethical description of the kingdom . . . a description of the palace and of everyday life at court; and, finally, information outlining the nature of his title" (Ramos 31).

Within that organizational structure, the interpolations swerve between classical lore (gold-digging giant ants [D]) and schoolboy silliness (a "Cavern of Dragons . . . whose depth is most deep, and most cavernly and full of secret places" [E]). The interpolations, recently translated by Keagan Brewer, mostly offer entertaining anecdotes yet fail to provide information that would help a reader locate the kingdom of Prester John. Of the interpolations, only redaction C includes material that alters LOPJ's underlying thrust, offering a millenarian warning that the world's monstrous races will soon be loosed on Europe (133–34).

When reading the fully interpolated version of LOPJ, a reader can see that these variations transform it into a communally authored textual tradition (or even a genre) rather than a singular text. Its open-source orientation also meant that its textual material could be readily incorporated into other texts and contexts. It is not surprising to see how quickly LOPJ was translated from Latin into vernaculars and from prose to poetry. Although copies of LOPJ continued to circulate hundreds of years after the Letter's original appearance—Brewer notes that nearly 100 of the 232 Latin manuscripts were produced in the fifteenth century—European authors began to integrate Prester John into more literary narratives, even as the historical expectations for his arrival endured.

Influence and Durability

Sober efforts to seek out the land of Prester John lasted through the eighteenth century (Brooks 174–83). Prester John has even become an American popular culture touchstone, featured in the Marvel comic universe as well as contemporary fantasy novels, travel narratives, and historical fiction. Prester John's legacy can be felt globally as well. Since 2003, the Instituto de Preste João in Portugal has served as Royal and Imperial Council of Foreign Nobility. A statue of Prester John graces Port Elizabeth, South Africa.[3] These contemporary reprisals vary in their treatment and use of the legend but collectively attest to an abiding interest in a figure of unreachable power through whom readers might orient their futures. Although it is unsurprising that no one was ever able to find Prester John, the resilience of his legend despite pressures to disbelieve attests to a persistent faith in (and desire for) the unknown.

Teaching Prester John

The legend of Prester John fits well into recent developments in medieval studies, a field that has taken a global turn over the past two decades. As scholarly interest in medieval travel writing, *mappae mundi*, cosmopolitanism, empire, and nation building continues to grow, the demand for teachable texts that reflect these interests also increases.

I outlined above five focal points for those who wish to teach the legend of Prester John. In an attempt to capture something of the vastness of Prester John's impact on medieval and early modern Europe, I may have complicated the matter of how exactly this legend might fit in the classroom. In what follows below, I hope to anticipate some of the questions about teaching Prester John and offer advice on how to teach this legend in a classroom context.

What to Teach

Any classroom treatment of the legend of Prester John should begin with a version of LOPJ. As a short, lively text, LOPJ makes for an engaging in-class reading assignment or a useful take-home annotation project. The uninterpolated urtext is about five pages long and Brewer's fully interpolated translation runs around twenty-five pages. Without a stand-alone edition of the letters of Prester John, Michael Uebel's translation of the uninterpolated letter (155–60) and Brewer's translation of the interpolated material (67–91) are best used.

After reading LOPJ, students will require some context to understand the wider purposes to which this letter was put, along with the desires it came to signify—though it should be made clear that even the most basic facts about the legend, such as the reasons for its generation, its provenance, and the intentions of its creator, remain unclear and under scholarly dispute. Scholarship on the legend is vast and varies in approach from compiling material related to the letter to collating hundreds of years of writing on Prester John to searching for the legend's origins to reimagining John's utopian kingdom.

In addition to reading LOPJ and surveying related scholarship, students might turn to primary texts that touched on the legend, be they travel narratives, universal histories, or romance tales. Some of the most compelling treatments of the Prester John legend can be found in Pope Alexander III's Letter to Prester John (1177), Wolfram von Eschenbach's *Parzival* (early thirteenth century), Marco Polo's *Le Devisement du Monde* (circa 1299), Jordanus of Severac's *Mirabilia* (circa 1330), *Mandeville's Travels* (circa 1360s), Johannes Witte de Hese's *Itinerarium* (circa 1389), Bertrandon de la Broquiere's *The Voyage to Outremer* (1457), Ludovico Ariosto's *Orlando Furioso* (1516), Antonio de Torquemada's *The Garden of Curious Flowers* (1570), Samuel Purchas' *Pilgrimage* (1613), Balthazar Tellez's *The Travels of the Jesuits in Ethiopia* (1680), and John Buchan's adventure novel for boys *Prester John* (1910). Brewer has excerpted and translated nearly fifty texts that helped develop the legend, including nearly all of those mentioned above. His book proves an indispensable resource for anyone interested in the adaptations of the Prester John legend.

Lastly, I point teachers toward "The International Prester John Project." My digital project was designed in part to help teachers immerse students in the making of this legend. The digital project presents five chapters or paths, organized chronologically, each concerned with the spread of the legend during a particular era. Each path offers a short overview of that era, interactive maps that reflect the spread of the legend during that era, and individual entries containing primary and secondary material particular to each author and text within the author's era. The annotated maps and interactive framework allow users to get lost in the archive as they forge paths through the legendary material for research and teaching purposes.

How to Teach

To introduce the legend of Prester John into the classroom, I have found success in giving students copies of the uninterpolated LOPJ (Uebel 155–60), along with a blank world map. From there, I break up the text into five relatively equal parts and assign groups to work through each part. Then, based on what they ascertain from the material in their section (using their own knowledge of medieval lore or the annotated LOPJ found in "The International Prester John Project"), students identify and sketch where they would search for Prester John on the blank map as if reading LOPJ as a medieval European. At the end of this first class, the groups present on the findings and justify their targets for exploration. Ideally, these maps vary quite a bit among the groups, and the activity bears witness to the multiplicity and ambiguity built (purposefully or not) into LOPJ.

For the next class, I supply additional context about the translation and dissemination of LOPJ while introducing students to some of the interpolated material (again, perhaps assigning groups one of the interpolations to report back to the class on). From there, to emphasize something of the durability and adaptability of the legend, I provide readings on the political context of the early phase of the legend and selections from Polo, *Mandeville's Travels*, and Witte de Hese, on the one hand, or Wolfram, Jordanus, and Buchan's *Prester John*, on the other.

Teachers can extend this strategy into a more involved assignment focused on having students identify, read, research, and report on one of the key secondary texts involved in proliferating LOPJ. Likewise, teachers might provide a list of all the places identified with the kingdom of Prester John (real and imaginary) and ask students to research how Prester John became associated with these locations.

More broadly speaking, when bringing the legend of Prester John into the classroom, consider focusing on one or more of the following questions, which can be explored using my database:

How did the legend spread geographically and linguistically over time?
Where did people locate Prester John's kingdom and how did this change over time?
Who wrote about Prester John: when, where, and for what purposes?
As the legend changed over time, by what names did writers identify Prester John and to what degree were these names location-dependent?
Is there a relationship between where texts situated Prester John and where these texts were themselves written?
Is there any correlation between the putatively historical texts mentioning Prester John (travel narrative, chronicle, geographic treatise) and the reflexively fictional accounts of his kingdom?

In the activities I outline above, the goal is to help students understand LOPJ in the context of the larger legend it was responsible for producing, but the legend can also be integrated into courses with other or more specific foci. For example, in a unit or course on medieval race, Prester John testifies to the ways medieval race can be understood as adaptable or as nonessentialist. Surveying visual depictions of Prester John among maps, frontispieces, and travel narratives in which John varies from a white European to a Black African, and even a supposed white Ethiopian in Johan Boemus's ethnographic encyclopedia *Omnium Gentium Mores, Leges, et Ritus* (1520) can help buttress or complicate theoretical frameworks on medieval and early modern race, especially when studied alongside the larger cultural-political motives surrounding the Prester John legend at the time and place where each text was produced.

Likewise, courses focused on global medieval literature could have students investigate how theories about Prester John helped shape European views of a number of non-European places (as I discuss above). Teachers can also create projects that compare European depictions of other areas of the globe with those areas' understandings of Europe.

Where to Teach

Courses on travel writing, East-West interactions; medieval monsters; and studies of nonhuman, non-European, non-Christian, or nonwhite identities have now become standard course topics at the undergraduate and graduate levels. In some of these courses, LOPJ is already an established core text, included in bibliographies and course syllabi concerned with a more globally focused vision of the Middle Ages. The legend has not yet, however, attained its deserved status among the most canonical of medieval myths, such as the Arthurian legends. Given its astounding medieval popularity, its unique perspective on contemporary academic conversations, and its easy appeal for undergraduates, the legend of Prester John should find a place within courses focused on early global literatures, travel literature, the Crusades, utopian literature, and European colonial history, in addition to wider surveys of medieval literature, history, art history, and religious history.

Notes

1. I follow Brewer's manuscript count and Wagner's manuscript classification. The languages, with the first date in which a version in that tongue appears (if known), are as follows: French (early thirteenth century), Anglo-Norman (early thirteenth century), Occitan (thirteenth century), Welsh (1346), Hebrew (1371), Italian, Catalan (fifteenth century), English (fifteenth century), Irish (fifteenth century), Swedish (fifteenth century), Serbian (fifteenth century), Old Church Slavonic (fifteenth century), Danish (early sixteenth century), Dutch (1506), Spanish (1515), Portuguese (1515), German, and Russian.

2. Pope Alexander III sent a letter to Prester John in 1177, the same year that the Peace of Venice ended the power struggle between the two leaders and forced Frederick to recognize papal supremacy. Eight hundred years later, Nicholas Jubber attempts to retrace the emissary's route and deliver Alexander's reply, despite the obvious facts standing in the way of this feat, in *The Prester Quest.*

3. The inscription reads, "In memory of those seafarers who searched for Prester John, 1145–1650."

Works Cited

Beckingham, C. F. "An Ethiopian Embassy to Europe, c. 1310." *Prester John: The Mongols and the Ten Lost Tribes*, edited by Beckingham and Bernard Hamilton, Variorum, 1996, pp. 197–206.

Brewer, Keagan, compiler and translator. *Prester John: The Legend and Its Sources.* Ashgate, 2015.

Brooks, Michael. *Prester John: A Reexamination and Compendium of the Mythical Figure Who Helped Spark European Expansion.* 2010. U of Toledo, PhD dissertation.

Heng, Geraldine. *The Invention of Race in the European Middle Ages.* Cambridge UP, 2018.

Jubber, Nicholas. *The Prester Quest.* Doubleday, 2005.

Ramos, Manuel João. *Essays in Christian Mythology: The Metamorphosis of Prester John.* UP of America, 2006.

Taylor, Christopher. "The International Prester John Project." *Global Middle Ages*, globalmiddleages.org/project/peregrinations-prester-john-creation-global-story-across-600-years.

Uebel, Michael. *Ecstatic Transformations: On the Uses of Alterity in the Middle Ages.* Palgrave, 2005.

Wagner, Bettina. *'Die Epistola presbyteri Johannes' lateinisch und deutsch: Überlieferung, Textgeschichte, Rezeption und Übertragungen im Mittelalter.* De Gruyter, 2000.

Part II

Zones and Geographies of the Global

Michael A. Gomez

The Epic of Sunjata and the Changing Worlds of Trans-Saharan Africa

Arguably the most famous representation of African oral traditions are those accounts associated with Sunjata, also known as Sundiata, Sundjata, Soundjata, and so on, a consequence of the name appearing in multiple Mande languages, as well as translations from French to English. The most famous compilation of these accounts is Djibril Tamsir Niane's Sundiata: *An Epic of Old Mali*. Long a staple in the Longman African Writers series, a revised edition of the 1965 English translation was then republished in 2006 by Pearson Publishing Company.

The *Sunjata* epic is an account within which reside multiple stories, told for a variety of reasons. At one level it conveys the dawn of an imperial tradition, explaining the origins of a far-flung polity. The rise of Malian imperialism would require the implementation of a theory of governance, as well as the identification of those who would govern provinces and towns, and, as such, the epic is a study of the qualities of Sunjata's contemporaries, who became his lieutenants. But the imperial tradition is also very much tethered to the internal dynamics and rivalries of royal clans, such that the epic is an exploration of which factions win and which ones lose. In examining the reasons for failure and success, the traditions become a vehicle through which those values and principles deemed exemplary are touted while those deemed antithetical to the best interest of the society are also underscored. Undergirding these multiple tales and objectives are familial relations, the foundation for which are mothers, while infusing all are spiritual forces and beliefs. As such, the *Sunjata* epic attempts to recount the past, but in so doing also uses that past as a blueprint to organize future generations. As prescriptive as descriptive, the epic can be viewed as a political charter.

Oral Transmission

The temporal focus of the epic is early thirteenth-century West Africa and the progenitor of the Malian empire, Sunjata, who dies around 1258 CE. Niane's *Sundiata* is but the most famous among dozens of either partial or complete compilations, in different West African languages, which altogether are referred to as an "epic," containing sufficient points of correspondence and formulaic substance to more or less constitute a composite, generalized account.

These various accounts constitute an approach to recalling the past that is arguably the most representative of Africa's oral tradition genre—it is certainly one of the best known in West Africa. Oral tradition, in turn, is a marvelous mechanism that treats the past as a canvas on which past developments and enduring values can be painted. Orality occasionally employs imagery more mythical than factual, at which moments the didactic purpose of the story merits careful attention.

Central to the oral tradition genre is the person telling the story—the *griot*, referred to as the *jeli* (pl., *jeliw*) in Mande languages. Griots or *jeliw* are born into that status; that is, whole families belong to griot formations, within which the craft is learned and perfected, and, as such, form a caste. (Austen; Conrad; Conrad and Condé; Niane,"Histoire"). To be sure, nowadays anyone can pay money to have a griot sing praises, but there are griots and there are griots, and those in the past charged with dynastic, royal histories took their craft and responsibilities very seriously.

Those responsible for the *Sunjata* epic over the centuries inhabit the highest rung of griot artistry. The griot's task is to recreate the past, and this is accomplished through a live performance. In this way, to read the *Sunjata* epic is at cross-purposes with its design, as the idea is for the story instead to be heard and experienced. English readers are several degrees removed from the effect of the griot's artistry, as the epic is translated from the French, and the French is in turn a translation from Mande and other African languages.

As a performance, the griot's account is a balance of historical content and artistic dexterity. We certainly need to be concerned with the limitations of memory, especially when the account is transmitted over centuries, but consideration of the epic's components helps address some of these concerns. To begin, at the core of the epic are songs, melodies created to commemorate events deemed the most important. The songs themselves are connected by way of narrative strategies that speak to key episodes, consisting of dialogue, speeches, recounting battles, and so on. These narrative links between songs will vary from version to version, but as the most archaic element of the epic, the songs themselves tend to be stable, their metric structure rendering them more resistant to alteration.

These songs often require musical accompaniment, and, in the case of the *Sunjata* epic, can be classified as a specific type of performance, a *foli*, with songs commemorating ancestors called *fasaw* (sing. *fasa*). The *janjon* is the highest form of the *fasa*. The specifics of the epic may drift over time and vary in performance, but the faithful reproduction of the songs has remained a priority throughout the centuries, placing constraints on any intentional improvisation. In this way, the songs police the process of transmission and performance, and serve as anchors to which narration is moored.

The griots who were contemporaries of Sunjata are considered the "first-singers" (Wilks 33). Their presence is independently verified by Ibn Baṭṭūṭa who, during his fourteenth-century visit to Mali paid close attention to "Dūghā the interpreter," who performed before dignitaries and sang poetry in which he praised the sultan and commemorated the sultan's expeditions and exploits. Dūghā was next followed by the *jeliw*, who declared to *Mansā* Sulaymān (the ruler at the time) that upon his royal seat (*bambī/banbī*) once sat "such-and-such a king and of his good deeds were so-and-so . . . so you do good deeds which will be remembered after you" (Hopkins and Levtzion 293). Although we do not know the specifics of their performance, as it concerned former rulers, Sunjata himself may have featured, especially as Ibn Baṭṭūṭa later actually mentions "Sāriq Jāṭa," the grandfather of *Mansā* Mūsā, likely the same person as Sunjata, or Mārī Jāṭa (Hopkins and Levtzion 295).

No thirteenth-century records of Sunjata have surfaced, and collections that focus on him date back no earlier than the late seventeenth century, when crafted under *Mansā* Saman of Kangaba (in the contemporary state of Mali; Niane, "Histoire" and "Recherches"). Kangaba town had become a last refuge for Malian rulers reduced to a small state called Minijan, as they were reeling from the incursions of the Bambara (or Bamana) of Segu. It was at that time that *Mansā* Saman initiated a tradition of reroofing the *Kama-Bolon* every seven years, a structure allegedly built by the aforementioned *Mansā* Sulaymān, following a purported return from the Ḥijāz in 752/1352.

Mansā Sulaymān's pilgrimage is probably fictitious, but the reroofing ceremony indeed took place, becoming over time the occasion for the gathering of representatives from the branches of the royal Keita clan (to which Sunjata belonged), along with the leaders of other Mande clans who were accompanied by their "traditionalists." At Kangaba they would listen to the Sunjata traditions as conveyed by the Jabate-Gberela griots of Keyla (five kilometers away), apparently in a concerted effort to recall the splendors of an earlier Mali. The language used to recount the *Sunjata* epic was distinctive, as the seventeenth-century griots regarded it as archaic, from the time of Sunjata himself—so-called *kuma koro* ("ancient speech").

Over time, Mande griots were joined by griots from all over the western Sudan during the reroofing of the *Kama-Bolon* and would host an instructional period lasting from six months to a year. This explains the preservation of the epic in various non-Mande languages, such as Pulaar, Wolof, Soninke, Zarma, and so on. The *Kama-Bolon* reroofing was not the only occasion for reciting the *Sunjata* epic, but it was apparently the most critical. From Kangaba, the Keyla master griots oversaw a process by which traditions were standardized, regulated, and disseminated, resulting in a measure of uniformity reinforcing the order imposed by the songs themselves (Camara 59–60).

We cannot know the ways in which the *Sunjata* epic may have been altered from the fourteenth to the late seventeenth century, and then into the late nineteenth century, when they are finally recorded by the French. But through the latter's imperial activity, the traditions celebrated at Kangaba may have been further disseminated.

Mali's Dawn in the Thirteenth Century

We do not have internally written records that provide insight into Mali's early years, but we do have externally written sources (in Arabic) that shed light on the place and period and corroborate the essential elements of the oral traditions. These traditions reveal a scene of destruction and mayhem in the early thirteenth century, in which Manden, or Old Mali, the land of Mande speakers who called themselves Maninka (or Mandinka) in the upper Niger valley, was reeling from pressures brought by the Susu, a related Mande group.

Unidentified in the external Arabic sources, the oral accounts name the Susu leader as Sumaoro or Sumanguru Kante, to whom Mali becomes subject. Sumaoro the Cruel is depicted as a "plunderer," robbing "merchants of everything when he was in a bad mood" (Sisòkò 7). He is further characterized as "an evil demon" who "forcibly abducted girls" and flogged "venerable old men" (8). The general picture is one of duress and is consistent with the rise of slaving activity (for transport through the Sahara) as described by Ibn Sa'īd, who wrote in the thirteenth century, and Ibn Khaldūn, who wrote in the fourteenth century (Hopkins and Levtzion 333).

If the oral and written sources concur on the rise of the Susu and war, they align even more on Sunjata as military conqueror. The oral accounts are unanimous in celebrating him as the person who defeats Sumaoro and ends Susu rule. Mention has been made of Ibn Baṭṭūṭa's reference to Sāriq Jāṭa, who was most probably Sunjata, a likelihood further strengthened by the fact that just forty years later, in 1394, one *Shaykh* ʿUthmān, a West African legal expert, arrived in Egypt and shared information with Ibn Khaldūn. Having once more noted a context of instability through slaving and the rise of the Susu, *Shaykh* ʿUthmān said, "Later the people of Mālī outnumbered the peoples of the Sūdān [and] vanquished the Ṣūṣū. . . . Their greatest king, he who overcame the Ṣūṣū, conquered their country, and seized the power from their hands, and was named Mārī Jāṭa . . ." (Hopkins and Levtzion 295, 333). If there is uncertainty as to whether the Sāriq Jāṭa of Ibn Baṭṭūṭa is Sunjata, there is no question that the Mārī Jāṭa of Ibn Khaldūn and Sunjata are one and the same.

Sogolon

Traditions focusing on Sunjata's birth and early life may provide insight into actual events, but they certainly address a deep contextual setting. Themes that emerge include the critical nature of a mother's connection to her children, sibling rivalry, and conflict between wives within polygamous households. Beyond the familial, the epic addresses the question of women and political power.

The story begins in crisis, for in neighboring Sangara (or Sankara), either adjacent to or conflated with the land of Do (or Daw), a buffalo or *koba* (in some traditions, a "horse-antelope") has been ravaging the land, killing farmers and terrorizing its twelve villages. But the buffalo is in fact Do-Kamissa, a woman who, undergoing transmogrification, has been unrelenting in killing twelve people every night in each of the twelve villages. Do's ruler Domògò Nyamògò Jata is desperate, recruiting hunters from surrounding lands to kill the *koba*. The hunters are all unsuccessful, and conditions continue to deteriorate until the arrival of two young Traore brothers, Dan *Mansā* Wulani and Dan *Mansā* Wulan Tamba. With a motif found elsewhere in West African folklore, they consult with an old woman in Do.

Initially rude, the old woman finally reveals that she is in fact the *koba*, having assumed the form "because my twelve brethren always treated me so vilely. My brethren have all the good things, villages, slaves and riches; but they gave me not one single slave to bring me water or wood for my hearth" (Cissé and Kamissòko, *La grande geste* 51). Gender asymmetries are therefore the reason for the difficulties, as the sister was excluded from sacrificial rites by her younger brother, the ruler Domògò Nyamògò Jata, simply because she is a woman. The grievance has to do with political power and privilege, such that this conflict in Sangara or Do (Daw) represents a moment in which the gender fluidity of political power is shifting and becoming more masculinized. The transition is unacceptable to Do-Kamissa, and the result is lethal protest. She proceeds to lay waste to the realm by mystical and magical means, further signaling the shift in the power of women from the political and material to the supernatural, a compensatory development.

For reasons not explained, Do-Kamissa tells the Traore brothers how to kill the buffalo. As a reward, the ruler offers them any of his nine daughters, but not the tenth, Sogolon. This is because she is extremely unattractive, "ugly," with "monstrous eyes" (Niane, Sundiata 6) and seven large, distinct bodily protuberances, with one eye higher than the other, one leg longer than the other, one arm shorter than the other, and one buttock larger than the other. She is otherwise described as a hairless "hunchback" (8) in mimicry of a buffalo. Although the ruler protests, the Traore brothers are instructed by Do-Kamissa to request Sogolon as their reward, as Sogolon is Do-Kamissa's "double" (8). The brothers comply, but as neither succeeds in consummating a relationship, they bring her to Manden's (Old Mali's) Maghan Kon Fatta the Handsome, who had been previously alerted that the woman was unattractive, but would become "the mother of him who will make the name of Mali immortal forever. The child will be the seventh star, the seventh conqueror of the earth. He will be more mighty than Alexander" (6).

The fantastical nature of these interactions underscores a celestial orchestration on the grandest of scales, the birth of Sunjata a cosmic event. The mention of Alexander the Great may reflect emendation, but it may also simply reveal the spread of the latter's fame as far as West Africa by the thirteenth century.

The story of Sunjata unfolds in a manner that underscores a remarkable closeness to his mother, then later with his sister, showing that his success depended on these relations. Women were largely responsible for who he would become, and not just in the biological sense, as their spiritual abilities would prove to be indispensable. Their bonds illustrate Mande society's high regard for women while gendering differentiated political and spiritual spheres of power.

A Child Is Born and Rejected

Niane's collection identifies Niani as Manden's capital (actually in contemporary Guinea, near the border with Mali), where Maghan Kon Fatta would marry Sogolon and have a son by her. But from birth through adolescence, Sunjata is hostage to rivalries between Maghan Kon Fatta's co-wives, as well as among his siblings. The ever-escalating levels of vitriol are interdependent, with the former rivalries in the interests of the latter. Sunjata and his mother and sister offer little resistance to various affronts and intrigues, testimony to their character.

Sogolon's initial reception among Mali's royals is characterized by rejection, led by Maghan Kon Fatta's first wife Sassuma Berete. Having "cast every kind of evil spell" to prevent the marriage, she warns Maghan, "I cannot live with her because she is too ugly" (Laye 90). Sassuma will also have a child, Dankaran Tuman, but the traditions differ as to whether he is older than Sunjata. In some, the name *Sunjata* means "lion thief," but the most popular interpretation is that *Sunjata* conjoins *Sogolon* and *Jata* (thus, "Sogolon's lion"), in any event a name assigned to him over time, since he was originally "called Maghan after his father, and Mari Djata, a name which no Mandingo prince has ever borne" (Niane, Sundiata 14). Sources other than Niane emphasize that *Sunjata* takes hold because, as a child, he stole a great deal—cattle, gold, jewelry—and became known as "a thief like a lion" (Sisòkò 51). This characterization should be understood as previewing his subsequent, imperial behavior (Zeltner 13–14; Sisòkò 51–52).

Walking as Divine Intervention

According to some accounts, Sunjata was so angry over not being recognized as the firstborn that he became "hot-tempered and violent," his temperament so intense that he refused to walk for years. Taciturn, perpetually angry, and braining other children, Sunjata crawls on all fours throughout his childhood. A large, heavy infant who crushed midwives and then grew into a "large bull," his huge head and large eyes connect him to the *koba*, Do-Kamissa of Sangara. The son of Maghan Kon Fatta the Handsome, Sunjata is even more the son of Do-Kamissa's "double" Sogolon, having received the Islamically influenced concept of *baraka* ("communicable spiritual power") from his father, whereas his *nyama* ("life force") and true Mande core came from his mother (Sisòkò 9). In some traditions, Sogolon also has *dalilu* 'powers of sorcery,' and it is from mothers that male heroes receive such powers (Conrad and Condé, xxi–xxii). In this way, Sunjata becomes the vessel within which *baraka*, *nyama*, and *dalilu* are reconciled.

Sunjata's inability or refusal to walk also defines his mother, subjecting them both to harsh ridicule. Sogolon's ugliness is no longer mentioned after Sunjata's birth; instead she becomes the long-suffering mother. In exasperation she laments to Sunjata, "I am so ashamed of you. . . . You can't even take yourself to the toilet, you son of misfortune!" (Ly-Tall et al. 37). In contrast, Sassuma's son Danakan Tuman is by age eleven a "fine and lively boy," a hunter (Sisòkò 64). Sogolon will have a daughter by Maghan, Sogolon Kolokon, who, as mentioned, will also play a critical role in Sunjata's life.

Sogolon's humiliation becomes the impetus for Sunjata's decision to walk, as one day she asks Sassuma Berete for baobab leaves to prepare a meal, to which Sassuma Berete contemptuously suggests she send Sunjata to retrieve the leaves instead. Sogolon's grief greatly impacts a seventeen-year-old Sunjata (in some accounts); enraged, he eventually enlists his father's smiths, bending and breaking one iron bar after another until one of enormous size and strength is forged, taking one year to make, and with which he finally stands. "Allah Almighty, you never created a finer day," he exclaims in one version (Niane, Sundiata 21), combining Islamic influence with ancestral belief in forces associated with metallurgy. He returns not simply with a few leaves, but with the entire tree (Conrad and Condé 74–78).

Sunjata's newfound ability to walk is a divine appointment, after which he is said to develop a youthful following that includes Fran Kamara of Tabon and Kamanjan of Sibi, sons of rulers of their respective lands, along with "other princes whose fathers had sent them to the court of Niani" (Niane, Sundiata 22–23). The celebration of such individuals underscores their bonds as well as their subsequent preeminence in the empire's founding, and establishes Sunjata as their leader early on. The traditions also claim that Sunjata becomes a *simbon* or master hunter very early in life. But his rise reignites rivalries and stokes fears. A number of versions identify Sassuma Berete as the person behind efforts to destroy or expel Sunjata. Maghan the Handsome dies, Dankaran Tuman succeeds him, and Sassuma Berete acts to safeguard her son's interests. Few versions present Dankaran as aggressively hostile to Sunjata, but he nonetheless advises him to leave the capital, with which Sogolon concurs as Sassuma Berete warns: "Go and seek a place to die, if not, I will chop through your necks" (Sisòkò 65).

An Exilic Corridor to Power

Sunjata's exile is subject to multiple interpretations, each contributing to the establishment of his claims to power. Although political exile has been a universal experience, in the case of Sunjata it operates between verity and fiction, as it imagines the dawn of a process by which sovereign states are subsumed by an empire as dependent provinces. One probable fiction is that the empire was fully accomplished during Sunjata's lifetime, but the truth is that Mali was indeed an imperial formation by the late fourteenth century, made up of the very provinces identified in the tale of exile, with Ibn Khaldūn asserting that Mali's "rule reached from the Ocean and Ghāna in the west to the land of Takrūr in the east" (Hopkins and Levtzion 334). What is therefore uncertain is the duration of this remarkable accomplishment. As such, the mythical qualities of Sunjata's sojourn attempt to account for a very real political transformation.

The exile also has the objective of ordering political relations by enshrining them in an auspicious story of origination, legitimizing claims of central authority. In this way, Sunjata's banishment is a primer in early Mande geography, as he moves from kingdom to kingdom, establishing an arterial network through which flow alliances, hierarchies of power and privilege, and relations of subservience. In addition to serving as the memory of Manden, the traditions become a critical mechanism of Manden's political apparatus, a political charter. Yet another possibility is of exile as a well-trod path to greatness. Examples abound in sacred writ, and in addition to Ishmael (or Ismāʾīl) in the Hebrew Old Testament there is the *hijra* ("flight") of the Prophet Muḥammad himself. Perhaps more relevant to the traditionists may have been the example of Joseph (Yūsuf) in the Qur'an, whose brothers sell him into slavery (*Sūra Yūsuf* 12).

But parallel to these examples, and arguably even more compelling, is the Mande requirement that hunters enter wilderness places for considerable periods to learn their craft, practice survival skills, and "harness occult power" (Johnson 14–20). During the *dali-ma-sigi* ("quest"), the hunter navigates spaces with reservoirs of spiritual power, constituting a "sacred geography" (14). Though already a *simbon*, Sunjata learns much during this peripatetic phase.

Sassuma Berete's threat to behead Sunjata also targets his mother Sogolon, his sister Sogolon Kolokon, and his half brother Manden Bukari (or Manding Bori), son of Maghan Kon Fatta's third wife Namanje (of legendary beauty). Oralists assert that, destined to be the right hand "of some mighty king," Manden Bukari becomes Sunjata's best friend, and they form a close bond with Fran Kamara of Tabon and Kamanjan (or Nan Koman Jan) of Sibi, with whom they grow up. Sogolon, Sogolon Kolokon, Manden Bukari, and an assorted host accompany Sunjata into exile.

According to Niane, Sunjata's sojourn begins with Jedeba, two days from Niani; then Tabon, "inhabited by the Kamara blacksmiths and the Djallonkés" in what is now Futa Jallon, where he is received by its ruler, Fran Kamara's father (Niane, Sundiata 31). Tabon's mention grounds an important alliance in the very origins of the Malian empire, but it is also anticipatory, as Fran Kamara informs Sunjata "the blacksmiths and the Djallonkés are excellent warriors," to which Sunjata vows he will make Fran Kamara "a great general" (32) underscoring the point that, in addition to soldiering, smiths also make weapons.

Niane records that Sunjata next travels to Ghana; in so doing, Niane introduces the critical merchant community of the Jula, who conduct commerce throughout the West African savanna, while he associates Sunjata with Ghana as an ancient land of renown led by the Sisse dynasty, thus establishing ties between the Soninke (the people of ancient Ghana) and the Maninka (the people of Mali) (Niane, Sundiata 28–34). Sunjata next goes to Mūsā Tunkara, ruler of Mema. Mema was a premier land of settlement, and therefore plays a similar role to Ghana's in the memory of the Mande as a source of political authority. In fact, it is in Mema that Sunjata accepts his destiny as Mali's eventual leader, as Niani sends for him to come lift the siege of Sumaoro, to which he responds only after the death of his mother Sogolon.

Sumaoro and Legendary War

As leader of the Susu, Sumaoro is consistently (though not universally) depicted as a malevolent force, an "evil demon" unlike other men (Niane, Sundiata 41), sprouting seven or eight heads in the midst of battle while able to metamorphize into sixty-nine different bodies. He is said to have had either a jinn or a gorilla for a father and two mothers, going back and forth between their wombs (Innes, *Sunjata* 73–77). As to his human background, he descends from the Jarisu family, smiths from the *numu* in the caste system of the Mande, having once served Ghana's rulers (Cissé and Kamissòko, *La grande geste* 126–29). A hunter and great warrior, Sumaoro has encyclopedic knowledge of the supernatural.

The external Arabic sources speak of war between the Susu and the Maninka but provide no specifics, so that what follows is purely from the orature. By the time Sunjata returns to Manden, Sumaoro is in control of both banks of the Niger River, having conquered at least half of all Mande territory and establishing his "iron rule" (Ly-Tall et al. 93). The traditions make an immediate transition from Sunjata's return from Mema to war with Sumaoro.

With Manden Bukari at his side, Sunjata reverses the stages of his exile, picking up support as he goes along, beginning in Mema and ending in Tabon. Half his cavalry is said to come from Mema, the other half from Ghana. From Tabon and Fran Kamara he receives the bulk of his infantry or *sofas*, made up of smiths and "the mountain-dwelling Djallonkés" (Niane, Sundiata 49), while 1,500 archers are provided by the king of the Bobo. The image of Sunjata gliding from kingdom to kingdom is certainly romantic but contains the certain truth that military victory was premised on manufacturing arms (thus the smiths), and that the introduction of horses into the West African savanna revolutionized the calculus of combat (Tymowski 37–47).

Horses were already present in Ghana, having been introduced into the middle Niger region between the seventh and tenth centuries and were a source of "great prestige" (Brooks 99). They became much more important in the thirteenth and fourteenth centuries when deployed as cavalry, during which time large herds were actually bred in Mali. If Sunjata did not initiate what amounts to a technological innovation, he certainly benefitted from it. Indeed, one of the meanings of the term Susu is "horse" or "horseman" (99; see also Law).

Sunjata's ensuing exploits include his famous generals, namely Kamanjan, Fran Kamara, and Tiramakan. None, however, are as intriguing as Fakoli Koroma. The nephew of none other than Sumaoro, he was known for his "large head and wide mouth." Trained by his uncle as a skilled warrior, he grew up to serve as one of his "great commanders," and, as the general who actually conquers Niani, he takes the *mansā*'s wife, Niuma Demba as his own (Jansen 39). Niuma Demba will lead to Fakoli's defection, for Sumaoro will take her as his own, telling Fakoli, "You have a wife, but she is not a wife for a child" (Ly-Tall et al. 58). Fakoli responds by swiftly joining forces with Sunjata.

The protracted war between Sunjata and Sumaoro only turns in the former's favor following Sogolon Kolokon's risking (or actually sacrificing) her virtue. Skilled in spiritual arts, she enters Sumaoro's bedchamber and learns "the secret of his *tana*" (Innes 72)—the object that would prove disastrous if discovered by enemies, in this instance the spur of a white rooster (Innes 72–77; Zeltner 28–29). With this secret in hand, a series of clashes culminate in the Battle of Krina on the Niger, where Sumaoro is decisively defeated. Two constants thread throughout the various descriptions of these battles: animal sacrifice to the Mande deities, and Sunjata's organization of hunters into a fighting force, based upon his status as not only a *simbon*, but a *donso karamoko* ("master hunter") (Cissé and Kamissòko *La grande geste*, 358–59).

Though the Battle at Krina involves unprecedented numbers, the real struggle is waged between Sunjata and Sumaoro as sorcerers, beginning either with the killing of Sumaoro's protective, twenty-seven-headed jinn Susufengoto, or his monstrous, forty-four-headed snake (Niane, Sundiata 59–69; Cissé and Kamissòko, *Soundjata* 13–17; Zeltner 30–31). Grazed by an arrow armed with his *tana*, Sumaoro immediately "felt his powers leave him" (Niane, Sundiata 64) and flees, meeting one of two ends: either he and those with him turn into pillars of stone; or he escapes, "disappearing" (67) into the mountains of Kulikoro never to be heard from again.

The Role of Islam

Although the epic generally depicts both Sunjata and Sumaoro as sorcerers, the theme of Islam also recurs in the accounts, as Islam was being established in Mali in the thirteenth century. Islam had previously entered ancient Ghana as well as other lands and polities along the West African Sahel through commercial activity as early as the eighth century, though it was largely confined to merchant elites until the eleventh century. By that time, Islam was making inroads among the peasantry, and Muslims were beginning to rule small Sahelian states.

Islam's influence continued to grow, and, whereas the majority of West African peasants would not convert until the seventeenth and eighteenth centuries, clans such as the Keitas—to which Sunjata belonged—embraced Islam early and reimagined their origins in ways that connected directly to the central Islamic lands. In fact, the Keitas claimed descent from Bilāl (or Bilali Bunama), a reference to the Nubian (or possibly Ethiopian) Bilāl b. Rabāḥ, Companion of the Prophet and first *mu'adhdhin* ("summoner to prayer") in Islam. Having claimed one of the most illustrious figures in Islam, these same traditions maintain Bilāl's descendant, Mamadi Kani, became a hunter king, establishing the title of *simbon* or *donso karamoko* ("master hunter") achieved through a special relationship with the jinn of "the forest and bush" (Cissé 78) and the special favor of *Kondolon Ni Sané*, twinned deities of the chase. Mamadi Kani will rule a following of hunters, connoting the Mande idea of polity developing from hunter guilds, the *donson ton*.

By claiming Bilāl b. Rabāḥ, the Keitas specifically and the Maninka generally asserted an ancient, powerful Muslim pedigree, for which they are revered throughout West Africa as one of the first to embrace Islam. At the same time, the elevation of Mamadi Kani as a master hunter acknowledges a connection to local realities. The traditions therefore present bona fides both Islamic and non-Islamic, perhaps by design, ingeniously reflecting an accommodation between Islam and anterior beliefs. Such negotiation can be observed throughout the life of Sunjata himself, who at times engages in non-Islamic activities while at other moments speaks and conducts himself as a Muslim.

Empire

With the defeat of Sumaoro, Sunjata is said to have convened an assembly of allies to create a new political framework, with the first order of business ensuring his generals' loyalty. It was Kamanjan who is said to have declared, "Henceforth it is from you that I derive my kingdom for I acknowledge you my sovereign. I salute you, supreme chief, I salute you, Fama of Famas ["King of Kings"]. I salute you, Mansa!" (Niane, Sundiata 75). Though the declaration cannot be corroborated, it underscores that until the Battle of Krina, the early Malian state had probably consisted of villages grouped into *kafus* or townships. The Keita may have established their authority after the eleventh century, taking the title of *mansā* ("ruler"). In bearing the titles of *mansā* as well as *fama* of *famas* (with *fama* signifying "chief" or "governor"), Sunjata was accepting recognition not only as a Mande ruler but also as someone who transcends other rulers, an "emperor." The transformation of the title *mansā* may therefore represent the extension of Malian power over previously independent polities, its association with Sunjata critical to its substantiation.

Ibn Khadūn records that Mārī Jāṭa (i.e., Sunjata) ruled for twenty-five years, and that his successor Walī performed hajj during the reign of the Mamluk ruler al-Ẓāhir Baybars (658–76/1260–77). If used to date the beginning of Sunjata's rule, the Battle of Krina would have taken place around 1233, and Sunjata would have died around 1258 (Hopkins and Levtzion 333). He is said to have either succumbed to natural death on the banks of the Sankarani River, or to have drowned in it, and was buried in either the town of Balandugu or the forest of Nora near the same river (Cissé and Kamissòko, *La grande geste* 82–83). Elaborate funeral rites delayed the burial some three months. The full bloom of Malian imperial power may not have been achieved during Sunjata's lifetime, but it was certainly on full display by the time *Mansā* Mūsā ascended to power in 1312, only fifty-four years after Sunjata's death.

The *Sunjata* epic invites an involved discussion of sources, the result of which is to tier the details of the account into categories of high probability, plausibility, and contextual framing. This layering is critical to uncovering Mali's imperial transformation, as in the instance of Sunjata's exile, where the question of historicity fades in comparison with its purpose as a charter for central and provincial power. Similarly, the conquest of the Susu, though highly probable, also establishes the basis for Mali's enduring regional claims.

The traditions contain key insights into early Mali's relationship to Islam, evincing a careful balancing act between ancestral and Islamic principles and forces. As such, the Keitas celebrate descent from Mamadi Kani as much as from Bilāl b. Rabāḥ, and the *dali-ma-sigi* is as generative as the hajj. Islam's role at imperial Mali's beginning is therefore limited. Accounts of Maghan Kon Fatta the Handsome's praying in the mosque or of Sunjata's exchanging the garb "of a Muslim" (Niane, Sundiata 73) for that of a hunter demonstrate, if anything, an accommodation between Islam and ancestral religion. The oral corpus is replete with sorcery and sacrifices that include those of Fakoli, leader of the *komo* society of smiths dedicated to non-Islamic practices.

Even so, Islam was on the move, and would only grow stronger, eventually ushering in an era of cosmopolitanism in the fifteenth and sixteenth centuries never before witnessed in the region.

Works Cited

Austen, Ralph A., editor. *In Search of* Sunjata*: The Mande Epic as History, Literature, and Performance.* Indiana UP, 1999.

Brooks, George E. *Landlords and Strangers: Ecology, Society and Trade in Western Africa, 1000–1630.* Routledge, 1993.

Camara, Seydou. "The Epic of *Sunjata*: Structure, Preservation, and Transmission." Austen, pp. 59–68.

Cissé, Yousouf Tata. *La confrérie des chasseurs Malinké et Bambara: Mythes, rites et récits initiatiques.* Éditions Nouvelles du Sud, 1994.

Cissé, Youssouf Tata, and Wâ Kamissòko. *La grande geste du Mali: Des origines à la fondation de l'Empire.* Karthala, 1988. Traditions de Krina au colloque de Bamako.

———. *Soundjata, la gloire du Mali.* Karthala, 1991. Vol. 2 of *La grande geste du Mali.*

Conrad, David C. "Searching for History in the *Sunjata* Epic: The Case of Fakoli." *History in Africa*, vol. 19, 1992, pp. 147–200.

Conrad, David C., and Djanka Tassey Condé. Sunjata*: A West African Epic of the Mande Peoples.* Indiana UP, 2004.

Hopkins, J. F. P., and Nehemia Levtzion. *Corpus of Early Arabic Sources for West African History.* Cambridge UP, 1981.

Innes, Gordon. Sunjata*: Three Mandinka Versions.* SOAS, 1974.

Jansen, Jan. *Siramuri Diabaté et ses enfants: Une étude sur deux generations des griots Malinké.* ISOR, 1991.

Johnson, John William. "The Dichotomy of Power and Authority in Mande Society and in the Epic of *Sunjata.*" Austen, pp. 9–23.

Law, Robin. *The Horse in West African History: The Role of the Horse in the Societies of Pre-colonial Africa.* International African Institute, 1980.

Laye, Camara. *The Guardian of the Word: Kouma Lafôlô Kouma.* Translated by James Kirkup. Vintage Books, 1984.

Ly-Tall, Madina, et al. *L'histoire du Mandé d'après Jeli Kanku Madi Jabaté de Kéla.* SCOA, 1987.

Niane, Djibril Tamsir. "Histoire et tradition historique du Manding." *Présence africaine*, vol. 89, 1974, pp. 59–74.

———. "Recherches sur l'Empire du Mali au Moyen Age." *Recherches africaines*, 1959, pp. 6–56.

———. Sundiata*: An Epic of Old Mali.* Translated by G. D. Pickett, Longman, 1965.

Sisòkò, Fa-Digi. *The* Epic of Son-Jara*: A West African Tradition.* Translated by John William Johnson, Indiana UP, 1992.

Tymowski, Michal. *The Origins and Structures of Political Institutions in Pre-colonial Black Africa: Dynastic Monarchy, Taxes and Tributes, War and Slavery, Kinship and Territory.* Edwin Mellen Press, 2009.

Wilks, Ivor. "The History of the *Sunjata* Epic: A Review of the Evidence." Austen, pp. 9–20.

Zeltner, Franz de. *Contes du Sénégal et du Niger.* Éditions Ernest Leroux, 1913.

Timothy May

Teaching the Mongols, Eurasia, and the World

In most classes, with the mere mention of the Mongols, students' ears prick up. They may not know much about them, but I find students are always curious about the Roman Empire, the Crusades, World War II, and the Mongols. In my classes, regardless of topic, it is generally a question of when the Mongols will appear. This appearance is not simply because of my own interest in the Mongols but also for the very fact that the Mongols serve as a wonderful device for demonstrating the interconnectedness of Eurasia, and the Mongol Empire is world history, providing a truly global aspect to the study of the Middle Ages. One cannot discuss the Mongol Empire effectively by only examining a particular region without considering what else is happening in the empire, and this is true at any phase of the Mongol Empire. Yet, the Mongols should not be reserved only for upper-level courses. They merit considerable attention at the survey level as well.

In surveys of world history, I end World History I with the Mongols and begin World History II with them, as, in my mind, they serve as the perfect transition point into the modern era. They also appear when I teach History of World Religions for their fundamental roles in spreading religion and concepts of religious tolerance and indifference. And then there are the upper-level courses. Beyond courses on the Mongol Empire, Mongols play an integral role in other courses, such as the Crusades and the medieval Middle East. Yet all these courses have their inherent challenges in presenting material. Since most universities offer world history in their curriculum, whether as a required course (which it should be) or as an elective, it would be best to start there.

Teaching the Mongols at the Survey Level

Throughout World History I (pre-1500), I emphasize the role of nomads in history, particularly in terms of connections with the Silk Road, but also as a bridge between the various empires and states. Although I have not taught world history in a few years because of my working in administration, most texts are shockingly weak in granting any agency to nomadic powers in world history and largely lump them together as a generic trope, especially for post-1500. Mongols still remain locked in as a one-dimensional other, seen as so-called barbarians in many textbooks. As textbooks update frequently, there remains hope for improvement and some have made strides in these areas.[1]

In taking the time to discuss the nomads properly and in some depth, I can accomplish a couple of goals. First, I can demolish claims of supposed cultural appropriation—that is to say, the transfer of cultural concepts from one culture to another. No culture stays uninfluenced by outside forces except those that exist in complete isolation. By focusing on nomads, we can discuss the transfer of culture and technology all over Eurasia. When discussing transfers of culture and technology, we cannot ignore the medium of nomads—not only as agents of transmission but also for their influences on culture itself.

Most ancient and medieval innovations in equine technology originated with nomads, as horses were such a fundamental part of their culture. An easy example is to ask students, "Do you wear pants?" If they respond, "Yes," I jokingly accuse them of cultural appropriation—unless they can demonstrate their Eurasian nomadic roots. This leads to a discussion of why people wear trousers: riding horses is much easier in trousers than in a toga or robe. I then connect riding to technology. In many books discussing military innovations, the stirrup is said to have originated in China, but the earliest stirrup artifact was found among the Northern Wei dynasty (386–534), founded by the Tuoba, a branch of the Xianbei nomads of Mongolia, but in what is now considered the modern People's

Republic of China. The Tuoba certainly did not consider themselves Chinese.

By giving other nomadic states attention, the ground has been set for the Mongols. A discussion of the basics of nomadic society has already occurred. Due to having only a week or two, I skim over the rise of Chinggis Khan, but my students receive a stern reminder that Temüjin's title is Chinggis Khan and not the dreaded G-word (Genghis Khan), and I explain why this is (May, *Simply Chinggis*). I spend the first day on the Mongol conquests. I present the more dramatic primary sources, so as to give students some inkling of the sense of dread that swept the world with the appearance of Mongols.

Besides, who doesn't like Chinggis Khan's "Punishment from God" speech from Ata Malik Juvaini's account of the sack of Bukhara (105)? Or Ibn al-Athir's lugubrious prologue where he says he is hesitant to write about the Mongols, for why would he want to record the destruction of Islam (202)? There is a great line where Ibn al-Athir says the Mongols were worse than al-Dajjal, the Antichrist, for even the Antichrist spared people, but the Mongols spared no one (202). Of course, I would be remiss if I neglected the Nikon Chronicle's account in which the Battle of Kalka is described (Zenkovsky 290). Here, we learn that no one knew who the Mongols were, where they originated, or where they went. Across cultures, the Mongols were described as punishment for sins. Sometimes in class this leads to a discussion of how the Mongols were viewed as the Borg are in the *Star Trek* franchise or, perhaps for the current generation, Thanos in the *Avengers* movies—an unstoppable force of unimaginable power. Throughout our discussion of the Mongols, I remind students never to forget these initial impressions, as they will continually influence how the Mongols will be viewed by not only their subjects but also their neighbors.

Now that I have established an apocalyptic sense of doom, we move on to what else was happening in the Mongol Empire and Eurasia. The second day I spend discussing the Mongol government, including the establishment of Qaraqorum (the Mongol capital) and its impact on trade, as well as how the Mongols controlled their territories. In this section, I try to emphasize the role of Mongol women as well, particularly in governing, as it serves as a nice contrast with what happened in most of world history thus far. Now the door is open for a conversation on why women wielded visible power and influence in the Mongol world more regularly than in the Christian, Islamic, and Confucian regions.

I then discuss the impact of the Mongols in world history. For this, I introduce my Silk Road–merchant exercise. In this exercise, we have a merchant in China with pepper, and a merchant from England who wants to find a way to make English food . . . well, more pleasant. The key for the students—who play the role of traveling merchants—is to figure out how to get the pepper from China to England. Many student-merchants in the game die along the way, as they learn that they need guards before encountering bandits and that taking shortcuts across a desert is unwise (#geographysaveslives). My game is first set in 1200 CE, and then in 1258 CE, to provide a perspective of what the period before the Mongol Empire was like for merchants and travelers in comparison to the changes later instituted by the Mongols.

This then allows me to set up a lecture on the dissolution of the Mongol Empire and show why trade routes became more difficult. With the dissolution of the empire, we then discuss how Eurasia has changed. Politically and geographically, change can be seen simply by my listing on the whiteboard the states that existed prior to the Mongols and then what happens afterward. I also use before and after maps (see figs. 1 and 2 for

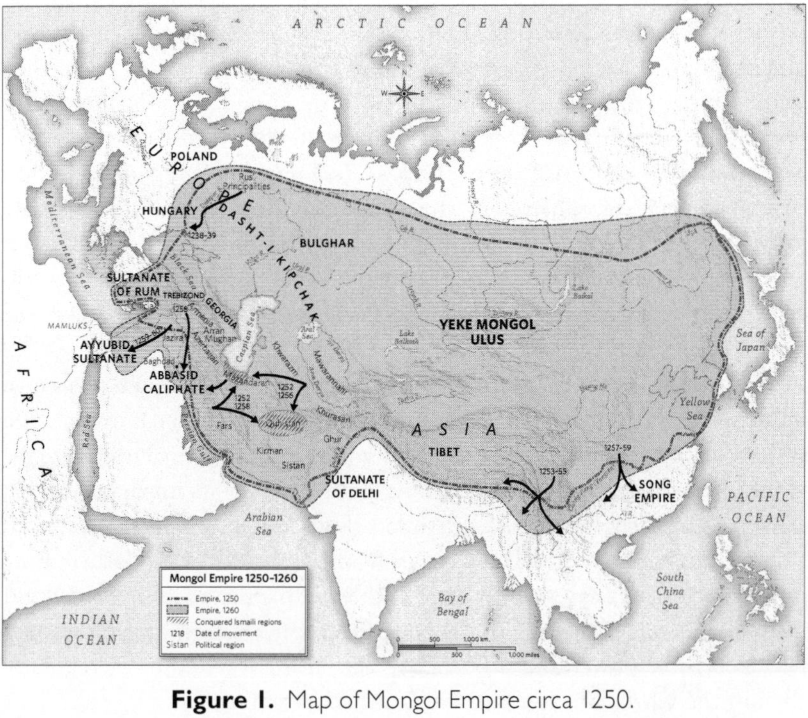

Figure 1. Map of Mongol Empire circa 1250.

examples). I like to map this over stages, say in increments of fifty years. We transition to a discussion of regional ramifications, which moves us into what I call the "Chinggis Exchange," or the Mongols' impact on world history, allowing me to tie the changes to a global level. I provide immediate examples but demonstrate how the Mongol Empire continues to affect the modern world, particularly in media, and sometimes I am able to connect current events to historical ones (Allsen; May, *Mongol Conquests* and "Chinggis Exchange").

For my World History II course, the Mongols serve as the foundation for discussions of later history, including how the dissolution of the Mongol Empire influenced Christopher Columbus's voyages. Playing the Silk Road–merchant game again helps demonstrate the rising cost of spices without *Pax Mongolica*. For the second half of world history, the past becomes prologue, and I use the Mongols as a backdrop for the rise of various states and people such as the Ottomans, Safavids, Mughals, Uzbeks, Kazakhs, the Ming, the Qing, and even the Russian Empire. All had to address their Mongol past as well find new routes to legitimacy by attempting

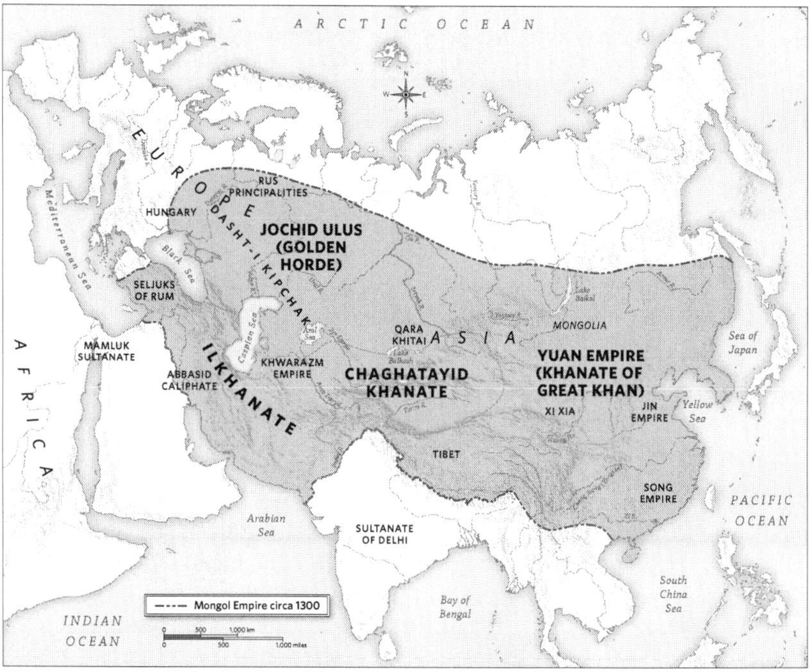

Figure 2. Map of Mongol Empire circa 1300.

to overcome the Chinggisid principle, in which only a descendant of Chinggis Khan had the right to rule.

The Mongols are always lurking in the background. Whether it is discussing the rise of the Russian Empire or the Qing Empire (1636–1911), and relations between the two states and the struggle to control the Eurasian steppes, some reference to the Mongol Empire is necessary to explain not only motives but also other actors who are present (Kazakhs, Zhungars, and other nomadic groups). I also discuss how the Mongol Empire facilitated the onset of the Renaissance by their intercontinental contacts and the Chinggis Exchange. Although I would not go so far as to say the Renaissance was caused by the Mongols, I argue that the Renaissance would look much different had there never been a Mongol Empire (May, *Mongol Conquests,* 244).[2]

When I teach the History of World Religions, the nomads are a nice tool to demonstrate how a single society can interact with a number of religions and have different outcomes. Indeed, this is true for much of Central Eurasia and offers some unique teaching moments: one is a discussion of how the Uighur Khanate (744–840) adopted Manichaeism, making it the only kingdom to ever do so. Yet, after the fall of their empire in 840, the Uighurs who moved into the Tarim Basin also adopted Buddhism as well as a form of Christianity. The Khazar Khanate (650–969) also serves as an interesting case study of a group converting to Judaism, a religion not known for proselytizing. In both cases, we see two Central Eurasian powers adopt religions that were generally the religions of often persecuted minorities. Why? What was the benefit? Discussions of syncretism and the maintenance of identity evolve from this.

The Mongols are an excellent case study for studying religion in history, as their empire contained virtually every religion of the medieval Eurasian world. One can compare and contrast the Mongols' reaction to various religions or examine each religion as a distinct case study. Christianity provides one example of the Mongol attitude to religion. Central Eurasia had significant numbers of members of the Church of the East, more popularly known as Nestorians; the aforementioned Uighurs are among these. Nestorianism also spread into Mongolia and parts of eastern Kazakhstan with the Naiman, Kereits, Önggüd, and possibly others. Christianity declined by the end of the Mongol Empire, whether in the form of the Church of the East or the Roman Catholic church (May, "Converting" and "Attitudes"). Eurasian religions also entered a world of shamanism—how did Christianity or other religions coexist in this context? Whereas the three universal religions of Christianity, Islam, and Buddhism eventually become the Mongol religions of choice, the inclusion of Central Eurasia demonstrates how a variety of religions interacted and coexisted in the same space and that the territorial map of religions is not static.

The Mongols were a society that decreed religious tolerance (or indifference) while practicing primal or Indigenous religions. At the same time, Mongol rulers also enjoyed religious debates while resisting the allure of a universal religion for decades. In the end, the Mongols largely converted to Islam and Buddhism, but the factors involved in their conversions make their situations suitable for discussions concerning syncretism, identity, and conversion processes, as well as how the Mongols fostered and helped spread their new religions while also contributing to the demise of another religion (Christianity) in Asia (see Elverskog; Jackson; May, *Mongol Empire*).

The appearance of Catholic missionaries aided the demise of Christianity in Asia, as Catholic missionaries were primarily successful in converting members of the Church of the East rather than the infidels and pagans they hoped to convert. Furthermore, the Catholic church in the East did not develop a native clergy: thus, when new priests did not come from Rome, the religion gradually faded away (May, "Converting" and "Attitudes"). The chaos related to the end of the Yuan Empire and the xenophobia connected to the Ming dynasty hastened this.

Teaching Upper-Level Courses on the Mongols

There are a number of complications in teaching a course on the Mongols, some of which would be found with any upper-level history class: sources, coverage, and the inevitable lack of background knowledge by students.[3] We should never belittle students for this: after all, they are attending university for an education. There are several challenges that arise when teaching the Mongols. One is the multiplicity of languages for primary materials, with Chinese and Persian among the most important, but also Latin, Old French, Church Slavonic, Georgian, Armenian, Turkic, Japanese, Korean, Arabic, Syriac, Tibetan, and Mongolian. Russian, Chinese, Japanese, Mongolian, German, Rumanian, French, and Magyar are rather handy for the secondary literature. Few students can learn more than a handful.

In an era with little emphasis on learning a foreign language and in a society in which learning a foreign language is viewed as scary, despite an ever increasingly globalized world, this obstacle is considerable. Although I don't expect undergraduates to do research in a foreign language, lacking foreign languages does limit their perspective. And few will have the temerity to pursue advanced study and pick up three or more languages, which makes it difficult to educate the next generation of scholars of the Mongol Empire. Beyond the language barrier, the greatest challenge in teaching the Mongol Empire is its geographic expanse. As with any vast empire, how does one include it all? With the world's largest contiguous empire, this becomes, quite honestly, a judgment call. Much like teaching world history, at some point, some area will receive only cursory coverage. It cannot be avoided.

Furthermore, most scholars stumble onto the Mongol Empire—very few start off studying the Mongol Empire per se. Instead, they enter the field originally as a historian of China, Russia, South Asia, the Middle East, or other regions, before emerging as a historian of the Mongol Empire. Thus, whereas their knowledge of a particular region will be strong, it is likely to be weaker in other areas. I maintain, however, that one cannot understand the Mongols without looking at the entire empire and connecting events in one area to another. It is nevertheless a challenge, and often one that one must work up to by building one's knowledge base, much like when teaching world history—one cannot and does not become an expert in all areas in a single semester.

Where and when to begin the course also poses a challenge. Does one begin with the life of Chinggis Khan or does one skip to 1206 when the steppes are united and Temüjin officially becomes Chinggis Khan? Or perhaps just before? There are valid reasons for all. Starting with 1206 is nice because at this point Chinggis Khan is there and you can skip forty years of chaotic events where history mingles with myth. Our most detailed information about the life of Chinggis Khan comes from *The Secret History of the Mongols*. The dating of events is often confused, and the work was written (and redacted) for a Mongol audience, so many events and statements would have been understood by a thirteenth-century Mongol, but not by anyone else.

There is also some question as to whether some events actually took place or whether some people were real. Although scholars continue to debate *The Secret History*'s value as a source, I find it indispensable, as it provides us a true understanding of how the Mongols viewed events—what was and was not important—and the development of Chinggis Khan's character. The standard comment on the value of *The Secret History* is that it reveals Chinggis Khan, warts and all. After all, it mentions he was afraid of dogs as a child and that he murdered his half brother, was enslaved, and was unable to prevent the kidnapping of his wife. Nonetheless, like any source, whether an official document or a private letter, *The Secret History* requires a careful approach. One must understand the context in order to begin to understand the text. But *The Secret History* gives us something to compare with other sources when examining the depiction of Chinggis Khan's life. The jury is still out on what sources are the most accurate, but the discussion of this continues to be productive.

I prefer to start before the life of Chinggis Khan, with an overview of Mongolia in the eleventh and twelfth centuries. My primary goal is not only to lay the foundations for the rise of Chinggis Khan but also to demonstrate that Mongolia did not exist in isolation, and plenty of activity happened there prior to the rise of Chinggis Khan. To that end, I briefly discuss the rise of the Liao Empire (916–1125) and its fall in order to explain the geopolitical context that existed in the aftermath of its end. The discussion remains general so as to not to become bogged down in rulers and dates: I want students to focus on the big picture. After that, we move to the birth of Chinggis Khan. I follow the narrative in *The Secret History* because it allows me to examine points of dispute, discuss the culture of the steppe, and move students out of their sedentary-civilization-centric perspective and appreciate how nomadic societies viewed the world. From there we move into the formation and expansion of the Mongol Empire.

Besides *The Secret History*, what else do we use for readings? When I started teaching the Mongols, the only real option was David O. Morgan's *The Mongols* and biographies such as Paul Ratchnevsky's *Genghis Khan: Life and Legacy* and Morris Rossabi's *Khubilai Khan*, plus a number of specialist monographs or popular histories of varying quality. For primary sources, the essentials were Christopher Dawson's *Mission to Asia* (previously called *The Mongol Mission*) and of course various editions of Marco Polo (see *Description* and *Travels*)—a very Western-centric approach.

What frustrated me in my initial years of teaching was the lack of an affordable *Secret History of the Mongols*. Urgunge Onon's translation is useful but not affordable; Paul Kahn's translation of Francis Cleaves's translation was serviceable, but that he omitted the *begats* often made it difficult to discuss concepts of identity, lineage, and how tribes were fluid.[4] Most of the really good translations were beyond the wallet of a student and even of some libraries. Today, however, there is much more to choose from in books. For a main text, I strongly recommend a book that came out in 2018: *The Mongol Empire* by a chap named Timothy May. This book is largely based on my own lectures, and writing it forced me to reconsider many elements of how I teach and what I was omitting. I like it quite a bit, particularly because recent scholarship means that earlier works such as Morgan's *The Mongols*, even with a second edition published, have grown outdated because of the explosion of scholarship on the Mongols (much of it inspired by Morgan's book), although it remains required reading for graduate students to understand historiography.

Another option is George Lane's lively *Short History of the Mongol Empire*. Since his is a short history, after discussing the rise of the Mongol Empire, Lane focuses on the two regions he knows best, the Middle East and China. Rossabi's *The Mongols: A Very Short Introduction* is also serviceable when accompanied by other works to provide depth.

For primary sources, we now have a free version of *The Secret History*. This is an e-book and an abridged version of Igor de Rachewiltz's masterful translation (the abridgment only affects the number of notes, not the actual translation). Of equal importance is that the number of sources on Mongols that have been translated keeps increasing. Many of them are also available freely and without copyright infringement on the internet.[5] The number of monographs and articles have also allowed instructors to have a great deal more variety in what they offer as readings as well, allowing them to focus emphasis where they desire.

The United Mongol Empire (as Michal Biran terms it) or *Yeke Monggol Ulus* (as the Mongols called it) ends at 1260. It has a brief reunion in the early fourteenth century but then quickly breaks apart again in four or more (depending on how one counts them), separate Mongol Empires: the Yuan Empire (East Asia), the Ilkhanate (Middle East); the Jochid Ulus or Golden Horde (Russia is part of this, but this really spans the Pontic and Caspian steppes), and the Chaghatayid Khanate (Central Asia). As these khanates all end at different times, it is difficult to pinpoint a true end date for the Mongol Empire. So, when does one declare the empire over? The dissolution of the *Yeke Monggol Ulus* (what the Mongols called the Mongol Empire) in 1260? This, however, then excludes Khubilai Khan and the Yuan Empire. With Khubilai's death in 1291? Then priority is placed on East Asia and ignores everything else that takes place in the fourteenth century.

There is no good answer, so I go until each successor empire can be said to be truly over. For the Jochid Ulus or Golden Horde, that means around 1526. In a one-semester course, that means much will not be covered. I used to apportion a week to each of the four khanates. After doing this for ten years, I finally decided to split my Mongol course into two semesters. When I first taught the Mongols, one semester seemed reasonably sufficient (remember my earlier point about building knowledge and competency?). Quite frankly, I have always been a *Yeke Monggol Ulus* or United Mongol Empire kind of a guy. My expertise of the post-1300 history of the Mongol Empire was general knowledge. As my own knowledge expanded, however, my frustration with my one-semester course grew. I have now taught the Mongols over two semesters and am much happier, as I have been able to add four weeks to the predissolution era, thus allowing for more discussion and to venture into thematic aspects of the empire that I had not really taught before or only mentioned fleetingly.

When I tell people that I teach the Mongol Empire in two semesters as opposed to one, I sometimes receive looks of incredulity. I am not sure why. Courses on Russia are usually in two semesters. My colleagues teach English history, not only based on early modern and modern but also in terms of Tudors and Stuarts; they do not just collapse everything into British history. The history of the United States as a survey is always taught in two semesters for an empire that has only a short history. Then again, Americanist colleagues sometimes bemoan that they have no one who can teach a particular decade, whereas their non-American and nonmodern colleagues are expected to cover hundreds of years of material. To tell the truth, in my idle moments I sometimes yearn to teach the two courses in one year and then add a seminar onto one of the postdissolution khanates in the next and perhaps something more thematic the following semester, such as a course on trade or perhaps a semester on Marco Polo or *The Secret History*—all Mongols all the time. Why not? At the moment, however, I lack the time to develop new courses because of administrative duties. But why not seminars on the postdissolution khanates? Or if a department can have three medievalists covering Europe, why not multiple Mongolists? After all, they will have some other regional specialization as well, thus broadening their medieval course offerings.

In many ways, it is easier to teach the postdissolution period, as one has Rossabi's *Khubilai Khan* as well as Marco Polo to serve as a nice foundation. In addition, the plethora of publications on the Yuan Empire and the Ilkhanate make both regions highly accessible for teaching purposes. The Golden Horde still tends to be elusive outside of its relations with the Russians, as demonstrated by Charles J. Halperin and Donald Ostrowski, respectively, although the amount of material on the Black Sea trade is ever growing due to the efforts of Virgil Ciociltan and others. Marie Favreau's *The Horde,* however, is quite promising. I think the most frustrating part is that the focus on the Horde still tends to center around regions west of the Volga. I am still trying to incorporate more of the Blue Horde (the region from the Volga to the Irtysh Rivers). The Chaghatayids will always be tough to teach, due to the paucity of sources. Nonetheless, there is enough material for discussing the major themes and events of those two regions with confidence while also saying, "This would make a great dissertation topic," and, with hope, embedding an idea in an enthusiastic student's mind.

Notes

1. See McKay et al.; Smith et al.; Bentley et al. Exceptions to this are Dunn and Mitchell; Tignor et al.; Bulliet et al.

2. For a different perspective, see Weatherford.

3. The latter point is something that haunts every class, and I always keep my own experience in the back of my mind. In 1995, as a graduate student at Indiana University, I took Professor Christopher P. Atwood's seminar on Inner Mongolian history. It was masterful and remains one of the best courses I have ever taken. I will never forget, however, when we flummoxed him with our complete ignorance of the Chinese Communist Revolution. The next class he gave us a brilliant lecture on this topic, veering (perhaps a left turn?) from the syllabus schedule. Without Atwood's improvisation, the course would have been much weaker.

4. The term *tribe* always causes debate. I use the definition found in Lindner.

5. In particular, see Daniel Waugh's Silk Road resource website: depts.washington.edu/silkroad/texts/texts.html.

Works Cited

Allsen, Thomas T. *Culture and Conquest in Mongol Eurasia.* Cambridge UP, 2001.

Bentley, Jerry H., et al. *Traditions and Encounters.* McGraw Hill, 2011.

Bulliet, Richard W., et al. *The Earth and Its Peoples.* Houghton Mifflin, 2005.

Ciociltan, Virgil. *The Mongols and the Black Sea Trade in the Thirteenth and Fourteenth Centuries.* Brill, 2012.

Dawson, Christopher, editor. *Mission to Asia.* U of Toronto P, 1980.

Dunn, Ross E., and Laura J. Mitchell. *Panorama: A World History.* McGraw Hill, 2015.

Elverskog, Johan. *Buddhism and Islam on the Silk Road.* U of Pennsylvania P, 2010.

Favreau, Marie. *The Horde: How the Mongols Changed the World.* The Belknap Press of Harvard UP, 2021.

Halperin, Charles J. *Russia and the Golden Horde: The Mongol Impact on Medieval Russian History.* Indiana UP, 1985.

———. *The Tatar Yoke: The Image of the Mongols in Medieval Russia.* Corrected ed., Slavica, 2009.

Ibn Al-Athir. *The Chronicle of Ibn al-Athir for the Crusading Period from al-Kāmil fi'l-ta'rīkh.* Translated by D. S. Richards, part 3, Ashgate, 2008.

Jackson, Peter. *The Mongols and the Islamic World from Conquest to Conversion.* Yale UP, 2017.

Juvaini, Ata Malik. *The History of the World Conqueror.* Translated by J. A. Boyle, U of Washington P, 1997.

Kahn, Paul. *The Secret History of the Mongols: The Origin of Chingis Khan.* Cheng and Tsui, 1998.

Lane, George. *A Short History of the Mongols.* I. B. Tauris, 2018.

Lindner, Rudi Paul. "What Was a Nomadic Tribe?" *Comparative Studies in Society and History*, vol. 24, no. 4, 1982, pp. 689–711. *JSTOR*, www.jstor.org/stable/178435.

May, Timothy. "Attitudes towards Conversion among the Elite in the Mongol Empire." *E-ASPAC: The Electronic Journal of Asian Studies on the Pacific Coast*, 2002–03, pp. 1–23.

———. "The Chinggis Exchange: The Mongol Empire and Global Impact on Warfare." *World History Connected*, vol. 12, no. 1, Feb. 2015, worldhistoryconnected.press.illinois.edu/12.1/forum_may.html.

———. "Converting the Khan: Christian Missionaries and the Mongol Empire." *World History Connected*, vol. 12, no. 2, June 2015, worldhistoryconnected.press.illinois.edu/12.2/forum_may.html.

———. *The Mongol Conquests in World History.* Reaktion, 2012.

———. *The Mongol Empire.* Edinburgh UP, 2018.

———. *Simply Chinggis.* Simply Charly, 2020.

McKay, John P., et al. *A History of World Societies.* 10th ed., Macmillan Education, 2015.

Morgan, David O. *The Mongols.* 2nd ed., Blackwell, 2007.

Onon, Urgunge, translator. *The Secret History of the Mongols: The Life and Times of Chinggis Khan.* Routledge, 2001.

Ostrowski, Donald. *Muscovy and the Mongols: Cross-Cultural Influences on the Steppe Frontier, 1304–1589.* Cambridge UP, 1998.

Polo, Marco. *The Description of the World.* Translated by Sharon Kinoshita, Hackett, 2016.

———. *The Travels.* Translated by Nigel Cliff, Penguin Books, 2015.

Rachewiltz, Igor de, translator. *The Secret History of the Mongols: A Mongolian Epic Chronicle of the Thirteenth Century.* Brill, 2004.

———, translator. *The Secret History of the Mongols: A Mongolian Epic Chronicle of the Thirteenth Century: Shorter Version*. Edited by John C. Street, Western Washington U, 2016, cedar.wwu.edu/cgi/viewcontent.cgi?article=1003&context=cedarbooks.

Ratchnevsky, Paul. *Genghis Khan: His Life and Legacy*. Translated by Thomas Nivison Haining, Blackwell, 1991.

Rossabi, Morris. *Khubilai Khan: His Life and Times*. 20th anniversary ed., U of California P, 2009.

———. *The Mongols: A Very Short Introduction*. Oxford UP, 2012.

Smith, Bonnie G., et al. *World in the Making, A Global History*. Oxford UP, 2019.

Tignor, Robert, et al. *Worlds Together, Worlds Apart*. W. W. Norton, 2013.

Waugh, Daniel. "Silk Road Narratives: A Collection of Historical Texts." depts.washington.edu/silkroad/texts/texts.html. Accessed 9 July 2019.

Weatherford, Jack. *Genghis Khan and the Making of the Modern World*. Crown, 2004.

Zenkovsky, Serge A., editor. *The Nikonian Chronicle*. Translated by Serge A. Zenkovsky and Betty Jean Zenkovsky, vol. 2, Kingston Press, 1984.

Emma J. Flatt

The Worlds of South Asia

The idea of the "Middle Ages" as a discrete period is not one that holds much traction in South Asian history. When the British began writing the history of India, they conceived of a tripartite schema, dividing India's pasts into ancient, medieval, and modern.[1] The specific historical periods to which these labels applied, however, were determined on the basis of the religion that was judged to be in the ascendant: the ancient epoch mapping onto the *Hindu period* (judged to stretch from the earliest times to the Ghurid invasions of ca. 1192); the medieval era mapping on to the *Muslim period* (from 1192 to the British victory at the Battle of Plassey in 1757); and the modern age being identified by the colonialists, self-declared bringers of so-called civilization and modernity, as the *British period* (1757–1947). Both the disjuncture of this imagined chronology, with the well-established time line of Western chronology, and the assumption that religion constituted the most salient factor of political life demonstrate the extent to which the British conceived of premodern India as outside of the chronology of (Western) history.

Although scholars have been challenging this tripartite division of Indian time since at least the 1980s, it has remained surprisingly persistent in popular discourse, as have simplistic assumptions about the religious and cultural homogeneity of Indian society within these time periods. The supposed Hindu period is popularly assumed to be defined by a timeless and unchanging temple Hinduism, supported by an inflexible caste system, with Sanskrit as the language of politics, religion, and high culture.[2]

The so-called Muslim period, by contrast, is popularly said to be defined by an expansionist and aggressive Islam, with Persian as the language of court, politics, and culture. Both survey courses and college textbooks, in simplifying the vast complexity of Indian history into a focus on the most powerful states, can tend unintentionally to reinforce the narrative of an early period when the most important and powerful states were Hindu (with a brief Buddhist ascendancy under Asoka), followed by an era of expansionist Muslim empires.

Inevitably, this obscures the multiplicity of religious traditions (including Buddhism and Jainism) practiced and given state patronage, as well as the wide diversity (both regional and caste-based) in the ways in which Hinduism itself was practiced and understood throughout both periods. Similarly, this periodizing narrative overshadows continuities with the older period, including the continued existence of flourishing Hindu states in the so-called Muslim period, as well as obscuring the dynamism and far-reaching significance of Hindu-Muslim encounters in multiple domains of political, religious, social, and cultural life.

Linguistic training has also contributed to such periodization: scholars have tended to acquire linguistic expertise in either the languages, literary traditions, and source types written in Indic scripts (particularly Sanskrit, Tamil, Telugu, and Kannada) or those written in Arabic scripts (particularly Persian, and for the later period, Urdu), but rarely in both scripts, until recently. This has meant the majority of scholars tend to research in one linguistic area to the exclusion of the other and to focus on distinct time periods: those working in Indic scripts have mostly worked on the period before 1192, whereas those working in Arabic scripts have focused on the period after 1192.

As a result, teaching South Asia in the global Middle Ages requires the majority of professors, even those trained in some aspect of South Asian history, to straddle the boundaries of what have traditionally been considered two distinct periods, with two different evidentiary bases, requiring different linguistic skills. The challenge then is to work against a well-established if contentious popular chronology that locates a significant disjuncture in the middle of this period, as well as against a master narrative that tends to privilege homogeneity over heterogeneity. Nevertheless, realigning South Asian chronology with the accepted chronological breaks of Western history—although problematic in some regards—does present an interesting opportunity to reflect on continuities as well as change within the region, look beyond the lens of religion as the sole way of understanding South Asian society, and examine linkages with the rest of the world.

In this essay, I discuss several historical events and nodes that provide a window into important themes and questions in the period of so-called medieval India. All the sources I recommend are to be read in translation: at the undergraduate level, students are not expected to read the sources in the original, particularly given the range of linguistic expertise required to cover all the relevant sources. Nevertheless, the question of when, why, and how sources have been translated—what has been excluded, occluded, assumed, added, and lost by the act of translation—should always form a crucial part of the pedagogical process, particularly in the light of the way translations of earlier documents were used to provide a rationale for British colonial rule and how they continue to inform present understandings of India's past.

Political Culture of Early Medieval India

The period between circa 500 to 1200 is characterized by the proliferation of powerful regional kingdoms in nearly every part of the Indian subcontinent. Unlike the preceding period, whose history is often told through the fortunes of two geographically extensive and long-lasting empires, the Mauryans (circa 322–187 BCE) and the Guptas (circa 319–543 CE), no single center emerged in this period that we can easily use to focus students' understanding. Therefore, rather than focusing on the specific details of the plethora of dynasties and kingdoms that emerged, it is more effective to consider the enduring shared political culture that emerged. Many elements of this political culture were already apparent in the Gupta Empire, and can be seen in both political and normative literature written over a wide range of time, from the third to at least the tenth centuries.

According to contemporary thought, the duty (*dharma*) of kings was to assure the very specific ordering of people, places and things, through the establishment of hierarchical relationships.[3] Texts like the *Arthasastra* (Kautalya) envision a vast hierarchy of kings organized into a concentric set of circles called a *rajamandala*, where the central king sought to develop alliances by circumventing his enemies and developing alliances with more distant kings.[4] In order to be considered a *cakravartin* ("universal king"), a ruler had to undertake a massive military campaign called a *digvijaya* ("conquest of the corners") to gain the submission of other, lesser kings. Instead of annihilating the incumbent kings and annexing their territory, however, defeated kings were reinstalled as rulers of their kingdoms and brought into the hierarchical system of the universal king, where they were required to offer tribute, gift their daughters, and attend court.

Scholars once dismissed the idea of the *rajamandala* as nothing more than a theoretical ideal, but more recently, Ronald Inden and Daud Ali have argued that the idealized political theory of normative texts should be taken seriously and suggest that a study of inscriptions demonstrates the existence of an elaborate political vocabulary, such as titles, that expressed a carefully ranked hierarchy. Similarly, this hierarchical conception of the political world can also be seen in the emergence of a complex courtly culture, widely depicted in literary and artistic works, in which hierarchy was openly displayed and strictly maintained. The holding of highly regulated courtly assemblies and the emergence of sumptuary rules governing the use of every type of courtly accoutrement from jewelry, fans, umbrellas, and flywhisks to crowns, thrones, and musical instruments are two examples of a whole series of practices scholars are only recently beginning to take seriously as political behavior (Ali, *Courtly Culture* 103–82).

Although political rhetoric does not reflect the complex reality of politics, understanding this hierarchical theory of sovereignty and power does help explain the plethora of regional kingdoms that emerged in this time period and the way in which they negotiated their position vis-à-vis neighboring and more distant states. Students need to see this as a period with a complex diplomatic patchwork of overlapping sovereignties and divided loyalties in which particular rulers often recognized one or more hierarchies of kings.

The Reign of Harsavardhana

A good way to demonstrate this political culture to students is to look at the description of a court assembly of King Harsavardhana (ruled circa 606–47) also known as Harsa, the Pushyabhuti ruler of Northern India.[5] I use an extract from the *Harsacarita*, an ornate Sanskrit biographical poem based on the life of Harsa written by his court poet Bana Bhatta.[6] Before I discuss this particular text, I also assign a reading on the Sanskrit genre of *kavya* ("poetry") to help comprehension of this unfamiliar genre (Ingalls 1–30).

The extract I assign describes Bana's first meeting with Harsa and, in its metaphor-filled description of the vast camp surrounding the king's court, gives a good sense of the idea of courtly hierarchy, with its descriptions of the multitude of defeated kings waiting attendance on King Harsa (Bana 44–69). Bana passes through three courts; in each he is overwhelmed by the multitude of subordinate kings, until he finally reaches the inner fourth court where he is presented to the king. Bana's awestruck reaction when he sees Harsa—and his detailed description of Harsa's beauty—can lead to a discussion of the importance of physical beauty in kingship (see below), whereas Bana's account of the king's disapproval of him due to his bad reputation demonstrates the extent to which success in this courtly world depended on preserving one's reputation. Bana's account also gives a sense of Harsa's court as a place of exotic and rare goods, with his description of the stables full of horses from Persia and other countries to the northwest of India, which provides a good opportunity to discuss trade routes.

Bana's account of Harsa's reign is complemented by the writings of a Chinese Buddhist pilgrim to India, Xuanzang, whose account is commonly used to illuminate the links between China and India in the seventh century, for example by Stewart Gordon (1–20). Xuanzang's account of his meeting (in circa 637–38) with Harsa (whom he calls Siladitya) demonstrates Harsa's awareness of Tang China, although Harsa's fulsome praise of Emperor Taizong may well have been added by Xuanzang to flatter his imperial audience (121–31).

According to Chinese sources, Xuanzang played a role in convincing Harsa to explore diplomatic ties with Tang China: between 641 and 658, at least three embassies were sent from Kanauj to Chang'an (Xi'an), and four were sent from Chang'an to Kanauj, a fact that Tansen Sen attributes to expansionism in the Tibetan plateau, which both kings would have considered a threat (18–24). Although the precise details are obscure, the final embassy seems to have led to Chinese military action in support of one contender to Harsa's throne. As well as geopolitical objectives, these diplomatic exchanges had spiritual objectives for the Chinese, who hoped to visit sacred sites associated with the Buddha and acquire sacred texts and relics. These exchanges also stimulated the transfer of goods, such as silk and Indian drugs purported to promote longevity; of personnel, such as

Indian physicians; and of technology, including the transmission of Indian sugar-making techniques to China and Chinese alchemical techniques to India (Sen 32–46).

Xuanzang describes Harsa as a Buddhist king, but a careful reading of his account shows that Harsa, despite his clear interest in and patronage of Buddhism, also continued to patronize Hindu gods, temples, and festivals, dressing as Indra in the huge spring festival, for instance, while his lower-ranked neighboring king also participated, dressed as Brahma. Such details demonstrate the fluidity of religious practices in this period and challenge students' assumptions about the fixity and exclusive nature of religions and religious practices.

In Xuanzang's account, we also get an outsider's view of the workings of the political system described above, particularly the hierarchical relationships a more powerful king like Harsa established with his smaller neighboring kings. Harsa's command to the king of Magadha, Kumara, with whom Xuanzang was staying, to attend his court and present his visitor, clearly casts Kumara in the role of a subordinate king whose duties include attendance at his overlord's court and participation, along with a host of other subordinate kings and important religious men—both Buddhist and Brahmin—in the spring festival.

Beauty and Pleasure

Another significant idea that scholars have argued runs through political rhetoric in the early Middle Ages in South Asia is the importance attributed to beauty and pleasure (Ali, *Courtly Culture* 142–262). This is seen in inscriptions, literature, and contemporary sculpture from the Gupta period, but continues after the demise of the Guptas.

We start by reading an extract from the *Kama Sutra*, a treatise on erotic love—one of the four aims of human life in early Hinduism—usually dated to the third or fourth century CE. Contrary to popular assumptions that this text is nothing more than a catalogue of highly acrobatic sexual positions, the *Kama Sutra* is actually a sophisticated guide for the courtly man about town to the intricacies of ancient Indian sociopolitical relations and the art of living well. I ask students to look at the description of the lifestyle of the man about town from book 1, with its detailed account of the precise ways a man should beautify himself, which demonstrates the extent to which adornment was an important part of an elite man's lifestyle (Vatsyayana 17–21).

We discuss what kind of society such a description presupposes: an urbanized, largely peaceful society, where a class of wealthy individuals have the time to devote themselves to self-fashioning instead of concerning themselves with earning a living or defending the kingdom. I direct attention to the luxurious commodities that form part of this daily lifestyle, and, with the help of several essays by James McHugh (see "*Blattes de Byzance* in India" and "Incense Trees"), we discuss the provenance of various material goods and what the presence of such goods tells us about global trade in the early Middle Ages.

The *Kama Sutra* also sheds light on the importance of the political use of pleasure in early medieval South Asia.[7] The book's focus on establishing and maintaining intimate relations with various women should be seen in the context of a society in which marriage between ruling families and with the women of subordinates was a crucial political strategy, and polygamy was an accepted part of elite society. That this remained an important concern of elite society long after the *Kama Sutra* was composed can be seen in many of the Sanskrit plays, including one by Harsa himself: *Priyadarsika* (*The Lady Who Shows Her Love*), which is short enough to assign to students in its entirety (Harsavardhana 282–487).[8] Drawing on recent scholarship, Harsa's play can be seen as an exaggerated and stylized depiction of courtly society and allows attention to be directed to the role of marital politics and the potential, if limited, agency of women in courtly society (Ali, "Courtly Love").

To demonstrate the overwhelming cultural focus on ornamentation in the early Middle Ages, I draw on Ali's analysis of beauty in courtly culture, which frames beauty as the "root idea" (175) of courtly life in this period, inextricably intertwined with ethical development, rather than a frivolous fascination with luxury that historians once saw as typical of a state in decline (Ali, *Courtly Culture* 175–82). We examine a series of primary sources before discussing this theorization.

First, we look at two extracts from the *Harsacarita*: a description of Harsa that reaches Bana before he visits the court, where the emperor's body is praised by the absence of various physiological diseases and symptoms correlated with moral vices (Bana 42–43) and Bana's awestruck description of his first glimpse of the emperor (56–61). The latter extract demonstrates various Sanskrit poetic conventions of describing the body. The poet will generally start from the feet and work upwards, describing each bodily part with a plethora of metaphorical phrases, frequently using plant-based imagery. Although students find this extract challenging, it is a good example of the way in which Sanskrit poetry is concerned with generating particular emotions—or *rasa*—in the reader rather than with character or plot development. We note which areas of the body are most fully described, the gait or bearing associated with Harsa, as well as the presence of adornments such as jewelry and flowers.

Second, using extracts from the *Natyasastra*, a circa third-century Sanskrit treatise on the performing arts, we discuss the importance of bearing, gait, and comportment in this courtly world, and the students act out specific poses, strides, and ways of bowing that were associated with specific types and classes of character in the performing arts (Natyasastra 514–21). Although the *Natyasastra* was clearly not intended to be a simple reflection of reality, it does give us a sense of how an idealized hero, heroine, or villain would be portrayed in Sanskrit: an exaggerated refraction of reality, which the audience would expect to recognize.

Using examples from Ali, we consider the extent to which these conventions are dispersed beyond the performing arts by looking at images of coins and statues from the Kushana, Gupta, and post-Gupta period, which show increasingly greater fluidity, and how the stance associated with a king moves from martial—standing with legs akimbo—to playful and graceful—reclining with one foot on the other knee, or on a footstool (Ali, *Courtly Culture* 144–62).

Hindu-Muslim Encounters

A second major theme in teaching the Middle Ages in South Asia is the history of the encounter between Hindus and Muslims. This is still a hotly contested and politicized topic in contemporary India, to an extent that is extremely difficult to convey to students unfamiliar with the country. As a result, I usually commence my discussion of this historical process, which began as early as the seventh century, with a brief explanation of the trauma of the partition (1947) of the subcontinent into the modern-day nations of India and Pakistan, and the way in which both partition and the subsequent communalization of religious identity has informed the way the past is understood.

In brief, I want my students to understand that a complex history of trade, invasion, conflict, coexistence, and cohabitation that connected the inhabitants of India (in all their regional, linguistic, religious, and cultural diversity) with individuals from a wide variety of geographic regions and ethnicities (including Arabs, Iraqis, Persians, Turks, and Afghans) in the so-called Islamic world has been simplified into a single narrative of Hindu and Muslim conflict. In that narrative, Hindus are said to be the authentic Indians (obscuring the existence and history of other communities espousing Jainism, Buddhism, and various Indigenous religions), whereas Muslims (the differences of ethnicity, country of origin, and religious sect elided into one single community)—despite over a millennium of habitation in parts of the subcontinent—are said to be the aggressive, invading foreigners.

To highlight the power and persistence of this narrative, I often find an issue currently in the news and bring it to the attention of my students.[9] The aim is to direct students' attention to the way medieval history is weaponized in contemporary India and to demonstrate the importance of constantly questioning simplistic assumptions or analyses and the value of making nuanced arguments.

One of the key strands in the popular narrative of Muslim aggression is the argument that Muslim conquerors routinely destroyed Hindu temples and enforced conversion at the point of the sword. Supporters of this argument rely on evidence from a range of Persian chronicles (translated into English) that regularly describe temple destruction during expansionist wars conducted by a victorious sultan—often the patron or the ancestor of the chronicler's patron.

The use of such accounts to make political points dates back to the British: one of the motivations of the administrator-scholars of the nineteenth century who undertook the translation of Persian chronicles was to emphasize supposed Muslim despotism as a counterfoil to alleged enlightened British rule. As Richard M. Eaton's article on temple destruction shows, however, we cannot always take such claims at face value: often architectural evidence directly contradicts the textual claims of temple destruction.[10]

Persian chronicles need to be read not as a simple, objective factual accounts, but rather as complex rhetorical documents written according to a whole series of generic conventions that reflect the understanding of history as a subject intended to form ethical readers, and the aim of a chronicle as the glorification of one's patron (or his ancestors), often by presenting evidence of his piety so as to shore up his claims to legitimacy, a frequent need in a period when succession disputes were common.

Somnath

The attack on the temple city of Somnath in Gujarat is a useful event for exploring some of these issues. Between 1001 and 1026, the Ghaznavid sultan Mahmud bin Sabuktigin launched a series of raids from his capital of Ghazna east into the Indian subcontinent, impelled largely by a need to finance his ambitions toward westward expansion but justified in contemporary sources—which describe it as a jihad—as a quest for religious glory. One of these raids, in 1026, focused on the temple of Somnath from which Mahmud carried off a significant amount of gold, and, according to later accounts, the main icon of the temple, a lingam.

To demonstrate the complexity and the variety of accounts from across the so-called Islamic world, I assign, inspired by Romila Thapar, a series of different accounts of the attack on Somnath in a variety of genres, languages, and from different regions (Thapar 73–100). The first account is from al-Biruni's *Tahqiq al-Hind* (written circa 1030), a learned narrative in Arabic of Indian systems of knowledge, social norms, and religion written by an erudite Khwarazmian polymath employed at the Ghaznavid court who had accompanied Mahmud on one of his raids into India and remained there, learning Sanskrit from some Brahmin pandits (399–401).

Al-Biruni's sophisticated explanation of Indian religions was motivated by a conviction that Sanskrit texts were saturated with philosophical doctrines recognizable to educated Muslims. Although disdainful attitudes toward India and Indians are present in his work, these are usually reserved for the supposed ignorant masses and their misunderstanding of their faith. In the extract I use, al-Biruni embeds a brief mention of the destruction of the lingam at Somnath and its removal to Ghazna by Mahmud in a chapter on Indian understandings of cosmography, particularly the influence of the moon over the tides (Sachau 398–401).

The second account (originally in Arabic) is from the thirteenth century Persian geographer al-Qazvini's cosmography *The Wonders of Creation* and focuses on the icon at Somnath as a wonder that floats suspended and unsupported in the air (Elliot and Dowson 97–99). The account of the attack on Somnath—said to be motivated by the sultan's religious piety—is followed by a section that focuses on the scientific curiosity of the sultan and his followers at the suspension of the lingam and the various experiments they undertook to solve the mystery of how it is suspended.

The final account was written by the Persian chronicler of the sultanate of Bijapur in the Deccan, Muhammad Qasim Firishta, in about 1608, nearly six-hundred years after the event (Briggs). Firishta greatly increases the military details of the attack on Somnath and focuses on the attempt by the Brahmins to stop the destruction of the idol by offering a large amount of money. Mahmud's pious refusal to be "an idol-seller" is rewarded by the discovery of a great store of valuable jewels hidden inside the broken idol.[11]

I ask students to read each of these different narratives of the same event and notice how each author has a different focus and the way the details of the attack change as the authors become further removed (both in time and geography) from the event. We think about how specific genres, audiences, and historical contexts may have contributed to the differences in these accounts. We then read and discuss Thapar's analysis of the contemporary Sanskrit epigraphical sources, which highlights their surprising silence concerning the Ghaznavid attack on Somnath (Thapar 76–104). Considering these sources together allows for a discussion about how historians negotiate multiple primary sources that offer such different accounts of an event and the dangers of relying on merely one account to the exclusion of others.

The Qutb Minar

Another useful node in teaching focuses on a close reading of the Qutb Minar, a mosque complex in Delhi, built during the Delhi Sultanate (1192–1526).[12] In 1192, to celebrate his success against the Chauhan Raja, Qutb al-Din Aybek, one of Sultan Muizz al-Din Ghuri's favorite slaves, whom posterity names as the first sultan of Delhi, commenced work on the first congregational mosque of Delhi, now known as the Qutb mosque, using pillars from plundered Jain and Hindu temples.

This mosque included a minaret, modeled on and intending to surpass other freestanding minarets in the Ghurid heartlands, including the newly built minaret at the Ghurid capital of Firuz Kuh (now Jam). In about 1229, Sultan Iltutmish added new courtyards, doubling the size of the mosque, and added three stories to the minaret, making it the tallest brick minaret in the world at that time. He also brought a fourth-century iron pillar from a Gupta period Vishnu temple, and reerected it in the courtyard of the mosque.

Finally, in 1300, Ala al-Din Khilji undertook significant renovations to the mosque and added a spectacular entrance hall, known as the *Alai Darwaza*. Focusing on a building rather than a text, I highlight the ways architecture played a significant part in the development of a political ideology in the Middle Ages and demonstrate the different types of histories we can glimpse through the use of the built environment as a historical source.

Students examine four different sets of sources that center around architectural details in the Qutb complex. The first set contains images of spolia (reused architectural elements) from the Qutb site, including temple columns, *kritimukha* ("lion faces"), and *apsaras* ("celestial females"), all of which came from Indic religious sites (Hindu and Jain temples) (Flood, *Objects* 137–226). The second source is a translation of what appears to be a foundation inscription above the main entrance to the Qutb mosque (Flood, Introduction xl). The third set contains an image of the Gupta period iron pillar installed in the Qutb by Iltutmish and details about the series of inscriptions that adorn it (Flood, "Pillars" 96, 98, 107). The fourth source is a description of the pillar by the fourteenth-century Moroccan traveler Ibn Battuta, who visited Delhi in 1333 (622).

Students are encouraged to consider why specific architectural details were incorporated into the mosque, who chose to include them, where they were positioned, and how these details have been understood by various observers in different regional and temporal proximity to the mosque. The point of this close reading of individual elements of the Qutb complex is to get students to understand that multiple individuals are involved in constructing meaning in a building, including a patron (or several patrons); the builders, artists, and epigraphists; and the users and observers of the building (worshippers, inhabitants of surrounding area, Muslims elsewhere in the Islamic world, tourists, scholars). As a result, Qutb al-Din Aybek's construction of this mosque needs to be set in the context not only of newly conquered India but also of the Ghurid Sultanate and the wider Islamic world.

The use of spolia in this mosque, particularly temple columns, many defaced, is often taken as a sign of the violent triumphalist irruption of Islam into India. I problematize this by using Finbarr Flood's argument that iconoclasm has a much more complex history in Islamicate societies, and the use of figural and anthropomorphic imagery has inspired a wide range of responses, not all of which have been violent (Flood, "Between Cult and Culture"). If we look at evidence carefully, we can see that there has been a selective approach to figuration in the Qutb mosque, ranging from total erasure to gouging the face and careful retooling to crude chiseling in the case of anthropomorphic images, and from defacing to leaving unaltered in the case of zoomorphic images.

A particularly important example is the *kirttimukha*, which is generally left untouched in the Qutb mosque, and even the Indic conventions for its use are retained, with it being positioned above windows and doors as prescribed in Sanskrit texts. The clear attempt to hierarchize space and to differentially deploy figural imagery suggests both a complex response to the available spolia and continuities in architectural idioms and construction labor between the pre-Ghurid and sultanate period (Flood, *Objects* 137–226). The foundation inscription, with its explicit reference to the use of spolia and the monetary value of that spolia, has often been seen as a transparent statement of fact, but as Flood's reading suggests, a closer examination suggests a much more nuanced interpretation (Flood, Introduction xl–xliii). The use of the iron pillar can also be read in multiple ways, including as a continuity of preconquest Indic practices. Ibn Battuta's reaction to it—more of wonder at the achievements of Indians than of Islamic triumphalism—highlights the nuanced reactions of contemporaries (Flood, "Pillars" 105).

Conceptual Commensurabilities

A final theme that must be taught in any course on South Asia in the global Middle Ages is the persistence of what I like to call "conceptual commensurabilities." Whereas episodes of conquest and conflict, such as those of Somnath and the establishment of a sultanate in Delhi that was the precursor to the building of the Qutb Minar, are a common part of the popular narrative of the Indian Middle Ages that require problematizing by walking students through nuanced analysis, it is equally important to investigate the ways medieval Indians of a variety of ethnicities, religions, and cultures cohabited in a less antagonistic way.

Although there are plenty of primary sources available that demonstrate such intermingling of traditions, I have found that undergraduate students—generally unfamiliar with almost every aspect of India—cannot be expected to possess enough knowledge about Indic and Islamicate cultural or religious traditions to be able to identify which elements belong to different traditions, or how they are being used or combined in an unusual way. As a result, I find using secondary sources that deconstruct a single inscription, building, or individual's life more effective than asking students to do this analysis themselves.

One useful extract is a discussion of a bilingual Sanskrit-Arabic inscription from Veraval near Somnath, dated 1264 (Chattopadhyaya, 70–78). This inscription concerns a merchant from Hormuz (Iran) who had acquired land to build a mosque near the temple of Somnath. Brajadulal Chattopadhyaya discusses how the Sanskrit portion of this inscription frames both the mosque (and the deity who is worshipped in it) in vocabulary and concepts comprehensible to the local Hindu population.

A similar sense of a shared vocabulary of elite practices and conceptual commensurabilities emerges from Phillip Wagoner's essay on "transcultural political elites," which challenges assumptions about the fixity of Hindu-Muslim (or Indic-Persianate) identities or cultural products by tracing the ways cultural code-switching and boundary crossing was a familiar part of everyday life for elite individuals in the late medieval Deccan region of South India. Flood's essay on "Arab Sind" uses material culture from the eighth to eleventh centuries, and from a region often sidelined in the typical master narrative of Indian history, to problematize the standard art historical taxonomic categories of "Indic" and "Islamic" ("Conflict").

After reading these essays, we discuss why such dynamic processes of cohabitation are less well known than the dramatic episodes of conflict that dominate the popular narrative on India.

Notes

1. This essay, which necessarily draws on scholarship by others, is not documented extensively. Where possible, however, I indicate the names of relevant scholars. For readers seeking a general introduction to this region I would recommend Trautmann (chs. 1–8); and Asher and Talbot.

2. The appropriateness of the terms *Hindu* and *Hinduism* to describe the religions of ancient India is a matter of debate. Although many of the texts and practices used in this period still have some place in modern Hinduism, they have often been dramatically and unrecognizably reinterpreted. Some argue that the term *Hinduism* flattens the complexity and antagonism of the various strands of religious practice and anachronistically implies a unified, theistic religion, something that many scholars argue only came into being in the nineteenth century. For more on this, see Gottschalk.

3. Since this essay is aimed at nonspecialists, I have not used diacritics in the transliteration of titles or names.

4. I will not discuss the issues over dating the various early Indian texts I mention here, most of which, like the *Arthasastra*, are given vast possible date ranges. Suffice to say that many modern commentators agree that it had assumed its present form by about the third century CE.

5. I am not a Sanskritist, and some may disapprove of my use of Sanskrit literary texts in translation and without due attention to teaching the highly com-

plex philosophy or mechanics of the language. I started teaching these early medieval literary sources, however, out of a sense of frustration that there was a huge body of complex and fascinating Indian literature about which my students knew nothing, and that gives an unparalleled window into the type of society idealized in early medieval India. My hope is this brief exposure serves to stimulate them to deeper studies.

6. There are various versions of the *Harsacarita*, including a recent scholarly translation from 2008; however, I use the 1897 version.

7. I often assign chapters 3 and 5 of book 1 of the *Kama Sutra*, to draw attention to this fact.

8. Three important Sanskrit plays are traditionally attributed to Harsa. Although we cannot prove this attribution definitively, it does demonstrate that literary accomplishment was seen as an integral part of ideal kingship.

9. In recent years, examples have included the controversy over a film, *Padmaavat*, whipped up by rumors that the film would feature a love affair between the fictional Rajput princess Padmavati and the invading Muslim sultan Ala al-Din Khilji (it did not) and the renaming of various places associated with Muslims (including Aurangzeb Road in Delhi, the city of Allahabad, etc.). The Indian news website www.scroll.in is a reliable and balanced source of current events.

10. I often assign Eaton's essay to students, along with an extract from Goel's bile-ridden but influential account.

11. On "Islamic Iconoclasm," see Flood (*Objects*). On Firishta's account and Briggs's translation, see Malagaris.

12. This lesson draws heavily on the works by Flood given in the works-cited list.

Works Cited

Ali, Daud. *Courtly Culture and Political Life in Early Medieval India*. Cambridge UP, 2004.

———. "Courtly Love and the Aristocratic Household in Early Medieval India." *Love in South Asia: A Cultural History*, edited by Francesca Orsini, Cambridge UP, 2006, pp. 43–60.

Asher, Catherine, and Cynthia Talbot. *India before Europe*. Cambridge UP, 2006.

Bana. *The Harṣa-carita of Bāṇa*. Translated by E. B. Cowell and F. W. Thomas, Royal Asiatic Society, 1897.

Biruni, al-. *Alberuni's India: An Account of the Religion, Philosophy, Literature, Geography, Chronology, Astronomy, Customs, Laws and Astrology of India about A.D. 1030*. Translated by Edward C. Sachau, Trübner, 1888.

Briggs, John, translator. "Sooltan Mahmood Ghiznevy." *History of the Rise of the Mahomedan Power in India Till the Year 1612*, by Mahomed Kasim Ferishta, vol. 1, Cambridge UP, 2013, pp. 27–31.

Chattopadhyaya, Brajadulal. *Representing the Other? Sanskrit Sources and the Muslims*. Manohar, 1998.

Eaton, Richard M. "Temple Desecration and Indo-Muslim States." *Journal of Islamic Studies*, vol. 11, no. 3, Sept. 2000, pp. 283–319.

Elliot, H. M., and John Dowson. *The History of India, as Told by Its Own Historians: The Muhammadan Period*. Vol. 1, Cambridge UP, 2013.

Flood, Finbarr. "Between Cult and Culture: Bamiyan, Islamic Iconoclasm, and the Museum." *The Art Bulletin*, vol. 84, no. 4, Dec. 2002, pp. 641–59.

———. "Conflict and Cosmopolitanism in Arab Sind." *A Companion to South Asian Art*, edited by Deborah Hutton and Rebecca Brown, Blackwell, 2011, pp. 365–97.

———. Introduction. *Piety and Politics in the Early Indian Mosque*, edited by Flood, Oxford UP, 2008, pp. xi–xviii.

———. *Objects of Translation: Material Culture and the "Hindu-Muslim" Encounter*. Princeton UP, 2009.

———. "Pillars, Palimpsests, and Princely Practices: Translating the Past in Sultanate Delhi." *RES: Anthropology and Aesthetics*, vol. 43, 2003, pp. 95–116.

Goel, Sita Ram. *The Story of Islamic Imperialism in India*. Voice of India, 1994.

Gordon, Stewart. *When Asia Was the World*. Da Capo Press, 2008.

Gottschalk, Peter. *Religion, Science, and Empire: Classifying Hinduism and Islam in British India*. Oxford UP, 2012.

Harsavardhana. The Lady of the Jewel Necklace *and* The Lady Who Shows Her Love. Translated by Wendy Doniger, New York UP, 2006.

Ibn Battuta. *The Travels of Ibn Battuta, AD 1325–1354*. Translated by H. A. R. Gibb, vol. 3, Cambridge UP, 1971.

Inden, Ronald B. *Text and Practice: Essays on South Asian History*. School of Oriental and African Studies, 2006.

Ingalls, Daniel H. H. *Sanskrit Poetry from Vidyākara's "Treasury."* Harvard UP, 2000.

Kautalya. *King, Governance, and Law in Ancient India: Kauṭilya's* Arthaśāstra*: A New Annotated Translation*. Translated by Patrick Olivelle, Oxford UP, 2016.

Malagaris, George. "Firishta's Sultan Mahmud: On Beauty and Gold." *Iran*, vol. 56, no. 1, 2018, pp. 21–33.

McHugh, James. "*Blattes de Byzance* in India: Mollusk Opercula and the History of Perfumery." *Journal of the Royal Asiatic Society*, vol. 23, no. 1, Jan. 2013, pp. 53–67.

———. "The Incense Trees of the Land of Emeralds: The Exotic Material Culture of Kāmasāstra." *The Journal of Indian Philosophy*, vol. 39, 2011, pp. 63–100.

The Natyasastra *of Bharatamuni*. Sri Satguru Publications, 2006.

Sachau, Edward C. *Alberuni's India*. Indialog Publications, 2003.

Sen, Tansen. *Buddhism, Diplomacy and Trade: The Realignment of India-China Relations, 600–1400*. Rowman and Littlefield, 2016.

Thapar, Romila. *Somanatha: The Many Voices of a History.* Verso, 2005.

Trautmann, Thomas. *India: Brief History of a Civilisation.* 2nd ed., Oxford UP, 2015.

Vatsyayana. Kamasutra*: A New, Complete English Translation of the Sanskrit Text.* Edited and translated by Wendy Doniger and Sudhir Kaka, Oxford UP, 2009.

Wagoner, Phillip. "Fortuitous Convergences and Essential Ambiguities: Transcultural Political Elites in the Medieval Deccan." *International Journal of Hindu Studies*, vol. 3, no. 3, Dec. 1999, pp. 241–64.

Xuanzang. *The Great Tang Dynasty Record of the Western Regions.* Translated by Rongxi Li, Numata Center for Buddhist Translation and Research, 1996.

Yuanfei Wang

Chinese Literature and the World: The Tang, Song, and Yuan Dynasties

One can see at least three types of relationships between Chinese literature and the world during the Tang (618–917), Song (960–1279), and Yuan (1271–1368) dynasties: three periods in Chinese history where China's openness to the rest of the world is well-documented and incontrovertible.

First, the introduction of Buddhism to China through Buddhist scripture translation had a profound impact on the lexicon of the Chinese language and the genres of Chinese literature. Second, Chinese literary representations of foreign goods, cultures, and peoples and literary transmission resulted from China's contact with the world during these three periods. Third, Chinese ethnocentric and protonationalistic sentiments produced some dramas, histories, and lyrics on China's war and diplomacy with its foreign neighbors.

In this essay, I classify the course materials I specify according to these three types of relations. The syllabus I outline below is for a twelve-week semester system. For the readings mentioned, see the works-cited list at the end of the essay for full bibliographic details.

Buddhism, Chinese Language, and Chinese Literature

Week 1: Buddhism, Translation, and Chinese Language

Beginning in the first or second century CE, Iranian and Tocharian people traveling along the Silk Road introduced Buddhism to the Chinese. Some of the earliest notable monks and translators entering China include the Parthian prince An Shigao (安世高) and his countryman An Xuan (安玄), Indo-Scythian Zhi Qian (支谦), Zhi Lou Jia Chen or Lokaksema (支婁迦讖) of the Kushan Empire, and Kumarajiva (鳩摩羅什) of Indian (Kashmiri) and Tocharian parentage. In the Tang dynasty, the famous monk Xuanzang (玄奘) also traveled to India (including to the famous Nalanda center of scholarship) to study Buddhism and translate scriptures.

Translation was done through collaboration and oral transmission. Whereas the early medieval foreign monks recruited teams of as many as ten people to translate a single text, Xuanzang established an emperor-sponsored translation bureau in the capital of the Tang dynasty, Chang'an (Xi'an), gathering students and collaborators from all over East Asia. In many cases, the translators simply dictated their translations to the scribes. The sutras translated into Chinese include the *Lotus Sutra* and the *Diamond Sutra*. Xuanzang's translation of the *Heart Sutra* has become the standard version in East Asia.

These Buddhist translations greatly influenced the lexicon, grammar, and syntax of the Chinese language. Examples of lexiconic changes include a big number of Chinese transliterations and translations of the Sanskrit names of Buddhist genres, terms, and concepts: for instance, *fanbai* (梵呗; *Brahma-patha* 'hymns'), *jie* (偈; *gatha* 'verses'), *niepan* (涅槃; "nirvana"), *yinyuan* (因緣; "karma"), and *shijie* (世界; "cosmos"). Some original Chinese phrases were used to convey new meaning in Buddhism: for instance, *yingxiang* (影響; its modern meaning is "influence") originally meant "shadow and sound" but was later borrowed to signify emptiness and karma in Buddhism.

Week 1 Readings

Victor Mair, "Buddhism and the Rise of Written Vernacular in East Asia: The Making of National Languages"

Zhu Qingzhi [朱慶之]. 佛典與中古漢語詞彙研究 [*Fodian yu zhonggu hanyu cihui yanjiu*]

Haun Saussy, "The 'First Age' of Translation"

Tansen Sen, "The Emergence of China as a Central Buddhist Realm." Sen, *Buddhism*, pp. 55–101.

Tansen Sen, "The Circulation of Knowledge." Sen, *India*, pp. 29–82.

Week 2: Buddhism and the Transformation Text

The introduction of Buddhism brought forth new literary genres to the Chinese. The transformation text is one of them. Preserved and discovered at Dunhuang, the transformation text or *bianwen* (變文) is a type of popular Buddhist literature in prosimetric format meant to be performed or chanted during a ritual or festive occasion. The word *transformation* signifies the manifestations of the Buddha, bodhisattvas, and the miracles they perform. The language of the genre is an alternation between verse and prose.

Usually, a story is chanted together with a painting scroll. As the storyteller tells the story, he or she moves the scroll. In the earliest extant fragmented painting scroll P4524 (circa ninth century) of "Subduing the Demons," six pictures show six rounds of a magical contest between the Buddha's disciple Śāriputra and his rival. The multicultural and multiracial audience portrayed as South Asians, Chinese, Tibetans, Uighurs, Khotanese, Sogdians, and Tocharians reflects the local population of Dunhuang, which was ruled by the Chinese emperor.

The other transformation text to be read is called the "Transformation Text on Maha-Maudgalyayana." It recounts how after attaining sainthood, Maudgalyayana wants to know whether or not his deceased parents have ascended to heaven. Knowing that his mother is suffering from punishments in hell, the filial son then immediately visits the underworld to rescue his mother. The topography and the torments of the hells are recounted in detail as the protagonist's eyewitness account. The story blends well Buddhist concepts with native Chinese culture that values filial piety. This text was performed during the Buddhist Ghost Festival of the fifteenth of the Seventh Month of the Chinese lunar calendar.

Week 2 Readings

Wilt Idema, "Dunhuang Narratives"

Victor Mair, "Śāriputra Defeats the Six Heterodox Masters: Oral-Visual Aspects of an Illustrated Transformation Scroll (P4524)"

Victor Mair, "Transformation Text on Mahamaudgalyayana Rescuing His Mother from the Underworld, with Pictures, One Scroll, with Preface"

Victor Mair, *Painting and Performance: Chinese Picture Recitation and Its Indian Genesis*, pp. 1–16.

Week 3: Monkey and The Story of How the Monk Tripitaka of the Great Country of Tang Brought Back the Sutras

Legends about the Tang monk Xuanzang's pilgrimage to India abounded, so much so that eventually they paved the way for the composition and publication of the great Ming novel *Journey to the West*. In the Song dynasty, a story entitled *The Story of How the Monk Tripitaka of the Great Country of Tang Brought Back the Sutras* fictionalized the monk's pilgrimage in the vernacular storytelling tradition of the transformation text.

In the story, Tripitaka and his disciples travel to India "since the sentient beings of the Eastern Land are ignorant of the Buddha's Law" (Wivell 1182). They visit an array of fantastic kingdoms, most of which are related to Buddhist, Hindu, Tantric, and Daoist deities. They visit the dwellings of Mahābrahmā Devarāja (the king of the eighteen Brahmalokas, a deity in the Hindu pantheon), the Deep Sand Deity (likely a Tantric deity), the Incense Temple of Avalokitesvara (also known as Guanyin, or the goddess of compassion) and Manjusri (Buddhist god of wisdom), the Queen Mother of the West (a Chinese Daoist goddess), the country of Hariti, and the Utpala and Magadha kingdoms in India.

Monkey appears for the first time in the story cycle as a novice and a helper of Tripitaka in the lyrics. He greatly resembles Hanuman in Valmiki's *Ramayana*. Both these characters shared unruly experiences in their youth, an aptness for shapeshifting and cloud soaring, and a common role as a counselor. Their commonalities have led scholars to speculate on the *Ramayana*'s transmission to China via the overland Silk Road and the maritime trade routes, and about the Indian epic's influence in shaping the Chinese cultural icon.

The Story suggests a cosmos decentered or multicentered or both. At the end of the story, the dharma teacher in India admonishes Tripitaka: "We of Prosperous Immortals Temple, for countless thousands of years and myriads of generations, have yet to hear of the Buddha's law. You say you seek that law, yet where is it to be found? Where is Buddha? You are a fool" (Wivell 1199). This indicates Buddhism's emphasis on emptiness. That very desire to seek truth through pilgrimage needs to be renounced in Buddhism. *The Story* also emphasizes that the Buddhist center is not a particular geographic location but rather is connected to enlightened minds and may be located in multiple places.

Week 3 Readings

Glen Dudbridge, *The* Hsi-yu chi*: A Study of Antecedents to the Sixteenth-Century Chinese Novel*

Hera S. Walker, "Indigenous or Foreign? A look at the Origins of the Monkey Hero Sun Wukong"

Victor Mair, "Suen Wu-kung=Hanumat? The Progress of a Scholarly Debate"

Charles J. Wivell, "The Story of How the Monk Tripitaka of the Great Country of Tang Brought Back the Sutras"

Anthony C. Yu, *The Monkey and the Monk: An Abridgement of* The Journey to the West

Week 4: Chan Buddhism and Tang Poetry

Chan Buddhism became popular in the Tang dynasty. It then was introduced into Japan. Some great Tang poets like Wang Wei (王維) wrote poems in the spirit of Chan Buddhism. Some Buddhist monks like Hanshan (寒山), living at the Tiantai Mountain, also composed great Chan Buddhist verses. Hanshan was especially loved by the Japanese, who knew him as Kanzan. Chan Buddhist poetry and Buddhism can also be appreciated in conjunction with the Chan Buddhist paintings by the southern Song Chan Monk Muqi or Muxi (牧谿), also known as Fa Chang (法常).

Week 4 Readings

Wang Wei, "Zhongnan Mountain," "The Deer Fence," "Calling Bird Brook." Cai, pp. 177, 207, 209.

Charlie Egan, *Clouds Thick, Whereabouts Unknown: Poems by Zen Monks of China*

Paul Rouzer, *Cold Mountain: A Buddhist Reading of the Hanshan Poetry*

Representations of Exotica, Foreign Cultures, and Peoples, and Literary Transmission

Week 5: Dragon Horses and Black Enslaved People in Tang Romances and Poems

In the Tang dynasty, luxurious and precious species of living creatures, such as goshawks, peacocks, cockatoos, rhinoceroses, and elephants came to China through the tributary trade routes or through the emperor's need for gifts and treasure. The famous Tang poet Li Bai wrote a couplet to praise these remarkable creatures: "The Horses of Heaven come out of the dens of the Kushanas / Backs formed with tiger markings, bones made for dragon wings" (Schafer 60). Such legends about the "Horses of Heaven" may have originated in Iranian art and myth. Emperor Xuanzong (玄宗) loved his six Turkic horses so much that their images were carved on the murals of his tomb. The beautiful Chinese names of his warhorses were transcriptions from the Old Turkic language.

Plants, woods, aromatics, drugs, textiles, pigments, industrial minerals, jewels, metals, and music scores also entered into Tang China. The finger bone of Shakyamuni was brought to China and enshrined in the celebrated Famen Temple in Xi'an. The "Sogdian Whirl" (*huxuan wu*; 胡旋舞) originated in Uzbekistan and Samarkand and became popular in the Tang courts. Poets Bai Juyi and Yuan Zhen depicted this mesmerizing exotic dance as foreshadowing the decadence of the Tang Empire.

A few Tang tales depict Black slaves and Central Asian people. For instance, the subservient, exotic, and benignly magical image of *kunlun nu* ("enslaved people of Kunlun" or "dark-skinned enslaved people") is portrayed in a Tang romance called *Mo He*. In the story, the Black enslaved person named Mo He is so intelligent that he helps his Chinese enslaver to decipher the mime of a beautiful courtesan and so adroit that he carries his enslaver and the courtesan to elope beyond the mountains, flying high above the walls like an eagle.

Week 5 Readings

Edward H. Schafer, *The Golden Peaches of Samarkand: A Study of T'ang Exotics*
Pedro Acosta, "The K'un-lun Slave"
Don J. Wyatt, *The Blacks of Premodern China*
Julie Wilensky, "The Magical Kunlun and 'Devil Slaves': Chinese Perceptions of Dark-Skinned People and Africa before 1500"

Week 6: Monk Xuanzang's Travelogue on India

Chinese literary representations of the foreign are quite scattered and miscellaneous. But we can broaden our definition of literature by including genres of travelogues and histories. Monk Xuanzang's prominent travelogue on India entitled *The Great Tang Dynasty Record of the Western Regions* (*Datang xiyu ji*; 大唐西域記), for instance, can be used as a text to study Chinese literary representations of India and Buddhism.

Week 6 Readings

Rongxi Li, *The Great Tang Dynasty Record of the Western Regions*
Samuel Beal, *Si-Yu-Ki: Buddhist Records of the Western World*
Anthony C. Yu, introduction to *The Journey to the West*

Week 7: Du Fu's Poetry Written during the An Lushan Rebellion

An Lushan (安祿山) was a military officer of Sogdian descent. He quickly rose to hold powerful posts and was the military governor of the Fanyang defense region on the Manchurian border. His rebellion that began on 16 December 755 marked the downturn of the Tang Empire. We see how China's greatest poet Du Fu (杜甫) responded to the historic event in world history in poems on warfare, frontiers, and political incidents during this crucial time period. For instance, Du Fu's well-known poem "The View in Spring," with its lexical economy, portrays the interrelationship between human suffering and nature in wartime.

Week 7 Readings

Du Fu, "The View in Spring" and "Lament by the River"

James Liu, "Some Chinese Concepts and Ways of Thinking and Feeling"

Zong-qi Cai, "Recent-Style Poetry: Heptasyllabic Regulated Verse." Cai, pp. 181–97.

William Hung, "The Rebellion of the Eastern Tatars Has Not Come to an End"

Week 8: Chinese Literary Transmission in Heian Japan

Chinese written scripts, a prestigious and cosmopolitan language circulating in East Asia, not only facilitated communication among East Asian peoples but also helped non-Chinese peoples recreate their own literary canon and traditions. For instance, the *Tale of Genji*, a mid-Heian court work, cites and appropriates Chinese poet Bo Juyi's poem on the romance between the Tang emperor and his favorite consort Yang Guifei.

Week 8 Reading

Brian Steininger, *Chinese Literary Forms in Heian Japan: Poetics and Practice*

Representations of Alliance Marriages and Cross-Border Wars

Week 9: The Repentance of Zhaojun

In the Chinese literary imagination on cross-cultural encounters, a popular trope is the alliance marriage between a beautiful Chinese court lady named Wang Zhaojun (王昭君) and the chieftain of the Huns, Huhan Ye (呼韓邪). In Han dynasty official history, the Chinese palace lady bitterly resents that she never had the chance to meet Emperor Yuan of the Han dynasty, so she volunteers to marry the so-called barbarian king who requested a bride from the emperor as an exchange for peace at the Han Empire's borders.

The marriage and the two daughters she bore for this king pleased him so much that he promised perpetual peace in the northwestern region of the Han Empire, between Dunhuang and the pass. But Wang Zhaojun's self-pitying melancholy and the Chinese fear of non-Chinese and nomadic culture took hold in Chinese literature and music as the topos of "the repentance of Zhaojun" (*Zhaojun yuan*; 昭君怨) or "Zhaojun goes beyond the pass" (*Zhaojun chusai*; 昭君出塞). The Ming dynasty artist Qiu Ying (仇英) painted this perennial story.

This story can be contrasted with written narratives and visual images of the marriage of the Tang dynasty Princess Wencheng (文成) with Songzän Gambo of the Tubo dynasty. The well-known Tang artist Yan Liben (顏立本) portrays the Turfan envoy *ga tong zain yü sung* paying tribute to the Tang emperor for the alliance marriage ceremony. A kind of Tibetan Buddhist painting, *Thangka*, also contains beautiful images of Songzän Gambo and his two wives.

Week 9 Readings

Stephen H. West and Wilt L. Idema, *Monks, Bandits, Lovers and Immortals: Eleven Early Chinese Plays*

Cameron David Warner, "A Miscarriage of History: Wencheng Gongzhu and Sino-Tibetan Historiography"

Brandon Dotson, "The 'Nephew-Uncle' Relationship in the International Diplomacy of the Tibetan Empire (7th–9th Centuries)"

Week 10: Imagining the World through Confucian Culturalism (I): Jurchens and Imagined Communities

The loss of sixteen prefectures to the Khitans during the Northern Song (960–1127) and the loss of the entire heartland to the Jurchen Jin during the Southern Song (1127–1279) created traumatic historical and social memories for Han Chinese communities. The unofficial history, *Proclaiming Harmony* (*Xuanhe yishi*; 宣和遺事), furnishes examples of such collective cultural memory. This plain narrative tale, on which the Ming novel *Water Margin* was loosely based, rationalizes the downfall of the Southern Song through Confucian moralism.

Proclaiming Harmony displays China as an all-encompassing empire. The emperor's "good and evil intention" determines the yin-yang balance of the empire and the cosmos (Hennessey 4). The rising of bandits and rebels signifies the emperor's moral corruption. To bring peace to the world, the ruler needs to cultivate benevolence, self-determination, and conscientious judgment in order to eliminate bandits, enemies, and bad ministers alike.

Such a Confucian notion of the empire verges on conservatism. It examines the empire through a Confucianist moral lens, considering communities outside China as barbarians and threatening to Chinese civilization. *Proclaiming Harmony* may be read in comparison with two schools of thought in the Song dynasties. The idealistic school of culturalism noted that sage kings always emphasized internal affairs, and only when the domestic realm was stabilized were remote regions to be pacified.

This kind of thinking supposed that the labels "Chinese" and "barbarian" were cultural designations rather than ethnic, social, or geographic distinctions. The other much more pragmatic view warned against the dangers of an eventual barbarian invasion and urged a strengthening of national defenses.

Week 10 Readings

William O. Hennessey, *Proclaiming Harmony*

Ari Daniel Levine, "The Reigns of Hui-Tsung (1100–1126) and Ch'in-Tsung (1126–1127) and the Fall of the Northern Song"

Hoyt C. Tillman, "Proto-nationalism in Twelfth-Century China? The Case of Ch'en Liang"

Week 11: Imagining the World through Confucian Culturalism (II): Khitans and Imagined Communities

A drama we could use to teach about Confucian culturalism and Chinese protonationalism is the *Theft of Bones.* This text is part of the oral and literary family compound of plain tales, plays, and vernacular fiction of the saga of Yang family generals. The saga relates how the loyal marshal Yang Ye (楊業), along with his sons and grandsons, fights an ongoing series of campaigns to defeat the hostile states of Khitan Liao and Western Xia in order for the Northern Song to restore a unified Chinese Empire. In the *Theft of Bones*, Yang Yanzhao dispatches his servants to retrieve his father's bones, which have been humiliated daily by the Khitans in the Bright Sky Pagoda, at Youzhou (幽州).

Zhang Zeduan's (張澤端) famous painting scroll *Along the River During the Qingming Festival* (*Qingming shanghe tu*; 清明上河圖) can be used in class to demonstrate the economic and cultural prosperity of the Song capital, Kaifeng. The scene of camels entering the city gate of Kaifeng shows how China was connected to the non-Chinese world through land routes, probably via the Silk Road.

Week 11 Readings

Wilt Idema, *Generals of the Yang Family: The Four Early Plays*
Valerie Hansen, *The Open Empire: The History of China to 1800*

Week 12: Chinese Muslims and Ape Babies in Yuan Drama and Painting

Muslims migrated from Central and West Asia to China and settled down in China during the Mongol conquests. They were classified into the *semu* (色目) and cast as administrators and merchants to rule the Han Chinese population during the Yuan dynasty. Under the early Ming, the concept of Chinese Muslim and Mongol communities in China also emerged. *The Drama of the Journey to the West*, the late Yuan to early Ming *zaju* dramatic adaptation of the legend of Tripitaka's pilgrimage to India was composed by the sinicized Mongol Yang Jingxian (楊景先), who wrote in literary Chinese, just like an educated Chinese author. In the drama, the character Deep Sand is a Muslim. In the play, the Muslim is easily converted to Buddhism and participates in his Buddhist master's pilgrimage. Also in the play, the depiction of the denigrating mockery of Islamic customs by onlookers might additionally indicate racial prejudice against Muslims in early Ming China.

A literary trope of fear of interspecies miscegenation can be glimpsed in *The Picture of Searching the Mountain* (*soushan tu*; 搜山圖), produced in the Song-Yuan period by an anonymous author. The painting scroll depicts women abducted by a lustful monkey demon holding his ape babies, evidently suggesting that the monkey demon needs to be captured and eliminated by the hunter deity Erlang (二郎).

Week 12 Readings

Michael Dillon, *China's Muslim Hui Community: Migration, Settlement, and Sects*
Yang Jingxian [楊景先], 西遊記雜劇 [*Xiyou ji zaju*]

Works Cited

Acosta, Pedro. "The K'un-lun Slave." *Classical Chinese Tales of the Supernatural and the Fantastic*, edited by Karl Kao, Indiana UP, 1985, pp. 351–56.

Beal, Samuel, translator. *Si-Yu-Ki: Buddhist Records of the Western World.* Reprint ed., Oriental Books Reprint Corporation, 1884.

Cai, Zong-qi, editor. *How to Read Chinese Poetry: A Guided Anthology.* Columbia UP, 2008.

Dillon, Michael. *China's Muslim Hui Community: Migration, Settlement, and Sects.* Curzon Press, 1999.

Dotson, Brandon. "The 'Nephew-Uncle' Relationship in the International Diplomacy of the Tibetan Empire (7th–9th Centuries)." *Contemporary Visions in Tibetan Studies*, edited by Dotson et al., Serindia, 2009, pp. 223–38.

Dudbridge, Glen. *The* Hsi-yu chi*: A Study of Antecedents to the Sixteenth-Century Chinese Novel.* Cambridge UP, 1970.

Du Fu. "The View in Spring" and "Lament by the River." *An Anthology of Traditional Chinese Literature: Beginnings to 1911*, edited by Stephen Owen, W. W. Norton, 1996, pp. 420, 422–23.

Egan, Charlie, translator. *Clouds Thick, Whereabouts Unknown: Poems by Zen Monks of China.* Illustrated by Charles Chu, Columbia UP, 2010.

Hansen, Valerie. *The Open Empire: The History of China to 1800.* W. W. Norton, 2000.

Hennessey, William O. *Proclaiming Harmony.* Center for Chinese Studies / U of Michigan P, 1981.

Hung, William. "The Rebellion of the Eastern Tatars Has Not Come to an End." 1952. *Tu Fu: China's Greatest Poet*, Russell and Russell, 1969, pp. 90–118.

Idema, Wilt. "Dunhuang Narratives." *The Cambridge History of Chinese Literature*, edited by Kang-I sun Chang and Stephen Owen, vol. 1, Cambridge UP, 2010, pp. 373–80.

———. *Generals of the Yang Family: The Four Early Plays.* World Scientific Publishing Company, 2013.

Levine, Ari Daniel. "The Reigns of Hui-Tsung (1100–1126) and Ch'in-Tsung (1126–1127) and the Fall of the Northern Song." *The Sung Dynasty and Its Precursors, 907–1279*, edited by Denis Twitchett and John K. Fairbank, Cambridge UP, 2009, pp. 556–643. Vol. 5, part 1 of *The Cambridge History of China.*

Li, Rongxi, translator. *The Great Tang Dynasty Record of the Western Regions.* Numata Center for Buddhist Translation and Research, 1995.

Liu, James. "Some Chinese Concepts and Ways of Thinking and Feeling." *The Art of Chinese Poetry*, U of Chicago P, 1983, pp. 162–80.

Mair, Victor. "Buddhism and the Rise of Written Vernacular in East Asia: The Making of National Languages." *Journal of Asian Studies*, vol. 53, no. 3, Aug. 1994, pp. 707–50.

———. *Painting and Performance: Chinese Picture Recitation and Its Indian Genesis.* U of Hawai'i P, 1988.

———. "Śāriputra Defeats the Six Heterodox Masters: Oral-Visual Aspects of an Illustrated Transformation Scroll (P4524)." *Asia Major*, vol. 8, no. 2, 1995, pp. 1–55.

———. "Suen Wu-kung=Hanumat? The Progress of a Scholarly Debate." *Proceedings of the Second International Conference on Sinology*, Academia Sinica, 1989, pp. 659–752.

———. "Transformation Text on Mahamaudgalyayana Rescuing His Mother from the Underworld, with Pictures, One Scroll, with Preface." *Columbia Anthology of Traditional Chinese Literature*, edited by Mair, Columbia UP, 1994, pp. 1093–1127.

Rouzer, Paul. *Cold Mountain: A Buddhist Reading of the Hanshan Poetry.* U of Washington P, 2015.

Saussy, Haun. "The 'First Age' of Translation." *Translation as Citation: Zhuangzi Inside Out.* Oxford UP, 2018, pp. 61–94.

Schafer, Edward H. *The Golden Peaches of Samarkand: A Study of T'ang Exotics.* U of California P, 1963.

Sen, Tansen. *Buddhism, Diplomacy, and Trade: The Realignment of Sino-Indian Relations, 600–1400.* U of Hawai'i P, 2004.

———. *India, China, and the World: A Connected History.* Rowman and Littlefield, 2017.

Steininger, Brian. *Chinese Literary Forms in Heian Japan: Poetics and Practice.* Harvard University Asia Center, 2017.

Tillman, Hoyt C. "Proto-nationalism in Twelfth-Century China? The Case of Ch'en Liang." *Harvard Journal of Asiatic Studies*, vol. 39, no. 2, Dec. 1979, pp. 403–28.

Walker, Hera S. "Indigenous or Foreign? A look at the Origins of the Monkey Hero Sun Wukong." *Sino-Platonic Papers*, vol. 81, Sept. 1998, pp. 1–117.

Warner, Cameron David. "A Miscarriage of History: Wencheng Gongzhu and Sino-Tibetan Historiography." *Inner Asia*, vol. 13, 2011, pp. 239–64.

West, Stephen H., and Wilt L. Idema, editors and translators. *Monks, Bandits, Lovers and Immortals: Eleven Early Chinese Plays.* Hackett, 2010.

Wilensky, Julie. "The Magical Kunlun and 'Devil Slaves': Chinese Perceptions of Dark-Skinned People and Africa before 1500." *Sino-Platonic Papers*, vol. 122, July 2002, pp. 1–45.

Wivell, Charles J., translator. "The Story of How the Monk Tripitaka of the Great Country of Tang Brought Back the Sutras." *The Columbia Anthology of Traditional Chinese Literature*, edited by Victor Mair, Columbia UP, 1994, pp. 1181–1207.

Wyatt, Don. *The Blacks of Premodern China.* U of Pennsylvania P, 2013.

Yang Jingxian [楊景先]. 西遊記雜劇 [*Xiyou ji zaju*]. 全元曲 [*Quanyuan qu*], edited by Sui Shusen [隋樹森], Zhonghua shuju, 1964.

Yu, Anthony C. Introduction. *The Journey to the West*. Edited and translated by Yu, U of Chicago P, 1980, pp. 1–96.

———. *The Monkey and the Monk: An Abridgment of* The Journey to the West. U of Chicago P, 2006.

Zhu Qingzhi [朱慶之]. 佛典與中古漢語詞彙研究 [*Fodian yu zhonggu hanyu cihui yanjiu*]. Wenjin chubanshe, 1992.

Derek Heng

Teaching the *Malay Annals*, or Southeast Asia in the World

The *Sejarah Melayu*, or *Malay Annals*, is perhaps one of the most important literary works of Southeast Asia. Straddling the late classical and early modern period of Island Southeast Asian history, the text records, and in turn has a significant influence on, the history and sociopolitical culture of the Malay world, particularly the region of the Straits of Melaka and the Malay Peninsula.

The *Sejarah Melayu* in World History

What is the *Sejarah Melayu*? Originally named *Sulalat us-Salatin* and translated as *Genealogy of the Kings*, this Malay epic is a record of the origins and history of the rulers of the sultanate of Melaka and the sultanate of Johor up to the end of the sixteenth century. The text traces this history of the rulers back into deep history, beginning with the genealogical origins of the rulers from Alexander the Great through to the rulers of the Chola dynasty in South India (848–1279), including the consummate relationship between Raja Chulan, the ruler of the Chola kingdom, with the princess of the sea world in the southern half of the Straits of Melaka and the resulting three princes of that union that led to the beginnings of the rulerships of the Minangkabau in upland Sumatra, Tanjongpura in South Borneo, and Palembang in coastal southeast Sumatra. It is from the third of these rulership lines that the rulers of Melaka and Johor trace their direct lineage.

Narrated as the chronological history of the rulers, the *Sejarah Melayu* is in fact the only significant account of the history of three important and connected Malay kingdoms in the Melaka Straits region—Singapura (late thirteenth–early fifteenth century; located on Singapore at the southern end of the Malay Peninsula), Melaka (1405–1510; located on the west coast of the Malay Peninsula), and Johor (established in 1528; located upriver of the Johor River, in present-day Johor State). It provides a historical narrative about the formation and growth of the body politic of Singapura, Melaka, and Johor; the formation of the courts and courtly protocol of the three kingdoms; the role that religion played in conferring political legitimacy and supremacy in the Malay region; and the differing degrees of membership and belonging of the people of the three kingdoms, particularly in regard to the place of the different groups of people inhabiting the land and maritime environments of the region.

In addition, the text canonizes specific physical landscapes, deeply etched in the mental landscape of the region's inhabitants while imbuing these specific landmarks with deep history and moral meaning. Extending over three centuries, this text attempts to record the changes over time of the various aspects of a Malay sociopolity, memorializing the deep history of that polity and codifying the social memory of the Malays in the lower Malay Peninsula. The *Sejarah Melayu* was therefore the culmination of efforts to articulate why the Johor Sultanate and the Malays of the region were special.

According to the preface of the *Sejarah Melayu*, the epic was set down in 1612 by Tun Bambang, a son of the one of the courtiers of the Johor Sultanate court. The preface also indicates that, although it is likely Tun Bambang composed significant parts of the text, he was also collating many of the oral traditions concerning the kingdoms of Singapura, Melaka, and Johor that were already circulating among the people of Johor at the beginning of the seventeenth century. In this regard, the *Sejarah Melayu* is not only a historical document that was intended for the consumption of the court of Johor, it was also an epic literary work of its cultural world, akin to the *Thousand and One Nights* (*Alf layla wa-Layla*), *Journey to the West* (西游记) by Wu Cheng En (circa 1592), and *Les Fables de La Fontaine* (circa 1668), in terms of the cyclical narrative structure, as well as a reflection of the social memories of the people of a sociocultural sphere.

The result is a text unique in the world literary landscape. One of the characteristics of the *Sejarah Melayu* is that, whereas it is a text containing historical information that can be cross-referenced to historical documents from other traditions such as those of Europe and China, the historical narrative is interwoven with fantastical mythical stories. Physical landmarks and features mentioned in the *Sejarah Melayu*, which were still in existence up to the early nineteenth century in Singapore and up to the present in Melaka, are mentioned as the setting of events and outcomes of a fantastical nature and narrated utilizing traditional Malay literary tropes. The result is a text that defies accepted conventions of what a historical document should be like.

Of the different renditions of the text, the version that has been relied on the most is the Raffles MS 18 (British Library), accepted to be the earliest known rendition of the text. There has been substantial scholarship on this rendition, which provides in-depth discussions of the *Sejarah Melayu*, the literary tradition it represents, the historical context in which it was composed and codified, and its various themes. For the purpose of this paper, we will be utilizing the Raffles MS 18 version, primarily because of the availability of two English translations of this text—by John Leyden and by C. C. Brown. The translation that will be referred to in this paper is the one by Brown, primarily because of its ready availability.

Approaching the *Sejarah Melayu*

How, then, should the *Sejarah Melayu* be approached? First, it is critical to locate the *Sejarah Melayu* in the context of Maritime Asian and world history. The early sixteenth century witnessed the advent of the early modern era in Maritime Southeast Asia. The Portuguese, who had circumnavigated the African continent in 1498 and established a factory on the eastern seaboard of India soon after that in 1505, arrived in Melaka in 1510. In 1511, they captured Melaka and from that point on established, along with the Spaniards, a commercial presence in the Malay Peninsula, West Sumatra, Thailand, coastal Vietnam, Luzon (in the Philippines), South China, and southern Japan. The Dutch, on the other hand, began to establish themselves in West Sumatra, North Java, the eastern Indonesian Archipelago, Taiwan Island, and southern Japan. By the beginning of the seventeenth century, when the *Sejarah Melayu* was set down, the European presence in Island Southeast Asia, and the Malay region in particular, was firmly established.

This European presence brought disruptions of a substantive nature. The introduction of new technologies in such areas as warfare, navigation, astronomy, and architecture characterized this period of Southeast Asian history. The European presence also changed the notion of the world that had long been held in Maritime Asia. For the first time, the New World was connected to Maritime Asia, and Europe, which had been the end terminus of the international trade networks that thrived for at least the last two millennia, began to interact directly with Maritime Southeast Asia.

Along with these developments, the nature of diplomacy, trade, and social interaction also changed in fundamental ways. Economic interaction, which had been a variable-sum game, became a zero-sum game with the Europeans' mercantilist approach, resulting in the instituting of monopolistic trade practices. Sectoral and multinetwork trade and shipping, a key feature of Maritime Asian trade, came to be challenged by long-distance shipping trade conducted by the Europeans.

In the face of such changes, the *Sejarah Melayu* may be understood as an attempt by the court of the Johor Sultanate, which was attempting to continue the tradition of a classical port kingdom, to assert its place in a changing world, where the old, and in some instances fantastical, was starting to give way to the modern. This shift may in fact be discerned as the narrative of the *Sejarah Melayu* progresses, for example, from the origin story at the beginning, involving fictitious connections to ancient historical characters such as Alexander the Great and Raja Chulan of the Chola kingdom, as well as mythical figures such as the princess of the underwater people of the Melaka Straits, to the fall of Melaka and the subsequent activities of the rulers, predominated by issues of realpolitik and geopolitical concerns.

Second, the *Sejarah Melayu* has to be located in the context of the regional vicissitudes of the Melaka Straits region during the sixteenth and seventeenth centuries. The fall of the port city of Melaka to the Portuguese in 1511 coincided with the establishment of the sultanate of Aceh (North Sumatra) at the end of the fifteenth century. While the Melakan court retreated to establish a new court at the Johor River, Aceh experienced a period of expansion, during which time it grew to include most of the coastal areas of Sumatra, and Pahang and Kedah in the Malay Peninsula by the early seventeenth century. During this time, Aceh establish diplomatic relations with the Ottoman Empire and became a center of Islamic learning in Southeast Asia, as well as a major trading center in the Bay of Bengal region through the export of pepper and camphor. Aceh and Johor became rivals in the Melaka Straits region, both for geopolitical and economic supremacy, as well as for the mantle of the seat of Islamic learning in the region and the attendant political status that such a mantle conferred.

As such, the *Sejarah Melayu* may also be read as a means by which the Johor Sultanate—the newly incarnated Melaka Sultanate—to articulate its moral superiority over the sultanate of Aceh. Three key themes may be noted in the text. The mantle, both political and economic, and therefore cultural, of being the epicenter of the Malay region, is articulated through the direct historical legacy of the Johor Sultanate, placing Johor as the direct inheritor of the mantle that passed on from Palembang, Singapura, and Melaka through to Johor.

Finally, the mantle of Johor as the true Islamic center of the Malay world is expressed through the direct genealogy of Johor's rulers all the way to Alexander the Great, who was understood to have been from the vicinity of the epicenter of Islam. The proximity of Alexander the Great's sphere of influence—the Hellenistic world, and its closeness and overlap with the Muslim Middle East and the Ottoman Empire's sphere of influence—was also likely not a coincidence in the *Sejarah Melayu*. That genealogy is then interspersed with key events narrated in the text, which reinforce this legacy and confer additional legitimacy to Melaka and Johor's Islamic credentials, including the adoption of an Islamic name by the founding ruler of Melaka and the voluntary transfer of the Islamic mantle from Pasai (North Sumatra) to Melaka.

Class Exercises

For the purpose of introducing what may be a relatively obscure Southeast Asian text to students, the following class activities address three pertinent issues that the *Sejarah Melayu* touches on: its historicity as a historical record; its role as a means of codifying membership and belonging to a social group; and its uniqueness as a genre of historical documents, particularly in comparison to cultures that maintain a tradition of archival histories as understood in the Western historiographical tradition.

Although any part of the *Sejarah Melayu* could be used for such exercises, the following classroom activity exercises utilize the first six chapters of the text, as they form a coherent section of the history of Melaka, from the genealogy of the rulers and the antecedent kingdom of Singapura to the founding of the sultanate of Melaka by the last ruler of Singapura.

Historicity of the Sejarah Melayu *as a Historical Record*

This exercise has three learning objectives. The first is to have students engage the *Sejarah Melayu* through a close-reading exercise, utilizing their own lens of what historicity should be in a historical record. The second is to compare the historicity of a document with what may be scientifically recovered from the ground—primarily through archaeological means—particularly for the history of a place where there is a scarcity of other historical materials to test the document against. The third is to try to have students experience and appreciate a different cultural approach to recording and remembering the past.

Begin by having students read the first six chapters of C. C. Brown's translation of the *Sejarah Melayu.* This section of the text pertains to the genealogical origins of the rulers of Melaka and the history of the five rulers of Singapura, the precursor kingdom to Melaka. Have students write down two lists of information drawn from the six chapters. The first list (list A) would comprise information from the *Sejarah Melayu* that would be plausible as historical facts, whereas the second list (B) would comprise information that would not be plausible as historical facts. Have students provide the reasons they selected the information included in lists A and B, respectively.

Once the lists are completed, have students read chapter 1 of *Seven Hundred Years: A History of Singapore* (Kwa et al. 18–50). This chapter is almost entirely reliant on archaeological information obtained from a former settlement site in Singapore, which was the site of Singapura. Have students identify which information in lists A and B corresponds with the historical information noted in chapter 1 of *Seven Hundred Years.*

Once the process of cross-referencing is complete, have students answer the following questions: (1) Do the so-called historical facts in the *Sejarah Melayu* coincide with the archaeological record? (2) Why were certain features of the settlement of Singapura recorded the way they were in the *Sejarah Melayu*? (3) How would you rate the *Sejarah Melayu* as an effective historical record and why?

The Sejarah Melayu *as a Means of Codifying Membership and Belonging to a Social Group*

With the key component of a Malay social polity being the number of people who were loyal to and could be mobilized by a ruler, as opposed to the extent of land under a ruler's administrative control, membership and belonging, or protocitizenship, was articulated differently in Malay society. The objective of this classroom exercise is to encourage students to develop a greater appreciation for how membership and belonging was articulated in Malay courtly literature. Instructors may wish to assign Heng ("Socio-political Structure") as a reading to assist with this exercise.

Brown's translation of the *Sejarah Melayu* contains full descriptions of the layout of the courts of Singapura (31) and Melaka (44–49), respectively, both occurring shortly after the founding of the respective kingdoms. The convocation of the two courts would have occurred less than one century apart. Bearing in mind that Melaka was established by the last ruler of Singapura, who fled northward to Muar following a Javanese attack on the city of Singapura, the convocation and layout of the two courts therefore reflect the initial nature of the respective member groups of the Singapura body politic and the changes that subsequently occurred.

The descriptions of the courts have to be read in the context of chapters 3 to 6 (Brown 23–59). These chapters provide the narratives of the different types of activities, varying oaths of loyalty, location of habitation, and processes of co-optation of the different groups of people who came to constitute the Singapura and Melaka populations.

Begin by having students read chapters 3 to 6 of Brown's translation of the *Sejarah Melayu*. Next, have students focus on the descriptions of the courts of Singapura (31) and Melaka (44–49). Have students draw the layout of each court according to these descriptions, the various locations of the office holders vis-à-vis the ruler, and the regalia associated with the different office holders. Also have the students identify which offices were hereditary and which were not.

Once the above exercise is complete, have students answer the following questions: (1) What do you think were the ways the relative closeness or distance of a particular social group to the ruler of the kingdom were expressed through the layout of the court? (2) If you were a foreigner, what were some ways through which you could become a member of the kingdom?

Comparing Different Genres of Historical Documents

This exercise involves comparing the same account of the founding of Melaka found in two different historical records—the *Sejarah Melayu* and the *Suma Oriental* by Tomé Pires (see Cortesão). The *Suma Oriental* was written between 1512 and 1515 as a means by which the Estado da India, located at Melaka, could lobby the Portuguese Crown to increase its involvement and commitment to the Portuguese commercial and administrative presence, both in the Straits of Melaka, as well as in Island Southeast Asia in general, as the trade between Europe and Asia was growing. The *Suma Oriental*'s record of the founding of the Melaka Sultanate, based on information obtained from those who were resident at Melaka at the time the Portuguese took over the port city in 1511 while echoing the *Sejarah Melayu*'s overall narrative, differs significantly in its details.

Traditionally, the *Suma Oriental* has been regarded by historians of Southeast Asia as the more dependable source of information, not least because of the stature of documentary veracity that European records have in general been accorded as part of the bias that has come with Western historiographical training and the privileging of Western historical archives over Indigenous sources of information. More recently, however, scholarship on Southeast Asian history has begun to relook at the place of Indigenous records and accounts as a viable source of historical information, recorded from the Indigenous perspective.

This exercise will allow students to explore the different approaches to the recording of the past, in terms of cultural differences pertaining to European and Malay histories, the differences between late medieval and early modern historical texts, and the lens by which information is either elevated and embellished or marginalized and censored.

To begin, have students read chapter 6 of the *Sejarah Melayu* (Brown 40–59) and fols. 164r–166v of the *Suma Oriental* (Cortesão 229–38) Have students draw two event time lines, one based on the *Sejarah Melayu* and the other on the *Suma Oriental*, from the events leading up to the founding of Melaka to the reign of Iskandar Shah. Once that is done, have students answer the following questions: (1) What are the critical differences between the two accounts of the founding of Melaka? (2) Why do you think the accounts are different? (3) Why does Parameswara appear only in the Portuguese account, whereas Iskandar Shah appears in both accounts?

Additional Resources

Because the *Sejarah Melayu* is a fairly obscure text for students in the West, additional resources may be needed to help students to be introduced to Island Southeast Asia and Maritime Asia in the late first to middle second millennium CE. For introductory readings on the region's culture, economy and society during the late first millennium CE onward, refer to Regina Krahl, John J. Guy, Keith Wilson, and Julian Raby, *Shipwrecked: Tang Treasures and Monsoon Winds*. For a reading that provides an overview of Island Southeast Asian history in the first half of the second millennium CE, refer to Barbara Watson Andaya and Leonard Y. Andaya, *A History of Early Modern Southeast Asia*.

For a more in-depth look at the history of Melaka and Johor, refer to chapters 1 and 2 of Andaya and Andaya, *A History of Malaysia* (10–83). Finally, for a detailed discussion of the nature of trade and statecraft in Island Southeast Asia and the Malay world in the first half of the second millennium CE, refer to Kenneth R. Hall, *A History of Early Southeast Asia*.

There are a number of online resources, including online videos, that are open access for students. A lecture by Heng on the economic relations between Island Southeast Asia and the larger maritime Asian world, entitled "Trans-regionalism and Economic Co-dependency across the South China Sea," would help provide the general context of the larger region and economic world involving Island Southeast Asia.

A workshop organized by the Tang Center for Early China (Columbia University) and sponsored by the Asia Society (New York) and centered on the late first millennium CE economic relations between China and Southeast Asia, provides more detailed information on various aspects of the economic relations between Southeast Asia and China (see www.youtube.com/channel/UCJOYzb3MyPoxecuRquHXN_g).

A lecture given by Peter Borschberg, sponsored by the Singapore Bicentennial Exhibition, provides an overview of the Malay world in the sixteenth century or the century leading up to the composition of the *Sejarah Melayu*. Finally, there is also an interactive multimedia website, entitled *700years.sg*, that contains very accessible information and discussions on the kingdom of Singapura and the Melaka Sultanate that are recorded in the *Sejarah Melayu* (www.700years.sg).

Apart from historical information, archaeological data may be useful in illuminating the nature of material culture in the Malay world from the fourteenth through the seventeenth centuries. At present, archaeological research based in Singapore into the fourteenth-century Malay world remains the main research conducted so far. For those interested in a detailed look at the material culture recovered from one of the sites of the Singapura kingdom, there are online excavation reports published by the Nalanda-Sriwijaya Centre (Institute of Southeast Asian Studies-Yusof Ishak

Institute, Singapore) Archaeological Report Series (see www.iseas.edu.sg/articles-commentaries/nsc-au-archaeology-report-series). In particular, reports 5 and 9 are of direct relevance to the *Sejarah Melayu*.

Additionally, an online database includes detailed descriptions and images of the small finds pertaining to an area of the settlement of the Singapura kingdom in the *Sejarah Melayu* that were recovered from an excavation conducted at the Singapore Cricket Club in Singapore (epress.nus.edu.sg/sitereports/).

In conclusion, located at the intersection between the premodern and early modern eras, the *Sejarah Melayu* is a text that has retained the tone, embellishments, and narrative style that characterize medieval texts, even as the subject and content, as well as the period during which the text itself was composed, are of an early modern period. Realpolitik, mundane economic issues, and sociocultural matters are articulated through stories of individuals and their acts of chivalry or treachery, loyalty versus betrayals, superhuman achievements and deeds of witchcraft, and embarkation on quests. The *Sejarah Melayu* can therefore be read alongside such literary early modern texts as *Don Quixote* (circa 1605 and 1615) and *Journey to the West* (circa sixteenth century) as a means of comparing this critical transition in human history.

The *Sejarah Melayu* may ultimately be seen as a window into the Indigenous zeitgeist of the Malays in the Melaka Straits region, and how they reacted to the events and changes that were occurring around them and in the wider world at the turn of the seventeenth century. As a literary work, it has been regarded by scholars as the most important classical literary work of the Malay world.

Works Cited

Andaya, Barbara Watson, and Leonard Y. Andaya. *A History of Early Modern Southeast Asia, 1400–1800.* Cambridge UP, 2015.

———. *A History of Malaysia.* Palgrave, 2017.

Borschberg, Peter. "Sixteen-Century Singapore: Lecture by Peter Borschberg." *YouTube*, www.youtube.com/watch?v=gxYwoQko4-0.

Brown, C. C. *Sejarah Melayu or Malay Annals.* Oxford UP, 1970.

Cortesão, Armando, editor. *The* Suma Oriental *of Tomé Pires: An Account of the East, from the Red Sea to China, Written in Malacca and India in 1512–1515 and the Book of Francisco Rodrigues.* Asian Educational Services, 2005.

Hall, Kenneth R. *A History of Early Southeast Asia: Maritime Trade and Societal Development, 100–1500.* Rowman and Littlefield, 2010.

Heng, Derek. "Socio-political Structure, Membership and Mobility in the Pre-modern Malay World: The Case of Singapore in the Fourteenth Century." *Migration and Membership Regimes in Global Perspective*, edited by Ulbe Bosma et al., Brill, 2013, pp. 113–39.

———. "Trans-regionalism and Economic Co-dependency across the South China Sea." Tang Center for Silk Road Studies, U of California, Berkeley. *YouTube*, www.youtube.com/watch?v=LbVRZRLq8os.

Krahl, Regina, et al. *Shipwrecked: Tang Treasures and Monsoon Winds.* Arthur M. Sackler Gallery / Smithsonian Institution, 2010.

Kwa Chong Guan et al. *Seven Hundred Years: A History of Singapore.* National Library Board of Singapore, 2019.

Leyden, John. Malay Annals *(Translated from the Malay Language).* Longman, Hyurst, Rees, Orme, and Brown, 1821.

Eva Haverkamp-Rott

Jewish History or History of the Jews as Global History

In 1099, Jerusalem was taken by the crusader armies who came mainly from France and Germany to the Middle East; the First Crusade and the establishing of the crusader states marked the beginning of transnational, transcultural, and violent movements from the west to the east, having been first attempted in Spain against the Muslims. Even before the official crusader armies had started marching eastward, bands of French and Germans under the leadership of a few nobles pursued the same goals, though they declared Jews enemies who had not only (allegedly) crucified Jesus but were living among Christians next door. As a result, Jewish communities along the Moselle, Rhine, and Danube were attacked by crusaders and local citizens; they were either immediately murdered or forcibly baptized, under threat of their life. Jews responded by committing martyrdom in order to prevent baptism or being killed by the attackers; they took their own lives and the lives of their loved ones. Among the victims were many scholars, especially in Worms and Mainz (E. Haverkamp, "Martyrs" 319–22).

The transnational movement of the First Crusade—in which Christians of all social strata participated—and the events taking place in the Middle East had thus a tremendous impact on the Jewish communities in medieval Germany. They demonstrate how transnational movements can change the life of Jews lying in their paths. The progress of the Crusades remained of interest to Jews as being relevant to them not only for their own security.

On a different but related level, anti-Judaism and medieval anti-Semitism—being transnational and transcultural—had a direct and often deadly impact on Jewish life in all regions of the known world. The history of the Jews is equivalent to a history of anti-Judaism or anti-Semitism, even for places where no Jews lived. The persistent way of persecuting Jews through actions, ideas, and propaganda over many centuries until today created a coherent, unified history, it seems. Simultaneously a history of Jews and part of Jewish history, it is also a history of the perpetrators, who often used anti-Jewish and anti-Semitic rhetoric and persecutions for their purpose of masking, enabling, and enhancing conflicts about new developments in politics, economy, theology and all manner of social changes (Nirenberg; Heng).

Around the time of the First Crusade, in Troyes, the highly regarded scholar Rashi (Shlomo ben Isaak) wrote his commentary on the Pentateuch, a commentary that is studied by religious Jews up to the present day. In his explanation of the first words of Genesis, Rashi included the following statement:

> In the Beginning. . . . What is the reason, then, that it commences with the account of the Creation? Because of the thought expressed on the text (Ps. CXI.6) "He declared to His people the strength of His works (i.e. He gave an account of the work of Creation), in order that He might give them the heritage of the nations." For should the peoples of the world say to Israel, "You are robbers, because you took by force the lands of the seven nations of Canaan", Israel may reply to them, "All the earth belongs to the Holy One, blessed be He; He created it and gave it to whom he pleased. When He willed, He gave it to them, and when He willed He took it from them and gave it to us" (Yalk. Exod. XII.2). (Silbermann and Rosenbaum 2)

Rashi's words read like a commentary on the occupation of the Holy Land by the crusaders or at least about their motives to take the land from the Muslims and supposedly liberate the Christian holy places. Rashi refers to God's will to give the land to whom He pleases—and notes that He gave it to the Jews. Even when crusaders were marching, committing atrocities during the conquest of Jerusalem, and claiming to fulfill God's will, it was God's will to give the Holy Land to the Jews, despite the actual situation of the Jews—they were living in the Diaspora and only a small number were in the Holy Land. This promise was an intrinsic part of the relationship with God; the destruction of the Second Temple in 70 CE by the Romans had not changed that.

For Jews, moving or emigrating to the Promised Land was not principally a result of political, economic, or religious pressures. Especially for French, German, and Spanish scholars, the decisive argument was the opportunity to keep additional mitzvoth (religious precepts) specific to the Holy Land while in Israel. Several scholars—among them Judah ben Samuel of Regensburg (d. 1217) and Meir of Rothenburg (d. 1293)—advised against settling in Israel since "the fulfillment of marital obligations, and even studying and praying properly were judged to be impossible" (Kanarfogel 206). Moreover, scholars argued that the harsh conditions in Israel preventing Jews from studying and praying in order to be able to make a living might even lead the immigrant to sin (Kanarfogel 205–10; Cuffel 85–87).

Despite the precarious economic conditions in Israel—and the continued fighting between crusaders and Muslims until the fall of Acre in 1291—a group of Jewish scholars as well as nonrabbinic figures and their families moved to Israel in the thirteenth century. The famous immigration of "three hundred rabbis" in 1211 was probably also motivated by messianic theology and remained exceptional. Around the same time, the wars between Muslims and Christians were interpreted as God's punishment for mistreatment of the Jews (Cuffel 90). According to messianic expectations, Spanish and southern French scholars saw "the wars between Edom and Ishmael/Egypt as harbingers of the final age in which Jews would reclaim the Promised Land" (Cuffel 100). Northern European scholars viewed the immigration of a select few to the Land of Israel as a precondition for the coming of the Messiah, who—in imitation of a crusader king—would lead a Jewish army successfully in fighting against crusader and Muslim armies (Yuval, *Two Nations* 268–70).

The decision to move to the Holy Land remained a personal choice; there was no religious obligation or communal pressure. The expectation to receive forgiveness for one's sins by staying in the Holy Land attracted Jews from both Muslim and Christian lands. Wishing to come together in Jerusalem where families united from different parts of the world was a very emotional and still often unrealistic hope (Cuffel 64).

Only a very few Jews immigrated for religious reasons to the Promised Land; pilgrimage to the holy places was considered to have a similar effect for oneself. By contrast, Jews in the Islamic world—not inhibited by language barriers as their northern European coreligionists were—settled in Israel and the Middle East because of persecutions in Spain under the Almohads (since the middle of the twelfth century), the majority in the wake of general migrations due to political instabilities and economic changes. With the decline of Abbasid power (in the tenth century), Jews (and Muslims) moved from Baghdad and Mesopotamia further east, that is, to Persia, Khorasan Province, and India or to North Africa, Sicily, Tunisia, Egypt, and Israel, becoming part of already existing communities or establishing new ones. Under Fatimid rule, Tunisia and Egypt, in particular Fustat, became the new economic hubs for the Mediterranean trade that expanded into the Indian Ocean extending to the coast of Malabar. Migrations to Egypt from northern African and even a few European Jewish communities since the eleventh century reflected the migrants' hope for prosperity (Stillman 40–63; Cuffel 63–69).

This short introduction gives a glimpse into the complexity of the Jews' relation to Jerusalem and the Holy Land in the Middle Ages, which differs not only from their relation in the modern or ancient era but also among Jews in different parts of the world. Jerusalem and the Holy Land still play an important role in conceptualizing Jewish history when the term *diaspora* is applied, however, and this application is common in the field of global or world history. In a recent publication, John Tolan defines *diaspora* as referring to "dispersed communities originating from a single homeland (real or imagined) and loosely connected through institutional, ethnic, linguistic or cultural ties" (Tolan, "Exile" 24).

This definition already cautions against the emphasis on a "return movement" or a "dispersal" or "expansion from a homeland" as common features of the diaspora model, not only applied to the Jewish Diaspora but even derived from it (see, e.g., R. Cohen in *Global Diasporas*). As Shlomo Sand pointed out, the implied assumption that all Jews are descendants of those expelled from ancient Israel—the ostensible homeland—is false (Tolan, "Exile" 25). Furthermore, the idea of a general exile of all Jews from the Land of Israel as result of the destruction of the Second Temple in 70 CE is a myth (Yuval, "Myth"). The assumed link of all Jews to a territorial center at all times of history or the description of Jewish existence as "victim diaspora" is as much problematic as it is tendentious. One might say it all depends on the definition of the term *diaspora* when applied to Jewish history.

To choose the other end of the scale and define Jewish Diaspora in terms of dispersion only—without any center—is also incorrect, since it glosses over the clearly religious component in the relation of medieval Jews to Jerusalem and the Holy Land, who in their vast majority decided to stay where they were and be pious in the exile.

Nearly all Jewish scholars in the Middle Ages considered themselves to be living in the *galuth*, the Hebrew word for "exile" (Koryakina 115). Despite this clearly negative connotation, Jewish scholars in Europe had emancipated themselves from the authority and directives of the geonim in the academies of Palestine and Mesopotamia/Babylonia from the beginning of the eleventh century, although keeping cultural links with both centers (Grossman, "Medieval Jewish Legends" and "Communication" 121–122; Menache, "Communication" 20–22). This development coincided with the decline of the Babylonian authority and the growing independence of the Jewish communities in Egypt, Tunisia, Yemen, Syria, and Palestine from the gaon in Baghdad (Stillman 40–53).

Foundational myths and legends from Spain, Italy, Ashkenaz, northern France, and Provence served "to legitimize leadership of learning and other administrative leadership" (Fishman 6) by claiming direct lineage with the elites of ancient Palestine—even descendants of the exiles from Jerusalem, following the destruction of the Second Temple—or Hai Gaon's family of Baghdad. Although scholarly elites from the thirteenth century onward counted much less on such foundational myths, these stories still characterized the ambivalent relation with the centers of scholarship in Babylonia and Palestine, as well as with the Land of Israel in general in the High Middle Ages (Grossman, "Medieval Jewish Legends").

The second foundation for Jewish existence, in particular in medieval Ashkenaz, France and Spain, was the concept of the autonomy of each Jewish community. Already in the tenth century, scholars defined a community as a beth din, a court of law, and gave communities the right to govern themselves. The authority, autonomy, and self-confidence of Jewish scholars in Europe had its equivalent in the rights and agency of Jewish communities. In the wake of the persecution of the Jews during the First Crusade, the communities affected even gained the status of sacred communities: "These communities were virtual Jerusalems, wherein the synagogue stood in place of the Holy Temple" (Woolf 181).

When Jews became martyrs in imitation of the Binding of Isaac, their offering to God transformed the synagogue into the Holy Temple (Yuval, *Two Nations* 144–54; Wolfson, "Sacred Space"). The synagogue became a holy space, which also defined new concepts and standards of purity to which in particular Jewish women adhered (Baumgarten, *Practicing Piety*

21–50). Instead of considering pilgrimages to the Holy Land, Jews undertook pilgrimages to the graves of famous scholars, for instance, in the Jewish cemeteries of Worms and Regensburg (Raspe). Thus, Jews developed local and regional identities that changed the relevance or even the contents of diaspora and galuth concepts.

To add briefly another aspect of the *diaspora* concept in the context of global history: in the second century, Christians had adopted the Greek term *diaspora* in their polemics against Jews. They interpreted the destruction of the Second Temple and the subsequent dispersal (the Diaspora) as a punishment from God for the Jews' rejection of Jesus as the Messiah and for having crucified him.

The church father Augustine (354–430) even elevated *exile* and *diaspora* to the core statement in his approach to Jews, which throughout the Middle Ages became the basis of a widely applicable but rather questionable policy of tolerance towards Jews. His interpretation of Psalm 59.12, summarized from *City of God* (bk. 18, ch. 46), reads something like this: Do not kill the Jews so that they may continue to follow the Old Testament. Disperse them so that the whole world may know that their exile and the conditions of their survival are punishment for their rejection of Christ (E. Haverkamp, "Jüdische Diaspora" 131). *Diaspora* thus received a theological meaning and function within Christian theology that could be turned against Jews on any occasion (Yerushalmi, "Exile"; E. Haverkamp, "Jüdische Diaspora" 131–32). Considering this anti-Jewish interpretation in Christian traditions, applying *diaspora* as a central concept to the history of the Jews and to Jewish history as global history becomes problematic.

Despite the different connotations and contexts of the term *diaspora* since antiquity—even in the discourses of Diaspora studies today—the term does allude to and combine two central and traditional directions of writing history: Jewish history and the history of the Jews.

Jewish history highlights the common and shared characteristics of all Jews, mainly based on their religion, Judaism, but also based on genealogy, education, cultural memory, rituals, and the study of canonized texts (the Bible, Talmud, etc.). Jewish history is often categorized as part of the history of religion or intellectual history or even the history of inner-Jewish worlds and based mainly on the interpretation of Jewish sources. The history of the Jews, in contrast, highlights the history of individual Jewish communities in their diverse relations with non-Jews and their political, economic, social, and religious conditions and structures and is perceived mainly in terms of political, economic, and social history.

Historians study in addition archival sources of mainly Christian provenience. The study of anti-Semitism and anti-Judaism falls mainly into the latter category, except the study of Jewish-Christian theological polemics and debates, especially on the Talmud, and topics such as the Messiah and prophecy.

This divide of histories has always been highly constructed, with many shades of intersection, but it has turned out to be untenable, especially since the mid-1990s. In 2007, Moshe Rosman summarized the questions that scrutinized this divide and had always prompted different answers since the beginning of the *Wissenschaft des Judentums* in the nineteenth century: "What is the relationship between the Jewish past and the Jewish present? Is there some definable key to Jewish history across periods, or is there an infinite number of meta-historical interpretations of its meaning? . . . What is the relationship between Jewish culture and history and the culture and history of the non-Jews among whom the Jews lived and live?" (Rosman 1–2). Relating to recent approaches and insights, Rosman answered these questions in a bold and provocative way:

> Postmodernity has led to the emergence of a new, as yet not fully articulated, metahistory that can be termed "multicultural." Its proponents view the various historical contexts of Jewish existence as not only significant, but determinative. In each historical context, Jewish society and culture are not seen to be cells of some worldwide Jewish community "in dialogue" with "surrounding" or "host" societies and cultures, as the acculturationist school had it, but to be a "hybrid" component of the "hegemonic" society and culture whose frameworks set the templates according to which, and the parameters within which, Jewish identity, culture, and society are "constructed"—differently—in each time and place. The engine of Jewish self-definition is the encounter with the non-Jewish Other. (Rosman 53)

It is obvious how relevant such judgments are for conceptualizing—and teaching—the global history of the Jews in the Middle Ages. What were the previous insights of historians? And what are the more current terminologies that try to grasp the complex relationships between Jews and non-Jews, which also affect the conceptual relations between Jewish history and the history of the Jews?

The greatest of the nineteenth-century historians, Heinrich Tzi Graetz, published between 1853 and 1855 his four-volume *Geschichte der Juden von den Ältesten Zeiten bis auf die Gegenwart*, encompassing the history of the Jews from 1500 BCE to 1850 CE in the Islamic as well as Christian world (a work he expanded and reworked until his last edition, published in 1888). He differentiated between the external history of the Jews as *Leidensgeschichte*, a history of suffering, and its inner history as *Literaturgeschichte*, a literary history of religious knowledge (Rosman 38).

Only a few decades later, in 1906, the Gesamtarchiv der deutschen Juden (Central Archives of German Jewry) was founded, and in 1908 Eugen Taeubler, the founder of this archive, defined the research approach to this history as follows: "Die Erkenntnis der Geschichte der Juden in Deutschland muss . . . in einer Mittellinie vorwärts streben, die ihre Richtung ebenso von der allgemeinen deutschen Geschichte wie von der allgemeinen Geschichte der Juden erhält" ("The knowledge of the history of the Jews in Germany must . . . strive forward along a middle line that takes its direction from both general German history and general Jewish history"). The defining terms he chose were "Siedlung, Assimilation und Eigenart" ("settlement, assimilation, and specific individual character") (A. Haverkamp 5; my trans.). Such an attitude and position characterized most of the German-Jewish scholars of Jewish history before the rise of the Nazis and the subsequent elimination of Jewish scholarship and the research of Jewish history all over Europe.

In light of the indescribable suffering of the Jewish people during the Shoah and since 1933 in Germany, it is astounding that Salomon Wittmayer Baron wrote his three-volume edition in 1937 and the expanded eighteen-volume second edition of *A Social and Religious History of the Jews* between 1952 and 1983 not as *Leidensgeschichte*. To the contrary, he wrote: "All my life I have been struggling against the hitherto dominant 'lacrymose conception of Jewish history'" (Baron, "New Emphases" 96)—and he continued the programmatic approach of the German Jewish scholars from the first decades of the twentieth century.

Gerson D. Cohen, Baron's successor as Professor of Jewish History at Columbia University, expounded the acculturationist metahistory implied by Baron: "Acculturation, adaptation, and even assimilation have been constant features of Jewish history . . ." (Rosman 52–53). Baron's global history of the Jews is not superseded and remains distinctive and singular not only for being written by just one author but also for its encompassing perspective and the breadth of Jewish and archival sources incorporated. In 1969, one of the leading scholars in the Israeli academy, Haim Hillel Ben-Sasson, added his perspective on medieval Jewish history to the available global history narratives; his contribution was part of his edited collection *A History of the Jewish People.*

On the basis of Genizah documents, Shlomo Goitein provided a monumental work for the Mediterranean world (reaching to the Indian Ocean) comparable to Baron's work, with the five-volume edition of *A Mediterranean Society* published between 1967 and 1988: *Economic Foundations, The Community, The Family, Daily Life, The Individual.*

The years 1993 to 1996 are marked by three important—even revolutionary—contributions to the historiography on medieval Jews in general, which are also groundbreaking from the perspective of the global history of the Jews. In 1993, Israel Jacob Yuval published his article "Vengeance and Damnation, Blood and Defamation: From Jewish Martyrdom to Blood Libel Accusations" in *Zion*, the leading periodical of Jewish history in Israel. He made the following general but highly innovative and revolutionary observation: "Just as the Jewish position towards Christianity was influenced by Christian attitudes towards Jews, so we must assume that the Christian stance was influenced by Jewish attitudes towards Christianity" (VI; see also Volkov 192).

Even though severely attacked by leading scholars of the Israeli academy in the next edition of *Zion* (1994), Yuval successfully defended his statements about blood libel accusations and more ("'The Lord will take Vengeance'"). In the same year, *Under Crescent and Cross: The Jews in the Middle Ages* by Mark R. Cohen appeared. Cohen provided a thematic and condensed comparison of Jewish existence in the Islamic and Christian medieval worlds, covering a great variety of topics: myth and countermyth, religion and law, economy, social order, polemics, and persecution. Students and professors in universities worldwide are studying this book, and it is the leading monograph on Jewish history as world history.

Only two years later, Sophia Menache published the edited collection *Communication in the Jewish Diaspora: The Pre-modern World* and wrote what she termed in her introduction "the pre-history of communication" (see Menache, "Pre-history"). She tackled one of the core issues in the global history field, namely communication among centers and people over great distances. In this volume, the communication that emerged in the Jewish Diaspora was "outlined according to three main interacting categories; namely (1) the Diaspora—which dictated the sociopolitical framework; (2) the *halachah*—the codex of religious law and behavior regulating Jewish life; and (3) trade—the basic livelihood of many Jews" (Menache, "Communication" 15). Avraham Grossman not only contributed to this volume, with his essay "Communication among Jewish Centers during the Tenth to the Twelfth Centuries," but had also previously addressed relations between Spanish and Ashkenazi Jewry ("Relations"), as well as the relation of Ashkenazi Jews to Babylonia and Palestine ("Relationship").

The work of Yuval changed the concepts scholars developed about the relations between Jewish and Christian cultures. Even though discussion on ideas such as *acculturation*, *assimilation*, *influence*, and *inward acculturation* had made great progress under the leadership of Jacob Katz (*Exclusiveness*) and Ivan Marcus ("Rituals"), Yuval opened the doors wide to reconceptualize and rethink. The extent to which scholars assume not only interconnections but also the quality of those interconnections has changed. Scholars are pointing to Jews and Christians as sharing a common conceptual language of religious images and symbols while each of the two cultivated a reasonably detailed, albeit if somewhat distorted picture of the other (E. Haverkamp, "Martyrs" 320.)

Along these lines, in 1999, Jeremy Cohen pointed out "a common ground in the language and thought of medieval Judaism and Christianity," and in reference to the Hebrew crusade chronicles on the persecution of 1096, he stated: "In service of both goals, polemical and recuperative, these narratives drew on a wealth of traditions, symbols, and concepts that medieval Ashkenazic Jews evidently shared with their Christian neighbors, considerably more extensive than previous generations of scholars have recognized" (23, 34).

These works of scholarship opened avenues of research in two new directions: reciprocal relations among Jewish centers separated by great distances and reciprocal relations between Jews and non-Jews and between Jewish and non-Jewish cultures. These two layers and levels of interactions constitute the global history of the Jews, and they will determine any further research. These two layers of scrutiny—as thick layers—are interwoven or entangled; they might even have hybrid elements. They affect each other: to the extent that there are changes on one level, it will affect the other. Or, to be more concrete, reciprocal relations between Jews and Christians in different regions change the Jewish culture of that region, for they create or influence what might be thought of as *subcultures.* These reciprocal relations also have an impact on the relations of the Jews of a given subculture with Jews of other regions—as well as vice versa.

How can we go about studying and teaching these complex relations in global history perspectives? Since 2000, a number of collections and handbooks have been published, with contributions by scholars as experts on different regions or intellectual topics. *Cultures of the Jews* is the programmatic title of one such collection, edited by David Biale in 2002. In 2016, a conference on "Interwoven Regional Worlds: Jews and Christians in Bavaria, Bohemia and Austria, 1349–1648," conceptualized by Eva Haverkamp, explored the various interwoven life worlds of the Jews by applying the concepts of global history to the history of three larger regions.

In 2018, the collection *Regional Identities and Cultures of Medieval Jews* (Castaño et al.) likewise led the way to a new framework for global history perspectives. Contrary to the general assumption, medieval Jewish cultures did not form larger entities composed mainly of Ashkenazim and Sephardim until the early modern period. For the Middle Ages, a great variety of cultural entities—coined "subcultures" by the editors of *Regional Identities and Cultures*—developed. For instance, one can differentiate between Jewish cultures of southern Italy, northern Italy, Provence, northern France, England, the Byzantine Empire, Egypt, Tunisia, Persia, and Southeast Asia, to name but a few. Furthermore, regional distinctions and different Jewish identities even developed within Spain, that is, Sepharad, or within Ashkenaz; regional cultural entities emerged, for instance, when adhering to a particular tradition of minhagim (customs), such as *minhag Austria* (Austria, Bavaria, and Bohemia) or *minhag Rhenus* (Rhineland) (E. Haverkamp, "Jüdische Diaspora" 132; Fishman 1–4).

Moreover, all these regional cultures—or macroregions (Mann 28)—were not stable entities. They were threatened, weakened, or even destroyed by persecutions and expulsions. Jews were expelled from England in 1290; from France in 1182, 1306, 1321, and again in 1394; from Spain and Sicily in 1492; from Portugal in 1496 to 1497. In addition, in the German Empire, Jews were expelled from cities and territories from the end of the fourteenth century on into the sixteenth century. This list of expulsions is not complete; the subsequent migrations of Jewish people through expulsion were sometimes taking place concomitant with migrations of Jews for scholarly or economic reasons. By the beginning of the sixteenth century, new centers of Jewish life developed along the Mediterranean, the Ottoman Empire, in northern Italy, and eastern Europe.

In light of these constant changes and upheavals, studies of regional identities and cultures turn out to be rather complex. Researchers have to "consider how Jewish regional identities were fashioned, propagated, reinforced, contested, and reformed" (Fishman 3). The essays in *Regional Identities and Cultures* point toward directions for research: identity claims;

the impact of non-Jewish cultures on regional traditions; geopolitical boundaries and their impact on Jewish regional identities; cultural content as a marker of Jewish regional identities (Fishman 4).

Other scholarly works in recent decades have added to the discussion on shared cultures between Christians and Jews, initiated by Yuval about twenty-five years ago. Terms under discussion are *embeddedness*, *exchange*, *acculturation*, *appropriation*, *overlap*, *interpenetration*, *hybridity*, and *entanglement*. These terms are never thought of as describing only positive relations, not the least the term *shared culture*, which describes a common space and common language that, for instance, created one of the most calamitous accusations against Jews, that of the blood libel. All these terms include the ideas of *exclusion*, *difference*, *distinctiveness*, *isolation*, *hostility*, *persecution*, *intolerance*, and *alienated* within their spectrum of meaning (compare Baumgarten et al., Introduction 4.). Instead of excluding or preferring one term over the other, researchers should embrace the variety of their meanings, since they can describe and define the multiple realities of Jewish-Christian relations.

The turn toward regional and local studies of Jewish cultures has resulted in great benefits (E. Haverkamp, "Martyrs" 322; Rosman 53; and several monographs and collections published by the Trier school, i.e., Alfred Haverkamp, Christoph Cluse, Jörg Müller, and others). For the sake of preparation of an overview and insight into potential global history topics to teach, the appendix to this essay provides a syllabus offering an extensive overview of the current state of research. The proposed modules suggest smaller topics; they all provide the two dimensions of transcultural studies, regionally or locally with non-Jewish cultures and, over greater distances, with other Jewish centers and scholars.

"Jewish history offers a prime test case for writing transnational history" (Perry and Voß 5). (The article by Perry and Voß is also very instructive as an overview dealing with cultural transfer and transnational studies; for an overview of the discussion about the term *appropriation*, see Baumgarten, "Appropriation"). This remains true. Moreover, by interpreting *transnational* in two directions—as "transcultural" between Jews and Christians and as "transcultural" between Jewish cultures—Jewish history and the history of the Jews provide exceptional challenges and opportunities. The chances are that Jewish history and the history of the Jews will be accepted as part of general history all over the world.

Works Cited in the Essay and in the Appendix

Baron, Salomon Wittmayer. "Newer Emphases in Jewish History." *History and Jewish Historians: Essays and Addresses*, by Baron, Jewish Publication Society, 1964, pp. 90–106.

———. *A Social and Religious History of the Jews.* Jewish Publication Society of America, 1952–83. 18 vols.

Baumgarten, Elisheva. "Appropriation and Differentiation: Jewish Identity in Medieval Ashkenaz." *AJS Review*, vol. 42, 2018, pp. 39–63.

———. *Practicing Piety in Medieval Ashkenaz: Men, Women, and Everyday Religious Observance.* U of Pennsylvania P, 2014.

Baumgarten, Elisheva, et al., editors. *Entangled Histories: Knowledge, Authority, and Jewish Culture in the Thirteenth Century.* U of Pennsylvania P, 2017.

———. Introduction. Baumgarten et al., *Entangled Histories,* pp. 1–20.

Ben-Sasson, Haim Hillel. "A History of the Jewish People: Part V: The Middle Ages." *A History of the Jewish People*, edited by Ben-Sasson, Harvard UP, 1976, pp. 385–723.

Berend, Nora, et al., editors. *Religious Minorities in Christian, Jewish and Muslim Law (Fifth–Fifteenth Centuries).* Brepols, 2017.

Biale, David, editor. *Cultures of the Jews: A New History.* Schocken Books, 2002.

Boustan, Ra'anan S., et al., editors. *Jewish Studies at the Crossroads of Anthropology and History: Authority, Diaspora, Tradition.* U of Pennsylvania P, 2011.

Buc, Philippe, et al., editors. *Jews and Christians in Medieval Europe: A Historiographical Legacy of Bernhard Blumenkranz.* Brepols, 2016.

Budde, Gunilla, et al., editors. *Transnationale Geschichte: Themen, Tendenzen und Theorien*, Vandenhoeck and Ruprecht, 2006.

Carlebach, Elisheva, and Jacob J. Schacter, editors. *New Perspectives on Jewish-Christian Relations.* Brill, 2012.

Castaño, Javier, et al., editors. *Regional Identities and Cultures of Medieval Jews.* Littman Library of Jewish Civilization, 2018.

Cohen, Jeremy. "The Hebrew Crusade Chronicles in Their Christian Cultural Context." *Juden und Christen zur Zeit der Kreuzzüge*, edited by Alfred Haverkamp, Thorbecke, 1999, pp. 17–34.

Cohen, Mark R. *Under Crescent and Cross: The Jews in the Middle Ages.* 1994. Princeton UP, 2008.

Cohen, Robin. *Global Diasporas: An introduction.* University College London P, 1997.

Cuffel, Alexandra. "Call and Response: European Jewish Emigration to Egypt and Palestine in the Middle Ages." *The Jewish Quarterly Review*, vol. 90, 1999, pp. 61–101.

Fishman, Talya. Introduction. Castaño et al., pp. 1–17.

Fox, Yani, and Yosi Yisraeli, editors. *Contesting Inter-religious Conversion in the Medieval World.* Routledge, 2017.

Goitein, S. D. *A Mediterranean Society: The Jewish Communities of the Arab World as Portrayed in the Documents of the Cairo Geniza.* U of California P, 1967–88. 5 vols.

Grossman, Avraham. "Communication among Jewish Centers during the Tenth to the Twelfth Centuries." Menache, *Communication*, pp. 107–25.

———. "Medieval Jewish Legends on the Decline of the Babylonian Centre and the Primacy of Other Geographical Centres." Castaño et al., pp. 37–45.

———. "Relations between Spanish and Ashkenazi Jewry in the Middle Ages." *Moreshet Sepharad: The Sephardi Legacy*, edited by Haim Beinart, vol. 1, Hebrew University / Magnes Press, 1992, pp. 220–39.

———. "The Relationship of Early Ashkenazi Jewry to the Land of Israel." *Shalem*, vol. 4, 1981, pp. 57–92.

Haverkamp, Alfred. "Juden im Mittelalter: Neue Fragen und Einsichten." *Alfred Haverkamp: Neue Forschungen zur mittelalterlichen Geschichte (2000–2011): Festgabe zum 75. Geburtstag des Verfassers*, edited by Christoph Cluse and Jörg R. Müller, Hahnsche Buchhandlung 2012, pp. 1–20.

Haverkamp, Eva. "Die Jüdische Diaspora." *Weltdeutungen und Weltreligionen 600 bis 1500*, edited by Johannes Fried and Ernst-Dieter Hehl, WBG, 2010, pp. 131–44, 472–73. Vol. 3 of *WBG Weltgeschichte: Eine Globale Geschichte von den Anfängen bis ins 21. Jahrhundert.*

———. "Martyrs in Rivalry: The 1096 Jewish Martyrs and the Thebean Legion." *Jewish History*, vol. 23, 2009, pp. 319–42.

Heng, Geraldine. *The Invention of Race in the European Middle Ages.* Cambridge UP, 2018.

Kanarfogel, Ephraim. "The 'Aliyah of 'Three Hundred Rabbis' in 1211: Tosafist Attitudes toward Settling in the Land of Israel." *The Jewish Quarterly Review*, vol. 76, 1986, pp. 191–215.

Katz, Jacob. *Exclusiveness and Tolerance: Studies in Jewish-Gentile Relations in Medieval and Modern Times.* Oxford UP, 1961.

Koryakina, Nadezda. "'The First Exile is Ours': The Terms *Golah* and *Galut* in Medieval and Early Modern Jewish *Responsa*." Tolan, *Expulsion*, pp. 103–16.

Mann, Michael. "Globalization, Macro-regions and Nation-States." Budde et al., pp. 21–31.

Marcus, Ivan G. *Rituals of Childhood: Jewish Acculturation in Medieval Europe.* Yale UP, 1998.

Menache, Sophia. "Communication in the Jewish Diaspora: A Survey." Menache, *Communication*, pp. 15–57.

———, editor. *Communication in the Jewish Diaspora: The Pre-modern World.* Brill, 1996.

———. "Introduction: The Pre-history of Communication." Menache, *Communication*, pp. 1–13.

Nirenberg, David. *Anti-Judaism: The Western Tradition*. W. W. Norton, 2013.

Perry, Micha J., and Rebekka Voß. "Approaching Shared Heroes: Cultural Transfer and Transnational Jewish History." *Jewish History*, vol. 30, 2016, pp. 1–13.

Raspe, Lucia. "'The Lord Was with Them, and They Were Not Found Out': Jews, Christians, and the Veneration of Saints in Medieval Ashkenaz." *Jewish History*, vol. 30, 2016, pp. 43–59.

Rosman, Moshe. *How Jewish Is Jewish History?* Littman Library of Jewish Civilization, 2007.

Silbermann, A. M., and M. Rosenbaum, translators and annotators. *Bereshith*. Feldheim Publisher, 1934. Vol. 1 of *Chumash with Targum Onkelos: Haphtaroth and Rashi's Commentary*.

Stillman, Norman. *The Jews of the Arab Lands*. Jewish Publication Society of America, 1979.

Toch, Michael, editor. *Wirtschaftsgeschichte der mittelalterlichen Juden: Fragen und Einschätzungen*. R. Oldenbourg Verlag, 2008.

Tolan, John. "Exile and Identity." Tolan, *Expulsion*, pp. 9–30.

———, editor. *Expulsion and Diaspora Formation: Religious and Ethnic Identities in Flux from Antiquity to the Seventeenth Century*. Brepols, 2015.

Wolfson, Elliot R. "Sacred Space and Mental Iconography: Imago Templi and Contemplation in Rhineland Jewish Pietism." *Ki Baruch Hu: Ancient Near Eastern, Biblical, and Judaic Studies in Honor of Baruch A. Levine*, edited by Robert Chazan et al., Eisenbrauns, 1999, pp. 593–634.

Woolf, Jeffrey R. *The Fabric of Religious Life in Medieval Ashkenaz (1000–1300): Creating Sacred Communities*. Brill, 2015.

Yerushalmi, Yosef H. "Exile and Expulsion in Jewish History." *Crisis and Creativity in the Sephardic World, 1391–1648*, edited by Benjamin R. Gampel, Columbia UP, 1997, pp. 3–22.

Yuval, Israel Jacob. "'The Lord will take Vengeance, Vengeance for the Temple'—*Historia sine Ira et Studio*." *Zion*, vol. 59, 1994, pp. 351–414 [Hebrew], XVII–XX [English summary].

———. "The Myth of the Jewish Exile from the Land of Israel: A Demonstration of Irenic Scholarship." *Common Knowledge*, vol. 12, 2006, pp. 16–33.

———. *Two Nations in Your Womb: Perceptions of Jews and Christians in Late Antiquity and the Middle Ages*. U of California P, 2006.

———. "Vengeance and Damnation, Blood and Defamation: From Jewish Martyrdom to Blood Libel Accusations." *Zion*, vol. 58, 1993, pp. 33–90 [Hebrew], VI–VIII [English summary].

Volkov, Shulamit. "Jewish History: The Nationalism of Transnationalism." Budde et al., pp. 190–201.

Appendix: Syllabus and Recommended Reading

Theoretical Approach, State of Research, Global History in Jewish History

Baumgarten, Elisheva. "Appropriation and Differentiation: Jewish Identity in Medieval Ashkenaz." *AJS Review*, vol. 42, 2018, pp. 39–63.

Fishman, Talya. Introduction. Castaño et al., pp. 1–17.

Baumgarten, Elisheva, et al. Introduction. Baumgarten et al., *Entangled Histories*, pp. 1–20.

Perry, Micha J., and Rebekka Voß. "Approaching Shared Heroes: Cultural Transfer and Transnational Jewish History." *Jewish History*, vol. 30, 2016, pp. 1–13.

Halevi, Leor. "Religion and Cross-Cultural Trade: A Framework for Interdisciplinary Inquiry." *Religion and Trade: Cross-Cultural Exchanges in World History, 1000–1900*, edited by Francesca Trivellato et al., Oxford UP, 2014, pp. 24–61.

Lasker, Daniel J. "Jewish Knowledge of Christianity in the Twelfth and Thirteenth Centuries." *Studies in Medieval Jewish Intellectual and Social History: Festschrift in Honor of Robert Chazan*, edited by David Engel et al., Brill, 2012, pp. 97–110.

Carlebach, Elisheva, and Jacob J. Schacter. Introduction. Carlebach and Schacter, pp. 1–9.

Boustan, Ra'anan S., et al., editors. Introduction. Boustan et al., pp. 1–28.

Schwartz, Yossef. "Images of Revelation and Spaces of Knowledge: The Cross-Cultural Journeys of Iberian Jewry." *Christian North—Moslem South*, edited by Alexander Fidora and Matthias Tischler, Aschendorff Verlag, 2011, pp. 267–87.

Haverkamp, Eva. "Martyrs in Rivalry: The 1096 Jewish Martyrs and the Thebean Legion." *Jewish History*, vol. 23, 2009, pp. 319–42.

Soifer Irish, Maya. "Beyond Convivencia: Critical Reflections on the Historiography of Interfaith Relations in Christian Spain." *Journal of Medieval Iberian Studies*, vol. 1, 2009, pp. 19–35.

Steer, Martina. "Kultureller Austausch in der jüdischen Geschichte der Frühen Neuzeit." *Kultureller Austausch: Bilanz und Perspektiven der Frühneuzeitforschung*, edited by Michael North, Böhlau Verlag, 2009, pp. 25–41.

Rosman, Moshe. *How Jewish Is Jewish History?* Littman Library of Jewish Civilization, 2007.

Volkov, Shulamit. "Jewish History: The Nationalism of Transnationalism." Budde et al., pp. 190–201.

Yuval, Israel Jacob. *Two Nations in Your Womb: Perceptions of Jews and Christians in Late Antiquity and the Middle Ages.* U of California P, 2006.

Marcus, Ivan G. "A Jewish-Christian Symbiosis: The Culture of Early Ashkenaz." Biale, pp. 449–516.

Menache, Sophia. "Communication in the Jewish Diaspora: A Survey." Menache, *Communication*, pp. 15–57.

Yuval, Israel Jacob. "'The Lord will take Vengeance, Vengeance for the Temple'—*Historia sine Ira et Studio*." *Zion*, vol. 59, 1994, pp. 351–414 [Hebrew], XVII–XX [English summary].

Yuval, Israel Jacob. "Vengeance and Damnation, Blood and Defamation: From Jewish Martyrdom to Blood Libel Accusations." *Zion*, vol. 58, 1993, pp. 33–90 [Hebrew], VI–VIII [English summary].

Periodization of the Jewish Middle Ages—Eurocentric?

Ruderman, David. "Looking Backward and Forward: Rethinking Jewish Modernity in the Light of Early Modernity." *The Early Modern World, 1500–1815*, edited by Jonathan Karp and Adam Sutcliffe, Cambridge UP, 2018, pp. 1089–1109. Vol. 7 of *The Cambridge History of Judaism*.

Rosman, Moshe. "Jewish History across Borders." *Rethinking European Jewish History*, edited by Jeremy Cohen and Moshe Rosman, Littman Library of Jewish Civilization, 2009, pp. 15–29.

Skinner, Patricia. "Confronting the Medieval in Medieval History: The Jewish Example." *Past and Present*, vol. 181, 2003, pp. 219–47.

Meyer, Michael. "Where Does Modern Jewish History Begin?" *Judaism*, vol. 23, 1975, pp. 329–38.

Overviews and State of Research

"Cultures" and "Subculture"

Chazan, Robert, editor. *The Middle Ages: The Christian World*. Cambridge UP, 2018. Vol. 6 of *The Cambridge History of Judaism*.

Chazan, Robert. *The Jews of Medieval Western Christendom, 1000–1500*. Cambridge UP, 2006.

Biale, David, editor. *Cultures of the Jews: A New History*. Schocken Books, 2002.

Cluse, Christoph, editor. *The Jews of Europe in the Middle Ages (Tenth to Fifteenth Centuries): Proceedings of the International Symposium Held at Speyer, 20–25 October 2002*. Brepols, 2004.

Goodman, Martin, et al., editors. *The Oxford Handbook of Jewish Studies*. Oxford UP, 2002.

Stow, Kenneth. *Alienated Minority: The Jews of Medieval Latin Europe*. Harvard UP, 1992.

Studies of "Cultures" (Selection, in English)

ASHKENAZ

Haverkamp, Alfred. *Jews in the Medieval German Kingdom*. Translated by Christoph Cluse, 2015, ubt.opus.hbz-nrw.de/frontdoor/index/index/docId/671.

Woolf, Jeffrey R. *The Fabric of Religious Life in Medieval Ashkenaz (1000–1300): Creating Sacred Communities*. Brill, 2015.

Malkiel, David. *Reconstructing Ashkenaz: The Human Face of Franco-German Jewry, 1000–1250*. Stanford UP, 2009.

BYZANTIUM

Kohen, Elli. *History of the Byzantine Jews: A Microcosmos in the Thousand Year Empire*. UP of America, 2007.

THE EAST

Rustow, Marina. *Heresy and the Politics of Community: The Jews of the Fatimid Caliphate.* Cornell UP, 2008.

Gil, Moshe. *A History of Palestine, 634–1099.* 1992. Cambridge UP, 2010.

Stillman, Norman. *The Jews of the Arab Lands.* Jewish Publication Society of America, 1979.

SEPHARAD

Soifer Irish, Maya. *Jews and Christians in Medieval Castile: Tradition, Coexistence, and Change.* Catholic U of America P, 2016.

Corfis, Ivy A., editor. *Al-Andalus, Sepharad and Medieval Iberia: Cultural Contact and Diffusion.* Brill, 2009.

Alfonso, Esperanza. *Islamic Culture through Jewish Eyes: Al-Andalus from the Tenth to Twelfth Century.* Routledge, 2008. Routledge Studies in Middle Eastern Literatures 20.

Nirenberg, David. *Communities of Violence: Persecution of Minorities in the Middle Ages*, Princeton UP, 2015.

Beinart, Haim, ed. *Moreshet Sepharad: The Sephardi Legacy.* Magnes Press, The Hebrew University, 1992. 2 vols.

Global History Narratives and Comparative Approach

Nirenberg, David. *Anti-Judaism: The History of a Way of Thinking.* W. W. Norton, 2013. Chapters 3–6, pp. 87–245.

Abulafia, David. *The Great Sea: A Human History of the Mediterranean.* Oxford UP, 2011.

Haverkamp, Eva. "Die Jüdische Diaspora." *Weltdeutungen und Weltreligionen 600 bis 1500*, edited by Johannes Fried and Ernst-Dieter Hehl, WBG, 2010, pp. 131–44, 472–73. Vol. 3 of *WBG Weltgeschichte: Eine Globale Geschichte von den Anfängen bis ins 21. Jahrhundert.*

Cohen, Mark R. *Under Crescent and Cross: The Jews in the Middle Ages.* 1994. Princeton UP, 2008.

Menache, Sophia, editor. *Communication in the Jewish Diaspora: The Pre-modern World.* Brill, 1996.

Ben-Sasson, Haim Hillel. "A History of the Jewish People: Part V: The Middle Ages." *A History of the Jewish People*, edited by Ben-Sasson, Harvard UP, 1976, pp. 385–723.

Baron, Salomon Wittmayer. *High Middle Ages.* Jewish Publication Society of America, 1957–1958. Vols. 3–8 of *A Social and Religious History of the Jews.*

Baron, Salomon Wittmayer. *Late Middle Ages and Era of European Expansion.* Jewish Publication Society of America, 1965–1980. Vols. 9–17 of *A Social and Religious History of the Jews.*

Selected Studies of Entangled Jewish Societies: Collections and Monographs

Castaño, Javier, et al., editors. *Regional Identities and Cultures of Medieval Jews.* Littman Library of Jewish Civilization, 2018.

Clemens, Lukas, and Christoph Cluse, editors. *The Jews of Europe around 1400: Disruption, Crisis, and Resilience*. Harrassowitz, 2018.

Baumgarten, Elisheva, et al., editors. *Entangled Histories: Knowledge, Authority, and Jewish Culture in the Thirteenth Century*. U of Pennsylvania P, 2017.

Berend, Nora, et al., editors. *Religious Minorities in Christian, Jewish and Muslim Law (Fifth–Fifteenth Centuries)*. Brepols, 2017.

Fox, Yani, and Yosi Yisraeli, editors. *Contesting Inter-religious Conversion in the Medieval World*. Routledge, 2017.

Buc, Philippe, et al., editors. *Jews and Christians in Medieval Europe: A Historiographical Legacy of Bernhard Blumenkranz*. Brepols, 2016.

Echevarria, Ana, et al., editors. *Law and Religious Minorities in Medieval Societies: Between Theory and Praxis*. Brepols, 2016.

Shoham-Steiner, Ephraim, editor. *Intricate Interfaith Networks in the Middle Ages: Quotidian Jewish-Christian Contacts*. Brepols, 2016.

Tolan, John, editor. *Expulsion and Diaspora Formation: Religious and Ethnic Identities in Flux from Antiquity to the Seventeenth Century*. Brepols, 2015.

Tolan, John, et al., editors. *Jews in Early Christian Law: Byzantium and the Latin West, Sixth–Eleventh Centuries*. Brepols, 2014.

Boissellier, Stéphane, and John Tolan, editors. *La cohabitation religieuse dans les villes européennes, Xe-XVe siècles / Religious Cohabitation in European Towns (Tenth–Fifteenth Centuries)*. Brepols, 2014.

Fierro, Maribel, and John Tolan, editors. *The Legal Status of Ḏimmī-s in the Islamic West*. Brepols, 2013.

Carlebach, Elisheva, and Jacob J. Schacter, editors. *New Perspectives on Jewish-Christian Relations*. Brill, 2012.

Boustan, Ra'anan S., et al., editors. *Jewish Studies at the Crossroads of Anthropology and History: Authority, Diaspora, Tradition*. U of Pennsylvania P, 2011.

Chazan, Robert. *Reassessing Jewish Life in Medieval Europe*. Cambridge UP, 2010.

Toch, Michael, editor. *Wirtschaftsgeschichte der mittelalterlichen Juden: Fragen und Einschätzungen*. R. Oldenbourg Verlag, 2008.

Elukin, Jonathan. *Living Together, Living Apart: Rethinking Jewish Christian Relations in the Middle Ages*. Princeton UP, 2007.

Yuval, Israel Jacob. *Two Nations in Your Womb: Perceptions of Jews and Christians in Late Antiquity and the Middle Ages*. U of California P, 2006.

Menache, Sophia, editor. *Communication in the Jewish Diaspora: The Pre-modern World*. Brill, 1996.

Modules

Module 1: Exile, Diaspora, Redemption, and Stories of Identity

PART I: AT THE CENTER AND ON THE MARGINS OF DIASPORA

Kogman-Appel, Katrin. "Eschatology in the Catalan Mappa Mundi." Buc et al., pp. 227–52.

Koryakina, Nadezda. "'The First Exile is Ours': The Terms *Golah* and *Galut* in Medieval and Early Modern Jewish *Responsa*." Tolan, *Expulsion*, pp. 103–16.

Yuval, Israel J. "The Myth of the Jewish Exile from the Land of Israel: A Demonstration of Irenic Scholarship." *Common Knowledge*, vol. 12, 2006, pp. 16–33.

PART 2: IDENTITIES BY ORIGIN STORIES AND STORIES OF LINEAGE

Grossman, Avraham. "Medieval Jewish Legends on the Decline of the Babylonian Centre and the Primacy of Other Geographical Centres." Castaño et al., pp. 37–45.

Franklin, Arnold E. *Noble House: Jewish Descendants of King David in the Medieval Islamic East.* U of Pennsylvania P, 2012.

Marcus, Ivan. "Judah the Pietist and Eleazar of Worms: From Charismatic to Conventional Leadership." *Jewish Mystical Leaders and Leadership in the Thirteenth Century*, edited by Moshe Idel and Mortimer Ostow, Jason Aronson, 1998, pp. 97–154.

Marcus, Ivan G. "The Foundation Legend of Ashkenazic Judaism." *Hesed ve-Emet: Studies in Honor of Ernest S. Frerichs*, edited by Jodi Magness and Seymour Gitin, U of Michigan P, 1998, pp. 409–18.

Module 2: Migrations and "New Identities"

PART 1: MIGRATIONS, SETTLEMENT, AND MYTHS OF ORIGIN

Toch, Michael. "The Emergence of the Medieval Jewish Diaspora(s) of Europe from the Ninth to the Twelfth Centuries, with Some Thoughts on Historical DNA Studies." Castaño et al., pp. 21–35.

Haverkamp, Alfred. "The Beginning of Jewish Life North of the Alps with Comparative Glances at Italy (c. 900–1100)." *"Diversi angoli di visuale": Fra storia medievale e storia degli ebrei, in ricordo di Michele Luzzati*, edited by Anna Maria Pult Quaglia and Alessandra Veronese, Pacini Editore, 2016, pp. 85–102.

Migration to Italy

Raspe, Lucia. "Minhag and Migration: Yiddish Custom Books from Sixteenth-Century Italy." Castaño et al., pp. 241–59.

Veronese, Alessandra. "Ashkenazi Immigrants in Northern Italy and their Relations with the Italian Jewish Population, c. 1380–1420." *The Jews of Europe around 1400: Disruption, Crisis, and Resilience*, edited by Lukas Clemens and Christoph Cluse, Harrassowitz, 2018, pp. 157–70.

Haverkamp, Alfred. "Jüdische Kultur beiderseits der Alpen in kulturlandschaftlichen Differenzierungen." *Die Staufer und Italien: Essays*, edited by Alfried Wieczorek et al., Curt-Engelhorn-Stiftung / Wissenschaftliche Buchgesellschaft, 2010, pp. 325–32.

Möschter, Angela. *Juden im venezianischen Treviso (1389–1509).* Hahnsche Buchhandlung, 2008.

Migrations, Boundaries, and Cultural Entities

Castaño, Javier. "The Peninsula as a Borderless Space: Towards a Mobility 'Turn' in the Study of Fifteenth-Century Iberian Jewries." Buc et al., pp. 315–32.

Schwartz, Yossef. "Images of Revelation and Spaces of Knowledge: The Cross-Cultural Journeys of Iberian Jewry." *Christian North—Moslem South*, edited by Alexander Fidora and Matthias Tischler, Aschendorff Verlag, 2011, pp. 267–87.

PART 2: FORCED MIGRATIONS (EXPULSIONS AND PERSECUTIONS) AND THE BUILDING OF NEW COMMUNITIES

Tolan, John. "Exile and Identity." Tolan, *Expulsion*, pp. 9–30.

Tolan, John, editor. *Expulsion and Diaspora Formation: Religious and Ethnic Identities in Flux from Antiquity to the Seventeenth Century*. Brepols, 2015.

Mundill, Robin A. *The King's Jews: Money, Massacre and Exodus in Medieval England*. Bloomsbury Publishing, 2010.

Mentgen, Gerd. "Die Judenvertreibungen im mittelalterlichen Reich." *Aschkenas*, vol. 16, 2006, pp. 367–403.

Burgard, Friedhelm, et al., editors. *Judenvertreibungen in Mittelalter und früher Neuzeit*. Hahnsche Buchhandlung, 1999.

Persecutions: Impact of the Black Death on Ashkenazi and Sephardi Jews; Reception of Medical Literature and Intellectual Interactions between Jewish, Christian, and Muslim Scholars

Einbinder, Susan L. *After the Black Death: Plague and Commemoration among Iberian Jews*. U of Pennsylvania P, 2018.

Clemens, Lukas, and Christoph Cluse, editors. *The Jews of Europe around 1400: Disruption, Crisis, and Resilience*. Harrassowitz, 2018.

Vici, Tamás. "Plague, Persecution, and Philosophy: Avigdor Kara and the Consequences of the Black Death." *Intricate Interfaith Networks in the Middle Ages: Quotidian Jewish-Christian Contacts*, edited by Ephraim Shoham-Steiner, Brepols, 2016, pp. 85–117.

PART 3: MIGRATION TO THE HOLY LAND

Cuffel, Alexandra. "Call and Response: European Jewish Emigration to Egypt and Palestine in the Middle Ages." *The Jewish Quarterly Review*, vol. 90, 1999, pp. 61–101.

Kanarfogel, Ephraim. "The ʿAliyah of 'Three Hundred Rabbis' in 1211: Tosafist Attitudes toward Settling in the Land of Israel." *The Jewish Quarterly Review*, vol. 76, 1986, pp. 191–215.

Module 3: Economic Networks, Exchanges, and Contacts

PART 1: INTRODUCTION

Toch, Michael. "Economic Activities." *The Middle Ages: The Christian World*, edited by Robert Chazan, Cambridge UP, 2018, pp. 357–79. Vol. 6 of *The Cambridge History of Judaism*.

Halevi, Leor. "Religion and Cross-Cultural Trade: A Framework for Interdisciplinary Inquiry." *Religion and Trade: Cross-Cultural Exchanges in World History, 1000–1900*, edited by Francesca Trivellato et al., Oxford UP, 2014, pp. 24–61.

Soloveitchik, Haym. "The Jewish Attitude to Usury in the High and Late Middle Ages (1000–1500)." *Collected Essays*, by Soloveitchik, vol. 1, Littman Library of Jewish Civilization, 2013, pp. 44–56.

Toch, Michael, editor. *Wirtschaftsgeschichte der mittelalterlichen Juden: Fragen und Einschätzungen*. R. Oldenbourg Verlag, 2008.

Toch, Michael. *Peasants and Jews in Medieval Germany*, Ashgate, 2003. Chapter 15, "Jews and Commerce: Modern Fancies and Medieval Realities."

Le Goff, Jacques. *Your Money or Your Life: Economy and Religion in the Middle Ages*. Zone Books, 1988.

Goitein, S. D. *Economic Foundations*. U of California P, 1967. Vol. 1 of *A Mediterranean Society: The Jewish Communities of the Arab World as Portrayed in the Documents of the Cairo Geniza*.

PART 2: ECONOMIC ACTIVITIES OF ASHKENAZI JEWS, SLAVE TRADE, AND CONNECTIONS TO THE EAST

Keil, Martha. "Jewish Business Contracts from Late Medieval Austria as Crossroads of Law and Business Practice." Berend et al., pp. 353–68.

Haverkamp, Eva. "Jewish Images on Christian Coins: Economy and Symbolism in Medieval Germany." Buc et al., pp. 189–226.

Toch, Michael. *The Economic History of European Jews: Late Antiquity and Early Middle Ages*. Brill, 2013, especially part 2: "Economic Functions and Significance," pp. 177–257.

Soloveitchik, Haym. "Pawnbroking: A Study in *Ribbit* and of the Halakhah in Exile." *Collected Essays*, by Soloveitchik, vol. 1, Littman Library of Jewish Civilization, 2013, pp. 57–166.

Shatzmiller, Joseph. *Cultural Exchange: Jews, Christians, and Art in the Medieval Marketplace*. Princeton UP, 2013, part 1: Pawnbrokers: Agents of Cultural Transmission, pp. 5–58.

Toch, Michael. "Netzwerke im jüdischen Handel des Früh- und Hochmittelalters?" *Netzwerke im europäischen Handel des Mittelalters*, edited by Gerhard Fouquet and Hans-Jürgen Gilomen, Jan Thorbecke Verlag, 2010, pp. 229–44.

Toch, Michael. "Economic Activities of German Jews in the Middle Ages." Toch, pp. 181–210.

Müller, Jörg R. *Beziehungsnetze aschkenasischer Juden während des Mittelalters und der frühen Neuzeit*. Hahnsche Buchhandlung, 2008.

Burgard, Friedhelm, et al., eds. *Hochfinanz im Westen des Reiches, 1150–1500*. Trierer Historische Forschungen, 1996.

Shatzmiller, Joseph. *Jews, Medicine, and Medieval Society*. U of California P, 1994.

PART 3: INDIAN TRADE

Ray, Himanshu Prabha. "Trading Partners across the Indian Ocean: The Making of Maritime Communities." *Expanding Webs of Exchange and Conflict, 500 CE–1500 CE*, edited by Benjamin Z. Kedar and Merry E. Wiesner-Hanks, Cambridge UP, 2015, pp. 287–308. Vol. 5 of *The Cambridge World History*.

Goitein, S. D., and Mordechai A. Friedman. *India Traders of the Middle Ages: Documents from the Cairo Geniza ("India Book")*. Brill, 2008.

Silverstein, Adam. "From Markets to Marvels: Jews on the Maritime Route to China, ca. 850–ca. 950 CE." *Journal of Jewish Studies*, vol. 58, 2007, pp. 91–103.

PART 4: MEDITERRANEAN TRADE

Winer, Rebecca. "Jews in and out of Latin Notarial Culture: Analyzing Hebrew Notations on Latin Contracts in Thirteenth-Century Perpignan and Barcelona." Baumgarten et al., *Entangled Histories*, pp. 113–33.

Balard, Michel. "European and Mediterranean Trade Networks." *Expanding Webs of Exchange and Conflict, 500 CE–1500 CE*, edited by Benjamin Z. Kedar and Merry E. Wiesner-Hanks, Cambridge UP, 2015, pp. 257–86. Vol. 5 of *The Cambridge World History*.

Ackerman-Lieberman, Phillip I. *The Business of Identity: Jews, Muslims, and Economic Life in Medieval Egypt*. Stanford UP, 2014.

Goldberg, Jessica L., *Trade and Institutions in the Medieval Mediterranean: The Geniza Merchants and their Business World*. Cambridge UP, 2012.

Holo, Joshua. *Byzantine Jewry in the Mediterranean Economy*. Cambridge UP, 2009.

Jacoby, David. "The Jews in Byzantium and the Eastern Mediterranean: Economic Activities from the Thirteenth to the Mid–Fifteenth Century." Toch, pp. 5–48.

Abulafia, David. "The Jews of Sicily and Southern Italy: Economic Activity." Toch, pp. 49–62.

Mueller, Reinhold C. "The Status and Economic Activity of Jews in the Venetian Dominions during the Fifteenth Century." Toch, pp. 63–92.

Goitein, S. D. *Letters of Medieval Jewish Traders*. Princeton UP, 1973.

Module 4: Politics and Law: Law and Interreligious Communities

PART 1: NEGOTIATING THE LEGAL STATUS OF JEWISH COMMUNITIES IN CHRISTIAN AND MUSLIM WORLDS

Matheson, Anna. "Muslims, Jews, and the Question of Municipal Membership in Twelfth- to Fifteenth-Century Portugal." Berend et al., pp. 191–218.

Koryakina, Nadezda. "Jewish Citizens versus Jewish Foreigners: The Legal Status of a Minority within the Minority in Medieval Catalonia." Berend et al., pp. 219–32.

Tartakoff, Paola. "Segregatory Legislation and Jewish Religious Influence on Christians in the Thirteenth Century." Berend et al., pp. 265–76.

Fierro, Maribel, and John Tolan, editors. *The Legal Status of Ḏimmī-s in the Islamic West*. Brepols, 2013.

Mueller, Christian. "Non-Muslims as Part of Islamic Law: Juridical Casuistry in a Fifth/Eleventh-Century Law Manual." *The Legal Status of Ḏimmī-s in the Islamic West*, edited by Maribel Fierro and John Tolan, Brepols, 2013, pp. 21–63.

Sapir Abulafia, Anna. *Christian-Jewish Relations, 1000–1300: Jews in the Service of Medieval Christendom*. Pearson Education Limited, 2011.

Cluse, Christoph, et al., editors. *Jüdische Gemeinden und ihr christlicher Kontext in kulturräumlich vergleichender Betrachtung*. Hahnsche Buchhandlung, 2003.

Goitein, S. D. *The Community*. U of California P, 1971. Vol. 2 of *A Mediterranean Society. The Jewish Communities of the Arab World as Portrayed in the Documents of the Cairo Geniza*.

Servi Camerae

Haverkamp, Alfred. "'Kammerknechtschaft' und 'Bürgerstatus' der Juden diesseits und jenseits der Alpen während des späten Mittelalters." *Die Juden in Schwaben*, edited by Michael Brenner and Sabine Ullmann, Oldenbourg, 2013, pp. 11–40.

Abulafia, David. "The King and the Jews—the Jews in the Ruler's Service." *The Jews of Europe in the Middle Ages (Tenth to Fifteenth Centuries): Proceedings of the International Symposium Held at Speyer, 20–25 October 2002*, edited by Christoph Cluse, Brepols, 2004, pp. 43–54.

Abulafia, David. "The Servitude of Jews and Muslims in the Medieval Mediterranean: Origins and Diffusion." *Mélanges de l'École Française de Rome—Moyen Âge*, vol. 112, 2000, pp. 687–714.

PART 2: GOING TO COURT—JEWS IN FRONT OF JEWISH AND NON-JEWISH COURTS

Jews in the Christian World

Furst, Rachel. "Marriage before the Bench: Divorce Law and Litigation Strategies in Thirteenth-Century Ashkenaz." *Jewish History*, vol. 31, 2017, pp. 7–30.

Roth, Pinchas. "Jewish Courts in Medieval England." *Jewish History*, vol. 31, 2017, pp. 67–82.

Olszowy-Schlanger, Judith. "'Meet you in Court': Legal Practices and Christian-Jewish Relations in the Middle Ages." Buc et al., pp. 333–47.

Baumgarten, Elisheva. "Seeking Signs? Jews, Christians, and Proof by Fire in Medieval Germany and Northern France." Carlebach and Schacter, pp. 205–25.

Jews in the Islamic World

Lieberman, Phillip I. "One Question, Two Answers: Rabbinic Responsa as Legal Advocacy in the Medieval Islamic World." *Jewish History*, vol. 31, 2017, pp. 47–65.

Serrano, Delfina. "*La yajuz li-hukm al-muslimin an yahkum bayna-huma*: Ibn Rushd al-Jadd (Cordoba, d. 1126 CE) and the Restriction on Dhimmis Shopping for Islamic Judicial Forums in al-Andalus." Berend et al., pp. 395–412.

Cohen, Mark R. "Defending Jewish Judicial Autonomy in the Islamic Middle Ages." *Law and Religious Minorities in Medieval Societies: Between Theory and Praxis*, edited by Echevarria et al., Brepols, 2016, pp. 13–33.

Wasserstein, David J. "Straddling the Bounds: Jews in the Legal World of Islam." *Law and Religious Minorities in Medieval Societies: Between Theory and Praxis*, edited by Echevarria et al., Brepols, 2016, pp. 73–80.

Goldish, Matt. *Jewish Questions:* Responsa *on Sephardic Life in the Early Modern Period*. Princeton UP, 2008.

Module 5: Cultural Identity, Religion, and Leadership: Contacts and Communication among Jewish Scholars

Baumgarten, Albert I., and Marina Rustow. "Judaism and Tradition: Continuity, Change, and Innovation." Boustan et al., pp. 207–37.

Goldberg, Sylvie Anne. "In the Path of Our Fathers: On Tradition and Time from Jerusalem to Babylonia and Beyond." Boustan et al., pp. 238–49.

Goldin, Simha. "'Companies of Disciples' and 'Companies of Colleagues': Communication in Jewish Intellectual Circles." Menache, *Communication*, pp. 127–39.

PART 1: BETWEEN ASHKENAZ AND SEPHARAD: NORTHERN AND SOUTHERN EUROPE

Idel, Moshe. "Prophets and Their Impact in the High Middle Ages: A Subculture of Franco-German Jewry." Castaño et al., pp. 285–337.

Kanarfogel, Ephraim. "Between Ashkenaz and Sefarad: Tosafist Teachings in the Talmudic Commentaries of Ritva." *Between Rashi and Maimonides: Themes in Medieval Jewish Thought, Literature and Exegesis*, edited by Kanarfogel and Moshe Sokolow, Yeshiva UP, 2010, pp. 237–73.

Grossman, Avraham. "Communication among Jewish Centers during the Tenth to the Twelfth Centuries." Menache, *Communication*, pp. 107–25.

Grossman, Avraham. "Relations between Spanish and Ashkenazi Jewry in the Middle Ages." *Moreshet Sepharad: The Sephardi Legacy*, edited by Haim Beinart, vol. 1, Magnes Press, 1992, pp. 220–39.

PART 2: BETWEEN BYZANTIUM (ITALY) AND FRANCO-GERMAN JEWISH CULTURE

Mandel, Paul. "The Sacrifice of the Soul of the Righteous upon the Heavenly Altar: Transformations of Apocalyptic Traditions in Medieval Ashkenaz." Castaño et al., pp. 49–72.

Steiner, Richard C. "A Jewish Theory of Biblical Redaction from Byzantium. Its Rabbinic Roots, its Diffusion and its Encounter with the Muslim Doctrine of Falsification." *JSIJ*, vol. 2, 2003, pp. 123–67.

PART 3: THE EAST, THE WEST, AND THE MEDITERRANEAN

Cohen, Mordechai Z. "A New Look at Medieval Jewish Exegetical Constructions of *Peshat* in Christian and Muslim Lands: Rashbam and Maimonides." Castaño et al., pp. 93–121.

Decter, Jonathan. "Mediterranean Regionalism in Hebrew Panegyric Poetry." Castaño et al., pp. 193–219.

Stroumsa, Sarah. *Maimonides in His World: Portrait of a Mediterranean Thinker.* Princeton UP, 2009.

Brody, Robert. *The Geonim of Babylonia and the Shaping of Medieval Jewish Culture.* Yale UP, 1998. Chapter 8, "Ties with the Diaspora," pp. 123–34.

PART 4: BETWEEN MEDIEVAL FRANCE AND GERMANY

Reiner, Avraham [Rami]. "From Rabbenu Tam to R. Isaac of Vienna: The Hegemony of the French Talmudic School in the Twelfth Century." *The Jews of Europe in the Middle Ages (Tenth to Fifteenth Centuries): Proceedings of the International Symposium Held at Speyer, 20–25 October 2002*, edited by Christoph Cluse, Brepols, 2004, pp. 273–82.

Kanarfogel, Ephraim. "From Germany to Northern France and Back Again: A Tale of Two Tosafist Centres." Castaño et al., pp. 149–71.

Kanarfogel, Ephraim. "Ashkenazic Talmudic Interpretation and the Jewish-Christian Encounter." *Medieval Encounters*, vol. 22, 2016, pp. 72–94.
Kanarfogel, Ephraim. *"Peering through the Lattices": Mystical, Magical, and Pietistic Dimensions in the Tosafist Period.* Wayne State UP, 2000.

PART 5: SPAIN, PROVENCE, AND NORTHERN FRANCE

Roth, Pinchas. "Rabbinic Politics, Royal Conquest, and the Creation of a Halakhic Tradition in Medieval Provence." Castaño et al., pp. 173–91.
Mack, Hananel. "The Bifurcated Legacy of Rabbi Moses Hadarshan and the Rise of *Peshat* Exegesis in Medieval France." Castaño et al., pp. 73–91.
Cohen, Mordechai Z. "Nachmanides' Four Senses of Scriptural Signification: Jewish and Christian Contexts." Baumgarten et al., *Entangled Histories*, pp. 38–58.
Reiner, Avraham [Rami]. "Bible and Politics: A Correspondence between Rabbenu Tam and the Authorities of Champagne." Baumgarten et al., *Entangled Histories*, pp. 59–72.

Module 6: Women and Family Life

Kanarfogel, Ephraim. "Rabbinic Conceptions of Marriage and Matchmaking in Christian Europe." Baumgarten et al., *Entangled Histories*, pp. 23–37.
Kaplan, Debra. "'Because Our Wives Trade and Do Business with our Goods': Gender, Work, and Jewish-Christian Relations." Carlebach and Schacter, pp. 241–61.
Goldin, Simha. *Jewish Women in Europe in the Middle Ages: A Quiet Revolution*, Manchester UP, 2011.
Baumgarten, Elisheva. *Mothers and Children: Jewish Family Life in Medieval Europe*, Princeton UP, 2004.
Marcus, Ivan G. *Rituals of Childhood: Jewish Acculturation in Medieval Europe.* Yale UP, 1998.
Goitein, S. D. *The Family.* U of California P, 1978. Vol. 3 of A *Mediterranean Society: The Jewish Communities of the Arab World as Portrayed in the Documents of the Cairo Geniza.*

PURITY

Shahar, Uri. "Pollution and Purity in the Near Eastern Jewish, Christian and Muslim Crusading Rhetoric." Baumgarten et al., *Entangled Histories*, pp. 229–47.
Baumgarten, Elisheva. *Practicing Piety in Medieval Ashkenaz: Men, Women, and Everyday Religious Observance.* U of Pennsylvania P, 2014. Chapter 1, "Standing Before God: Purity and Impurity in the Synagogue," pp. 21–50.
Constable, Olivia Remie. "From Hygiene to Heresy: Changing Perceptions of Women and Bathing in Medieval and Early Modern Iberia." *La cohabitation religieuse dans les villes européennes, Xe-XVe siècles / Religious Cohabitation in European Towns (Tenth–Fifteenth Centuries)*, edited by Stéphane Boissellier and John Tolan, Brepols, 2014, pp. 185–206.
Horowitz, Elliott. "Between Cleanliness and Godliness: Aspects of Jewish Bathing in Medieval and Early Modern Times." Tov Elem*: Memory, Community and Gender in Medieval and Early Modern Jewish Societies: Essays in Honor of Robert*

Bonfil, Bialik Institute and Mandel Institute of Jewish Studies, 2011, pp. 29*–54*.

Module 7: Crossing Boundaries: Converts, Apostates, and Race

PART 1: CONVERTS AND APOSTATES

Tartakoff, Paola. “Conversion and Return to Judaism in High and Late Medieval Europe: Christian Perceptions and Portrayals.” Fox and Yisraeli, pp. 177–94.

Resnick, Irven. “Conversion from the Worst to the Best: The Relationship between Medieval Judaism, Islam, and Christianity.” Fox and Yisraeli, pp. 197–209.

Kanarfogel, Ephraim. “Returning Apostates and Their Marital Partners in Medieval Ashkenaz.” Fox and Yisraeli, pp. 160–76.

Yagur, Moshe. “The Donor and the Gravedigger: Converts to Judaism in the Cairo Geniza Documents.” Fox and Yisraeli, pp. 115–34.

Perry, Craig. “Conversion as an Aspect of Master-Slave Relationships in the Medieval Egyptian Jewish Community.” Fox and Yisraeli, pp. 135–59.

Stocking, Rachel. “Forced Converts, ‘Crypto-Judaism,’ and Children: Religious Identification in Visigoth Spain.” *Jews in Early Christian Law: Byzantium and the Latin West, Sixth–Eleventh Centuries*, edited by John Tolan et al., Brepols, 2014, pp. 243–66.

Domínguez, Oscar Prieto. “The Mass Conversion of Jews Decreed by Emperor Basil I in 873: Its Reflection.” *Jews in Early Christian Law: Byzantium and the Latin West, Sixth–Eleventh Centuries*, edited by John Tolan et al., Brepols, 2014, pp. 283–310.

Kanarfogel, Ephraim. “Changing Attitudes toward Apostates in Tosafist Literature, Late Twelfth–Early Thirteenth Centuries.” Carlebach and Schacter, pp. 297–327.

Schwartz, Yossef. “Images of Revelation and Spaces of Knowledge: The Cross-Cultural Journeys of Iberian Jewry.” *Christian North—Moslem South*, edited by Alexander Fidora and Matthias Tischler, Aschendorff Verlag, 2011, pp. 267–87.

PART 2: CONVERSION AND RACISM

Heng, Geraldine. *England and the Jews: How Religion and Violence Created the First Racial State in the West*. Cambridge UP, 2019.

Heng, Geraldine. *The Invention of Race in the European Middle Ages*. Cambridge UP, 2018. Chapter 1, “Inventions/Reinventions,” pp. 15–54.

Nirenberg, David. “Was there Race Before Modernity? The Example of ‘Jewish Blood’ in Late Medieval Spain.” *The Origins of Racism in the West*, edited by Miriam Eliav-Feldon et al., Cambridge UP, 2009, pp. 232–64.

Nirenberg, David. “Mass Conversion and Genealogical Mentalities: Jews and Christians in Fifteenth-Century Spain.” *Past and Present*, vol. 174, 2002, pp. 3–41.

Module 8: Disputes over Interpretation, Disputations, Polemics

Ben-Shalom, Ram, and Israel Jacob Yuval. “‘There Is No Hatred in Polemics—and Liberty Is Granted.’” *Conflict and Religious Conversation in Latin Christendom: Studies in Honour of Ora Limor*, edited by Israel Jacob Yuval and Ram Ben-Shalom, Brepols, 2014, pp. 1–22.

Ragacs, Ursula. "Christian-Jewish or Jewish-Jewish, That's My Question." *European Journal of Jewish Studies*, vol. 5, 2011, pp. 93–114.

CHRISTIANS AGAINST JEWS

Capelli, Piero. "Jewish Converts in Jewish-Christian Intellectual Polemics in the Middle Ages." *Intricate Interfaith Networks in the Middle Ages: Quotidian Jewish-Christian Contacts*, edited by Ephraim Shoham-Steiner, Brepols, 2016, pp. 33–83.

Sapir Abulafia, Anna. *Christian and Jews in the Twelfth-Century Renaissance.* Routledge, 1995.

Chazan, Robert. *Barcelona Beyond: The Disputation of 1263 and Its Aftermath.* U of California P, 1992.

Maccoby, Hyam. *Judaism on Trial: Jewish-Christian Disputations in the Middle Ages.* Fairleigh Dickinson UP, 1982.

JEWS AGAINST CHRISTIANS

Grossman, Avraham. "Rashi's Position on Prophecy among the Nations and the Jewish-Christian Polemic." Carlebach and Schacter, pp. 399–417.

Lasker, Daniel J. *Jewish Philosophical Polemics against Christianity in the Middle Ages.* Littman Library of Jewish Civilization, 2007.

Trautner-Kromann, Hanne. *Shield and Sword: Jewish Polemics against Christianity and the Christians in France and Spain from 1100–1500.* Mohr Siebeck, 1993.

PART 1: AT THE TURN OF THE JEWISH MILLENIUM (1240) IN EUROPE: POLEMICS, THREATS AGAINST JEWS AND THE TALMUD, RITUAL MURDER ACCUSATION, THE MONGOLS, MESSIANISM, AND IMMIGRATION TO THE LAND OF ISRAEL

Heng, Geraldine. *The Invention of Race in the European Middle Ages.* Cambridge UP, 2018. Chapter 6, "The Mongol Empire: Global Race as Absolute Power," pp. 287–416.

Tolan, John. "Royal Policy and Conversion of Jews to Christianity in Thirteenth-Century Europe." Fox and Yisraeli, pp. 96–111.

Capelli, Piero. "Nicolas Donin, the Talmud Trial of 1240, and the Struggles between Church and State in Medieval Europe." Baumgarten et al., *Entangled Histories*, pp. 159–78.

Galinsky, Judah. "The Different Hebrew Versions of the 'Talmud Trial' of 1240 in Paris." Carlebach and Schacter, pp. 109–40.

Limor, Ora, "Polemical Varieties: Religious Disputations in 13th Century Spain." *Iberia Judaica*, vol. 2, 2010, pp. 55–79.

Yuval, Israel Jacob. *Two Nations in Your Womb: Perceptions of Jews and Christians in Late Antiquity and the Middle Ages.* U of California P, 2006. Chapter 6, "The End of the Millenium (1240)," pp. 257–96.

Kanarfogel, Ephraim. "The 'Aliyah of 'Three Hundred Rabbis' in 1211: Tosafist Attitudes toward Settling in the Land of Israel." *The Jewish Quarterly Review*, vol. 76, 1986, pp. 191–215.

PART 2: POLEMICS AGAINST CHRISTIANS AND JEWS AROUND 1400

Žonca, Milan. "The 'Imagined Communities' of Yom Tov Lipmann Muehlhausen: Heresy and Communal Boundaries in Sefer Niẓẓaḥon." *The Jews of Europe around 1400: Disruption, Crisis, and Resilience*, edited by Lukas Clemens and Christoph Cluse, Harrassowitz, 2018, pp. 119–43.

Limor, Ora, and Israel Yuval. "Scepticism and Conversion: Jews, Christians, and Doubters in 'Sefer Ha-Nizzahon.'" Hebraica veritas? *Christian Hebraists and the Study of Judaism in Early Modern Europe*, edited by Allison Coudert and Jeffrey S. Shoulson, U of Pennsylvania P, 2004, pp. 159–90.

Module 9: Liturgy

Kanarfogel, Ephraim. "Prayer, Literacy, and Literary Memory in the Jewish Communities of Medieval Europe." Boustan et al., pp. 250–70.

PART 1: LITURGICAL PRAYERS, MARTYRDOM, AND THEIR TALES: "ALENU LE-SHABEAH" AND "UNETANE TOKEF"—FROM PALESTINE TO ASHKENAZ

Gross, Abraham. "Liturgy as Personal Memorial for the Victims in 1096." *Death in Jewish Life: Burial and Mourning Customs among Jews of Europe and Nearby Communities*, edited by Stefan C. Reif et al., De Gruyter, 2014, pp. 155–70.

Langer, Ruth. "The Censorship of Aleinu in Ashkenaz and Its Aftermath." *The Experience of Jewish Liturgy. Studies Dedicated to Menahem Schmelzer*, edited by Debra Reed Blank, Brill, 2011, pp. 147–66.

Kimelman, Reuven. "*U-n'taneh Tokef* as a Midrashic Poem." *The Experience of Jewish Liturgy. Studies Dedicated to Menahem Schmelzer*, edited by Debra Reed Blank, Brill, 2011, pp. 115–46.

Yuval, Israel Jacob. *Two Nations in Your Womb: Perceptions of Jews and Christians in Late Antiquity and the Middle Ages.* U of California P, 2006, pp. 192–202.

Yuval, Israel Jacob. "The Silence of the Historian and the Ingenuity of the Storyteller: Rabbi Amnon of Mayence and Esther Minna of Worms." *Common Knowledge*, vol. 9, 2003, pp. 228–40.

PART 2: LITURGICAL POEMS: FROM SEPHARAD TO ASHKENAZ

Hollender, Elisabeth. "Attraction and Attribution: Framings of Sephardi Identity in Ashkenazi Prayer Books." Castaño et al., pp. 221–39.

Dealings with Christianity in Jewish Liturgy

Langer, Ruth. *Cursing the Christians? A History of the Birkat Haminim.* Oxford UP, 2011.

Poetry and Martyrdom

Einbinder, Susan L. *Beautiful Death: Jewish Poetry and Martyrdom in Medieval France.* Princeton UP, 2002.

Module 10: Communication through Letters

Goldberg, Jessica L. *Trade and Institutions in the Medieval Mediterranean: The Geniza Merchants and their Business World.* Cambridge UP, 2012. Chapter 3, "Merchants in Their Community," pp. 56–92; and chapter 7, "The Geography of Information," pp. 187–210.

Goldberg, Jessica L. "The Use and Abuse of Commercial Letters from the Cairo Geniza." *Journal of Medieval History*, vol. 38, 2012, pp. 127–54.

Carlebach, Elisheva. "Letter into Text. Epistolarity, History, and Literature." *Jewish Literature and History: An Interdisciplinary Conversation*, edited by Eliyana R. Adler and Sheila E. Jelen, UP of Maryland, 2008, pp. 113–33.

Goitein, S. D., and Mordechai A. Friedman. *India Traders of the Middle Ages: Documents from the Cairo Geniza ("India Book").* Brill, 2008.

Cohen, Mark R. "On the Interplay of Arabic and Hebrew in the Cairo Geniza Letters." *Studies in Arabic and Hebrew Letters: In Honor of Raymond R. Scheindlin*, edited by Jonathan P. Decter and Michael Rand, Gorgias Press, 2007, pp. 17–35.

Gil, Moshe. "The Flax Trade in the Mediterranean in the Eleventh Century A.D., as Seen in Merchants' Letters from the Cairo Geniza." *Near Eastern Studies*, vol. 63, 2004, pp. 81–96.

Gertwagen, Ruthi. "Geniza Letters: Maritime Difficulties along the Alexandria-Palermo Route." Menache, *Communication*, pp. 73–91.

Grabois, Aryeh. "The Use of Letters as a Communication Medium among Medieval European Jewish Communities." Menache, *Communication*, pp. 93–105.

Goitein, S. D. *Letters of Medieval Jewish Traders.* Princeton UP, 1973.

Module 11: Jewish Historiography (Knowledge about the Other and Collective Memory)

Haverkamp, Eva. "Historiography." *The Middle Ages: The Christian World*, edited by Robert Chazan, Cambridge UP, 2018, pp. 836–59. Vol. 6 of *The Cambridge History of Judaism.*

Ben-Shalom, Ram. *Medieval Jews and the Christian Past: Jewish Historical Consciousness in Spain and Southern France.* Littman Library of Jewish Civilization, 2016. Especially chapter 1, "Genres and Motives," pp. 13–63.

PART I: TRANSCULTURAL KNOWLEDGE

Ben-Shalom, Ram. *Medieval Jews and the Christian Past: Jewish Historical Consciousness in Spain and Southern France.* Littman Library of Jewish Civilization, 2016. Chapter 5, "History of the Iberian Monarchies," pp. 177–238.

Decter, Jonathan P. *Iberian Jewish Literature: Between al-Andalus and Christian Europe.* Indiana UP, 2007. Chapter 4, "Context: Imagining Hebrew Fiction between Arabic and European Sources," pp. 99–124.

Jacobs, Martin. *Islamische Geschichte in juedischen Chroniken: Hebraeische Historiographie des 16. und 17. Jahrhunderts.* Mohr Siebeck, 2004. Chapter 6, "Ha-Kohens Darstellung islamischer Geschichte," pp. 128–220 (about the author and his work, see also pp. 82–108).

PART 2: HISTORIOGRAPHY, MARTYROLOGY, AND HAGIOGRAPHY

Barzilay, Tzafrir. "Retelling the Crusaders' Defeat in Hungary: Cultural Contact between Jewish and Christian Chroniclers." *Jewish History*, vol. 31, 2018, pp. 173–96.

Einbinder, Susan. "A Death in Wisdom's Court: Poetry and Martyrdom in Thirteenth-Century Castile." *Christianity and Culture in the Middle Ages: Essays in Honor John van Engen*, edited by David C. Mengel and Lisa Wolverton, U of Notre Dame P, 2015, pp. 253–79.

Haverkamp, Eva. "Martyrs in Rivalry: The 1096 Jewish Martyrs and the Thebean Legion." *Jewish History*, vol. 23, 2009, pp. 319–42.

Raspe, Lucia. *Juedische Hagiographie im mittelalterlichen Aschkenas.* Mohr Siebeck, 2006. Chapter 5, "Schimon von Mainz und der juedische Papst," pp. 242–322.

Module 12: Travel to the East: Benjamin of Tudela

Raspe, Lucia. "'The Lord Was with Them, and They Were Not Found Out': Jews, Christians, and the Veneration of Saints in Medieval Ashkenaz." *Jewish History*, vol. 30, 2016, pp. 43–59.

Jacobs, Martin. *Reorienting the East: Jewish Travelers to the Medieval Muslim World.* U of Pennsylvania P, 2014.

Raspe, Lucia. "Sacred Space, Local History, and Diasporic Identity: The Graves of the Righteous in Medieval and Early Modern Ashkenaz." Boustan et al., pp. 147–63.

Shoham-Steiner, Ephraim. "Jews and Healing at Medieval Saints' Shrines: Participation, Polemics, and Shared Cultures." *HTR*, vol. 103, 2010, pp. 111–29.

Reiner, Elchanan. "A Jewish Response to the Crusades." Juden und Christen zur Zeit der Kreuzzüge, edited by Alfred Haverkamp, Jan Thorbecke Verlag, 1999, pp. 209–22.

Jacoby, David. "Benjamin of Tudela in Byzantium." *Palaeoslavica*, vol. 10, 2002, pp. 180–85.

Shatzmiller, Joseph. "Jews, Pilgrimage, and the Christian Cult of Saints: Benjamin of Tudela and His Contemporaries." *After Rome's Fall: Narrators and Sources of Early Medieval History: Essays Presented to Walter Goffart*, edited by Alexander Callander Murray, U of Toronto P, 1998, pp. 337–47.

The Itinerary of Benjamin of Tudela: Travels in the Middle Age. Joseph Simon / Pangloss Press, 1983.

Part III

Habitus: Mapping, Environments, Disease, Animals

Asa Simon Mittman, Karen Pinto, and Cordell D. K. Yee

Mapping the Worlds of the Global Middle Ages

Maps are amalgams of words and images, of history, myth, and religion, of art and science—and as such, they highlight the arbitrary divisions we have created between modern disciplines that have little or no relevance to the study of medieval artifacts. Maps therefore can be of great use in courses across many disciplines. Two of us have been using old maps in our teaching for many years and have found that they provoke some of the richest class discussions each semester. Maps are gripping, consuming things; they draw us in, orient us in space and time, invite us to explore their extents, and create whole worlds anew.

We wish to place particular stress on the value of teaching cartographic materials in the context of the effort to engage with a global Middle Ages. For this important project, maps are obvious, appropriate, and highly effective pedagogic tools. If we wish to understand what a global Middle Ages might mean, one place we could start is with our subjects' understanding of what the globe looked like (Yee, "Chinese Cartography," "Chinese Maps," "Reinterpreting," "Taking," "Traditional Chinese Cartography"; Pinto, *Medieval Islamic Maps*, "Capturing Imagination," "Fit for an Umayyad Prince," "In God's Eyes," "Interpretation," "It's a Bird,"

“Passion and Conflict,” “Searchin’ His Eyes,” “Surat Bahr al-Rum,” “Maps”; Mittman, “Mapping Global Middle Ages”). Many of the myriad cultures that coexisted throughout the world in the era loosely gathered under the Eurocentric rubric of the “Middle Ages” had their own mapping traditions and conventions, some in dialogue with one another and others wholly separate. We will here focus on only three cultures—China, the Islamicate world, and Christian Europe—so we can only gesture toward the potentiality of this material here, but eventually we hope to explore the power of medieval maps in greater detail and with more geohistorical breadth in our next collaborative undertaking.

Reorientation

In the spring of 2019, Karen Pinto and Asa Simon Mittman tested the possibilities of teaching across traditional boundaries through maps. Mittman always includes a unit of medieval cartography in his medieval art survey course, but had only covered European Christian maps—indeed, really only English and French Christian maps. Mittman is currently undertaking an effort to globalize this unit en route to a new, semester-long course called Global Medieval Worldviews. As a first tentative step in this direction, he invited Pinto to Skype into his course after a week in which students examined Christian mapping, with a focus on T-O maps, and the Psalter (circa 1265, London) and Hereford (circa 1305, Hereford) maps.

Pinto brought to the class a series of Islamic maps that served several purposes. First and foremost, they are important and interesting in their own right. Second, they expanded the scope of this unit and therefore of the course as a whole. Third, and most potent, they inspired a reorientation of the course in a way that lasted throughout the semester. In the most literal sense, medieval Islamic maps are, in general, oriented differently than Christian ones. Whereas Christian maps are usually oriented to the east (toward the so-called Orient), Islamic maps are usually oriented to the south. This is the most obvious but far from the only difference. (Pinto, *Medieval Islamic Maps;* “Capturing Imagination,” “Fit for an Umayyad Prince,” “In God’s Eyes,” “Interpretation,” “It’s a Bird,” “Passion and Conflict,” “Searchin’ His Eyes,” “Surat Bahr al-Rum,” “Maps”).

In confronting medieval Christian maps, students must first adjust themselves to the eastern orientation. Many tilt their heads to the left while looking at the screen, and squint a bit, before seeming to become again comfortable, as if they have found again the world they know. When we presented them with medieval Islamic maps, the students again tilted, squinted, and eventually settled into the new conventions. What they achieved, in each case, however, was a false sense of comfort; medieval maps do not present the world we know today, not only because the world has changed so much but also because maps do not show the world as it is. As Denis Wood writes, "There is nothing natural about a map. It is a cultural artifact, a cumulation of choices made among choices every one of which reveals a value: Not the world, but a slice of a piece of the world; not nature but a slant on it; not innocent, but loaded with intentions and purposes; . . . not, in a word, as it is" (*Rethinking* 108). What we see, then, when we look at maps—including the most current maps produced with the latest satellite and GIS (geographic information system) technology—is not the world but the worldview of the map's creators. Each time we disorient students, we reveal anew the ideological underpinnings of our own maps, and in so doing, reveal some of the ideological underpinnings of our current historical and political moment.

A Brief Social History of Cartography

For much of the twentieth century, historians of cartography were concerned with movement toward greater mimesis (imitation of the real world), with demonstrating progress toward greater purported accuracy, and therefore saw early maps as crude and later maps as superior. The critical cartography movement shifted the focus of the discipline by suggesting that scholars should evaluate each period and each map on its own merits, based on the goals of its creators. J. Brian Harley was the generative figure in this movement (Edney; Wood, "Deconstructing"; Terkla), and the multivolume landmark *The History of Cartography* series he edited with David Woodward (begun in 1987 and ongoing with new editors) remains the field standard.

Harley drew from "information-theory, linguistics, semiotics, structuralism, phenomenology, developmental theory, hermeneutics, iconology, Marxism, and ideology" (Andrews 2). J. H. Andrews sums up the "positivist" school of cartographic thought that Harley challenged as "maintain[ing] that cartography can be, and usually is, objective, detached, neutral (in all disputes except that between truth and falsehood), and transparent . . . [and] can be exact and accurate" (5). Harley, instead, advocated for "a social history of cartography" (Harley 1), a "nonpositivist alternative [that] entails looking not through the map at the world it depicts but inwards or backwards to its maker and outwards or forwards to its readers" (Andrews 6).

How to Read a Map

Before proceeding, we should try to define the key term in play here: what is a map? Harley and Woodward "adopted an entirely new definition of 'map,' one that is neither too restrictive nor yet so general as to be meaningless . . . Maps are graphic representations that facilitate a spatial understanding of things, concepts, conditions, processes, or events in the human world" (xvi). Responding to Harley and Woodward, David Turnbull offers two important refinements: "Firstly, maps are *selective*: they do not, and cannot, display all there is to know about any given piece of the environment. Secondly, if they are to be maps at all they must directly represent at least *some* aspects of the landscape" (3).

The process of analyzing a map is deeply aligned with the process of close visual analysis used in art history. Maps rely on all the same formal and compositional elements as any other visual material. In looking at a map, we can consider any of the following: material support, size, scale, orientation, centering, borders, colors, languages, scripts, symbols, visual hierarchy, and the vital choices underlying inclusions and exclusions. Turnbull reminds us: "the mapmaker determines what *is*, and equally importantly, what is *not* included" (5; emphasis in original). Whether or not a mapmaker deliberately considers each of these choices (e.g., Should rivers appear? If so, what color should they be painted? Should they be labeled, and if so, in what language, in what script?) or whether the mapmaker is merely reproducing what seems to be standard conventions, these remain choices with important consequences, both for the map and for the territories it describes. ("Cartography Guide" provides a more extensive series of considerations for the cartographer.)

As Turnbull argues, "The map, if it is to have authority . . . , must have the appearance of 'artless-ness'; that is, it must appear simply to exhibit the landscape, rather than describe it with artifice or in accordance with the perceived interests of the mapmaker" (8). Propaganda is more effective when it is not clearly positioned as such, and all the more so when it hides under the guise of something like scientific neutrality (less operative in the Middle Ages than after, perhaps) or religious authority (omnipresent in Christian maps of the period). Turnbull continues, "The power of maps lies not merely in their accuracy or their correspondence with reality.

It lies in their having incorporated a set of conventions that make this combinable in one central place, enabling the accumulation of both power and knowledge at its center" (26).

Preconceived Notions of Maps

Pinto has developed a useful exercise for her history of cartography courses. She asks her students to make a map—any map they choose—and gives them thirty minutes. They place their maps on a common table and students pick one another's maps to discuss without knowing whose they are, attempting to figure out the intention of the cartographer. After presenting their readings, the students who made the maps reveal themselves and discuss the deductions of their peers. This exercise is crucial for an introductory course on the history of cartography because most students come with the typical modern map of the world, with the United States of America in the middle, emblazoned in their minds.

On the first day of history of cartography courses, Pinto uses another exercise to help students understand Islamic world maps that would be helpful in grappling with many forms of premodern mapping. Since Islamic maps (like most medieval Christian maps and some medieval Chinese maps) do not point in the usual northerly direction of most modern maps, Pinto asks students to turn all maps that they consult to face any direction but north. She recommends that they pin up paper maps on their walls oriented in different directions in order to learn to see the world in anything but a northerly direction. This is a key entry-level exercise for being able to understand medieval maps from around the globe. Exercises like these help students to break out of their world views and learn the basics of map analysis, which they can build on through the course. It makes them more open and receptive to medieval maps that initially look very strange to their eyes. It takes work to coax students into understanding and appreciating all the amazing things premodern maps have to tell us.

Most discussions of medieval cartography are studies limited to medieval Christian cartography (though they are rarely framed as such). To foster a broader perspective on global medieval mapping, we decided to alter the usual order and begin with Chinese mapping instead, continue with Islamicate mapping, and end with medieval European mapping. Mapping in the Chinese tradition presents a variety of practices and ways of engaging with the world: mimetic, nonmimetic, quantified, nonquantified, linguistic, nonlinguistic, emotive, and nonemotive. The section on Chinese mapping is followed by one on maps of the Islamicate world, which begins in the shadows of the seventh-century Arab lightning conquests and comes into early contact with the Chinese mapping tradition and adopts and adapts elements of it to create the *Kitāb al-masālik wa-al-mamālik* (*Book of Routes and Realms*)—shorthand KMMS mapping tradition—which is used with the accompanying geographical text to administer the gigantic and far-flung Islamic Caliphate of the Middle Ages. It is through the Muslims that Europe acquired a hybrid, global carto-geographical tradition of Chinese origin bundled with the paper to make them ubiquitous. This transfer of technology broadened Christian mapmaking so that alongside seemingly simple Isidorean T-O maps more detailed *mappaemundi* types flourished, especially as the onset of the Crusades gave their creators and audiences a view of the world with greater detail. It was the richness of detail, along with the technological advances in shipbuilding that the Crusades inspired, that led to active Christian (especially Italian) exploration of the Mediterranean. Inspired by the development of *mappaemundi*, mapmakers began charting the coast of the Mediterranean, creating the genre of isolarii, thereby stimulating further maritime exploration that culminated in a Renaissance in cartography with more and more mimetic maps. It thus seems fitting to end our account with a description of medieval European mapping, which actually belongs at the end of the medieval story about mapping, though it has been customary to address it first.

The Story of the Stone: The Middle Kingdom in the Middle?

Two of the most famous Chinese maps are carved on opposite sides of the same stone slab. One is the *Yu ji tu* (*Map of the Tracks of Yu* [a legendary emperor], from 1136). What attracts interest is the square scaling grid superimposed on this map of China (fig. 1). Each grid increment represents one hundred Chinese miles. Geographic space thus seems to have been mathematized. In large part because of this map, Chinese mapmaking during the global Middle Ages has been regarded as moving toward modern cartography. Thus, it might at first seem that China is out of place in an account of medieval cartography.

The map on the other side of the stone on which the *Yu ji tu* is engraved alters that potential counternarrative somewhat (fig. 2). This map bears the title, *Hua yi tu* (*Map of China and Barbarian Lands*; from 1136). Unlike its companion, the *Hua yi tu* does not have a scaling grid. It represents more topographic features but in some ways seems more general-

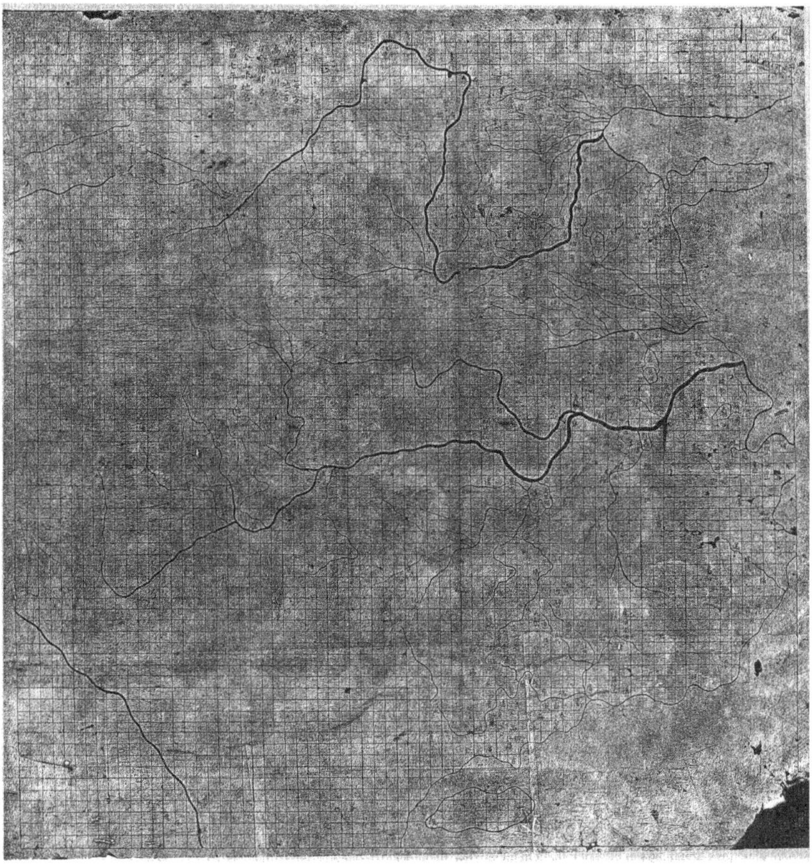

Figure 1. *Yu ji tu (Map of the Tracks of Yu).* A reversed image of an ink rubbing at the Library of Congress. North is at the top. Courtesy of the Geography and Map Division, Library of Congress, Washington, DC, G7821.C3 1136 .Y81, loc.gov/item/gm71005080.

ized than its companion map. The line representing the coastline, for example, is not as nuanced. It also does not bear an expressed scale (Cao, vol. 1; Harley and Woodward, *Cartography in the Traditional East and Southeast Asian Societies*).

The two maps are often classed as Chinese world maps. *World* here should be understood in a somewhat restricted sense. In the context of the global Middle Ages, the notion of a Chinese world map should be separated from that of a globe. For Chinese mapmakers, the earth was not a sphere: they generally treated the earth as flat or perhaps with a curve so

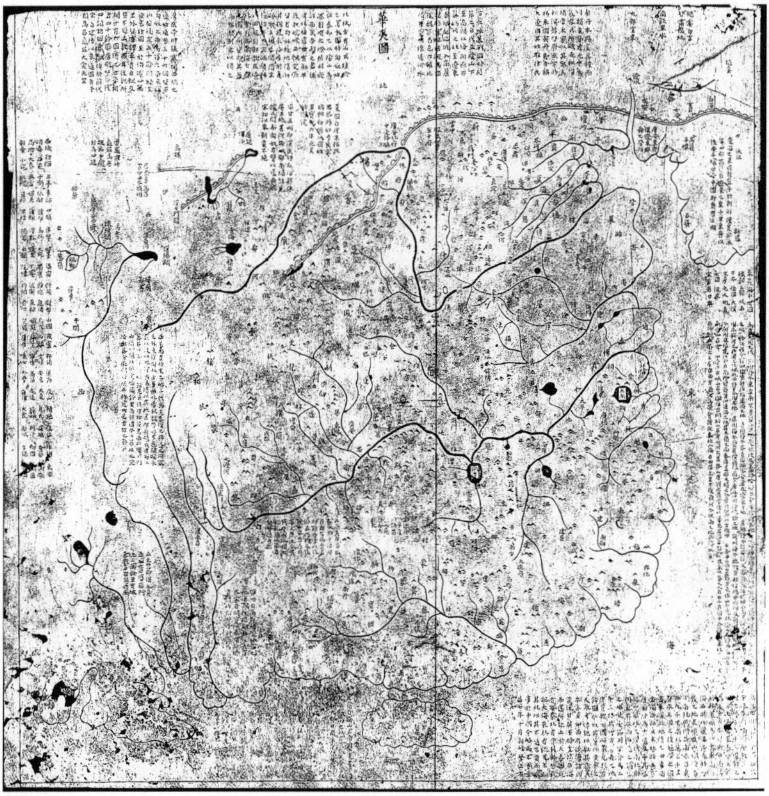

Figure 2. *Hua yi tu (Map of China and Barbarian Lands).* A reversed image of an ink rubbing at the Library of Congress. North is at the top. Courtesy of the Geography and Map Division, Library of Congress, Washington, DC, G7820 1136 .H81, loc.gov/item/gm71005081.

slight that representing the earth's surface on a flat sheet would not result in much distortion. They did not have a clear conception of the earth's dimensions. The boundaries of the *Yu ji tu* and *Hua yi tu* may not have corresponded to notions about the limits of the earth. Nevertheless, the territory shown on these two maps represents much less of the earth's surface than appears even in earlier Western geographic works, such as Ptolemy's *Geography.*

The two maps are oriented in opposite directions on the stone on which they appear, suggesting they were not meant for display. Instead, engraved intaglio, they served as the originals of copies made by ink rubbing. That the stone engravings were used to produce copies serves as a reminder that for at least part of the global Middle Ages, printing was already in use.

Beyond its lack of an expressed scale, the *Hua yi tu* differs from the *Yu ji tu* in being heavily annotated. On Chinese maps before the twentieth century, the image was generally not the primary bearer of quantitative information, such as direction and distance. More often such information was contained in accompanying text. Focus on maps like the *Yu ji tu*, however, has contributed to a general disregard for nonmathematized maps. Taking the nonmathematical seriously would detract from a narrative that has modern cartography as its end (e.g., Needham). The popularity of that narrative belies the much greater number of nonmathematical maps among the extant body of works. Such maps lack a scaling grid or an expressed scale, and their directional orientation may be inconsistent. Instead of abstraction, their mode of representation tends toward the pictorial.

As an example, we shall consider the *Shu chuan tu* (*Map of the Shu River*), which dates perhaps to the early thirteenth century, drawn in ink on six sheets of paper mounted on silk to form a handscroll. It depicts the courses of two waterways in Sichuan. From right to left, the first three sheets show the north-south stretch of the Min River from Maozhou to Meishan (circa 200 km). The second three sheets show the Yangzi River from east to west, from Zhongzhou to the Diaoshi Rapids (circa 200 km). Between the two sections, there is a gap representing the roughly two-hundred-kilometer stretch from Jiazhou to Fengdu (Documentation on the *Shu chuan tu* 35n2).

Along the waterways, the names of 189 places—mountains, caves, administrative seats, and temples—are listed. The map does not have an expressed scale, so one cannot read distances from the image. Since text was the primary carrier of such information, some distances between places are noted on the map.

Despite the lack of an expressed scale, the rough equality between the lengths of the waterways and between the length of their representations (376.0 cm and 377.5 cm) suggests the mapmaker paid some attention to actual physical geography. The order of the places named lines up with geographic fact, and some of the inscriptions cite geographic works. Some inscriptions note changes in toponyms (place-names) in accord with practices of historical geography.

Directional orientation is not consistent across the length of the map. The straightness of the scroll suppresses a change of direction in the waterways, from north toward the right to north toward the top. In addition, the uniformity in the height of the scroll limits the variation in width across the water that can be depicted.

Unlike the *Hua yi tu* and *Yu ji tu*, the *Shu chuan tu* is not meant to be seen whole with a single look. In order to see it in its entirety, one would have to unroll it and then step back to the point where the work would appear to be a long band, represented here as a rectangle to suggest the work's proportions (fig. 3). One would be unable to discern much of the detail shown on the map, which has been executed in the manner of landscape paintings: landforms and architectural elements are represented in a pictorial manner (figs. 4–6). To view the map as intended, one would scroll through the map section by section, as if one were moving alongside the water and viewing the scenery. Looking at the map would thus be a way of simulating a journey along the waterways. The Qianlong emperor was moved to inscribe on the work:

> 尋丈間有萬里之勢, 脱盡筆墨痕, 与造物者游矣.
>
> . . . in the space between a span and ten feet, there are ten thousand miles of scenery; one completely casts off the marks of brush and ink, and roams with the maker of things.
>
> (our trans.)

The emperor also inscribed the poetic sequence "Autumn Meditations," by Du Fu (712–70), who once lived near the Min River in Chengdu. Among the verses are these two lines that describe a river scene and evoke the dynamism that is lost in a still picture:

> 江間波浪兼天湧,
> 塞上風雲接地陰.
> In the River waves join the frothing skies;
> Above the passes, wind and clouds touch the
> shadows on the ground.
>
> (our trans.)

The toponyms not only serve to identify places but also are themselves a display of artistic skill. An inscription by the artist Dong Qichang (1555–1636) praises the "calligraphy fine as a fly's head" (蠅頭細書), the "small characters written as if they were large" (小字如大字).

The inscriptions serve in part to record readers interacting with and contributing to the work. They show the work was appreciated as the site of three arts: painting, poetry, and calligraphy, known as the "three perfections" (三絕). As such, the work also achieves a temporal unity going beyond the global Middle Ages and spanning ten centuries: poetry from

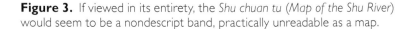

Figure 3. If viewed in its entirety, the *Shu chuan tu (Map of the Shu River)* would seem to be a nondescript band, practically unreadable as a map.

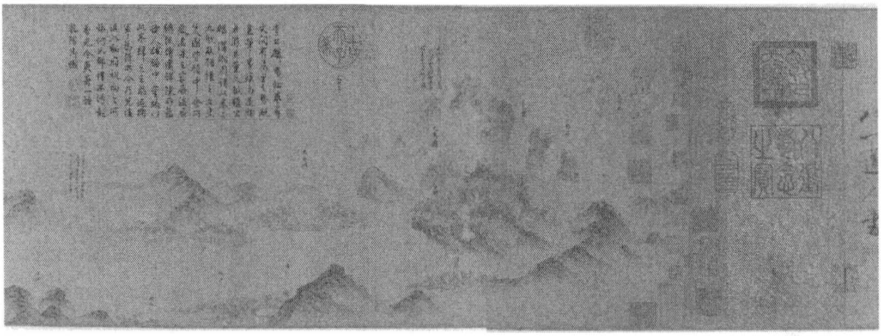

Figure 4. Opening section of the *Shu chuan tu*. Shows a part of the Min River, with an inscription by the Qianlong emperor (detail). Freer Gallery of Art, Smithsonian Institution, Washington, DC, gift of Charles Lang Freer, F1916.539.

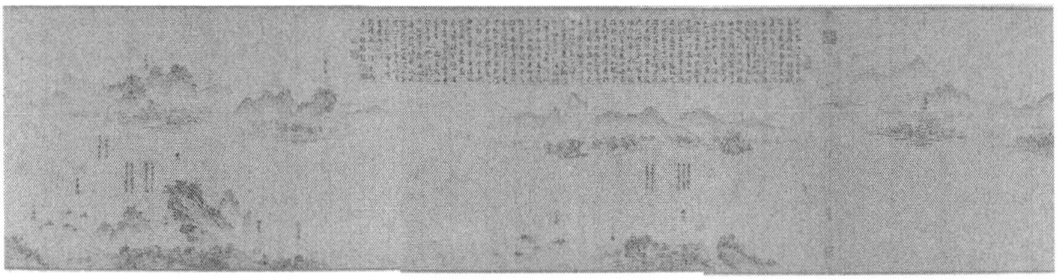

Figure 5. Section of the *Shu chuan tu*. Shows a part of the Yangzi River, with an inscription by the Qianlong emperor (detail). Freer Gallery of Art, Smithsonian Institution, Washington, DC, gift of Charles Lang Freer, F1916.539.

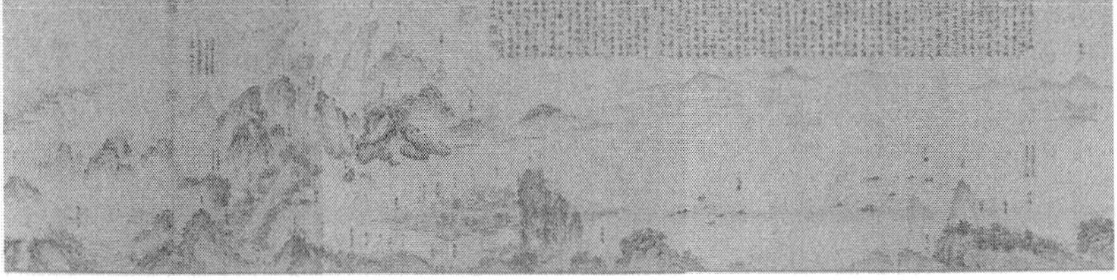

Figure 6. Section of the *Shu chuan tu*. Shows a part of the Yangzi River, with an inscription by the Qianlong emperor (detail). Freer Gallery of Art, Smithsonian Institution, Washington, DC, gift of Charles Lang Freer, F1916.539.

the eighth century, painting from the thirteenth century, and script from the eighteenth century. When one tries to take in the map as a whole in a single look, one loses sight of its perfections and unity. The whole is in some ways less than the sum of the parts.

The extant maps from the twelfth through the nineteenth centuries do not suggest a mathematical tradition but a movement away from the mathematical (Woodward et al. 172–73). An emphasis on the mathematization of space, on horizontal linear distances, leads to a falsification. The result is an impression of homogeneity, even a lack of features of interest. Faced with the nonmathematical, those seeking to mathematize Chinese mapmaking deny that works like the *Shu chuan tu* are maps, arguing that maps have practical uses and paintings have artistic intent (Hu 48). The toponyms and notes on distances on works like the *Shu chuan tu*, however, indicate they were intended at least in part to serve as geographic references. Otherwise, there would be no need to provide such information. In addition, it is not clear why artistic intent disqualifies a work from maphood, and it is clear that maps from all the cultures represented in this essay were products of artistic intent. It is not difficult to conceive of practical purposes for an attempt to convey the appearance of a place or region.

From Chinese mapmaking, one can begin to see that the global Middle Ages is not simply an incipient global modernity. Maps like the *Shu chuan tu*, made centuries after the invention of printing, suggest the resilience of the practices of manuscript culture. If there was a print revolution in China, it proceeded more slowly than the one that marked the end of the Middle Ages in Europe. In addition, instead of looking forward to modern cartography, much of Chinese mapmaking looks back to Ptolemy's *Geography*. There, *geography*, the making of maps of large areas, is distinguished from *chorography*, a type of mapmaking that focuses on smaller areas and requires the skills of a painter. The maps with which our treatment of China began, the *Hua yi tu* and *Yu ji tu*, are often read as leading outward toward the edges and beyond, as if in anticipation of expanded foreign contacts and further imperial expansion. The prominence of rivers on the two maps, however, directs one inward to riverscapes such as those shown on the *Shu chuan tu*. There are worlds worth exploring there as well.

Medieval Islamicate Cartography

From the eleventh century onward, many maps survive from the medieval Islamicate world comprising Islamic Caliphates governing a hybrid, transcultural body of peoples (this section is based on Pinto, *Medieval Islamic Maps* 1–2, 59–66). Developed originally sometime in the seventh or eighth century, maps showing the shape and organization of the world—and especially that of Islamic regions—were used by medieval Islamicates composed of a hybrid of Muslims, Christians, Jews, Hindus, Buddhists, Tibetans, and Africans. The Islamicate maps were thus born of an intense hybridity of transcultural traditions, which are reflected in their maps (Pinto, *Medieval Islamic Maps*). They became a cultural cornerstone of the Muslim rulers translating from Arabic to Persian as the primary language of the rulers changed and eventually Turkic. In fact, it is through the incredible artistic influences of the Mongols and Turks who brought with them both a nomadic form of mapping and a formal administrative form through the Middle Kingdom that the painting of Islamicate maps improved in leaps and bounds.

Scoffing at the exactitude of uneven coasts (because they did not have sophisticated telescopes with which to stare back at the earth as we do now through satellites), the Islamicate maps employ deliberately stylized images made up of a series of curious geometric shapes that look like birds, eyes, fingers, shoe prints—to signify the earth. Arabia as the head of a bird, Asia as its body, Europe as its tail, all protected under the generous overarching protective wing of Africa, oriented with South on top (Pinto, "It's a Bird"). In doing so, medieval Islamicate maps tapped into a crucial greater Mediterranean medieval belief, best preserved in the anonymous *Ad Herrenium*, that to be able to transport an image in one's memory one had to relate it to a form that one could remember easily, which explains why these maps continued to be copied in manuscripts in the Islamic world well into the nineteenth century. That and the cosmographic symbolism with which they came to be associated (Pinto, "In God's Eyes").

Thus, the world in the form of a bird could have been transported easily by all conquerors, soldiers, traders, and travelers in their heads as an approximate layout of the world and the specific province in which they found themselves (Pinto, "It's a Bird"). Straddling the nexus point of the Old World, the Muslims were able to avail themselves of a multitude of earlier mapping traditions. Over the course of eleven centuries from the rise of Islam in the seventh century and the lightning Arab conquests following the death of the Prophet Muhammad in 632 CE to trade and military contacts with the Chinese and the coming of the Turkic tribes, Mongols, and eventually the Ottoman Empire, scholars in the medieval Islamicate world honed their interests and skills in mapping the world.

They were among the chief conquerors, traders, travelers of the medieval world that transmitted back to Europe many advantageous inventions from the Chinese, such as paper and maps, that Islamicate scholars generously shared with Europe, never thinking of establishing copyrights. Europe was able to use these inventions to propel itself into the Renaissance and onto a new stage of knowledge and skills.

Instead of attempting to produce an image of the world as it is, to convey the shape of landforms and waterways as they actually are, stylized images function as mnemonic and contemplative devices that help the viewer understand the world, which involves more than just the world's outward form. A world map from a late twelfth-century copy of al-Iṣṭakhrī's *Kitāb al-masālik wa-al-mamālik* (*Book of Routes and Realms*) made in late Arabo-Norman Sicily, and possibly browsed by the emperor Frederick II in his youth (Pinto, "Interpretation"), provides a good example (fig. 7). Within the encircling ocean, the world is geometric, with compass-drawn circles of red, blue, and gold. To see how this can even be a map, we will first look at a slightly simpler example, another al-

Figure 7. "Ṣūrat al-Arḍ" ("Picture of the World"). Siculo-Norman, 589/1193, abbreviated copy of al-Iṣṭakhrī's *Kitāb al-masālik wa-al-mamālik* (*Book of Routes and Realms*). Gouache and ink on paper. Diameter 37.5 cm. Courtesy of Leiden University Libraries, Cod. Or. 3101, fols. 4–5.

Iṣṭakhrī map, this time from a late fifteenth-century copy commissioned for the Fatih library complex established by Mehmet II following his conquest of Constantinople in 1453 (Pinto, "Maps") (fig. 8). Minus elaborate calligraphy and illumination, the form of the Islamic map emerges clearly (fig. 9).

First, we must find the mimesis that is actually present, to make these works more accessible to students; then, we can consider their meanings. We start with a map that shows the world as we are used to seeing it. We then turn the map so that south is on top—instead of north as is the modern Western practice (which must be broken; see exercise cited above). As a result, Africa looms large at the top of the map, as on medieval Muslim maps. Because the maps under consideration predate contact with the Americas, they need to be cut off from the modern map (fig. 10). In order to align the medieval Islamicate map with the increasingly altered modern map, we have to skew the projection (fig. 11), enlarging and stretching Africa so it merges with Australia, in keeping with the concept of an overextended Africa that dominated medieval Islamic and Christian geographic thought. At this point, the modern and medieval maps become alike (Pinto, "Maps" and "In God's Eyes").

It is possible to connect various choices reflected in the orientation, arrangement, and scale of the geographic features with cultural values and experiences. The southern orientation of most maps produced by medieval Muslims, for example, is likely the result of these maps having been designed in the Abbasid Caliphate's major centers, which were to the north of Mecca and Medina. A south-facing orientation would therefore privilege the holiest cities of Islam, much as medieval Christian maps privileged Jerusalem and Eden through their eastern orientation.

By contrast to Christian maps, however, the exaggeration of Africa might result not from religious concepts but from navigational experience. Muslim sailors frequented the coasts of East Africa, and did not circle the Horn of Africa, resulting in the foreshortening of the continent. Records suggest Muslim ships—like most medieval ships—did not stray from the coasts, and therefore, though they did visit Sofāla (in present-day Mozambique) and Madagascar, they did not sail to India by crossing the Indian Ocean but by following the coastlines around Arabia. This could account for the diminishment of the distance from Africa to India. Therefore, although medieval Islamic maps give the initial impression to modern eyes of being entirely divorced from the natural world, there are strong elements of mimesis present.

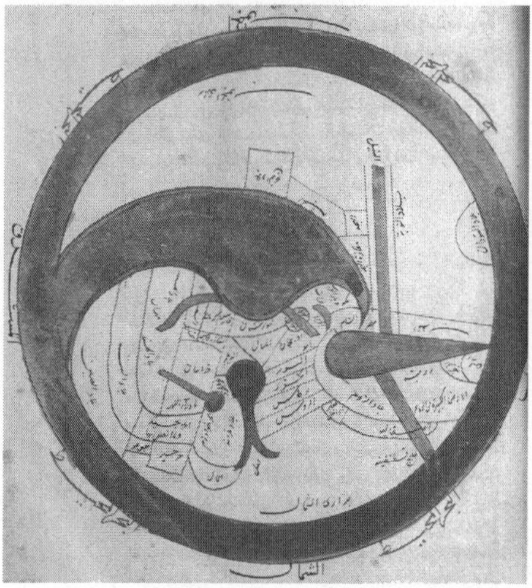

Figure 8. KMMS World Map from Ottoman Cluster. Ottoman, 878/1473. Light-blue gouache and red and black ink on paper. Diameter 19.5 cm. Courtesy of Sülemaniye Camii Kütüphanesi, Istanbul, Aya Sofya 2971a, fol. 3a. Photograph by Karen Pinto.

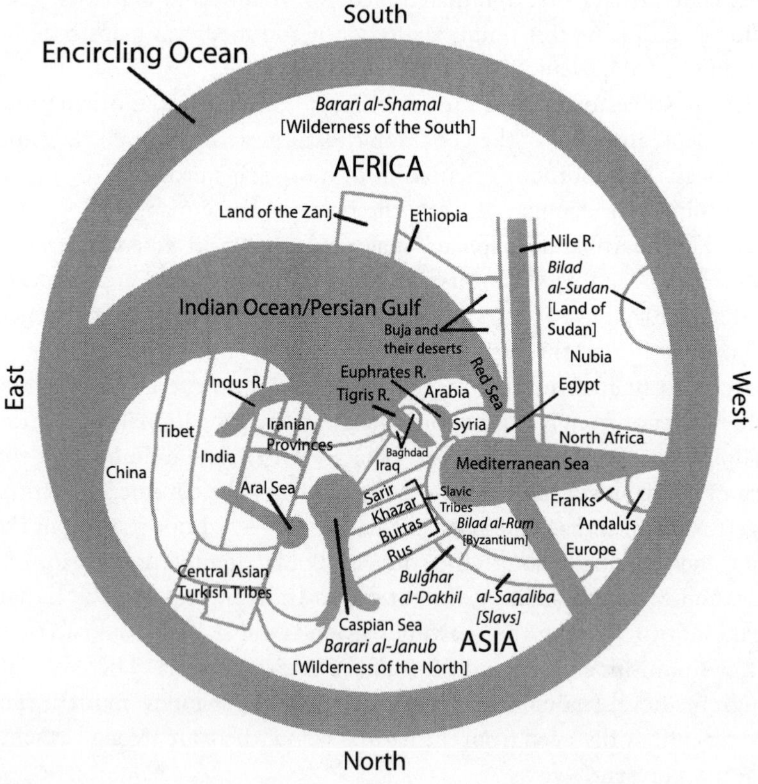

Figure 9. Translation of KMMS World Map. Based on Ottoman Cluster map (fig. 8). Source: Karen Pinto with assistance from Damien Bovlomov.

Figure 10. Relief map of the world with south on top and the Americas removed. Prepared by Karen Pinto.

Figure 11. Skewed south-facing relief map of the world. Prepared by Karen Pinto.

On most Islamic maps (like the Christian T-O map described above) the world is surrounded by an encircling ocean, which is in turn surrounded by the names of the eight cardinal and intermediate directions. The Indian Ocean and Persian Gulf become dominant, curling into the center of the ecumene, whereas the Mediterranean—dominant on Christian maps—is small and peripheral. The extended mass of Africa forms the large, pointed arched wing at the top of the map, as in our altered map of the modern world (fig. 11). The landmass to the lower left is Asia, the body of the mass and the bird, and the mass that connects them is no less than the head of Arabia. This means that the small, rather unobtrusive landmass in the lower right is Europe, representing no less than the tail of the bird (with all the connotations that implies), obviously far less central to medieval Islamic religion, politics, culture, trade, and travel. The scale of Africa and Asia on these maps therefore reflects their relative cultural importance to Islamicate society because they were central territories for trade and conquest. According to Muslims, the heart of the world lay in Arabia, Asia, and Africa, so why bother with insignificant Europe?

A few other bodies of water are significant: the keyhole-shaped Caspian and Aral Seas, the rectangular Nile running into Africa, and the Bosporus dividing off Europe. Other rivers, such as the Tigris and Euphrates, Indus, Oxus, and Volga appear, but as smaller and less significant elements. The wastelands of the poles are noted, boundaries between territories are often drawn in, and toponyms abound alongside rare ethnonyms (names for groups of people).

This brings us back to the elaborately illuminated late twelfth-century al-Iṣṭakhrī map with which this section began (fig. 7). Helping students work through the somewhat more mimetic al-Iṣṭakhrī map from the Ottoman cluster allows them to understand the basic features that make up the classical medieval Islamic world map, and the worldview it represents (Pinto, "Maps"). In order to fully understand medieval Islamicate maps, however, the viewer must consider the way in which these medieval maps open windows onto medieval spatial studies (Pinto, "Capturing Imagination," "Searchin' His Eyes," and "Surat Bahr al-Rum"), medieval patronage (Pinto, "Maps"), medieval cosmography (Pinto, "In God's Eyes"), medieval philosophy (Pinto, "It's a Bird"), and especially the bridges they build between medieval European and East Asian cartography (Pinto, *Medieval Islamic Maps*; Park) thus enriching the early modern development of the history of cartography.

Medieval Christian Cartography

The preponderance of maps that appear in all the standard texts on the subject of "Medieval Cartography" were produced by Christians, for Christians, from explicitly Christian perspectives, and defined by Christian ideologies (see, e.g., Woodward 286). Mittman is direct in addressing this in class discussions, as it is essential for understanding the ideologies within these maps. By far, the most common map type from medieval Christian culture is the T-O map (fig. 12). This surprises students, who struggle even to recognize these as maps. These maps are uniquely suited to classroom teaching, owing to their deceptive simplicity and clarity. On screen, every detail is visible to a classroom of students.

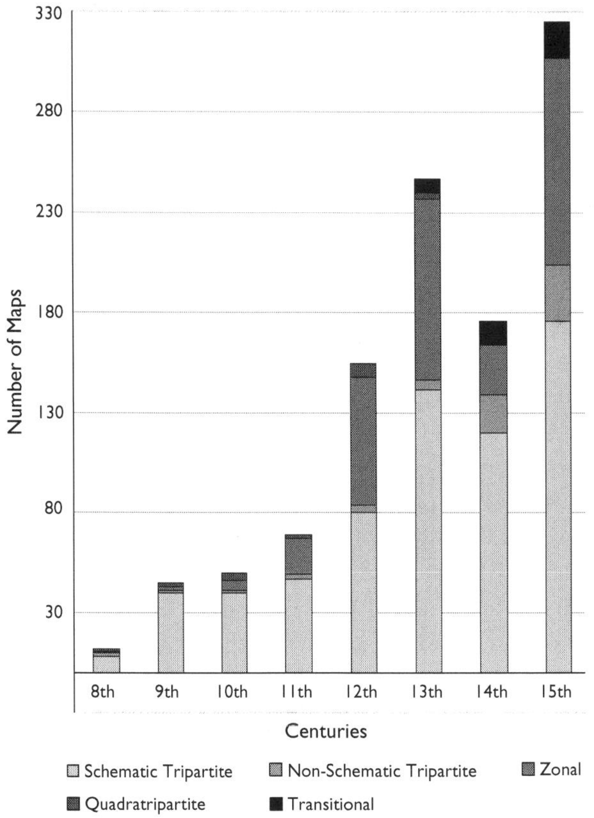

Figure 12. Extant *mappaemundi* by category. Based on figure 18.8 in David Woodward, "Medieval *Mappamundi.*" Graph by Asa Simon Mittman.

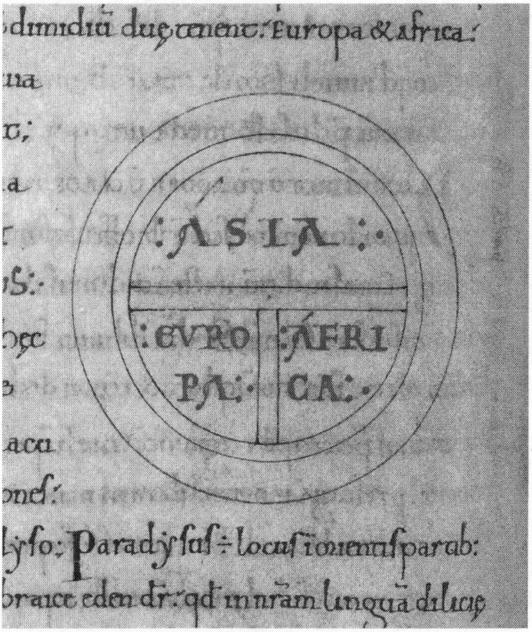

Figure 13. T-O Map. England, tenth century, in Isidore's *Etymologies*. British Library, London, Royal MS 6 C I, fol. 108v. © The British Library Board.

A T-O map that appears, as many do, in a copy of Isidore of Seville's popular *Etymologies* will serve as our paradigmatic example (fig. 13). Mittman often spends the majority of a three-hour class session on this map, an exercise that initially strikes students as implausible, and yet, semester after semester, three hours prove inadequate to unpack all that is happening within its small circle. This serves to demonstrate not only the power of mapping but also of "deceleration and immersive attention" to objects (Roberts). This T-O map is a relatively bare-bones version of the type, though there are yet simpler versions that are nothing but a circle inscribed with a *T*.

Mittman begins by asking the class: What choices did the mapmaker make in designing this map? The Isidorian version reproduced here is standard in all major features (Mittman). Oriented to the east (the location of Jerusalem and, medieval Christians believed, the Garden of Eden and all major biblical events), it is composed of three outer rings defining the universe, and then the great world ocean that encircles the three parts of the earth, each labeled in red, in a majuscule display script: Asia above, filling half the ecumene (inhabitable world); Europe to the lower left; and Africa to the lower right. Each Latin toponym is preceded by two *puncti*—a medieval form of punctuation—and followed by three more, suggesting these individual words are intended as complete grammatical units, as, somehow, complete thoughts (Mittman). The parts are divided by rectilinear bands schematically representing waterways: the vertical Mediterranean dividing Europe and Africa; the Nile dividing Africa and Asia; and the Tanais (the River Don) dividing Asia from Europe. The linearity of these waterways, the *T* of the T-O, transforms the waters into the cross of Christ, reaching from one end of the ecumene to the other, generating an image of a globe encompassed by Christ and therefore established for the use of Christians.

The apparent simplicity of this map makes it seem increate, like it was always there, given, natural. It is in no way thus. Every line, every dot, the ink colors, the language choice, the script, every element represents, as Wood reminds us, "choices made among choices." As an experiment to reveal these choices anew, we commissioned an artist to produce a series of variations on this T-O map, tweaking properties in a range of ways (fig. 14). This series stands in for the many variations that Mittman has drawn on whiteboards during class discussions. These variations are all deliberately close to the original.

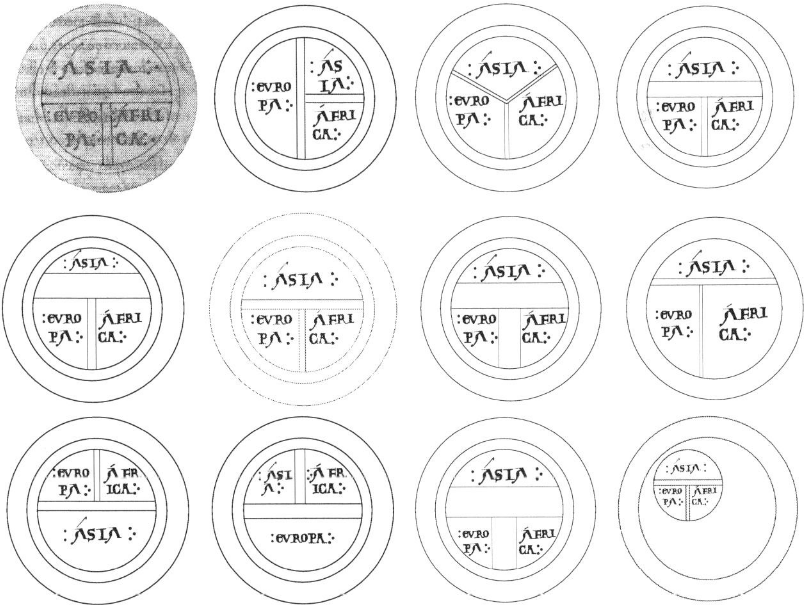

Figure 14. T-O map variations. Digital images by Misty Findley.

All are circular, though it is possible to make world maps in any shape, and medieval examples survive that are rectangular (Chekin 393, 491, 492; Woodward 347, 351, 357), oval (Chekin 454, 352), almond-shaped (Woodward 313, 353), diamond-shaped (Woodward 335), multilobed (Chekin 388, 389; Woodward 321), and so on. All show and label the three parts of the world. They maintain the language, script, and punctuation. And yet, each presents a different world, a different worldview, each of the "choices made among choices" resulting in distinct meanings. What is privileged through orientation (*superior* is Latin for "above") or hieratic scale (since scale here is not based on some factual accounting of landmass areas)? What is equated? How close or distant are these lands? How vast and uncrossable or narrow and easily forded do the waterways appear to be?

The T-O map is based on a few lines of text in Isidore's *Etymologies* that can be put on screen beside the map. The text is imprecise, and what details there are, are not necessarily conveyed in the map. What does Isidore mean where he writes that the central sea is "called the Mediterranean because it flows through the 'middle of the land' (*media terrae*) all the way to the East, separating Europe, Africa, and Asia" (Barney et al. 277)? The answer presented in the T-O format is a possible reading of this, but not the only possible one.

Some of our modern variations on the T-O form appear in surviving medieval cartography. There are west-facing maps (Chekin 333, 339), south-facing maps (341), maps that give less ground to Asia (327, 332), and so-called Y-O maps (Chekin 495; Woodward 346, 347) that divide the ecumene evenly. The most apparently subversive of our modern variants is that which denies the ecumene pride of place in the center of God's divine creation, and yet there are medieval maps (hybrids of the east-facing T-O map type and the north- or south-facing zonal map type that presents five climate zones, from the frigid poles through the temperate regions to the scorching equatorial zone; Chekin 395–445) that decenter the lands in similar fashion. Presenting students with our variant models, or inviting them to read the texts and draw their own, draws attention to the deliberate nature of this most popular of medieval Christian map types.

For reasons of space, our case studies are brief, but they suffice to open up a number of questions that warrant further discussion. What is a map or, perhaps better, what are maps? Above, we discussed attempts to broaden the definitions of a map. It may be that maps do not reduce to a single, all-encompassing definition, but instead have what Wittgenstein calls "family resemblances": they may have "no one thing in common" but are "related to one another in many different ways," to the point that "similarities crop up and disappear" across examples (Wittgenstein 1.65–66). There are also forms, conventions, and purposes to consider. The examples presented here differ in governing principles, spatial organization, format, medium, and technique, and these differences imply differences in how users understood the world and their relation to it. This is just one reason why maps like these are crucial to the project of globalizing the Middle Ages.

Works Cited

Andrews, J. H., "Meaning, Knowledge, and Power in the Map Philosophy of J. B. Harley." Introduction. *The New Nature of Maps: Essays in the History of Cartography*, by J. B. Harley, edited by Paul Laxton, Johns Hopkins Press, 2002.

Barney, Stephen A., et al., editors. *The Etymologies of Isidore of Seville*. Cambridge UP, 2006.

Cao Wanru et al., editors. *Zhongguo gudai ditu ji* [*An Atlas of Ancient Maps in China*]. Wenwu chubanshe, 1990–97. 3 vols.

"Cartography Guide." *Axis Maps*, 2017, www.axismaps.com/guide/.

Chekin, Leonid S. *Northern Eurasia in Medieval Cartography: Inventory, Texts, Translation, and Commentary*. Brepols, 2006.

Documentation on *Shu chuan tu* (F1916.539). Freer Gallery of Art, www.freersackler.si.edu/wp-content/uploads/2017/10/F1916-539_Documentation.pdf.

Edney, Matthew H. "The Origins and Development of J. B. Harley's Cartographic Theories." *Cartographica*, vol. 40, nos. 1–2, 2005, pp. v–143.

Harley, J. B. "Cartography, Ethics and Social Theory." *Cartographica*, vol. 27, no. 2, summer 1990, pp. 1–23.

Harley, J. B., and David Woodward, editors. *Cartography in Prehistoric, Ancient, and Medieval Europe and the Mediterranean*. U of Chicago P, 1987. Vol. 1 of *The History of Cartography*.

———, editors. *Cartography in the Traditional East and Southeast Asian Societies*. U of Chicago P, 1994. Vol. 2, book 2 of *The History of Cartography*.

Hu, Bangbo. "Art as Maps: Influence of Cartography on Two Chinese Landscape Paintings of the Song Dynasty (960–1279 CE)." *Cartographica*, vol. 37, no. 2, 2000, pp. 43–55.

Mittman, Asa Simon. "Mapping Global Middle Ages." *Toward a Global Middle Ages: Encountering the World through Illuminated Manuscripts*, edited by Bryan C. Keene, Getty Publications, 2019, pp. 99–101.

Needham, Joseph, with Wang Ling. *Mathematics and the Sciences of the Heavens and the Earth*. Cambridge UP, 1959. Vol. 3 of *Science and Civilisation in China*.

Park, Hyunhee. *Mapping the Chinese and Islamic Worlds: Cross-Cultural Exchange in Pre-modern Asia.* Cambridge UP, 2012.

Pinto, Karen. "Capturing Imagination: The *Buja* and Medieval Islamic Mappamundi." *Views from the Edge: Essays in Honor of Richard W. Bulliet*, edited by Neguin Yavari et al., Columbia UP, pp. 154–83.

———. "Fit for an Umayyad Prince: An Eighth-Century Map or the Earliest Painting of the Moon?" *The Medieval Globe*, vol. 4, no. 2, 2018, pp. 29–68.

———. "In God's Eyes: The Sacrality of the Seas in the Islamic Cartographic Vision." *Espacio, tiempo, y forma, serie VII, Historia del arte*, vol. 5, no. 1, 2017, pp. 55–79.

———. "Interpretation, Intention, and Impact: Andalusi Arab and Norman Sicilian Examples of Islamo-Christian Cartographic Translation." *Knowledge in Translation: Global Patterns of Scientific Exchange, 1000–1800 CE*, edited by Patrick Manning and Abigail E. Owen, U of Pittsburgh P, 2018, pp. 41–57.

———. "It's a Bird. It's a Plane. No, it's the World! An Exploration of the Spiritual Meaning Underlying the Bird Forms Used in Islamicate Maps." *Geography and Religious Knowledge in the Medieval World*, edited by Christoph Mauntel, De Gruyter, 2021, pp. 39–56.

———. "The Maps Are the Message: Mehmet II's Patronage of an 'Ottoman Cluster.'" *Imago Mundi*, vol. 63, no. 2, 2011, pp. 155–79.

———. *Medieval Islamic Maps: An Exploration.* U of Chicago P, 2016.

———. "Passion and Conflict: Medieval Islamic Views of the West." *Mapping Medieval Geographies*, edited by Keith Lilley, Cambridge UP, 2014, pp. 201–24.

———. "Searchin' His Eyes, Lookin' for Traces"*:* Piri Reis' World Map of 1513 and Its Islamic Iconographic Connections (a Reading through Bağdat 334 and Proust)." *Journal of Ottoman Studies*, vol. 39, no. 1, 2012, pp. 63–94.

———. "Surat Bahr al-Rum (Picture of the Sea of Byzantium): Possible Meanings Underlying the Forms." *Eastern Mediterranean Cartographies: The Cartography of the Mediterranean World: Proceedings of the 18th International Conference on the History of Cartography, Athens, 11–16 July 1999*, edited by George Tolias and Dimitris Loupis, Institute for Neohellenic Research, 2004, pp. 234–41.

Ptolemy. *Ptolemy's* Geography*: An Annotated Translation of the Theoretical Chapters.* Translated by J. Lennart Berggren and Alexander Jones, Princeton UP, 2000.

Roberts, Jennifer L. "The Power of Patience: Teaching Students the Value of Deceleration and Immersive Attention." *Harvard Magazine*, Nov.–Dec. 2013, pp. 40–43.

Terkla, Dan. "Where to Fix Cadiz?" Introduction. *A Critical Companion to English* Mappae Mundi *from the Twelfth and Thirteenth Centuries*, edited by Terkla and Nick Millea, Boydell, 2019, pp. 1–19.

Turnbull, David. *Maps Are Territories: Science Is an Atlas.* U of Chicago P, 1993, territories.indigenousknowledge.org/.

Wittgenstein, Ludwig. *Philosophical Investigations.* Translated by G. E. M. Anscombe, 3rd ed., Blackwell, 2001.

Wood, Denis. "Deconstructing the Map: Twenty-Five Years on This Is Not about Old Maps." *Cartographica*, vol. 50, no. 1, 2015, pp. 14–17.

———. *Rethinking the Power of Maps.* Guilford Press, 2010.

Woodward, David. "Medieval *Mappaemundi.*" Harley and Woodward, *Cartography in Prehistoric, Ancient, and Medieval Europe*, pp. 286–370.

Woodward, David, et al. *Approaches and Challenges in a Worldwide History of Cartography.* Institut Cartogràfic de Catalunya, 2001.

Yee, Cordell D. K. "Chinese Cartography among the Arts: Objectivity, Subjectivity, Representation." Harley and Woodward, *Cartography in the Traditional East and Southeast Asian Societies*, pp. 128–69.

———. "Chinese Maps in Political Culture." Harley and Woodward, *Cartography in the Traditional East and Southeast Asian Societies*, pp. 71–95.

———. "Reinterpreting Traditional Chinese Geographical Maps." Harley and Woodward, *Cartography in the Traditional East and Southeast Asian Societies*, pp. 35–70.

———. "Taking the World's Measure: Chinese Maps between Observation and Text." Harley and Woodward, *Cartography in the Traditional East and Southeast Asian Societies*, pp. 96–127.

———. "Traditional Chinese Cartography and the Myth of Westernization." Harley and Woodward, *Cartography in the Traditional East and Southeast Asian Societies*, pp. 170–202.

Jeffrey J. Cohen

Deserts, Cities, and Frozen Poles: Teaching Ecology in Early Texts

The essays gathered in this volume make clear the challenges and possibilities of articulating the contours of a global Middle Ages, a bustling expanse with multiple centers, long histories of conflict and coexistence, cultures in transit and transformation, diverse languages and stories full of challenge.[1] Such a globe requires multiple perspectives, none of which is likely to capture anything approaching a total picture. Frequent shifts between divergent scales are required in order to bring on-the-ground, lived realities into an analysis that can achieve something more than explication of the intensely local. Historicism, the study of how texts and artifacts reflect and reveal the contextual conditions of their emergence, continues to reside at the heart of medievalist training, so local frames come easily to most scholars of the period, regardless of the geography in which they specialize. But because a global Middle Ages demands a more expansive ambit, I start with the question of what some medieval people would have imagined themselves beholding when they traveled in their minds to the outer reaches of space and looked back at the home they had left behind. How did the globe of the global Middle Ages appear when viewed from afar?

The fourteenth-century English poet Geoffrey Chaucer offers an answer that might seem rooted in the regional and Anglocentric but that opens a wide world in motion. Like many medieval authors who have been tied in later ages to the births of singular nations, Chaucer's works open up polyglot and expansive worlds, even though he is mainly writing from London. This expansiveness applies to both geography and time. Chaucer ends his narrative poem *Troilus and Criseyde* with the death in battle of the male protagonist. The soul of the lovelorn Trojan warrior rises from his body upward through heavens, leaving the walls of his native city below. As he passes through the orbits of the wandering planets, Troilus turns back for a moment toward his former home, a city soon to be devastated by the Greeks. He beholds his place of origin as "this litel spot of erthe that with the see / Embraced is" ("This little spot of land that is embraced by the sea"; 5.1815–16). He beholds a total vision of the globe as radiant sphere, the medieval version of present-day images like the Blue Marble and Spaceship Earth (Cohen and Elkins-Tanton; Crane). Though this moment of lingering is conveyed through lyrical language, the effect of seeing the place in which his life was spent reduced to a "spot" distances Troilus from its value: "and fully gan despise / This wrecched world, and held al vanite" ("and [he] began to completely despise this wretched world and consider it mere vanity"; 5.1816–17). Literally superior to a globe that once held him too tightly in its difficult grasp, Troilus now laughs at its pettiness, at its celestial insignificance (5.1821). What had seemed an all-consuming milieu when he dwelled within its confines now dwindles in his estimation to a "wrecched" dot.

But let us stay with the vastness of the globe for a moment and resist Troilus's diminution of its expansiveness. That the earth is both formidable and round is easy to apprehend. A ship sailing over the ocean's curve or a caravan sinking beneath a sandy horizon is proof enough. More people living today likely believe the planet on which they dwell is flat than have ever thought so in the past. The Internet is well designed to persuade us of so-called facts at which ancestors would have scoffed. Chaucer inherited his frame for imagining an aloof perspective on the *orbis terrarum* ("sphere of lands," "circle of the world," "globe") from the *Dream of Scipio.* This story was related by the Roman orator Cicero in the sixth book of his *De re publica* (*Treatise on the Republic*).

Throughout the European Middle Ages, the dream was known only through a detailed fifth-century commentary by Macrobius, who used the narrative to describe with precision the configuration of the cosmos. Cicero and Macrobius relate how the Roman general Scipio the Younger was once visited in his sleep by his adoptive grandfather, an accomplished military man. From the edges of the Milky Way the elder Scipio grants to his relation a view of Rome, looking distantly down on his city from above. The varied climates of the globe resolve into five distinct bands: two polar ice fields, north and south; two temperate and habitable zones hugging the equator; and a scorching expanse of desert dividing the Northern and Southern Hemispheres from each other. In medieval manuscript illustrations this Macrobian earth often resembles Jupiter, vivid in its orderly stripes. Each of these thermal bands represents a *climate*, a medieval noun that designates an ecological environing as well as an inclination induced through living in place. Whether you inhabit a torrid desert, a city within some more temperate expanse, an island near the frozen poles, or somewhere in between, climate was thought to implant itself in the body at the moment of birth. Climate is an inclination shared by living things across species and kingdom, the ecological coexistentiveness of plants, animals, humans, air, weather.

But the place binding of climate does not diminish human restlessness. People and their animate and inanimate companions wandered the world and proliferated in regions to which they were not indigenous, often to the great harm of those already dwelling in them. The Middle Ages were truly global, with flows of bodies and goods and languages constantly crossing seas and continents, as the many essays collected in this volume well illustrate. Sometimes this travel was, like Scipio's journey to the edges of the galaxy, imaginative—but even then such stories possessed worldly effects. As the British Empire forcefully expanded, Chaucer's literary works wandered Europe, Asia, the Middle East. Once canonized as the Father of English poetry, his local orientation to these geographies became foundational, difficult to realign. The author of the book of world travels published under the name of John Mandeville may never have visited any of the countries he so meticulously describes, but he nonetheless gifted many Europeans with a mode of viewing India, Africa, and China that remains tenaciously rooted in the Western imagination. Sometimes an invasive species is a story that only appears to have arrived from some distant elsewhere and proliferates in ways that both expand and inhibit modes of knowing the globe.

Scale and the Environmental Humanities

The first lesson of teaching the environmental humanities is that the scale of the world is at once vast and small. This insight resonates profoundly with how the global Middle Ages might best be studied. Every small story opens to a larger one; every large narrative is embedded in extensive particulars. Medieval theorists of the cosmic expressed this entangled simultaneity whenever they described the human as a microcosm, a world within a world. Gregory the Great, Ibn Ḥaddik, Ibn Gabirol, Maimonides, Hildegard of Bingen, and John Gower emphasized that every human body, no matter where on the expansive earth that body dwelled, enmeshed within itself a universal system, the "less world" within the greater. Like the rest of the natural realm, bodies were thought to be composed of flows of itinerant force and matter impressed by climate, a medieval term that (as we have seen) designates "inclination" as much as "zone of inhabitation."

Place matters profoundly within this frame. Human corporeality and culture operate differently within torrid deserts, temperate cities, or the frigid extremes of the distant North and South. Yet even the most precise of locations (Acre, Rome, Jerusalem, Paris, Cairo) will open continuously to wider scales. This doubled conceptualization was shared by a variety of thinkers across languages, faiths, and cultures, but especially by those who had read the Greek philosophers and their Roman literary and philosophical inheritors. Whether the idea was expressed in Greek (*mikros kosmos*), Arabic (*ʿālam ṣaghīr*), Hebrew (*olam katan*), Latin (*mundus minor*), or a proliferation of vernaculars, a *microcosm* means that in every small world a greater one unfolds. For thinkers influenced by Greek and Roman tradition this microcosm-macrocosm nexus usually involves entangling a resolutely material body composed of four humors with astrological influences that act as gravitational pulls on them. In the spleen, kidney, and heart is evidence of the impress of Mars, Venus, Mercury, organs as doorways to the whole of the sky. In lightness or darkness of skin is a story of weak or weighty solar intensity, as well as a story of psychology, corporeality, and race.

In the less world may be discerned the greater. Contemporary ecologists know this truth well. That the scale of the world is at once minute and nearly infinite is made clear whenever environmental writers describe the human microbiome as a world within a world, or when emphasizing what Stacy Alaimo has described as *transcorporeality*, the permeability of all bodies to changing climatic and toxic environs (Alaimo). Transcorporeality in fact has deep affinities with what is often called geohumoralism, the medieval and early modern belief that place actively impresses itself on human and nonhuman bodies. No matter the time or place you are investigating with an ecological bent, your critical methodology and mode of argument will likely combine *close reading* (examination of the textual world through its deployment of words, sounds, metaphors, and intertextuality) with *close looking* (examination of the world's vibrancy with that same intensity of regard, activating the full human sensorium through that practice of observation).

As an environmental humanist and a medievalist trained within a mainly European archive, I teach a variety of ecologically themed classes, from undergraduate general education courses that are open to all who are interested (Ecocriticism; Environment and Literature; Desert Thinking) to graduate seminars that dive deeply into emergent themes within these burgeoning fields (The New Materialism; Ecological Approaches to the Middle Ages; Environ Body Object Veer). Some of these classroom investigations are anchored fully in medieval texts of diverse origin, but most combine literary and historical work that roves a millennium.

Ecological thinking invites long-duration contemplation. The twelfth-century romance writer Chrétien de Troyes has more in common with Rachel Carson than you might think. Chrétien's gripping tale of sudden, catastrophic climate change induced by a magic fountain in *Le Chevalier au Lion* (*The Knight with the Lion*) is intimate in surprising ways to Carson's famous introduction to *Silent Spring*, "A Fable for Tomorrow." With its narration of a town rendered silent through mysterious agency, eventually revealed to be the work of a commonly used pesticide with dire environmental consequences, Carson's "Fable" owes its otherworldly frame to Arthurian romance as mediated through Victorian medievalism. Both Chrétien's and Carson's stories are more global in their ambit than they might at first appear. Carson's vivid illustration of the effects of DDT toxicity deploys the intensely local ("There was once a town in the heart of America") to critique the internationally distributed manufacture and utilization of this so-called wonder chemical, a magical modern substance with unintended consequences not unlike those of the catastrophic fountain in *The Knight with the Lion*.

Chrétien de Troyes wrote at a nexus where a transnational and rapacious *Franj* (as medieval authors writing in Arabic called the people whom scholars writing in English now label the Normans, the French, or Europeans) connected London to Jerusalem through turbulent movements of bodies, objects, words, violence, story. When later in the same narrative Chrétien describes enslaved women workers in a silk weaving factory, he is "close looking" at a lucrative and geography-spanning commodity trade, lingering with the labor conditions under which such luxury items circulate into and around the global market. Silk, like the gemstones that trigger the tempest earlier in the tale and like so many of the romance's objects mentioned in passing, demonstrates the romance's entanglement within a geographically vast Middle Ages. Scholars such as Geraldine Heng (*Empire*, *Invention*), Shirin A. Khanmohamadi, and Sharon Kinoshita have amply detailed the wide and troubled worlds that medieval romance and their fellow travelers reveal—and that have been the very condition of its formation as a genre.

Close reading and close looking open up the globe.

Tiny Ecology I: Ibrahim

Ibrahim chose for his required daily observation a tree that was a sapling when his family moved to Northern Virginia from Iran.[2] By the time he enrolled in college, the skinny mulberry was about ten feet high. When the little forest behind his house was being cut back by a landscaper, Ibrahim asked that the tree be preserved, even though a nonnative species. He had learned through his research that its flourishing connected his family's yard to Japan and Taiwan, as well as to the wide aerial routes of the birds who devour its berries. Ibrahim's daily observations of the young tree invited him to note that the sheen of its bark differed depending on the time of day, the angle of the sun, and whether it had rained. He noticed lichens just beginning to flourish near its base, a signal of the relative lack of air pollution in his neighborhood. He admitted in class that when he came to speak of the story of this unplanned mulberry in a suburban yard that the plant came to remind him of his family's story of uprootedness and adaption. Ibrahim told us how in his twelve weeks of spending time with the tree he often thought about his own unlikely flourishing in a place where cultures mix. His presentation ended with a montage of iPhone pictures he had taken of the mulberry over the semester, and a statement that he hoped to see the mulberry bear fruit for the first time next year, since this spring had disappointed that hope.

Ecological Attending

No matter the precise geographical or temporal ambit of the class, my environmental humanities pedagogy is built around an exercise called the Tiny Ecology. This semester-long regimen of sustained attentiveness inculcates the pleasures of "staying with the trouble" (Haraway), of companioning a tightly bounded space that in time will reveal a roiled cosmos. I do not give my students all that much information on this key component of the semester-long endeavor that we undertake together—in fact, nothing more than a succinct paragraph, all in the hope that they will quickly make this project and practice their own. Here is what they receive attached to their syllabus:

> By the end of the first week of class you will choose a small nearby place for the daily practice of intense and sustained ecological attentiveness. During the course of the semester, you will make ten-minute visits and note daily, weekly, monthly changes within this space. There are no special requirements for the ecosystem you choose: a built environment, a natural expanse, a carefully curated site (park, garden, river walk), an abandoned corner or lot, a creek, or a fountain. Best is an area close to where you live or work that you have passed by for some time without paying much regard to what unfolds within its little biome. The area can be as small as a concrete planter by a Metro station or as large as a single tree and its immediate environs. Attention should be paid to human influence and neglect, nonhuman forces (weather, sunlight, microclimates, pollution, decay, gentrification), and the surfacings of particular histories (especially but not limited to the species of animals and plants evident; you may have to learn the difference between kudzu and dandelion, starling and wren, and research how this flora and fauna came to be within your Tiny Ecology). Take ample notes that include any questions that your observations elicit. Make sketches if possible and write poems or songs if you feel so inclined. During the course of the semester, you will be asked to create various narratives from these observations: vignettes, short essays, journalism, and a public presentation of your findings. Your notes and narratives will also be used for eleven weekly oral presentations, and then as the basis of your culminating presentation on Tiny Ecology Day.

Most students are immediately enthralled by the possibilities that this endeavor invites. They select lovely and lively locations: a bench in a nearby park, a university rose garden, a water feature near the library, a beloved oak tree sheltering the bus stop where they catch the campus shuttle. Others throw up their hands and select without much thought an expanse that seems impossible: a mossy crack in the cement of their apartment's balcony, a rubbish-strewn drainage ditch near a convenience store, a patch of mold flourishing on a dormitory shower curtain. Whether drawn to this space through incipient love or a sense of weary obligation, students by the end of the semester inevitably discover in their tiny expanse a map of the globe. In Washington, DC, for example, any patch of ground long observed is likely to birth kudzu, "the vine that ate the South" (as the monsterizing rhetoric around the plant goes). Indigenous to the subtropical regions of Korea, China, and Japan (its English name derives from Japanese 葛 [*kuzul*]), this vigorous plant was introduced to the United States for erosion control as well as ornamental beauty. The vine grows rapidly and tends to smother the trees and bushes that become its unwilling support. Like many humanly introduced plants and animals, kudzu is often described as an invasive species. Considering its presence in the American Southeast dates back to around 1876, however, that description—always followed by the phrase "native to Asia"—is itself a problem, given that the vine has been thriving in these ecosystems for so long. Vines and trees, like humans and other animals, move around a lot, and perpetually raise the question of what constitutes the foreign, the familiar, the indigenous, the invader, the ornamental, the weed.

Even plants know the first lesson of ecological scale, that the world is at once vast and small. Stare long enough at the mulch beneath an oak in Washington, DC, and the tendrils of a sudden vine will want to talk to you about American desires for Japan, Orientalism and its botanical consequences. To capture the small scale with the large, two modes of looking have to unfold at once: down at ground from close quarters, and the same view but at an almost inhuman remove. Without both perspectives in simultaneity, global interconnection can be difficult to discern.

Tiny Ecology 2: Michal

Never a fan of cities, Michal challenged herself to observe for twelve weeks a desolate courtyard behind her urban dormitory. The space had little to recommend it: dark, wet, often strewn with garbage (especially on Sunday morning, the aftermath of student weekends). She was surprised at how much the light changed as the weeks progressed. Late August's dappled sun yielded to November's unbroken shade. The few weeds that clung to the brick paths vanished after the first hard frost, whereas the green moss on one wall became radiant after rain. Starlings, swallows, ants, and rats knew that Sunday was a day to feast, and by the first light of dawn the courtyard was a scavenger's festival. On a week in class dedicated to race and space (a fraught conversation anywhere, but especially in a Washington, DC, that is rapidly gentrifying by pushing to its margins a vibrant African American community that had long made Chocolate City its home), Michal observed that the same man who cleaned the lobby of her dorm was also charged with ensuring that the weekend's detritus was removed by Monday. When she was speaking in class about these cleanings a fellow student asked her the man's name. She was embarrassed to admit that she had never addressed him, that she had been satisfied somehow to allow his labor to be unattached to a biography. She told us she was reminded of Margery Kempe, who after having been a pilgrim in the Holy Land had written about how her journey was enabled by handsome Saracens but never thought to record their names. In time Michal unfolded to the class a narrative that connected the dormitory courtyard to Europe and New York (through the starlings, descendants of the one hundred birds shipped from the United Kingdom and released in Central Park in the 1890s to ensure that every bird Shakespeare mentions would have a home in the United States) and to Central America through the man who cleaned it. He imparted to Michal a troubled story that he did not want shared of how he arrived in DC and asked her not to convey his name. Instead, he told her it would be enough to tell anyone who wanted to hear that citizens of the United States ought to think more deeply about what their government is doing in their name in distant countries, places that they prefer not to think about because they have the privilege to consider themselves removed from what is in fact intimate.

Case Study: The Voyages of the Ark

Teaching ecology in early texts is all about close looking as well as close reading. I will close this essay with a few words about a story my students and I spend time with in almost every environmentally themed class I teach. As the semester progresses, we observe that ecological narratives tend towards the apocalyptic, with humans reaping the fruit of their own misdeeds in the form of storms, sea surge, fires, toxic land and poisoned water, smothering air, warming atmosphere. The stories we tell, just like the stories medieval authors told, do not come from nowhere, but activate a deep and polyglot archive of tales that from early recordations we know have long haunted imaginations. Cuneiform tablets speak of survival against terrible floods in Mesopotamia. Such ecocatastrophe narratives cross time and cultures, opening not just a global Middle Ages but also a global human epoch, the Anthropocene. The first lesson of the environmental humanities again: the scale of catastrophe is at once vast and small, and its narratives unfold a multilingual, multitemporal, heterogeneous, and violence-ridden cosmos.

The most familiar story of ecological catastrophe within the Abrahamic religions is that of Noah and his ark. This tale of survival against the ruin of the world is the dominating trope for imagining life within anthropogenic (human-caused) climate change. I therefore teach the story of Noah in most of my environmental humanities classes, but I start by telling students it is a tale that everyone thinks they know but do not. The form of the narrative familiar to most involves happy animals processing into a gargantuan boat, two by two; forty days and nights at sea; and joyful culmination in a rainbow. But that is not really how it happens, not in Genesis. To emphasize that point I begin with a version of the Noah story familiar only to some in my class:

> And Nuh did certainly call upon Us, and most excellent answerer
> of prayer are We.
> And We delivered him and his followers from the mighty distress.
> And We made his offspring the survivors . . .
> Then we drowned the others.

When I project this text in Arabic and in English, several students will make the educated guess that these words are from the Quran, and sometimes one of them will even know the precise source to be sura 37 (verses 75–82, in fact), God's description of the proper submission that Nuh (Noah) modeled for Ibrahim (Abraham).[3] Because I have always taught in institutions where some of my students will have grown up with a knowledge of Islamic tradition and may well be observant themselves, someone in the course will often volunteer to inform their classmates that the story of Noah is spread throughout the Quran (131 verses mention the man, sixteen refer to his ship, and nowhere is the narrative told in a straightforward way). A messenger on behalf of Allah, Nuh attempted to return a wayward and idolatrous people to obedience. Despite his impassioned preaching, few listened to his words. When he came to realize that disbelief was endemic to the world, he prayed for a purging of all humankind ("For surely if Thou leave them they will lead astray Thy servants, and will not beget any but immoral, ungrateful [children]," 71.27). Nuh was then instructed by God to build a boat ("safina"; 29.15) and await the Flood (11.37). He takes his family onboard the vessel with him, along with some fellow believers and two of every animal. Left to the ark's exterior are his oldest son, who thought a mountaintop secure enough refuge; his disbelieving wife (at least according to some commentators, based on an obscure reference in 66.10); and a world that jeered and mocked while worshipping false gods. When the waters swiftly rose, all perished. Nuh's son was overwhelmed even as his father begged him to enter the boat: "And the wave came in between them, so he was among the drowned" (11.43). After the Flood receded, the ark came to rest on a mountain. There is no mention of ravens, doves, olive branches, or rainbows. As Nuh mourned his drowned child, Allah informed him that the righteous are his true family (11.46), and the world begins anew.

The Christian tradition is similar in many ways, emphasizing Noah's perfect obedience to God. Commanded to build an ark, Noah constructed the three-level vessel to a precise number of cubits. The Roman African bishop Augustine of Hippo wrote in the fifth century that when Noah immediately undertook the building of the ark he prefigured the perfect obedience of Jesus to his father (*City of God* 15.26). Following Augustine's lead, most medieval Christians read the story typologically, so that if Noah is Christ, then the ark is the cross, the church, or a tomb; the Flood is baptism; the end of the disaster is the resurrection; and the dove is the Holy Spirit.

Jewish interpreters of Torah were more ambivalent when it came to Noah and his divine compliance. Born into the large Jewish community that flourished in Troyes during the eleventh century, the renowned commentator Rashi wondered if Noah was righteous only comparatively, since he was born in a generation of wicked men. It was an open question for him whether, if Noah had lived at the same time as Abraham, he would have been considered to be of any importance. Noah is perhaps even culpable for the Flood because he did not appeal for mercy on the world's behalf. When the impending destruction of Sodom and Gomorrah is declared, for example, Abraham asks God if he intends to destroy the righteous along with the wicked (Genesis 18.33). God relents, granting Abraham the opportunity to seek out those who do not deserve to perish. Jewish writers pointed out that the God of Genesis likes challenge. Recalling the promises made to Abraham, Isaac, and Jacob, Moses on Sinai refuses to allow God to destroy the golden calf-worshipping Israelites and start again. Those who argue with God are often rewarded for their efforts. Noah is told to build an ark and silently complies. Unhesitating obedience can be an ideal (Islamic and Christian tradition) or a fault (Jewish commentary).

Yet even in Christian narration Noah's ship is not always a place of peaceful coexistence, as the late medieval introduction of a boisterous version of Mrs. Noah or the smuggling aboard of the devil will make clear. In some Jewish traditions the raven even rebukes Noah for classifying him as unclean and thereby allotting space for two rather than seven of his kind aboard the ark. When told he must depart the vessel and search the flooded world for signs that the water might be receding, the bird accuses Noah of risking the extinction of all ravens and wonders how Noah can live with the risk of an earth impoverished by loss. When I raise all these points in class, the inevitable result is that students admit that they cannot believe how much has been added to the Genesis narrative.

It is at this point I have them look at the story themselves, and I ask them: What happened to the giants who were there before the Flood, and how can they be back later as Joshua and his people move into Canaan? Why were seven of some animals brought on board, and what does it mean that many of these former ark-mates are sacrificed or consumed under the rainbow of covenant? Why do we always tell the story as if it concludes with the disembarkation from the ark, when in fact we next witness Noah becoming drunk, passing out naked, and cursing the progeny of one of his sons to eternal slavery? These three sons found the peoples of the world: what does it mean for later ages that Noah places a malediction on one of them? Why is it that in Genesis the world after the Flood is just as wicked as the world that preceded ecocatastrophe?

We examine the Noah story so closely in class not only because it continues to offer the frame (for better and for worse) for survival in a gated community against floods of every kind but also because it emphasizes three points central to any understanding of the global Middle Ages: scale is both local and vast; every small world when examined with enough attention reveals a multicultural, multilingual, place-spanning cosmos in motion; and the complicated stories that connect deserts, cities, and frozen poles across time are there, right before us, ready to be told.

Notes

1. The Global Middle Ages platform phrases the charge as "to see the world whole in a large swathe of time—as a network of spaces braided into relationship by trade and travel, mobile stories, cosmopolitan religions, global cities, cultural borrowings, traveling technologies, international languages, and even pandemics, climate, and wars" ("About GMAP").

2. All accounts of Tiny Ecology assignments contained in this chapter are anonymized and composite descriptions of student participation that draw from my teaching of this exercise across a decade.

3. In class I typically use the version of the Quran made available through The Perseus Project because it is free to all readers and collates the Arabic with three very different English translations. I quote here from Pickthall's translation.

Works Cited

"About GMAP." *Global Middle Ages*, www.globalmiddleages.org/about.

Alaimo, Stacy. *Bodily Natures: Science, Environment, and the Material Self.* Indiana UP, 2010.

Carson, Rachel. *Silent Spring.* 1962. Houghton Mifflin, 2002.

Chaucer, Geoffrey. *The Riverside Chaucer.* Edited by Larry D. Benson, 3rd ed., Houghton Mifflin, 1987.

Chrétien de Troyes. *Yvain; or, The Knight with the Lion.* Translated by Ruth Harwood Cline, U of Georgia P, 1984.

Cohen, Jeffrey Jerome, and Lindy Elkins-Tanton. *Earth.* Bloomsbury, 2017.

Crane, Susan. "'The Lytel Erthe That Here Is': Environmental Thought in Chaucer's Parliament of Fowls." *Studies in the Age of Chaucer*, vol. 39, 2017, pp. 1–30.

Haraway, Donna. *Staying with the Trouble: Making Kin in the Chthulucene.* Duke UP, 2016.

Heng, Geraldine. *Empire of Magic: Medieval Romance and the Politics of Cultural Fantasy.* Columbia UP, 2003.

———. *The Invention of Race in the European Middle Ages.* Cambridge UP, 2018.

Khanmohamadi, Shirin A. *In Light of Another's Word: European Ethnography in the Middle Ages.* U of Pennsylvania P, 2014.

Kinoshita, Sharon. *Medieval Boundaries: Rethinking Difference in Old French Literature.* U of Pennsylvania P, 2006.

Macrobius. *Commentarii in somnium Scipionis.* Edited by James Willis, B. G. Teubner, 1970.

Quran. Edited and translated by Muhammad M. Pickthall, Perseus Project, www.perseus.tufts.edu/hopper/text?doc=Perseus%3Atext%3A2002.02.0006.

Wan-Chuan Kao

The World Is an Inn: *Habitus* in the Global Middle Ages

Marco Polo, in his *Travels*, takes careful note of the lavish hostels that play host to foreign ambassadors and merchants in the fabled city of Cambalac during the reign of Kubilai Khan. Radiating from the imperial center is a network of post stations that serve the messengers in the Great Khan's postal system. At every post (*yizhang*), called *yam* (from the Mongolian *jamci*, Chinese *zhanchi*), is a "palatial hostelry" worthy of royalty (151). Elsewhere, Polo observes that "in every suburb or ward, at about a mile's distance from the city [Cambalac], there are many fine hostels which provide lodging for merchants coming from different parts: a particular hostel is assigned to every nation, as we might say one for the Lombards, another for the Germans, another for the French. Merchants and others come here on business in great numbers, both because it is the Khan's residence and because it affords a profitable market" (29). More exotic is Polo's next observation that in these hotel spaces, "the number of public women who prostitute themselves for money, reckoning those in the new city as well as those in the suburbs of the old, is twenty-five thousand" (29).

These textual moments from Polo's *Travels*—depicting premodern, Eastern institutions of a postal courier system, travel accommodations, political embassy, trade and exchange, and even brothels—make up one of the core cultural praxes I examine in my teaching of the global Middle Ages. Specifically, I am interested in exploring with students the various representations of inns or hostels—what we might today call *hotels*—in medieval texts. This critical inquiry constitutes a unit in my lower-level English literary survey course, in an upper-level English seminar titled Hotel Orient, and in another upper-level English seminar on Chaucer's *Canterbury Tales.* All the iterations of the hotel unit have been taught at the undergraduate level. Although my classes strive to be as global as possible within the time permitted during a regular semester, they do not claim to be comprehensive in coverage. Furthermore, my method is grounded in both historicism and critical theory.

Multipurpose Hotels

Geraldine Heng, in her 2014 article on early globalities, asks Euromedievalists, as well as medieval and transhistorical globalists, to consider questions of methods, concepts, and objectives in their scholarship. Specifically, Heng challenges the field to reflect critically on its "animating terms" and theoretical frames (236). Such self-reflexive examinations are important because "[u]ndergirding all this—the convergence between how we read a text and how we study the past—lie the larger ramifications of the politics of endeavor" (235). Similarly, moving from scholarship to pedagogy, questions of methods, concepts, objectives, and politics also animate the teaching of the global Middle Ages in higher education.

In terms of my focus, Hotel Orient, pedagogical questions of framework and methodology are always fraught, tricky, if not always already problematic. Above all, it is the metaphoricity of *hotel*—as a sign and a narrative—that is the most complicated to navigate in the classroom. Hotel, as a conceit, seems to launch its own cultural narrative and interpretation. And in the particular case of Hotel Orient, the analytics of its workings do not escape easily, if at all, from the alleged logic of the ethnographic encounter. A hotel may be one of the oldest clichés, a universal experience shared by everyone. "Everyone has been to a hotel of some sort, right?" The rhetorical question, when posed to students, precludes critical thinking. Presentist assumptions about the hotel experience limit the critical field of our investigation. In the end, our universalizing and modernizing impulses, when lurking behind our approach to the cultural praxes of hotel, are nothing but the colonization of space by another name. Hotel is never a universal experience.

Other forms of pedagogical trickiness involve transhistoricism and diachronicity, globality vis-à-vis globalism, resemblance and difference, and system thinking. It is important not to produce, in the class, a simplistic version of a world-system that reinscribes reductive liberal relativism, undifferentiated interconnectedness, and meaningless globality if not globalization. Two important keys to navigating successfully these kinds of pedagogical trickiness surrounding hotel teaching, I think, are through social geography and language. Specifically, in my lower-level survey courses and upper-level English seminars, I put to work two pedagogical imperatives: cartography and philology.

Cartography provides an effective point of entry and introduction to medieval spatial practices. Visual materials, especially maps, often function as an effective hook to stimulate student interest and engage their attention. T-O maps, cosmological schema, and portolan charts are some possible materials for this purpose. Although a simple *Google* search quickly yields many images of medieval maps, it is not my preferred source of medieval visual materials. A more effective approach is to use a single map as a paradigm, such as the Hereford *mappamundi*; an interactive map is available on the site *Hereford Mappa Mundi* hosted by the Hereford Cathedral (www.themappamundi.co.uk). Another possibility is the scholarly site *Virtual Mappa 2.0* (sims2.digitalmappa.org/36).

With an eastward orientation on top and Jerusalem at the center, T-O maps quickly defamiliarize students from the comfort of Cartesian spatiality, with its northward orientation, and allow them to shed a related set of modern assumptions about space, time, and travel (see the essay in this volume by Asa Simon Mittman, Karen Pinto, and Cordell D. K. Yee, "Mapping the Worlds of the Global Middle Ages," for further discussion of how to use medieval maps in teaching). At the same time, one must be careful in the classroom to avoid exoticizing and sensationalizing medieval practices of space.

The seeming strangeness of medieval spatiality helps foreground the historical difference of hotel practices then and now. Whereas a *mappamundi* decenters a particular modern Eurocentric logic of space and point of view, philology may further defamiliarize medieval hotel experiences. By philology, I do not mean the sort of endeavor rooted in nationalism. Instead, I deploy philology as a mode of comparative study that puts in play related words from a variety of languages that cluster around premodern hotel architecture and experience.

A key methodological concept, for me, is best expressed by Olivia Remie Constable in her book, *Housing the Stranger in the Mediterranean.* "Words," Constable contends, "are important, and tracing a spreading network of cognate terms is more than merely an exercise in philology. People use words to indicate specific things and to convey ideas" (5). By tracing a cluster of words in medieval texts that would fall under the rubric of *hotel* today, students can grasp the diversity of premodern hotel practices. Unlike modern accommodations, what functioned as hotels in the Middle Ages encompassed a diverse range of spaces from institutions of learning (such as the Muslim madrassas) to places of worship (synagogues, mosques, and Buddhist temples), hospices, hospitals, khans or caravansaries, *funduqs* (fonduks), and government-operated post stations. Rather than simply a place of rest and pleasure, the premodern hotel was a multipurpose venue of encounter that served a variety of functions, some of which might seem alien to students today: as lodging, restaurant, supply station, school, storage, marketplace, prison, embassy, customs house, and even brothel.

In a lower-level undergraduate literature survey course, it would be difficult to expect students, many of whom are not humanities majors, to engage in an in-depth, graduate-level linguistic, cultural, and historical analysis. Yet an accessible engagement with medieval texts and historical materials is effective in conveying the richness and complexity of the premodern hotel experience across the globe. In my survey class, we begin with Marco Polo's *Travels.* A useful pedagogical tool is the web page "Imagining Medieval Narrative: The Travels of Marco Polo" hosted by Vanderbilt University, and available through the platform www.globalmiddleages.org. The site not only provides an interactive map that charts Polo's itinerary but also usefully annotates select places he visited and their importance.

The first type of accommodation my class examines is the Mongol *yam*, a hybrid institution that is part postal station and part hostel. This unit of the course is based on my research and published essay "Hotel Tartary," which the students read as preparation for class discussions. As I explain in the essay, the origins of the Mongol *yam* system remain obscure. In antiquity, the Chinese had their own postal relay systems that rivaled those of the Persians and the Romans.

During the Tang dynasty (618–907), the postal system in China became truly comprehensive and organized. The Tang system would become the basis and model for future dynasties' networks. Traditionally, the postal traffic was supported by wealthy and influential families, while poorer families provided the personnel, worked the fields that belonged to the station, and watched the postal animals. Later, during the Song dynasty (960–1279), the imperial government militarized the postal service in the year 961, and soldiers served as runners. The network was used primarily for the transport of official documents and mercantile goods.

As a comparison to a European perspective, students would find it useful to read excerpts from the Chinese travelogue, *Wuchuan lu* (*Diary of a Boat Trip to Wu*), by a Song governmental official and poet Fan Chengda, in which he describes his travels throughout China in 1177. As James M. Hargett points out, lodging options for traveling Chinese officials were limited to private inns, Buddhist temples, and government-operated guesthouses (*guan*). The *guans* formed "an empire-wide lodging or hostel system for traveling officials and their entourages" (Hargett 18). Song guesthouses were uneven in quality, unlike those in the later Yuan dynasty. Fan, in fact, complains about the guesthouse in Xinjin (in Sichuan): "In the Xinjin town office the roof leaks and the walls are drafty. There is not a single, open, clean spot [in the building] . . . we joyfully passed the entire day and forgot about the vulgar nature of their accommodations" (Hargett 50).

The Mongols who conquered China thus inherited an old and established tradition of postal relay systems. The *yams* served a variety of functions: communication throughout the vast empire, defense of borders, bureaucratic administration of the realm, escort for visiting envoys, transport of materials, and the gathering of intelligence. And a great diversity of facilities and amenities became associated with the *yams*: official rest houses, private inns or hostelries attached to the stations for those who lacked the right to use government facilities, restaurants, granaries, and prison cells for the transport of prisoners. The network of hostels qua postal network, as both Polo and the Persian historian Rashid al-Din Hamadani note, is one of the great achievements of *Pax Mongolica*. The very sameness—or, rather, familiarity and recognizability—of the hostels renders them interchangeable, hence conducive to traffic and to circulation of people and goods. That is, good hostels mean good trade. In effect, medieval Mongols' *yams* and hostels were an institution that, like paper money, mediated trade and globalized the reaches of premodern capital.

Mongol rulers actively courted foreign merchants, and hospitality became key to attracting global capital. Polo observes many lavish hotels in the suburbs of Cambalac, each assigned to a specific ethnic or racial category. What Polo describes might be the special accommodation quarters, the *huitong guan*, set up by the Yuan government to lodge foreign envoys and merchants visiting Cambalac. In Chinese, *huitong* means "to convene" and also refers to the meeting of government officials and the emperor; *guan* denotes accommodation and a place for cultural activities.

As the principal agency for receiving both foreign envoys and feudal lords visiting the capital, the *huitong guan* was established in 1276, discontinued in 1288, and reestablished in 1292. The *huitong guan* was more than a lodging place; it was in effect the Yuan government's agency for collecting data on foreign geography, postal stations, pastorage, products, and maps: a kind of intelligence-gathering hub. Moreover, the *huitong guan* was the center of language studies, as many interpreters worked there to facilitate the exchange of trade and diplomacy.

Years before the establishment of the *huitong guan* in Yuan China in 1276, the Mongols already had a similar institution for the reception of foreign ambassadors and merchants. Friar William of Rubruck, in 1254, observed in Qaraqorum a prototype of the later *huitong guan* in China: "Ambassadors at Baatu's court and at that of Mangu are treated differently. At Baatu's camp there is a *iam* on the west side who receives all who arrive from the west, and there is the same arrangement regarding the other directions. In Mangu's camp, however, they are all together under one *iam* and may visit and see one another" (183). In addition, William noted the presence of numerous interpreters in these *yams* during his meetings with Mongol officials and their wives. The *huitong guan* in Yuan China was therefore a later crystallization of an earlier Mongol institution designed specifically to facilitate the flow of trade, culture, and intelligence.

It is important that students read non-European travel narratives alongside canonical accounts by Western missionaries and merchants. Medieval non-European travelogues, such as those by Ibn Battutah, Ibn Jubayr, and Benjamin of Tudela, record not only similar types of accommodations but also those that European travelers would never visit. Like Polo, Ibn Battutah observes similar lodging options for foreigners in China: "When a Muslim merchant arrives in a Chinese town he chooses whether to stay with one of the Muslim merchants designated among those domiciled there, or in the *funduq*" (263). He then uses the term *funduq* again to describe the hostels attached to *yams* in China: "A man may travel for nine months alone with great wealth and have nothing to fear. What is responsible for this is that in every post station in their country is a *funduq*, which has a director living there with a company of horse and foot" (264).

The Arabic *funduq* means a hostel or inn in North Africa, and it is the cognate of the Italian *fondaco*. As Constable has shown, both the *funduq* and the *fondaco* are rooted in the Greek *pandocheions*, which were inns in the Mediterranean in antiquity and the early Middle Ages. During the twelfth century, the *funduq* was primarily an urban hostel and storage facility for Muslim and Jewish traders. At the same time, the *fondaco* began to appear in Muslim cities like Alexandria, that served as an enclave for the lodging and commercial activities of Christian merchants. The *fondaco* was dedicated to serving a specific clientele, a particular community of foreign merchants and their goods, with certain negotiated rights and restrictions.

So entrenched was the *fondaco* in the psyche of European travelers that Giovanni Battista Ramusio, in his Italian translation of Marco Polo's *Travels*, calls the hostels (*huitong guan*) in Cambalac that Polo depicts *fondaci*. The *fondaco* thus "remained the term of choice in Italian (and particularly Venetian) usage to designate an enclave for cross-cultural business activities" (Constable 293). Students should note, however, that the Mongol *yam* and the Chinese *huitong guan*, because they were tightly maintained and regulated by the government, did not function in precisely the same ways as the *funduq* and the *fondaco*, where communities of foreign merchants often enjoyed various degrees of self-regulation within the host cities.

Beside *funduqs*, Arab travelers like Ibn Battutah and Ibn Jubayr had access to places of accommodation, such as the madrassa, that were off-limits to European Christians. Ibn Battutah stayed in the College of the Booksellers, a madrassa, in Tunis; when in Cairo, he remarked that the city had so many madrassas that it was impossible to count. And Ibn Jubayr, while in Alexandria, noted the city's "colleges [madrassas] and hostels erected there for students and pious men from other lands. There each may find lodging where he might retreat, and a tutor to teach him the branch of learning he desires, and an allowance to cover all his needs" (33).

Moreover, the sultan of Alexandria provided traveling scholars with baths, a hospital, and servants. A hospice is another type of lodging that Muslim travelers could seek. Ibn Battutah, in Tabriz, describes "a hospice in which food is supplied to all wayfarers, consisting of bread, meat, rice cooked in ghee, and sweetmeats. The amir arranged for my lodging in this hospice, which is situated among rushing streams and leafy trees" (79). And in Yanija (in Asia Minor), Ibn Battutah lodged in a hospice where a local student served him.

In addition to Christian and Muslim accounts, medieval Jewish travel writing is a significant tradition of which students should be aware.

Benjamin of Tudela, like his Arab counterparts, visited Alexandria and observed the diverse range of travelers passing through and the segregated accommodations there, not unlike those that Polo observed in Cambalac: "The city is full of bustle and every nation has its own *fondaco*" (Benjamin 272). Medieval Jewish travelers moved within a tight network of hospitality. Lodging options included synagogues and *funduqs*. As Sandra Benjamin points out, Jewish travelers found safety and refuge in synagogues: "At synagogue he would be received warmly. Some local man—often the cantor—would invite him home, offer him bed and meals for the duration of his sojourn, and, as he prepared to move on, furnish him with victuals, an animal, and detailed directions for reaching the next town" (46).

And for travelers with means, they either rented a place or stayed in Jewish hospices, or *funduqs*, that were often located near or next to synagogues. The Jewish hospices were "pious endowments, and their administration and purpose were similar to those of Muslim *funduqs*. . . . They sometimes provided free lodging to the needy, sick or homeless, but they also produced rent revenues for other worthy community endeavors" (Constable 86).

A unit on premodern hotels in the global Middle Ages can be part history, part cultural studies, and part philology. Through a series of primary and secondary readings, undergraduate students gain an understanding of the complex global networks of travel accommodations in the Middle Ages, institutions and practices that, though they may appear similar to hotels today, were in fact different in fundamental ways. One crucial difference is the flexibility of many premodern hostels and inns that in practice were multipurpose facilities. Another important feature is how, despite the traffic of people and goods, medieval hotel spaces in general remain stubbornly segregated and self-selecting. Students should recognize the material force of categorical thinking that undergirds these institutions. In places that experienced the global circulations of bodies and commodities, religious difference—which was also code for bodily difference—was the primary determinant of who got to stay where.

Hotel Theory

In the rest of this essay, I would like to describe briefly, first, the place of the medieval in a transhistorical course on hotel and, second, the place of critical theory in the teaching of premodern hotel praxes. In my upper-level undergraduate English seminar, titled Hotel Orient, the coverage is broader geographically and temporally, spanning the medieval to the postmodern. In addition to medieval historical and literary materials, the class also examines contemporary texts such as Graham Greene's *The Quiet American*, David Henry Hwang's *Chinglish*, V. S. Naipaul's *An Area of Darkness*, Yoko Ogawa's *Hotel Iris*, and Tennessee Williams's *In the Bar of a Tokyo Hotel*. While the postmodern globalities these texts examine do not necessarily reflect or align with the early globalities found in the writing of medieval travelers such as Marco Polo and Ibn Battutah or in the fictive medieval compilation *The Travels of Sir John Mandeville*, I have found that reading the medieval, in fact, offers students a firmer theoretical and historical grounding in analyzing texts from later periods. The medieval is an important site that affords a firmer grasp of the culture from later iterations of itself. For instance, Polo's observation of the Mongol *yam* system raises questions about the nature and idea of empire and its communications apparatus in the works of Greene, Hwang, Naipaul, and even Williams.

I have found that careful deployments of critical theory are useful for students in thinking through the space of Hotel Orient. My key theorists include Wayne Koestenbaum (*Hotel Theory*), Matteo Pericoli ("Writers" and *Laboratory*), Jacques Derrida (*Of Hospitality* and "Hostipitality"), and Edward Said (*Orientalism*). For students, some productive theoretical insights into hotel praxes include hotel as a sign and as a text; the uncanny relation between home and hotel; homelessness and hotel; textual architecture; and biopolitics that turns hotel into a tool of control and surveillance. Theory is productive in students' careful reading of the premodern and modern hotel experience. Derrida's concept of "hostipitality," for instance, correlates provocatively with non-European biopolitical regimes in the Middle Ages. For the Mongols, compulsory census and maintenance of *yams* (post stations qua hostels) were instrumental to their rule over subjugated populations—a policy that effectively converted the subjects' living bodies into political resources, assessed taxes, identified craftsmen and technicians, and recruited military personnel.

Immediately following his praise of the Mongols' achievement in hotel and postal management, Polo abruptly shifts to questions of how the Eastern idolaters are able to sustain their vast system. The answers, Polo suggests, lie in Cathay's large population and cereal production. Polo's turn to population is in effect a turn toward biopolitics that first reduces the Mongols and their conquered subjects into bodies, what Giorgio Agamben terms the bare life (*zoē*), that lives only to support the sovereignty of the

Great Khan. The systematization of population through census, in fact, was a method actively utilized if not perfected by the Mongols to fully regulate and exploit subject peoples.

Michel Foucault, in his 1977 to 1978 lectures at the Collège de France titled *Security, Territory, Population*, theorizes that a population is a "political subject" (42) and "the very source of . . . the dynamic of the strength of the state and sovereign" (68). In other words, for Foucault, population is managed by the government's *dispositif* of control. Of course, Foucault is discussing the emergence of biopolitics and modernity, specifically in the fields of medicine and statistics. But Foucault's insight that a correlation exists between population and techniques of security finds an uncanny premodern parallel in medieval Mongols' practices of *yams* and census. Among the Mongol demands for full submission of subject populations was the agreement of these populations to census and the maintenance of the *yam* system. Hence, Juvaini remarks that "each two *tumen* has to supply one *yam*. Thus, in accordance with the census, they so distribute and exact the charge" (Boyle 599). The subject states' participation in the census and the *yam* was a sign of their active support of the Mongol Empire and its continual military campaigns.

Hotel, Koestenbaum argues, "represents a failed relation to space" (20) because it is an artificial refuge that mimics the home but is nonetheless unhomely. The traveler, staying ever so long, fails to find any permanent comfort in the transient space and must continue the life of an exile. What hotel embodies is therefore a particular institutionalized hospitality that, as A. K. Sandoval-Strausz observes, figures "a complex set of possibilities and tensions" (1). As much as it is predictable and therefore reassuring, hotel also offers opportunities for transgression and play, behavior that might not be ventured at home.

The multiple and conflicting associations of hotel, or more broadly, of hospitality itself, have been examined by Derrida, who contends that hospitality's contradiction lies in the act of welcoming a stranger into an alien and possibly constraining space; that is, the gesture involves as much hospitality as hostility. Derrida's own term "hostipitality" seeks to reflect medieval French etymology connecting the word *hospes* 'host-guest-stranger,' with *obses* 'hostage.' Derrida argues: "Hospitality gives and takes more than once in its own home. It gives, it offers, it holds out, but what it gives, offers, holds out, is the greeting which comprehends and makes or lets come into one's home, folding the foreign other into the internal law of the host [*hôte* (host, *Wirt*, etc.)] which tends to begin by dictating the law of its language and its own acceptation of the sense of words, which is to say, its own concepts as well" (7). What welcomes and gives shelter to the stranger also holds the guest hostage. The Middle English *hoste* denotes simultaneously a host, a place of lodging, and an army. Hospitality, ironically, is a failed relation to space. Reading Derrida with undergraduates is a challenge, but it can be done with more careful pacing and attention.

In contrast to Polo's glowing praise in the *Travels*, the reality of the Mongols' postal and hostel system was far from perfect. While surviving and thriving in China, the *yam* network in the western Ilkhanate suffered systemic corruption and was on the verge of collapse by the early thirteenth century. Modernity, Heng argues, "is a repeating transhistorical phenomenon," and "the phenomenon is never coincidental with its expression" (239). Therefore, multiple modernities have emerged asynchronously around the globe, not coinciding with Western modernity. Likewise, if a plurality of modernities were possible, might we not think that multiple forms of premodern biopowers also existed among various early globalities? I would like to think of them as *bioglobalities*.

But thinking the Hotel Orient through early bioglobalities is not without its complications. First, as Heng and others have pointed out, in academia, framing the Middle Ages as "global" has always been easier than framing it as "racial." Things are changing, but we still feel the battle lines. Words are important, Constable reminds us. To think of the Hotel Orient through globality and biopolitics is to think of it through race. The premodern hotel is an important site of racialization: this is what students must recognize and consider carefully.

Foucauldian biopolitics has been critiqued for its narcissistic provinciality. As Elizabeth A. Povinelli points out, "This provinciality becomes apparent when biopolitics is read from a different global history—when biopolitics is given a different social geography" (3). Similarly, when hotel theory is read from a different global history within a non-Eurocentric social geography, it demands a different political science of life and nonlife.

This brings me to Chaucer's Squire's Tale, a popular teaching moment in *The Canterbury Tales*, that is rich in hotel psyche and tonality. Whatever you think of the tale, it is concerned with premodern globality, even with the teaching of a version of early globality. The Squire draws attention to his incompetence and, deploying false modesty, to his poor "English"; picks an Oriental setting for his story that is as global as it could get; and reimagines the biopowers of a racialized Tartar regime after the real Mongol Empire had already collapsed in history. Students of Chaucer should keep this fact in mind.

Hotel figures a failed spatial relationality because it is an artificial refuge that mimics the home but is nonetheless unhomely. The Squire's Great Khan inhabits a palace not dissimilar to a luxury hotel, except on a grand scale. You can teach the *Squire's Tale* as a hotel precisely because of its racial, aristocratic mimicry. And racialization in the *Squire's Tale* is indistinct from the logic of Hotel Orient, that is, the *habitus* of bioglobality.

Works Cited

Agamben, Georgio. Homo Sacer*: Sovereign Power and Bare Life.* Translated by Daniel Heller-Roazen, Stanford UP, 1998.

Benjamin, Sandra. *The World of Benjamin of Tudela: A Medieval Mediterranean Travelogue.* Fairleigh Dickinson UP, 1995.

Boyle, John Andrew, translator. *Genghis Khan:* The History of the World Conqueror *by Ala-ad-Din Ata-Malik Juvaini.* U of Washington P, 1958.

Chaucer, Geoffrey. *The Riverside Chaucer.* Edited by Larry D. Benson, Houghton Mifflin, 1987.

Constable, Olivia Remie. *Housing the Stranger in the Mediterranean World: Lodging, Trade, and Travel in Late Antiquity and the Middle Ages.* Cambridge UP, 2003.

Derrida, Jacques. "Hostipitality." Translated by Barry Stocker and Forbes Morlock. *Angelaki*, vol. 5, no. 3, 2000, pp. 3–18.

Derrida, Jacques, and Anne Dufourmantelle. *Of Hospitality.* Translated by Rachel Bowlby, Stanford UP, 2000.

Foucault, Michel. *Security, Territory, Population: Lectures at the Collège de France 1977–1978.* Translated by Graham Burchell, Picador, 2009.

Greene, Graham. *The Quiet American.* Penguin, 2004.

Hargett, James M. *Riding the River Home: A Complete and Annotated Translation of Fan Chengda's (1120–1193)* Diary of A Boat Trip to Wu (Wuchuan lu). Chinese UP, 2008.

Heng, Geraldine. "Early Globalities, and Its Questions, Objectives, and Methods: An Inquiry into the State of Theory and Critique." *Exemplaria*, vol. 26, nos. 2–3, 2014, pp. 234–53.

Hwang, David Henry. *Chinglish.* Theatre Communications, 2012.

Ibn Battutah. *The Travels of Ibn Battutah.* Translated by C. F. Beckingham, Picador, 2000.

Ibn Jubayr. *The Travels of Ibn Jubayr.* Translated by R. J. C. Broadhurst, Goodword Books, 1952.

"Imagining Medieval Narrative: *The Travels of Marco Polo.*" *Global Middle Ages*, globalmiddleages.org/project/imagining-medieval-narrative-travels-marco-polo.

Kao, Wan-Chuan. "Hotel Tartary." *Mediaevalia*, vol. 32, 2011, pp. 43–68.

Koestenbaum, Wayne. *Hotel Theory*. Soft Skull Press, 2007.

Naipaul, V. S. *An Area of Darkness*. Vintage, 2002.

Ogawa, Yoko. *Hotel Iris*. Picador, 2010.

Pericoli, Matteo. *The Laboratory of Literary Architecture*, lablitarch.com.

———. "Writers as Architects." *The New York Times*, 4 Aug. 2013, p. SR12.

Polo, Marco. *The Travels of Marco Polo*. Translated by Ronald Latham, Penguin, 1958.

Povinelli, Elizabeth A. *Geontologies: A Requiem to Late Liberalism*. Duke UP, 2016.

Said, Edward. *Orientalism*. Vintage, 2003.

Sandoval-Strausz, A. K. *Hotel: An American History*. Yale UP, 2007.

The Travels of Sir John Mandeville. Translated by C. W. R. D. Moseley, Penguin, 1983.

William of Rubruck. *The Mission of Friar William of Rubruck: His Journey to the Court of the Great Khan Möngke, 1253–1255*. Edited by Peter Jackson and David Morgan, translated by Jackson, Hakluyt Society Publications, 1990.

Williams, Tennessee. In the Bar of a Tokyo Hotel *and Other Plays*. New Directions Books, 1994.

Monica H. Green and Jonathan Hsy

Disability, Disease, and a Global Middle Ages

This essay considers ways to teach globally about questions of disability and disease in an interconnected and globalized Middle Ages. As an example of disease and disability, we focus on leprosy because it was widespread in the premodern Old World (Eastern Hemisphere) and Oceania. Though its presence in the precontact Americas remains to be confirmed, leprosy was certainly among the diseases brought to the Americas through what has been called the "Columbian Exchange." Leprosy is, in other words, a global disease, offering us a means to examine how different societies, in different cultural circumstances, reacted to a common physical condition.

Our contribution demonstrates the importance of collaborative and multidisciplinary approaches to the global. Monica H. Green brings expertise as a medical historian and Jonathan Hsy brings a perspective from literary and cultural disability studies. We use our divergent disciplinary approaches to explore connections and parallel developments, asking ourselves, In what ways might we see major parts of the world between about 300 CE to 1500 CE as sharing challenges and concerns? Different forms of evidence (material, textual, and visual) allow us to tell a global history of leprosy and can invite students to ask informed questions about historical evidence that is increasingly available to us in a digitally interconnected world.

Global Diseases

After 1500 CE, when European colonialist expansion connected the Americas with Africa and Eurasia, trade networks readily carried infectious diseases across the Atlantic and Pacific, creating global disease pools. Before that period, beyond certain viruses and microparasites that humans throughout the world had shared for hundreds of thousands of years, most infectious diseases that afflicted humans would have had only regional or hemispheric reach. Malaria, for example, which originated in Africa many thousands of years ago, spread from there into Asia and Europe. But there is no evidence that it passed through Beringia during the migration of the First Peoples, circa twenty thousand years ago, perhaps because the mosquitos needed for its transmission could not survive the Arctic. The Americas, therefore, were malaria-free until the disease was brought over by Europeans and Africans after 1500.

Similarly, plague, a disease of northern Eurasian origin, caused massive mortality during the First and Second Plague Pandemics (sixth to eighth centuries CE and thirteenth to nineteenth centuries CE, respectively) in both Eurasia and Africa. Yet plague has only afflicted human populations for about six thousand years; it is, in other words, too young a disease to have been involved in the Beringia crossing about twenty thousand years ago. Tuberculosis (TB), whose age as a pathogen is somewhat younger than plague's, also was too young to have been involved with the Beringia crossing. Originating in East Africa perhaps about four thousand years ago, TB spread to West Africa and, in different strains, to all of Eurasia. We know that it reached the New World in the Middle Ages, and this through a most unlikely source: it was transmitted by seals and sea lions from Africa to the western coast of South America, whence it then spread to North America as well. It may have also reached parts of Oceania. TB, therefore, is the one disease that can now be proven to have been truly global in the Middle Ages (Goble, "Globalisations"; Green and Jones; McDonald et al.).

Although TB often causes both disease (physical destruction of the body) and disability (impaired use of the body), this essay focuses on yet another disease, leprosy.[1] Leprosy, which usually maims rather than kills, is a useful model for approaching the concept of a global Middle Ages precisely because it creates such recognizable physical symptoms when it has advanced to extreme states, particularly in the face, hands, and feet, making it a social disease because of its visibility. For leprosy, we are not yet sure whether it existed in both hemispheres before 1500 CE, as we will explain below. Yet leprosy is valuable to teach with nonetheless because it can tell us so much about how societies reckon with illness and disability.

Leprosy has struck virtually every population in the world at one time or another. If leprosy has at times been associated with certain ethnic groups or regions, it is necessary to look into the historical reasons for such associations. Leprosy is also important to teach with because of the false belief that the disease died out with the Middle Ages themselves, with no modern repercussions. In fact, leprosy persists in the world today, with about 200,000 people newly diagnosed each year. Leprosy's role in the stigmatization and segregation of racialized others has had enduring consequences in imperial and colonial contexts across the globe (Amundson and Ruddle-Miyamoto [Hawai‘i]; Deacon [South Africa]; Kim [Korea]; Leung [China]; Mesele [Ethiopia]; Obregón [Colombia]; Burns [Japan]). Knowledge of leprosy's global history can help address the stigma that persists against currently infected individuals; indeed, its history has been critical in identifying the causes and consequences of stigma for other diseases, most notably HIV/AIDS.

Leprosy's Biology

There are two species of the bacterium that causes leprosy. The one most widely distributed throughout the world, and the one most people are probably thinking of when they hear the word *leprosy*, is *Mycobacterium leprae*. The organism itself is likely many millions of years old. Yet the strains that have thus far been documented in humans only seem to be about five to six thousand years old: about the same timeframe as plague's effects on humans. This kind of leprosy existed throughout most of the Old World (the Eastern Hemisphere) in the Middle Ages. The other type of leprosy, caused by *Mycobacterium lepromatosis*, was only discovered in 2008 and has primarily been documented in the New World. We do not yet know when it arrived, though its evolutionary age leaves open the possibility that it came with the First Peoples' migrations. Both forms of leprosy, crucially, can cause significant levels of disability (Roberts). *M. leprae* in particular can cause blindness, loss of voice, loss of use of the feet and hands, and general disfigurement. *M. lepromatosis* is particularly associated with a syndrome called Lucio and Lapati's phenomenon, causing necrosis (cell death) of the skin and extremities so severe that sufferers have been mistaken for burn victims.

Although it is believed that leprosy is transmitted primarily from person to person through sneezing, coughing, and touching open sores, there may also be transmission through soil in areas surrounding places where persons infected with leprosy live. (The leprosy bacillus seems to be able to survive for a while within amoebae that live in the soil.) The leprosy bacillus, or at least *M. leprae*, is one of the slowest-reproducing bacteria known to science, replicating only once every two weeks. Hence, leprosy is very slow to develop: persons may be infected for two to ten years before they show any symptoms at all.

How leprosy manifests in the body can vary considerably, in part depending on how much of a fight the individual's immune system puts up against the infection. Hence, leprosy can manifest with a wide range of symptoms. Keeping in mind that range of symptoms, and the variable length of time it takes for the disease to develop, will be helpful in reading literary accounts, especially those that raise issues of concealment or attempts at disguising symptoms of leprosy.

Leprosy's History and Geographic Distribution

Although it is often claimed that leprosy is the oldest human disease, as we noted above, *Mycobacterium leprae*—the leprosy bacillus discovered by Hansen, who was working in Norway in the later nineteenth century—seems to have been circulating in humans for only the past five to six thousand years, at most.[2] In evolutionary terms, the organism must have been at least fourteen million years old when it diverged from its so-called cousin, *M. lepromatosis*. But if the disease has only circulated in humans for the past five thousand years or so, that puts it within the period of the world's major writing systems. We should expect, therefore, that leprosy would have seemed to be a new disease when it arrived in different places during the ancient and medieval periods. We should expect to see the development of vocabularies to talk about the disease; the formation of social attitudes toward the disease; and the creation, at least in some situations, of moral or religious responses to the disease. Again, this is a disease that maims, not kills. Learning to live with leprosy—both as an individual and as a society—is what it demanded of all the cultures it affected.

The new evolutionary understanding of leprosy that has come from genetics is beginning to give us a road map of how we should think about leprosy's arrival into human populations. The oldest strains of *M. leprae* are found on the Pacific Rim: in Japan, China, and Oceania (Blevins et al.). Among the Pacific Island nations, we have no historical records that date back to the medieval period. The only written evidence for leprosy here, as in many other parts of the world, comes from European or American colonial accounts, mostly from the nineteenth and twentieth centuries (Luker and Buckingham). The evidence from genetics, however, suggests the strains of leprosy found in the Philippines and Oceania, which belong to Lineage 0, diverged about 4,600 years ago from other strains within Lineage 0 that are now found in Japan, Korea, and China, on the one hand, but also in Hungary and Denmark, on the other. The strains from the Philippines and Oceania are thus the oldest living strains of leprosy in the world today. But the other strains within Lineage 0 also have important stories to tell because the split between the cluster of strains that stayed in East Asia and those that ended up in Europe occurred about four thousand years ago. And in Africa, too, leprosy may have arrived before the beginning of the Common Era. What is most interesting about the evidence genetics now gives us, however, is that in Asia, Africa, and Europe we see marked divergences starting around 500 CE. For reasons we cannot yet explain, leprosy seems to have been increasingly spreading in all these areas in the Middle Ages.

When we turn to the documentary records for leprosy in both Japan and Korea, we find that their histories of reckoning with a disease they would eventually associate with the words *rai* (Japanese) and *mundungbyong* (Korean) seem to have begun in the early Middle Ages (Burns; Kim). Europe seems likewise to have been wrestling with the new arrival of leprosy in the early Middle Ages. In fact, the burden of leprosy may have been most intense in northern Europe. We know of the spread of particular strains of *M. leprae* in medieval Europe because of aDNA—ancient DNA, retrieved from buried human remains—which currently has shown that at least four of the six lineages of *M. leprae* were in circulation (Schuenemann et al.). For western Asia and Africa, we have no aDNA yet, save for one Egyptian sample from the Ptolemaic period, but for the medieval period in the Islamic world we have scattered legal pronouncements and medical treatises that discuss the condition in passing (Neukamm et al.;

Dols). We thus have ample material for a truly global historical analysis, comparing how different societies, at more or less the same time, wrestled with the same physical conditions.

Reading Leprosy across Cultures

Medieval societies wrestled with leprosy in the same way all societies have faced disease and disability: through the medium of their culture. Language, religious concepts, moral beliefs, living spaces, visual representations: all these have functioned as tools for controlling, or trying to make sense of, this debilitating disease. The range of materials that might be assembled on the topic of medieval leprosy—seen now from a global perspective—is staggering. Since methods of bacteriological identification of any disease did not exist before the late nineteenth century, we should not assume that every instance where a historical source names a case of *lepra* (the Latin term), *elephancia* (Greek), *al-baraṣ* (Arabic), *lai* (Chinese), *rai* (Japanese) or *mundungbyong* (Korean), is in fact a case of leprosy as we would define it now. The bacteriological disease's presence in medieval Africa and Eurasia, however, means that the cultural records of these societies—medical texts, literature, and visual arts—allow us to examine how the disease was perceived and experienced by people of the past.

Consider, for example, how a text such as the following might be taught from a global perspective. This excerpt comes from a Latin medical text from the eleventh century CE, called the *Passionarius* (*The Book of Sufferings*), which in turn synthesizes two earlier works. The first part, with the description of symptoms, probably comes from North Africa in the fourth century CE, though it is perhaps based on an earlier source from the first or second century CE. The second part, with an ethnography of leprosy, derives from a work by the Greek physician Galen who lived in the second century CE:

> On leprosy (the elephant disease). We discern those suffering from leprosy by the blemishes, which in the beginning arise like freckles, both yellowish and without any itching, and without any treatments applied they disappear spontaneously, but then arise again and then persist as bumps. And now, having become extensive and solid, they turn black, producing pus from the wounded part. [Leprosy] is also indicated by raspiness of the voice, small coughs, and loose bowels. It is called *elephantia* from "elephant." For just as the elephant is the

> greatest of all animals, so this disease is the greatest of all diseases, and more pernicious.

After a further description of symptoms and a section on therapy, the text continues:

> These and conditions similar to them proliferate especially in Egypt and Alexandria from a defect of the air and from the consumption of foods, because they [Egyptians] eat . . . many sauces, and snails, and the meat of donkeys, and other such foods which are greasy and which generate a melancholic humor or make it grow. Such conditions are also found in Germany and Cappadocia and Misia [parts of modern-day Turkey], but rarely do they last long; they are also easier to cure. Among the Scythians, however, the disease is difficult to find, because of the amount of milk that they drink and the moderate temperature of the air.[3]

One approach to teaching leprosy in a global Middle Ages is to help students think carefully about ideas of disease and disability in a historical context, and to use evidence (among them textual and visual sources) to examine how stories of bodily difference, including theories of health and disease transmission, are shaped by local environments. The text above invites many questions. How are physical symptoms and the progression of leprosy described? Why is the elephant a useful metaphor? Is a disease understood to be caused by behavior, diet, environment, or some combination thereof? What social attitudes does one adopt toward a person with leprosy (sympathy, wonder, disgust, pity)?

Scholarship on medieval evidence from the Old World reveals recurring themes. Throughout medieval European, Islamic, and East Asian contexts, signs of leprosy can be associated with social stigma and perceived as a deserved punishment for some transgression, and across disparate societies the establishment of leprosaria (leper houses), hospitals, or similar communities suggests a desire to segregate people and contain disease while also building environments for collective care (Burns; Hsy; Leung; Orlemanski; Pearman; Rawcliffe; and Richardson). Although many cultures associated leprosy with a supposedly deserved punishment for immorality, many medieval sources, including most medical ones, do not dwell on these aspects of leprosy and instead seek to describe its physical symptoms, theorize its modes of transmission, and adapt to its social realities.

Noting similarities across cultural responses to leprosy is important, but so is attending to local understandings. Kristina L. Richardson notes that "disability" in medieval Islamicate societies was framed through the classical Arabic term *'āha* ("blight" or "damage"), a word that suggests a spoiling of an assumed wholeness or integrity of a living thing; in this context "blights" could include "leprosy, lameness, deafness, amputation, cross eyes, blue eyes[,] . . . halitosis[,] . . . and blindness" (Richardson 123). Physician Ibn Qayyim al-Jawziyya "interpret[s] the Prophet's command to flee the leper as medically sound advice," since "leprosy was transmitted through shared air and physical contact" and thus the "Prophet could not have been advocating the social isolation of lepers" but was seeking to "protect non-afflicted individuals" (Richardson 24).

In her history of leprosy in China, Angela Ki Che Leung notes (in respects parallel to the Latin West and Islamicate societies) that notions of disease and contagion were expressed through religious frameworks. Medieval Chinese doctors associated what we now call leprosy with *dafeng* ("malignant Wind"), denoting contagion, and *li* or *lai* emerging as names for the skin sores (Leung 18), as well as forms of stigma, segregation, and association with sexual immorality "mediated by religion [and] possibility of redemption through Buddhist or Daoist salvation or Confucian good works" paralleled the "medieval history of leprosy in Christian Europe" (Leung 214).

In their scholarship on leprosy and medicine in medieval Japan, Susan L. Burns and Andrew Edmund Goble, respectively, note how Japanese understandings of leprosy (*rai*) drew on and synthesized earlier Chinese systems of knowledge (Burns; Goble, *Confluences*). The *Ton'ishō* (*Book of the Simple Physician* or *Jottings on Medicine*) by the Buddhist monk and clinical physician Kajiwara Shōzen does not just present *rai* as a "deserved punishment" or "karmic illness" but recognizes it as carrying "multiple meanings" and that "perceptions of it were not monolithic" (Goble, *Confluences* 68).

One example (from the Latin West) from a digital resource can be useful for teaching students to think carefully about social contexts even within one cultural setting. An illustration from a chapter of *Omne bonum* (*All That is Good*), an encyclopedia compiled by fourteenth-century London clerk James le Palmer, asks if clerics should lose their benefices due to infirmity or illness (including chronic conditions such as leprosy). The red spotted skin is a common strategy for depicting leprosy in European art (including English literature and art specifically), and the text and image allow students to ask new questions about medieval ideas of leprosy and its relation to what we might now call "disability" (see Le Palmer in the list of course materials in the appendix; Green and colleagues provide a complete translation and analysis of the accompanying text).

The primary issue regarding leprosy in *Omne bonum* is a practical one: its slowly debilitating effects on the body and the capacity of a cleric to perform professional duties. The responses to clerical debilitation differ by circumstances. Depending on the rank of the cleric, a coadjutor (assistant) is appropriate rather than full removal and replacement; and the issue of whether leprosy is naturally occurring or acquired through a moral (sexual) transgression is a diagnosis left to a physician to determine. In asking what issues a practical resource presents as most urgent to its audience, we see disease and disability framed not simply as a matter of social stigma, sin, or segregation but rather in terms of accommodation. How does the medieval term *debilitatus* ("debilitated") differ from the modern term *disabled*? Is leprosy or disability a social category or identity in this context, or is it something else?

Reading Sources, Asking Questions

This essay includes an appendix consisting of a list of medieval sources (texts and images) for possible use in a medieval studies classroom (including courses in history or literature); the sources encompass an array of geocultural traditions and artistic genres. In a global medieval context, thinking cross-culturally generates new kinds of knowledge. To what purpose do different cultures use stories about disease acquisition and transmission? How does the mutability of disease and disability interact with gender, class, ethnicity, and religion? What might cultural attitudes about disease and disability from the historical past reveal about social structures of support and care today?

Our case study of medieval leprosy illustrates the benefits of approaching the same condition through divergent disciplinary frameworks. In studying a global Middle Ages, we encourage scholars and students to be attentive and inquisitive in using evidence: material, textual, and visual. We would also stress that one type of evidence is not more true than another. A biological understanding of leprosy's nature or mode of progression need not supplant a literary account that attributes the disease to sin or sexual behavior.

Readings of a literary or artistic work about leprosy (or whatever seemingly equivalent medieval word is used) can explore social and cultural dimensions that complement or contradict paradigms of modern biology. Indeed, we would strongly encourage pairing medieval sources with patients' accounts from leprosaria in the nineteenth through mid–twentieth centuries, before modern antimicrobial therapies made the disease curable.[4]

The conceptual world our medieval writers and artists inhabited was as real as any bacteria, and students can appreciate the global dimensions of medieval disease and disability by seeking to understand the worldviews of our medieval guides.

Notes

1. Starting in the 1940s, it became common to refer to *Hansen's disease* rather than *leprosy*. The name *Hansen* refers to Gerhard Henrik Armauer Hansen, who first isolated the *Mycobacterium leprae* bacillus in 1873. *Hansen's disease* was deemed preferable because so much stigma had accrued to the term *leprosy* and its associated form *leper*. Here, we eschew the latter term, which identifies individuals solely by their disease status. Because a second kind of leprosy has now been discovered (by the microbiologist Xiang-Yang Han in 2008), however, that term is now the more inclusive and accurate to refer to the disease. Roberts provides an excellent summary of the disease's history.

2. Developments in genetics in the past twenty years have revolutionized the ability to gauge the age of human diseases. The estimated age of *M. leprae* as a human pathogen (disease-causing agent) is a matter of ongoing debate; for our comments here, we draw on the latest work, Neukamm et al. For teaching purposes, one should note that many of these studies are open-access publications, accompanied by visual materials (phylogenetic trees, photographs showing skeletal lesions, maps) that can be helpful in conveying the material record of the disease and the methods used to investigate them.

3. This comes from bk. 5, cap. 5 of the *Passionarius* attributed to Gariopontus of Salerno. The translation was made by Monica H. Green from Cologny, Fondation Martin Bodmer, Cod. Bodmer MS 177, s. xii in. (Northern Italy), where it appears on pp. 121–23, www.e-codices.unifr.ch/en/fmb/cb-0177/121/0/Sequence-891. The *Passionarius* is a composite text. The first half of this excerpt comes from a late antique Latin work on chronic diseases known as the *Esculapius*, which was probably made in late antique North Africa and derives from the writing of the first- to second-century Greek physician, Soranus of Ephesus. The latter half comes from the *Methodus medendi ad Glauconem* (*The Method of Healing for Glauco*) by the second-century Greek physician, Galen of Pergamon.

4. See, for example, the accounts drawn on for the special issue of *Journal of Pacific History* (Luker and Buckingham).

Works Cited

Amundson, Ron, and Akira Oakaokalani Ruddle-Miyamoto. "A Wholesome Horror: The Stigmas of Leprosy in Nineteenth-Century Hawaii." *Disability Studies Quarterly*, vol. 30, no. 3/4, 2010, http://dx.doi.org/10.18061/dsq.v30i3/4.1270.

Blevins, Kelly E., et al. "Evolutionary History of *Mycobacterium leprae* in the Pacific Islands." *Philosophical Transactions of the Royal Society B*, vol. 375, no. 1812, 2020, http://dx.doi.org/10.1098/rstb.2019.0582.

Burns, Susan L. *Kingdom of the Sick: A History of Leprosy and Japan.* U of Hawai'i P, 2019.

Deacon, Harriet. "Racial Segregation and Medical Discourse in Nineteenth-Century Cape Town." *Journal of South African Studies*, vol. 22, no. 2, 1996, pp. 287–308.

Dols, Michael W. "Leprosy in Medieval Arabic Medicine." *Journal of the History of Medicine and Allied Sciences*, vol. 34, no. 3, July 1979, pp. 314–33.

Goble, Andrew Edmund. *Confluences of Medicine in Medieval Japan: Buddhist Healing, Chinese Knowledge, Islamic Formulas, and Wounds of War.* U of Hawai'i P, 2011.

———. "The Globalisations of Disease." *Human Dispersal and Species Movement: From Prehistory to the Present*, edited by Nicole Boivin et al., Cambridge UP, 2017, pp. 494–520.

Green, Monica H., and Lori Jones. "The Evolution and Spread of Major Human Diseases in the Indian Ocean World." *Disease Dispersion and Impact in the Indian Ocean World*, edited by Gwyn Campbell and Eva-Marie Knoll, Palgrave Macmillan, 2020, pp. 25–57. Palgrave Series in Indian Ocean World Studies.

Green, Monica H., et al. "Diagnosis of a 'Plague' Image: A Digital Cautionary Tale." *Pandemic Disease in the Medieval World: Rethinking the Black Death*, edited by Green and Carol Symes, special issue of *The Medieval Globe*, vol. 1, no. 1, pp. 309–25.

Hsy, Jonathan. "'Be More Strange and Bold': Kissing Lepers and Female Same-Sex Desire in *The Book of Margery Kempe*." *Early Modern Women Journal*, vol. 5, fall 2010, pp. 189–99.

Kim, Jane Sung Hae. *Leprosy in Korea: A Global History.* 2012, U of California, Los Angeles, PhD dissertation.

Leung, Angela Ki Che. *Leprosy in China: A History.* Columbia UP, 2009.

Luker, Vicki, and Jane Buckingham. "Histories of Leprosy: Subjectivities, Community and Pacific Worlds." *Journal of Pacific History*, vol. 52, no. 3, 2017, pp. 265–86.

McDonald, S. K., et al. "'TB or not TB': The Conundrum of Pre-European Contact Tuberculosis in the Pacific." *Philosophical Transactions of the Royal Society B*, vol. 375, no. 1812, 2020, https://doi.org/10.1098/rstb.2019.0583.

Mesele, Terecha Kebede. *Leprosy, Leprosaria and Society: A Historical Study of Selected Sites, 1901–2001.* Armauer Hansen Research Institute, 2005.

Neukamm, Judith, et al. "Two-Thousand-Year-Old Pathogen Genomes Reconstructed from Metagenomic Analysis of Egyptian Mummified Individuals." *BMC Biology*, vol. 18, article no. 108, 2020, https://doi.org/10.1186/s12915-020-00839-8.

Obregón, Diana. "The Social Construction of Leprosy in Colombia, 1884–1939." *Science Technology Society*, vol. 1, no. 1, 1996, pp. 11–23.

Orlemanski, Julie. "How to Kiss a Leper." *Postmedieval*, vol. 3, no. 2, May 2012, pp. 142–57.

Pearman, Tory V. *Women and Disability in Medieval Literature.* Palgrave, 2010.

Rawcliffe, Carole. *Leprosy in Medieval England.* D. S. Brewer, 2006.

Richardson, Kristina L. *Difference and Disability in the Medieval Islamic World: Blighted Bodies.* Edinburgh UP, 2014.

Roberts, Charlotte A. *Leprosy: Past and Present.* U of Florida P, 2020.

Schuenemann, Verena J., et al. "Ancient Genomes Reveal a High Diversity of *Mycobacterium Leprae* in Medieval Europe." *PLOS Pathogens*, vol. 14, no. 5, 2018, https://doi.org/10.1371/journal.ppat.1006997.

Appendix

TEACHING ACTIVITIES AND QUESTIONS

1. How does this source describe or depict the symptoms of leprosy or somatic features associated with the condition?
2. Does the source offer (or assume) a theory of disease transmission or geographical spread?
3. What clues does the source provide about social attitudes regarding leprosy?
4. Can this source offer evidence of lived experience of leprosy?
5. How might this source challenge ideas of leprosy as a deserved punishment (in whichever cultural or religious context this work is situated)?
6. What other forms of corroborating evidence would be helpful to offer a fuller story about this source?
7. Compare two sources (from the same geocultural background or from different parts of the globe). Can one source help you understand the other? How do the sources differ in addressing the symptoms or understandings of leprosy? What do the sources suggest about leprosy's geographical spread?

COURSE MATERIALS: TEXTS AND IMAGES

The Arabian Nights, circa fourteenth century CE. "The Tale of King Yunan and the Sage Duban." King with leprosy is cured. *The Arabian Nights: A Norton Critical Edition*, translated by Husain Haddawy, edited by Daniel Heller-Roazen, W. W. Norton, 2009, pp. 36–41.

Chaucer, Geoffrey. General Prologue to *The Canterbury Tales*, circa 1387–1400 CE. Portrait of Summoner, lines 623–68. Interlinear translation, sites.fas.harvard.edu/~chaucer/teachslf/gp-par.htm. Image of Summoner from the Ellesmere manuscript, circa 1410 CE, Huntington Library, San Marino, CA, MS EL 26 C 9, fol. 81r, hdl.huntington.org/digital/collection/p15150coll7/id/2526. (See also Bridget Whearty, "The Leper on the Road to Canterbury: The Summoner, Digital Manuscripts, and Possible Futures," *Mediaevalia*, vols. 36–37, 2015–16, pp. 223–61.)

Henryson, Henry. *Testament of Cresseid*, late fifteenth century CE. Edited by Robert Kindrick, *The Poems of Robert Henryson*, Medieval Institute Publications, 1997, d.lib.rochester.edu/teams/text/kindrick-poems-of-robert-henryson-testament-of-cresseid. Abridged modern spelling edition by Michael Murphy, academic.brooklyn.cuny.edu/webcore/murphy/troilus/testamen.pdf.

Ibn Farroukh, Shayban. *Sahih Muslim* (*The Famous Authentic Compilation of the Prophet's Traditions*), n.d. "The Tale of the Leper, the Bald Man, and the Blind Man." English translation in *Classical Arabic Stories: An Anthology*, edited by Salma Khadra Jayyusi, Columbia UP, 2010, pp. 179–81.

Jo gdan Bsod nams bzang po (1341–1433 CE) et al., hagiographies of Tibetan Buddhist nun Gelongma Palmo. English translations in Ivette M. Vargas-O'Brian, "The Life of dGe slong ma dPal mo: The Experience of a Leper, Founder of a Fasting Ritual, a Transmitter of Buddhist Teachings on Suffering and Renunciation in Tibetan Religious History," *Journal of the International Association of Buddhist Studies*, vol. 24, no. 2, 2001, pp. 157–86.

Kajiwara Shōzen. Ton'ishō (Book of the Simple Physician or Jottings on Medicine), 1304 CE. Ch. 34. English excerpts in Andrew Edmund Goble, *Confluences of Medicine in Medieval Japan: Buddhist Healing, Chinese Knowledge, Islamic Formulas, and Wounds of War*, U of Hawai'i P, 2011), pp. 68–79.

Kempe, Margery. *The Book of Margery Kempe*, circa 1436 CE. Ch. 75. Edited by Lynn Staley, Medieval Institute Publications, 1996, d.lib.rochester.edu/teams/text/staley-book-of-margery-kempe-book-i-part-ii. Translated by Anthony Bale, *The Book of Margery Kempe*, Oxford UP, 2015.

Le Palmer, James. *Omne Bonum* (*All That is Good*), circa 1350–75 CE. "De clerico debilitate ministrante sequitur videre" ("On Ministration by a Disabled Cleric"), www.bl.uk/manuscripts/FullDisplay.aspx?ref=Royal_MS_6_E_VI/1&index=0. Image with Latin text and English translation in Monica H. Green et al., "Diagnosis of a 'Plague' Image: A Digital Cautionary Tale," *Pandemic Disease in the Medieval World: Rethinking the Black Death*, edited by Green and Carol Symes, special issue of *The Medieval Globe*, vol. 1, no. 1, 2014, pp. 309–26, scholarworks.wmich.edu/medieval_globe/1/.

Life of Saint Alice of Schaerbeek, circa 1260–1275 CE. Also known as the *Vita* of Alice the Leper. Translated by Martinus Crawley, Guadalupe Translations, 1994. Excerpts online, www2.kenyon.edu/projects/margin/alice.htm.

Nawawī, al-. *Kitāb al-adhkār* (*Book of Remembrances*), late thirteenth century CE. Q 49.11. Excerpt from advice manual discusses nicknames relating to physical impairment. Translated by Kristina Richardson, *Difference and Disability in the Medieval Islamic World: Blighted Bodies*, Edinburgh UP, 2012, p. 113.

St Elzéar Curing the Lepers, circa 1373 CE. Alabaster statue, art.thewalters.org/detail/25661/saint-elzcar-curing-the-lepers/.

Teresa de Cartagena. *Arboleda de los enfermos* (*Grove of the Infirm*), after 1450 CE. Deaf Spanish nun describing fleshly mortification and afflictions as "the stamp of our suffering" with the "body and face of the suffer" as a symbolic "coat of arms." *The Writings of Teresa de Cartagena*, translated by Dayle Seidenspinner-Núñez, D. S. Brewer, 1998, pp. 63–64.

Denise A. Spellberg

The Camel in Early Global Literatures

The camel connected people across the medieval globe, from China to Europe, as a beast of burden. Beyond its pivotal role in overland travel, this curious creature also appeared in religious texts, art, and literary imagination across continents. Educating students about the camel's important role in history allows them a point of entry into the connectivity of global cultures. The camel's particularly prominent presence in the history of the medieval Middle East offers a unique view of Arab environmental challenges and agency, before and after the rise of Islam.

This essay follows the template of a camel's trek, providing a tour of possible approaches to the beast's importance in human history. Scientific details about the animal's origins establish the basis for understanding its centrality to the Silk Road and Arabia. The species first appeared on the one continent where it also first became extinct in prehistoric times. This tour of the camel's history, unique assets, and global impact on commerce and culture will conclude with the story of its attempted reintroduction to North America in the mid–nineteenth century, a tale that takes the camel's global history full circle.

First Steps: Origins and Evolution

Camels first appeared during the Eocene era—roughly forty million years ago—in North America. In this then toasty environment, the earliest camelids were tiny and appeared to resemble llamas. A cooling atmosphere in the late Eocene era probably wiped out the smallest versions of these creatures in North America by 10,000 BCE. *Camelus*, the animal recognized today, however, escaped extinction by earlier, dual paths of migration. Around 2.5 million years ago, the progenitors of the species we recognize today found warmer climes via two different land bridges that no longer exist. The species migrated to South America, where it evolved into the llama and alpaca. Moving eastward via the Bering Strait, the species arrived in Asia. There, the Bactrian (two-humped) and the dromedary (one-humped) camel varieties both evolved. Scientists believe the single-humped camel appeared after its dual-humped progenitor. The dromedary spread west into the Middle East six to seven thousand years ago. Ill-equipped to fend off predators, camels followed the evolutionary path of horses and dogs in early domestication, trusting humans to protect them (Irwin 37–45).

Long before the dromedary became synonymous with the Arabs during the Roman era, the Bactrian found a place in the ancient religions of India and Iran. It is mentioned as a valuable domestic animal in the Sanskrit *Rig Veda*, one of the four sacred texts of Hinduism, which may originate as far back as 1700 BCE. As in the Hindu text, the camel is also designated by the same word, *ushtra*, in the Zoroastrian holy book, the *Avesta* (Bulliet, *Camel* 153). The Prophet Zarathushtra's (Zoroaster's) very name means "he who can manage camels." This moniker invokes the importance of the animal among the ancient Indo-Iranians (Boyce 182–183). Although his dates are uncertain, many historians believe that Zarathustra lived in the early seventh to the mid–sixth century BCE.

The Zoroastrian Achaemenids (559–330 BCE), the greatest ancient Iranian dynasty, depicted Bactrian camels as part of the homage of tribes from northeastern Iran to their ruler on stone friezes that still stand at the great palace complex of Persepolis, located near Shiraz, Iran. The dromedary camel appears on these same walls only in connection with the Arab delegation's visit to the ruler (Bulliet, *Camel*, figs. 74–75). According to Herodotus, the Achaemenid shah, Cyrus the Great, who ruled an empire stretching from the Indus to the Aegean, employed camels as military pack animals, using them in a successful 547 BCE charge against the enemy

Lydian forces in order to frighten their horses (Clutton-Brock 159). Before the Arab Muslim invasion, Bactrians were the single camel type in Iran.

One Hump or Two? Differences between the Bactrian and the Dromedary

Camels evolved to meet challenging environments in unique physiological ways. The Bactrian and the dromedary are the same species but differ by more than their distinct number of humps.

The Bactrian camel is named after the province of Bactria in northern Afghanistan, where they once flourished. Its homeland also may have included Mongolia or northwestern China (Bulliet, *Camel* 143). It was first domesticated in Turkestan around 1000 BCE (Irwin 197). This type of camel is physiologically distinguished from the dromedary in several key ways. It has the following features: shorter legs, but the ability to carry loads of a thousand pounds, almost twice as much as the dromedary; a double coat, with a furry undercoat which insulates while the outer hairy topcoat reflects sunlight for cooling; and a gestational period of thirteen months, one month longer than a dromedary. The Bactrian camel proved to be the "single most important animal used over the Silk Road" (Olsen 22), linking China to the Mediterranean, from the second century BCE to the thirteenth century CE: "No travel corridor is more important in world history" (Liu 1). For an image of a Bactrian camel pulling a cart along the Amur river in northeastern China, see the Library of Congress website: loc.gov/pictures/item/2004708090/.

In China this two-humped creature became a beast of burden as early as the western Han dynasty (206 BCE–24CE). Ceramic images of camels have been found frequently in Tang dynasty tombs, dating from the seventh to the tenth centuries CE (fig. 1). A Muslim account about trade with China from 851 CE details the Chinese possession of "numerous beasts of burden," which included "donkeys and the two-humped camels in plenty," but no Arabian horses (Liu 145). The Bactrian camel linked trade from China through Central Asia to Iran.

In contrast, the dromedary boasts features unique in the animal world that make it ideal for desert travel:

A third eyelid may close to protect its eyes from sand.
The slit nose is protected by flaps that may close at will.

It can survive thirty days without water, and five to seven days without either food or water.
It can consume up to twenty-eight gallons of water at one time.
It prefers to graze six to eight hours a day and will eat thorn and scrub other ruminants will not.
It can tolerate a six-degree rise above its body heat.
Its hump does not store water but fat, which produces water when metabolized.
It moves three miles an hour normally, but twelve to fourteen at a gallop.
It may carry six hundred pounds.
Gestation takes a bit more than twelve months.
A she-camel will mother her calf for a year, though it is weaned after four months.
A female camel will weep and mourn for ten days when her offspring are taken from her. (Bulliet, *Camel* 30–35; Irwin 17–30)

For an image of a mother and baby dromedary with a bedouin in the Transjordan, see the Library of Congress website: www.loc.gov/pictures/item/2019693716/.

Likely first domesticated in southern Arabia around 4000 BCE, the dromedary predominated in hot and arid climes (Irwin 197). As a beast of burden in southern Arabia, the camel is mentioned in the Hebrew Bible as part of the queen of Sheba's delegation to King Solomon. She "arrived in Jerusalem with a very large retinue, with camels bearing spices, a great quantity of gold, and precious stones" (1 Kings 10.2). Sheba's king-

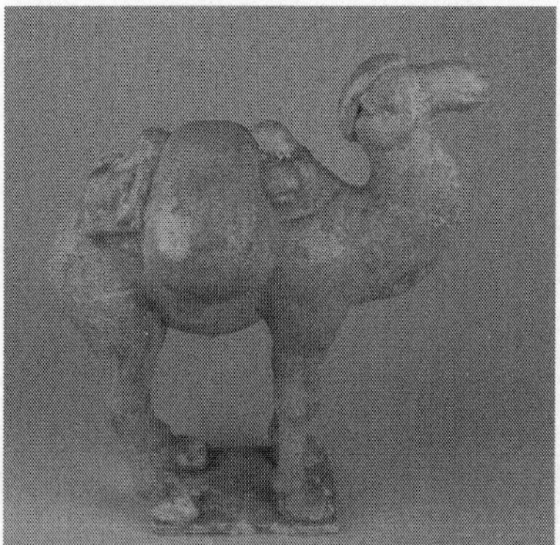

Figure 1. *Bactrian Camel Funerary Object*. Tang dynasty (618–907 CE). Metropolitan Museum of Art, New York. Source: Creative Commons Zero.

dom of *Saba* is thought to be either located in southern Arabia or the Horn of Africa (today's Somalia or Ethiopia). The wealth the queen of Sheba offers King Solomon, who reigned 965–31 BCE, includes spices. Sheba's kingdom encompassed the only environs on earth where the commodity frankincense, used as both a spice and a perfume, grew on trees. These are the same locations where what came to be known as the South Arabian camel saddle originated (fig. 2). This earliest dromedary camel saddle allowed the rider to sit behind the hump.

In the year 77 CE, the Roman historian Pliny described commodities flowing westward from China and India, which included silk, ebony, and cotton. Frankincense, much in demand for religious rites and embalming, arrived in the Roman world via southern Arabia along a 1,500-mile overland route to Gaza and the Mediterranean, "divided into 65 stages with halts for camels" (Liu 65). The Roman demand for frankincense had ebbed long before the seventh-century rise of Islam, but the camel remained ubiquitous in Arabia, tied to the subsistence of pastoral nomads and trade routes north to Palestine and Syria. Scholars of technology argue about when they were first domesticated in southern Arabia, one putting the earliest date at 4000 BCE (Irwin 197), another estimating 3000 BCE (Bulliet, *Camel* 56).

Figure 2. *Bedouin in the Sinai Mounted on a South Arabian Saddle.* Circa 1900. Library of Congress, Washington, DC, Prints and Photographs Division, LC-M31-A-371.

Camels in the Bible

The camel's presence is notable in the sacred texts of the three great monotheisms: Judaism, Christianity, and Islam. What follows is a template for searching sacred texts that contain camel references. Students may be interested in these cited examples but should be urged to find additional references in multiple sacred texts.

The camel is mentioned a total of sixty-two times in the Bible, the vast majority, fifty-six, appearing in the Hebrew Bible (Irwin 140). Scholars believe the mention of camels in the life of Abraham, patriarch of the Arabs and the Hebrews, and through the latter's Davidic line, Jesus, however, to be an anachronism. Recent archeological finds of camel bones in Israel now date the animal's domestication in that region to the latter part of the tenth century BCE. In contrast, Abraham, Joseph, and Jacob, all associated with verses including camels, are supposed to have existed in a much earlier era, between 2000 and 1500 BCE (Wilford, "Camels"). This inaccuracy suggests camels were added to these texts ex post facto, as symbols of wealth. Additionally, unlike Muslims, for whom the camel may be eaten, Jews are forbidden its consumption: ". . . you shall not eat: the camel—although it chews the cud, it has no true hoofs: it is unclean for you" (Leviticus 11.4).

In Europe, camels were used by Roman armies as pack animals. Although the animal's remains have been found at archeological sites in Spain, Italy, France, Germany, and in the Balkans, it is unlikely that these one-humped camels would have survived long in these cold climates. One naturalist posits that Roman troops originally stationed in Asia may have tested the animal's durability in Europe as an experiment (Clutton-Brock 159). Although the bones of the one-humped dromedary have been found in western Europe, some two-humped, or Bactrian, remnants have been recovered in eastern Europe. The discovery of camel's teeth at a Roman archeological site in Greenwich Park, near London, suggests the Romans may have brought some camels as far north as England (Bond).

Even after the collapse of the Roman Empire, there is sporadic archeological evidence of camel presence in western Europe. Gregory of Tours mentions them as beasts of burden in his sixth-century *History of the Franks* (290). The Merovingian ruler Clotaire II "paraded his Queen Brunehaut on a camel before having her executed" (qtd. in Irwin 157–58). Camels crossed into Spain with the Islamic conquest but did not flourish there. They also were used in thirteenth-century Sicily by Frederick II. These animals were possibly remnants of camels brought by ninth-century Muslim conquerors of the island.

Although it is not impossible that a handful of medieval Europeans observed live camels, it is more likely that the animal became best known as a type of fauna featured in the Bible. By 950 CE, the Old English translation of the *Lindisfarne Gospels* featured the words *camella*, *camelles*, and *camel*. The *Oxford English Dictionary* contains multiple medieval references to camels in religious and literary sources beyond these earliest tenth-century Gospel evocations ("Camel, *N.*"). The Gospels of both Matthew and Mark refer to the "camel hair" clothes of John the Baptist (Matt. 3.4; Mark 1.6).

In the most famed New Testament reference to a camel, Jesus admonishes his followers with a pivotal analogy about wealth as an obstacle to salvation: "And again, I tell you, it is easier for a camel to go through the eye of a needle than for a rich man to enter the kingdom of God . . ." (Matt. 19.24). A slight variation of this admonition may be found in Mark 10.25. The Qur'an contains a similar camel-based warning, not for the wealthy, but for the disbeliever: "Lo! They who deny Our revelations and scorn them, for them the gates of Heaven will not be opened nor will they enter the Garden until the camel goeth through the needle's eye. Thus do we requite the guilty" (7.40).

One particular incident in Genesis served as inspiration for European Christian artists' visual depiction of camels in the medieval era. The story of Abraham's plan to find a wife for his son Isaac includes a test for the prospective bride involving these creatures. Abraham sends his servant (later named Eliezer), who "took ten of his master's camels" (Gen. 24.10) on his trip to the patriarch's homeland. Stopping outside the city of Nahor by the well, the servant asked God to select as Isaac's future bride a woman who would not only draw water for him but also offer to "water [his] camels" (Gen. 24.14).

The beautiful Rebecca did precisely this (Gen. 24.46). Her gesture would have proved labor intensive, since each of the stranger's ten camels might consume up to twenty-eight gallons of water at one time. This test, observes historian Richard Bulliet, proved therefore "a truly extraordinary token of potential wifely submission" (Bulliet, *Camel* 35). Rebecca's gesture also revealed her kindness and generosity toward a complete stranger—and his thirsty beasts. These positive feminine qualities marked her as preferred for Isaac as a future wife above all other women. In describing his master's wealth for Rebecca's family, Abraham's servant lists the patriarch's ownership of "sheep and cattle, silver and gold, male and female slaves, camels and asses" (Gen. 24.35). When Rebecca returns with Abraham's servant, she first glimpses her future husband, Isaac, as she "alighted from the camel" (Gen. 24.64).

The pivotal moment in the tale when Rebecca waters the camels became a visual motif in Christian churches and religious texts. A striking twelfth-century fresco of the scene graces the Norman cathedral of Monreale, near Palermo, Sicily (fig. 3). The camels featured may have been inspired by the propinquity of real beasts. Farther north, however, even without live examples, European Christian artists drew this same Genesis story with beautifully illustrated camels in the thirteenth-century French Psalter of Saint Louis. The text now resides at the Bibliothèque Nationale de France. Camels were also featured in illustrations of Jesus's Nativity and the visit of the Magi, which Giotto depicted in a fourteenth-century fresco in Padua, Italy. Although exotic and foreign in western Europe, camels were enshrined in Christian religious texts and the art their faith inspired. Students may be invited to search for additional art historical images of camels in medieval global art using the online search engine *ArtStor*.

Myriad Arabic Words for Camels

Contrary to the idea that all camels appear alike, each creature had individual traits and purposes. All these nuances were evoked in the Arabic language, a sign of the intimacy of this animal-human history. The importance of the dromedary camel resonates in the nearly six thousand terms in Arabic

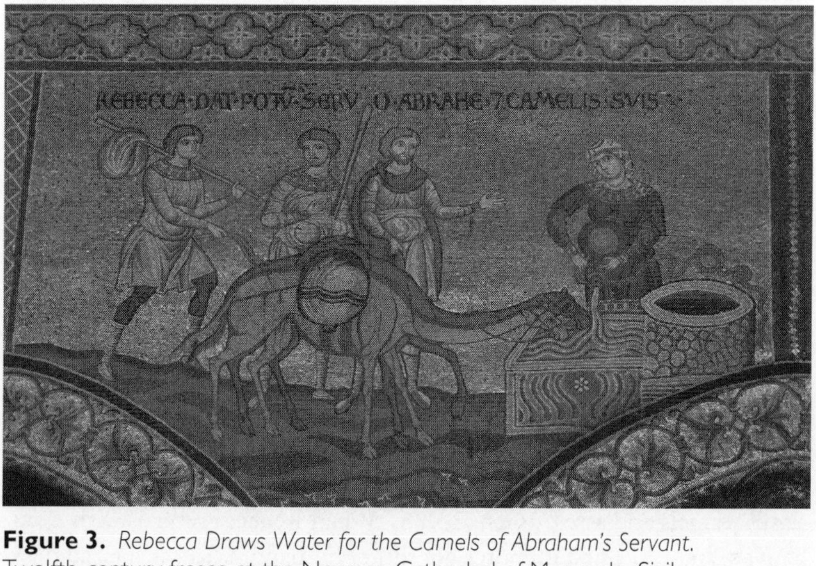

Figure 3. *Rebecca Draws Water for the Camels of Abraham's Servant.* Twelfth-century fresco at the Norman Cathedral of Monreale, Sicily. Photograph by Allan Langdale.

for camel types, including gender, meat, milk, and saddle paraphernalia (Irwin 79). For example, *ibil* is the collective noun used in Arabic for both the one-humped dromedary camel and the two-humped Bactrian (Pellat).

In contrast, *jamal*, an Arabic noun drawn from the same root as the word "beautiful," indicates a male camel, between its sixth and twentieth year (Irwin 80). When poets praised the prized female riding camel, however, the more common term was *naqa* (Khoury 286). In contrast, a newborn camel would be termed a *saqb* ("male") or *saqba* ("female") (ad-Damiri 2: 53). A she-camel of advanced age would be termed *sharif* (2: 97), whereas a she-camel that has her young with her is termed *'aidh* (2: 280). The camel could also be described by its gait as a heavy-treading female *'athamthama* or a male with a similar tread, *'athamtham* (2: 282). These terms are distinct from the designation for camels on which kings ride, *'asjadiyya* (2: 293) or a he-camel with small legs and a high hump, *'aqid* (2: 343), or a camel (male or female) with a large head, *'andal* (2: 393). And the myriad varieties continue, according to al-Damari, a fourteenth-century author from Cairo.

Camels in Pre-Islamic Arabia: Advances in Saddle Technology

The historian Richard Bulliet's classic study of Arab breakthroughs in camel technology asserts a pivotal thesis about an important change in camel saddles: "Sometime between 500 and 100 B.C. a camel saddle was invented that transformed the economic, political, and social history of the Middle East" (Bulliet, *Camel* 87). Bulliet terms this advancement in technology the North Arabian saddle, positing that when Arabs in this part of the peninsula learned to ride seated above the single hump, they transformed the ubiquitous animal into a military mount.

The North Arabian saddle consists of inverted *V* sticks, one in front of the hump and one behind, linked by straight or crossed wooden boughs. These framed the hump, distributing the rider's weight evenly on the animal's rib cage. A pad below this contraption and above it, anchored by girths, allowed the rider to sit securely on the single hump of the dromedary (Baum). The name for the new saddle, *shadad*, refers to its firmness. Bulliet theorized that unlike the South Arabian saddle, which relegated the rider to a perch behind the hump, the new North Arabian saddle allowed the rider better vision and superior control of his mount's head for military purposes (fig. 4).

This new saddle translated into greater power for the Arabs over the sedentary peoples to the north with whom they were linked by trade. Arab

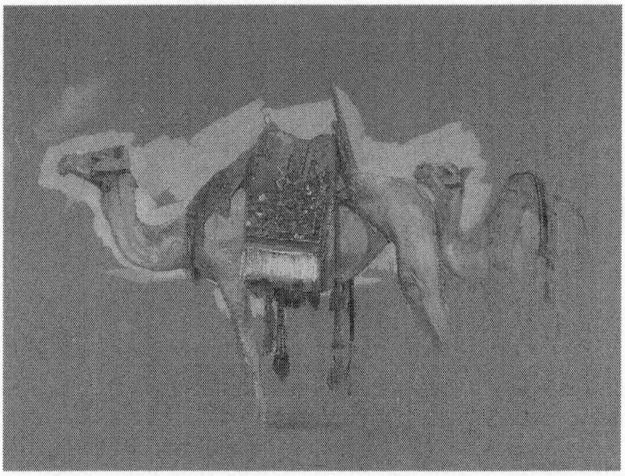

Figure 4. *The North Arabian Saddle in Two Camels*. Circa 1843, John Frederick Lewis. The Metropolitan Museum of Art, New York. Source: Creative Commons.

bows and arrows were replaced by more damaging swords and spears. These new weapons, in turn, could be used to demand greater protection money for camel caravans. These funds allowed Arabs to purchase the most costly and coveted of Arab military mounts: the horse, the Arabian variety of which remains prized worldwide (Bulliet, *Camel* 90–99).

Pre-Islamic Arab Poetry and Sacrifice

When pre-Islamic Arabs declaimed their odes, a standard part of the panegyric included a section boasting about the poet's camel mount. The *wasf al-jamal*, the camel theme, stood alone or introduced the *rahil*, the desert journey of the poet. Among the most famed pre-Islamic poems were those known as the *Mu'allaqa*, the annual prizewinning verses hung on the Ka'ba, the cubicle shrine of Mecca, which was a site of veneration even before the rise of Islam. Tarafa ibn al-'Abd's famed ode dates from the sixth century and includes vivid language in praise of his fleet female camel:

> Ah, but when grief assails me, I ride it off
> mounted on my swift, lean-flanked camel, night and day racing,
> sure footed, like the planks of a litter; I urge her on
> down the bright highway, that back of a striped mantle;
> she vies with the noble hot-paced camels, shank on shank
> nimbly plying over a path many feet have beaten.
>
> (Qtd. in Arberry 83)

The poet's description of this beloved creature continues in praise of her beauty and power. He evokes the "[p]erfectly firm flesh of her two thighs," her "tightly knit spine-bones," and "swift legs, smooth swinging gait."

Tarafa lauds her "long neck," which he compares to "the rudder of a Tigris-bound vessel," and "her cheek . . . smooth as Syrian parchment" (Arberry 84). These references to places far north of the poet's Arabian home suggest the considerable reach of camel-borne Arabs into the urban Middle East, tied by trade—and the endurance of their trusty mounts. The camel theme evolved over time in Arabic poetry. By the rise of the Abbasid dynasty in 750 during the Islamic era, the poet's journey with his beloved camel was often replaced by allusions to the horse, the mount of the settled Muslim urban elite (Jacobi 22).

Pre-Islamic Arabs originally believed that wild camels (*hush*) lived in the mythical country of Wabar, somewhere in southern Arabia. When the people there were destroyed by God for their disobedience, their land was given over to the jinn, supernatural air or flame-born spirits. These wild Wabar camels then mated with the jinn's camels. Their offspring are still known as the best riding camels, among them the prized Mahri and Omani varieties (Bulliet, *Camel* 48).

Pre-Islamic religious practices included the annual sacrifice of camels slaughtered at the Ka'ba. In this period the practice of *baliyya* allowed for a camel to be tethered to its master's grave and left there to starve as a sacrifice to the deceased (Pellat).

Arabs found in camels sources of sustenance (meat, milk, and hair for tents), transportation, and wealth. These beasts could provide payment to quell a vendetta with the family of a murdered tribal enemy or support a dowry for an Arab bride. The ninth-century proverb of the Muslim author Ibn Qutayba, a native of Baghdad, records an anecdote which demonstrates the superiority of the camel in the hierarchy of pastoral animals in Arabia, before and after the rise of Islam:

> The daughter of al-Khuss was asked,
> "What would you say to a hundred goats?"
> "Sufficiency!"
> "To a hundred sheep?"
> "Wealth."
> "To a hundred camels?"
> "Fulfillment." (Lewis 271)

Camels in the Qur'an and Islamic Sacred History

The camel in the Qur'an is designated as a demonstration of God's creation: "Do they consider the camels [*ibil*], how they are created?" (88.17). As a token of God's wisdom and power, the camel's strength ultimately yields to human direction, just as the believing human yields to God in Islamic tradition. In contrast, verses about signs of the end of the world include the moment "when the camels big with young are abandoned" (81.4). The world and known animal husbandry practice had indeed gone awry with apocalyptic threat if owners would abandon these highly valued creatures and their offspring. The word *'ishar* in the sacred text specifically indicates a camel in the tenth month of her twelve-month pregnancy.

An even more extensive role in the Qur'an for the animal unfolds in the story of the Arabian prophet Salih, sent by Allah to the Arabian people of Thamud. The divine endorsement of this prophet's monotheistic mission is made manifest as "a sign" from God in the form of *naqat Allah* 'the she-camel of Allah' (7.73, 11.64, 26.155). The people of Thamud, believed to occupy the area of western Arabia between the Hijaz and Syria, were warned to accept Salih's guidance in showing deference to this she-camel: "so let her feed in Allah's earth, and touch her not with hurt lest painful torment seize you" (7.73). Elsewhere they were warned that this camel was sent as a test (*fitna*), and that "the water is to be shared between [her and] them . . ." (54.27–28), but on alternating days (26.155). The people of Thamud, however, heeded neither the prophet Salih nor deferred to God's she-camel with kindness; instead, they chose to defy divine injunction and killed the camel by hamstringing it, or cutting off its legs between the hip and the knee (26:157; 54.29). For their defiance of God and his messenger—and their bloody destruction of the divinely-designated female camel—the people of Thamud were annihilated by an earthquake (7.78). This account parallels the fate of other people in the Qur'an who denied divine messengers, such as Lot and Noah, and were punished accordingly.

Beyond the Qur'an, the Prophet's precedent, preserved orally over generations and then set down in writing as *hadith*, included directives about how to treat camels. In one ninth-century collection authored by the traditionist named Muslim, the Prophet upbraids his wife 'A'isha for treating her camel too harshly: "It behooves you to treat the animal gently" (qtd. in Foltz 20). This injunction, as we will see, predates 'A'isha's involvement in the politics of succession after her husband's death, when her name fused eternally with that of her camel mount (Spellberg 101–49). Among the prophetic precedents preserved by the Shi'i Muslim minority is an account of the Prophet's compassion for a camel about to be slaughtered by its owner. The camel protested that this seemed a harsh sentence for a lifetime of devoted service, and the Prophet agreed, enjoining the owner to free the beast: "For my sake, spare him and don't sacrifice him."

Whereupon, the camel freely wandered ever after throughout Medina, cared for by all the new Muslim converts there (qtd. in Foltz 22–23).

In al-Tabari's tenth-century universal history, the prophet Adam was taught the camel's name: "God taught him the name of everything down to the camel [*ba'ir*], cow, and sheep." *Ba'ir*, is the term for a male one-humped camel (al-Tabari, *From the Creation* 267). In this same history, we learn why the snake, who aided the angel Iblis/Satan in inveigling Adam and Eve to disobey God in Paradise, lost its feet—and its original resemblance to a camel: "Now, when Iblis wanted to cause their downfall, he entered inside the snake. The snake had four feet as if it were a Bactrian camel and was one of the most beautiful animals created by God" (al-Tabari, *From the Creation* 277). As a punishment, God cursed the snake and severed its feet, ending its original resemblance to the lovely two-humped camel forever.

In a different section of al-Tabari's tenth-century world history, an account of the Prophet's death in 632 CE is followed by lists of his wives, formerly enslaved persons, scribes, horses, mules, and camels. The named camels are divided into mounts and "milch" camels. The latter provided the Prophet's family with considerable quantities of liquid protein: two big waterskins full every evening. One of Muhammad's contemporaries reported that the "greatest part of the diet" of the Prophet and his family came from this source. The Prophet's wife 'A'isha owned one of these camels named *al-Qaswa'*, described as a "slit-eared she-camel (al-Tabari, *Last Years* 150)." The Prophet purchased her from 'A'isha's father, Abu Bakr, for eight hundred silver *dirhams* (150). (Abu Bakr would become the first successor to the Prophet after his death.) This milch camel "remained with him [the Prophet] until he died." Significantly, this was the same camel on which the Prophet made the *hijra*, the pivotal 622 emigration from Mecca to Medina (151).

In the earliest eighth-century biography of the Prophet, this same she-camel figured in choosing the site for the construction of the first mosque in Medina. One observer declared, "Let her go her way," for this camel was "under God's orders." After several stops at the residences of Medinan Muslims, the camel finally knelt at a place that had been used for drying dates. The Prophet "did not alight, and it [the camel] got up and went a short distance." He "left its rein free, not guiding it, and it turned in its tracks and returned to the place where it had knelt at first and knelt there again. It shook itself and lay exhausted with its chest upon the ground." At this point, the Prophet dismounted his camel and asked who owned the property. He was told that two orphans owned the site, and "that he could take it for a mosque and he would pay the young men for it." (Ibn Hisham 228).

A Battle Named after a Camel: The Prophet's Wife and Gender in Islamic Politics

This conflict referenced not just any camel, but the beast on which the Prophet's favorite wife, ʿA'isha bint Abi Bakr, rode to war as a widow. The first armed conflict between Muslims, known ever after as the Battle of the Camel, pitted ʿA'isha against her brother-in-law, the caliph ʿAli ibn Abi Talib (d. 661). Near Basra, Iraq, ʿA'isha's troops challenged ʿAli's caliphate, decrying him as unfit to rule because he refused to punish the murderers of the previous caliph, 'Uthman.

The purchase of ʿA'isha's male camel named *ʿAskar* ("Army") occurred en route to this first battle of the first Islamic civil war. Its owner demanded a thousand silver *dirhams*. Haggling ensued, with the owner proudly affirming its exorbitant price, because the animal proved so fleet of foot that it always caught up with enemies or outran them. When told that his camel should cost less because it was intended as the mount of "your mother," the owner exclaimed: "But I left my mother sitting in her tent, not wanting to go anywhere" (al-Tabari, *Community* 50).

All Muslims knew, however, that as one of the Prophet's wives ʿA'isha merited the honorific "Mother of the Believers." The camel owner's insistence that his biological mother did not wish to leave her home contains an unsubtle but unstated gendered rebuke of ʿA'isha's unfeminine march to battle, the very reason for the purchase of her new and expensive mount. The camel owner's remark invokes implicitly a Qur'anic verse that enjoins all the Prophet's wives to remain in their homes (33.33). Clearly, ʿA'isha did not follow this injunction, but not all the Prophet's widows did. Some left their homes in Medina for religious pilgrimage to Mecca or other reasons. In defense of her political actions as a widow elsewhere, ʿA'isha claimed that she had challenged ʿAli's fitness to rule as a representative of her deceased husband's *sunna* or precedent. In support of her political opposition to ʿAli, she invoked another Qur'anic command for *islah*, the necessity to make peace between two conflicting Muslim factions (49.9–10).

ʿA'isha purchased the magnificent camel for half its proposed price. As part of the deal, its original owner received a *Mahriyya* she-camel, a breed famed for their smarts and speed. The camel's owner, who implicitly critiqued ʿA'isha's maternal status and behavior, served as a guide for her troops on their way to the battle. This led to yet another gendered critique of her march to war.

When the camel's owner led ʿA'isha to the spring of al-Hawaʾab, she heard dogs barking. This caused her to yell "at the top of her voice and hit the upper foreleg of her camel to make it kneel down." She cried out three times: "By Allah, I'm the one the dogs of al-Hawʾab have barked at, at night! Take me back!" (al-Tabari, *Community* 50). The howling of dogs had been considered an ill omen in Arabia. At this juncture, ʿA'isha suddenly recalled her husband's warning in the presence of all his wives: "I wish I knew at which of you the dogs of al-Hawʾab will bark" (68). The memory caused ʿA'isha distress. She halted her march to war for twenty-four hours because of her husband's utterance, which along with the howling dogs, she took as a warning. Although she stopped, eventually she continued her journey, but only after another male ally urged her to flee from enemy troops, a ruse to propel her forward (50).

At the Battle of the Camel: Bloodshed and Defeat

ʿA'isha's camel became the enduring symbol of her absence from home and her presence at the soon-to-be named first battle of the first civil war. The word used in Arabic for her mount was *jamal*, meaning a male camel. She did not fight in the battle, but she presided over the day's bloodshed from behind the lines. Some describe her "on a red camel in a red howdah," or *howdaj*, a palanquin or covered litter used by women atop her mount. So many enemy arrows became stuck in her *howdaj* that observers compared its appearance to a hedgehog (al-Tabari, *Community* 156). Both her male allies had been killed by noon, but ʿA'isha continued to urge her troops forward in battle.

Thus, the heaviest fighting continued close to ʿA'isha's mount. The bravest but most vulnerable of her defenders died holding the camel's nose ring bridle. Their members of the Banu Dabba tribe proudly described themselves as "allies of the camel." They declaimed poetry in the *rajaz* meter, one linked since pre-Islamic times to the depiction of camels. They fought and proclaimed their loyalty to the Prophet's wife in verse:

> Mother of ours, ʿA'isha! Do not fear!
> All of your sons are heroes brave.
> Mother of ours, wife of the Prophet,
> Wife of the blessed and the guided!"
> (al-Tabari, *Community* 138)

It is said that forty men were killed holding the nose rope of ʿAʾisha's camel, defending her (al-Tabari, *Community* 138). Members of the Azd tribe, also fighting for the Mother of the Believers, picked up her camel's dung, and, after smelling it, exclaimed, "The dung of our mother's camel smells of musk!" (al-Tabari, *Community* 144). The implication that this refuse had somehow become perfumed reflects the elevated, sacred status of ʿAʾisha and her famed mount.

Only when the caliph ʿAli insisted that ʿAʾisha's camel be hamstrung did the battle cease. The bellowing of the dying camel announced an end to the fighting. Her enemies lifted ʿAʾisha's palanquin off her deceased mount. She was unhurt, but as many as ten thousand Muslims fighting "around the camel" died that day, half in defense of the Prophet's wife, half fighting for her opponent, the caliph ʿAli (al-Tabari, *Community* 164).

ʿAʾisha's presence atop her camel at this deadly battle would become synonymous with her participation in the first civil war. Debates among medieval Muslims about her culpability endured. The conflict rent the Muslim community into sectarian disputes, with the Shiʿi Muslim minority lauding ʿAli and condemning ʿAʾisha ever after. In the sixteenth century, a Sunni Ottoman manuscript of the Prophet's life featured a miniature which captured ʿAʾisha's visage and red palanquin upon her mount (fig. 5). The artist rendered her camel's massive head almost twice the size as the flanking and opposing horses, a point of emphasis on her important presence. The more accurate designation of the battle should not be the Battle of the Camel, but rather the unstated and implicitly enduring: the Battle of ʿAʾisha's Camel. Even without invoking her name explicitly, all Muslims always remembered which wife of the Prophet had been present at the commencement of the first Islamic civil war.

Consequences of the Battle of the Camel, and a Battle of the Mule?

ʿAli treated the defeated ʿAʾisha respectfully after her defeat, ordering her to return to Medina. ʿAʾisha wept for the dead and never participated actively in politics again. Her defeat set a negative precedent for future Muslim women's political engagement. While Sunni Muslims defended her reputation, blaming her political culpability on her two male allies, Shiʿi Muslims, who revere ʿAli, condemned ʿAʾisha as his eternal enemy.

One supposedly humorous anecdote underscored how Muslims feared that ʿAʾisha might once again participate politically after the Battle of the

Figure 5. *ʿAʾisha in Her Red Palanquin atop Her Camel.* Circa 1595, in *Siyer-i Nebi,* biography of the Prophet in Ottoman Turkish. Topkapi Sarayi Museum Library, Istanbul. Source: Wiki Commons.

Camel: "the story goes that once when a dispute had broken out between two clans of Quraish, ʿAʾisha, Mother of the Faithful, left her home mounted on a mule. Ibn Abi ʿAtiq met her and asked: 'Where are you going?' 'To reconcile the two clans.' 'By God,' he exclaimed, 'we have hardly done washing our heads after the "Day of the Camel", and now we shall have to start talking of the "Day of the Mule!"' She laughed and went on her way" (Jahiz 185).

The famed ninth-century Sunni scholar, al-Jahiz, critiqued this as a "forged tradition" (Jahiz 185). He attributed it to Shiʿi partisans. His Sunni defense of ʿAʾisha included the observation that if ʿAʾisha had indeed "taken to the saddle," the "whole of the populace" of Muslims would have accompanied her. Al-Jahiz also offered an observation about the importance of mules as animals who were needed by "everybody" and "ridden by great men" (Jahiz 186). It is doubtful that 'A'isha would have found this anecdote about her meddling in Islamic politics amusing.

Islamic Literary Visions of the Camel, and Praise for a Hybrid

Al-Jahiz, a ninth-century scholar of East African origin famed for his multivolume encyclopedia, *Kitab al-hayawan* (*The Book of Animals*) described the origins of the giraffe as the result of a cross between the hyena and the camel (Jahiz 127). He also wrote that the bedouin, "with his rustic ignorance," once came before a Persian king and made an argument for the camel's superiority. He claimed the camel's cry carried the furthest, its meat was the tenderest, and it carried the heaviest burdens. The Persian king countered on all points, emphasizing the strength of the elephant to bear loads (Jahiz 184).

Al-Jahiz also described the advent of a new camel, which resulted from the Arab Muslim invasion of eastern Iran. There, the Muslim invaders crossed their native dromedary with a Bactrian. The result, the *bukht*, created a bigger and stronger pack animal. The hybrid appeared to be a single-humped camel but actually displayed "a 2- to 6-inch indentation approximately a third of the way back from their shoulders, representing the missing gap between humps" (qtd. in Bulliet, *Cotton* 110). Al-Jahiz praised the female *bukht*, which resulted from a male Bactrian and a female dromedary: "For the confirmation of these two species does not get any nobler, more glorious, more pleasing, or more costly" (qtd. in Bulliet, *Cotton* 110).

Unfortunately, these hybrids did not replicate the same strengths when bred with other camels. Whereas the Bactrians continued their dominance in China's overland trade, moving goods westward, they were unloaded at Bukhara (a city in today's Central Asian country of Uzbekistan), where the hybrid *bukhts* then carried the loads through Iran and Iraq (Bulliet, *Cotton* 111). Their breeding allowed them to thrive in warmer climes than the Bactrian.

Two hundred years later, a Nestorian Christian doctor who attended to the Abbasid caliphs, wrote the text for a bestiary illustrated in the thirteenth century that included the dromedary. The author, Ibn Bakhtishu, wrote of this camel's nature that it is "malevolent, extremely spiteful and bitter." He also wrote: "It has a long retentive memory and forgets nothing. It will look for an opportunity to be alone with someone who has beaten or maltreated it to take revenge on him, and when the chance comes it will not spare him" (qtd. in Contadini 86). The author then draws a dubious analogy between the camel's character and that of all Arabs: "It is said that among all the beasts of burden it is the one most like the Arab in character" (qtd. in Contadini 87).

The Camel in Tenth-Century Baghdad: On and in Bowls

The dromedary camels in Islamic decorative art not only appear circling a tenth-century bowl (fig. 6) but also might be prepared to fill these bowls—as meat, in the same century! Recipes designed for the Abbasid dynasty (750–1258 CE), who at their zenith ruled the Islamic world from Iran to North Africa from their capital at Baghdad, included camel meat.

Ibn Sayyar al-Warraq's tenth-century cookbook celebrated royal cuisine in a text of 132 chapters. Among the featured dishes were those which included *jazur*, the meat of a slaughtered camel. It is described as beneficial in the diet of people who are "physically active," along with the meat of beef and horse (Nasrallah 103). In most recipes for camel, the hump is the preferred portion, probably because that part of the anatomy is considered the most succulent. In one recipe, cooks are enjoined to crush

Figure 6. *Ceramic Bowl with the Image of Four Camels*. Iraq, tenth century (probably Abbasid dynasty). Metropolitan Museum of Art, New York, Joseph Pulitzer Bequest. Source: Creative Commons.

onions, add salt, and fry until "the hump releases all its fat." The meat is then seasoned with vinegar, black pepper, coriander, and caraway seeds, brought to a boil, then simmered. All the recipes conclude: "God willing," which suggests the outcome of the culinary mission relies ultimately on divine direction (Nasrallah 320).

The Bedouin and the Camel in Ibn Khaldun's Theory of Civilization

In his *Muqaddimah* (*Introduction*) to a multivolume fourteenth-century history of Muslim North Africa, the diplomat and scholar Ibn Khaldun theorized about the rise and fall of human civilization. He asserted, in contrast to the Islamic ideal that history has a divine beginning and an end, that all civilizations rise and fall in stages. The cycle begins, he asserted, in the desert, among pastoral nomads. According to Ibn Khaldun, these peripatetic people's lives focus upon their need to maintain one pivotal animal in a harsh environment:

> Those who make their living raising camels move around more. They wander deeper into the desert, because the hilly pastures with their plants do not furnish enough subsistence for camels. They must feed on the desert shrubs and drink the salty desert water. They must move around the desert regions during the winter, in flight from the harmful cold and the warm desert air. In the desert sands, camels can find places to give birth to their young ones. Of all animals, camels have the hardest delivery and the greatest need for warmth in connection with it. [Camel nomads] are therefore forced to make excursions deep [into the desert]. (92)

Ibn Khaldun theorized that when these camel nomads harnessed *ʿasabiyya* 'group will,' they could organize to conquer urban civilization. He asserted, "The toughness of desert life precedes the softness of sedentary life," and he thus tied the rise of civilization to the compulsions of conquering camel nomads. Once they successfully overwhelmed urban civilization, these newly sedentary conquerors inevitably succumbed to laziness and decadence after four generations. Ibn Khaldun tied this eternal cycle of civilizational rise and fall to his bedrock belief that "Bedouins are prior to sedentary people" and that "[t]he desert is the basis and reservoir of civilization and cities" (93).

Linking the desert to the conquest of settled cultures would be the pastoral nomad's mount: the camel. As an homage to this pivotal animal's important role in the arts, Ibn Khaldun observed that poetry and song originated among the Arabs when driving their camels: "Now, camel drivers sang when they drove their camels, and young men sang when they were alone. They repeated sounds and hummed them. When such humming was applied to poetry, it was called singing" (330). A *hadi*, or camel driver, sang to urge camels along. In the twenty-first century, an ethnographic film entitled *The Story of the Weeping Camel* (2004) documented the important role of music used by Mongolian herdsmen to cause a female Bactrian camel first to weep, then to suckle a calf she had earlier rejected. (Irwin 31–32)

The Camel Returns to North America: Texas, 1856–57

Camels as a species originated in North America fourteen million years ago but died out with cooling climate change around 10,000 BCE. Although camels since the prehistoric era have not been native to the continent, there were two separate early-eighteenth-century attempts to bring two camels each to the colonies of Virginia and Massachusetts (Bulliet, *Camel* 244–45). Neither effort was intended to or resulted in the creation of a domestic camel population in North America.

In the mid–nineteenth century, a more serious program to introduce camels to the United States found support from the administration of President Franklin Pierce. His then secretary of war, Jefferson Davis, promoted the idea of a camel corps suitable for exploring the American southwest in 1853. Two years later, thirty thousand dollars was allotted by congress for the importation of camels (Bulliet, *Camel* 247–54).

Thirty-three or thirty-four camels arrived in Matagorda Bay, Texas, twenty miles south of Galveston, in May 1856. All the camels were purchased in Egypt, and all were dromedaries, except for two Bactrians, which did not survive their ocean voyage. An additional forty-four more dromedaries arrived in Texas the next year from the Ottoman Levant.

The first and last American camel corps was headquartered at Camp Verde, Texas, sixty miles northwest of San Antonio (fig. 7). The camels were tested first on a five-month surveying trek from New Mexico to the California border in 1857 and back the next year. They braved river crossings and snow, bearing up beautifully as pack animals, although they did sometimes frighten mules and horses (Irwin 162–63).

Lieutenant Edward Fitzgerald Beale, leader of the expedition, dubbed it an unqualified success. He requested government backing for the

Figure 7. *The Surprising Arrival of Camels at the United States Army's Camp Verde, Texas.* Mural on a lumber company's wall, Ingram, Texas. Library of Congress, Washington, DC, Prints and Photographs Division. Photograph by Carol M. Highsmith, 2014, LC-DIG-highsm- 29583.

purchase of a thousand more camels repeatedly through 1860. Unfortunately, the advent of the Civil War the following year, and the fact that Jefferson Davis, now president of the Confederacy, had supported the initial purchase, put an end to the creation of a permanent United States camel corps (Irwin 162–63).

Most of the camels were sold off to mining companies, circuses, and zoos, whereas others were turned loose or escaped and turned feral. Sightings of camels in Arizona persisted into the 1890s, and in West Texas continued through 1931 (Irwin 163). The last member of the original United States camel corps died in a zoo in 1934 (Gingold).

The camels that landed in Texas had been accompanied by Muslim camel experts. One, named Hajji ʿAli, a native of Syria, remained in the United States after the failure of the government experiment with the animals he knew so well. He continued to work for the army for 30 years and then became a miner, marrying a Sonoran Mexican woman, with whom he had two daughters. When he died in 1902, he was destitute. The U.S. government never allotted him the pension he repeatedly requested for his services (Gingold).

A monument to ʿAli—topped by a camel figurine—remains a tribute to him in Quartzite, Arizona, where he died. Because the Americans who relied on his camel expertise could not pronounce his name, they referred to him by the absurd moniker "Hi Jolly." This inaccurate designation is etched on his monument.

The camels' provisional presence in the history of the United States resulted in two works of fiction. One, *Army Camels: Texas Ships of the Desert* by Doris Fisher, is nicely illustrated and accessible for elementary school students. It details how the camels endured their transoceanic voyage from Egypt to Texas and documents their hijinks in the Lone Star State. There, the creatures avidly consumed the prickly pear cacti that the United States Army thought would suffice for their fence!

An unusually poignant novel for children of all ages, *Exiled: Memoirs of a Camel*, by Kathleen Karr, attempts to view the world through the eyes of ʿAli, a camel in the camel corps. He, like most of Egyptian origin, professes the faith of Islam. Written in ʿAli's first-person narration, the novel describes the camel's varied encounters with "men-beasts" (Karr 12), documenting their cruelty, kindness, and stupidity toward him. Despite the demise of the United States Army's plans, ʿAli finds love with a female member of the camel corps and, in the end, both freedom and fatherhood. In a final demonstration of animal agency, ʿAli rescues his human friend, Hajji ʿAli, whose "hand," the camel swears, "I would never need to bite" (238). In the end, this eloquent protagonist recalls "words once spoken by my mother. Wise words about our destiny being tied to that of human-kind" (238).

And so this trek with and about camels returns to the North American place of their prehistoric origins, concluding a global survey of their enduring impact in history.

Works Cited

Arberry, A. J. *The Seven Odes*. Allen and Unwin, 1957.

Baum, Doug. "The Art of Saddling a Camel." *Saudi Aramco World*, vol. 69, no. 6, Nov.–Dec. 2018, www.aramcoworld.com/en-US/Articles/November-2018/The-Art-of-Saddling-A-Camel.

Bond, Sarah. "Were There Camels in Roman Britain? New Evidence Suggests Camels Were Common across the Empire." *Forbes*, Nov. 17, 2017, www.forbes.com/sites/drsarahbond/2017/11/17/were-there-camels-in-roman-britain-new-evidence-suggests-camels-were-common-across-the-empire/#381dae8f23f8.

Boyce, Mary. *A History of Zoroastrianism*. E. J. Brill, 1975.

Bulliet, Richard W. *The Camel and the Wheel*. 1975. Reprint ed., Columbia UP, 1990.

———. *Cotton, Climate, and Camels in Early Islamic Iran: A Moment in World History*. Columbia UP, 2009.

"Camel, N." *Oxford English Dictionary*, Oxford UP, Mar. 2019, www.oed.com/view/Entry/26665.

Clutton-Brock, Juliette. *A Natural History of Domesticated Mammals.* Cambridge, 1999.

Contadini, Anna. *A World of Beasts: A Thirteenth-Century Illustrated Arabic Book on Animals (the* Kitab Na'at al-Hawayan*) in the Ibn Bakhtishu' Tradition.* E. J. Brill, 2012.

Damiri, ad-. *Hayat al-Haywan (A Zoological Lexicon).* Translated by A. S. G. Jayakar, 2 vols., Luzac and Company, 1908.

Fisher, Doris. *Army Camels: Texas Ships of the Desert.* Pelican Publishing, 2013.

Foltz, Richard C. *Animals in Islamic Tradition and Muslim Cultures.* Oneworld, 2006.

Gingold, Naomi. "One of America's First Syrian Immigrants Helped Conquer the West—with Camels." PRI's *The World*, 15 May 2017, www.pri.org/stories/2017-05-12/one-americas-first-syrian-immigrants-helped-conquer-west-camels.

Gregory of Tours. *History of the Franks.* Translated by Lewis Thorpe, Penguin, 1974.

Ibn Hisham. *The Life of Muhammad: A Translation of Ishaq's* Sirat Rasul Allah. 1955. Translated by A. Guillaume, reprint ed., Oxford UP, 1967.

Ibn Khaldun. *The* Muqaddimah*: An Introduction to History.* Translated by Franz Rosenthal, Princeton UP, 1967.

Irwin, Robert. *Camel.* Reaktion, 2010.

Jacobi, Renate. "The Camel Section of the Panegyrical Ode." *Journal of Arabic Literature*, vol. 13, 1982, pp. 1–22.

Jahiz, al-. *The Life and Works of Jahiz.* Translated by Charles Pellat, U of Berkeley P, 1969.

Karr, Kathleen. *Exiled: Memoirs of a Camel.* Marshall Cavendish, 2004.

Khoury, R. J. "Camel." *Encyclopaedia of the Qur'an*, edited by Jane McAuliffe, vol. 1, E. J. Brill, 2001, pp. 286–87.

Lewis, Bernard, editor and translator. *Islam: From the Prophet to the Capture of Constantinople.* Vol. 2, Harper, 1974.

Liu Xinru. *The Silk Roads: A Brief History with Documents.* Bedford/St. Martin's, 2012.

The Meaning of the Glorious Qur'an: Text and Explanatory Translation. Translated by Muhammad Marmaduke Pickthall. Muslim World League, 1977.

Nasrallah, Nawal. *Annals of the Caliphs' Kitchens: Ibn Sayyar al-Warraq's Tenth-Century Baghdadi Cookbook.* Translated by Nawal Nasrallah, E. J. Brill, 2007.

Olsen, Stanley J. "The Camel in Ancient China and an Osteology of the Camel." *Proceedings of the Academy of the Natural Sciences*, vol. 140, no. 1, 1988, pp. 18–58.

Pellat, Charles. "Ibil." *Encyclopaedia of Islam*, edited by P. Bearman et al., 2nd ed., 2012, http://dx.doi.org/10.1163/1573-3912_islam_SIM_3020.

Spellberg, D. A. *Politics, Gender, and the Islamic Past: The Legacy of ʿAʾisha bint Abi Bakr.* Columbia UP, 1994.

Tabari, al-. *The Community Divided.* Translated by Adrian Brockett, State U of New York P, 1997. Vol. 16 of Bibliotheca Persica *[Taʾrikh al-rusul waʾl-muluk].*

———. *General Introduction and From the Creation to the Flood.* Translated by Franz Rosenthal, State U of New York P, 1989. Vol. 1 of Bibliotheca Persica *[Taʾrikh al-rusul waʾl-muluk].*

———. *The Last Years of the Prophet.* Translated by Ismail Poonawala, State U of New York P, 1990. Vol. 9 of Bibliotheca Persica *[Taʾrikh al-rusul waʾl-muluk].*

Tanakh, the Holy Scriptures, The New JPS Translation according to the Hebrew Text. The Jewish Publication Society, 1988.

Wilford, John Noble. "Camels Had No Business in Genesis." *The New York Times,* 10 Feb. 2014, www.nytimes.com/2014/02/11/science/camels-had-no-business-in-genesis.html.

Part IV

Modalities of Culture, Technologies of Culture

Lars Christensen and Gabriela Currie

Soundscapes in the Global Middle Ages

Unless sounds are remembered by many, they perish, for they cannot be written down.

—Isidore of Seville

There is no way in writing to make people clear on a precise tone.

—Jing Fang

An often noted property of music is its ephemerality. In lucky cases, an original visual or textual artifact from long ago might survive intact and in good enough condition to bear direct examination, but the analogous situation could never obtain with music, since the original product is lost as soon as its last echo has died away. A musical performance might be repeated, but before recording technology, this second performance could not be directly compared with the original in the way that texts or images can. Even after the advent of recording technology, the reproduction of music must be mediated through playback devices that can never provide more than a simulacrum of the original sounds, in contrast to the more direct evidence of the painting or the page. For these reasons, sounds can only be imperfectly and incompletely impressed on the historical memory.

And yet, none of this is to say that we cannot profitably learn something about the music of the distant past. Even if the trace of sounds in the historical memory is necessarily fragmentary, they still survive in words, images, objects, and downstream living traditions that can tell us something about bygone musical practices. Though we can seldom be as confident about our representations of past musics as those who deal with visual and literary evidence, constructing them forces us to remember that in lived experience the past was not silent. Like our own world, it was full of sounds, and those sounds meant something to those who created them and listened to them. Our goal in this essay is to demystify these representations to reveal an often neglected facet of the past so we can imagine more completely and accurately what it was like to be there.

Our representations of past musics can be arrayed on a continuum, ranging from the products of pure imagination about the past and an ideal, perfect reconstruction of the sounds of the past. The former need not concern us, as it has no basis in scholarship, whereas the latter is an impossible target. In between, however, are various combinations of imagination and evidence that we can use to build a representation of past musical activity and knowledge.

There are essentially five kinds of evidence we can draw on to make our representations of music of the past: verbal accounts, visual depictions, physical objects, specialized symbolic visual systems known as music notation, and oral-aural transmission preserved in present-day traditions. Verbal accounts can be further divided into those that discuss theoretical aspects of music and those that mention music in some other context, such as a travelogue or literary work. Physical objects preserve actual remains, such as preserved musical instruments or the architecture of a performance space. Though all these may provide evidence for our representations, each is best suited at conveying rather different kinds of information. For that reason, our representations will be more faithful when they are constructed from an overlap between different kinds of evidence.

Devising such representations may seem daunting, and in many ways it is, but our argument here is simply a plea that when these kinds of evidence are encountered, in texts or images presented in the classroom, they not be brushed aside.

Instead, take a moment to have students consider what they tell us about the musical characteristics of the culture that produced them, as well as what they do not. Use this as an opportunity to bring in a sonic dimension, to remind students that the past was not as silent as their textbooks or slide decks imply, even if it is impossible to know as much about that dimension as we would like. We aim to provide some tools to be able to talk about the silences of the sources, or some ideas of what to look for. Whereas a full exploration of the music of a certain time and place requires considerable expertise, a modular approach could allow for a unit on music to be incorporated into a wide variety of classes, such as courses that treat travel literature, court traditions, religion, history of science, archaeology, gift exchanges, or area studies. Music is not merely present but is even an important part of all these contexts in nearly any time or place. Omitting mention of it because it is difficult to deal with robs students of the opportunity to engage more fully with the past and develop their historical imaginations.

In the present essay, we begin with a discussion of musical instruments, whose tangibility (not to say frequent beauty) makes them obvious touchstones for students, even those with little experience with music. The existence of instruments as objects and their frequent appearance in depictions and descriptions make them useful—if problematic—proxies for musical styles and contexts, indicating larger patterns in cultural history. But instruments are also rich in meaning and fundamentally connected to the systems of thought in which music traffics. They can even embody philosophical concepts that take us well beyond the domain of sound into the most elaborate intellectual products of their societies.

Afterward, we turn to that bugbear for those without musical training, music notation. Ignorance of notation is often used as justification for entirely omitting discussion of music, though, as we show in the previous section, it is hardly a necessary part of incorporating music into a course. Nevertheless, since early music notation provides the most detailed information we have for building musical representations, it is worth confronting. Like paleography, it is easy to get bogged down in the many details and quandaries about early notation. Thinking more broadly, though, about how various kinds of notation work and why some (far from all) cultures have used it reveals a great deal about the life of music in a society. We discuss the issues of notation from the broadest possible perspective, to clarify the issues in its interpretation and suggest productive ways nonexperts can engage with it.

Musical Instruments and Thought

Not all objects that produce sound are musical instruments. The introductory distinction is that beyond the capacity to make a sound, musical instruments are signifying objects that carry cultural meaning, symbolism, mythology, and cosmology beyond their purely physical form. By and large, whereas a mere sound-producing object makes a sound during everyday behavior, a musical instrument is used to make humanly organized sound in a context removed from everyday behavior and one that can be fully understood only in direct relation to its function and meaning in a cultural space or transcultural milieu. One could argue thus that the morphologies, functions, and meanings that musical instruments carry in the premodern world are among the most accessible and rewarding music-related components to be incorporated in most courses concerning early globalities.

Providing answers to the apparently simple question "what is a musical instrument?" involves investigating culturally specific taxonomies, untangling embedded cultural symbolism and cosmologies, and tracing patterns of transcultural circulation, and thus can seem daunting at first. Yet addressing these issues either as independent from one another or in any possible combination can clarify and concretize the larger theme of a given teaching project. To an extent, this is largely the consequence of the fact that, ultimately, the information pertaining to musical instruments comes from diverse sources, primarily the visual representations that survive in manuscripts; murals; carvings; and texts of a wide variety of types, including religious and literary writings, travel literature, and diplomatic documents.

Moreover, though only in rare cases do musical instruments from the premodern era survive, most have been found, wholly or fragmentarily, in burials that attest to their status in their respective cultures where they had been sufficiently valued to be interred in the company of corpses and treasures. The archaeological analysis and documentation of such artifacts—including dating, morphological description, and explanation of archaeological and cultural contexts—complements the investigative methods developed in art historical and text-anchored disciplines. Educators can choose to explore information pertaining to musical instruments and their related practices from the medium of their choice or expertise. As such, archaeological, iconographic, and textual analysis together render musical instruments viewed as objects of material culture as one of the most versatile and interdisciplinary subjects in the study of the past that can inhabit our curricula.

Musical instruments are also an illustrative example of technologies that can be investigated from different angles. In the vernacular sense, the technology they embody—precise engineering, metallurgy, and so on—can say something about the protoscientific knowledge of the instrument makers. From a hermeneutic perspective, they can be seen as tools to be interpreted (morphologically and technologically) as texts, something we have to read in their culturally specific use. They can also be explored as technological manifestations that enable an embodiment relation to the world, as extensions of human cognition, through which trained musicians were able to express themselves through nonconceptual, embodied knowledge. Musical instruments, as well as their visual and textual representations, are all interlinked cultural objects that ultimately mediate between the spheres of musical conceptualization and performance, and as such their exploration transcends their materiality.

Individual musical instruments are often sorted in conceptual categories that only make sense within a specific cultural context. Organological taxonomies are in fact a consequence of the ways musical cultures understand their instruments and group them in categories meaningful to them and, at times, to no one else. Though these taxonomic schemes are sometimes morphological in nature, there are often examples that reflect extrainstrumental concerns pertaining to societal function, mythology, or cosmology (Kartomi). Exploring the organological classification of instruments, in either their local or transcultural manifestations, underscores the link between their materiality and their societal and cultural interpretation.

Three organizational systems illustrate the issues pertaining to specific modes of conceptualizing classes of objects in the larger context of cultural preferences. Western organology, for example, traces its origins in part to the distinction between animate instruments (human voice) and inanimate instruments (string and wind instruments) characteristic of Hellenic musical thought. More systematic classifications that prevailed throughout the medieval period were introduced by the third-century philosopher Porphyry, who divided musical instruments into three categories: wind, strings, and percussion. Moreover, an influential gender-based interpretation of musical instruments, which resurfaces in Europe throughout the medieval period in various hypostases, was offered in the third to fourth century by

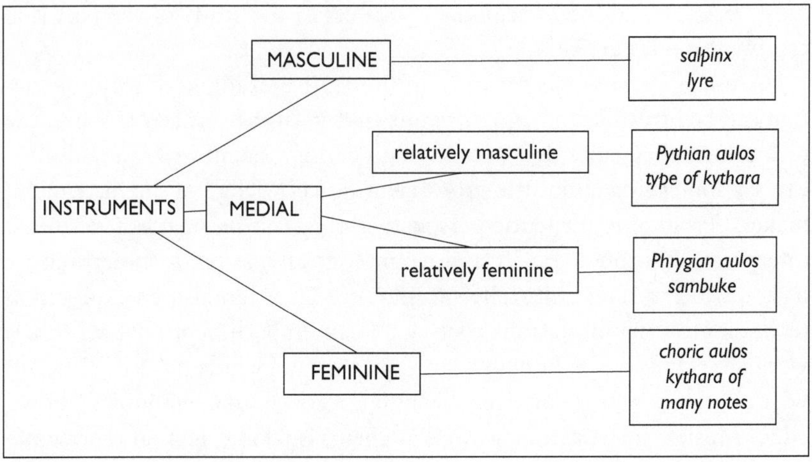

Figure 1. Classification of instruments, by Aristide Quintilianus. Third to fourth century.

Aristide Quintilianus, who grouped the then extant instrumentarium into three categories: masculine, medial, and feminine (fig. 1).

The roughly contemporaneous scheme featured in the Sanskrit *Nāṭyaśāstra* (200 BCE–200 CE) on the other hand, groups the instruments according to the morphological categories of "stretched" (the *vīṇā*, a string instrument); "covered" (drums); "hollow" (flutes); and "solid" (bells and cymbals). In addition, however, the *Nāṭyaśāstra* classification maps onto this morphological grouping two additional taxonomic layers: one pertaining to performance practice (solo vs. accompanying instrument) and an overarching one based on the notion of "lower" and "higher" status that may reflect the normative social status of their performers at that time (fig. 2).

In addition to morphology, gender, and status, other extramusical concerns are operational in the construction of instrumental categories. At the foundation of the Chinese classification system known as *bayin* ("eight sounds"), for example, lay ideas about the nature of sound, including the concept of *qi* ("subtle matter," "human breath," "spirit") and the notion that sounds were manifestations of the equilibrium and disequilibrium of nature and political power. Attested in classical texts, this system remained influential over the centuries, and it is still familiar today. The eightfold division in the *bayin* was according to the material from which the instruments were made. Arrived at only gradually, the standard version features as sources for sound eight materials: metal, stone, skin, gourd, bamboo,

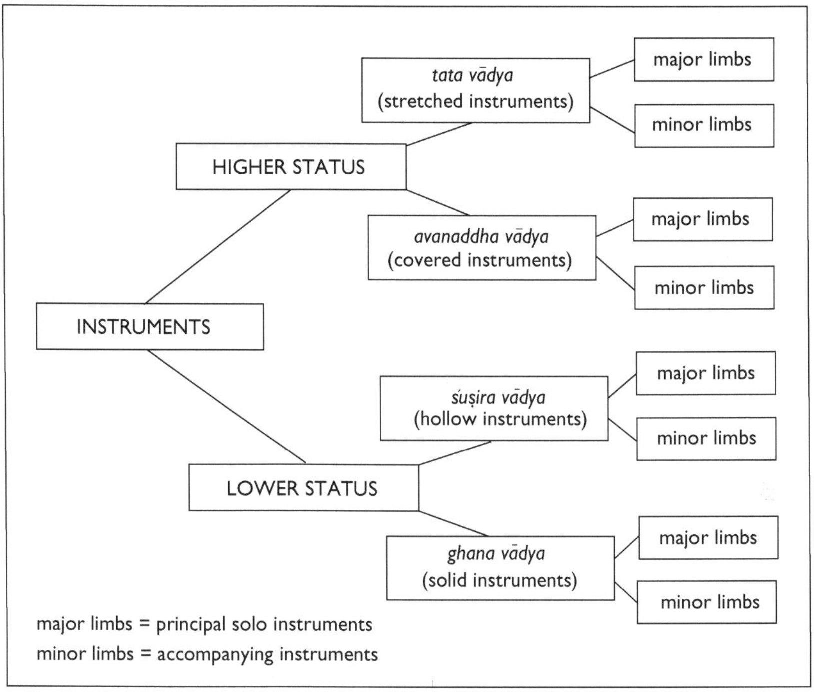

Figure 2. Classification of instruments, based on *Nāṭyaśāstra*. First century BCE to third century CE.

wood, silk, and clay. The character of the various categories was established in conformity with the perceived link in the sphere of cosmology and ritual between the materials and the seasons, winds, and by extension, human welfare and political power:

Bayin	**Seasons**	**Cardinal points**
silk	summer	southwest
clay	summer-autumn	west
metal	autumn	northwest
stone	autumn-winter	north
skin	winter	northeast
gourd	winter-spring	east
bamboo	spring	southeast
wood	spring-summer	south

Classes of musical objects were not alone in being linked to micro- and macrocosmic categories. Particular instruments themselves were often seen as embodiments of nature and of cosmological perfection. Fairly often, not only their morphology but also their tuning, the pitches and scales such tuning favors (an intrinsic part of what we generally call musical thought), and the manner of performance were perceived as expressions of the perfection of the universe and of the principles governing the natural world.

Not surprisingly, it was those instruments that came to be seen in cosmological terms that emerged as central to the construction of the early musical identity of a given culture. In the Islamicate world, the *ʿūd*—the ancestor of the European lute and the relative of the Chinese pipa—was regarded as the perfect instrument, whose excellence was due to its perfect morphological proportions that were of the same (Pythagorean) essence as the harmonious proportions of other cosmic manifestations. Its four strings, for example, as well as the set of pitches produced on each string, were correlated with the topography of the heavens and earth, the four groups of zodiac signs, the directions of the winds, the four elements in nature (earth, water, air, fire) and their corresponding bodily humors among others (Klein 111–27; Farmer 97–102; see table 1).

Traces of analogous cosmological interpretations are found in Chinese writings discussing the pipa, beginning with the *Fengsu Tongyi* (*Common Meanings in Customs*) by Ying Shao and touched on in various writings up through the Qing period. The cosmological instrument par excellence in early China, however, was the *guqin*, a seven-stringed instrument in the zither family. Virtually every morphological aspect of this instrument is interpreted in terms of cosmology or nature and was identified by an anthropomorphic or zoomorphic name in an ever-present cosmological context: the upper board symbolizes heaven, for example, whereas the lower board symbolizes earth. In performance, the *guqin* symbolizes the coming together of humankind, earth, and heaven and is echoed in the three types of sound that the performer produces when plucking a string: an open string represents earth, string harmonics represent heaven, and a stopped string represents humans. Moreover, the music of the *guqin* is thought to directly imitate natural sounds, such as the flowing of water or the singing of birds (Kouwenhoven 46; DeWoskin 33–35, 138).

Table 1. Music as cosmic ingredient in Al-Kindī's *Risāla* (from Farmer, p. 98; modified).

String of the lute	Bamm	Mathlath	Mathnā	Zīr
Quarter of the Zodiac	Capricorn to Pisces	Libra to Sagittarius	Aries to Gemini	Cancer to Virgo
Element	water	earth	air	fire
Wind	west	north	east	south
Season	winter	autumn	spring	summer
Quarter of the day	midnight to sunrise	sunset to midnight	sunrise to midday	midday to sunset
Humor	phlegm	black bile	blood	yellow bile
Quarter of life	old age	middle age	infancy	youth
Faculty of the soul	masculine	preserving	*fantāsiyya*	thinking
Faculty of the body	resisting	prehensile	assimilative	attractive
External actions	mildness	goodness	intellect	courage

Inevitably, the morphology of musical instruments might be seen by some educators as a field-specific approach; their symbolic, mythological, or cosmological positioning in a given culture, however, as well as their role in producing sounds that in turn are conceptualized according to specific cultural practices, should afford a context that proves of interest to any cultural or art historian, as well as to scholars of text, gender, and political structures, among others. Moreover, the exploration of many music-making instruments and practices of musical conceptualization from a transcultural perspective is well suited to courses focused on transcultural circulation and as subjects of cultural encounters (Strohm). For indeed, the interactions among people from diverse cultures enabled musical contact in manners that were as varied as they were complex, driving the movement of musical concepts and instruments, together with performance practices and repertoires, back and forth along routes of intense transcultural commerce.

The lute, for example, morphologically identified as a short-necked string instrument with an almond-shaped body, originated sometime near the beginning of our era in the Bactrian-Gandharan space (present-day Afghanistan and Pakistan) and over several centuries came to be part of musical cultures spanning from Europe to Japan. Its eastward dissemination maps the spread of Buddhism along the Eurasian trade routes; iconographical and archeological records as well as literary references suggest it reached China most likely by the late Han dynasty (206 BCE–220 CE), where it starts to be known as the *Han-pipa*.

From China, several centuries later and apparently via Korea, it entered Japan, where it is known as *biwa*; a couple of these lutes are still part of the Japanese imperial Shōsōin Repository in Nara. A morphologically related instrument crossed from Gandhara into the Tarim Basin, possibly via India, where it was enthusiastically integrated in the organologic world of Kucha (the oasis on the northern branch of the Silk Road as it straddles the Taklamakan Desert); from here, together with a number of musicians, it entered the Chinese musical world possibly not much earlier than the Sui (581–618 CE) and Tang (618–907 CE) dynasties, where it becomes known as the *wuxian-* or *Kuchean pipa*.

In a westward direction, through cultural mechanisms that remain to be fully ascertained, the first version enters the Sasanian cultural core territories, where it becomes known as *barbat*, whence it is adopted with enthusiasm in the Islamicate world as *al ʾud*, and through Arab contacts arrived in Europe as the lute (Currie 68).

One needs to keep in mind, however, that musical instruments and thought do not travel alone. A cultural encounter with a foreign object, such as an instrument or a system of scales, does not have any necessary consequences, but is instead variously appropriated, reworked, or ignored by the networking cultures in ways contingent on the local situation. In the aftermath of a cultural encounter, as visual and textual sources can demonstrate, musical instruments or conceptualizations can be appropriated by other cultures, but in doing so, those cultures become changed by that very object or system, all through various forms of agency.

In general terms, the impact of an imported object, especially a hitherto-unknown foreign instrument, on the new host culture raises important questions of whether and how presumably embodied meanings from cultures of origin travel with instruments across cultural boundaries and become lost, replaced, or transformed in transit. Intrinsic physical features of the instrument and their embedded music-related conceptualizations are often the artifactual characteristics most readily modified, adapted, or removed to suit local practices. This phenomenon can offer students the challenge of assessing, through the study of the iconographic and textual records, the extent to which aspects of an entire superstructural complex of meanings, values, and associations an object once evoked in its previous sociocultural context are retained or changed among members of its new adoptive communities.

An additional layer in the analysis of cultural encounters and transcultural dynamics with which students can engage comes from considering the various components of what we generally understand as "musical thought." The textual sources providing the necessary information are not only the commonly labeled "music theoretical treatises" but also a wide array of writings that can be selected by educators to suit their expertise or interests from the range of materials chosen for a specific course: philosophical, religious, and literary texts; official administrative documents; as well as travel accounts, among others.

The poetry of Amīr Khosrow, for example, is an important resource for exploring the musical and cultural entanglements of Persian and Indian traditions at the time of the Delhi Sultanate (Karomat; Wade). Persian philosophical writings, significant in their own right, stand witness to the transmission of Hellenistic musical thought in the Islamicate world (Hicks; Wright). Meanwhile, Korean and Japanese texts such as *Samguk sagi* or *Kyōkunshō* bear witness to the interrelationship of East Asian musical cultures and the significant dependence of musical practices, instrumentaria, and conceptualization on the Chinese traditions of the Sui, Tang, and Song eras (Kato; McQueen Tokita and Hughes; Picken and Nickson; Provine).

Music Notation

Turning to writing of a different kind, a surprising amount of music notation from across medieval Eurasia survives. (In sub-Saharan Africa, the Americas, and Oceania, however, we are not aware of any before the colonial period, though it is possible that poorly understood systems of communication, such as the Andean *khipu*, may sometimes encode musical information.) In most cases, music notation was an outgrowth of the codification of playing techniques and theoretical knowledge when they appeared in a culture that had established writing as an important means of preserving and transmitting information. Unlike writing, however, music notation seems to have developed independently multiple times and shows a remarkable diversity in how information is encoded, what information is encoded, and why it was used. Below we explore these three dimensions, which we call the notation's system (the how), parameters (the what), and function (the why). In so doing, we illustrate why the interpretation of a piece of notation can be controversial or vary widely, which are important considerations for the teacher who wishes to share recordings.

Systems of music notation can be broadly divided into two classes, digital and analog. A digital system uses discrete symbols to encode musical information, most often by representation of their pitch or rhythmic value. A simple and familiar example are the letters that represent the notes A, B, and so on, which represent pitches. Digital systems struggle to indicate transitions between these notes, which might in practice sound like a precise change, a slide from one pitch to another, or a variety of other articulations. Digital music notation is most like glottographic writing, which indicates phonemes with precision but similarly struggles with representing prosodic features. The earliest surviving music notation in the world, a Hurrian hymn notated using cuneiform, is digital, as are other systems that are based on a system of writing.

There are two special cases of digital notation that should be mentioned, in which the symbols do not refer to musical parameters but are instead mediated through the practice of a specific instrument. The first, discursive notation, is simply ordinary writing that describes in words the process of playing a piece of music. The earliest music notation in China, a piece for the *guqin* zither, was written in this way, carefully noting which fingers should touch which strings and where (Kaufmann 269–71). The second is a kind of notation called tablature that directly encodes performance instructions for a specific musical instrument rather than universal musical properties. Both types are instrument-specific; whereas the notated music could be reproduced on other instruments or voices (and may well have been in early times), one needs a complete understanding of the design of the intended instrument in order to decode them. The obscurity of the internal anatomy used in the voice makes it impossible to use these kinds of notations for vocal music.

Analog systems, on the other hand, base their representation on a gestural contour. These systems lack the precision of digital notation but can better convey the sorts of information that do not neatly fit into digital categorizations. A good example is the contours of Tibetan chant, about which more below (fig. 3).

We have already alluded somewhat to musical parameters. These are the building blocks of music, including such aspects as pitch, duration, timbre (sound quality), loudness, articulation, and directionality (location). This listing is in approximate order of how commonly they appear in notational systems. Pitch, the parameter that often synecdochically represents

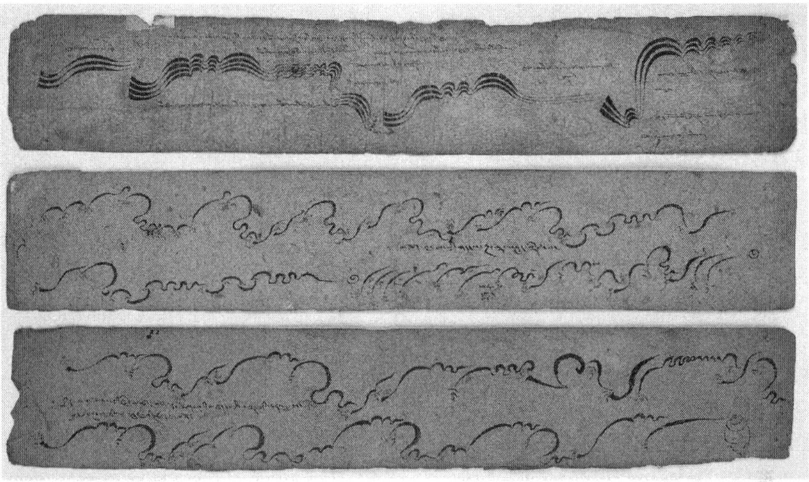

Figure 3. Three folios of Tibetan chant notation. Wellcome Collection Tibetan MS 42. Photograph: Wellcome Collection (reproduced under CC-BY-4.0).

music as a whole, is the most common, though it is entirely absent in some forms of notation as well.

Notations are inherently incomplete, since they can never fully capture every detail about a musical performance; moreover, to maintain legibility, they generally choose a small set of parameters to encode. Which parameters appear in musical notation depends on cultural priorities. Though in principle all these parameters are objectively present in any set of sounds themselves, if they are deemed unimportant in the musical culture in which the notation arises, they are unlikely to be notated. In practice, because of their complex timbre, drum and percussion parts are often considered unpitched and not notated with pitch information.

For instance, Tibetan chant, which sonically emphasizes continuous modulations of sound quality, uses lines of increasing thickness to indicate timbral and dynamic characteristics. Furthermore, although time roughly goes from left to right, it is not measured with rhythmic precision, and seemingly impossible overlapping lines occur. If you have never heard Tibetan chant, it might be hard to imagine how this would function as music because the parameters of timbre and dynamics are so subordinate in many other musical systems and the sense of time so distinctive.

The availability of parameters in notation can have significant effects on musical thought or even practice. Because certain parameters will be notationally prominent, they may gain an outsized role when the music is considered visually because the notational patterns channel the creative process in particular directions. Since the notation was usually developed based on salient parameters in the first place, this can snowball, as what were perceived as important parameters are further discursively emphasized, whereas those that were perceived as unimportant remain ignored or even invisible.

Finally, we turn to the function of notation. This is an important consideration because considerations of function control how detailed and precise the notation should be. Moreover, it provides an obvious explanation for why our concerns do not match those of the people who made the notation. An investigator into ancient music might wish notation to be as detailed and precise as possible, to assist in their recreation of it, but medieval scribes were not writing for the benefit of twenty-first-century musicologists.

But who were they writing for? The literacy of musical cultures spans a continuum, and notation can fulfill a range of possible functions appropriate to more or less literate musical situations. The most oral-based notation would be very simple jottings that might help one remind a fully competent musician of minute, easily forgotten details. The least helpful to us of such notation might be a list of pieces of music, to remind the performer of the order in which they should be performed. Another common mnemonic is the text of vocal music, with no musical notation attached. Competent singers can often reliably reproduce a seldom sung tune themselves with just the words to jog their memories. Whether these count as musical notation is a semantic distinction; they certainly do convey to us some information about long-lost musical performances, though not in a way that allows us to easily imagine the sound (e.g., Picken, "Shapes").

More detailed mnemonic aids might give some indication of pitch or rhythm without providing much detail, as certain complex or difficult-to-notate parts would require oral training. But if these aids were used in transmitting music, even informally, we might expect more detail, as the person they are intended for no longer already knows the tune but must find ways of learning it. The less access the student had to the teacher, the more detail we might expect; this generalization may explain in part the phenomenon of marginal survival.

Another function of notation might be to aid in discussions of music theory. Sometimes, an analytical treatise would like to include a musical example as an illustration, in which case it can turn to whatever notational systems are available or make up new ones. Though such newly created ones may be entirely ad hoc, if the treatise was intended to be comprehensible, it must include keys to deciphering the system. Not infrequently, such treatises then provide clues for other instances of notation in the surrounding culture, for even if it was different from the system otherwise used, it may imply something about underlying principles or which parameters were considered important. Needless to say, the treatise itself will often provide important means for understanding the musical practices.

More highly literate cultures are often concerned about the preservation of cultural artifacts, perhaps for religious or ritual reasons, and thus may endeavor to produce notation to record music. The notation may be deliberately obscure even in such cases of preservation, however, since the recorded music may be of esoteric importance and not intended for ordinary people to understand.

Ultimately, a fully literate music culture can use notation to disseminate music to those who have not heard it before. This is the familiar function of music notation in modern times, but it was rare in premodern times. In this luckiest case, if we can recover how the notational code worked, as well as the intended recipients, we can recreate the music as well as they can. That remains a big *if*, however, as the interpretation of the inherently limited notation can still vary tremendously, and the unnotated aspects remain open to interpretation.

Other pitfalls of music notation will be familiar to those who study literature and visual culture. There are very few copies of notated works; before printing, instances of music notation usually exist in only a single exemplar, which could certainly contain the errors of its human maker or have been partially damaged. Only rarely are multiple copies available for collation and philological emendation.

Another fraught question is how closely the performance of music notated in ancient times should conform to parallel or descendent traditions about which we know much more. Some early music practitioners pay a great deal of attention to such traditions. If these traditions are conservative, then this can tell us a great deal about performance practices that were too obvious for writers to bother describing. There is no a priori reason to assume that these traditions are conservative, however, and it is quite possible to mistake a later innovation as an ancestral trait because of the paucity of information. Here, references in literature or art may be very helpful, though not infrequently the evidence is ambiguous.

In some cases, surviving notation yields the possibility of experiencing historical music more directly. Though recreations are never perfect, as they are inevitably based on limited information and reflect the concerns of the present-day performers, they can nonetheless greatly enhance our capacity to imagine past societies. When using recordings, one should carefully examine the accompanying materials to better understand how to frame them for students, so they appreciate what decisions the performers have made. If possible, finding multiple different recordings will make the diversity of possibilities more salient to the students. This exercise may even better attune them to the issues that are at stake in the interpretation of any source in any field of humanities.

Notation is not just useful in recreating forgotten music but can also help us better understand patterns of intercultural transmission. For instance, Buddhist chant seems to have been a rather conservative tradition, even as it spread from India through Central Asia to China and Japan, given the parallels between notated sources from Japan and Tibet (Duran). The implication that the practice of chant was passed down without interruption over the centuries helps us better understand the development and spread of monastic culture in these different social environments.

In other cases, we can discern significant changes within a transmitted repertoire. Consider the music of the Tang court in Chang'an (modern Xi'an), China. No notated sources survive from there, but pipa notation from some tunes was found among the manuscripts in the library of Dunhuang Cave 17. The same repertoire was transmitted to Japan, where it was performed in Heian times (794–1185). Laurence Picken and his numerous students worked for many years collating these and other sources and found significant commonalities that have greatly improved their interpretation (Picken and Nickson). According to their findings, though some of the repertoire continues to be played as gagaku music in Japan today, the performance practice has changed enormously, so that the tunes are now performed unrecognizably slowly and seemingly constructed around what was once mere embellishment to the original tunes (Marett).

Regardless of what aspect of music or what musical evidence we choose to focus on in our respective courses, we have shown how specific musicological analysis is only a part of the story, and one that can be set aside or de-emphasized in most courses. Musical instruments form a special node in our narrative, however. They concretize both the musical properties (for instance, those necessary to make sense of tablature) and the philosophical properties that place music in its broader intellectual setting (the symbolism of the morphology of a single instrument or a taxonomic scheme). Moreover, instruments are probably the easiest way to engage students without assuming any cultural familiarity, both because of their recognizability in images without reference to words or codes and because of their unambiguous connection to music. Together, the domains of instruments, notation, and concepts lend themselves to many and diverse scholarly approaches and interdisciplinary perspectives, and in the end, even if the sound of musics past cannot ever be perfectly recaptured, their material and conceptual aspects can be effectively integrated in curricular practices.

Works Cited

Currie, Gabriela. "Sonic Entanglements, Visual Records and the Gandharan Nexus." *The Music Road: Coherence and Diversity in Music from the Mediterranean to India*, edited by Reinhard Strohm, Oxford UP, 2019, pp. 41–70.

DeWoskin, Kenneth J. *A Song for One or Two: Music and the Concept of Art in Early China*. U of Michigan Center for Chinese Studies, 1982.

Duran, Stephen. "In Search of Svarasvasti: Re-envisioning the Liturgy of Seventh-Century Buddhist Chant Using Medieval Japanese and Tibetan Sources." Paper delivered at the Society for Ethnomusicology 63rd Annual Meeting, Albuquerque, New Mexico, 2018.

Farmer, Henry George. "The Influence of Music: From Arabic Sources." *Proceedings of the Musical Association*, vol. 52, 1925, pp. 89–124.

Hicks, Andrew. "The Regulative Power of the Harmony of the Spheres in Medieval Latin, Arabic and Persian Sources." *The Routledge Companion to Music, Mind and Well-Being*, edited by Penelope Gouk et al., Routledge, 2018, pp. 33–45.

Karomat, Diloram. "Roots of Persian Parda System in Hindustani Music: A Conclusion from the Works of Amir Khusrau." *Jashn-e-Khusrau 2013: Celebrating the Genius of Khusrau*, edited by Shakeel Hossain, Aga Khan Trust for Culture / Mapin Publishing, 2015, pp. 88–95.

Kartomi, Margaret J. *On Concepts and Classifications of Musical Instruments*. U of Chicago P, 1990.

Kato, Yuri. *The Role of Music in the Politics and Performing Arts as Evidenced in a Crucial Musical Treatise of the Japanese Medieval Period, the* Kyōkunshō 教訓抄. 2018. PhD dissertation, University of Edinburgh.

Kaufmann, Walter. *Musical Notations of the Orient*. Indiana UP, 1967.

Klein, Yaron. *Musical Instruments as Objects of Meaning in Classical Arabic Poetry and Philosophy*. 2009. PhD dissertation, Harvard University.

Kouwenhoven, Frank. "Meaning and Structure: The Case of Chinese Qin (Zither) Music." *British Journal of Ethnomusicology*, vol. 10, no. 1, 2001, pp. 39–62.

Marett, Allan. "Togaku: Where Have the Tang Melodies Gone, and Where Have the New Melodies Come From?" *Ethnomusicology*, vol. 29, no. 3, 1985, pp. 409–31.

McQueen Tokita, Alison, and David Hughes. "Context and Change in Japanese Music." *The Ashgate Research Companion to Japanese Music (SOAS Musicology Series)*, edited by McQueen Tokita and Hughes, 2008, pp. 1–33.

Picken, Laurence E. R. "The Shapes of Shi Jing Song Texts and Their Musical Implications." *Musica Asiatica*, vol. 1, 1977, pp. 111–65.

Picken, Laurence E. R., and Noël J. Nickson. *Some Ancient Connections Explored*. Cambridge UP, 2000. Vol. 7 of *Music from the Tang Court*.

Provine, Robert C. "The Treatise on Ceremonial Music (1430) in the Annals of the Korean King Sejong." *Ethnomusicology*, vol. 18, no. 1, Jan. 1974, pp. 1–29.

Strohm, Reinhard, editor. *Studies on a Global History of Music: A Balzan Musicology Project*. Routledge, 2018.

Wade, Bonnie C. "Indian Music History in the Context of Global Encounters." *The Cambridge History of World Music*, edited by Philip V. Bohlman, Cambridge UP, 2011, pp. 125–54.

Wright, Owen. "Music and Musicology in the Rasāʾil Ikhwān Al-Ṣafāʾ." *Epistles of the Brethren of Purity: Ikhwān Al-Ṣafāʾ and Their Rasāʾil: An Introduction*, edited by Nader El-Bizri, Oxford UP, 2008, pp. 216–49.

Kristen Collins and Bryan C. Keene

Teaching a Global Middle Ages through Manuscripts

The title of this essay emphasizes our classroom, the objects we have to work with, and the members of the general public we teach. As manuscripts curators at the J. Paul Getty Museum, we contribute to a robust program that yields three to four exhibitions a year. Our collection consists entirely of manuscripts, light-sensitive objects that require frequent rotation when on display.

Manuscripts produced in Europe and the greater Mediterranean world are handwritten books on animal skin parchment or paper,[1] and they often feature painted decoration or embellishment with gold or other metallic leaf.[2] Our students are the general public and online audiences around the world. As curators who stage the lesson plan, we are often not present to see how our information is being received by roughly 150,000 to 200,000 visitors per exhibition that enter our gallery.

As public medievalists, we know we have the opportunity to offer a corrective to Eurocentric or nationalistic tropes of Crusades, castles, and cathedrals (codified by nineteenth-century scholarship and reinforced by Hollywood productions and other avenues of popular culture). To the degree that our collection allows, we also try to nuance the ways medieval Europeans were connected to and concerned about the world beyond their doorsteps. This essay provides strategies for presenting global narratives through local collections, leveraging the Getty's western European collections to expand outward into the greater medieval world through object case studies focused on manuscripts, materials, and the movements thereof.

Illuminated manuscripts allow us to glimpse the real and imagined worlds of medieval artists, patrons, thinkers, writers, pilgrims, and travelers. In a time before the borders of cities, nations, and even continents were clearly defined or established, individuals could turn to texts—including epics, romances, world histories, encyclopedias, travel literature, and sacred writings—to learn about distant lands and peoples. Many of these accounts were accompanied by stunning illuminations, which gave life to a world that was otherwise accessible only to indomitable travelers or a vibrant imagination.

Collections and Interactions: Finding the Global in the Local

Curators are charged with the care and display of art objects, and the sharing of histories that are directly tied to the objects in a particular collection. The Getty acquired the Peter and Irene Ludwig collection of manuscripts in 1983, making possible the display of important illuminated books from the major European schools of book production during the High Middle Ages and the Renaissance. This group of objects included as well significant examples from major centers of the Byzantine world, historic Armenia, Tunisia, Safavid Isfahan (Iran), and the colonial Andes. From that time forward, the institution has continued to expand the breadth of the collection with the purchase of texts from Coptic Egypt and Ethiopia, and the acquisition in 2018 of the Rothschild Pentateuch, a rare and remarkable northern European Hebrew manuscript from the late thirteenth century (fig. 1).

Since 2004, when the Getty first began digitizing this collection, we have come to radically rethink our audience and impact. The entire collection has been digitized, and high-resolution images of over six thousand illuminations (and growing) are available to download for fair use—a decision made in 2013 that has dramatically expanded the accessibility of the growing collection and fundamentally changed the way that we research and teach medieval manuscripts (see Cuno; Conway et al.).[3] The high quality of the photography available now enables, to a certain degree,

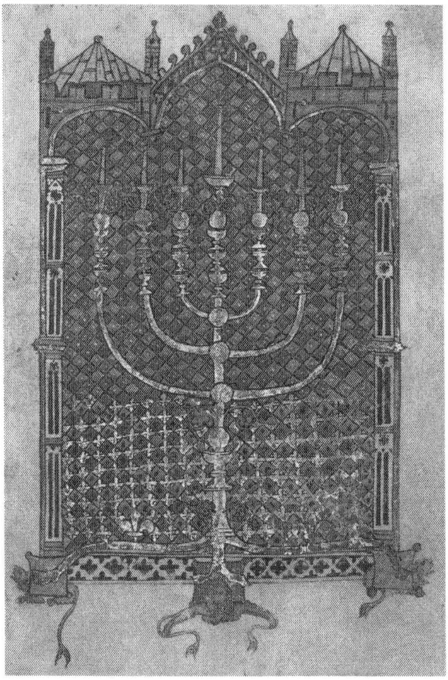

Figure 1. *Menorah.* France or Germany, 1296, in the Rothschild Pentateuch. The J. Paul Getty Museum, Los Angeles, MS 116 (2018.43), fol. 226v. Digital image courtesy of the Getty's Open Content Program.

the kind of close study that was formerly the purview of privileged connoisseurs who were granted physical access to these fragile works.

The democratization of scholarship through accessibility has changed the field of art history broadly and has ushered in a new era for manuscripts studies. Numerous museum, library, and archival collections around the world have contributed to the expanding corpus by sharing their digitized manuscript collections online (see the resources section of this volume). The Morgan Library and Museum and the British Library were early trailblazers in online cataloguing. The International Image Interoperability Framework has brought digital access and connectivity to the next level through linked open data and shared canvas viewers, making it possible to collaborate and research across geographies (see iiif.io/community/consortium/). One of the many communities we serve is the small but dedicated field of manuscripts specialists who in the past would have been constrained by the resources needed for a physical visit, but other communities include school groups, Pinterest enthusiasts, and members of the general public who would not otherwise have the opportunity to engage with medieval objects in a museum space.

Acquisitions provide one (slow) way to expand the narratives we present. Publications and public programming offer other opportunities to teach global narratives. Exhibitions are among the most impactful means of expanding the public view of the chronological and geographic horizons of the Middle Ages. *Holy Image, Hallowed Ground: Icons from Sinai* provides one example of the potential of an international loan show to explore global narratives and model inclusive histories (www.getty.edu/art/exhibitions/icons_sinai/; Nelson and Collins). *Icons from Sinai* presented Saint Catherine's Monastery in Egypt not simply as a repository of Byzantine icons, but as a site with global reverberations and as a nexus for transcultural interaction.

The exhibition considered how the identity of the Byzantine monastery evolved, from a site dedicated to the Virgin and the burning bush to an affiliation with Saint Catherine, at least in part because of expectations of pilgrims from the Latin West (Collins 95–119). It also considered how a monastery with a collection that has come to represent the art of a lost Byzantium in fact had distinctly local features, owing to its position at (and then beyond) the borders of the Byzantine Empire. The monastic community included Arabic-speaking Christians (as well as Muslims), and its cultural diversity is made powerfully apparent in the seventeenth-century image of the Heavenly Ladder of John Climacus that appears in the spiritual treatise by the same name (Nelson 248–49).

Created during Ottoman rule of the region, perhaps for Arabic-speaking monks, the manuscript image incorporates the core elements present in earlier examples of the image, as in a Sinai icon that showed the late sixth-century monk, John Climacus, ascending the thirty rungs to heaven (figs. 2 and 3). He is followed by Archbishop Antonios and his community of monks, who must resist the temptations of devils or be pulled from the rungs. In the seventeenth-century manuscript, the ladder slants to the left rather than the right, following the reading direction of Arabic. A flaming halo surrounding Christ's head and brightly colored demons further differentiate the work from the Byzantine example.

While containing distinctly Ottoman features, the illumination also includes aspects of the local Sinai landscape that became increasingly important for pilgrims in the centuries after Climacus's time. The early association of the site with the burning bush continues to be made with a small figure of Moses who crouches before a flaming teardrop-shaped mandorla encapsulating the Virgin and Christ. Whereas Constantinopolitan images represent the theophany with Christ in the flaming bush, the in-

Figure 2. *The Heavenly Ladder* (in Arabic). Sinai (?), 1612. The Holy Monastery of Saint Catherine, Sinai, cod. Arab 343, fol. 13. By permission of Saint Catherine's Monastery, Sinai, Egypt.

Figure 3. *The Heavenly Ladder.* Late twelfth century. The Holy Monastery of Saint Catherine, Sinai. By permission of Saint Catherine's Monastery, Sinai, Egypt.

clusion of Mary may allude to the iconography of the Virgin of the burning bush that emerged at Sinai (Collins 95–119). At the top of the mountain, on the right, two angels lay Saint Catherine's body to rest.

Much is possible with loans, and even small, low-budget exhibitions can expand beyond collection parameters if one is enterprising with objects that lie closer to hand. When curating exhibitions from the permanent collection, we often include loans from local collections to add dimension and depth to our presentations. *Traversing the Globe through Illuminated Manuscripts* combined loans from local Los Angeles collections with Getty manuscripts to connect broader premodern histories and to decenter Europe in our vision of a "Middle Ages" (see www.getty.edu/art/exhibitions/globe/). Adding to a core group of approximately forty permanent collections objects, the Getty borrowed an additional forty objects from local institutions.

Foremost among these loans were Indian and Islamic manuscripts from the Los Angeles County Museum of Art, the inclusion of which effectively expanded the geographic, artistic, and religious scope of premodern communities described as "medieval."[4] This exhibition took a connective approach to a global Middle Ages by grouping western European and Byzantine manuscripts from the Getty collection with loans of book arts from other confessional and literate traditions of Afro-Eurasia and the Americas.

The exhibition emphasized commonalities and linkages by considering cultural contacts and the movement of peoples, ideas, and materials. By grouping a ninth-century Qur'an from Tunisia with a contemporaneous ivory plaque from a Carolingian manuscript with purple-painted pages allowed for a consideration of trans-Saharan and Mediterranean trade routes in gold, ivory, and pigments or dyes. Elsewhere in the gallery, a seventh- to ninth-century Maya codex-style ceramic vessel showing a scribe was paired with a sixteenth-century pendant comprising a pearl (likely from the Caribbean) to address early colonial contacts and the grim results of trans-Atlantic trade, which ultimately resulted in the destruction of the Maya and the majority of their codices (some of which date back to earlier centuries).

The book arts of the Maya were also placed in proximal time with the long-held and canonical cultures such as the Carolingian Empire and Aghlabid or Fatimid dynasties. In this way, both diachronic and synchronic relations were established to demonstrate early globalities and the potential of studying manuscripts in deep time.

At times, with the Getty's one-room collection shows, a comparative or thematic approach to premodern visual, religious, and intellectual traditions can guide visitors to explore global themes in history. *Pathways to Paradise: Medieval India and Europe*, an exhibition hinging outward from the permanent collection, compared ideas of paradise through book arts and portable objects (coinage, jewelry, textiles, and votive offerings) across Eurasia. The themes addressed included gardens and arboreal imagery, the story of the Buddha and the Christianized tale of Prince Josaphat of India,[5] mapping heaven and earth, and the çintamani motif (see Folda 146–66). (This three-orbed or dotted design originated from the Hindu-Buddhist concept of a wish-granting or protective jewel and was found on textiles, sculptures, and in manuscripts across Eurasia.)

The centuries 500 to 1500 witnessed increased movement between Europe, Byzantium, the Islamicate world, and South and East Asia. One of the historical figures whose legacy links many of these cultures is Alexander the Great. Few contemporary accounts survive about the Macedonian world ruler, but classical and medieval writers in Europe, Central Asia, and India preserved his memory through histories, chronicles, and romances. Pairing stories about Alexander and his Persian avatar Iskandar, from central Europe and Persia, allowed visitors to encounter worldviews from two extremes of the medieval globe and encapsulated each of the exhibition's themes.[6] *Pathways to Paradise* and *Traversing the Globe* offered primarily positive stories (see www.getty.edu/art/exhibitions/pathways_paradise/).

Whereas the aforementioned exhibitions mapped outward from Europe (and from the collection), *Outcasts: Prejudice and Persecution in the Medieval World* presented the world within Europe (see www.getty.edu/art/exhibitions/outcasts/). Without loans to augment this show from the permanent collection, we used prejudice as a strategy for revealing diversity. For our general public, the presence of Jews, Muslims, Black Africans, Mongols, as well as female leaders and people perceived as gender or sexual deviants was revelatory. The twenty-two case studies presented in the exhibition drew on forty years of academic work on anti-Semitism, Islamophobia, critical race studies, feminism, queer and trans studies, disability studies, and more broadly on the global Middle Ages, but as these are narratives not often explored on the walls of collections of historical European art, the show proved surprising for some of our visitorship.

The case study model inspired new avenues of research about core objects in the collection. *The Life of the Blessed Hedwig*, a hagiographic account of the twelfth-century Silesian noblewoman (written and illuminated in 1353), contains a dynamic two-page composition showing the Battle of Liegnitz, in which the Mongol army combatted the Polish troops of Duke Heinrich II.[7] In the exhibition, we explained that the harsh realities of life in the Middle Ages, among them perpetual warfare and routine threats of violence, fanned the flames of xenophobia.

The first sequence of images shows the Golden Horde besieging the city of Liegnitz (Legnica, Poland), defended by an army of Poles, Czechs, and Germans under the command of Heinrich II, Hedwig's husband. When Heinrich is decapitated, the bloodshed intensifies, and his head is presented on a pike at the upper right on the facing page. The hellmouth at the lower left shows a demon swallowing the souls of the slain Mongols, consigning them to eternal damnation (fig. 4). This exact sequence of images was replicated in two later examples—a *Vita* diptych (fig. 5) and another manuscript copy of *The Life of the Blessed Hedwig* (fig. 6)—but with one significant

Figure 4. *Scenes from the Life of Saint Hedwig.* 1353, in the *Life of the Blessed Saint Hedwig of Silesia.* The J. Paul Getty Museum, Los Angeles, MS Ludwig XI 7 (83.MN.126), fols. 11v–12r. Digital image courtesy of the Getty's Open Content Program.

Figure 5. Diptych with *Scenes from the Life of Saint Hedwig.* Circa 1440, from the Church of Saint Bernardino of Siena in Wrocław. National Museum, Warsaw, inv. No. Sr. 28 MNW. Photograph by Bryan C. Keene.

Figure 6. *Scenes from the Life of Saint Hedwig.* Early 1400s. Wrocław University Library, Warsaw, inv. No. IV F 192, fols. 5v–6.

change. In the Getty 1353 manuscript, the Mongol pennant shows a king (white, bearded, and crowned), whereas the pennants on the diptych a century later contain stylized Mongol headdresses.

Most striking, the pennants in the 1451 manuscript have transformed the banner image representing the Mongol leader into a Black African man. This shift in representation fits into a larger European trend in which blackness became a visual strategy for depicting vanquished foreigners rather than an indicator of sub-Saharan African heritage. By the fifteenth century, heraldic images of black-skinned men wearing a crown came to signify Muslim adversaries from North Africa or the eastern Mediterranean: the sultans of Egypt and Syria during the crusader era of the eleventh through thirteenth centuries, followed by the Mongol and Turkish forces in the fourteenth and fifteenth centuries (see Seelig 181–209; Devisse and Mollat 31–82).[8] These peoples were not Black, but blackness became a sign for the non-European interloper.

Figure 7. Georges Trubert, *The Adoration of the Magi.* Circa 1480–90, in a book of hours. The J. Paul Getty Museum, Los Angeles, MS 48 (93. ML.6), fol. 59. Digital image courtesy of the Getty's Open Content Program.

Outcasts included a case study of a figure whose blackness was actually intended to point to sub-Saharan origins. A small book of hours contains an image of the African Magus (fig. 7), a figure who came to prominence in fifteenth-century art and continues to be seen in Nativity crèches even today. The late fifteenth-century Black African Magus was a paradoxical figure for the period. His presence reveals the racial diversity in Europe at a time when ecumenical church councils welcomed delegates from Ethiopia and the Coptic church of Egypt to Florence and Rome (see Kelly). At the same moment, however, Europeans began to engage in the brutal African slave trade.

The artist of the painting was Georges Trubert (active about 1469–1508), illuminator to René of Anjou and René II of Lorraine. According to

Figure 8. Georges Trubert, *The Adoration of the Magi*. 1480–1500, in the Breviary of René II de Lorraine. Bibliothèque de l'Arsenal, Paris, MS 601 réserve, fol. 124v.

Figure 9. Georges Trubert, *The Adoration of the Magi*. 1483–1503, in a book of hours. Bibliothèque Nationale de France, Paris, MS N.A.L. 3210, fol. 34v.

archival records first published by A. Lecoy de la Marche, René I owned a number of enslaved Black Africans, one of whom was called "Katherine la More," and he collected so-called Moorish objects (including a knife, sword, spurs, and decorative objects) and animals from Africa (camel, lions, ostriches, monkeys) (De la Marche 219–22; see also Kekewich 154–55). In 1448, René I established the *Order of the Croissant* (*Crescent*), whose patron saint was Maurice, who was often represented in art and described in literary works as a Black African; René I also owned a manuscript life of the saint (Reynolds 125–61; Gertz, 33–68, 163). Georges Trubert depicted Balthazar as a Black king in the breviary of René II of Lorraine (fig. 8)[9] and in two books of hours (one in Paris [fig. 9] and the other in Los Angeles [fig. 7]).[10] In the breviary, Balthazar is accompanied by an entourage of Black African attendants who do not feature in the Paris or Los Angeles books of hours. This African entourage, unseen but its presence felt, likely influenced the figure of the Black Balthazar in Trubert's work.

In *Outcasts*, the placement of this African figure in a fifteenth-century historical context rather than an imagined biblical past was perceived by some visitors as political and therefore a challenge to the implicit rules of engagement in an art museum (which often promises experiences predicated on beauty and positive emotional responses to the objects). Other visitors wanted to know more about race in the Middle Ages. With greater frequency, curators are called on to adopt an outside in approach that incorporates feedback from audiences in the gallery and online (see blogs .getty.edu/iris/tags/medieval-outcasts/). An essential component of *Outcasts* was a blog series inviting questions, comments, and critique of our work in progress.

One year later, building on questions from our public, we began to organize another collections-based exhibition called *Balthazar: A Black African King in Medieval and Renaissance Art*.[11] Taking Balthazar's blackness as a crucial theme, the exhibition emphasizes both European artists' interest in race and the racial (not to mention linguistic, religious, and cultural) diversity across the African continent. Including primarily western European, Christian works from the permanent collection, the exhibition comprises three sections: (1) African Kingship Real and Imagined, (2) Black Africans and the Paradox of the Renaissance, and (3) The Language of Slavery, Race, and Religion. These themes are explored through case studies of manuscripts in the collection and pairings with portable luxury objects.

In the section African Kingship Real and Imagined, which attempted to challenge the fiction of the Black African king promoted by fifteenth-century Europeans, we utilized maps and didactics to consider the theme of kingship from an African perspective. During the Middle Ages and Renaissance (500s to 1600s), the Mediterranean served as a major thoroughfare for trade and travel, transporting goods, peoples, and ideas between Africa and Europe. African Muslim and Christian rulers gained international fame, including the Mansa Musa of Mali; the kings of Axum (Eritrea and Ethiopia); and Qaitbay, the Mamluk sultan of Egypt. All the while, Europeans promulgated the belief that a mythical Christian priest-king called Prester John lived in Ethiopia, a tale that typified the European fantasy of a wealthy African ally (though one version places him in India; for teaching Prester John, see Christopher Taylor's essay in this volume). In the fifteenth century, religious embassies from the courts of Christian Ethiopia and Coptic Egypt journeyed to Europe for church councils.

The section Black Africans and the Paradox of the Renaissance sought to problematize commonly held narratives surrounding the Renaissance. Although the Renaissance is often called the Age of Exploration, when Europeans collected newly excavated antiquities as well as contemporary objects from distant lands, scenes of *The Adoration of the Magi* from the late fifteenth century offer us different, and painful, aspects of the period. Andrea Mantegna was court painter to Francesco Gonzaga and Isabella d'Este, rulers of Mantua (in northern Italy). Mantegna's position, like that of Trubert, may provide insight into the objects and people that he encountered in his everyday life and represented in his work. Isabella has long been lauded as an avid collector of antiquities, but only in recent decades have scholars acknowledged that she acquired enslaved people as well (Kaplan, "Isabella" 125–54). Letters document that she purchased Black African children to be raised as servants (who were nominally freed on baptism to Christianity) (Kaplan, "Isabella" 125–54; Lowe 65–76). Although Mantegna had encountered both enslaved and free Black Africans in the Veneto since the 1450s, he would have come into regular contact with servants at the Mantuan court near the end of the fifteenth century.

Mantegna's painting follows a thousand years of Christian thought regarding the origins of the mysterious Magi (fig. 10). The eldest king, Caspar, holds Chinese porcelain that identifies him with Asia. In the center, Melchior carries a Turkish incense burner and wears a turban associated with eastern Europe or Asia Minor. Balthazar wears a leopard-skin headdress evoking Africa. His vessel is made of banded alabaster or agate, recalling the containers used for precious myrrh-infused oil in antiquity. For decades this painting has been discussed for its early representation of Ming porcelain and for the other materials, such as Balthazar's alabaster or agate vessel (Carr; Sargent 4–5; Clunas and Harrison-Hall 11, 292–93, 307, no. 263; Christian and Clark, 45, 106, 168).

Only recently have contributions by scholars such as Paul Kaplan and Kate Lowe begun to disrupt positive narratives of Renaissance collecting by speaking plainly about the commodification of humans as living symbols of aristocratic luxury and power (Kaplan, "Isabella" 134; Lowe).[12] Porcelain and antiquities continue to serve as positive or benign globalities. When Isabella d'Este received a letter from her agent about the possible acquisition of a *negra*, or Black girl, the marchioness responded by calling her a *moreta*, another term employed inconsistently for both Muslims and Black Africans (Kaplan, "Isabella" 134).

Figure 10. Andrea Mantegna, *The Adoration of the Magi.* 1495–1505, the J. Paul Getty Museum, Los Angeles, 85.PA.417. Digital image courtesy of the Getty's Open Content Program.

Across Europe, documents regularly referred to Black "servants," enslaved individuals who were nominally freed once baptized into Christianity. One enslaved child who entered Isabella's household in 1499 was renamed Maystro Petro, or Master Peter. Could the figure of Balthazar in this work have been based on an individual that Mantegna encountered in these contexts? Just as Balthazar's African origin was intended to demonstrate the universal reach of Christianity, Black Africans among Isabella's or Francesco's retinue were meant to showcase the couple's worldliness and power.

The juxtaposition of the painting by Mantegna and the manuscript by Trubert in the galleries, together with ancient stone vessels and contemporaneous objects from Ethiopia, Egypt, and China encourages visitors to take a closer look at the relation between collecting and display in museums and in historic contexts. These groupings also serve to define globalisms in the premodern world.

It is not easy to condense the painful topic of enslavement into a single didactic panel for the museum public. In The Language of Slavery, Race, and Religion, we sought to contextualize the fifteenth-century moment within the longer tradition of enslavement in Europe from antiquity while making it clear that the systematic amplification of the practice during the premodern period dramatically altered the practice along racial lines. We also sought to emphasize the ways servitude and freedom were relative conditions in the fifteenth century and how language can obscure the true histories of Black African servants. Here is an example of a focus text that addresses these themes in a section made up of a handful of objects (manuscripts and decorative arts):

> Europeans and Africans engaged in the trade of captive humans since antiquity. But in the 1440s, with the Portuguese incursions into West Africa, the slave trade escalated in unprecedented ways, industrializing the practice and bringing thousands—ultimately millions—of subjugated Black Africans into Europe and the Americas. While there were small numbers of free Black Africans in fifteenth-century Europe, by about 1480–90 the vast majority were not free.
>
> It is difficult to parse the entangled language of slavery, race, and religion from written records, partly because the linguistic terms shift readily depending on context. The word "slave" comes from the Latin *sclava*, a term originally referring to enslaved Slavic peoples that was then used more broadly throughout the Roman Empire. In thirteenth-century northeastern Spain, in the kingdom of Aragon, "Saracen" and "Moor" were applied interchangeably and derogatorily to Muslims and Black Africans. In late fifteenth-century northern Italy, at the court of Mantua, Isabella d'Este received a letter about a *negra*, or Black girl, and responded by calling her a *moretta*, another term employed inconsistently for both Muslims and Black Africans.
>
> Across Europe, documents regularly referred to Black "servants," enslaved individuals who were nominally freed once baptized into Christianity. Scholars are now grappling with the full meaning of "servant," "slave," and "page" when seeking to uncover the realities of Black Africans living in medieval and Renaissance Europe. Their histories can be hard to trace, as forcibly Christianized individuals were given new—and often ironic—names. One enslaved child who entered Isabella's household in 1499 was renamed Maystro Petro, or Master Peter). (Lowe 65–76)

One of the challenges of teaching without prerequisites is that we as curators cannot assume knowledge and thus often spend limited didactic space dispelling commonly held stereotypes. Increasingly, we also have to contend with preconceptions about the purpose or function of the art museum. Many people come with expectations of what a museum should be, whether aesthetic temple, therapeutic experience, or informal learning environment (Burnham and Kai-Kee). There are those visitors who reject the telling of difficult histories in these spaces or those histories that are not as well known. Responding to this resistance or charting new territory for exploration for our publics is one of the challenges of presenting a global Middle Ages, and it is also one of the rewards.

Early Globalities: From the Museum to the Classroom

In the galleries and in the manuscripts study room at the Getty, we frequently lead seminars for university students with the focus on close looking and an exploration of a range of topics relevant to medieval studies. We also have opportunities to teach courses at local universities, and we have used the metaphor of mapping in order to encourage students to think globally, to look beyond the pages of manuscripts created in the greater Mediterranean for evidence of contact with or awareness of other peoples and ideas from throughout the medieval world.

Mapping as a methodology can allow students to consider a range of themes. A few successful examples include plotting the geographic origins of saints in calendars, litanies, or suffrages as a means of understanding the potential global imaginary of a book of hours or liturgical manuscripts; charting the journey or place names in a chronicle, romance, or history text onto a contemporaneous map from the same region to address relative geography and world views (or comparing contemporaneous maps from different places); and applying approaches from linguistics, such as translation, when examining spolia or materials and motifs borrowed from other traditions.

Mapping is a useful methodology for broadening the geographic and chronological scope of a global Middle Ages, and manuscripts are particularly well suited for the study of medieval notions of place and time. For example, an early fifteenth-century illuminated copy of Benoît de Sainte-More's twelfth-century *Chronique de Normandie* would have transported the Parisian reader of the text back in time to the tenth and eleventh centuries. The author recounted that this period was a time when "ferocious pagan warriors from Denmark known for their unmatched seafaring ways raided and eventually settled in the lands of northeastern France [Normandy]" (*Chronique*, fol. 2v; our trans.).

The manuscript's large opening miniature sets the stage for the text: Christian missionaries attempt to convert the king of Denmark, while a battle ensues outside. Despite the Norsemen's "pagan roots and ravenous ways," the chronicler celebrated their eventual adoption of Christianity (*Chronique*, fol. 2v; our trans.). Several pages later, on facing pages one sees at left workmen rebuild the Benedictine Abbey Church of Saint Wandrille, which the Norsemen burnt to the ground in 852 though the relics were preserved; at right, Robert I, grandson of the first Norse king of Normandy, Rollo, receives a diplomatic gift of a hunting hawk. These miniatures emphasize the duchy of Normandy's long lineage both temporally and territorially.

This manuscript allows us to peel back modern associations of French nationhood and examine the complex web of connections that can be discerned in the medieval histories of this region. We look forward to the opportunities for mapping outward from this object to consider materials and trade or knowledge networks of the Normans into Scandinavia, the Spanish Canary Islands, or Sicily.[13] A global Middle Ages offers possibilities for expanding, recentering, and decentering the field of medieval studies.

As curators, we are interested in interpreting and displaying collections of European art in inclusive and generous ways. Starting from where we are with the objects at hand has allowed us to present histories that connect Europe to the highlands of Ethiopia, the foothills of the Kathmandu Valley, the silver mines of the Andes, and beyond. Teaching global art history in the museum today is as much about changing method as it is about changing content; global is a methodology of inclusion. Collections change slowly, but as we have demonstrated through this case study, we can be responsive to the changes in scholarship and the world by being creative about the histories we present through our existing objects. Museums cannot change history. But museums can change art history and the stories told from the artworks in the collection.

Notes

We thank Geraldine Heng for the invitation to participate in the session Teaching the Global Middle Ages at the 2019 Medieval Academy of America Annual Meeting and Susan Noakes for moderating the discussion. Bryan is grateful to the students at Pepperdine University and Riverside City College for sharing their insights on the projects discussed herein.

1. Elsewhere across the globe, manuscript makers used palm leaves, birchbark, deerskin, and other surfaces for writing. For more on early globalities of manuscript cultures and networks, see Keene, *Toward*, "World," and "Bodies."

2. For an in-depth examination of metallic leaf and pigments in manuscripts, see Turner 77–92.

3. For the digitized manuscripts collection at the Getty, see www.getty.edu/art/manuscripts/.

4. These collections at the Los Angeles County Museum are largely drawn from the important Nasli M. Heeramaneck Collection, bequest of Joan Palevsky. Whereas the Getty's Ludwig collection comprises manuscript cultures of the medieval Mediterranean, the Heeramaneck Collection maps a considerable geography of Buddhist, Hindu, Jain, Islamic, and other religious manuscript traditions across Eurasia from roughly 1000 onward. For the Heeramaneck collection, see Pal; Heeramaneck.

5. For more on the Buddha-Josaphat story, see Keene, Prologue.

6. When teaching an undergraduate seminar at Loyola Marymount University entitled Manuscripts and a Global Middle Ages, we assigned students virtual exhibition projects that mapped common narratives, motifs, or materials across cultures. One of these topics was the Alexander-Iskandar texts, meticulously researched and creatively curated by Graciela Ramirez, who is now pursuing an MLS degree from UCLA. For more on teaching the Alexander romance, see the essay by Adam Miyashiro and Su Fang Ng in this volume.

7. A priority for the Getty Museum is to continually update online object records, including bibliography and provenance. For more on the Hedwig manuscript, go to www.getty.edu/art/manuscripts.

8. On the Mongols, see Heng, "Jews" 247–69 and *Invention* 287–416. On the topic of European engagement with the Mongol Empire in the thirteenth and fourteenth centuries, see Lomuto.

9. To view the entire digitized manuscript, see gallica.bnf.fr/ark:/12148/btv1b71006162/f252.item.

10. The owner of the Bibliothèque Nationale de France book of hours may have been Jean de Chasteauneuf, lord of Pixérécourt and *secrétaire du roi* to René. To view the entire digitized manuscript, see archivesetmanuscrits.bnf.fr/ark:/12148/cc71698t and gallica.bnf.fr/ark:/12148/btv1b10532602t/f74.item. The patron of the Getty manuscript has not been identified.

11. This show is heavily indebted to the groundbreaking work of Paul Kaplan, whose ongoing research continues to inform critical race studies for the visual arts. See Kaplan, *Ruler, Saint, and Servant* and *Rise of the Black Magus*. See also Keene, "Bodies"; Collins and Keene, *Balthazar*. We thank Sahar Tchaitchian for carefully reading our exhibition didactic texts and working with us to nuance the messages for the general public.

12. For more on Africans as living symbols of European power, see Earle and Lowe; Massing; Jordan; and Seelig.

13. For a reading that provocatively questions the nationalistic narratives about the canonical Gothic in art history, see Wicker.

Works Cited

Burnham, Rika, and Elliott Kai-Kee. *Teaching in the Art Museum: Interpretation as Experience.* Getty Publications, 2011.

Carr, Dawson W. *The Adoration of the Magi.* J. Paul Getty Museum, 1997.

Christian, Kathleen, and Leah R. Clark, editors. *Art and Its Global Histories: European Art and the Wider World, 1350–1550.* Manchester UP, 2017.

Chronique de Normandie. 1400–1415, J. Paul Getty Museum, Los Angeles, MS Ludwig XIII 4, www.getty.edu/art/collection/objects/1422.

Clunas, Craig, and Jessica Harrison-Hall, editors. *Ming: Fifty Years that Changed China.* British Museum, 2014.

Collins, Kristen. "Visual Piety." *Holy Image, Hallowed Ground*, edited by Robert S. Nelson and Kristen Collins, Getty Publications, 2006, pp. 95–119.

Collins, Kristen, and Bryan C. Keene, editors. *Balthazar: A Black African King in Medieval and Renaissance Art.* Getty Publications, 2022.

Conway, Mikka Gee, et al. "Open Content at the Getty: Three Years Later, Lessons Learned." *Getty Iris*, 16 Aug. 2016, blogs.getty.edu/iris/open-content-at-the-getty-three-years-later-some-lessons-learned/.

Cuno, Jim. "Open Content: An Idea Whose Time Has Come." *Getty Iris*, 12 Aug. 2013, blogs.getty.edu/iris/open-content-an-idea-whose-time-has-come/.

De la Marche, A. Lecoy. *Le roi René: Sa vie, son administration, ses travaux artistiques et littéraires d'après les documents inédits des archives de France et d'Italie.* Libraire de Firmin-Didot Frères, 1875.

Devisse, Jean, and Michel Mollat. "The Shield and the Crown." *From the Early Christian Era to the "Age of Discovery," Africans in the Christian Ordinance of the World*, edited by David Bindman and Henry Louis Gates, Jr., Harvard UP, 2010, pp. 31–82. Vol. 2, part 2 of *The Image of the Black in Western Art.*

Earle, T. F., and Kate Lowe, editors. *Black Africans in Renaissance Europe.* Cambridge UP, 2010.

Folda, Jaroslav. "Crusader Artistic Interactions with the Mongols in the Thirteenth Century: Figural Imagery, Weapons, and the Çintamani Design." *Interactions: Artistic Interchange between the Eastern and Western Worlds in the Medieval Period*, edited by Colum Hourihane, Pennsylvania State UP, 2007, pp. 146–66.

Gertz, SunHee Kim. *Visual Power and Fame in René d'Anjou, Geoffrey Chaucer, and the Black Prince.* Palgrave Macmillan, 2010.

Heeramaneck, Alice N. *Masterpieces of Indian Painting: From the Former Collections of Nasli M. Heeramaneck.* Advent Books, 1984.

Heng, Geraldine. *The Invention of Race in the Middle Ages.* Cambridge UP, 2018.

———. "Jews, Saracens, 'Black Men,' Tartars: England in a World of Racial Difference." *A Companion to Medieval English Literature, c. 1350–c. 1500*, edited by Peter Brown, Blackwell, 2007, pp. 247–69.

Jordan, Annemarie. "Images of Empire: Slaves in the Lisbon Household and Court of Catherine of Austria," Earle and Lowe, pp. 155–80.

Kaplan, Paul H. D. "Isabella D'Este and Black African Women." Earle and Lowe, pp. 125–54.

———. *The Rise of the Black Magus in Western Art.* UMI Research Press, 1984.

———. *Ruler, Saint, and Servant: Blacks in European Art to 1520.* 1983. Boston U, PhD dissertation.

Keene, Bryan C. "Bodies at the Borders: Momentum in Medieval Studies from 2020 Movements." *ICMA News*, Oct. 2020, pp. 18–23.

———. Prologue. Keene, *Toward*, pp. 1–4.

———, editor. *Toward a Global Middle Ages: Encountering the World through Illuminated Manuscripts.* The J. Paul Getty Museum, 2019.

———. "The World Beyond the Pages of the Book: Mapping Inclusive Literary, Oral, and Visual Traditions of Premodern Globalities." *Journal of Medieval Worlds*, vol. 2, nos. 1–2, 2020, pp. 44–56, https://doi.org/10.1525/jmw.2020.2.1-2.44.

Kekewich, Margaret L. *The Good King: René of Anjou and Fifteenth Century Europe.* Palgrave Macmillan, 2008.

Kelly, Samantha. "Ewosṭateans at the Council of Florence (1441): Diplomatic Implications between Ethiopia, Europe, Jerusalem and Cairo." *Afriques*, 29 June 2016, journals.openedition.org/afriques/1858.

Lomuto, Sierra. *Exotic Allies: Mongol Alterity in the Global Middle Ages, 1220–1400.* 2018. U of Pennsylvania, PhD dissertation.

Lowe, Kate. "Isabella d'Este and the Acquisition of Black Africans at the Court of Mantua." *Mantova e il Rinascimento italiano: Studi in onore di David S. Chambers*, edited by Philippa Jackson and Guido Rebecchini, Editoriale Sometti, 2011, pp. 65–76.

Massing, Jean Michel. "The Image of Africa and Iconography of Lip-Plated Africans in Pierre Desceliers's World Map of 1550." Earle and Lowe, pp. 48–69.

Nelson, Robert S. "Heavenly Ladder of John Climacus." Nelson and Collins, cat. no. 49, pp. 248–49.

Nelson, Robert S., and Kristen M. Collins. *Holy Image, Hallowed Ground: Icons from Sinai.* Getty Publications, 2006.

Pal, Pratapaditya. *Islamic Art: The Nasli M. Heeramaneck Collection, Gift of Joan Palevsky.* Los Angeles County Museum of Art, 1973.

Reynolds, Michael T. "René of Anjou, King of Sicily, and the Order of the Croissant." *Journal of Medieval History*, vol. 19, no. 1, 1993, pp. 125–61.

Sargent, William R. "Five Hundred Years of Chinese Export Ceramics in Context." *Treasures of Chinese Export Ceramics from the Peabody Essex*

Museum, edited by William R. Sargent and Rose Kerr, Peabody Essex Museum / Yale UP, 2012, pp. 4–5.

Seelig, Lorenz. "Christoph Jamnitzer's 'Moor's Head': A Late Renaissance Drinking Vessel." Earle and Lowe, pp. 181–209.

Turner, Nancy. "Reflecting a Heavenly Light: Gold and Other Metals in Medieval and Renaissance Manuscript Illumination." *Manuscripts in the Making: Art and Science*, edited by Stella Panayotova and Paola Ricciardi, vol. 1, Harvey Miller, 2018, pp. 77–92.

Wicker, Nancy. "Would There Have Been Gothic Art Without the Vikings? The Contribution of Scandinavian Medieval Art." *Medieval Encounters*, vol. 17, no. 1, 2011, pp. 198–229.

Robert W. Barrett, Jr., and Elizabeth Oyler

Medieval Drama, East and West

In this essay, we propose a sample course comparing medieval Japanese drama with that of England, a choice that immediately raises the questions: Why drama? Why Japan and England? Juxtaposing distinct theatrical forms—particularly ones as arcane as those developed in the Middle Ages—poses immediate difficulties for scholars trained along traditional national and disciplinary lines.

How do you gain competence in not one but two complex traditions from the opposite ends of the Eurasian continent? How do you even begin to reconstruct centuries-old performances attended by long-dead audiences? The medieval studies classroom amplifies these problems for drama-curious instructors: learning about medieval drama usually means reading play texts and screening recorded performances instead of attending a live production of a play or (even better) acting in one. When we study medieval theater, we are constantly confounded by our distance, historical and practical, from the object of our interest, and the addition of a second cultural and linguistic tradition on top of the first one heightens our sense of alienation. To study medieval drama is explicitly to confront the gap between our expectations and the artifacts in front of us. Few skills could be more immediately and obviously meaningful for contemporary students.

Why the plays of England and Japan, though? Beyond the obvious fact that these dramas are our personal areas of expertise, they share recognizable similarities that serve as foundations for meaningful comparative analysis. In their earliest days, plays from both traditions were performed in multiple locations and thus made do with impromptu stages. They were equally infused with religious practices and affiliated with religious institutions. In performance, both utilized minimal props and set pieces, establishing themselves as presentational rather than representational theaters. Both were experienced communally, and both were accessible to audiences of varying levels of literacy. The theaters of medieval Japan and England played similar roles in interpreting, presenting, and critiquing venerable cultural narratives, even as they intervened in contemporary concerns. The performance mode outlined here is certainly ad hoc, but its adaptability to varied staging conditions, acting levels, and material resources gives it the strength that makes these medieval plays relevant and entertaining in the twenty-first century.

Texts and Authors

In Japan, what we now identify as noh drama emerged in the fourteenth century from the patronage of the Ashikaga shoguns, especially Ashikaga Yoshimitsu. Captivated by the performance of Zeami, the adolescent son of the leader of the Yuzaki troupe, Yoshimitsu brought the young man into his household, providing him with the intellectual and material resources to create a new performing art. The provincial Yuzaki troupe originally operated outside the highly literate context of the aristocratic realm into which the Ashikaga—a clan of warrior arrivistes—was rapidly climbing. Yoshimitsu's patronage of Zeami brought noh drama into this rarefied realm as well, resulting in an archive that includes libretti of plays, records of performances, and even treatises written by Zeami himself.

Noh have been performed and written about continuously since Yoshimitsu's time. We know that the pace of performance has slowed dramatically since Zeami's day, and that formerly more props were used. Noh was originally performed outdoors, and the conventions of today's indoor stage only developed during the Edo period (1600–1868), during which the repertoire was winnowed, resulting in the set of approximately two hundred plays performed by the five extant noh schools. Most of the plays in this repertoire were written by a handful of playwright-actors and reflect a preference for the aesthetic ideals favored by Zeami: a rich layering of poetic allusion, an intellectual and artistic engagement with the strains of fifteenth-century Buddhist thought, and a constant striving toward the artistic goal of *yūgen*, a sense of depth and beauty. The plays included in the syllabus below favor Zeami, although those by Motomasa (Zeami's son) and Nobumitsu (Zeami's grandson) give some sense of the current canon's range in aesthetics, styles, and stagings.

Like noh, England's vernacular Bible and morality plays stem from the late fourteenth century: the first record of the York cycle dates to approximately 1376. Unlike noh, however, the vast majority of medieval English plays lack authors. (This is why we have not bothered to specify in the syllabus below when an English play selection is anonymous—they all are.) We can name many of the scribes who transmitted the plays in manuscript form, and we also know the names of many of the antiquarians who collected those manuscripts. But the playwrights' identities remain elusive, either lost by chance or subordinated to the needs of the organizations producing their scripts. (There have been attempts, largely New Critical, to create such author analogs as the "York Realist" or the "Wakefield Master," but these designations are largely outmoded.)

Moreover, there has been no continuous tradition of performance. Reformation-era religious controversy put paid to the great civic play cycles in the 1560s and 1570s (York ended in 1569, Chester in 1575), and medieval English drama went unperformed from the late sixteenth century until William Poel's revival of the morality play *Everyman* in 1901. The medieval shows flourishing in York, Chester, and elsewhere today are reconstructions based on the work of theater historians, performers, and laypersons making sense of the extant manuscripts and bureaucratic records.

The plays preserved in this archive are corporate works, expressions of group identity articulated at the local levels of parish, chapter, and commune. In larger towns (such as Chester, Coventry, and York), religious and trade guilds were given responsibility for individual plays, and complex systems of processional performance emerged. Smaller communities made do with smaller plays or pitched together to produce extravaganzas like the spectacular Digby *Play of Mary Magdalene*. Professional actors and musicians participated when the price was right, but much medieval English drama was the work of amateurs (albeit amateurs with extensive support networks and histories of performance). In its plays, the community was speaking to itself and for itself, oftentimes revealing that its voice was anything but unified—antipathy is expressed as often as amity.

The Religious Context

The Japan of the Ashikaga shogunate was a geographic area centered on the capital (modern-day Kyoto) and only just beginning to encompass the far eastern edges of the realm (depicted as a frontier zone in such plays as *Sumida-gawa*). Since the late twelfth century, the warriors expanding its borders had become increasingly central political and cultural actors; accompanying their violent rise to prominence was a widespread—and wholly unsurprising—interest in the apocalyptic Buddhist concept of *mappō*, the latter days of the law. Although Buddhism had long been the foundation for religious practice in Japan, new schools emerged in this period, and philosophers and theologians began to articulate more formally Buddhist beliefs in relation to the native religious practices known as *Shintō*, the way of the gods (kami).

For noh plays, the most important of these developments included the tenets, especially aesthetic ones, associated with Zen Buddhism; the popular faith-based schools focusing on the salvific power of Amida Buddha; and the syncretic *shinbutsu shūgō*, the harmonization of Buddhas and kami. Noh was strongly rooted in religious ritual and was thus often performed in temples, shrines, and other religious spaces. Zeami's plays reflect this context: his *fukushiki mugen nō* ("two-act dream noh") structure involves an encounter between a priest and a ghost haunting a site—the play enacts the priest's prayers for the enlightenment of the ghost. These dramas lie at the ritual end of the noh repertoire, whereas *genzai nō* ("present noh")—set in real time and ghost-free—tend to be more dramatic and theatrical. *Atsumori* and *Tadanori* are canonical examples of *mugen* noh; *Funa Benkei*, of *genzai* noh.

Medieval English drama is likewise obsessed with ritual and liturgy. Christian sacraments are staged either reverently or satirically; sacred music accompanies the action with an ear toward liturgical propriety; and the medieval church's calendar of feasts defined a theatrical season with summer and winter peaks. Adjacent to this core experience of ritual celebration was a powerful element of pastoral outreach. Originally aimed at Latinate priests, this program underwent vernacularization in 1357 with the publication of the archbishop of York's *Lay Folks' Catechism*. By the 1370s, the same decade as the York cycle's initial appearance in the archival record, widespread interest in vernacular theology had helped to generate Lollardy, England's first homegrown heresy. The English plays on our syllabus thus belong to a history of religious conversation and controversy, one in which laypersons felt authorized to teach doctrine to one another in dramatic form.

At the core of the theological debate was the status of the Eucharist, the sacramental wafer and wine that is, in orthodox belief, Christ's Body and Blood through transubstantiation. Lollards and their Protestant successors argued bitterly that the Eucharist was mere commemoration, symbol rather than identity. This point of contention has particularly fraught implications for drama: Can a human actor play God? Can mortal clay convey eternal truth? Is impersonation sinful presumption on the part of the actor? Or, given that Christianity is also a religion predicated on theories of incarnation and embodiment, do created beings have some capacity for divine instruction? Is theater not simply words made flesh, and is that not a good thing?

Sample Syllabus

This syllabus grows from a course taught by Robert Barrett at the University of Illinois, as well as our aforementioned interest in thinking about medieval theater in global terms and in searching for common ground from which to make meaningful comparisons.

Our textbooks are Royall Tyler's 1992 Penguin Classics edition of *Japanese Nō Dramas* and Christina M. Fitzgerald and John T. Sebastian's 2013 *Broadview Anthology of Medieval Drama*. Both collections are well annotated, introducing their play texts with headnotes that manage to provide context for students without squashing opportunities for discussion. The *Broadview Anthology* also has a companion website containing PDF versions of plays supplementing the print edition (broadviewpress.com/the-broadview-anthology-of-medieval-drama); instructors can take advantage of Broadview Press's "custom texts" option to include these plays in a class-specific print anthology. We suggest that the instructor purchase Karen Brazell's *Traditional Japanese Theater*, which contains invaluable introductory material, a translation of the play *Busu* (not included in the Tyler anthology), and several other plays that might substitute for the choices we have made below.

We have also included recommended readings for each unit of the class. Since we envision the course as focusing on close and comparative readings of our twenty-one plays, these secondary sources are primarily intended for instructors' use in producing lesson plans. They are chosen because of their ready availability and readability; they identify issues in each play that will sometimes be transferable to the other tradition but in all cases connect to the major research concerns of scholars working on the genre, period, or play in question. In the case of the noh, where much more scholarship is available in Japanese than in English, we include material that addresses broader contextual issues when essays specifically addressing a given play are untranslated. We have also included links to a small number of online play clips (or even full performances in several instances). These selections are not exhaustive (you can easily find recordings of other productions or other plays online), but they do come from relatively stable, authorized sources and are unlikely to vanish in the short term.

Short, regular reading responses on individual plays are one logical choice for assignments in this course. Our use of anthologies also means that there are numerous thematically related plays available for students to write about and thus demonstrate their command of course concepts as applied to new material. Creative assignments could include adaptations of characters and plots from one tradition to the performance traditions of the other: what would a noh version of the Crucifixion look like? Or an English-inflected take on the reconciliation between husband and wife at the end of *Kinuta*? Finally, resources permitting, students could stage a class performance of scenes or even complete plays—the point here would be less to produce a stellar show than to get students thinking about how to combine words and bodies theatrically.

Textbooks and Recommended Reading

Brazell, Karen, editor. *Traditional Japanese Theater: An Anthology of Plays.* Columbia UP, 1998.

Fitzgerald, Christina M., and John T. Sebastian, editors. *The Broadview Anthology of Medieval Drama.* Broadview, 2013.

Tyler, Royall, editor and translator. *Japanese Nō Dramas.* Penguin Classics, 1992.

Unit 1: Enter Stage Right

The two plays composing this first unit foreground the image of a cherry tree. In the case of *Saigyo-zakura*, it is the blooming springtime cherry celebrated in Japanese culture as an image of ephemeral beauty and the transience of all existence. In the N-Town *Nativity*, it is the paradoxical winter cherry laden with ripened fruit that offers succor to its human analog, the pregnant Virgin. The unusual animacy of these two trees—identical in material terms, disparate in devotional ones—is the starting point for a conversation on the conventions, contexts, and performance practices of our two medieval theaters.

Zeami, *Saigyo-zakura*

Brazell, Karen. "The Noh and Kyōgen Theaters: Elements of Performance." *Traditional Japanese Theater: An Anthology of Plays*, Columbia UP, 1998, pp. 115–25.

"Noh Reimagined 2018—Noh Mask, Noh Movement: Illusory Devices—Seminar." *YouTube*, uploaded by muartsproduction, 6 Jan. 2019, youtu.be/VrSwYBqWHvo.

Pinnington, Noel J. "The Classic Noh Plays." *A New History of Medieval Japanese Theater*, Palgrave Macmillan, 2019, pp. 113–45.

Yamanaka, Reiko. "Fraternizing with the Spirits in the Noh Plays *Saigyōzakura* and *Yamanba*." *Rethinking Nature in Japan: From Tradition to Modernity*, edited by Bonaventura Ruperti et al., 2017, pp. 133–40.

N-Town *Nativity*

Dillon, Janette. "Places of Performance." *The Cambridge Introduction to Early English Theatre*, Cambridge UP, 2006, pp. 1–64.

Farina, Lara. "Curl." *Veer Ecology: A Companion for Environmental Thinking*, edited by Jeffrey Jerome Cohen and Lowell Duckert, U of Minnesota P, 2017, pp. 434–54.

Novacich, Sarah Elliott. "Transparent Mary: Visible Interiors and the Maternal Body in the Middle Ages." *JEGP*, vol. 116, no. 4, 2017, pp. 464–90.

Twycross, Meg. "The Theatricality of Medieval Plays." *The Cambridge Companion to Medieval English Theatre*, edited by Richard Beadle and Alan J. Fletcher, 2nd ed., Cambridge UP, 2008, pp. 26–74.

Unit 2: Women in and out of Society

This unit addresses the location of women within their social contexts. Because these contexts are male-dominated, the female characters in these seven plays are initially defined by their marital status (or lack thereof). Thus, suspicious sexuality unites the unmarried protagonists of *Eguchi*, *Seki-dera Komachi*, and the Digby *Mary Magdalene*: Lady Eguchi is a known prostitute, Komachi has aged into obscurity after scandal drives her from the imperial court, and Mary loses her virginity offstage to the sweet-talking personification of Pride. Yet each woman also reveals a command of patriarchal discourse that belies her low status: the sex worker has a greater understanding of Buddhist doctrine than the monk Saigyo, Komachi's lecture on poetry earns her a place of honor at the Tanabata Festival, and the redeemed Mary's devotion to Christ makes her not only a saint but the *apostola apostolorum*, the "apostle to the apostles."

The women of *Kinuta*, the Chester *Play of Noah's Flood*, *Sumida-gawa*, and the Digby *Candlemas Day and the Killing of the Children of Israel* are wives (and, in the case of the latter three plays, mothers). Their position within patriarchal society seems secure, but all are tested over the course of their shows. Sometimes it is the husbands' work that drives the dramatic conflict: in *Kinuta*, the protagonist is an isolated woman driven to madness and death by her husband's three-year absence pursuing a legal case—when he finally does return home, he must confront the demon his abandonment has summoned.

Noah's wife has the opposite problem: she has a supportive group of drinking buddies, but now her husband is trying to split them up on the basis of some divine command. When she opts for feminist solidarity and refuses to board the ark, hijinks ensue. The takes on female suffering in *Sumida-gawa* and the Digby *Candlemas Day* are less personal but all the more chilling for their communal nature: both plays depict women stripped of their children by patriarchal systems—profitable enslavement of people in the noh play, political infanticide in the Bible drama. The women resist with performative madness (*Sumida-gawa*) and gender-marked violence (*Candlemas Day*), but they lose their children nonetheless.

Zeami, *Eguchi* and *Seki-dera Komachi*

Kawashima, Terry. "Authored Margins: The Prosperity and Decline of Komachi." *Writing Margins: The Textual Construction of Gender in Heian and Kamakura Japan*. Harvard University Asia Center, 2001, pp. 123–74.

Strong, Sarah M. "The Making of a Femme Fatale: Ono no Komachi in the Early Medieval Commentaries." *Monumenta Nipponica*, vol. 49, no. 4, 1994, pp. 391–412.

Terasaki, Etsuko. "*Eguchi*: Is Courtesan Eguchi a Buddhist Metaphorical Woman?" *Figures of Desire: Wordplay, Spirit Possession, Fantasy, Madness, and Mourning in Japanese Noh Plays*, University of Michigan Center for Japanese Studies, 2002, pp. 263–93.

Digby *Mary Magdalene* (Broadview PDF)

Coletti, Theresa. "'Courtesy Doth It Yow Lere': The Sociology of Transgression in the Digby *Mary Magdalene*." *ELH*, vol. 71, no. 1, 2004, pp. 1–28.

Findon, Joanne. "Napping in the Arbour in the Digby *Mary Magdalene* Play." *Early Theatre*, vol. 9, no. 2, 2006, pp. 35–55.

Zeami, *Kinuta*

Atkins, Paul S. "Figuring the Feminine Ideal." *Revealed Identity: The Noh Plays of Komparu Zenchiku*, University of Michigan Center for Japanese Studies, 2006, pp. 163–96.

Savas, Minae Yamamoto. "Voices from the Past: Symbolic Madness in the Noh Play *Kinuta, The Fulling Block*." *Japan Studies Association Journal*, vol. 11, 2013, pp. 144–57.

Chester *Play of Noah's Flood*

"The Chester *Noah Play*—Liverpool University Players." *YouTube*, uploaded by Sarah Peverley, 13 June 2013, youtu.be/Cn0pcYONuxc.

Novacich, Sarah Elliott. "*Uxor Noe* and the Animal Inventory." *New Medieval Literatures*, vol. 12, 2010, pp. 169–77.

Wack, Mary. "Women, Work, and Plays in a Medieval English Town." *Maids and Mistresses, Cousins and Queens: Women's Alliances in Early Modern England*, edited by Susan Frye and Karen Robertson, Oxford UP, 1999, pp. 33–51.

Kanze Motomasa, *Sumida-gawa*

Ishii, Mikiko. "The Weeping Mothers in *Sumidagawa*, *Curlew River*, and Medieval European Religious Plays." *Comparative Drama*, vol. 39, no. 3/4, 2005, pp. 287–305.

Nelson, Thomas. "Slavery in Medieval Japan." *Monumenta Nipponica*, vol. 59, no. 4, 2004, pp. 463–92.

Digby *Candlemas Day and the Killing of the Children of Israel* (Broadview PDF)

Coletti, Theresa. "Genealogy, Sexuality, and Sacred Power: The Saint Anne Dedication of the Digby *Candlemas Day and the Killing of the Children of Israel*." *Journal of Medieval and Early Modern Studies*, vol. 29, no. 1, 1999, pp. 25–59.

Ryan, Denise. "Womanly Weaponry: Language and Power in the Chester *Slaughter of the Innocents*." *Studies in Philology*, vol. 98, no. 1, 2001, pp. 76–92.

Unit 3: Masculinity and Embodied Violence

This unit focuses on violence and its relation to masculinities in both cultural traditions. In the noh *Atsumori* and *Tadanori*, the main characters are the ghosts of warriors killed on the battlefield, and both are valorized as the best of their kind: valiant, noble, and stoic in the face of inevitable defeat, and yet embodying as well the arts of peace, specifically music and poetry, that noh celebrates most. The ghosts' parallels in the Towneley

Killing of Abel and the York *Crucifixion* plays—Abel the shepherd and Christ the Good Shepherd—are similarly figures of peace, facing their deaths with equanimity. To compensate for the theatrical deficiencies of such idealized passivity, the English plays focus instead on male characters defined by violent action and aggressive action: Abel's disobedient brother Cain, Cain's profane servant Pickharness, and the anonymous soldiers who treat the Crucifixion as just another day at work.

Funa Benkei and the York *Resurrection* concentrate instead on hierarchical relations and the role of violence in sustaining the orders underpinning society: the increasingly rigid warrior ethos (which would later inform modern and contemporary ideas of the samurai) in Japan, and the overly comfortable alliance between church and aristocracy in England. *Funa Benkei* stages a world of exclusively male relationships celebrating the relationship between Lord Yoshitsune and his retainer Benkei. The *Resurrection* play takes an opposite tack, contrasting the self-serving machismo of Pilate, Caiaphas, Annas, and their soldiers with the loyalty and devotion shown to the risen Christ by the three Marys.

Zeami, *Atsumori* and *Tadanori*

"*Atsumori*: Final Scene." *YouTube*, uploaded by Theatre Nohgaku, 29 Aug. 2012, youtu.be/DhSbe4Ctq64.

Brazell, Karen W. "Subversive Transformations: *Atsumori* and *Tadanori* at Suma." *Currents in Japanese Culture: Translations and Transformations*, edited by Amy Vladeck Heinrich, Columbia UP, 1997, pp. 35–52.

Hare, Thomas Blenman. "Guntai: The Martial Mode." *Zeami's Style: The Noh Plays of Zeami Motokiyo*, Stanford UP, 1996, pp. 185–224.

Towneley *Killing of Abel* (Broadview PDF)

Davidson, Clifford. "Cain in the Mysteries: The Iconography of Violence." *Fifteenth-Century Studies*, vol. 25, 2000, pp. 204–27.

Evans, Ruth. "*Sir Orfeo* and Bare Life." *Medieval Cultural Studies: Essays in Honour of Stephen Knight*, edited by Ruth Evans et al., U of Wales P, 2006, pp. 198–212.

York *Crucifixion*

Fitzgerald, Christina M. "Acting Like a Man: The Solitary Christ and Masculinity." *The Drama of Masculinity and Medieval English Guild Culture*, Palgrave Macmillan, 2007, pp. 145–64.

Nakley, Susan. "On the Unruly Power of Pain in Middle English Drama." *Literature and Medicine*, vol. 33, no. 2, 2015, pp. 302–25.

Kanze Nobumitsu, *Funa Benkei*

Lim, Beng Choo. "(De-)Constructing Furyū Noh." *Kanze Nobumitsu and the Late Muromachi Noh Theater*, Cornell East Asia Program, 2012, pp. 157–84.

"Noh Funabenkei (with commentary in English)." *YouTube*, uploaded by Noh Open Course Ware [Doshisha University], 8 May 2018, youtu.be/rNiIB1IkMFs.

Pinnington, Noel J. "Noh in the Age of Chaos: 1450–1600." *A New History of Medieval Japanese Theater*, Palgrave Macmillan, 2019, pp. 147–78.

York *Resurrection*

Beckwith, Sarah. "Presence after Presentness: The Theater of Resurrection in York." *Signifying God: Social Relation and Symbolic Act in the York Corpus Christi Plays*, U of Chicago P, 2001, pp. 72–89.

Horner, Olga. "'Us Must Make Lies': Witness, Evidence, and Proof in the York *Resurrection*." *Medieval English Theatre*, vol. 20, 1998, pp. 24–76.

Unit 4: Time and the Boundaries of the Human

The plays in this unit confront the precariousness of the human condition in the face of all that is unknowable in our environment: more than human entities, both natural and supernatural, as well as timescapes that exceed our limited understanding. What does a human life encompass? What might lie beyond the temporal boundaries of that life? *Yamamba* and the Towneley *Judgment* are set at liminal times and places, albeit in different contexts: *Yamamba* depicts pilgrims crossing into the mysterious and magical space of the mountains, where they encounter a being who challenges ideas about identity, divinity, and monstrosity. The *Judgment*, by contrast, reminds its contemporary audience of the eternity that awaits them after death and at the end of history—even as it puts a satirical spotlight on a trio of demons moonlighting as fifteenth-century lawyers.

Kantan and *Mankind* also juxtapose the stasis of eternity with the mutability of human time. *Kantan* places its audience at two removes from the eternal, first by setting its action in China, where the protagonist travels from an inn to a heaven all too reminiscent of the Chinese imperial court, and then by revealing that this journey is nothing more than a transitory dream. *Mankind*'s eponymous protagonist also tarries in a tavern, seduced from a life of virtuous labor by the devil Titivillus and his three minions, the rogues Nowadays, Newguise, and Nought. Like his parallel in *Kantan*, Mankind seemingly learns a lesson about the perils of clinging to material existence—but both plays leave true reform an open-ended question on their conclusion.

Zeami, *Yamamba*

Bethe, Monica, and Karen Brazell. *Noh as Performance: An Analysis of the Kuse Scene of* Yamamba. Cornell China-Japan Program, 1978.

Klein, Susan Blakeley. "When the Moon Strikes the Bell: Desire and Enlightenment in the Noh Play *Dōjōji*." *Journal of Japanese Studies*, vol. 17, no. 2, 1991, pp. 291–322.

Towneley *Judgment*

Cawsey, Kathy. "Tutivillus and the 'Kyrkchaterars': Strategies of Control in the Middle Ages." *Studies in Philology*, vol. 102, no. 4, 2002, pp. 434–51.

Stevenson, Jill. "Playing with Time's End: Cultivating Sincere Contrition in Medieval Last Judgment Performances." *The Routledge Research Companion*, edited by Pamela King, Routledge, 2016, pp. 118–36.

Kantan

Tyler, Royall. "Buddhism in Noh." *Japanese Journal of Religious Studies*, vol. 14, no. 1, 1987, pp. 19–52.

Yip, Leo Shingchi. "Locating China in Noh: The Evolving Dynamics of the Other and Self." *China Reinterpreted: Staging the Other in Muromachi Noh Theater*. Lexington Books, 2016, pp. 1–34.

Mankind

Dinshaw, Carolyn. "Temporalities." *Middle English*, edited by Paul Strohm, Oxford UP, 2007, pp. 107–23.

Garrison, Jennifer. "*Mankind* and the Masculine Pleasures of Penance." *Exemplaria*, vol. 31, no. 1, 2019, pp. 46–62.

"PLS: *MANKIND* at the Festival of Early Drama, Toronto 2015." *YouTube*, uploaded by Matthew Sergi, 27 Feb. 2017, youtu.be/qQGji_BhrGQ.

Unit 5: Exit Stage Left

The course ends with this unit centered on two transgressive feasts: the "poison" that turns out to be delicious sugar in the *kyōgen* play *Busu* and the seemingly endless supply of meat consumed in the Chester *Shepherds' Play*. As a comic genre developing in tandem with the noh tradition, the *kyōgen* theater routinely relies on festive mockery, not only of noh tropes but also of elite culture. The bumbling servants Tarō Kaja and Jirō Kaja are thus perfect counterparts for the bickering Welsh shepherds of the English play.

Busu

"Bilingual Kyogen 'Busu.'" *YouTube*, uploaded by Doji Company Performance Information, 24 May 2017, youtu.be/DWxZhtPG0Nw.

Morley, Carolyn. "Kyōgen: A Theatre of Play." *Miracles and Mischief: Noh and Kyōgen Theater in Japan*, edited by Sharon Sadako Takeda, Los Angeles County Museum of Art, 2002, pp. 146–60.

Pinnington, Noel J. "Medieval Kyōgen." *A New History of Medieval Japanese Theater*, Palgrave Macmillan, 2019, pp. 179–208.

Chester Shepherds' Play

Fitzgerald, Christina M. "Male Homosocial Communities and Public Life." *The Drama of Masculinity and Medieval English Guild Culture*, Palgrave Macmillan, 2007, pp. 95–144.

Sergi, Matthew. "Festive Piety: Staging Food and Drink at Chester." *Medieval English Theatre*, vol. 31, 2009, pp. 89–136.

Teaching Other Performance Traditions from the Global Middle Ages

Instructors may wish to take advantage of medieval performance traditions beyond those of England and Japan, and there are a number of affordable translations to support such substitutions. For example, the University of Illinois course that served as the basis for our sample syllabus included a selection of *zaju* song-plays from Yuan-dynasty China (1279–1368). Staged for urban audiences by both male and female performers, these musical dramas engage with many of the same themes as the noh and Bible plays on our list: Guan Hanqing's *Injustice Done to Dou E* offers a female-centered take on the legal corruption that informs Christ's Passion, whereas *The Zhao Orphan* runs counter to *Atsumori* in its validation of revenge.

The female protagonists of our second unit would make excellent foils for two of the long-suffering heroines of Sanskrit drama: the foundling Śakuntalā (from Kālidāsa's *Recognition of Śakuntalā*) and the courtesan Vasánta-sena (from Śūdraka's *Little Clay Cart*). The scurrility of *Mankind* pairs nicely with the bawdy shadow plays of the thirteenth-century Cairene physician Ibn Dāniyāl, and noh's memorialization of the twelfth-century Genpei War has a fifteenth-century Mayan parallel in the dance-drama *Rabinal Achi* and its commemoration of the conflict between the Rabinal and Quiché peoples.

Arabic Drama

Ibn Dāniyāl. *Theatre from Medieval Cairo: The Ibn Dāniyāl Trilogy.* Translated and edited by Safi Mahfouz and Marvin Carlson, Martin E. Segal Center Theatre Publications, 2013.

Chinese Drama

Hsia, C. T., et al., editors. *The Columbia Anthology of Yuan Drama.* Columbia UP, 2014.

Idema, Wilt L., and Stephen H. West, editors and translators. *Battles, Betrayals, and Brotherhood: Early Chinese Plays on the Three Kingdoms.* Hackett Publishing, 2012.

Wang Shifu. *The Story of the Western Wing.* Edited and translated by Stephen H. West and Wilt L. Idema, U of California P, 1995.

West, Stephen H., and Wilt L. Idema, editors and translators. *Monks, Bandits, Lovers, and Immortals: Eleven Early Chinese Plays.* Hackett Publishing, 2010.

Mayan Drama

Rabinal Achi*: A Fifteenth-Century Maya Dynastic Drama.* Translated by Alain Breton, edited by Teresa Lavender Fagan and Robert Schneider, UP of Colorado, 2007.

Rabinal Achi*: A Mayan Drama of War and Sacrifice.* Translated by Dennis Tedlock, Oxford UP, 2003.

Sanskrit Drama

Kālidāsa. *The Recognition of Śakuntalā: A Play in Seven Acts.* Translated by W. J. Johnson, Oxford UP, 2001.

———. *Theatre of Memory: The Plays of Kālidāsa.* Edited by Barbara Stoler Miller, Columbia UP, 1994.

Śūdraka. *The Little Clay Cart.* Translated by Diwakar Acharya, New York UP, 2009.

———. *The Little Clay Cart: An English Translation of the Mṛcchakaṭika of Śūdraka as Adapted for the Stage by A. L. Basham.* Edited by Arvind Sharma, State U of New York P, 1994.

Lynn Ramey

Teaching the World through Digital Technology and Media

Digital and online resources have substantially expanded the viability of teaching the Global Middle Ages in a variety of classroom settings and disciplines. Teacher and student access to primary data and sources from researchers around the world is now limited only by the time required to process the information presented rather than measured in lengthy waiting for interlibrary loans or acquiring funding for visits to faraway archives. Digital maps, 3D models, video, audio, and online archives are just some of the resources available to give students a broad sense of the world from 500 to 1500 CE.

Experiencing the past through visualizations and immersive environments (including 3D, virtual, and augmented reality) brings new understanding as students and teachers come closer to seeing and experiencing the past as it may have been by those who lived it. Technology has not solved all the problems of accessing the past, of course; resources are still sometimes difficult to find and, as with all resources, attention must be given to selecting the best and most reliable materials. In this essay, I aim to highlight a selection of digital resources of various types in several disciplines and suggest how these might be used in a classroom, and the appendix includes syllabus resources organized by topic. Digital resources become dated while new sites are added daily, so attention will be given to searching for and selecting new, reliable, and exciting digital work for the classroom.

Finding Resources

Google and *Google Scholar* turn up a plethora of print resources, but platforms and articles devoted solely to aggregating digital medieval resources provide a better starting point for classroom media applications. Though one may encounter broken links or outdated materials, the aggregation platforms and articles point to the scholars working with digital tools, and finding their newest work requires little further searching. Provided that the scholars have cited their archival sources well, direct access to the data they used is also very useful in the classroom. The challenge for those teaching the global Middle Ages is locating sources of information about non-Western cultures, ideally authored by scholars from diverse backgrounds.

For instance, though the 2017 *Speculum* issue devoted to *The Digital Middle Ages* provides an overview of some of the ways that digital resources are being used by medievalists (manuscript studies, soundscapes, immersive environments, mapping, data science), none of the essays addresses truly global topics, with the boundaries of modern Europe circumscribing all "digital medieval" (Birnbaum et al.). Likewise, the Medieval Academy of America's curated "Medieval Digital Resources" provides short descriptions and links to many databases and digital projects, but non-Western resources figure sparsely.

In order to help focus attention on non-Western sources, the *Global Middle Ages* platform aggregates and curates digital resources and teaching materials from around the world in the period 500 to 1500 CE (see "Projects"). The twenty (as of 2021) core projects circle the globe, though South America and Australia are notably absent. Though not contained within the core projects that receive support from the platform, a section with links to external projects helps complete a wider picture of what was happening around the medieval world and resources are added regularly (see "External"). Project directors working with non-Western materials are encouraged to make contact through the platform to add their syllabuses and project sites.

The following sections provide an overview of selected resources by media type—some a part of the core projects, some figuring as external links, and others with no connection to the platform at all—each focused either on points of contact between cultures or on non-Western cultures.

Augmented and Virtual Reality

Virtual reality (VR) and augmented reality (AR) have become inexpensive enough to use in the classroom, and both technology and content are growing exponentially.[1] At the lowest entry point, some content is available for smartphones with the use of the *Cardboard* app and a simple holder for the phone, costing on average about eight dollars at the time of this writing. Much better viewers with access to more complex applications can range, at the time of this writing, from two hundred dollars for the Oculus GO to $1,600 for the HTC Vive Pro (and on up, but for classroom use, the costlier professional-quality apparatuses are unlikely to be available). Applications can be bought through the online stores for each device, as well as through the gaming platform *Steam* for selected devices.

Museums are excellent sources of educational AR and VR content related to the past, though sometimes their projects are only available onsite. The Museo Arqueológico Nacional in Spain has a VR experience, *Live the Past*, that includes a short segment on medieval Muslim Spain ("National Archeological Museum"). Available for the Oculus Rift, Quest, or Go, or Gear VR, students can choose Spanish or English language, and a guide will show them the village square, the exterior of the mosque, and the interior of a typical home. Free exploration is also possible.

Along with visits to BCE Rhodes and seventeenth-century India, *Wonders of the World* for Gear and Go provides a view of conquest-era Peru, with an educational game set in Machu Picchu in 1532 ("*Wonders*"). A young girl starts the quest for the user, who plays the role of Anko, an emissary for the Incan emperor, Atahualpa (fig. 1). As Anko, the user must learn about the area, including crops, herding practices, and record keeping in order to complete the emperor's mission, thus getting insight into the material conditions of life in medieval Peru at the last moment before the vibrant Incan civilization is annihilated.

Masterworks (for Vive, Go, and Rift) takes the user to the ruins of the fourteenth-century Thai capital of Ayutthaya ("*MasterWorks*"). Though the user does not play a role in the scenario, visiting various parts of the ruins and learning about the history of the capital city will reward the user with artifacts. Local experts provide the narration, which is translated into English.

Figure 1. An Incan girl teaches users about farming practices. In *Wonders of the World*'s VR game set in Machu Picchu.

As more, and affordable platforms for VR come to market, 3D content will continue to proliferate. *YouTube*'s VR content, viewable in 3D on most cell phones, is a good platform to check frequently for classroom-appropriate content. Most of the videos are shot live with a 360-degree camera and edited later but do not include additional 3D creations. These videos generally show the present-day state of a medieval site, or perhaps a live reenactment, while an expert explains the historical context.

Videos of non-Western medieval sites include fourteenth-century Tenochtitlan (now Mexico City) with narration in Spanish ("Tenochtitlan") and the eleventh-century temples of Bagan in Myanmar ("Restoring"). *VR DunHuang*, an experience in the Mogao Caves in China, provides a spectacular experience on the HTC Vive ("*VR DunHuang*"). Sarah Kenderdine's immersive exhibits of the Mogao Caves are highly praised for their engaging presentations. Her shows require 360-degree large-screen enclosures or location-based augmented reality and are thus available only as traveling museum exhibits (see her site for installations, "Pure Land AR").

Art historians and archeologists use laser scanning and modeling software to preserve the state of historical sites as well as to reconstruct digitally how a monument or object most likely looked in the past. Many of these models are available online; searching a site like *3D Warehouse* (3dwarehouse.sketchup.com) using the keyword "medieval" yields more than a thousand hits, but finding non-Western models requires using specific keywords, such as "Machu Picchu." Because of the popularity of the Middle Ages in popular culture, video-game-style models are quite common and can be bought inexpensively, but most lack any real historical basis in their construction. Sites that vet these models and provide documentation on their creation are preferable for classroom use. A scholarly database of open-access, 3D models that contains important metadata about the models' creation and that can be searched based on location and construction is sorely needed.

Users can freely explore a multicultural Middle Ages in Hiverlab's *Churches of Famagusta, Cyprus*, based on art historian Michael J. K. Walsh's work (Walsh et al.; Walsh and Bernardello). Hiverlab software developers describe the methods used to collect the data for the church models, and the criteria they used for data collection (Yi and Shutao 315–17). They explain as well how they used academic resources and photographs of the churches to create the texture maps to place over the digital framework the building derived from the laser scanning process. Their documentation of the process would give students insight into the choices that are made in the creation of a digital, virtual Middle Ages, and classroom activities could be developed to pull out the choices, problems, and promises of 3D digital reconstructions. The software used in the Famagusta project is readily available, and more adventuresome classes should try their hands at creating their own models of medieval sites (storyhive.com).[2]

Models of important heritage sites in Africa show the impressive architectural practices found throughout medieval Africa. The *Zamani Project* (www.zamaniproject.org/) presents 3D models of cultural heritage sites throughout Africa, the Middle East, and Southeast Asia (fig. 2). The architecture in the model is given a name and location, but unfortunately the site does not provide building dates or historical context, though the creation methods are documented, and the research team is identified. Thus, searching for medieval sites requires searching elsewhere to find the dates for the buildings (except for Bagan in Myanmar, where the buildings have dates from the second to the fifteenth centuries). Many of the sites are medieval, including rock-cut churches of the twelfth and thirteenth centuries in Lalibela, Ethiopia; the ruins of the coastal town Gedi in Kenya; the reconstructed old mosque at Djenné and the fourteenth-century Djinguereber Mosque in Mali; the ruins of Kilwa Kisiwani and Songo Mnara, medieval trading towns in Tanzania; and the Great Zimbabwe palace ruins dating from the eleventh century.

Figure 2. Animation of Kubyauk-gyi Temple in Bagan, Myanmar. *Zamani Project*'s Bagan temple models are explorable online at www.zamaniproject.org/.

Fortunately, other resources provide needed historical context within more complex online portals, simplifying the use of their digital materials in the classroom. The Kariye Camii church in Istanbul, for example, serves as the subject of a project that includes the history of the building, drawings and photographs of the church, virtual reality experiences, 3D animations, and a glossary of terms ("Restoring Byzantium"). The detail provided by this project team would facilitate in-depth research by faculty or graduate students, as well as sophisticated projects for students in middle and high school, along with appealing visual demonstrations for elementary school students.

In a similar vein and with the virtue of being partially gamified, Roger Martinez-Davila's app *Virtual Plasencia* integrates high-quality 3D models of reconstructed Plasencia, Spain, where Christians, Jews, and Muslims interacted in the local village square over centuries ("*Virtual Plasencia*"). Students in Martinez-Davila's class have contributed to the field as they use his web pages, creating crowdsourced transcriptions of medieval manuscripts in the archives of Plasencia. Like "Restoring Byzantium," Martinez-Davila's project features—in addition to a 3D immersive experience—a robust map of the area, historical background for the project, and an explanation of how the virtual world can help students understand the multicultural nature of the Middle Ages.

Figure 3. Simulation visualizing Angkor from above. The *Virtual Angkor* site has 360-degree videos that allow for immersive experiences (www.virtualangkor.com).

Finally, *Virtual Angkor* provides a complete teaching and learning site for thirteenth-century Cambodia (www.virtualangkor.com) in a beautiful, American Historical Association award-winning portal. The 360-degree video can be seen in a VR headset or on a computer screen, allowing students to immerse themselves in recreations of Angkor Wat (fig. 3). The site provides three teaching paths, "Power and Place," "Water and Climate," and "Trade and Diplomacy." Each theme gives bibliographical references for further reading and provides questions for students to address as they view the reconstruction. The "Sources" section is of particular interest, giving the scholarly apparatus for the site itself, as well as further documentation for a deeper dive into medieval Angkor and the Khmer Empire.

Online resources like *Virtual Plasencia*, "Restoring Byzantium," and *Virtual Angkor* aim to provide full contextualization of their subject matter for users. In many classrooms, these robust projects provide an opportunity for those beginning to learn about the global Middle Ages playfully to explore as they learn.

Interactive Maps

Though 3D experiences are visually appealing, one of their drawbacks is that users can sometimes become so immersed in other worlds that they may not make necessary connections and distinctions in the space-time of their own lives. Good pedagogical practice would have students learn from other times and places and make explicit connections with their here and now.

Online maps allow students to orient themselves spatially in the areas being studied. These resources can be linked to travel narratives telling of vast expanses in space, or the maps can focus on a particular community. A map hosted at the University of California, Davis, allows students to explore the map based on topics that include "trade routes," "religions," and "wind and ocean currents" ("Sites"). Travel routes used by explorers are mapped on a platform devoted to premodern travel (fictional and historical) to the Americas from points around the globe ("Explorers"). The "Mapping Mandeville Project" allows users to see the world as viewed through the eyes of fourteenth-century John Mandeville, who purportedly travels from England to the East, by mapping locations mentioned in *Mandeville's Travels* onto a reproduction of the circa 1300 Hereford *mappa mundi* (Greenlee).

Using a modern base map, Marco Polo's account is mapped in a multilingual English, French, and Franco-Italian project that uses the text of Polo's travels to illustrate what he reported of his encounters with peoples, economies, and religions of the East (Bailey et al.). All these maps can provide details to students looking for more information about the authors, their writings, and the lands through which they traveled. As a classroom project, students inspired by these scholarly maps can make their own maps of works they are studying using *Google Maps* (for instructions, see "About: *My Maps*"), working in groups to add data for each location, creating sophisticated resources that they can share with online.

Databases and Archives

Research-focused sites provide rich sources of primary data. *Digital Silk Road* is a Japanese-English resource with collections of images, maps, and digitized books (dsr.nii.ac.jp/). This rich site has some sections that may be of limited use in the classroom, such as place-name databases (gazetteers), but graduate students and faculty members could find these resources extremely useful in their research. Photographs of the routes are tagged with metadata and placed on a map showing where the photos were taken. Individual architectural models can be accessed for use in the classroom ("3D Digital Archives"). *Digital Silk Road* would require quite a bit more selection on the part of the instructor than, say, *Virtual Angkor*, where the learning path for users is clearly at the forefront of the portal design. The archived data and digitized primary sources, however, allow students to conduct their own research.

For instance, whereas *Virtual Angkor* and *VR DunHuang* provide a reconstruction that seems seamless and affords users a sense of telepresence, or feeling of being there, the database of Buddhist cave temples in China found within *Digital Silk Road* includes a stunning archive of new and historical photographs of the caves in Dunhuang, accessible via a table numbering each room in the cave system ("Dunhuang Mogao Caves"). Students could reconstruct their own versions, do their own readings of the murals, or make a diorama of a cave not featured in other projects.

Likewise, classes could work with digitized medieval (thirteenth to fifteenth century) manuscripts from the archive in Timbuktu (*Tombouctou Manuscripts Project*, www.tombouctoumanuscripts.org/). Those who can read the Arabic would do different work than those who could be asked to look for general information about learning and archival practices in medieval Africa. A compendium of resources in Syriac, *Syriaca.org*, provides multiple databases of primary materials—a gazetteer of place names, a biographical database of important historical figures, a catalog of saints, a handbook of authors writing in Syriac, and a database of hagiographical literature ("*Syriaca.org*"). A student project could involve looking at several of the thirty-five entries on John the Baptist, perhaps locating translations of the stories and comparing the differences in the tales, noting the place or time of composition (fig. 4). Instructors could use the interactive map to show the widespread use and importance of the Syriac language, underscoring its importance in global medieval interactions.

Cultural Resources

Reconstructions, 3D objects, and maps certainly qualify as resources to understand the culture of medieval peoples. Some aspects of medieval culture do not have material forms dating from the Middle Ages, but scholars are able to reimagine or reconstruct them. In the case of oral stories, the epic *Sundiata*, telling of the founding of the Mali Empire by Sundiata Keita, has been extracted from the stories of modern-day griots, or oral historians (for ideas on teaching the epic, see the essay by Michael J. Gomez in this volume). The University of California, Berkeley's collection of Sundiata resources for teaching includes historical contexts, a retelling of

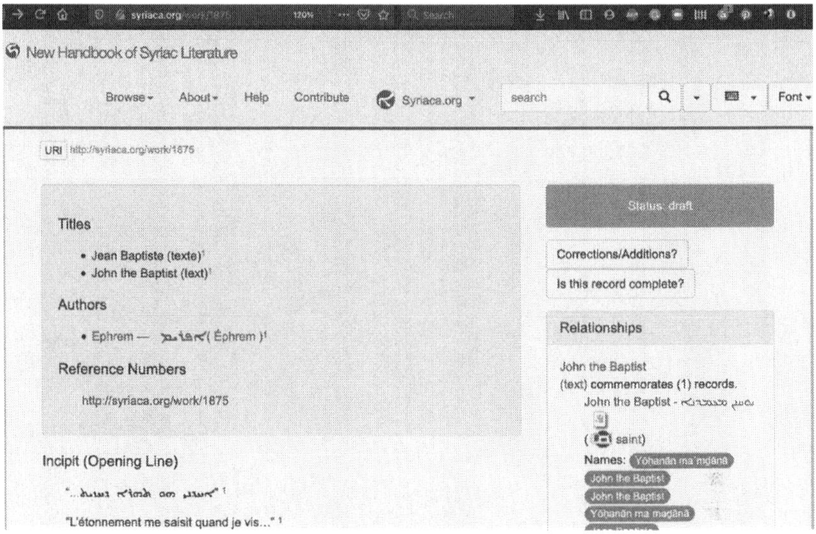

Figure 4. Screenshot of John the Baptist text. *Syriaca.org*'s robust databases allow students to search and cross-reference people, places, and things ("*Syriaca.org*").

the story, the script for a play to be performed by students, and questions for class discussion, providing a rich framework for a classroom at any level ("Sundiata"). Likewise, the travel narrative of fourteenth-century Moroccan Ibn Battuta as he explored the known world can be adapted to most classes. Maps and extracts from his writings make the Muslim scholar's life come alive in the classroom ("Travels").

Christopher Taylor's impressive multimedia Scalar project about the origins and uses of the Letter of Prester John details how a story about a mythical Christian priest-king in faraway Eastern lands became a recurring cultural touchstone for more than six centuries (Taylor). The story itself is fascinating, and Taylor provides images from manuscript pages, maps of the travels of real and fictitious voyagers who claimed to either meet Prester John or seek his kingdom, and historical contexts throughout the centuries (fig. 5; for more on teaching Prester John, see Taylor's essay in this volume).

"Imagining Medieval Narrative: *The Travels of Marco Polo*" (Bailey et al.) and "Mapping Mandeville" (Greenlee) likewise combine maps, textual data, and contextual essays about the author and work. All these sites lend themselves for use in classes where students read the texts *Sundiata*,

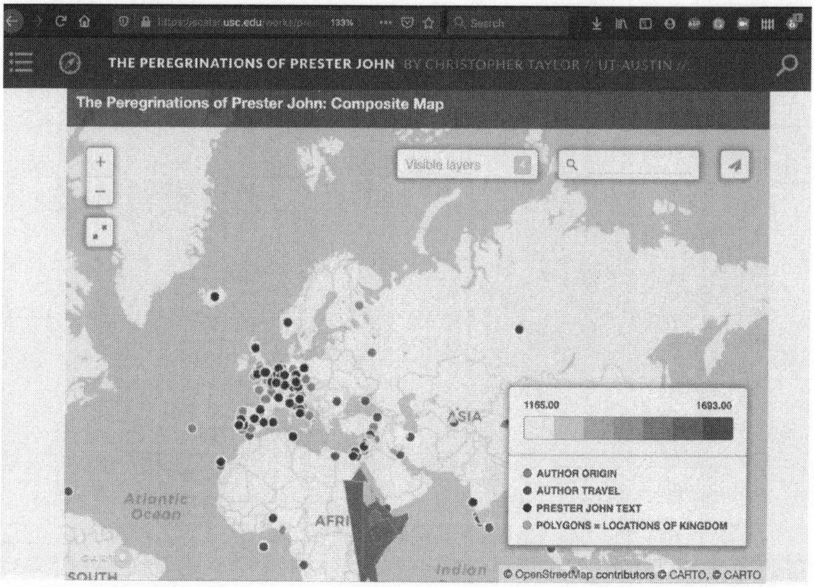

Figure 5. Composite map orientation to "International Prester John Project." The project includes a digital image of the manuscript letter, an English translation, maps, historical context, and more.

The Travels of Ibn Battuta, *The Travels of Marco Polo*, *Mandeville's Travels*, or the Letter of Prester John (multiple editions of all are available online in various languages) and use the websites to explore further about the historical contexts of their composition and the impact that these imaginative works had on later epics, travel stories, and political events.

Digital resources bring the past to the present and faraway lands to our doorsteps. As medievalists continually look for ways to foreground the diverse nature of medieval cultures around the globe, the use of technology offers new ways to approach medieval conceptions of embodiment, disembodiment, and religious differences. At the same time technology serves as a powerful tool for allowing modern users to experience the past in novel ways. Students can often not only use these ever-evolving digital resources but also create their own and share them, reinforcing their learning as they also produce new knowledge that advances the field. Fortunately, no teacher needs to master content creation in all digital methodologies available today; simply guiding students in the direction of the best online resources empowers students to discover and use them along a continuum, from basic cultural awareness to profoundly engaged research about another society.

Notes

1. VR sickness is fairly common when using VR equipment. Continued research in this area, however, has resulted in apps becoming much easier to use without discomfort. Students should be warned about this possible outcome before using any VR device or app for the first time, and they should be encouraged to stop immediately should they feel disoriented. Most apps can be used from a seated position, perhaps on a swivel chair to allow a full range of view. Students who are prone to nausea or dizziness may wish to consult with a health care professional if they experience discomfort. Higher-quality headsets that provide a clearer view and allow the lenses to be repositioned to fit the user's pupil distance can make a significant difference in the amount of discomfort experienced.

2. Storyhive can be downloaded from App Store or Play Store. After you log in, click on the magnifier button on the bottom right corner of the home page, and look for a project named Famagusta, which you can download, and explore models of the Armenian Church of Famagusta and the Church of St. Peter and Paul.

Works Cited

"About: *My Maps.*" *Google Maps*, www.google.com/maps/about/mymaps/.

Bailey, Cara J., et al. "Imagining Medieval Narrative: *The Travels of Marco Polo.*" *Global Middle Ages*, www.globalmiddleages.org/project/imagining-medieval-narrative-travels-marco-polo.

Birnbaum, David J., et al. "The Digital Middle Ages: An Introduction." *Speculum*, vol. 92, no. S1, Oct. 2017, pp. S1–S38.

"Dunhuang Mogao Caves." *Database for Buddhist Cave Temples in China, Digital Silk Road*, dsr.nii.ac.jp/china-caves/dunhuang/.

"Early Global Connections: East Africa between Asia, and Mediterranean Europe." *Global Middle Ages*, www.globalmiddleages.org/project/early-global-connections-east-africa-between-asia-and-mediterranean-europe.

"Explorers." *"Discoveries" of the Americas*, www.discoveriesoftheamericas.org/explorers/.

"External." *Global Middle Ages*, www.globalmiddleages.org/content/external.

Green, Monica H., et al. "Black Death Digital Archive Project." *Global Middle Ages*, www.globalmiddleages.org/project/black-death-digital-archive-project.

Greenlee, John Wyatt. "Mapping Mandeville Project." *Historia Cartarum*, historiacartarum.org/john-mandeville-and-the-hereford-map-2/.

"*MasterWorks*: Journey Through History in Virtual Reality." CyArk and Partners, masterworksvr.org/.

"Medieval Digital Resources: A Curated Guide and Database." Medieval Academy of America, mdr-maa.org/.

"National Archeological Museum: *Live the Past*." App developed by 3D Scenica, *Oculus from* Facebook, www.oculus.com/experiences/gear-vr/11442071 45676653/.

"Projects." *Global Middle Ages*, www.globalmiddleages.org/projects.

"Pure Land AR." *Sarah Kenderdine*, sarahkenderdine.info/installations-and-curated-exhibitions/pure-land-ar.

"Research at Songo Mnara." *Songo Mnara*, www.songomnara.rice.edu/songo.htm.

"Restoring Byzantium." *Columbia University*, www.columbia.edu/cu/wallach/exhibitions/Byzantium/.

"Restoring the Eleventh-Century Temples of Bagan." *The New York Times. YouTube*, uploaded by *The New York Times*, 11 May 2017, www.youtube.com/watch?v=u4MYedXDH7E&list=PLtZ7rcj9igDkXIcnWEw-lesQy7b4JMgBP&index=79. The Daily 360.

"Sites of Encounter in the Medieval World." *California History–Social Science Project*, U of California, Davis, chssp.ucdavis.edu/programs/historyblueprint/maps/medieval-map.

"Soundscape of a Medieval City in the Abbasid Caliphate: Audio Atmosphere." *Ambient-Mixer.com*, city.ambient-mixer.com/medieval-middle-eastern-city.

"The Story of Global Ivory in the Pre-modern Era." *Global Middle Ages*, www.globalmiddleages.org/project/story-global-ivory-pre-modern-era.

"Sundiata." *Berkeley ORIAS*, UC Regents, U of California, Berkeley, 2021, orias.berkeley.edu/sundiata.

"*Syriaca.org*: The Syriac Reference Portal." *Global Middle Ages*, www.globalmiddleages.org/project/syriacaorg.

"The Tang Shipwreck." *Global Middle Ages*, www.globalmiddleages.org/project/tang-shipwreck.

Taylor, Christopher. "The International Prester John Project: How a Global Legend was Created across Six Centuries." *Global Middle Ages*, www.globalmiddleages.org/project/international-prester-john-project.

"Tenochtitlan VR." *YouTube*, uploaded by AURA XR, 27 Sept. 2017, www.youtube.com/watch?v=2gEQGKRfQpw&list=PLtZ7rcj9igDkXIcnWEw-lesQy7b4JMgBP&index=82.

"3D Digital Archives: Virtual Reality, Virtual Worlds, and *Google Earth*." *Digital Silk Road*, dsr.nii.ac.jp/3D/.

"The Travels of Ibn Battuta." *Berkeley ORIAS*, UC Regents, U of California, Berkeley, 2021, orias.berkeley.edu/resources-teachers/travels-ibn-battuta.

"*Virtual Plasencia*." *Global Middle Ages*, www.globalmiddleages.org/project/virtual-plasencia.

"*VR DunHuang*." App developed by Gravity Wave VR, *Viveport*, www.viveport.com/apps/29d22c2d-c29c-4439-82aa-751120b91735?hl=en_US.

Walsh, Michael J. K., and Rachele Bernardello. "Heritage Visualisation and Potential Speculative Reconstructions in Digital Space: The Medieval Church of St. Anne in Famagusta, Cyprus." *Disegnarecon*, vol. 11, no. 21, 2018, pp. 1–11.

Walsh, Michael J. K., et al., editors. *The Armenian Church of Famagusta and the Complexity of Cypriot Heritage: Prayers Long Silent.* Springer International Publishing, 2017.

"*Wonders of the World*." App developed by MATTERvr, *Oculus from* Facebook, www.oculus.com/experiences/go/1251787591581936/.

Yi, Yuan, and Ender Jiang Shutao. "The Application of Virtual Reality Technology to Heritage Conservation in Famagusta's Armenian Church." Walsh et al., pp. 313–23. *Springer Link*, https://doi.org/10.1007/978-3-319-48502-7_16.

Appendix: The Digital Global Middle Ages: Syllabus Resources

Teachers of a global Middle Ages course can augment their syllabus with these resources and lesson ideas. These modules could be added to literary, cultural, or historically based course content.

Introduction to Early Globalism

What does early globalism look like? What interconnects the world? Begin by asking students to write a blog post about what the Middle Ages means to them. (Most institutions offer ways for students to write classroom blogs through content management services. If your students do not have access to class blogs, wordpress.com provides free blogging sites.) What images does the phrase evoke? Weekly blogging will allow students to chart their expanding vision of the global Middle Ages.

Digital resources: Introduce students to aggregation platforms like the Global Middle Ages Project (www.globalmiddleages.org). For homework, encourage them to explore the site and come to class prepared to discuss what surprised them.

Migration and Exploration

The period from 500 to 1500 CE was one of global movement. Vikings sailed to the Americas, the Chinese ventured throughout the Pacific, Muslim sailors ventured outside the Mediterranean around southern Africa and into the Pacific Ocean. Discuss the controversies surrounding the various discoveries of other worlds.

Digital resources: The *"Discoveries" of the Americas* site presents information on real and apocryphal travels to the Americas ("Explorers"). The site includes a useful bibliography, including Fuad Sezgin's work on Muslim navigators, the controversy over Zheng He's so-called discovery of America, and resources for the study of how Saint Brendan became associated with New World discoveries.

Trade and Material Objects

The Mali Empire was one of the greatest trading empires of all time. Where did this empire reach? How and where did it intersect with the trading communities of the Far East, the Mediterranean, and the rest of sub-Saharan Africa? What sorts of things were traded? What were some side effects of trade and travel (for example, spread of disease)?

Digital resources: Explore the trading routes of the Silk Road (*Digital Silk Road*, http://dsr.nii.ac.jp/; *International Dunhuang Project*, http://idp.bl.uk/) and learn about the founder of the Mali Empire ("Sundiata"). Have students explore Songo Mnara (*Research at Songo Mnara*) and other medieval African towns (*Zamani Project*, www.zamaniproject.org/) to get a sense of what African architecture and village life was like.

Watch a video interview of archeologist Chapurukha Kusimba and a documentary on early Swahili culture ("Early Global Connections"). Explore the interactive map to look at trade routes ("Sites"). Learn about the Tang shipwreck and watch Stephen Murphy's lecture on trade between China, Southeast Asia, and the Middle East ("Tang Shipwreck"). Read about the global ivory trade and discover some of the ivory items found around the world ("Story"). Have students create their own maps with *Google Maps* showing the locations where objects came from and where they were found.

This project could use data and images from any of the sites mentioned above, though "The Story of Global Ivory," *Digital Silk Road*, the *International Dunhuang Project*, and "The Tang Shipwreck" have particularly robust databases of objects. Have students use the bibliographical resources about the global reach of the plague (Green et al.) to create digital maps of plague sites. Do these maps intersect with trade maps?

Global Medieval Cities

What were cities like around the world? Did they have similarities? Which cities had diverse communities?

Digital resources: Though not a large town, Plasencia had communities of Christians, Jews, and Muslims in close contact. Explore those communities in a game-based environment ("*Virtual Plasencia*"). Explore the cities of Tenochtitlan and Angkor in VR ("Tenochtitlan"; *Virtual Angkor*, www.virtualangkor.com/). Using the *Wonders of the World* VR application, play the game in Machu Picchu ("*Wonders*"). What sorts of resources did South American cities have? How was South American city life similar or dissimilar to life in other medieval towns (Paris? London? Cairo?). Listen to the soundscape of a medieval city in the Abbasid caliphate ("Soundscape"). What do you hear? Would these same sounds be heard in Plasencia? In Angkor Wat? How are the sounds you hear emblematic of what took place in a medieval Islamic town? Have students create their own medieval city soundscapes using a soundscape mixer (e.g., ambient-mixer.com).

Religion

How did religions spread and change during the Middle Ages? How did religious people imagine other religions and how did they understand their own?

Digital resources: The Mogao Caves contain spectacular examples of Buddhist art. Have students use the VR application ("*VR DunHuang*") and explore online resources about the caves ("Dunhuang Mogao Caves"). Read the Letter of Prester John and use the digital map to discover how the story spread (Taylor). Look at the religious architecture and symbolism found in a Byzantine church ("Restoring Byzantium"), the temples of Bagan ("Restoring"), the mosque in Djenné (*Zamani Project*, www.zamaniproject.org/) and churches in Famagusta (storyhive.com). Use the interactive map at "Sites of Encounter in the Medieval World." What information can students glean from the map? What information do they wish the map provided? Give students a *Google Maps* group project to provide one piece of information on a map about medieval religion that the "Sites of Encounter" map did not give.

Kavita Mudan Finn and Helen Young

Teaching the Global Middle Ages through Popular Culture

Students who enter a medieval studies classroom at university likely bring with them ideas about the Middle Ages developed at least in part through exposure to the rampant medievalism of contemporary Western popular culture. The specifics of those ideas will vary depending on the interests, experiences, and backgrounds of individual students, but several interconnected themes dominate: the Middle Ages of popular culture can be reasonably summarized as muddy, bloody, geographically and culturally Eurocentric, and racially white.

This depiction is typical in productions from Europe, the United States, and the United Kingdom, and is not limited to realist historical fictions (in any medium) but is also a hallmark of medievalist fantasy, crime, romance, and other genres. The fantasy franchise built around George R. R. Martin's *A Song of Ice and Fire* novels, for example, is one of—if not the—most well known and widely consumed of twenty-first-century Western medievalisms and has garnered criticism for attempting to claim authenticity in defending its more problematic narrative choices (see Kennedy; Carroll; Young, *Race*).

Contemporary Western medievalisms are also highly influenced by those of the nineteenth century that encoded Eurocentric imperialist ideologies into cultural and historical engagements with, and representations of, the medieval past (see Young, "Whiteness"; Davis and Altschul). Discerning a global orientation in popular culture medievalism is possible but requires careful attention (D'Arcens and Lynch). Since Western popular medievalisms typically see Europe as either the whole world, or as the center of it, there may not seem to be an obvious space for a pedagogy of a globally interconnected and multilocational Middle Ages.

This essay and the accompanying syllabus (see appendix), however, aim to outline ways popular culture can be used to introduce and explore the globality of the Middle Ages. This can be accomplished by deconstructing Eurocentric ideologies of Western popular culture and challenging its authority and assumptions by placing it in dialogue with non-Western popular culture as well as with medieval source materials.

Why Teach Popular Culture and the Global Middle Ages

The study of medievalism (as opposed to the more traditional study of the medieval period) has grown in the past several decades. Medievalists writ large have been forced to grapple with the fact that what the mainstream public thinks is medieval has very little to do with what we know of the Middle Ages. In short, as Paul Sturtevant has observed, "[U]nderstandings of medieval history develop through childhood and are influenced by pop-culture depictions of the period" (8). These popular culture depictions are shaped not by the actual Middle Ages, but by nineteenth-century ideas about cultural purity and European superiority, "which imagine the medieval era as a pristine space in which whiteness and masculinity assume a prevalence naturalized by the soft focus of medievalism's pseudo-historical lens" (Kaufman 199).

What we as scholars and teachers must acknowledge is that medievalism is part of the social, cultural, and political present and has been particularly taken up by right-wing extremists. Dominant representations support those ideas, not least because they have the same foundations in racist imperialist discourses of the nineteenth century—namely, a white European mythological ancestry intended to enforce superiority over colonized peoples and refocus world history as that of Europeans and their interactions with everybody else. It is incumbent on us as educators to encourage and direct our students to what Margo Hendricks calls premodern critical race studies, an activist praxis that "pursues not only the study of race in the premodern, not only the way in which periods helped to define, demarcate, tear apart, and bring together the study of race in the premodern era, but the way that outcome, the way those studies can effect a transformation of the academy and its relationship to our world."

The unit proposed in this chapter is therefore not intended to correct or reclaim inaccurate misappropriations of the medieval; rather, it is to provide students with critical and conceptual tools and information so they can identify bigoted perspectives and representations for themselves. We are not writing as informed scholars correcting the errors and misapprehensions of popular culture (wherever it is from); we are writing against the practices of academic pedagogy and popular culture that make the Middle Ages Eurocentric and proposing counterstories to those Eurocentric assumptions (see Delgado).

Developing a pedagogy of a global Middle Ages through the medievalisms of popular cultures poses different challenges compared to a more traditional medieval studies approach in a literature, history, or interdisciplinary classroom. Among these challenges is the typically Eurocentric perspective of popular culture accessible to Anglophone audiences, whether or not they are in or from the global West, although the growing ubiquity of streaming services and the transnational reach of certain media properties, such as television dramas based on Chinese *wuxia* novels, illustrates a potential shift in accessibility (see Ng). Nor is translated material, whether popular or historical, without ideology in what is available, how it is framed, and the language used. This is also an issue for modern translations of European medieval sources that might be incorporated into a medievalism classroom (Otaño Gracia and Armenti).[1]

It is important to remember that there is no way to access a real global Middle Ages through popular culture—or, in a post-Derrida world, to do so at all—although numerous franchises claim to, whether or not they also include fantasy elements, as, for example, *Game of Thrones* (see Young, *Race* 63–87). So-called authenticity in popular culture has very little, if anything, to do with historical realities but is rather generated by audience expectations that are themselves shaped by genre, by the realities of commercial production and technical capabilities, and through discursive construction in publicity material (Elliott 214–16; Young, "Place" 1–5).

Even historical fiction authors who claim close adherence to known history acknowledge that the needs of the story will sometimes override research and fact (Polack). Until recently, scholars (see, e.g., Alexander) often dismissed popular medievalism as having no real relation with the Middle Ages at all; this position is reflected to a significant degree in theorizations of neomedievalism that typically focus on the popular domain and argue that the version of medieval history evoked in neomedievalist discourse is more obviously reflective of contemporary concerns.

Critical histories of medievalism—themselves often Anglo- or Eurocentric—tend to construct dichotomies between those medievalisms that claim to represent historical realities and those that do not (see, e.g., Matthews). Common threads between these areas, however, include nationalism, Eurocentrism, and whiteness (see Young, "Whiteness"), and there are those in both camps of medievalism who work to exclude marginalized people (see Whitaker, "Race-ing"; Finke and Shichtman). This is less a reflection of anything medieval than the larger tendency in Western popular culture to claim whiteness as the default (see Whitaker, *Black Metaphors*).

Nationalistic nostalgia is a common feature of popular culture medievalisms from around the globe, albeit not one that is uniformly present in them. Chinese and Turkish medievalisms, for example, construct purported historical golden ages that serve contemporary nationalistic purposes (Kurtz; Furlanetto), whereas Indian medievalisms often emphasize religious uniformity, particularly in the current conservative climate of Hindu nationalism. Western popular culture medievalisms display nostalgia (see, e.g., Aronstein) while attempting to position the medieval as somehow wholly antithetical to the modern day by way of a false narrative of progress.

Works produced, translated, or adapted for Western popular culture (often targeted to the United States as the largest audience within that market) may be significantly altered or shaped for that market. Suggestions for exploring this include a week comparing Kurosawa's *The Seven Samurai* (1953) with *The Magnificent Seven* (1960 or 2016), and a week on Elif Shafak's *The Forty Rules of Love*, a novel by a Turkish author written in English.

Challenges in Teaching

Although a course in popular medievalism is likely to attract students not otherwise interested in the medieval period, students are also reasonably likely to be fans of a medievalist narrative, be it *Game of Thrones*, Tolkien's *Lord of the Rings*, the tabletop role-playing game Dungeons and Dragons, or one of many medievalist video games. These fans can be resistant to critiques of the object of their fandom and even fall back on the tired assumptions that what those fandoms represent is somehow "how things were back then." Critical discussion of concepts of authenticity and engagement with medieval primary sources, as suggested in the syllabus, may help challenge their assumptions. Students who are highly engaged with fandoms are also very likely to have deep knowledge of texts and related genres and can be productively encouraged to bring this to class discussions.

Additionally, most works produced by authors or creators from marginalized non-European backgrounds are not understood as Western popular culture. Our suggested texts move outside Western popular culture where possible but may not always be available with subtitles or dubbing in English. Although this makes clear that these texts are not intended for an English-speaking audience and thus offer an alternative perspective, there are obvious issues of accessibility involved. For instance, in the syllabus, the Chinese drama based on the life of Zheng He is available only in Mandarin without subtitles, as is the Hindi-language drama based on the life of Noor Jehan. Larger-budget productions such as Sanjay Leela Bhansali's *Padmaavat* or Hayao Miyazaki's *Princess Mononoke* do have subtitles, as do several films and series that have been optioned by Netflix and other streaming services. Works that are not dubbed or subtitled may be accessible to multilingual students. Such works can also be a springboard for discussion of the multiplicity of modern global cultural perspectives on the medieval past.

Lastly, European colonial attempts to erase culture, including through the imposition of Christianity, looting of artifacts, and linguistic imperialism mean that the supposed medieval culture and history of many colonized places are not easily available to local people to be made into popular culture. The rise of popular European medievalism in the late eighteenth and nineteenth centuries dovetailed, not coincidentally, with the height of European colonialism. At a time when Europeans were increasingly enabled to access the medieval past and its artifacts and to see them as part of their cultural heritage, colonized peoples faced the destruction and denial of culture and heritage. As a result, precolonial pasts from outside Europe are frequently not as easily available to reimagine as medievalism. The week on Recovering African Medievalisms in the suggested syllabus (see appendix) opens up space for discussion of such issues.

Teaching a global Middle Ages through twenty-first-century popular culture is both challenging and rewarding. It opens up pathways for engaging with contemporary understandings and uses of the past that students may otherwise not encounter in medieval studies or humanities classrooms more broadly.

Our syllabus seeks to engage in decolonial pedagogy by deconstructing colonialist medievalist discourses and by offering counterstories from peoples who are typically marginalized, othered, or completely excluded from Western popular narratives. It aims to challenge the habitual Eurocentric lens through which Western popular culture views the medieval past and offer multiple perspectives from both the modern and the medieval to encourage teachers and students alike to engage meaningfully with the globality of the past, present, and future.

Note

1. Translations have historically occluded the presence of figures who exist outside the translator's idea of gender, sexual, and racial norms (Murray).

Works Cited

Alexander, Michael. *Medievalism: The Middle Ages in Modern England.* Yale UP, 2007.

Aronstein, Susan. *Hollywood Knights: Arthurian Cinema and the Politics of Nostalgia.* Palgrave Macmillan, 2005.

Carroll, Shiloh. *Medievalism in A Song of Ice and Fire and* Game of Thrones. Brewer, 2018, pp. 107–30.

D'Arcens, Louise, and Andrew Lynch. "The Medieval, the International, the Popular: Introduction." *International Medievalism and Popular Culture*, edited by d'Arcens and Lynch, Cambria, 2014, pp. xi–xxx.

Davis, Kathleen, and Nadia Altschul, editors. *Medievalisms and the Postcolonial World: The Idea of "the Middle Ages" Outside Europe.* Johns Hopkins UP, 2009.

Delgado, Richard. "Storytelling for Oppositionists and Others: A Plea for Narrative." *Critical Race Theory: The Cutting Edge*, edited by Delgado and Jean Stefancic, 2nd ed., Temple UP, 2000.

Elliott, Andrew B. R. *Remaking the Middle Ages: The Methods of Cinema and History in Portraying the Medieval World.* McFarland, 2011.

Finke, Laurie A., and Martin B. Shichtman. "Inner-City Chivalry in Gil Junger's *Black Knight*: A South Central Yankee in King Leo's Court." Ramey and Pugh, pp. 107–22.

Furlanetto, Elena. "'Imagine a Country Where We Are All Equal': Imperial Nostalgia in Turkey and Elif Shafak's Ottoman Utopia." *Cross / Cultures*, vol. 1982, no. 3, 2015, pp. 159–80.

Hendricks, Margo. "Coloring the Past, Rewriting Our Future: RaceB4Race." Folger Institute: Race and Periodization, Sept. 2019, folger.edu/institute/scholarly-programs/race-periodization/margo-hendricks. Lecture.

Kaufman, Amy S. "Purity." *Medievalism: Key Critical Terms*, edited by Elizabeth Emery and Richard Utz, D. S. Brewer, 2014.

Kennedy, Kathleen. "*Game of Thrones* Is Even Whiter Than You Think." *Vice*, 18 Oct. 2016, www.vice.com/en_us/article/8gexwp/game-of-thrones-is-even-whiter-than-you-think.

Kurtz, Joachim. "Chinese Dreams of the Middle Ages: Nostalgia, Utopia, Propaganda." *The Medieval History Journal*, vol. 21, no. 1, 2018, pp. 1–24, https://doi.org/10.1177/0971945817753874.

Matthews, David. *Medievalism: A Critical History*. D. S. Brewer, 2015.

Murray, Jacqueline. "Twice Marginal and Twice Invisible: Lesbians in the Middle Ages." *The Handbook of Medieval Sexuality*, edited by Vern L. Bullough and James Brundage, Routledge, 2013, pp. 191–222.

Ng, Jeannette. "The History and Politics of Wuxia." *Tor.com*, 29 June 2021, tor.com/2021/06/29/the-history-and-politics-of-wuxia/.

Otaño Gracia, Nahir, and Daniel Armenti. "Constructing Prejudice in the Middle Ages and the Repercussions of Racism Today." *Medieval Feminist Forum*, vol. 53, no. 1, 2017, pp. 176–201, ir.uiowa.edu/mff/vol53/iss1/11/.

Polack, Gillian. "Novelists and Their History." *Rethinking History*, vol. 18, no. 4, 2014, pp. 522–42, https://doi.org/10.1080/13642529.2014.893669.

Ramey, Lynn, and Tison Pugh, editors. *Race, Class, and Gender in "Medieval" Cinema*. Palgrave Macmillan, 2007.

Sturtevant, Paul B. *The Middle Ages in Popular Imagination: Memory, Film, and Medievalism*. I. B. Tauris, 2018.

Whitaker, Cord J. *Black Metaphors: How Modern Racism Emerged from Medieval Race-Thinking*. U of Pennsylvania P, 2019.

———. "Race-ing the Dragon: The Middle Ages, Race and Trippin' into the Future." *Postmedieval*, vol. 6, no. 1, 2015, pp. 3–11, link.springer.com/article/10.1057/pmed.2014.40.

Young, Helen. "Place and Time: Medievalism and Making Race." *The Year's Work in Medievalism*, vol. 28, 2013, dro.deakin.edu.au/eserv/DU:30106473/young-placeandtime-2013.pdf.

———. *Race and Popular Fantasy Literature: Habits of Whiteness*. Routledge, 2016.

———. "Whiteness and Time: The Once, Present, and Future Race." *Studies in Medievalism*, vol. 24, 2015, pp. 39–49.

Appendix: Syllabus for The Global Middle Ages in Popular Culture

The unit envisaged here is for a mid- to upper-level undergraduate course of twelve to fifteen weeks with students who have no assumed prior knowledge of medieval history. It does not cover all angles that might be considered or encompass the entirety of a truly global Middle Ages because the popular culture accessible to the largely Anglophone readers of this MLA volume of essays does not do so. Suggested texts have been selected with likely accessibility in mind and are representative examples of possible options. The particular texts or weeks within each module could be selected, reordered, or swapped out for other options according to the interests of teachers and students, availability of sources, and the production of new popular medievalist works.

Assessment options for this course could include short response papers for individual texts; reviews of medievalist texts not included on the syllabus; and longer papers addressing historical context, sources, and interpretations. Students might also be asked to create popular medievalist works (e.g., creative writing, a board game, or short animation) that reflect on course themes.

Introduction

Introduction to the unit, readings, structure, and so on. What are the "global Middle Ages"? Whose popular culture? What are common ideas about the Middle Ages in Western popular culture? What do we expect to encounter and why?

Readings

D'Arcens, Louise, and Andrew Lynch. "The Medieval, the International, the Popular: Introduction." *International Medievalism and Popular Culture*, edited by d'Arcens and Lynch, Cambria, 2014, pp. xi–xxx.

Heng, Geraldine. "Inventions/Reinventions: Race, Modernity, and the Middle Ages." Heng, *Invention*, pp. 15–54.

Lomuto, Sierra. "White Nationalism and the Ethics of Medieval Studies." *In the Middle*, 5 Dec. 2016, www.inthemedievalmiddle.com/2016/12/white-nationalism-and-ethics-of.html.

Module 1: The Global Middle Ages through a Eurocentric Lens

This module offers opportunities to explore ways Western popular culture takes up eighteenth- and nineteenth-century imperialist ideologies and presents Eurocentric perspectives. It aims to give students the tools to identify and deconstruct those ideologies in popular Western medievalisms.

Option 1.1: Medievalist, Eurocentric Fantasies

Medievalism is not limited to historical texts; the fantasy genre is also significant. This week students are encouraged to think about the ways Western popular culture medievalisms work to center white European perspectives and experiences.

Readings

PRIMARY

Assumed basic knowledge of the *Game of Thrones* franchise.

An Atlas of Ice and Fire. atlasoficeandfireblog.wordpress.com/.

Martin, George R. R., et al. *The World of Ice and Fire: The Untold History of Westeros and the Game of Thrones.* Bantam, 2014.
Mandeville, John. *The Travels of John Mandeville.* Edited by Anthony Bale, Oxford UP, 2012.

SECONDARY

Carroll, Shiloh. *Medievalism in A Song of Ice and Fire and* Game of Thrones. Brewer, 2018, pp. 107–30.
Kennedy, Kathleen. "*Game of Thrones* Is Even Whiter Than You Think." *Vice*, 18 Oct. 2016, www.vice.com/en_us/article/8gexwp/game-of-thrones-is-even-whiter-than-you-think.
Young, Helen. *Race and Popular Fantasy Literature.* Routledge, 2015. Chs. 1 and 3, pp. 15–39 and 63–87.

Option 1.2: Western Adaptations

Appropriations (generally understood as adaptations of medieval history and popular medievalisms of non-Western cultures) are common in Western popular culture. They typically have roots in, and are influenced by, Orientalism. This week would see students encounter Japanese medievalism alongside a Western adaption. Suggested texts and readings from option 2.5: China, centered on and adapting *The Journey to the West* might be used here instead.

Readings

PRIMARY

Kurosawa, Akira, director. *Seven Samurai.* Toho, 1954.
Fuqua, Antoine, director. *The Magnificent Seven.* MGM, 2016.
Sturges, John, director. *The Magnificent Seven.* Mirisch Company, 1960.

SECONDARY

Said, Edward. *Orientalism.* Routledge, 1979, pp. 1–48.
Schiff, Randy P. "Samurai on Shifting Ground: Negotiating the Medieval and the Modern in *Seven Samurai* and *Yojimbo.*" Ramey and Pugh, pp. 59–72.

Option 1.3: Counternarratives

Two cornerstones of white, Eurocentric medievalisms can be found in the Crusades and in representations of the Vikings. This week's readings offer counternarratives to both these visions of a racially and religiously homogenous Middle Ages seen through European eyes.

Readings

PRIMARY

Chahine, Youssef, director. *El Naser Salah Ad-Din* [*Saladin the Victorious*]. Assia, 1963.
Ahmed, Saladin. "Without Faith, without Law, without Joy." *Rags and Bones: New Twists on Timeless Tales*, edited by Melissa Marr and Tim Pratt, Little, Brown,

2013, pp. 314–27. Story starts at 5:20 in the podcast podcastle.org/2014/08/14/podcastle-324-without-faith-without-law-without-joy/.
Waititi, Taika, director. *Thor: Ragnarok*. Marvel Studios. 2018.

SECONDARY

Birnbaum, Sariel. "Egyptian Islamists Fight Back on Screen." *Middle East Quarterly*, winter 2019, www.meforum.org/7266/egyptian-islamists-fight-back-on-screen.

Cobb, Paul M. *The Race for Paradise: An Islamic History of the Crusades*. Oxford UP, 2014.

Ganim, John M. "Reversing the Crusades: Hegemony, Orientalism, and Film Language in Youssef Chahine's *Saladin*." Ramey and Pugh, pp. 45–58.

Halim, Hala. "The Signs of *Saladin*: A Modern Cinematic Rendition of Medieval Heroism." *Journal of Comparative Poetics*, no. 12, 1992, pp. 78–94.

Kim, Dorothy. "White Supremacists Have Weaponized an Imaginary Viking Past: It's Time to Reclaim the Real History." *TIME Magazine*, 15 Apr. 2019, time.com/5569399/viking-history-white-nationalists/.

Option 1.4: Recovering African Medievalisms

The great medieval civilizations of Africa were ignored, denigrated, looted, and erased by European colonizers, but traces remain and are increasingly being recovered. In recent years, the arts and culture of Mali, Songhai, and Ghana have been the subject of exhibitions and academic studies, and the genre of Afrofuturism has offered a reinvention and reimagining of what African medievalism might look like when paired with the trappings of science fiction.

Readings

PRIMARY

Adeyemi, Tomi. *Children of Blood and Bone*. Henry Holt, 2018.
Jemisin, N. K. *The Killing Moon*. Orbit, 2012.
Coogler, Ryan, director. *Black Panther*. Marvel Studios, 2018.

SECONDARY

Gates, Henry Louis, Jr., producer. *Africa's Great Civilizations*. Inkwell Films / McKee Media / Kunhart bFilms / WETA Washington, DC, 2017, www.pbs.org/weta/africas-great-civilizations/home/. Especially episodes 3 and 4.

Thomas, Ebony Elizabeth. *The Dark Fantastic: Race and the Imagination from Harry Potter to* The Hunger Games. NYU Press, 2019, pp. 1–31.

Module 2: Global Locations

This module aims to help students develop an understanding of the multilocational nature of the globe during the Middle Ages. Primary texts include contemporary popular representations as well as medieval sources and are selected to provide perspectives from around the globe.

General Readings

Global Middle Ages. globalmiddleages.org/.

Tignor, Robert, et al., editors. *Beginnings through the Fifteenth Century*. 5th ed., W. W. Norton, 2017. Vol. 1 of *Worlds Together, Worlds Apart: From the Beginnings of Humankind to the Present*.

Option 2.1: The Middle East

The Islamic world was multilocational and stretched from North Africa to Southeast Asia during the Middle Ages. Eurocentric perspectives typically focus on the Middle East and are filtered through the history of the Crusades, although these are only a small part of Islamic history. Texts suggested below are generally focused within the Islamic world rather than on the Crusades. Option 2.2: India and option 2.3: Mali might be taught in conjunction with this option as part of a minimodule on the Islamic world, depending on text selection.

Readings

PRIMARY

Ahmed, Saladin. *The Throne of the Crescent Moon*. DAW, 2012.

Mahmoud, Abdulaziz al-. *The Holy Sail*. Translated by Karim Taboulsi, Hamad Bin Khalifa UP, 2017.

Shafak, Elif. *The Forty Rules of Love: A Novel of Rumi*. Penguin, 2011.

The Arabian Nights. Translated by Husain Haddawy, edited by Daniel Heller-Roazen and Muhsin Mahdi, Norton, 2009.

SECONDARY

Furlanetto, Elena. "Imagine a Country Where We Are All Equal: Imperial Nostalgia in Turkey and Elif Shafak's Ottoman Utopia," *Cross/Cultures*, vol. 1982, no. 3, 2015, pp. 159–80.

Furlanetto, Elena. "The Rumi Phenomenon between Orientalism and Cosmopolitanism: The Case of Elif Shafak's *The Forty Rules of Love*." *European Journal of English Studies*, vol. 17, no. 2, 2013, pp. 201–13.

Heynders, Odile. "Popular Fiction, Elif Shafak." *Writers as Public Intellectuals: Literature, Celebrity, Democracy*, edited by Heynders, Palgrave Macmillan, 2016, pp. 160–81.

Qualey, M. Lynx. "The Paradoxes of Women and Freedom in Abdulaziz al-Mahmoud's 'The Holy Sail.'" *ArabLit: Arabic Literature and Translation*, 24 Nov. 2015, arablit.org/2015/11/24/the-paradoxes-of-women-and-freedom-in-abdulaziz-al-mahmouds-the-holy-sail/.

Option 2.2: India

Any attempt to pin down a monolithic medieval version of India is doomed to failure; the complex web of warring kingdoms, alliances, and invasions, not to mention the hundreds of languages for primary sources, pose a variety of challenges for instructors and students alike. Contemporary India also has a strong tradition of popular history in film, however, and this unit offers the opportunity to showcase to students how an instance of popular medievalism led to intense controversy, censorship, and even violence, thus operating as both a cultural lesson and a cautionary tale.

Readings

PRIMARY

Bhansali, Sanjay Leela, director. *Padmavaat*. Bhansali Productions / Viacom, 2018. Hindi with English subtitles.

Jayasi, Malik Muhammad. "Padmavathi." Circa 1540. Edited and translated by G. A. Grierson and Mahamahopadyaya Sudhakara Dvivedi, Asiatic Society of Bengal, 1896. *Internet Archive*, archive.org/stream/padumawatiofmali00maliuoft#page/n4/mode/1up.

The Forgotten Empress. 2015. *YouTube*, uploaded by Farah Yasmeen Shaikh, 21 Apr. 2017, www.youtube.com/watch?v=MVrPm71MKu4. Theatre/dance performance filmed live.

Kumar, Siddarth Anand, et al., directors. *Siyaasat* [*Politics*]. Green Light Productions, 2014. Hindi without subtitles. Forty-two-episode series aired on the EPIC Channel.

Sundaresan, Indu. *The Twentieth Wife*. Washington Square Press, 2003.

SECONDARY

Habib, Irfan. "Building the Idea of India." Edited by Naved Ashrafi, Lecture at Aligarh Muslim University, 7 Oct. 2015, awaam.net/building-the-idea-of-india-irfan-habib/.

Rajvi, Sabika. "Malik Muhammad Jayasi: The Poet Who Penned the Ballad 'Padmavat.'" *The Quint*, 30 Dec. 2017, www.thequint.com/entertainment/malik-muhammad-jayasi-poet-of-padmavat.

Rampal, Nitish. "Padmavati Controversy: History Is at Risk of Being Trapped between Left, Right Interpretations of the Past." *Firstpost*, 24 Nov. 2017, www.firstpost.com/india/padmavati-controversy-history-is-at-risk-of-being-trapped-between-left-right-interpretations-of-the-past-4225695.html.

Sreenivasan, Ramya. *The Many Lives of a Rajput Queen: Heroic Pasts in India, c. 1500–1900*. U of Washington P, 2007.

Option 2.3: Mali

The Mali Empire was a West African empire from the twelfth into the fifteenth century. Like most African empires other than the Egyptian, it does not feature often in Western contemporary popular fictions, but it was known throughout the medieval world as a location of legendary wealth and power.

Readings

PRIMARY

Kouyaté, Dani, director. Keïta!*: L'heritage de griot* [*Keita!: The Heritage of the Griot*]. Sahelis Productions, 1995. French and Jula with English subtitles.

Scott, Rafael. *Beyond Mali*. Independent, 2013.

Niane, Djibril Tamsir. Sundiata*: An Epic of Old Mali*. Translated by G. D. Pickett, 2nd ed., Longman, 2006.

"Sundiata." *Berkeley ORIAS*, UC Regents, U of California, Berkeley, 2021, orias.berkeley.edu/sundiata.

SECONDARY

Conrad, D. C. *Empires of Medieval West Africa: Ghana, Mali, and Songhay*. Revised ed., Chelsea House, 2010.

Cooksey, T. L. "'The Man of the Day to Follow': Dani Kouyaté's "Keita!" and the Living Epic." *Literature/Film Quarterly*, vol. 37, no. 4, 2009, pp. 262–69.

Garane, Jeanne. "The Future Emerges from the Past: Tradition and Modernity in Dani Kouyaté's Keita!*: The Heritage of the Griot*." *Women in French Studies*, vol. 2006, no. 1, 2016, pp. 204–19, https://doi.org/10.1353/wfs.2006.0050.

Gomez, Michael A. *African Dominion: A New History of Empire in Early and Medieval West Africa*. Princeton UP, 2018.

Option 2.4: The Americas

Pre-Colombian South and Central America are a staple of Anglophone historical fiction published in the United States, but few of the most well-known works are written by authors whose first language is Indigenous to those regions or Spanish, or who are from those places. The suggested text is an example of a recent translation of a Spanish-language novel by a Mexican author.

Readings

PRIMARY

Yaaron, Ernesto. *Obsidian Blood*. 2018. Originally published in Spanish as *Sangre de Obsidiana*, 2014).

SECONDARY

Altschul, Nadia. *Geographies of Philological Knowledge: Postcoloniality and the Transatlantic National Epic*. U of Chicago P, 2012.

Brading, D. A. "Monuments and Nationalism in Modern Mexico." *Nations and Nationalism*, vol. 7, no. 4, 2001, pp. 521–31.

Earle, Rebecca A. *The Return of the Native Indians and Myth-Making in Spanish America, 1810–1930*. Duke UP, 2007.

Option 2.5: China

Chinese historians have taken up the idea of a Middle Ages in their accounts of Chinese history; this allows students to think through what is global about the medieval in a new way. There are also issues around adaptation, genre, white-washing, translation, and white-savior narratives to discuss, depending on text selection.

Readings

PRIMARY

Cheng-en, Wu. *The Journey to the West.* Translated by Anthony C. Yu, U of Chicago P, 2012.

Johnstone, Gerard, director. *The New Legends of Monkey.* Written by Jacquelin Perske et al., ABC / Netflix, 2018. Ten-episode series.

Hark, Tsui, director. *Detective Dee and the Mystery of the Phantom Flame.* Huayi Brothers / Emperor Motion Pictures, 2010.

Hark, Tsui, director. *Young Detective Dee: Rise of the Sea Dragon.* Huayi Brothers, 2013.

Hark, Tsui, director. *Detective Dee: The Four Heavenly Kings.* Cine Asia, 2018.

Sa, Shan. *Empress.* Harper Perennial, 2009.

Zhang, Yimou, director. *The Great Wall.* Legendary East / Atlas Entertainment / China Film Group / Le Vision Pictures, 2016.

SECONDARY

Kurtz, Joachim. "Chinese Dreams of the Middle Ages: Nostalgia, Utopia, Propaganda." *The Medieval History Journal,* vol. 21, no. 1, 2018, pp. 1–24.

Li, Shuangyi. "Translingualism and Autoexotic Translation in Shan Sa's Franco-Chinese Historical Novels." *Essays in French Literature and Culture,* vol. 55, 2018, pp. 115–31.

Option 2.6: Japan

What the West considers medieval Japan—which usually encompasses both the Heian period (794–1185) and the Feudal period (1185–1600)—has been reinvented within Japan and appropriated by the West to Orientalize and exoticize Japanese culture. This unit therefore focuses primarily on popular medievalisms produced within Japan.

Readings

PRIMARY

Miyazaki, Hayao, director. *Princess Mononoke.* Studio Ghibli, 1997.

Shikibu, Murasaki. Selections from *The Tale of Genji.* Translated by Royall Tyler, Columbia UP, 2001.

Sugii, Gisaburō, director. *Genji Monogatori* [*The Tale of Genji*]. 1987. *YouTube,* uploaded by LoremasterMotoss, 28 Mar. 2008, www.youtube.com/watch?v=CYwJaO88mm4.

SECONDARY

Buruma, Ian. "The Sensualist: What Makes *The Tale of Genji* So Seductive." *The New Yorker,* 13 Jul. 2015, www.newyorker.com/magazine/2015/07/20/the-sensualist-books-buruma.

Smith, Nathanael. "Footprints of a God: *Princess Mononoke* Twenty Years On." *Little White Lies,* 11 Jun. 2017, lwlies.com/articles/princess-mononoke-studio-ghibli-hayao-miyazaki/.

Tyler, Royall. "Translating the *Tale of Genji*." 2003, nihongo.monash.edu/tylerlecture.html. Lecture.

Module 3: Medieval Travelers

This module aims to acquaint students with the challenges of reading and interpreting medieval travel narratives, both those of Westerners traveling away from Europe, and, more important for our purposes, travelers based in Asia and Africa making their own circuits and sometimes encountering the West.

General Readings

Phillips, K. M. "Travel, Writing, and the Global Middle Ages." *History Compass*, vol. 14, 2016, pp. 81–92, https://doi.org/10.1111/hic3.12301. Note: This is behind a paywall.

Thompson, Carl, editor. *The Routledge Companion to Travel Writing*. Routledge, 2016.

Option 3.1: Travelling in Eurasia and Africa

Abu Abdullah Muhammad Ibn Battuta (1304–1368/9) was a Muslim man from Morocco who traveled extensively in Africa, the Middle East, Asia, and Europe. He left an account of his travels, written in the last years of his life, that is an important historical source for the geography, society, and culture of the many places he visited.

Readings

PRIMARY

Dunn, Ross E. *The Adventures of Ibn Battuta: A Muslim Traveler of the Fourteenth Century*. Revised ed., U of California P, 2004.

Ibn Battuta: The Man Who Walked across the World. Produced by Tim Mackintosh-Smith, BBC Four, 2008.

Journey to Mecca: In the Footsteps of Ibn Batutta. Directed by Bruce Neibaur, Cosmic Picture / SK Films, 2009, www.journeytomeccagiantscreen.com/.

"The Travels of Ibn Battuta." Created by Nick Bartel and Ross Dunn, *Berkeley ORIAS*, UC Regents, U of California, Berkeley, 2021, orias.berkeley.edu/resources-teachers/travels-ibn-battuta.

The Travels of Ibn Battuta. Edited by Tim Mackintosh-Smith, revised ed., Pan Macmillan, 2003.

Unearthed: On the Trail of Ibn Battuta. Semaphore, 2012, www.unearthedgame.com/.

SECONDARY

Barsoum, Marlène. "The Traveller and His Scribe: In the Footsteps of Ibn Battuta and Their Rendering by Ibn Juzayy." *The Journal of North African Studies*, vol. 11, no. 2, 2006, pp. 193–203, https://doi.org/10.1080/13629380600704738.

Waines, David. *The Odyssey of Ibn Battuta: Uncommon Tales of a Medieval Adventurer*. U of Chicago P, 2010.

Israeli, Raphael. "Medieval Muslim Travelers to China." *Journal of Muslim Minority Affairs*, vol. 20, no. 2, 2000, pp. 313–21, https://doi.org/10.1080/713680367.

Option 3.2: Receiving Viking Visitors

Western popular culture has been littered with accounts of Viking exploration and settlement in North America since at least the beginning of the twentieth century.

Readings

PRIMARY

Bruchac, Joseph. "Ice Hearts." *Turtle Meat and Other Stories*, Holy Cross Press, 1993.
Kolodny, Annette. *In Search of First Contact: The Vikings of Vinland, the Peoples of the Dawnland, and the Anglo-American Anxiety of Discovery*. Duke UP, 2012. Especially the Penobscot stories.
Qitsualik-Tinsley, Rachel, and Sean Qitsualik-Tinsley. *Skraelings: Clashes in the Old Artic*. Inhabit Media, 2014.

SECONDARY

Evans, Michael. "Is Pre-Columbian America Medieval? Indigenous Absence in American Medievalisms." *This Year's Work in Medievalism*, vol. 30, 2015.
Harty, Kevin J. "Who's Savage Now?! The Vikings in North America." *The Vikings on Film: Essays on Depictions of the Nordic Middle Ages*, edited by Harty. McFarland, 2011, pp. 106–20.
Hsy, Jonathan. "Native, Norse, Other: Embodied Difference and Forms of First Contact." *In the Middle*, 25 Sep. 2014, www.inthemedievalmiddle.com/2014/09/native-norse-other-embodied-difference.html.

Option 3.3: Traveling North

Ahmad Ibn Fadlan was an emissary sent north from Baghdad into what is now Russia to treat with a variety of northern groups, including Vikings. His memoir of that journey offers a fascinating glimpse of the Volga Vikings through the eyes of a cosmopolitan traveler from Baghdad.

Readings

PRIMARY

Beowulf. Translated by Seamus Heaney, Fararr, Strauss, and Giroux, 2000.
Ibn Fadlan and the Land of Darkness: Arab Travellers in the Far North. Translated by Paul Lunde and Caroline E. M. Stone, Penguin Classics, 2011.
Crichton, Michael. *The Thirteenth Warrior*. Knopf, 1999. Originally published as *Eaters of the Dead*, 1976.
McTiernan, John, director. *The Thirteenth Warrior*. Touchstone Pictures, 1999.

SECONDARY

Hermes, Nizar F. *The [European] Other in Medieval Arabic Literature and Culture: Ninth–Twelfth Century AD*. Palgrave Macmillan, 2012.

Shutters, Lynne. "Vikings through the Eyes of an Arab Ethnographer: Constructions of the Other in the *Thirteenth Warrior*." *Race, Class, and Gender in "Medieval" Cinema*, edited by Lynn Ramey and Tison Pugh, Palgrave Macmillan, 2007, pp. 75–89.

Option 3.4: Traveling South

Al-Hasan ibn Muhammad, also known as Leo Africanus, was a Muslim trader and traveler whose family fled Spain in the late fifteenth century to avoid the Inquisition. He grew up in Fez, Morocco, and was educated at el-Quarawiyyin University before joining his uncle on diplomatic missions across Europe and Africa. His most famous text is *The Description of Africa*, first printed in Venice in 1550 and translated into English by John Pory in 1600.

Readings

PRIMARY

Maalouf, Amin. *Leo Africanus*. New Amsterdam Books, 1998.
Leo Africanus, *The Description of Africa*. Translated by John Pory. 1600. Hakluyt Society, 1896. *Reprinted*: Edited by Robert Brown, Cambridge UP. 3 vols.

SECONDARY

Wise, Christopher. "Leo Africanus and the Songhay Dynasty of the Askiyas." *Arena Journal*, vol. 39/40, no. 39, 2013, pp. 140–57.
Leo Africanus: A Sixteenth-Century Exploration of Morocco. LeoAfricanus.com. Website created using a Fulbright grant with maps of Leo's travels, biographical information, and bibliography.

Option 3.5: Traveling South and West

Based on the voyage of the Chinese admiral Zheng He (aka Cheng Ho, in the Wade-Giles system of transliteration). This week highlights some of the difficulty of studying the global Middle Ages through popular culture. The Chinese television series is not accessible to viewers who do not speak Mandarin. The English-language book, however, is American medievalism, not Chinese.

Readings

PRIMARY

Terrell, Heather. *The Map Thief*. Ballantine, 2009.
Xiao, Ma, and Liu Haitao, directors. *Zheng He Xia Xiyang* [*Zheng He Sails the Western Ocean*], 2009, ent.sina.com.cn/f/v/zhxxy/index.shtml.

SECONDARY

Bastiampillai, B. E. S. J. "China–Sri Lanka: Trade and Diplomatic Relations including the Voyages for Cheng Ho." *UNESCO Silk Roads: Dialogue, Diversity, and Development*.
Dewaraja, Lorna. "Cheng Ho's Visits to Sri Lanka and the Galle Trilingual Inscription in the National Museum in Colombo." *Journal of the Royal Asiatic Society of Sri Lanka*, vol. 52, 2006, pp. 59–74. *JSTOR*, www.jstor.org/stable/23731298.

Kurtz, Joachim. "Chinese Dreams of the Middle Ages: Nostalgia, Utopia, Propaganda." *The Medieval History Journal*, vol. 21, no. 1, 2018, pp. 1–24.
Wade, Geoff. "The Zheng He Voyages: A Reassessment." *Journal of the Malaysian Branch of the Royal Asiatic Society*, vol. 78, no. 1, 2005, pp. 37–58.

Option 3.6: Traveling West and Traveling East

Marco Polo is a common figure in Western popular culture. His travels east from Europe into Asia are extremely well known, in contrast to the journeys and experiences of those who made the opposite journey west, such as Rabban Bar Sauma. Their relative fame in Western Anglophone culture is the result of a Eurocentric lens that positions Europe as a center to travel out from, Europeans as explorers and discoverers, and so on.

Readings

PRIMARY

Rønning, Joachim, et al., director. *Marco Polo*. Netflix, 2015–16. Television series.
Polo, Marco. *The Travels of Marco Polo*. Edited by Peter Harris, translated by William Marsden, Everyman, 2008.
Rabban Bar Sauma. *The Monks of Kublai Khan Emperor of China; or, The History of the Life and Travels of Rabban Sawma*. Translated by E. A. Wallis Budge, Religious Tract Society, 1928, www.aina.org/books/mokk/mokk.htm.

SECONDARY

Heng, Geraldine. *The Invention of Race in the European Middle Ages*. Cambridge UP, 2018, pp. 323–49.
Wolfe, Alexander C. "Marco Polo: Factotum, Auditor: Language and Political Culture in the Mongol World Empire." *Literature Compass*, vol. 11, no. 7, 2014, pp. 409–22.

Part V

Resources

Colleen C. Ho

The following resources supplement the works-cited lists and bibliographies appearing in the volume's essays. Our intention was to include accessible sources in a variety of media with geographical breadth. The list below, though not exhaustive, will be useful for teachers and students interested in further exploring diverse source material.

Asia

Primary Sources

The Harsacarita. Translated by E. B. Cowell and F. W. Thomas, Royal Asiatic Society, 1897. *Internet Archive*, archive.org/details/harsacaritaofban00banaiala/page/n8.

Secondary Print Sources

Abramson, Marc. *Ethnic Identity in Tang China*. U of Pennsylvania P, 2008.

Allan, Sarah. *The Shape of the Turtle: Myth, Art, and Cosmos in Early China*. State U of New York P, 1991.

Allsen, Thomas T. "Command Performances: Entertainers in the Mongolian Empire." *Russian History*, vol. 28, nos. 1–4, 2001, pp. 37–46.

Atwood, Christopher. *Encyclopedia of Mongolia and the Mongol Empire*. Facts-on-File, 2004.

Becker, Judith. "The Migration of the Arched Harp from India to Burma." *The Galpin Society Journal*, vol. 20, Mar. 1967, pp. 17–23.

Bialock, David T. "From 'Heike to Nomori No Kagami': Onmyōdō and the Soundscapes of Medieval Japan." *Cahiers d'Extrême-Asie*, vol. 21, École française d'Extrême-Orient, 2012.

Cao Wanru, et al., editors. *Zhongguo gudai ditu ji* (*An Atlas of Ancient Maps in China*). Wenwu chubanshe, 1990–97. 3 vols.

Chekin, Leonid S. *Northern Eurasia in Medieval Cartography: Inventory, Texts, Translation, and Commentary*. Brepols, 2006.

Chong, Alan, and Stephen A. Murphy, editors. *The Tang Shipwreck: Art and Exchange in the Ninth Century*. Asian Civilisations Museum, 2017.

Christensen, Lars. "Imag(in)ing Musical Instruments: Prescriptive Iconography in the Northern Song Dynasty." *Music in Art: International Journal for Music Iconography*, vol. 43, 2018, pp. 101–12.

Clark, Mitchell. *Sounds of the Silk Road: Musical Instruments of Asia*. MFA Publications, 2005.

Condit, Jonathan. *Music of the Korean Renaissance: Songs and Dances of the Fifteenth Century*. Cambridge UP, 1984.

De Weerdt, Hilde. *Information, Territory, and Networks: The Crisis and Maintenance of Empire in Song China*. Harvard UP, 2016.

Drompp, Michael Robert. *Tang China and the Collapse of the Uighur Empire: A Documentary History*. Brill, 2005.

Feng, Linda Ruifeng. *City of Marvel and Transformation: Chang'an and Narratives of Experience in Tang Dynasty China*. U of Hawai'i P, 2015.

Filipiak, Yu. *Chen Yangs Darstellung der "barbarischen" Musikinstrumente im Buch der Musik (Yueshu): Ein Beitrag zur Erforschung des Musiklebens am Kaiserhof der Song-Dynastie (960–1279)*. Ostasien-Verl, 2015.

Forêt, Philippe, and Andreas Kaplony, editors. *The Journey of Maps and Images on the Silk Road*. Brill, 2008.

Fuller, Michael. *An Introduction to Chinese Poetry: From the Canon of Poetry to the Lyrics of the Song Dynasty*. Harvard U Asia Center, 2017.

Gole, Susan. *Indian Maps and Plans: From Earliest Times to the Advent of European Surveys*. Manohar, 1989.

Grame, Theodore. "The Symbolism of the 'Ūd." *Asian Music*, vol. 3, no. 1, 1972, pp. 25–34.

Hartman, Charles. *Han Yu and the T'ang Search for Unity*. Princeton UP, 1986.

Hong, Zaixin [洪再新]. 蒙古宮廷和江南文人——元代書畫藝術研究論集 [*Menggu gongting he Jiangnan wenren: Yuandai shuhua yishu yanjiu lunji*]. Zhongguo meishu xue yuan, 2018.

Hsia, C. T., Wai-yee Li, and George Kao, editors. *The Columbia Anthology of Yuan Drama*. Columbia UP, 2014.

Hu, Bangbo. "Cultural Images: Reflection of Political Power in the Maps of Chinese Administrative Gazetteers of the Song Dynasty." *Cartographica*, vol. 42, no. 4, 2007, pp. 319–34.

Hu, Jun. "Global Medieval at the 'End of the Silk Road,' circa 756 CE: The Shōsō-in Collection in Japan." *The Medieval Globe*, vol. 3, no. 2, 2017, pp. 177–202.

Hung, William. *Tu Fu: China's Greatest Poet*. Harvard UP, 1952.

Jao, Tsong-yi, and Paul Demieville. *Airs de Touen-Houang [Touen-Houang k'iu]: Textes à chanter des VIIIe–X^e siecles*. Éditions du Centre National de la Recherche Scientifique, 1971.

Karomat, Diloram. "Interrelations between India and Central Asian Music." *Central Asia on Display: Proceedings of the Seventh Conference of the European Society for Central Asian Studies*, edited by Gabriele Rasuly-Paleczek and Julia Katschnig, Lit Verlag, 2004, pp. 171–82.

Lam, Joseph S. C. "Music, Sound, and Site: A Case Study from Southern Song China (1127–1275)." *New Perspectives on the Research of Chinese Culture*, edited by P.-K. Cheng and K. W. Fan, Springer Verlag, 2013, pp. 99–118.

Lawergren, Bo. "Buddha as a Musician: An Illustration of a Jātaka Story." *Artibus Asiae*, vol. 54, no. 3/4, 1994, pp. 226–40.

Li, Yu-Jiuan. "The Legend of Miyako no Yoshika: A Canvass of Literary Relations between Heian Japan and Tang China." *Journal of Chinese Studies*, vol 56, Jan. 2013, pp. 81–100.

Lin, Miecun. "A Study on Court Cartographers of the Ming Empire." *Journal of Asian History*, vol. 49, nos. 1–2, pp. 187–228.

Ma Huan. *Ying-yai Sheng-lan: The Overall Survey of the Ocean's Shores [1433].* 1970. Translated by J. V. G. Mills, reprint ed., White Lotus Press, 1997.

Mair, Victor. *The Columbia Anthology of Traditional Chinese Literature.* Columbia UP, 1994.

Mierse, William E. "The Significance of the Central Asian Objects in the Shōsōin for Understanding the International Art Trade in the Seventh and Eighth Centuries." *Sino-Platonic Papers*, vol. 267, 2017, pp. 1–52.

Millward, James A. "Chordophone Culture in Two Early Modern Societies: A *Pipa-Vihuela* Duet." *Journal of World History*, vol. 23, no. 2, 2012, pp. 237–78.

———. *The Silk Road: A Very Short Introduction.* Oxford UP, 2013.

Murck, Alfreda. *Poetry and Painting in Song China: The Subtle Art of Dissent.* Harvard University Asia Center, 2000.

Needham, Joseph, with Wang Ling. *Mathematics and the Sciences of the Heavens and the Earth.* Cambridge UP, 1959. Vol. 3 of *Science and Civilisation in China.*

Nelson, Steven G. "Court and Religious Music (1): History of *Gagaku* and *Shomyo.*" *The Ashgate Research Companion to Japanese Music*, edited by Alison McQueen Tokita and David W. Hughes, Ashgate, 2008, pp. 35–48.

Nicolas, Arsenio. "Musical Exchange between India and Southeast Asia." *Early Interactions between South and Southeast Asia: Reflections on Cross-Cultural Exchange*, edited by Pierre-Yves Manguin et al., Institute of Southeast Asian Studies, 2011, pp. 343–65.

———. "Musical Terms in Malay Classical Literature: The Early Period (Fourteenth–Seventeenth Century)." *Nalanda-Sriwijaya Centre Working Paper*, vol. 24, 2017, pp. 1–51.

Owen, Stephen. *An Anthology of Traditional Chinese Literature: Beginnings to 1911.* W. W. Norton, 1996.

———. *The End of the Chinese "Middle Ages": Essays in Mid-Tang Literary Culture.* Stanford UP, 1996.

———. *The Great Age of Chinese Poetry: The High T'ang.* Yale UP, 1981.

———. *The Late Tang: Chinese Poetry of the Mid-Ninth Century (827–860).* Harvard U Asia Center, 2006.

Park, Hyunhee. *Mapping the Chinese and Islamic Worlds: Cross-Cultural Exchange in Pre-modern Asia.* Cambridge UP, 2012.

Picken, L. E. R. "T'ang Music and Musical Instruments." *T'oung Pao*, second series, vol. 553, no. 1/3, 1969, pp. 74–122.

Picken, Laurence, and Noël J. Nickson. *Some Ancient Connections Explored.* Cambridge UP, 2006. Vol. 7 of *Music from the Tang Court.*

Pratt, Keith. "Music as a Factor in Sung-Koryŏ Diplomatic Relations, 1069–1126." *T'oung Pao*, second series, vol. 62, 1976, pp. 199–218.

Rossabi, Morris. *The Mongols: A Very Short Introduction.* Oxford UP, 2012.

Saussy, Haun. *Texts and Transformation: Essays in Honor of the Seventy-Fifth Birthday of Victor H. Mair.* Cambria Press, 2018.

Sen, Tansen, and Victor H. Mair. *Traditional China in Asian and World History.* Association for Asian Studies, 2012.

Sha, Wutian. "An Image of Nighttime Music and Dance in Tang Chang'an: Notes on the Lighting Devices in the Medicine Buddha Transformation Tableau in Mogao Cave 220, Dunhuang." *The Silk Road*, vol. 14, 2016, pp. 19–41.

Sieber, Patricia Angela. *Theaters of Desire: Authors, Readers, and the Reproduction of Early Chinese Song-Drama.* Palgrave Macmillan, 2003.

Skaff, Jonathan Karam. *Sui-Tang China and Its Turko-Mongol Neighbors: Culture, Power, and Connections, 580–800.* Oxford UP, 2012.

Su, Qikang [蘇其康]. 文學, 宗教, 性別和民族: 中古時代的英國, 中東, 中國 [*Wenxue, zongjiao, xingbie, he minzu: Zhonggu shidai de Yingguo, Zhongdong, Zhongguo*]. Lianjing, 2005.

Tian, Qing. "The Ancient *Qin* 琴, Musical Instrument of Cultured Chinese Gentlemen." *Journal of Chinese Literature and Culture*, vol. 3, no. 1, Duke UP, Apr. 2016, pp. 108–36.

Van Gulik, R. H. "The Lore of the Chinese Lute: An Essay in Ch'in Ideology." *Monumenta Nipponica*, vol. 1, no. 2, 1938, pp. 386–438, and vol. 2, no. 1, 1939, pp. 75–99.

Wang, Ao. *Spatial Imaginaries in Mid-Tang China: Geography, Cartography, and Literature.* Cambria Press, 2019.

Wang, Zhenping. *Ambassadors from the Island of Immortals: China-Japan Relations in the Han-Tang Period.* U of Hawai'i P, 2005.

Widdess, Richard. *The Ragas of Early Indian Music.* Clarendon Press, 1995.

Wolpert, Rembrandt, et al. "'The Waves of Kokonor': A Dance-Tune of the T'ang Dynasty." *Asian Music*, vol. 5, no. 1, 1973, pp. 3–9.

Wong, Dorothy, and Gustav Heldt, editors. *China and Beyond in the Medieval Period.* Cambria Press, 2014.

Wright, Owen. "On the Concept of a 'Timurid Music.'" *Oriente Moderno*, new series, vol. 15, Istituto per l'Oriente C. A. Nallino, 1996, pp. 665–81.

Media Resources

Nadeem | Eran ud Turan [@eranudturan]. Tweets about Central Asian and East Iranian history, *Twitter.*

Photos of Silk Road [@PicsSilkRoad]. *Twitter.*

Saymou, Kelsey, and Peiyou Chang. "Visualizing Sound: A Lecture and Demonstration on the Notation System and Music of the Chinese Qin." Lecture-demonstration, Yale University, 15 Feb. 2019. *YouTube*, uploaded by Yale ISM, 11 Apr. 2019, www.youtube.com/watch?v=sbLO6uBMwwc&t=442s.

The Story of the Weeping Camel. Directed by Byambasuren Davaa and Luigi Falorni, ThinkFilm, 2004.

Web Resources

Digital Silk Road. Digital Silk Road Project, National Institute of Informatics, 2003–16, dsr.nii.ac.jp/.

Early Tibet. By Sam van Schaik, British Library, earlytibet.com.

Himalayan Arts Resources. 2021, www.himalayanart.org/.

"A Historical Atlas of South Asia." Edited by Joseph E. Schwartzberg, *Digital South Asia Library*, 2006, dsal.uchicago.edu/reference/schwartzberg/.

The Huntington Archive of Buddhist and Asian Art. 2021, Huntington Archive, huntingtonarchive.org/.

International Dunhuang Project. idp.bl.uk.

Islam in Asia: Diversity in Past and Present: The Silk Road and Islam Spread. Cornell U Library, guides.library.cornell.edu/IslamAsiaExhibit/SilkRoadIslam.

MIMO: Musical Instrument Museums Online. mimo-international.com/MIMO/accueil-ermes.aspx.

Mongols, China and the Silk Road: Archaeology and History of the Silk Road. By Hans van Room, mongolschinaandthesilkroad.blogspot.com.

"Resources." *The Sogdians: Influencers on the Silk Roads*, Freer Gallery of Art and Arthur M. Sackler Gallery, Smithsonian Institution, sogdians.si.edu/resources/. Annotated bibliography.

"Revitalizing Shashmaqâm: Court Music of Central Asia." *Smithsonian Folkways Recordings*, 2021, Smithsonian Institution, folkways.si.edu/revitalizing-shashmaqandacircm-court-music-central-asia/central-asia-spoken-word-world/music/video/smithsonian.

Sahapedia. 2018, www.sahapedia.org/. Resource on the arts, cultures, histories, and heritage of India.

Scroll. www.scroll.in. Indian news in English.

Silk Road Digressions. By Susan Whitfield, silkroaddigressions.com.

Silk Road Exhibition. By Susan Whitfield and Ursula Sims-Williams, *British Library*, idp.bl.uk/4DCGI/education/silk_road/index.a4d.

Silk Road Seattle. By Daniel C. Waugh, Walter Chapin Simpson Center for the Humanities, U of Washington, depts.washington.edu/silkroad/.

The Silk Road: Connecting Cultures, Creating Trust. Smithsonian Folklife Festival, Smithsonian Institution, festival.si.edu/2002/the-silk-road/smithsonian.

The Silk Roads Programme. UNESCO, en.unesco.org/silkroad/.

"The Tang Shipwreck." *Global Middle Ages*, www.globalmiddleages.org/project/tang-shipwreck.

Turfan Studies. 2007, Berlin-Brandenburg Academy of Sciences and Humanities, turfan.bbaw.de/bilder/Turfan_engl_07.pdf.

Africa and Near East

Primary Sources

Bulman, Stephen. "A Checklist of English and French Versions of the Sunjata Epic published before the Twenty-First Century." verbafricana.org/malinke-fr/griots/Bulman.pdf.

Ferdowsi, Abolqasem. *Shahnameh: The Persian Book of Kings*. Translated by Dick Davis, Viking / Penguin, 2006.

Persian Literature in Translation. The Packard Humanities Institute, persian.packhum.org.

Southgate, Minoo S., translator. *Iskandarnamah: A Persian Medieval Alexander-Romance*. Columbia UP, 1978.

Secondary Print Sources

Antrim, Zayde. *Routes and Realms: The Power of Place in the Early Islamic World*. Oxford UP, 2012.

Berlekamp, Persis. *Wonder, Image, and Cosmos in Medieval Islam*. Yale UP, 2011.

Berzock, Kathleen Bickford, editor. *Caravans of Gold, Fragments in Time: Art, Culture, and Exchange across Medieval Saharan Africa*. Princeton UP, 2019.

Biran, Michal. "Music in the Conquest of Baghdad Safi Al-Din Urmawi and the Ilkhanid Circle of Musicians." *The Mongols' Middle East: Continuity and Transformation in Ilkhanid Iran*, edited by Bruno De Nicola and Charles Melville, Brill, 2016, pp. 133–54.

Blum, Stephen. "Foundations of Musical Knowledge in the Muslim World." *The Cambridge History of World Music*, edited by Philip V. Bohlman, Cambridge UP, 2011, pp. 103–24.

Conrad, David C. *Epic Ancestors of the Sunjata Era: Oral Tradition from the Maninka of Guinea*. U of Wisconsin, 1999.

———. Sunjata*: A New Prose Version*. Hackett, 2016.

Delafosse, Maurice. *Historiques et légendaries du Soudan occidentale: Traduites d'un manuscrit arab inédit*. Comité de l'Afrique française, 1913.

Denny, Walter. "Music and Musicians in Islamic Art." *Asian Music*, vol. 17, no. 1, autumn-winter 1985, pp. 37–68.

Fallahzadeh, Mehrdad. *Persian Writing on Music: A Study of Persian Musical Literature from 1000 to 1500 AD*. Uppsala U, 2005.

Gomez, Michael A. *African Dominion: A New History of Empire in Early and Medieval West Africa*. Princeton UP, 2018.

Jeppie, Shamil, and Souleymane Bachir Diagne, editors. *The Meanings of Timbuktu*. Human Sciences Research Council Press, 2008.

Kamal, Youssouf. *Monumenta Cartographica Africae et Aegypti*. 1926–1951. Edited by Fuat Sezgin, facsimile reprint ed., Institut für Geschichte der Arabisch-Islamischen Wissenschaften, 1987. 6 vols.

Khazrai, Firoozeh. "Music in Khusraw va Shirin." *The Poetry of Nizami Ganjavi: Knowledge, Love, and Rhetoric*, edited by Kamran Talattof and Jerome W. Clinton, Palgrave, 2000, pp. 163–78.

King, David. *Islamic Astronomy and Geography*. Ashgate-Variorum, 2012.

———. *World-Maps for Finding the Direction and Distance to Mecca: Innovation and Tradition in Islamic Science*. Brill, 1999.

Manteghi, Haila. *Alexander the Great in the Persian Tradition: History, Myth and Legend in Medieval Iran*. I. B. Tauris, 2018.

Meisami, Julie Scott, and Paul Starkey, editors. *Encyclopedia of Arabic Literature*. Taylor and Francis, 1998.

Miquel, André. *La géographie humaine du monde musulman jusqu'au milieu du 11e siècle*. Mouton, 1967–1988. 4 vols.

Nielson, Lisa. "Gender and the Politics of Music in the Early Islamic Courts." *Early Music History*, vol. 31, 2012, pp. 235–61.

Pinto, Karen. *Medieval Islamic Maps: An Exploration*. U of Chicago P, 2016.

Rapoport, Youssef, and Emilie Savage-Smith, editors. *Eleventh-Century Egyptian Guide to the Universe: The* Book of Curiosities. Brill, 2013.

Savage-Smith, Emilie. *Islamicate Celestial Globes*. Smithsonian Institution, 1984.

Sawa, George. *Music Performance Practice in the Early ʿAbbāsid Era, 132–320 AH / 750–932 AD*. Institute of Mediaeval Music, 2004.

Sezgin, Fuat. *The Contribution of the Arabic-Islamic Geographers to the Formation of the World Map*. Institut für Geschichte der Arabisch-Islamischen Wissenschaften an der Johann Wolfgang Goethe-U, 1987.

Sidibé, B. K. Sunjata: *The Story of Sunjata Keita, Founder of the Mali Empire*. Oral History and Antiquities Division of the Vice-President's Office, 1980.

Zadeh, Travis. *Mapping Frontiers across Medieval Islam: Geography, Translation, and the ʿAbbasid Empire*. I. B. Tauris, 2011.

Web Resources

Bint al-Waha, Sherezzah. "Arabian Nights Images." *Beledy*, www.beledy.net/sherezzah/ARABNITE.HTM.

Camels and Culture: A Celebration. Special issue of *Saudi-Aramco World*, vol. 69, no. 6, Nov./Dec. 2018, www.aramcoworld.com/en-US/Articles/November-2018/Camels-and-Culture-A-Celebration.

Hannoosh Steinberg, Amanda. "Reclaiming the Women of Arabic Popular Epics." *ArabLit*, vol. 2, Aug. 2018, arablit.org/2018/08/02/reclaiming-the-women-of-arabic-popular-epics/.

Hoh, Anchi. "A Thousand and One Nights: Arabian Story-telling in World Literature." *Four Corners of the World International Collections*, Library of Congress, 26 Oct. 2017, blogs.loc.gov/international-collections/2017/10/a-thousand-and-one-nights-arabian-story-telling-in-world-literature/.

Lundell, Michael. *The Journal of the* Thousand and One Nights. journalofthenights.blogspot.com.

Marzolph, Ulrich. "The Arabian Nights Bibliography." *Ulrich Marzolph: Exploring the Narrative Culture of the Muslim World*, wwwuser.gwdg.de/~umarzol/arabiannights-b.html.

Mille et Une Nuits. Bibliothèque Nationale de France (BNF), expositions.bnf.fr/1001nuits/.

Razzaque, Arafat. "Who 'Wrote' Aladdin? The Forgotten Syrian Storyteller." *Ajam Media Collective*, 14 Sept. 2017, ajammc.com/2017/09/14/who-wrote-aladdin/.

The Thousand Nights and a Night. 2009, www.wollamshram.ca/1001/index.htm.

Tolder, Pamela D. "In Fragments from Fustat, Glimpses of a Cosmopolitan Old Cairo." *AramcoWorld*, vol. 67, no. 1, Feb. 2016, pp. 4–9, www.aramcoworld.com/en-US/Articles/January-2016/In-Fragments-from-Fustat-Glimpses-of-a-Cosmopolit.

The Tombouctou Manuscripts Project. University of Capetown, www.tombouctoumanuscripts.uct.ac.za/.

Zamani Project. www.zamaniproject.org.

Europe

Primary Sources

Stoneman, Richard, translator. *The Greek Alexander Romance*. Penguin Books, 1991.

Wagner, Von Bettina. Die *"Epistola presbiteri Johannis" lateinisch und deutsch: Überlieferung, Textgeschichte, Rezeption und Übertragunen im Mittelalter: Mit bisher unedierten Texten*. Max Niemeyer Verlag, 2000.

Zarncke, Friedrich. "Uber eine neue Redaction des Briefes des Priester Johannes." *Berichte uber die Verhandlungen der koniglich sachsischen Gesellschaft der Wissenschaften zu Leipzig, Phililogischen-historische Classe*, vol. 29, 1877, pp. 111–56.

Secondary Print Sources

Brooks, Michael E. "Visual Depictions of Prester John and His Kingdom." *Quidditas*, vol. 35, 2014, pp. 147–76.

Campbell, Mary Baine. "Prester John Writes Back: The Legend and Its Early Modern Reworkings." *A Knight's Legacy: Mandeville and Mandevillian Lore in Early Modern Europe*, edited by Ladan Niayesh, Manchester UP, 2012, pp. 155–72.

Cattaneo, Angelo. *Fra Mauro's* Mappa Mundi *and Fifteenth-Century Venice*. Brepols, 2011.

Connolly, Daniel K. *The Maps of Matthew Paris: Medieval Journeys through Space, Time and Liturgy*. Boydell and Brewer, 2009.

Delano-Smith, C., and R. Kain. *English Maps: A History*. Toronto UP, 1999.

Duzer, Chet van. "*Hic Sunt Dracones*: The Geography and Cartography of Monsters." *Research Companion to Monsters and the Monstrous*, edited by Asa Simon Mittman and Peter Dendle, Ashgate, 2012, pp. 387–436.

Edson, Evelyn. *Mapping Time and Space: How Medieval Mapmakers Viewed Their World*. British Library, 1999.

———. *The World Map, 1300–1492: The Persistence of Tradition and Transformation*. Johns Hopkins UP, 2007.

Gaullier-Bougassas, Catherine. "Alexandre le Grand et la conquête de l'Ouest dans les *Romans d'Alexandre* du XIIe siècle, leurs mises en prose au XVe siècle et le *Perceforest*." *Romania: Revue trimestrielle consacré a l'étude des langues et des littératures romanes*, vol. 118, no. 1, 2000, pp. 83–104.

Harvey, P. D. A., editor. *The Hereford World Map: Medieval World Maps and Their Context*. British Library, 2006.

Heng, Geraldine. *Empire of Magic: Medieval Romance and the Politics of Cultural Fantasy*. Columbia UP, 2003.

———. *The Invention of Race in the European Middle Ages*. Cambridge UP, 2018.

Kline, Naomi Reed. *Maps of Medieval Thought: The Hereford Paradigm*. Boydell Press, 2001.

Kupfer, M. *Art and Optics in the Hereford Map*. Yale UP, with the Paul Mellon Centre for Studies in British Art, 2016.

Lavezzo, Kathy. *Angels on the Edge of the World: Geography, Literature and English Community, 1000–1534*. Cornell UP, 2006.

Martin, Thomas R., and Christopher W. Blackwell. *Alexander the Great: The Story of an Ancient Life*. Cambridge UP, 2012.

Mittman, Asa Simon. *Maps and Monsters in Medieval England*. Routledge, 2006.

Rachewiltz, Igor de. *Prester John and Europe's Discovery of East Asia*. Australian National UP, 1972.

Ramos, Manuel João. *Essays in Christian Mythology: The Metamorphosis of Prester John*. UP of America, 2006.

Stoneman, Richard. *Legends of Alexander the Great*. I. B. Tauris, 2012.

Talbert, Richard. *Rome's World: The Peutinger Map Reconsidered*. Cambridge UP, 2010.

Talbert, Richard J. A., and Richard W. Unger, editors. *Cartography in Antiquity and the Middle Ages: Fresh Perspectives, New Methods*. Brill, 2008.

Terkla, Dan, and Nick Millea, editors. *A Critical Companion to English* Mappaemundi *of the Twelfth and Thirteenth Centuries*. Boydell, 2019..

Uebel, Michael. *Ecstatic Transformations: On the Uses of Alterity in the Middle Ages*. Palgrave, 2005.

Westrem, Scott. *The Hereford Map: A Transcription and Translation of the Legends with Commentary*. Brepols, 2001.

Williams, John. *The Illustrated Beatus*. Harvey Miller, 1994–2003. 5 vols.

Zarncke, Friederich. "Der Priester Johannes." *Abhandlungen der philologisch-historischen Classe der königlich sächsischen Gesellschaft der Wissenschaften*, vol. 7, 1879, pp. 831–1028.

Web Resources

Hereford Mappa Mundi. Hereford Cathedral, www.themappamundi.co.uk.

Huber, Emily Rebekah, compiler and annotator. "Medieval Alexander Bibliographies." *River Campus Libraries*, University of Rochester Libraries, www.library.rochester.edu/robbins/medieval-alexander.

Americas

Secondary Print Sources

Almqvist, Bo. "'My Name is Guðriðr': An Enigmatic Episode in *Grænlendinga saga*." In *Approaches to Vínland*, edited by Andrew Wawn and Þórunn Sigurdardóttir, Sigurður Nordal Institute, 2001, pp. 15–30.

Ebenesersdóttir, Sigríður Sunna, et al. "A New Subclade of mtDNA Haplogroup C1 Found in Icelanders: Evidence of Pre-Columbian Contact?" *American Journal of Physical Anthropology*, vol. 144, 2011, pp. 92–99.

McAleese, Kevin. "*Skrælingar* Abroad—*Skrælingar* at Home?" *Vinland Revisited: The Norse World at the Turn of the First Millennium*, edited by Shannon Lewis-Simpson, Historic Sites Association of Newfoundland and Labrador, 2000, pp. 353–64.

McGhee, Robert. "The *Skraellings* of Vinland." *Viking Voyages to North America*, edited by Max Vinner, Viking Ship Museum, 1993, pp. 43–53.

Sutherland, Patricia D. "The Norse and Native North Americans." *Vikings: The North Atlantic Saga*, edited by William W. Fitzhugh and Elisabeth I. Ward, Smithsonian Institution Press, 2000, pp. 238–47.

Wallace, Birgitta Linderoth. "An Archeologist's Interpretation of the Vinland Sagas." *Vikings: The North Atlantic Saga*, edited by William W. Fitzhugh and Elisabeth I. Ward, Smithsonian Institution Press, 2000, pp. 228–31.

———. "L'Anse aux Meadows: Gateway to Vinland." *The Norse of the North Atlantic*, edited by Gerald F. Bigelow, *Acta Archaeologica*, vol. 61, 1991, pp. 166–97.

———. "L'Anse aux Meadows and Vinland: An Abandoned Experiment." *Contact, Continuity, and Collapse: The Norse Colonization of the North Atlantic*, edited by James H. Barrett, Brepols, 2003, pp. 207–48.

Web Resources

"'Discoveries' of the Americas." *Global Middle Ages*, www.globalmiddleages.org/project/discoveries-americas.

"L'Anse aux Meadows National Historic Site." *Newfoundland and Labrador Tourism*, www.newfoundlandlabrador.com/top-destinations/lanse-aux-meadows.

"L'Anse aux Meadows National Historic Site." *UNESCO*, whc.unesco.org/en/list/4/.

"L'Anse aux Meadows National Historic Site." *Parks Canada*, Government of Canada / Gouvernement du Canada, www.pc.gc.ca/en/lhn-nhs/nl/meadows.

Global

Primary Sources

Beckingham, C. F., and B. Hamilton, editors. *Prester John, the Mongols, and the Ten Lost Tribes.* Variorum, 1996.

Brewer, Keagan. *Prester John: The Legend and Its Sources.* Ashgate, 2015.

Budge, E. A. Wallis, translator. *The History of Alexander the Great: Being the Syriac Version of the Pseudo-Callisthenes.* Reprint ed., Georgias Press, 2003.

———, translator. *The Life and Exploits of Alexander the Great: Being A Series of Translations of the Ethiopic Histories of Alexander by the Pseudo-Callisthenes and Other Writers.* C. J. Clay and Sons, 1896. *Internet Archive*, archive.org/details/cu31924091208573/page/n12.

Pseudo-Callisthenes. *The Romance of Alexander the Great.* Translated by Albert Mugrdich Wolohojian, Columbia UP, 1969.

Ullendorff, Edward, and C. F. Beckingham. *The Hebrew Letters of Prester John.* Oxford UP, 1982.

Zuwiyya, Z. David, editor and translator. *Islamic Legends Concerning Alexander the Great.* Global Publications, 2001.

Secondary Print Sources

Akbari, Suzanne Conklin. "Alexander in the Orient: Bodies and Boundaries in the *Roman de toute chevalerie.*" *Postcolonial Approaches to the European Middle Ages: Translating Cultures*, edited by Ananya Jahanara Kabir and Deanne Williams, Cambridge UP, 2005, pp. 105–26.

———. *Idols in the East: European Representations of Islam and the Orient, 1100–1450.* Cornell UP, 2009.

Bar-Ilan, Meir. "Prester John: Fiction and History." *History of European Ideas*, vol. 20, 1995, pp. 291–98.

Boyle, J. A. "The Alexander Romance in the East and West." *Bulletin of the John Rylands Library*, vol. 60, no. 1, 1977, pp. 13–27.

Brock, S. P. "The Laments of the Philosophers Over Alexander in Syriac." *Journal of Semitic Studies*, vol. 15, no. 2, 1970, pp. 205–18.

Cleaves, Francis Woodman. "An Early Mongolian Version of the Alexander Romance." *Harvard Journal of Asiatic Studies*, vol. 22, 1959, pp. 1–99.

Constable, Olivia Remie. *Housing the Stranger in the Mediterranean World: Lodging, Trade, and Travel in Late Antiquity and the Middle Ages.* Cambridge UP, 2003.

Denny, Walter. "Early Music from Around the World." Special Issue. *Early Music*, vol. 24, no. 3, 1996.

Doufikar-Aerts, Faustina. *Alexander Magnus Arabicus: A Survey of the Alexander Tradition through Seven Centuries: from Pseudo-Callisthenes to Ṣūrī.* Translated by Ania Lentz-Michaelis. Peeters, 2010.

Duncan, James S., and David Ley. *Place/Culture/Representation.* Routledge, 1993.

Eco, Umberto. *Baudolino.* Translated by William Weaver, Harcourt, 2002.

Edson, Evelyn, and E. Savage-Smith. *Medieval Views of the Cosmos: Picturing the Universe in the Christian and Islamic Middle Ages.* Bodleian Library, 2004.

Furtado, Antonio L. "From Alexander of Macedonia to Arthur of Britain." *Arthuriana*, vol. 5, no. 3, 1995, pp. 70–86.

Grame, Theodore C., et al. "Steed Symbolism on Eurasian String Instruments." *The Musical Quarterly*, vol. 58, no. 1, 1972, pp. 57–66.

Gumilev, L. N. *Searches for an Imaginary Kingdom: The Legend of the Kingdom of Prester John.* Translated by R. E. F. Smith, Cambridge UP, 1987.

Harley, J. B. "Cartography, Ethics and Social Theory." *Cartographica*, vol. 27, no. 2, 1990, pp. 1–23.

———. "Deconstructing the Map." *Cartographica*, vol. 26, no. 2, spring 1989, pp. 1–20.

Harley, J. B., and David Woodward, editors. *Cartography in Prehistoric, Ancient, and Medieval Europe and the Mediterranean.* U of Chicago P, 1987. Vol. 1 of *The History of Cartography.*

———, editors. *Cartography in the Traditional African, American, Arctic, Australian, and Pacific Societies.* U of Chicago P, 1998. Vol. 2, book 3 of *The History of Cartography.*

———, editors. *Cartography in the Traditional East and Southeast Asian Societies.* U of Chicago P, 1994. Vol. 2, book 2 of *The History of Cartography.*

———, editors. *Cartography in the Traditional Islamic and South Asian Societies.* U of Chicago P, 1992. Vol. 2, book 1 of *The History of Cartography.*

Heng, Geraldine. "Early Globalities, and Its Questions, Objectives, and Methods: An Inquiry into the State of Theory and Critique." *Exemplaria*, vol. 26, nos. 2–3, 2014, pp. 234–53.

———. "An Ordinary Ship and Its Stories of Early Globalism: Modernity, Mass Production, and Art in the Global Middle Ages." *The Journal of Medieval Worlds*, vol. 1, no. 1, 2019, pp. 11–54.

——— "Sex, Lies, and Paradise: The Assassins, Prester John, and the Fabulation of Civilizational Identities." *Differences*, vol. 23, no. 1, spring 2012, pp. 1–31.

Jacob, Christian. *The Sovereign Map: Theoretical Approaches in Cartography throughout History.* Translated by Tom Conley, U of Chicago P, 2006.

Kao, Wan-Chuan. "Hotel Tartary." *Mediaevalia*, vol. 32, 2011, pp. 43–68.

King, Geoff. *Mapping Reality: An Exploration of Cultural Cartographies.* St. Martin's Press, 1996.

Kinoshita, Sharon. "Medieval Mediterranean Literature." *PMLA*, vol. 124, no. 2, 2009, pp. 600–08.

———. "Translatio/n, Empire, and the Worlding of Medieval Literature: The Travels of *Kalila Wa Dimna.*" *Postcolonial Studies*, vol. 11, no. 4, Dec. 2008, pp. 371–85.

Koestenbaum, Wayne. *Hotel Theory*. Soft Skull Press, 2007.

Lefebvre, Henri. *The Production of Space*. Translated by Donald Nicholson-Smith, Blackwell, 1992.

Lewis, Martin W., and Kären E. Wigen. *The Myth of Continents: A Critique of Metageography*. U of California P, 1997.

Lilley, Keith, editor. *Mapping Medieval Geographies*. Cambridge UP, 2013.

Mittman, Asa Simon. "Mapping Global Middle Ages." *Toward a Global Middle Ages: Encountering the World Through Illuminated Manuscripts*, edited by Bryan C. Keene, Getty Publications, 2019, pp. 99–101.

Monmonier, Mark. *How to Lie with Maps*. U of Chicago P, 1996.

Ng, Su Fang. "The *Alexander Romance* in Southeast Asia: Wonder, Islam, and Knowledge of the World." *Alexander the Great in the Middle Ages: Transcultural Perspectives*, edited by Markus Stock, U of Toronto P, 2016, pp. 104–22.

———. *Alexander the Great from Britain to Southeast Asia: Peripheral Empires in the Global Renaissance*. Oxford UP, 2019.

Ptolemy. *Ptolemy's* Geography: *An Annotated Translation of the Theoretical Chapters*. Translated by J. Lennart Berggren and Alexander Jones, Princeton UP, 2000.

Ramey, Lynn, and Tison Pugh, editors. *Race, Class, and Gender in "Medieval" Cinema*. Palgrave Macmillan, 2007.

Salvadore, Matteo. *The African Prester John and the Birth of Ethiopian-European Relations, 1402–1455*. Routledge, 2016.

Scafi, Alessandro. *Mapping Paradise: A History of Heaven on Earth*. U of Chicago P, 2006.

Sezgin, Fuat. *Mathematical Geography and Cartography in Islam and Their Continuation in the Occident*. Translated by Guy Moore and Geoff Sammon, Institut für Geschichte der Arabisch-Islamischen Wissenschaften an der Johan Wolfgang Goethe-U, 2000–07. 3 vols.

Shiloah, Amnon. "Jewish and Muslim Traditions of Music Therapy." *Music as Medicine: The History of Music Therapy since Antiquity*, edited by Horden Peregrine, Ashgate, 2000, pp. 69–83.

Smith, Jonathan Z. *Map Is Not Territory: Studies in the History of Religions*. Brill, 1978. Reprint ed., U of Chicago P, 1993.

Stock, Marcus, editor. *Alexander the Great in the Middle Ages: Transcultural Perspectives*. U of Toronto P, 2016.

Stoneman, Richard, et al., editors. *The Alexander Romance in Persia and the East.* Barkhuis Publishing / Groningen University Library, 2012.

Taylor, Christopher. "Global Circulation as Christian Enclosure: Legend, Empire, and the Nomadic Prester John." *Literature Compass*, vol. 11, no. 7, 2014, pp. 445–59.

Tibbetts, Gerald R. *Arab Navigation in the Indian Ocean before the Coming of the Portuguese.* 1971. Reprint ed., Royal Asiatic Society of Great Britain and Ireland, 1981.

Tuan, Yi-Fu. *Space and Place: The Perspective of Experience.* 1977. U of Minnesota P, 2002.

Turnbull, David. *Maps Are Territories: Science Is an Atlas: A Portfolio of Exhibits.* U of Chicago P, 1993. Inventive Labs, 2008, territories .indigenousknowledge.org/home/contents.html.

Valente, Catherynne M. *The Habitation of the Blessed: A Dirge for Prester John.* Vol. 1, Night Shade Books, 2010.

Whitfield, Peter. *The Image of the World.* British Library, 1994.

Wood, Denis. *Rethinking the Power of Maps.* Guilford Press, 2010.

Zuwiyya, Z. David, editor. *A Companion to Alexander Literature in the Middle Ages.* Brill, 2011.

Media Resource

"Caravans of Gold, Fragments in Time at The Block Museum of Art." *Vimeo*, uploaded by Block Museum, Northwestern University, vimeo.com/ 307108617.

Web Resources

"Cartography Guide." *Axis Maps*, www.axismaps.com/guide/.

"Critically Endangered." *Wild Camel Protection Foundation*, www.wildcamels .com/.

"Dromedaries and Camels." *Livius.org: Articles on Ancient History*, www.livius .org/articles/misc/dromedaries-and-camels/.

Global Middle Ages. www.globalmiddleages.org.

Imagining Medieval Narrative: The Travels of Marco Polo. By Vanderbilt University Department of French and Italian, scalar.usc.edu/works/the -travels-of-marco-polo/index.

The International Prester John Project: How A Global Legend Was Created Across Six Centuries. By Christopher Taylor, scalar.usc.edu/works/prester-john/.

The Laboratory of Literary Architecture. By Mateo Pericoli, lablitarch.com/.

Razzaque, Arafat. "Who Was the 'Real' Aladdin? From Chinese to Arab in Three Hundred Years." *Ajam Media Collective*, 10 Aug. 2017, ajammc .com/2017/08/10/who-was-the-real-aladdin/.

Virtua Mappa *2.0: Digital Editions of Medieval Maps of the World.* British Library and Schoenberg Institute for Manuscript Studies, sims2 .digitalmappa.org/36.

Curriculum Guides and Material

"AFE Special Topic Guide: The Silk Road." *Asia for Educators*, Columbia University, afe.easia.columbia.edu/special/silk_road.htm.

"Curriculum Guide: From Silk to Oil." School of Chinese Studies, China Institute, New York, www.chinainstitute.org/school/educators/curriculum-guides-lesson-plans/.

"Gupta Game: Simulating Society in Ancient India." By Stewart Gordon, www.stewartgordonhistorian.com/teaching-materials.html.

A Level Delivery Guide: Genghis Khan and the Explosion from the Steppes, c. 1167–1405. OCR, www.ocr.org.uk/Images/182556-genghis-khan-and-the-explosion-from-the-steppes-delivery-guide.pdf.

"Resources Curriculum for *The Music of Strangers*." *SilkRoad*, www.silkroad.org/resources-tmos.

"Silk Road Activity: Is the Silk Road an Example of Globalization?" Field Museum Learning Center, Cyrus Tang Hall of China, Field Museum, Chicago, www.fieldmuseum.org/sites/default/files/silk_road_activity.pdf.

Notes on Contributors

Robert W. Barrett, Jr., is associate professor of English, medieval studies, theatre, and the Unit for Criticism and Interpretive Theory at the University of Illinois at Urbana-Champaign. He is the author of *Against All England: Regional Identity and Cheshire Writing, 1195–1656* (2009) and has also published essays on the Chester Pentecost and Shepherds plays. His current research project uses medieval English theatre, critical plant studies, and animacy theory to answer Mark Cody Poulton's question, "Can a play about anything so passive as a plant make for good theatre?"

Shahzad Bashir is Aga Khan Professor of Islamic Humanities at Brown University. He specializes in the intellectual and social history of Iran and Central and South Asia. He is the author of *Sufi Bodies: Religion and Society in Medieval Islam* (2011), *Fazlallah Astarabadi and the Hurufis* (2005), and *Messianic Hopes and Mystical Visions: The Nurbakhshiya Between Medieval and Modern Islam* (2003). He has coedited *Under the Drones: Modern Lives in the Afghanistan-Pakistan Borderlands* (2012). His publications also include *The Market in Poetry in the Persian World*, in the Cambridge Elements series in the Global Middles Ages (2021) and the digital monograph *A New Vision of Islamic Pasts and Futures* (2022).

Lars Christensen is an independent scholar based in Saint Paul, Minnesota. In 2019 he completed a PhD from the University of Minnesota with the dissertation, *The Time-Suturing Technologies of Northern Song Musicology*, which analyzed how eleventh-century Chinese music reformers used linguistic, mathematical, and visual resources to resolve textual ambiguities and establish a more direct connection with the past. He is the coauthor (with Gabriela Currie) of the *Eurasian Musical Journeys: Five Tales* (2022) in the Cambridge Elements series in the Global Middle Ages. His other research interests include the role of narrative in global premodern music history; connections between musical, philosophical, and protoscientific thought; and the early use of music notation worldwide.

Jeffrey J. Cohen is dean of humanities at Arizona State University and former copresident of the Association for the Study of Literature and the Environment. His research examines things that challenge the imagination. Cohen is widely published in the fields of medieval studies, monster theory, and the environmental humanities. His book *Stone: An Ecology of the Inhuman* received the 2017 René Wellek Prize in comparative literature from the American Comparative Literature Association.

Kristen Collins is curator of manuscripts at the J. Paul Getty Museum. She earned her BA from Mount Holyoke College; MA from Williams College; and PhD from the University of Texas at Austin, all in art history. Over the past eighteen years, she has curated and supervised more than twenty exhibitions from the Getty's permanent collection and cocurated two international loan shows: *Holy Image, Hallowed Ground: Icons from Sinai* (2006) and *Canterbury and St. Albans: Treasures from Church and Cloister* (2013). Recurring themes in her scholarship are transcultural exchange and resonance and reuse in the material culture of the Middle Ages and Renaissance. In addition to the catalogue for *Icons from Sinai*, she coedited and contributed to both *The St. Albans Psalter: Painting and Prayer in Medieval England* (2013) and *St. Albans and the Markyate Psalter: Seeing and Reading in Twelfth-Century England* (2017). Other essays appear in *British Art Studies* (2017) and *Toward a Global Middle Ages*, edited by Bryan C. Keene (2019).

Gabriela Currie is associate professor of musicology at the University of Minnesota. Her research interests and publications encompass a broad range of subjects, including the intersection of music, religion, philosophy, science, and visual arts in medieval Europe; and premodern and early modern Eurasian transcultural musical commerce. Her current work includes several projects on the entanglement of musical thought, instruments, and practices in premodern Eurasia under the theoretical umbrella of intersections and intercultural exchanges in early globalities. She is the coauthor (with Lars Christensen) of the *Eurasian Musical Journeys: Five Tales* (2022) in the Cambridge Elements series in the Global Middle Ages, and the coeditor (with Paola Dessí) of the forthcoming *Music Accounts in Travel Narratives from the Age of Exploration*.

Kavita Mudan Finn has taught literature, history, and gender studies at MIT, Georgetown University, George Washington University, the University of Maryland, College Park, and Simmons University. Her first book, *The Last Plantagenet Consorts: Gender, Genre, and Historiography, 1440–1627*, was published in 2012, and her work has appeared in *Viator*, *Shakespeare*, *Medieval and Renaissance Drama in England*, *Critical Survey*, *The Journal of Fandom Studies*, *Quarterly Review of Film and Video*, and a range of edited volumes. She has a forthcoming Cambridge Element in the Global Middle Ages series, *Global Medievalisms: An Introduction*, coauthored with Helen Young.

Emma J. Flatt is associate professor of history at the University of North Carolina, Chapel Hill, and visiting associate professor at the National University of Singapore. Her work focuses on the social and cultural history of early modern India. She is the author of *The Courts of The Deccan Sultanates: Living Well In The Persian Cosmopolis* (2019); the coauthor, with Daud

Ali, of *Garden and Landscape Practices in Precolonial India: Histories from the Deccan* (2011), as well as the author of various journal articles on the histories of astrology, wrestling, magic, friendship, and perfumes.

Marci Freedman completed her PhD at the University of Manchester (2016) and most recently held the Sava Ranisavljevic Postdoctoral Fellowship at Northwestern University. A scholar of textual and intellectual history with interests in Jewish travel narratives, pilgrimage, and the exchange of ideas between cultures, she is the author of "So Many Tall Tales: Constantijn L'Empereur's Polemical Reading of Benjamin of Tudela's *Book of Travels*" (2020) and "Moving Away from the 'Historical' Benjamin of Tudela" (forthcoming). Her current book project, *The Jewish Diaspora in the Global Middle Ages*, for the Cambridge Elements in the Global Middle Ages series, traces the diasporic experiences of medieval Jews from Spain to China and England to Africa.

Michael A. Gomez is currently Silver Professor of History and Middle Eastern and Islamic Studies at New York University, and the director of NYU's newly established Center for the Study of Africa and the African Diaspora (CSAAD), having served as the founding director of the Association for the Study of the Worldwide African Diaspora (ASWAD) from its inception in 2000 to 2007. He is also series editor of Cambridge Studies on the African Diaspora. He has chaired the history departments at both NYU and Spelman College and also served as president of UNESCO's International Scientific Committee for the Slave Route Project from 2009 to 2011. He is the author of *Pragmatism in the Age of Jihad: The Precolonial State of Bundu* (1992), *Exchanging Our Country Marks: The Transformation of African Identities in the Colonial and Antebellum South* (1998), *Reversing Sail: A History of the African Diaspora* (2005), and *Black Crescent: African Muslims in the Americas* (2005). He is the editor of the collection *Diasporic Africa: A Reader* (2006). Gomez's most recent book, *African Dominion: A New History of Empire in Early and Medieval West Africa* (2018), is a comprehensive study of polity and religion during the region's iconic moment and was awarded the 2019 African Studies Association's Book Prize (formerly the Herskovits Book Award), and the 2019 American Historical Association's Martin A. Klein Prize in African History. Gomez supports the struggles of African people worldwide.

Monica H. Green is a historian of medicine specializing in two areas. On the one hand, she has devoted much of her career to surveying the intellectual and social history of medicine in medieval western Europe, focusing on women and gender and on the adoption of Arabic medicine starting in the eleventh century. In the past decade and a half, she has also adopted a global approach to infectious disease history, using the findings of genetics to track the transmission of the world's most devastating diseases around the globe. Currently, she is working on a global history of the Black Death, as well as a focused study of the role the Tunisian Arabic translator, Constantine the African, played in formulating European medical education and theory.

Eva Haverkamp-Rott is professor of medieval Jewish history at Ludwig-Maximilians-University in Munich, Germany (since 2009). From 1999 to 2008 she was assistant professor and then associate professor of Jewish and medieval history at Rice University. Her research focuses on medieval Jewish historiography, economic history of the Jews, and areas of shared or entangled histories of Jews and Christians in medieval Ashkenaz. Her publications include the essay "Die Jüdische Diaspora" in *Weltdeutungen und Weltreligionen 600 bis 1500*, edited by Johannes Fried and Ernst-Dieter Hehl.

Derek Heng is professor and chair of the History Department at Northern Arizona University. He specializes in the transregional history of Maritime Southeast Asia and the South China Sea during the first and early second millennia CE, utilizing archaeological and textual data to advance our understanding of this important era of historical interaction. He is the author of *Sino-Malay Trade and Diplomacy in the Tenth Through the Fourteenth Century* (2009; 2012), coauthor of *Seven Hundred Years: A History of Singapore* (2019), and author of *Geography, Networks, and Trade in Southeast Asia* in the Cambridge Elements in the Global Middle Ages series.

Geraldine Heng is Perceval Professor of English and Comparative Literature, Middle Eastern Studies, Women's Studies, and Jewish Studies at the University of Texas at Austin. She is the author of *Empire of Magic: Medieval Romance and the Politics of Cultural Fantasy* (2003), *The Invention of Race in the European Middle Ages* (2018), which was the winner of four awards: the 2019 PROSE Prize in Global History, the 2019 Robert W. Hamilton Grand Prize, the 2019 American Academy of Religion Prize in Historical Studies, and the 2020 Otto Gründler Prize. She is also the author of *England and the Jews: How Religion and Violence Created the First Racial State in the West* (2018), and *The Global Middle Ages: An Introduction* (2021). Heng is founder and director of the Global Middle Ages Project (www.globalmiddleages.org) and coeditor of the Cambridge Elements series in the Global Middle Ages and of the University of Pennsylvania Press series RaceB4Race: Critical Studies of the Premodern. She is currently writing a new Cambridge Element, *Teaching Early Global Literatures*, and researching and writing *Early Globalities: The Interconnected World, 500–1500 CE*. Heng is a fellow in the Society of Fellows, Medieval Academy of America, and a member of the Medievalists of Color collective.

Colleen C. Ho is senior lecturer in the History Department at the University of Maryland, where she teaches courses on the medieval world and the

Mongol Empire. She has published on women's lay piety, Marco Polo, and European relations with the Mongol Empire. Research interests include the diffusion of artistic practices, trade relations, and travelers across medieval Eurasia.

Jonathan Hsy specializes in comparative literary and cultural studies, and his work explores manifold understandings of embodied difference in the global medieval past and our present-day world. He is coeditor of *A Cultural History of Disability in the Middle Ages* (2020), codirector of *Global Chaucers* and coeditor of its special issue of *Literature Compass* (June 2018), and the author of *Antiracist Medievalisms: From "Yellow Peril" to Black Lives Matter* (2021). He is completing a book on disability and life-writing in medieval European culture and present-day activist communities.

Wan-Chuan Kao is associate professor of English at Washington and Lee University. His research interests include whiteness studies, race, gender and sexuality, affect, aesthetics, and critical theory. His work has appeared in *Studies in the Age of Chaucer*, *Exemplaria*, *Journal of Lesbian Studies*, *Mediaevalia*, *postmedieval*, and several collected volumes. His forthcoming monograph, entitled *White before Whiteness in the Late Middle Ages*, examines late medieval representations of whiteness across bodily and nonsomatic figurations.

Bryan C. Keene (he/they/él/elle) is a curator and educator whose work promotes diversity and equity for the study and display of premodern visual arts as well as for the advocacy of the LGBTQIA2+ communities. At the J. Paul Getty Museum, he has curated or coorganized award-winning exhibitions on the topics of global manuscript cultures and on out-groups of the Middle Ages, in addition to over ten other projects. He edited and contributed essays to the volume *Toward a Global Middle Ages: Encountering the World through Illuminated Manuscripts* (2019), which features contributions by twenty-six authors on book arts from Afro-Eurasia, the Americas, and Austronesia. He is coauthor, with Larisa Grollemond, of *The Fantasy of the Middle Ages: An Epic Journey through Imaginary Medieval Worlds* (2022). He teaches at Riverside City College; serves on the board of directors of the International Center of Medieval Art, the mentoring committee of the Medieval Academy of America; and is an adjunct professor of art history and the humanities at Pepperdine University. He holds a PhD from the Courtauld Institute of Art.

Timothy May is professor of Central Eurasian history at the University of North Georgia. He is the author of *The Mongol Art of War* (2007), *The Mongol Conquests in World History* (2012), and the editor of *The Mongol Empire: A Historical Encyclopedia* (2016). He is also the author of *The Mongol Empire* (2018) and *The Mongols* (2019). He was named the University of North Georgia Alumni Distinguished Professor in 2014. When not teaching courses on the Mongol Empire, the Crusades, or Islamic history, he serves as associate dean of Arts and Letters.

Asa Simon Mittman is professor of art history at California State University, Chico. He is the author of *Maps and Monsters in Medieval England* (2006), coauthor of *Inconceivable Beasts: The Wonders of the East in the Beowulf Manuscript* (2013), and author of articles on monstrosity and marginality in the Middle Ages, including pieces on Satan and race in the Middle Ages. He edited the *Research Companion to Monsters and the Monstrous* (2012), and coedited *Monstrosity, Disability, and the Posthuman in the Medieval and Early Modern World* (2019) and *Demonstrare*, a two-volume monster studies reader (2018), and cocurated *Medieval Monsters: Terrors, Aliens, Wonders* at the Morgan Library.

Adam Miyashiro is associate professor of literature at Stockton University in New Jersey. He completed a PhD in comparative literature at Penn State and wrote a dissertation on medieval literature and the construction of race. He is on the advisory board of the journal *Early Middle English* and has published articles and reviews in *Literature Compass*, *postmedieval*, *Comparative Literature Studies*, *Journal of Law and Religion*, *Notes and Queries*, and *Neophilologus*.

Su Fang Ng is Cutchins Professor of English at Virginia Tech. She has held fellowships at the Radcliffe Institute at Harvard; the National Humanities Center; the University of Texas, Austin; Heidelberg University; All Souls College, Oxford; and the University of Wisconsin, Madison. The author of *Literature and the Politics of Family in Seventeenth-Century England* (2007), as well as numerous articles, she recently published *Alexander the Great from Britain to Southeast Asia: Peripheral Empires in the Global Renaissance* (2019), which won the Renaissance Society of America's 2020 Phyllis Goodhart Gordan Prize for best book in Renaissance Studies.

Elizabeth Oyler is associate professor of Japanese at the University of Pittsburgh. She specializes in medieval Japanese narrative and performing arts. Her publications include *Swords, Oaths, and Prophetic Visions: Authorizing Warrior Rule in Medieval Japan* (2006); a study of authority and voice in the *Tale of the Heike*, Japan's most prominent war tale; and articles about medieval narrative. She coedited *Like Clouds or Mists* (2013), a volume of translations and studies of noh plays derived from *Tale of the Heike*, and the forthcoming *Cultural Imprints: War and Memory in the Samurai Age*. She is involved in collaborative projects on traditional Japanese theater and world puppet theater traditions.

Karen Pinto was born and raised in Karachi, Pakistan, and is of Indian, Russian, and French descent, was educated at Dartmouth and Columbia, and is into maps of all kinds and sizes. She specializes in the history of

Islamic cartography and its intersections between Ottoman, European, and other worldly cartographic traditions and has spent the better part of two decades hunting down maps in Oriental manuscript collections around the world. She has a two-thousand-strong image repository of Islamic maps—many never before published. Her book *Medieval Islamic Maps: An Exploration* (2016) won a 2017 Outstanding Academic Title award from Choice. She has won numerous grants, including a National Endowment of the Humanities fellowship (2013–14) for her work on Islamic maps of the Mediterranean. She has published articles on medieval Islamic and Ottoman maps and is working on books on Islamo-Christian cartographic connections, the Mediterranean in the Islamic cartographic imagination, and what is Islamic about Islamicate maps.

Lynn Ramey is professor of French at Vanderbilt University, where she specializes in medieval French literature and digital humanities. She directs the Center for Digital Humanities and the Digital Cultural Heritage research cluster. Ramey is the author of *An Introduction to Jean Bodel* (forthcoming), *Black Legacies: Race and the European Middle Ages* (2014), and *Christian, Saracen and Genre in Medieval French Literature* (2001) She is currently working on recreations of medieval language, literature, and culture in video games.

Arafat A. Razzaque is assistant professor of Islamic history in the Department of Near and Middle Eastern Civilizations at the University of Toronto. He earned his PhD in history and Middle Eastern studies from Harvard University and specializes in medieval Islamic social and cultural history with a focus on religious and scholarly life in the early Abbasid Empire. His current project examines ideas about gossip and slander in the literature of early Islamic piety. He also maintains an interest in the textual history and reception of the *Arabian Nights* and has published on its first European edition: "Genie in a Bookshop: Print Culture, Authorship, and 'The Affair of the Eighth Volume' at the Origins of *Les Mille et une nuits*" in *The* Thousand and One Nights*: Sources and Transformations in Literature, Art, and Science* (2020).

Rachel Schine is a humanities research fellow at New York University, Abu Dhabi. She holds a PhD in Near Eastern languages and civilizations from the University of Chicago. Her work focuses on premodern Arabic literature, with interests in race and racialization, gender and sexuality, and orality and storytelling practices. Her current project analyzes racial logic and representations of Black heroes in the Arabic sīrahs, or popular epics. She has published on topics relating to race, kinship, and reproduction in Arabic narrative in, among others, the *Journal of Arabic Literature* and *al-ʿUṣūr al-Wusṭā: The Journal of Middle East Medievalists.*

Denise A. Spellberg is professor of history and Middle Eastern studies at the University of Texas, Austin. A medievalist trained in the study of gender and religion in early Islamic society, she now also writes on the presence of Islam and Muslims in Europe and America. She is the author of *Politics, Gender, and the Islamic Past: The Legacy of 'A'isha bint Abi Bakr* (1994), which won the support of a Fulbright-Hays and the National Endowment for the Humanities. Her most recent book, *Thomas Jefferson's Qur'an: Islam and the Founders* (2013), was awarded a Carnegie Scholarship for the study of Islam in the modern world. It has been translated into Indonesian, Turkish, and Arabic. She is currently working on *The Evil Eye: Global Fears, Global Protections*, for the Cambridge Elements series in the Global Middle Ages.

Christopher Taylor is an independent researcher whose work on the Prester John legend has appeared in *Literature Compass* and in several book chapters. He is the creator of "The International Prester John Project," an immersive digital narrative, database, and archive of Prester John lore, hosted by the Global Middle Ages Project (www.globalmiddleages.org). His work can also be found in *postmedieval* and *New Medieval Literatures*. He is currently working on *The Global Legend of Prester John: A Transhistorical Cultural History*, for the Cambridge Elements series in the Global Middle Ages.

Yuanfei Wang is visiting scholar at the University of Southern California and associate professor of Chinese literature at Lingnan University in Hong Kong (from 2022). Her research crosses the divides of world history, comparative literature, and Chinese literature in the medieval and early modern periods. She is an awardee of several grants, including the SSRC transregional research postdoctoral fellowship and the Chiang Ching-kuo Foundation scholar grant. In 2021 she published her first book, *Writing Pirates: Vernacular Fiction and Oceans in Late Ming China*. Currently she is working on two projects: one on women, material culture, and late imperial Chinese literature; the other on globalism and China's literature in the Qing dynasty. She is also working on a Cambridge Element in the Global Middle Ages series (with Victor H. Mair) entitled *Early Globalism and China's Literature*.

Susan Whitfield has been researching, traveling, and writing on the Silk Road for over three decades. As curator of over fifty thousand medieval Silk Road manuscripts at the British Library, she directed an international collaboration between museums, libraries, and other holders of Silk Road artifacts worldwide, led major research and educational projects, and curated two international Silk Road exhibitions. Her books are widely used in both university and school teaching, as well as finding a wider readership. She is now professor of Silk Road studies at the University of East Anglia and has an honorary position at the Institute of Archaeology, University College London.

Cordell D. K. Yee leads classes in science, mathematics, music, literature, and philosophy at St. John's College in Annapolis, Maryland. He was an assistant editor and contributing author to *Cartography in the Traditional East and Southeast Asian Societies* (1994; vol.2, book 2, of *The History of Cartography*) and coauthor of *Challenges in a World-Wide History of Cartography* (2001). His other works include *Space and Place: Mapmaking East and West: Four Hundred Years of Western and Chinese Cartography* (1996), *The Word according to James Joyce: Reconstructing Representation* (1997), and "Reading within the Lines: Henri Michaux and the Chinese Art of Writing" (2009). He is currently working on *From Local to Global: Maps and Mapmaking in the Middle Ages*, coauthored with Asa Mittman and Sonia Brentjes, for the Cambridge Elements series in the Global Middle Ages.

Helen Young is lecturer in the School of Communication and Creative Arts at Deakin University. Her current research interests include critical race studies, medievalism, and popular culture. She has recently published in *postmedieval*, *Literature Compass*, *Studies in Medievalism* and *Continuum*. Her latest book is *Race and Popular Fantasy Literature: Habits of Whiteness* (2016) and she has a forthcoming Cambridge Element in the Global Middle Ages series (with Kavita Mudan Finn), *Global Medievalisms: An Introduction*.